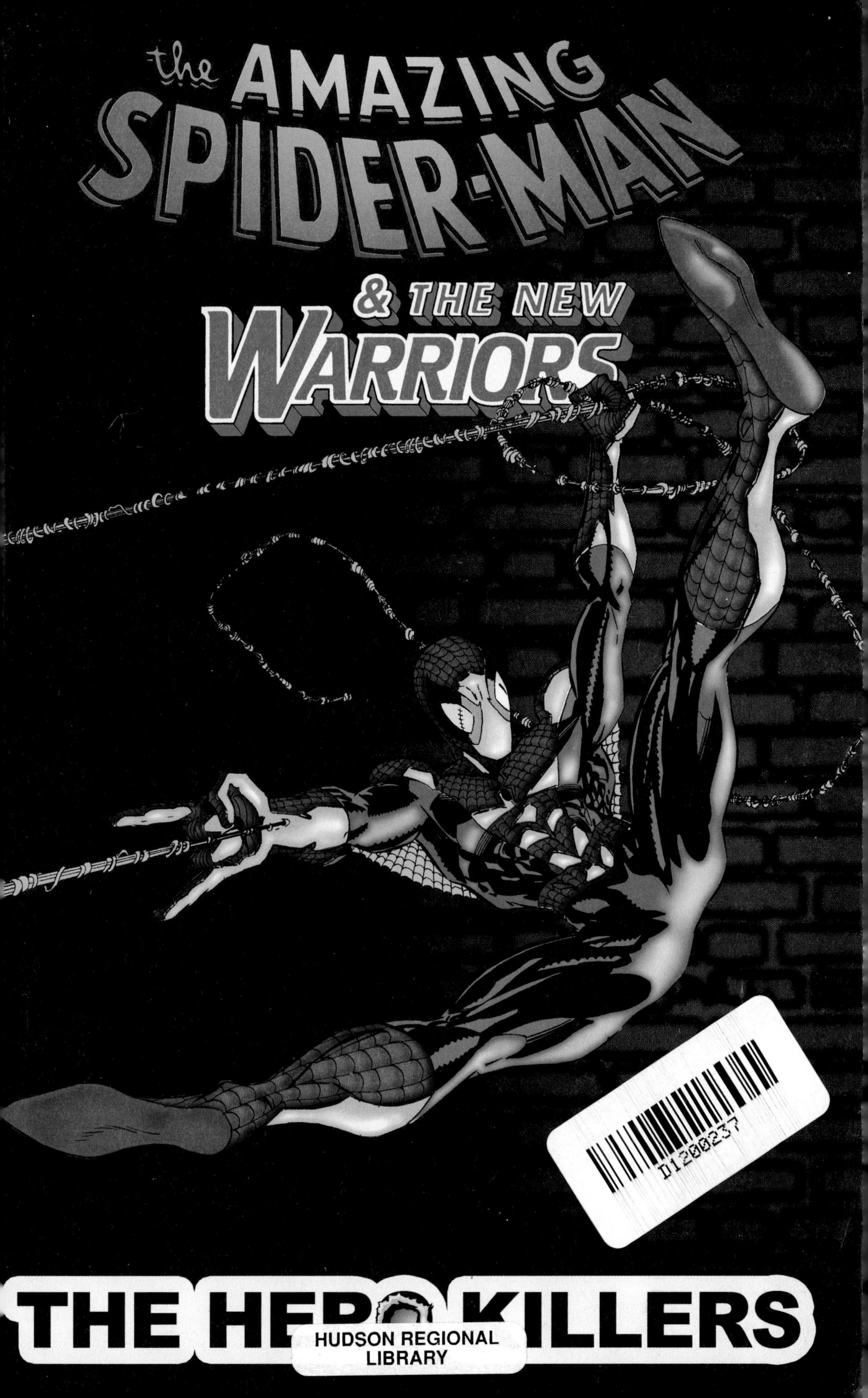
the AMAZING
SPIDER-MAN
& THE NEW
WARRIORS
THE HE
KILLERS

THE HERO KILLERS

WRITERS
DAVID MICHELINIE
& FABIAN NICIEZA

PENCILERS
SCOTT MCDANIEL
& BRANDON PETERSON

INKERS
KEITH WILLIAMS
WITH MARK STEGBAUER,
AL MILGROM
& JIMMY PALMIOTTI

COLORISTS
BOB SHAREN
WITH MARIE JAVINS
& SARRA MOSSOFF

LETTERER
STEVE DUTRO

VENOM: FIRST KILL!

WRITER
DAVID MICHELINIE

PENCILER
AARON LOPRESTI

INKER
BRUCE JONES

COLORISTS
KEVIN TINSLEY & BOB SHAREN

LETTERER
STEVE DUTRO

CLOAK AND DAGGER: EVIL'S LIGHT

WRITER
ERIC FEIN

PENCILER
VINCE EVANS

INKER
DON HUDSON

COLORIST
JOHN KALISZ

LETTERER
DAVE SHARPE

ADDITIONAL MATERIAL

WRITERS
ERIC FEIN, TOM BREVOORT, MIKE KANTEROVICH,
GLENN HERDLING, G. ALAN BARNUM & FABIAN NICIEZA

PENCILERS
SCOTT KOLINS, AARON LOPRESTI,
TOD SMITH & STEVE BUCCELLATO

INKERS
SAM DELAROSA, AARON LOPRESTI,
DON HUDSON & STEVE BUCCELLATO

COLORISTS
JOHN KALISZ, SARRA MOSSOFF,
MARIE JAVINS & STEVE BUCCELLATO

LETTERERS
CHRIS ELIOPOULOS, DAVE SHARPE,
JON BABCOCK & STEVE DUTRO

ASSISTANT EDITOR: ERIC FEIN · **EDITOR:** DANNY FINGEROTH
COVER ARTISTS: MARK BAGLEY & RANDY EMBERLIN
COVER COLORIST: TOM CHU

COLLECTION EDITOR: NELSON RIBEIRO · **ASSISTANT EDITOR:** ALEX STARBUCK
EDITORS, SPECIAL PROJECTS: MARK D. BEAZLEY & JENNIFER GRÜNWALD
SENIOR EDITOR, SPECIAL PROJECTS: JEFF YOUNGQUIST
SENIOR VICE PRESIDENT OF SALES: DAVID GABRIEL
SVP OF BRAND PLANNING & COMMUNICATIONS: MICHAEL PASCIULLO
PRODUCTION: COLORTEK & JOE FRONTIRRE
RESEARCH & LAYOUT: JEPH YORK
EDITOR IN CHIEF: AXEL ALONSO · **CHIEF CREATIVE OFFICER:** JOE QUESADA
PUBLISHER: DAN BUCKLEY · **EXECUTIVE PRODUCER:** ALAN FINE

SPIDER-MAN & THE NEW WARRIORS: THE HERO KILLERS. Contains material originally published in magazine form as AMAZING SPIDER-MAN ANNUAL #26, SPECTACULAR SPIDER-MAN ANNUAL #12, WEB OF SPIDER-MAN ANNUAL #8 and NEW WARRIORS ANNUAL #2. First printing 2012. ISBN# 978-0-7851-5967-4. Published by MARVEL WORLDWIDE, INC., a subsidiary of MARVEL ENTERTAINMENT, LLC. OFFICE OF PUBLICATION: 135 West 50th Street, New York, NY 10020. Copyright © 1992 and 2012 Marvel Characters, Inc. All rights reserved. $24.99 per copy in the U.S. and $27.99 in Canada (GST #R127032852); Canadian Agreement #40668537. All characters featured in this issue and the distinctive names and likenesses thereof, and all related indicia are trademarks of Marvel Characters, Inc. No similarity between any of the names, characters, persons, and/or institutions in this magazine with those of any living or dead person or institution is intended, and any such similarity which may exist is purely coincidental. **Printed in the U.S.A.** ALAN FINE, EVP - Office of the President, Marvel Worldwide, Inc. and EVP & CMO Marvel Characters B.V.; DAN BUCKLEY, Publisher & President - Print, Animation & Digital Divisions; JOE QUESADA, Chief Creative Officer; DAVID BOGART, SVP of Business Affairs & Talent Management; TOM BREVOORT, SVP of Publishing; C.B. CEBULSKI, SVP of Creator & Content Development; DAVID GABRIEL, SVP of Publishing Sales & Circulation; MICHAEL PASCIULLO, SVP of Brand Planning & Communications; JIM O'KEEFE, VP of Operations & Logistics; DAN CARR, Executive Director of Publishing Technology; SUSAN CRESPI, Editorial Operations Manager; ALEX MORALES, Publishing Operations Manager; STAN LEE, Chairman Emeritus. For information regarding advertising in Marvel Comics or on Marvel.com, please contact John Dokes, SVP Integrated Sales and Marketing, at jdokes@marvel.com. For Marvel subscription inquiries, please call 800-217-9158. **Manufactured between 2/8/2012 and 2/27/2012 by R.R. DONNELLEY, INC., SALEM, VA, USA.**

10 9 8 7 6 5 4 3 2 1

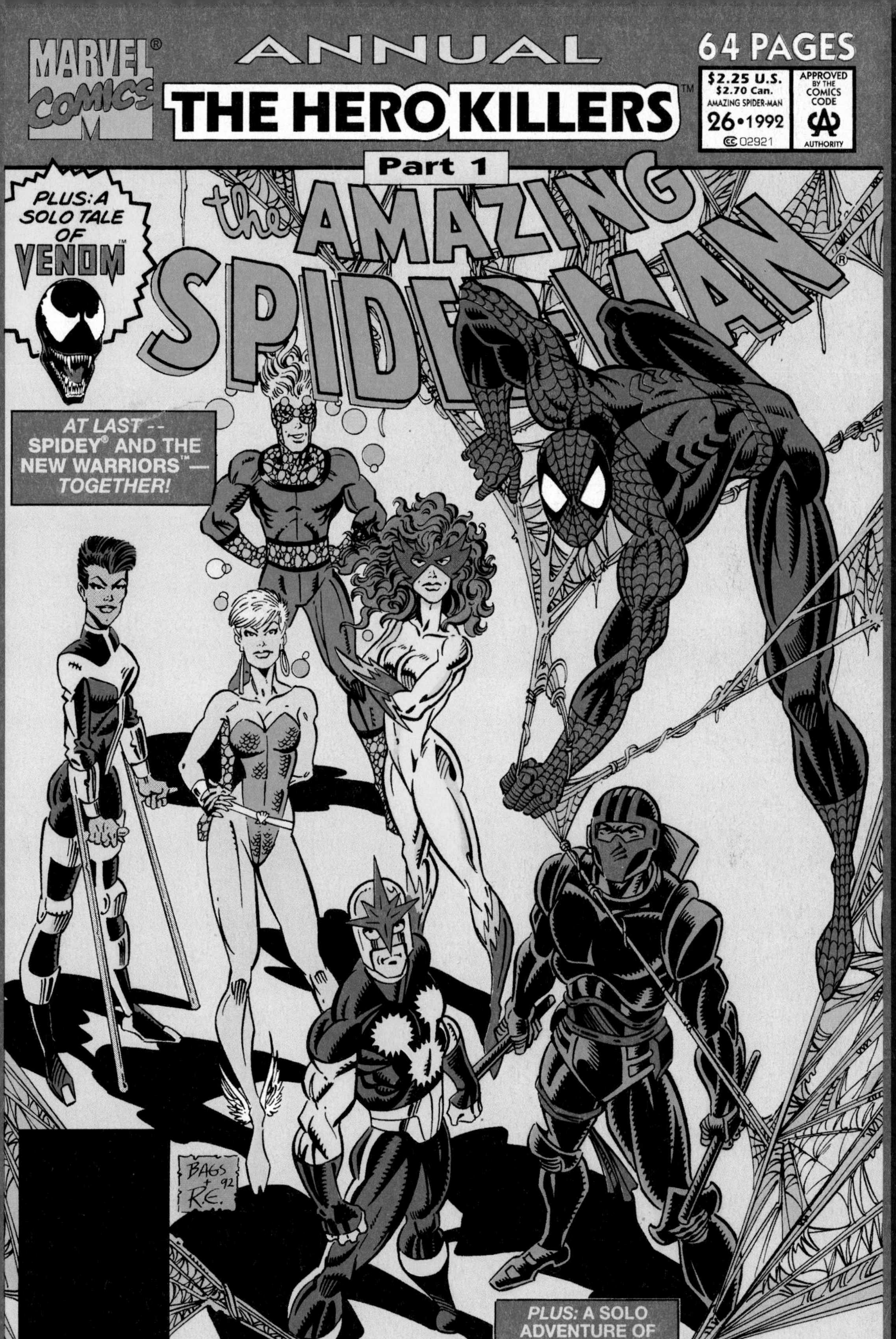
MARVEL® COMICS
ANNUAL
THE HERO KILLERS™
Part 1
64 PAGES
$2.25 U.S.
$2.70 Can.
AMAZING SPIDER-MAN
26 • 1992
CC 02921
APPROVED BY THE COMICS CODE AUTHORITY
the AMAZING SPIDER-MAN®
PLUS: A SOLO TALE OF VENOM™
AT LAST -- SPIDEY® AND THE NEW WARRIORS™ — TOGETHER!
BAGS + R.E. '92
PLUS: A SOLO ADVENTURE OF SOLO™! AND MUCH MORE!

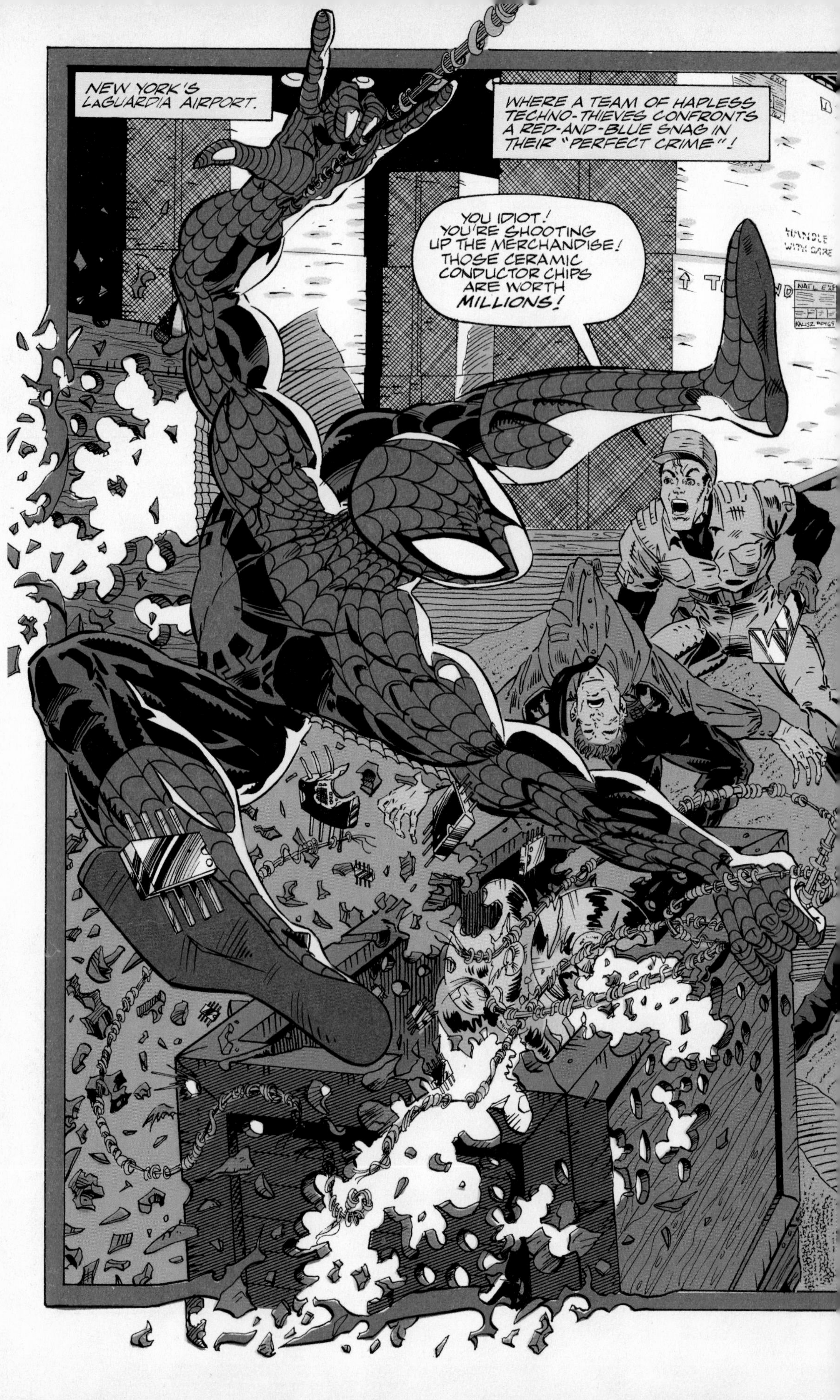
NEW YORK'S LAGUARDIA AIRPORT.
WHERE A TEAM OF HAPLESS TECHNO-THIEVES CONFRONTS A RED-AND-BLUE SNAG IN THEIR "PERFECT CRIME"!
YOU IDIOT! YOU'RE SHOOTING UP THE MERCHANDISE! THOSE CERAMIC CONDUCTOR CHIPS ARE WORTH MILLIONS!
HANDLE WITH CARE

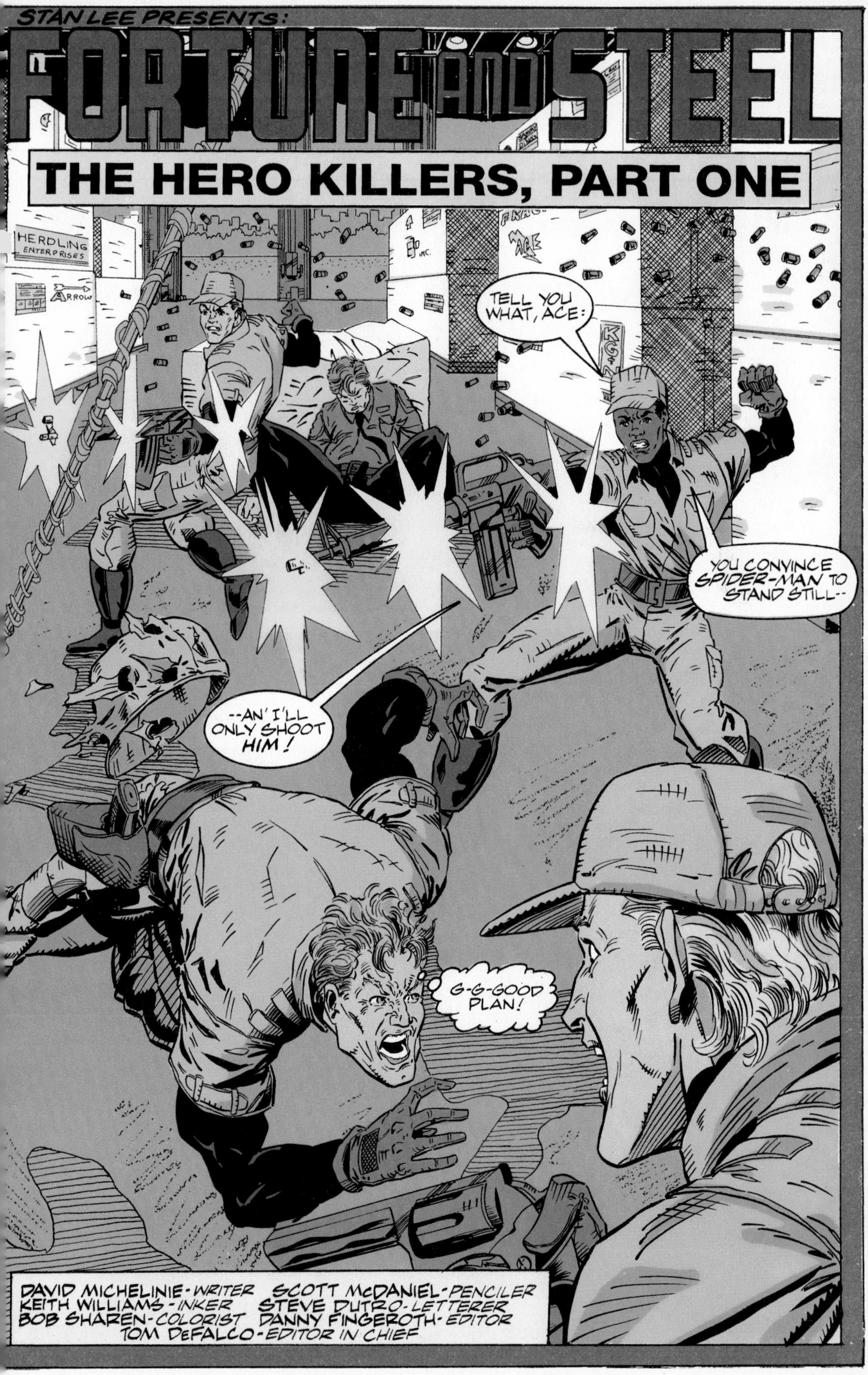

STAN LEE PRESENTS:
FORTUNE AND STEEL
THE HERO KILLERS, PART ONE
HERDLING ENTERPRISES
ARROW
ACE
TELL YOU WHAT, ACE:
YOU CONVINCE SPIDER-MAN TO STAND STILL--
--AN' I'LL ONLY SHOOT HIM!
G-G-GOOD PLAN!
DAVID MICHELINIE-WRITER SCOTT McDANIEL-PENCILER
KEITH WILLIAMS-INKER STEVE DUTRO-LETTERER
BOB SHAREN-COLORIST DANNY FINGEROTH-EDITOR
TOM DeFALCO-EDITOR IN CHIEF

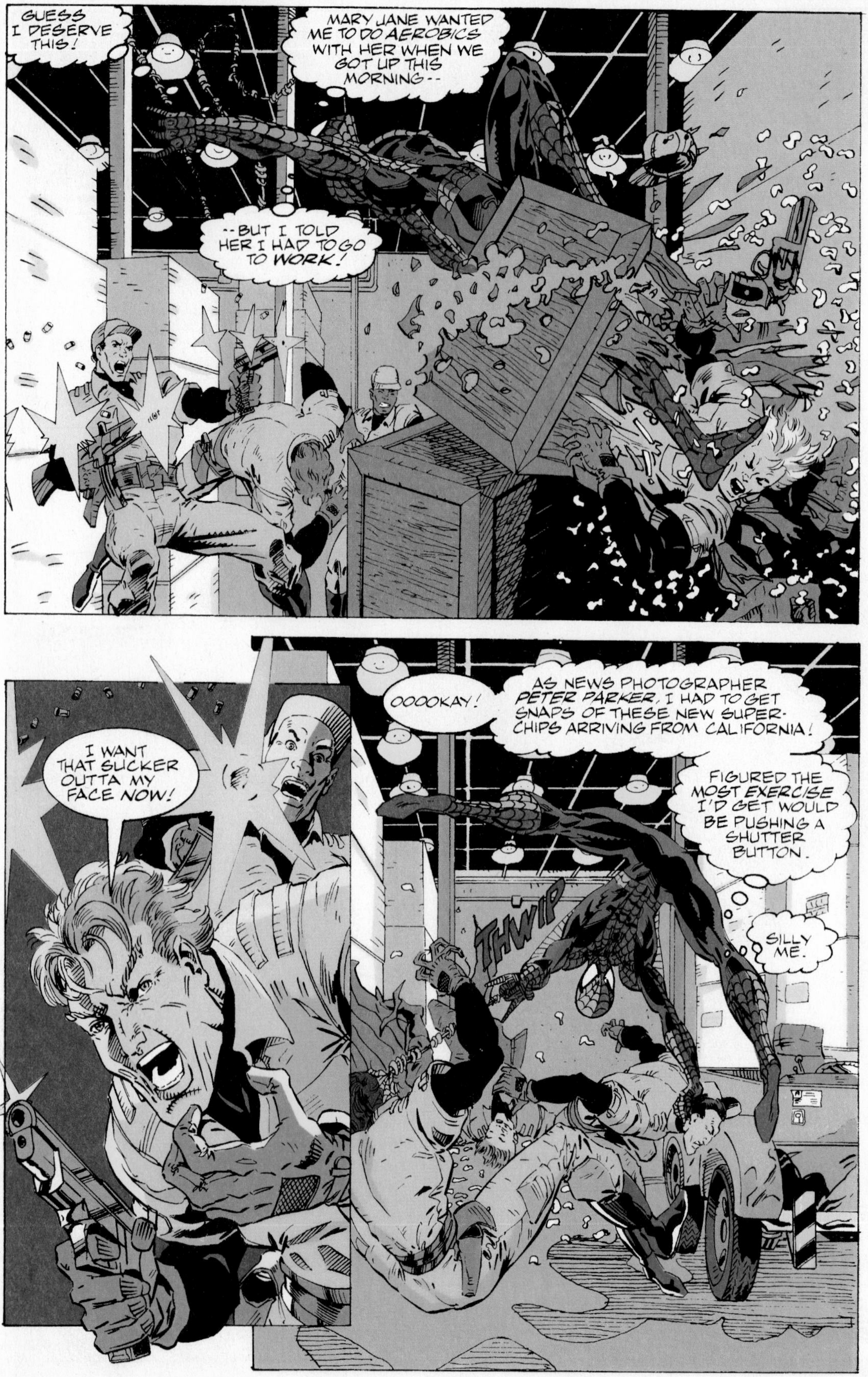
GUESS I DESERVE THIS!
MARY JANE WANTED ME TO DO AEROBICS WITH HER WHEN WE GOT UP THIS MORNING--
--BUT I TOLD HER I HAD TO GO TO WORK!
I WANT THAT SUCKER OUTTA MY FACE NOW!
OOOOKAY!
AS NEWS PHOTOGRAPHER PETER PARKER, I HAD TO GET SNAPS OF THESE NEW SUPER-CHIPS ARRIVING FROM CALIFORNIA!
FIGURED THE MOST EXERCISE I'D GET WOULD BE PUSHING A SHUTTER BUTTON.
THWIP
SILLY ME.

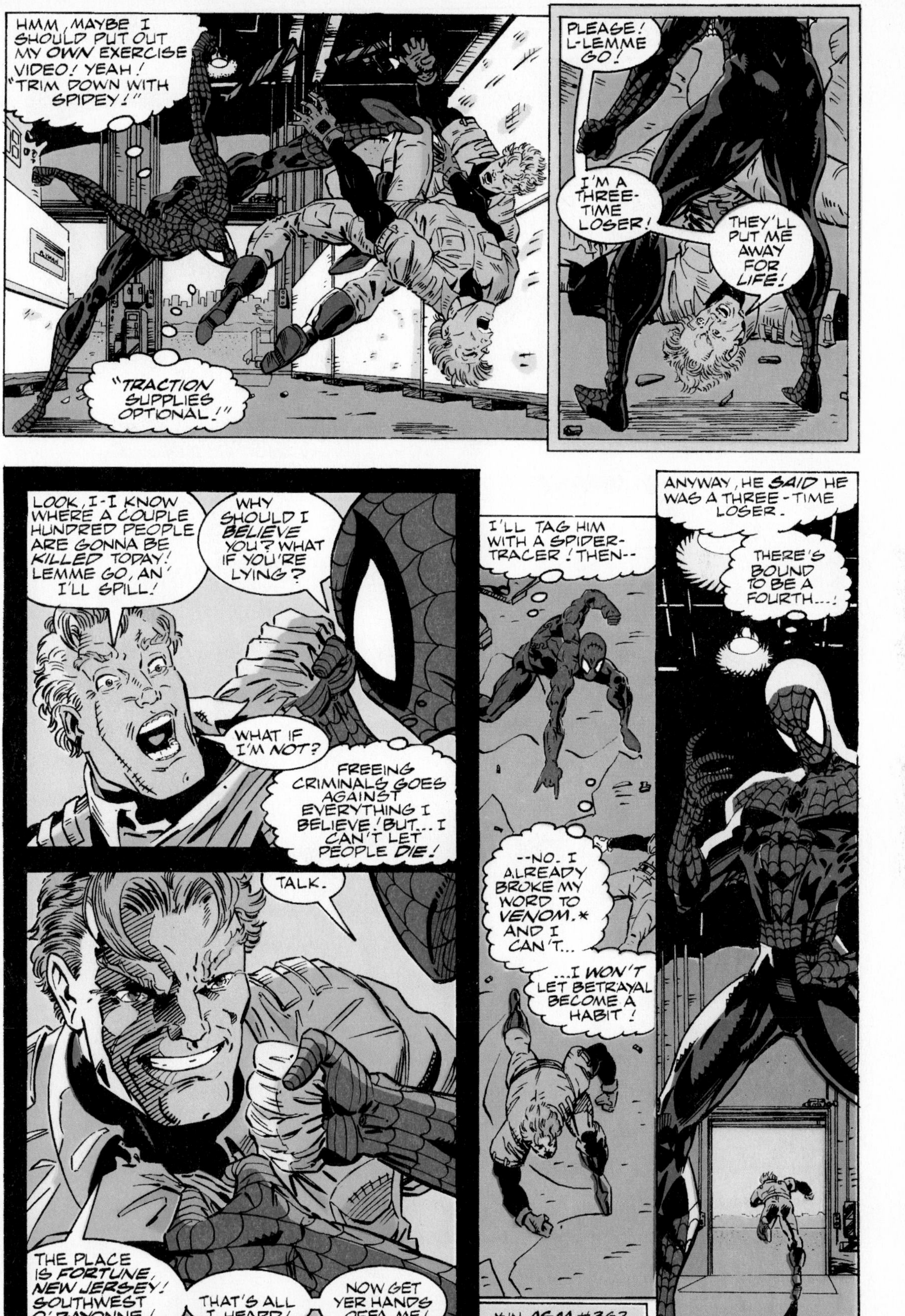

HMM, MAYBE I SHOULD PUT OUT MY OWN EXERCISE VIDEO! YEAH! "TRIM DOWN WITH SPIDEY!"
"TRACTION SUPPLIES OPTIONAL!"
PLEASE! L-LEMME GO!
I'M A THREE-TIME LOSER!
THEY'LL PUT ME AWAY FOR LIFE!
LOOK, I-I KNOW WHERE A COUPLE HUNDRED PEOPLE ARE GONNA BE KILLED TODAY! LEMME GO, AN' I'LL SPILL!
WHY SHOULD I BELIEVE YOU? WHAT IF YOU'RE LYING?
WHAT IF I'M NOT?
FREEING CRIMINALS GOES AGAINST EVERYTHING I BELIEVE! BUT... I CAN'T LET PEOPLE DIE!
TALK.
THE PLACE IS FORTUNE, NEW JERSEY! SOUTHWEST O' BAYONNE!
THAT'S ALL I HEARD!
NOW GET YER HANDS OFFA ME!
I'LL TAG HIM WITH A SPIDER-TRACER! THEN--
--NO. I ALREADY BROKE MY WORD TO VENOM.* AND I CAN'T...
...I WON'T LET BETRAYAL BECOME A HABIT!
*IN ASM #363. --DANNY
ANYWAY, HE SAID HE WAS A THREE-TIME LOSER.
THERE'S BOUND TO BE A FOURTH...!

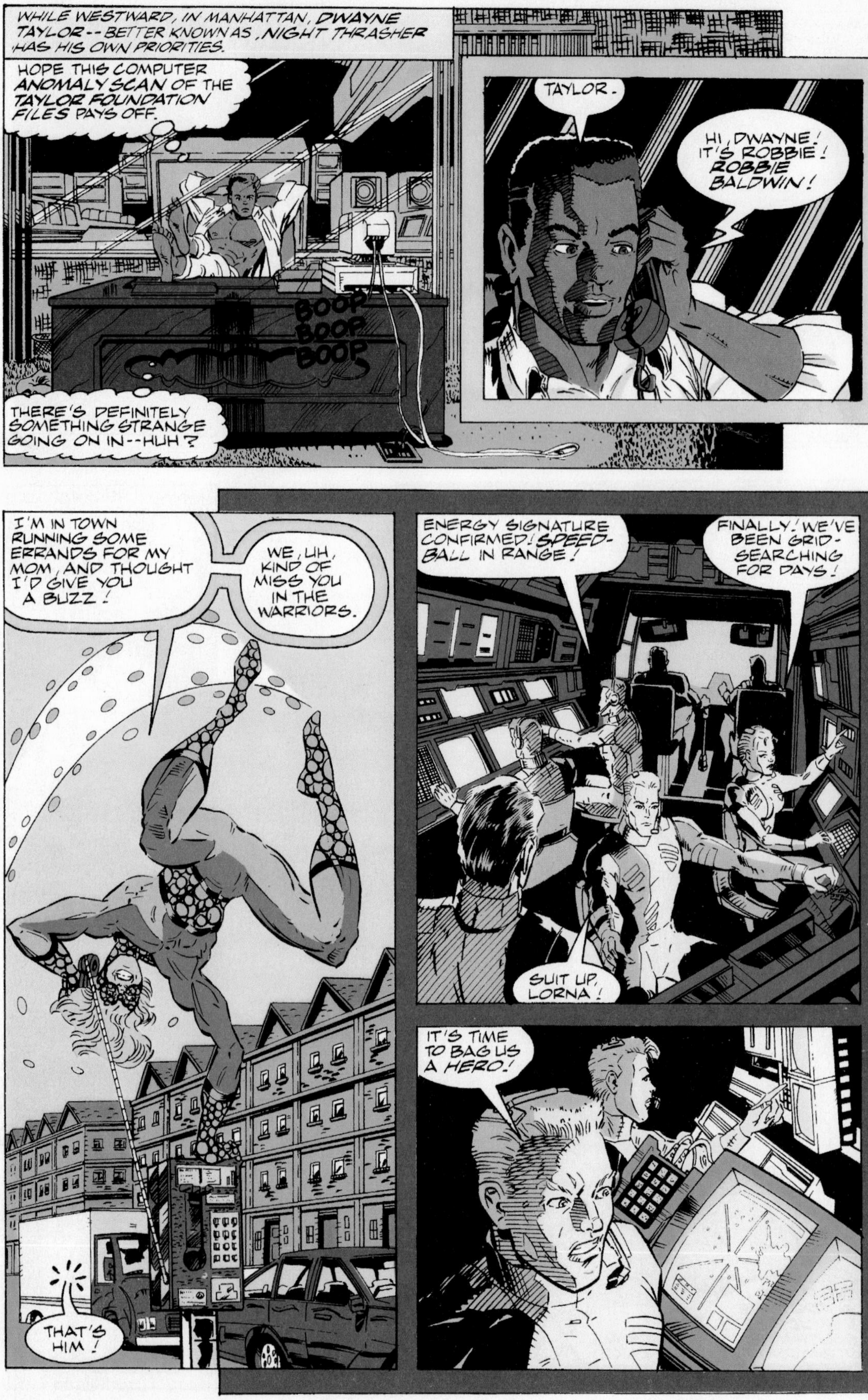
WHILE WESTWARD, IN MANHATTAN, DWAYNE TAYLOR -- BETTER KNOWN AS, NIGHT THRASHER HAS HIS OWN PRIORITIES.
HOPE THIS COMPUTER ANOMALY SCAN OF THE TAYLOR FOUNDATION FILES PAYS OFF.
BOOP BOOP BOOP
THERE'S DEFINITELY SOMETHING STRANGE GOING ON IN--HUH?
TAYLOR.
HI, DWAYNE! IT'S ROBBIE! ROBBIE BALDWIN!
I'M IN TOWN RUNNING SOME ERRANDS FOR MY MOM, AND THOUGHT I'D GIVE YOU A BUZZ!
WE, UH, KIND OF MISS YOU IN THE WARRIORS.
THAT'S HIM!
ENERGY SIGNATURE CONFIRMED! SPEEDBALL IN RANGE!
FINALLY! WE'VE BEEN GRID-SEARCHING FOR DAYS!
SUIT UP, LORNA!
IT'S TIME TO BAG US A HERO!

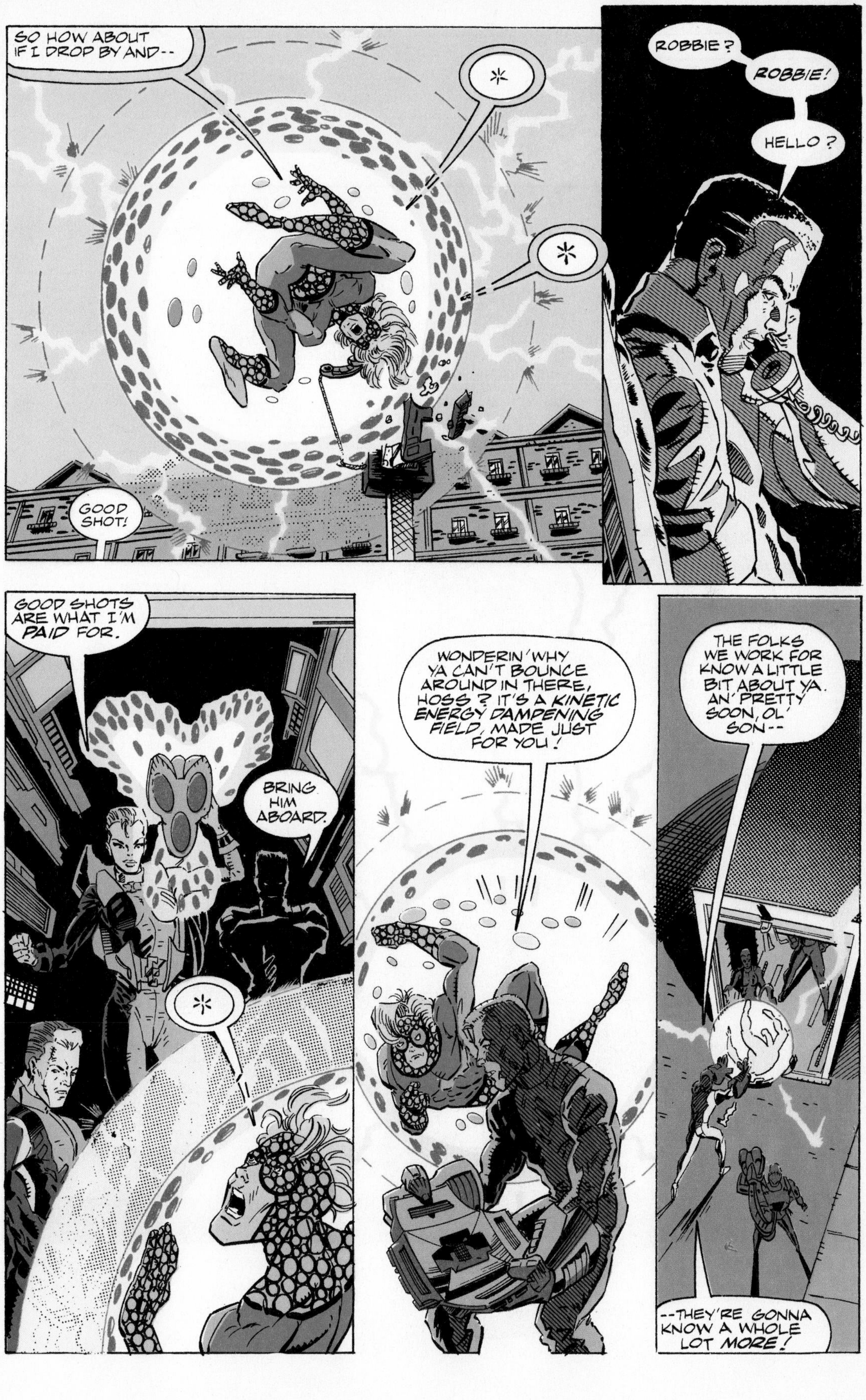
SO HOW ABOUT IF I DROP BY AND--
!
!
GOOD SHOT!
ROBBIE?
ROBBIE!
HELLO?
GOOD SHOTS ARE WHAT I'M PAID FOR.
BRING HIM ABOARD.
!
WONDERIN' WHY YA CAN'T BOUNCE AROUND IN THERE, HOSS? IT'S A KINETIC ENERGY DAMPENING FIELD, MADE JUST FOR YOU!
THE FOLKS WE WORK FOR KNOW A LITTLE BIT ABOUT YA. AN' PRETTY SOON, OL' SON--
--THEY'RE GONNA KNOW A WHOLE LOT MORE!

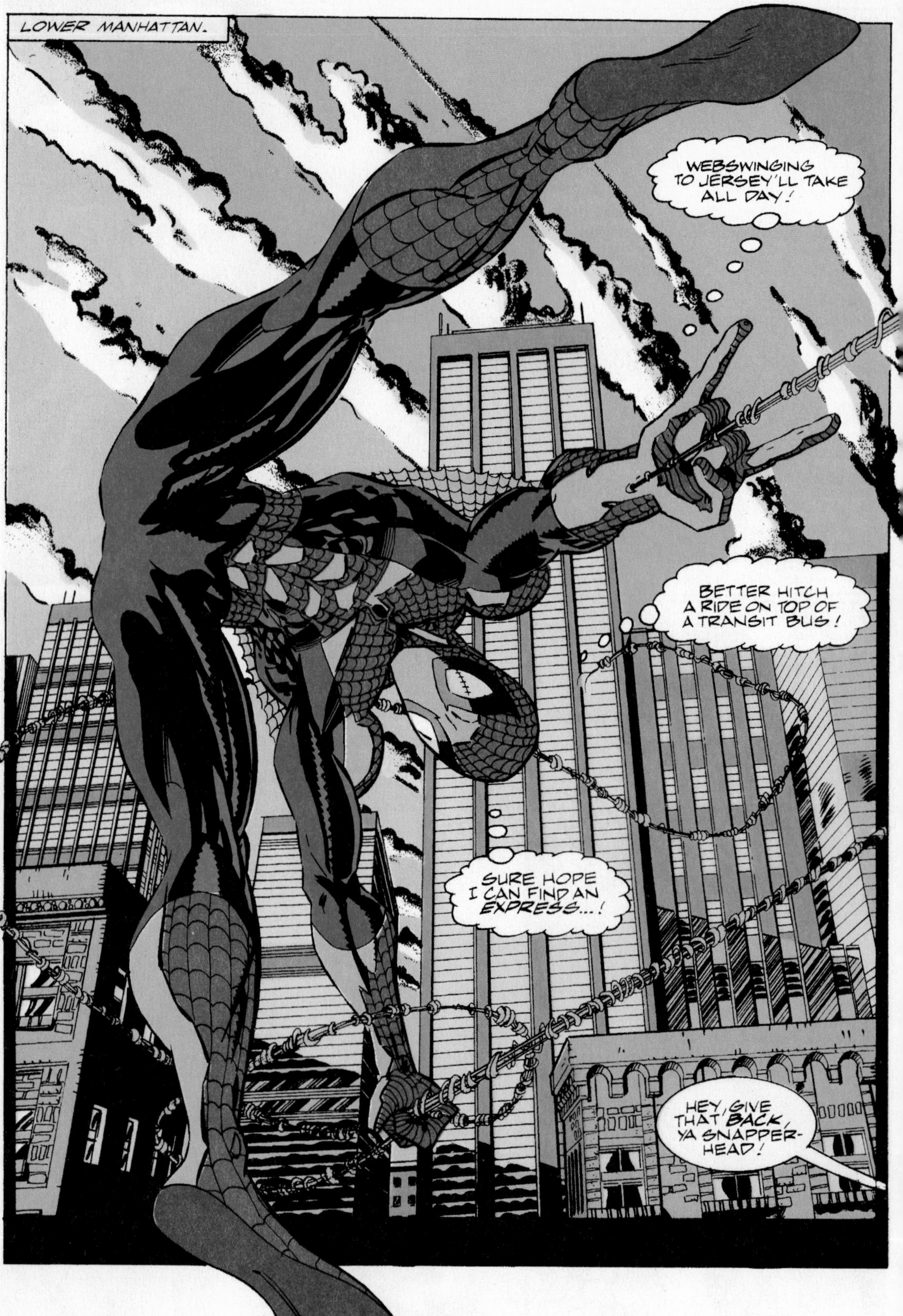
LOWER MANHATTAN.
WEBSWINGING TO JERSEY'LL TAKE ALL DAY!
BETTER HITCH A RIDE ON TOP OF A TRANSIT BUS!
SURE HOPE I CAN FIND AN EXPRESS...!
HEY, GIVE THAT BACK, YA SNAPPER-HEAD!

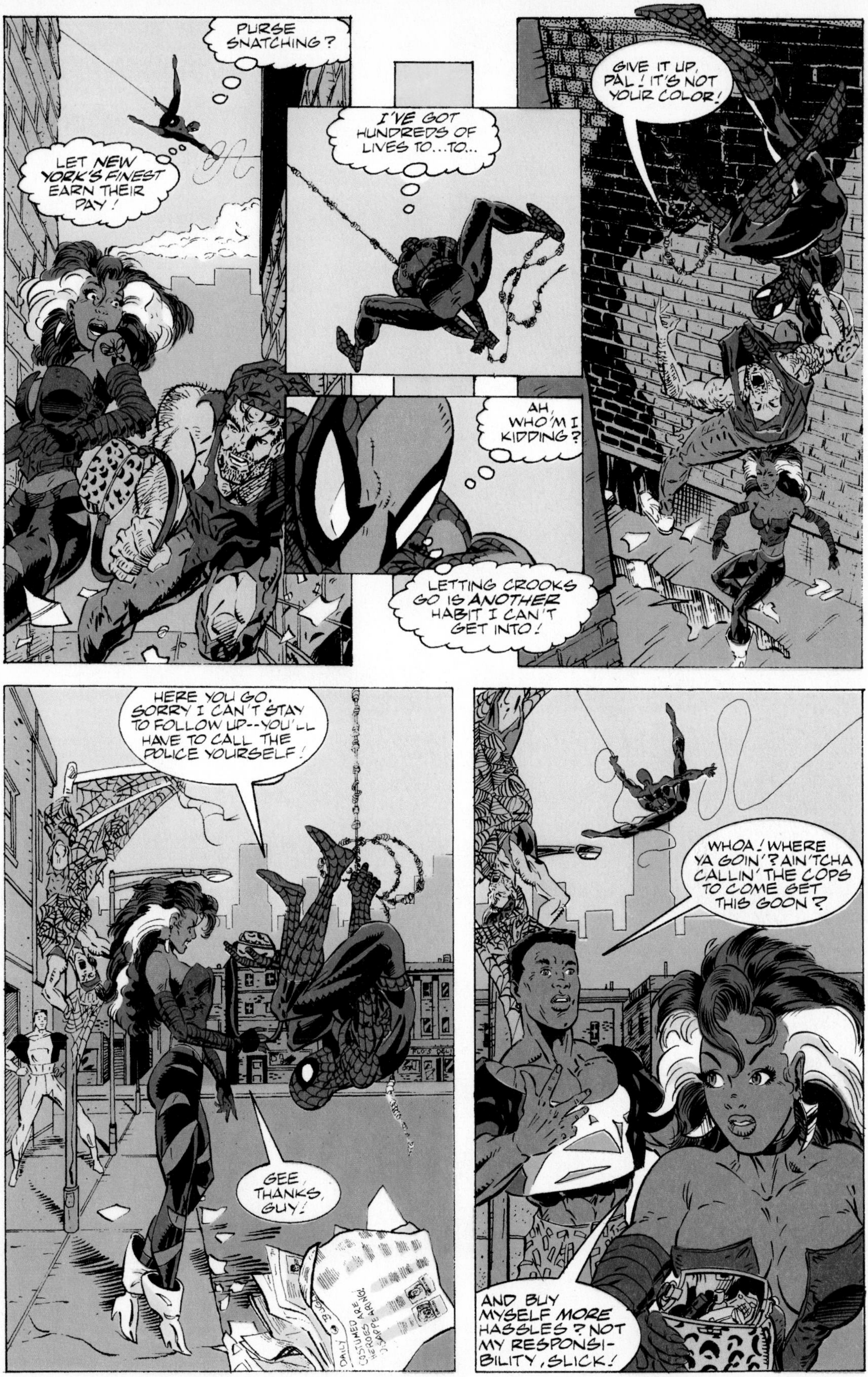
PURSE SNATCHING?
LET NEW YORK'S FINEST EARN THEIR PAY!
I'VE GOT HUNDREDS OF LIVES TO...TO...
AH, WHO'M I KIDDING?
LETTING CROOKS GO IS ANOTHER HABIT I CAN'T GET INTO!
GIVE IT UP, PAL! IT'S NOT YOUR COLOR!
HERE YOU GO. SORRY I CAN'T STAY TO FOLLOW UP--YOU'LL HAVE TO CALL THE POLICE YOURSELF!
GEE, THANKS, GUY!
WHOA! WHERE YA GOIN'? AIN'TCHA CALLIN' THE COPS TO COME GET THIS GOON?
AND BUY MYSELF MORE HASSLES? NOT MY RESPONSIBILITY, SLICK!

WHILE AT A PREVIOUSLY-PRESENTED PENTHOUSE...

SEARCHING SEARCHING
SEARCHING SEARCHING
SEARCHING SEARCHING
SEARCHING SEARCHING

UPDATE MODE - SCROLL QUERY LOCK ON LEVEL 7B.2 LIBR. ACC. 5 SUMMARY

HARD TO FOCUS MY MIND ON THE ANOMALY SCAN.

KEEP THINKING ABOUT ROBBIE.

I MEAN, PUBLIC PHONES AREN'T LEGENDARY FOR THEIR *RELIABILITY.*

BUT THERE'S A STORY GOING AROUND ABOUT COSTUMED HEROES DROPPING OUT OF SIGHT! IF--

BZZZT

--EH? SCAN'S FOUND SOMETHING UNUSUAL IN THE FOUNDATION FILES!

...UPDATE INTERRUPT...UPDATE INTERRUPT...UPDATE INTERRUPT...

PRIORITY MEMO

TAYLOR FOUNDATION
ELECTRONIC MESSENGER

RECEIVER: ALL TF EMPLOYEES   DATE: XX/YY/ZZ
SOURCE: UNTRACEABLE   CODE: UNKNOWN
SUBJECT: FORTUNE, NJ

ALL EMPLOYEES IN THE TRI-STATE AREA ARE TO REMAIN CLEAR OF FORTUNE, NJ AT THIS TIME. PROXIMITY TO THIS LOCATION COULD BE FATAL...
⟨END MEMO⟩

TIMESTAMP 10:54:21   WORK STATION MLELØA
LOC: UNKNOWN   STATUS: UNTRACEABLE
SCR. CODE: ASCII   TYPE: GLOBAL FLASH MEM
CNTR 2 TO ... - CNTR Q TO QUIT - CNTR S TO SA...

PAR
UPDAT
WIN.   APPE
LOCK   ERA
DATA   LIST
QUE   SEA
FILE   EDT
UTIL

"FATAL"?! BETTER CHECK THIS OUT--*FAST!* AND IF IT'S THAT DANGEROUS--

FATAL

--WELL, I MAY NOT BE AN OFFICIAL *WAR-RIOR*, BUT THAT DOESN'T MEAN I CAN'T CALL ON *FRIENDS* FOR FAVORS!

1	WARRIORS	SIL	11
2	DOMINOES	CHORD	12
3	EXEC OFF	VP SCHED	13
4	EXEC SEC	VP ACCT	14
5	DIR OFC	VP PR	15
6	DIR PDI	VP ADV	16
7	BOARD RM	VP MKT	17
8	BOARD RM	VP SALS	18
9			

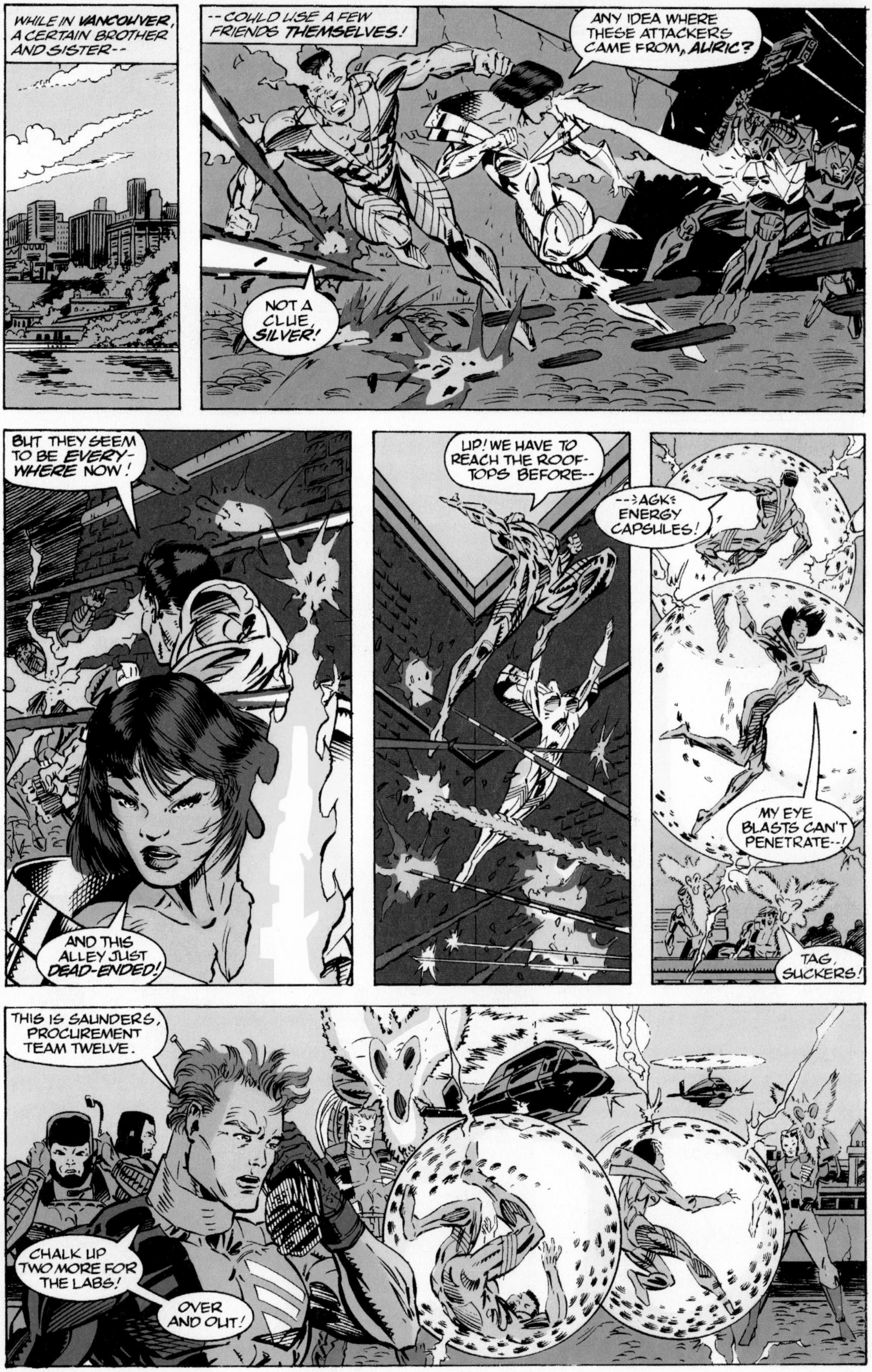
WHILE IN VANCOUVER, A CERTAIN BROTHER AND SISTER--
--COULD USE A FEW FRIENDS THEMSELVES!
ANY IDEA WHERE THESE ATTACKERS CAME FROM, AURIC?
NOT A CLUE, SILVER!
BUT THEY SEEM TO BE EVERY-WHERE NOW!
AND THIS ALLEY JUST DEAD-ENDED!
UP! WE HAVE TO REACH THE ROOF-TOPS BEFORE--
--AGK-- ENERGY CAPSULES!
MY EYE BLASTS CAN'T PENETRATE--!
TAG, SUCKERS!
THIS IS SAUNDERS, PROCUREMENT TEAM TWELVE.
CHALK UP TWO MORE FOR THE LABS!
OVER AND OUT!

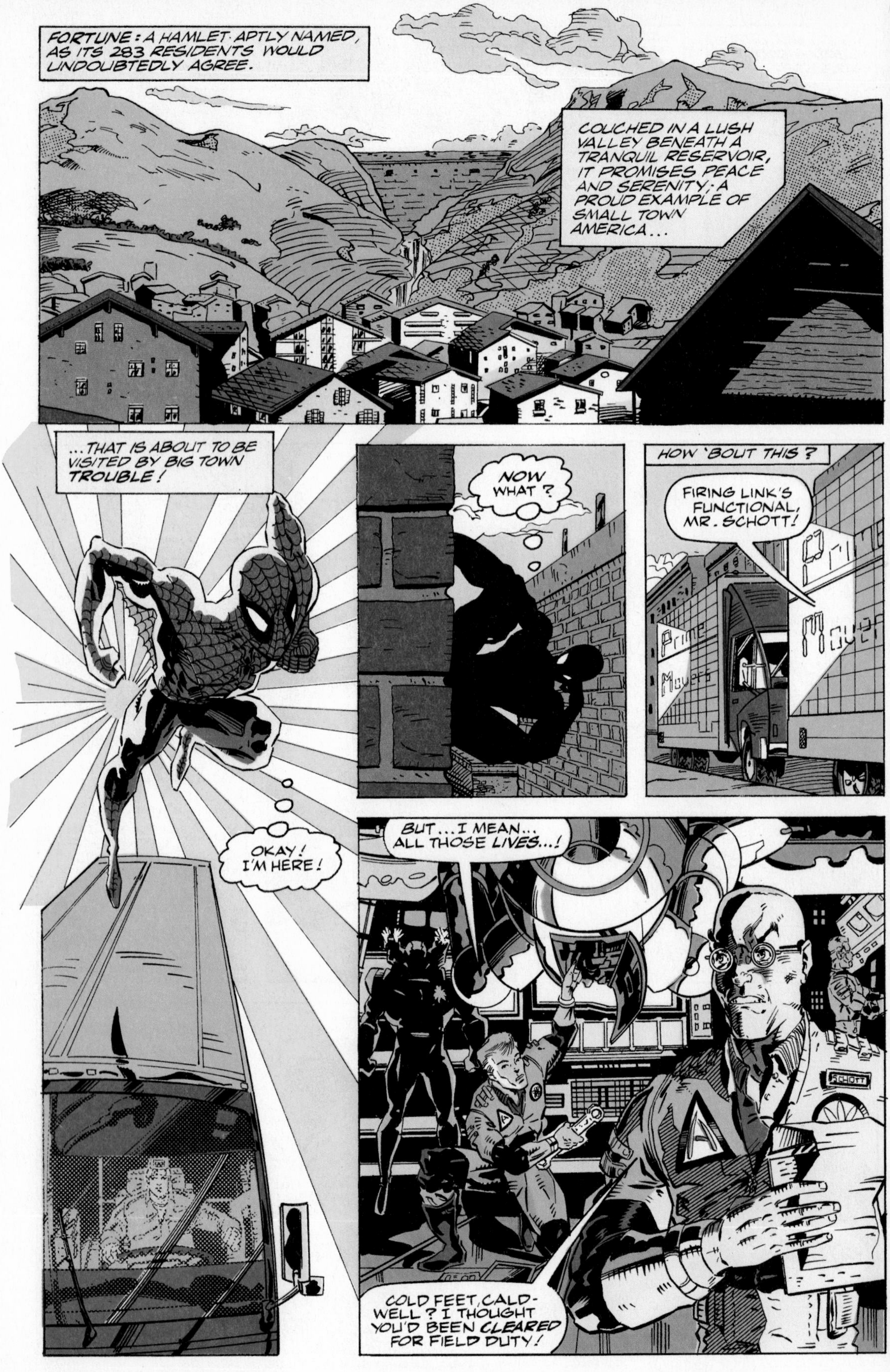
FORTUNE: A HAMLET APTLY NAMED, AS ITS 283 RESIDENTS WOULD UNDOUBTEDLY AGREE.
COUCHED IN A LUSH VALLEY BENEATH A TRANQUIL RESERVOIR, IT PROMISES PEACE AND SERENITY; A PROUD EXAMPLE OF SMALL TOWN AMERICA...
...THAT IS ABOUT TO BE VISITED BY BIG TOWN TROUBLE!
OKAY! I'M HERE!
NOW WHAT?
HOW 'BOUT THIS?
FIRING LINK'S FUNCTIONAL, MR. SCHOTT!
Prime Movers
BUT... I MEAN... ALL THOSE LIVES...!
SCHOTT
COLD FEET, CALD-WELL? I THOUGHT YOU'D BEEN CLEARED FOR FIELD DUTY!

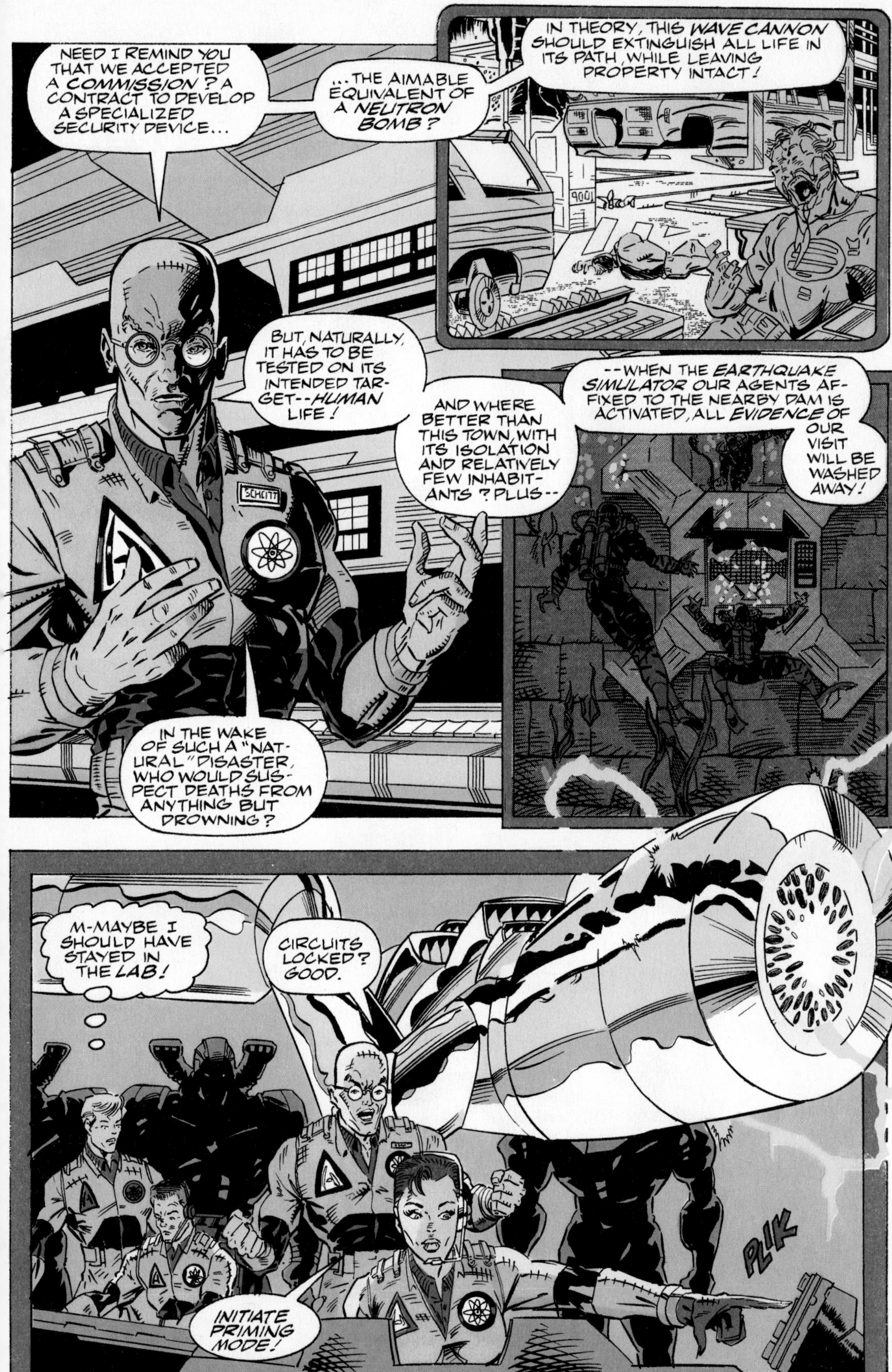

NEED I REMIND YOU THAT WE ACCEPTED A COMMISSION? A CONTRACT TO DEVELOP A SPECIALIZED SECURITY DEVICE...
...THE AIMABLE EQUIVALENT OF A NEUTRON BOMB?
IN THEORY, THIS WAVE CANNON SHOULD EXTINGUISH ALL LIFE IN ITS PATH, WHILE LEAVING PROPERTY INTACT!
BUT, NATURALLY, IT HAS TO BE TESTED ON ITS INTENDED TARGET--HUMAN LIFE!
AND WHERE BETTER THAN THIS TOWN, WITH ITS ISOLATION AND RELATIVELY FEW INHABITANTS? PLUS--
--WHEN THE EARTHQUAKE SIMULATOR OUR AGENTS AFFIXED TO THE NEARBY DAM IS ACTIVATED, ALL EVIDENCE OF OUR VISIT WILL BE WASHED AWAY!
IN THE WAKE OF SUCH A "NATURAL" DISASTER, WHO WOULD SUSPECT DEATHS FROM ANYTHING BUT DROWNING?
M-MAYBE I SHOULD HAVE STAYED IN THE LAB!
CIRCUITS LOCKED? GOOD.
INITIATE PRIMING MODE!
PLIK

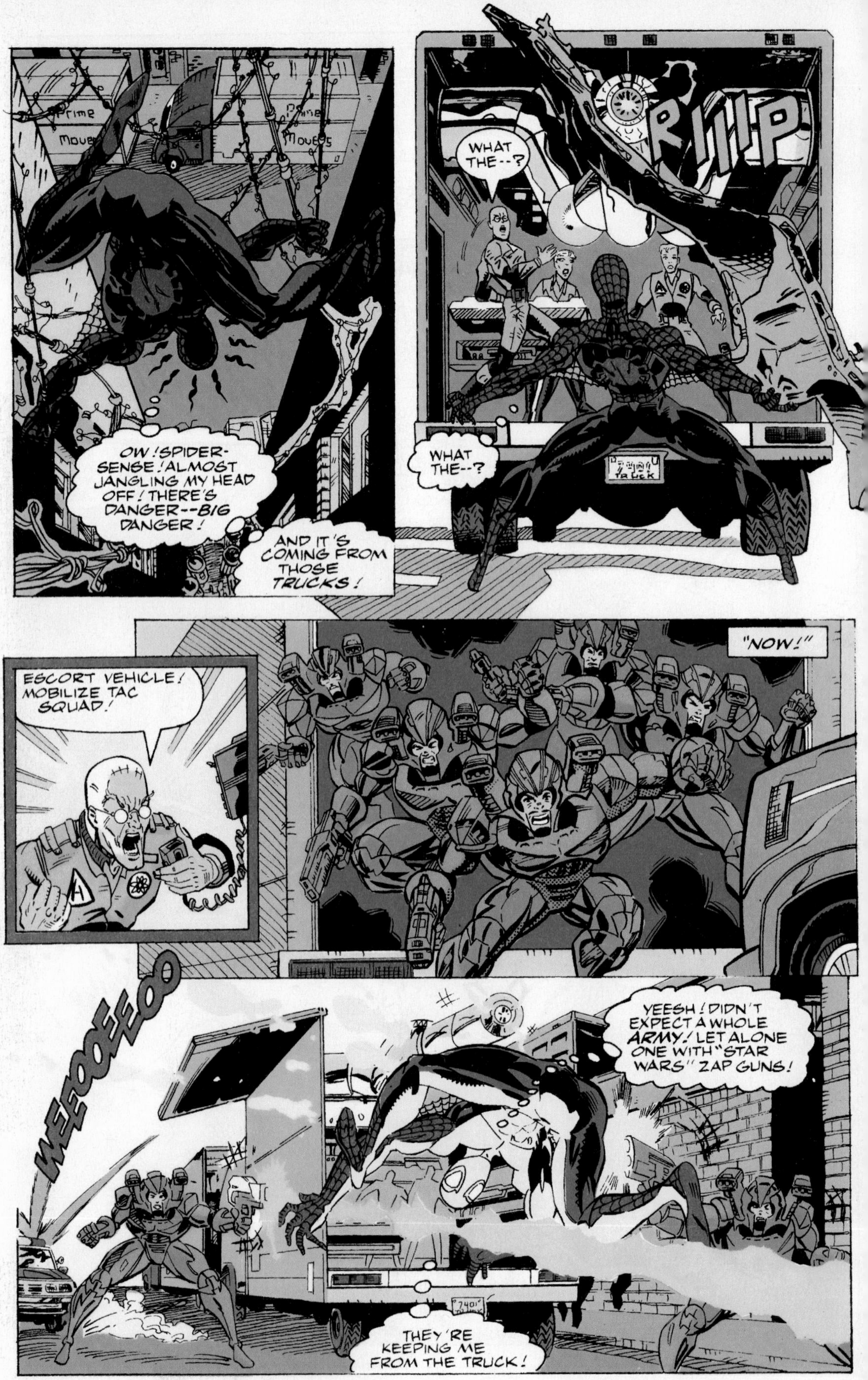
OW! SPIDER-SENSE! ALMOST JANGLING MY HEAD OFF! THERE'S DANGER--BIG DANGER!
AND IT'S COMING FROM THOSE TRUCKS!
WHAT THE--?
RIIIP!
WHAT THE--?
ESCORT VEHICLE! MOBILIZE TAC SQUAD!
"NOW!"
WEEOOEEOO
YEESH! DIDN'T EXPECT A WHOLE ARMY! LET ALONE ONE WITH "STAR WARS" ZAP GUNS!
THEY'RE KEEPING ME FROM THE TRUCK!

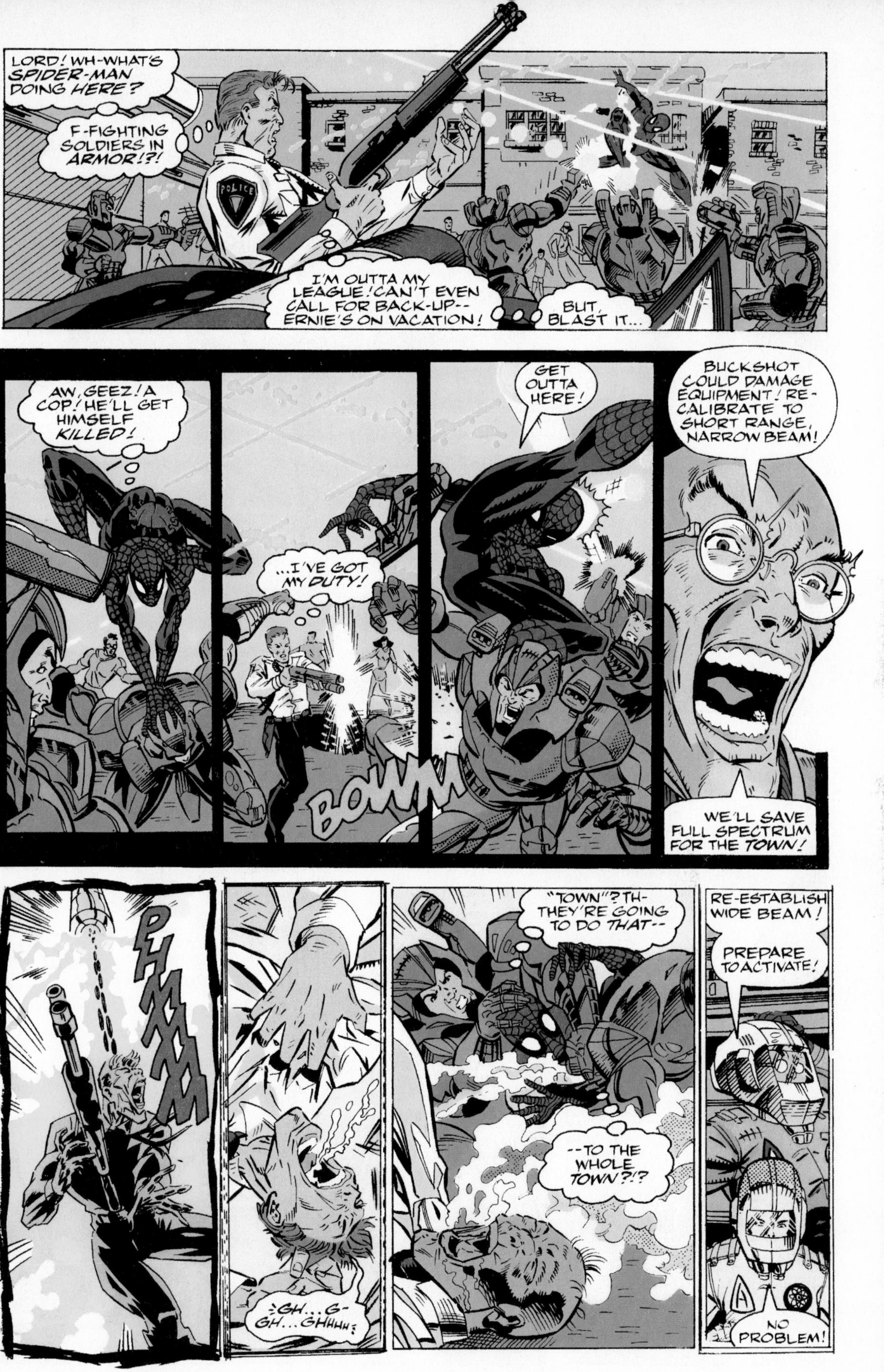
LORD! WH-WHAT'S SPIDER-MAN DOING HERE?
F-FIGHTING SOLDIERS IN ARMOR!?!
I'M OUTTA MY LEAGUE! CAN'T EVEN CALL FOR BACK-UP-- ERNIE'S ON VACATION!
BUT, BLAST IT...
AW, GEEZ! A COP! HE'LL GET HIMSELF KILLED!
...I'VE GOT MY DUTY!
BOWM
GET OUTTA HERE!
BUCKSHOT COULD DAMAGE EQUIPMENT! RE-CALIBRATE TO SHORT RANGE, NARROW BEAM!
WE'LL SAVE FULL SPECTRUM FOR THE TOWN!
PHMMM
GH... G-GH... GHHHH
"TOWN"? TH-THEY'RE GOING TO DO THAT--
--TO THE WHOLE TOWN?!?
RE-ESTABLISH WIDE BEAM!
PREPARE TO ACTIVATE!
NO PROBLEM!

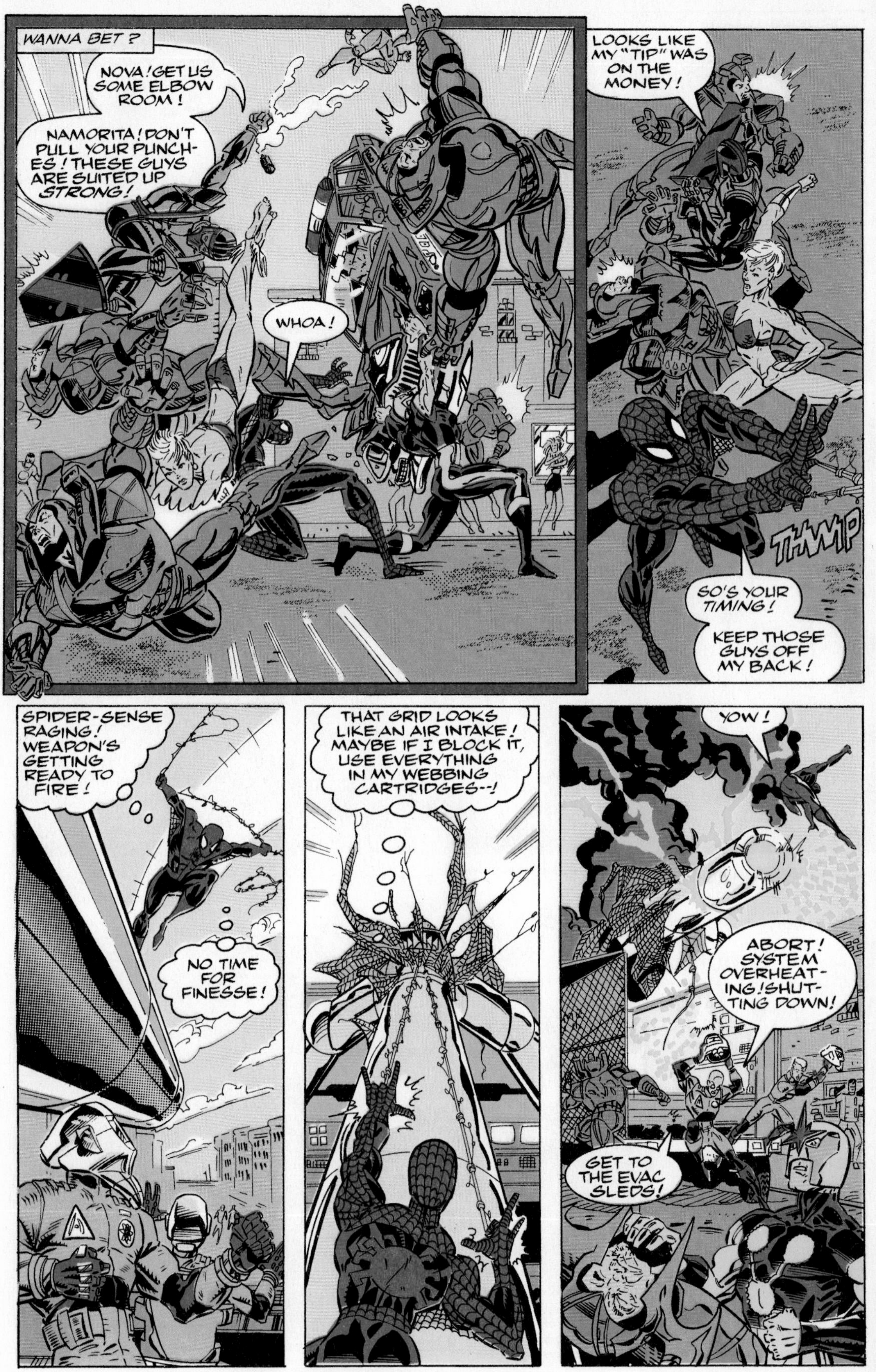
WANNA BET ?
NOVA! GET US SOME ELBOW ROOM!
NAMORITA! DON'T PULL YOUR PUNCHES! THESE GUYS ARE SUITED UP STRONG!
WHOA!
LOOKS LIKE MY "TIP" WAS ON THE MONEY!
THWIP
SO'S YOUR TIMING!
KEEP THOSE GUYS OFF MY BACK!
SPIDER-SENSE RAGING! WEAPON'S GETTING READY TO FIRE!
NO TIME FOR FINESSE!
THAT GRID LOOKS LIKE AN AIR INTAKE! MAYBE IF I BLOCK IT, USE EVERYTHING IN MY WEBBING CARTRIDGES--!
YOW!
ABORT! SYSTEM OVERHEATING! SHUTTING DOWN!
GET TO THE EVAC SLEDS!

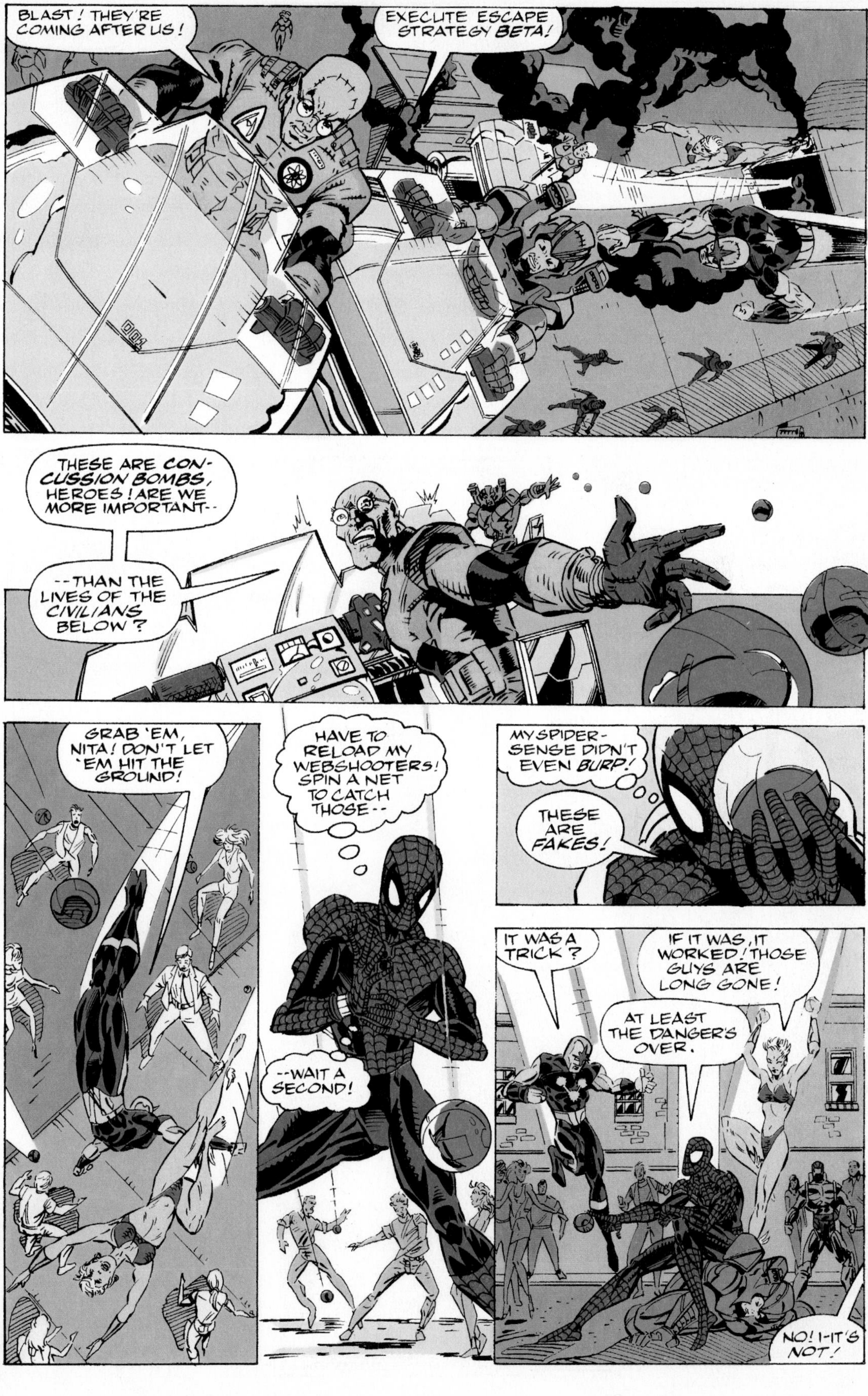

BLAST! THEY'RE COMING AFTER US!
EXECUTE ESCAPE STRATEGY BETA!
THESE ARE CONCUSSION BOMBS, HEROES! ARE WE MORE IMPORTANT--
--THAN THE LIVES OF THE CIVILIANS BELOW?
GRAB 'EM, NITA! DON'T LET 'EM HIT THE GROUND!
HAVE TO RELOAD MY WEBSHOOTERS! SPIN A NET TO CATCH THOSE--
--WAIT A SECOND!
MY SPIDER-SENSE DIDN'T EVEN BURP!
THESE ARE FAKES!
IT WAS A TRICK?
IF IT WAS, IT WORKED! THOSE GUYS ARE LONG GONE!
AT LEAST THE DANGER'S OVER.
NO! I-IT'S NOT!

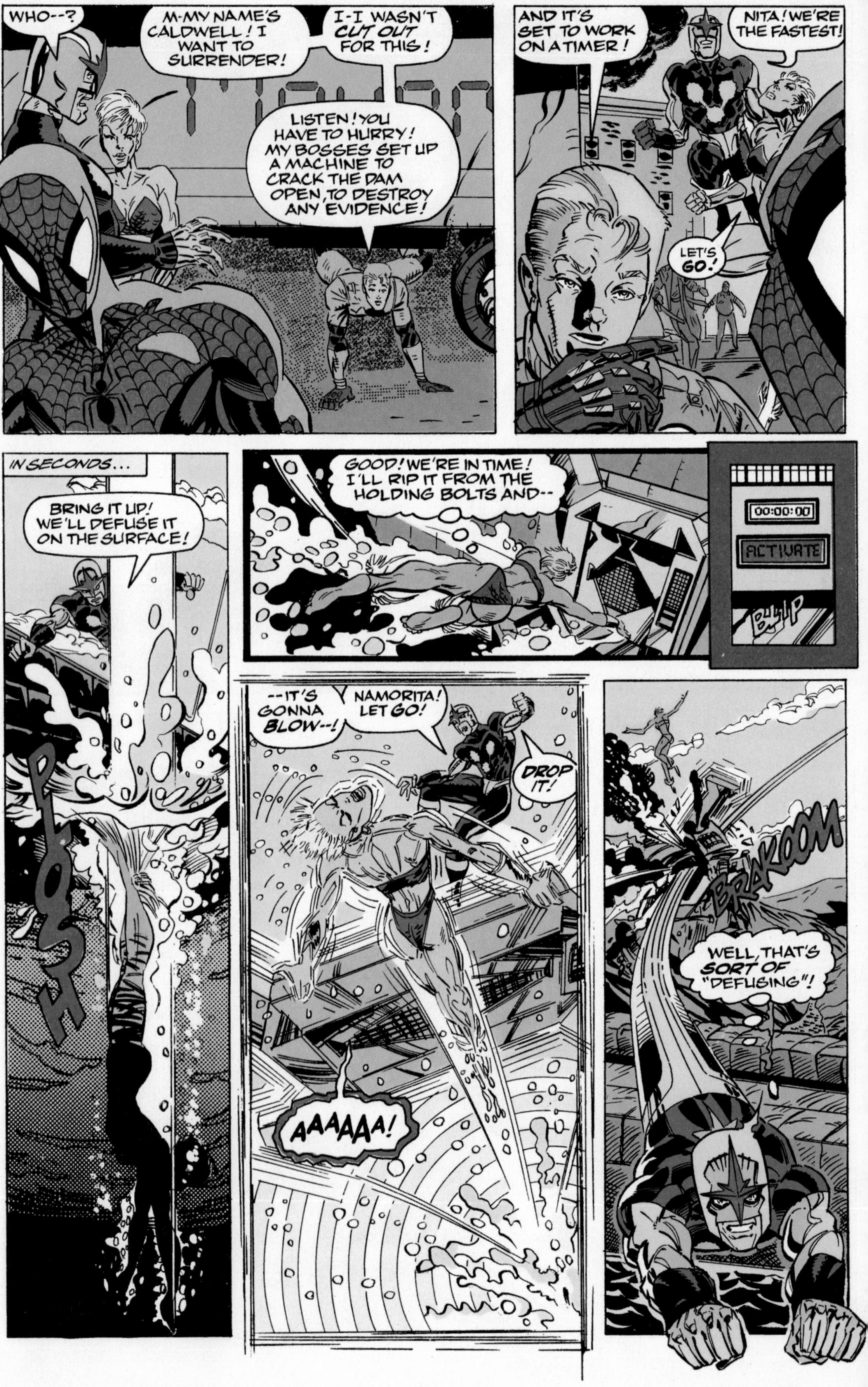
WHO--?
M-MY NAME'S CALDWELL! I WANT TO SURRENDER!
I-I WASN'T CUT OUT FOR THIS!
LISTEN! YOU HAVE TO HURRY! MY BOSSES SET UP A MACHINE TO CRACK THE DAM OPEN, TO DESTROY ANY EVIDENCE!
AND IT'S SET TO WORK ON A TIMER!
NITA! WE'RE THE FASTEST!
LET'S GO!
IN SECONDS...
BRING IT UP! WE'LL DEFUSE IT ON THE SURFACE!
PLOOSH
GOOD! WE'RE IN TIME! I'LL RIP IT FROM THE HOLDING BOLTS AND--
00:00:00
ACTIVATE
BLIP
--IT'S GONNA BLOW--!
NAMORITA! LET GO!
DROP IT!
AAAAAA!
BRAKOOM
WELL, THAT'S SORT OF "DEFUSING"!

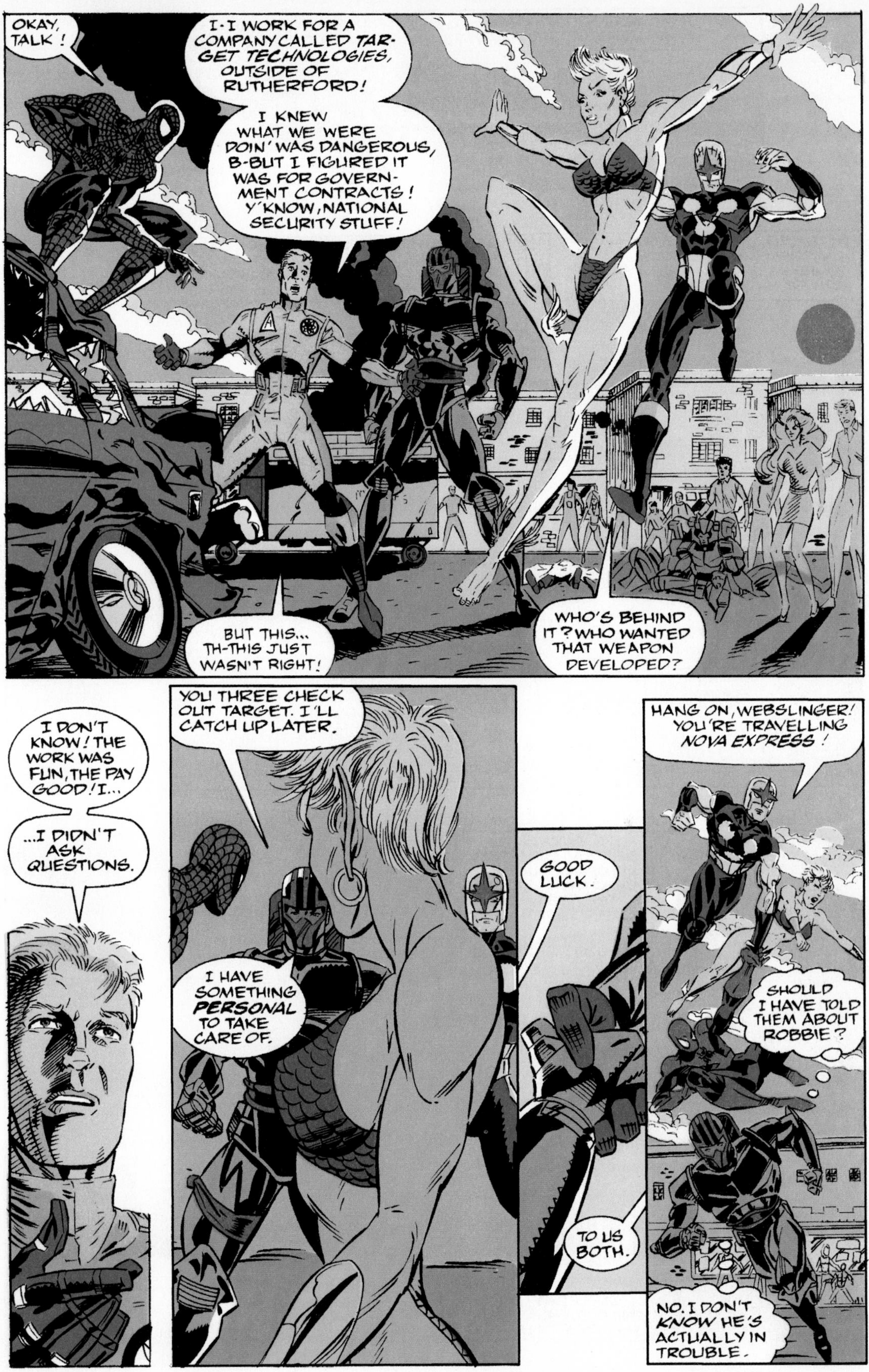
OKAY, TALK!
I-I WORK FOR A COMPANY CALLED TARGET TECHNOLOGIES, OUTSIDE OF RUTHERFORD!
I KNEW WHAT WE WERE DOIN' WAS DANGEROUS, B-BUT I FIGURED IT WAS FOR GOVERNMENT CONTRACTS! Y'KNOW, NATIONAL SECURITY STUFF!
BUT THIS... TH-THIS JUST WASN'T RIGHT!
WHO'S BEHIND IT? WHO WANTED THAT WEAPON DEVELOPED?
I DON'T KNOW! THE WORK WAS FUN, THE PAY GOOD! I...
...I DIDN'T ASK QUESTIONS.
YOU THREE CHECK OUT TARGET. I'LL CATCH UP LATER.
I HAVE SOMETHING PERSONAL TO TAKE CARE OF.
GOOD LUCK.
TO US BOTH.
HANG ON, WEBSLINGER! YOU'RE TRAVELLING NOVA EXPRESS!
SHOULD I HAVE TOLD THEM ABOUT ROBBIE?
NO. I DON'T KNOW HE'S ACTUALLY IN TROUBLE.

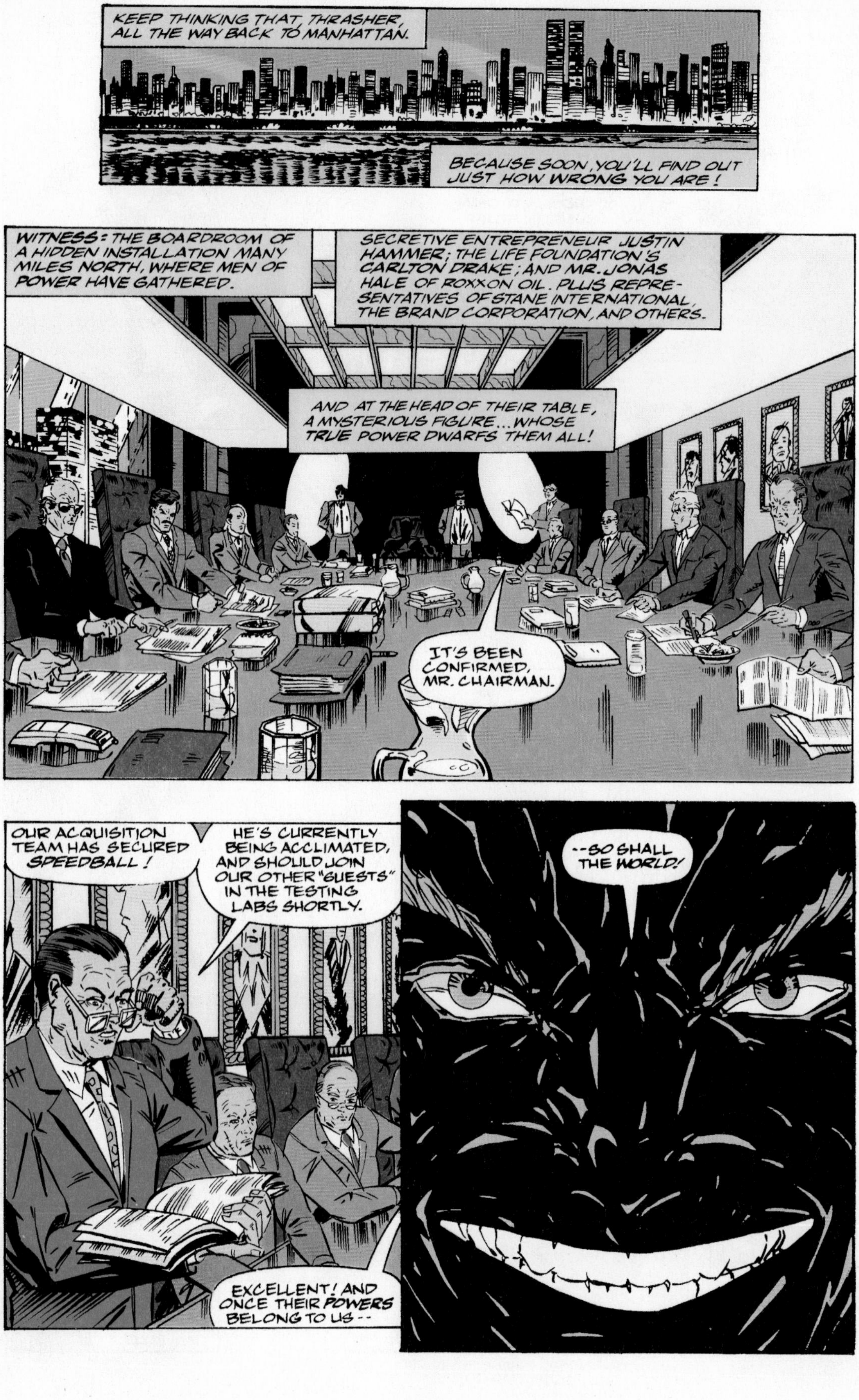

KEEP THINKING THAT, THRASHER, ALL THE WAY BACK TO MANHATTAN.
BECAUSE SOON, YOU'LL FIND OUT JUST HOW WRONG YOU ARE!
WITNESS: THE BOARDROOM OF A HIDDEN INSTALLATION MANY MILES NORTH, WHERE MEN OF POWER HAVE GATHERED.
SECRETIVE ENTREPRENEUR JUSTIN HAMMER; THE LIFE FOUNDATION'S CARLTON DRAKE; AND MR. JONAS HALE OF ROXXON OIL. PLUS REPRESENTATIVES OF STANE INTERNATIONAL, THE BRAND CORPORATION, AND OTHERS.
AND AT THE HEAD OF THEIR TABLE, A MYSTERIOUS FIGURE... WHOSE TRUE POWER DWARFS THEM ALL!
IT'S BEEN CONFIRMED, MR. CHAIRMAN.
OUR ACQUISITION TEAM HAS SECURED SPEEDBALL!
HE'S CURRENTLY BEING ACCLIMATED, AND SHOULD JOIN OUR OTHER "GUESTS" IN THE TESTING LABS SHORTLY.
EXCELLENT! AND ONCE THEIR POWERS BELONG TO US --
--SO SHALL THE WORLD!

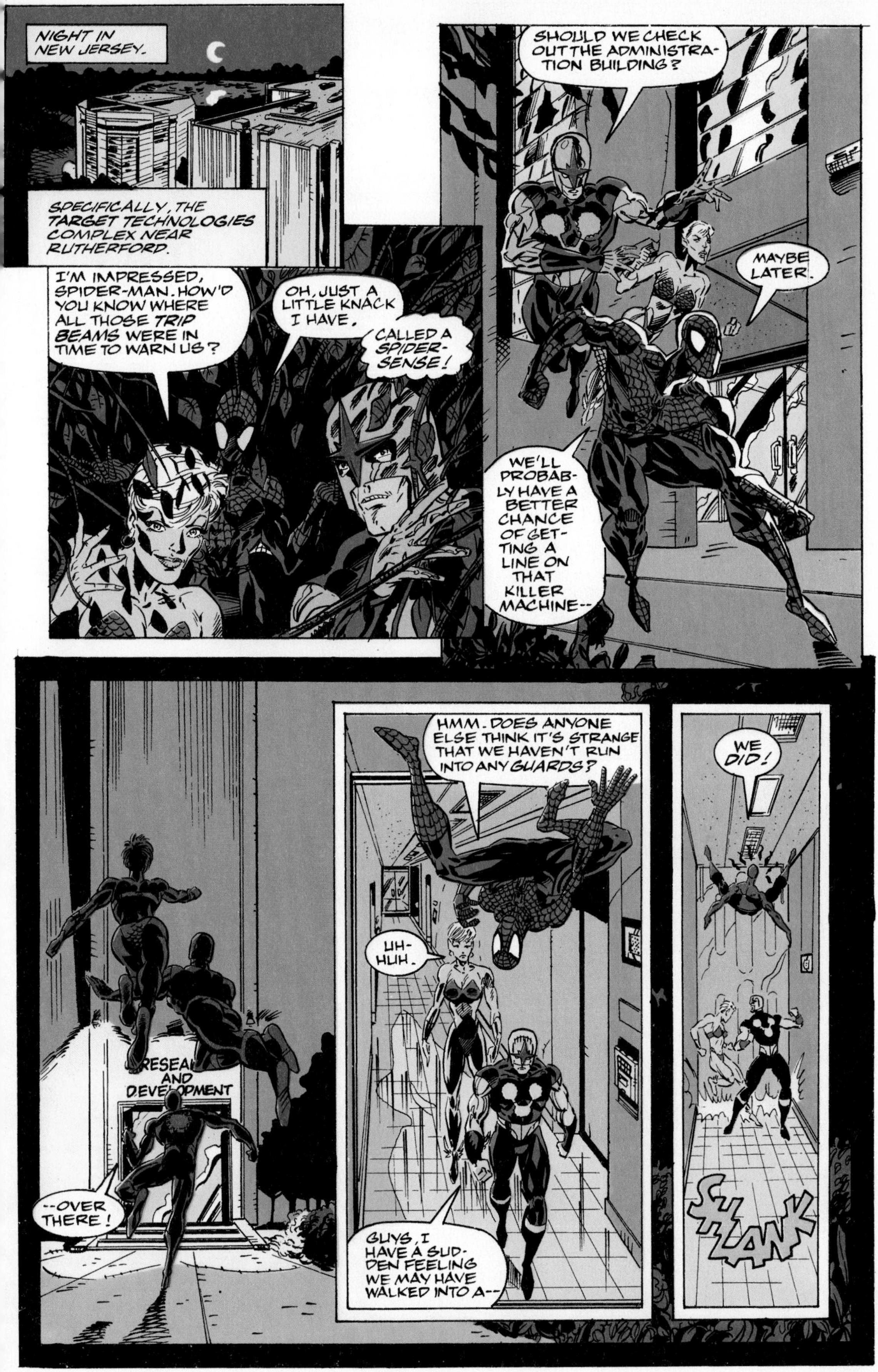
NIGHT IN NEW JERSEY.
SPECIFICALLY, THE TARGET TECHNOLOGIES COMPLEX NEAR RUTHERFORD.
I'M IMPRESSED, SPIDER-MAN. HOW'D YOU KNOW WHERE ALL THOSE TRIP BEAMS WERE IN TIME TO WARN US?
OH, JUST A LITTLE KNACK I HAVE.
CALLED A SPIDER-SENSE!
SHOULD WE CHECK OUT THE ADMINISTRATION BUILDING?
MAYBE LATER.
WE'LL PROBABLY HAVE A BETTER CHANCE OF GETTING A LINE ON THAT KILLER MACHINE--
RESEA AND DEVELOPMENT
--OVER THERE!
HMM. DOES ANYONE ELSE THINK IT'S STRANGE THAT WE HAVEN'T RUN INTO ANY GUARDS?
UH-HUH.
GUYS, I HAVE A SUDDEN FEELING WE MAY HAVE WALKED INTO A--
WE DID!
SHANK

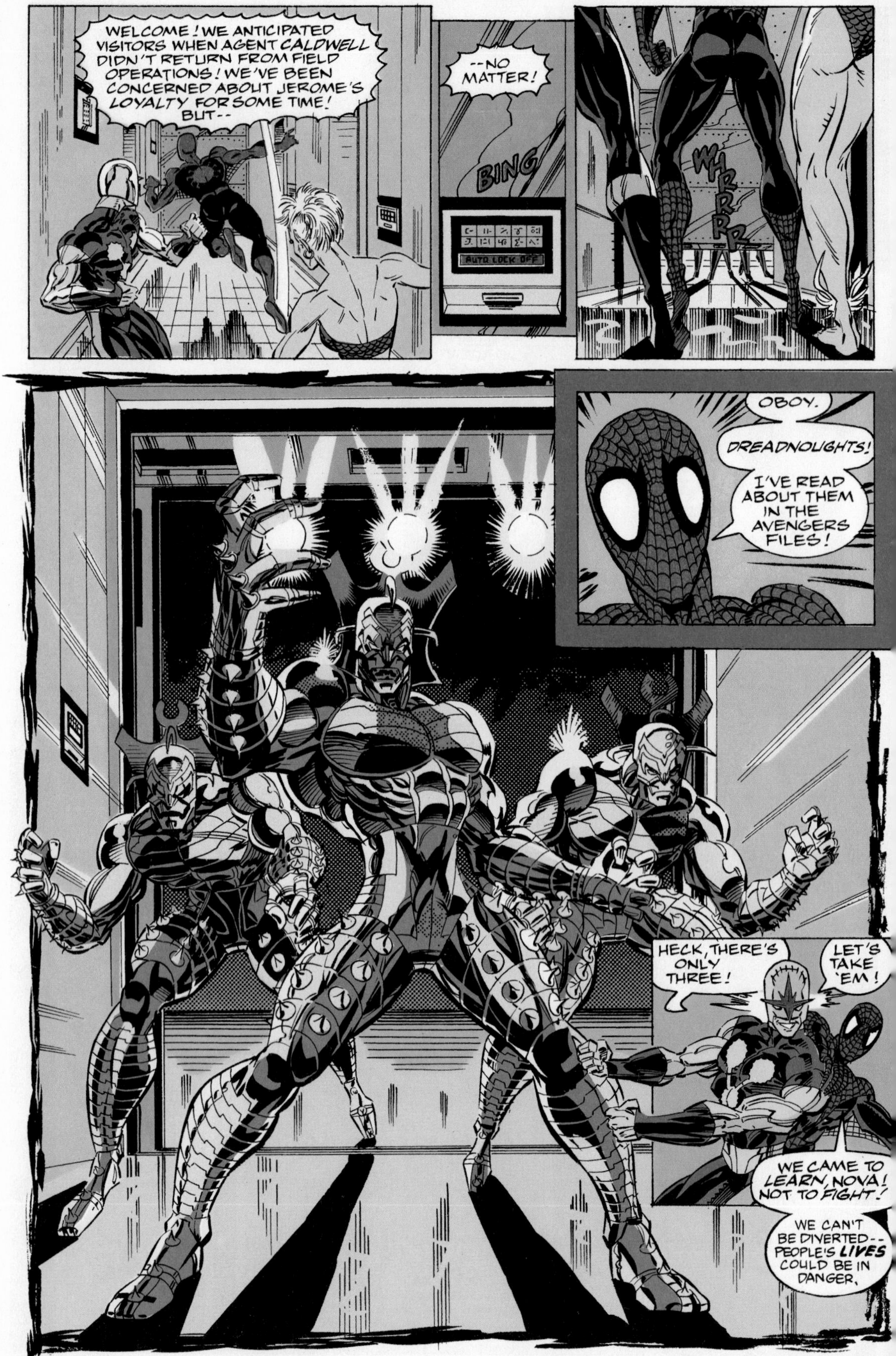
WELCOME! WE ANTICIPATED VISITORS WHEN AGENT CALDWELL DIDN'T RETURN FROM FIELD OPERATIONS! WE'VE BEEN CONCERNED ABOUT JEROME'S LOYALTY FOR SOME TIME! BUT--
--NO MATTER!
BING
AUTO LOCK OFF
WHRRRR
OBOY.
DREADNOUGHTS!
I'VE READ ABOUT THEM IN THE AVENGERS FILES!
HECK, THERE'S ONLY THREE!
LET'S TAKE 'EM!
WE CAME TO LEARN, NOVA! NOT TO FIGHT!
WE CAN'T BE DIVERTED--PEOPLE'S LIVES COULD BE IN DANGER.

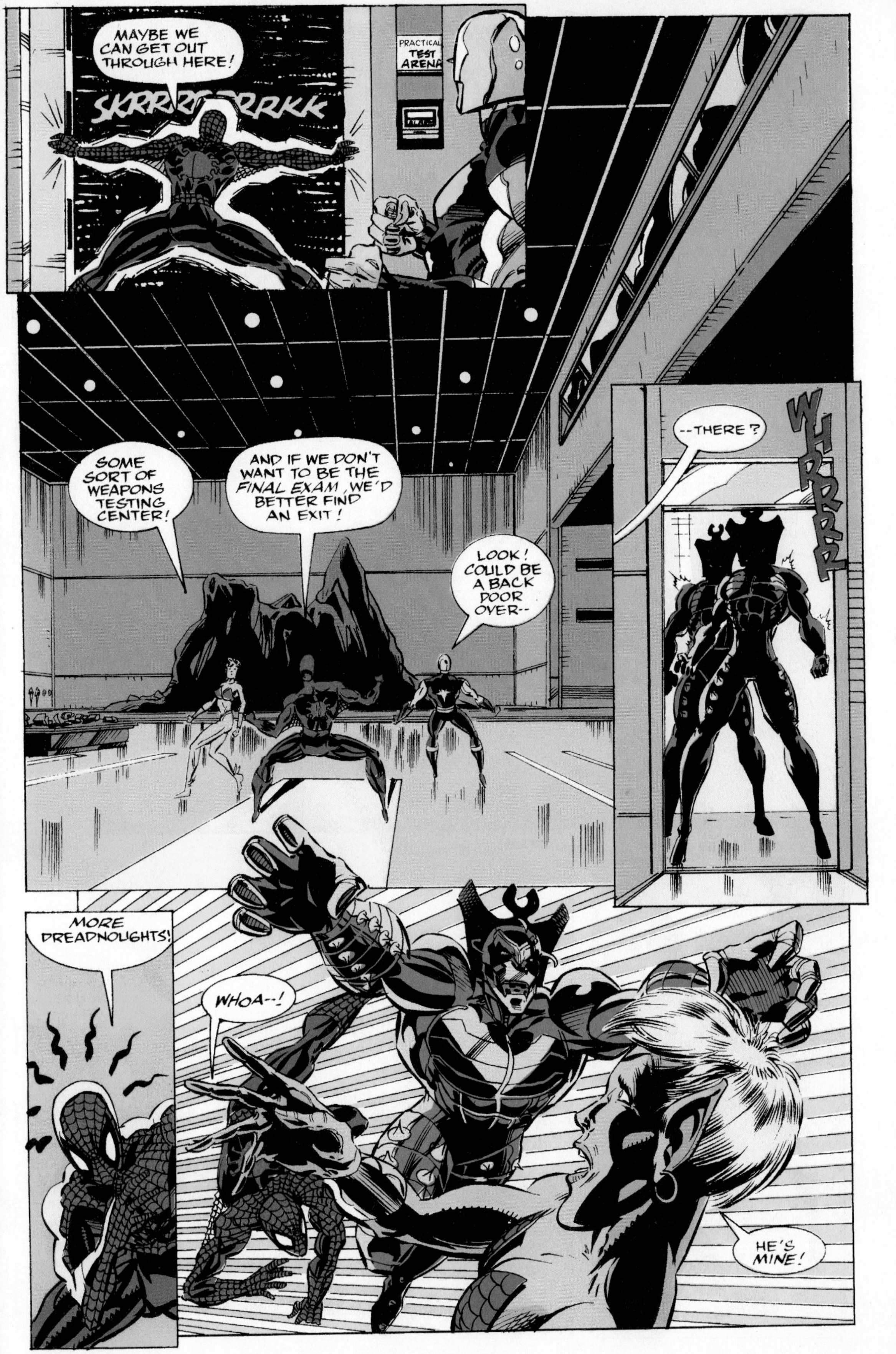
MAYBE WE CAN GET OUT THROUGH HERE!
SKRRRRRRRKK
PRACTICAL TEST ARENA
SOME SORT OF WEAPONS TESTING CENTER!
AND IF WE DON'T WANT TO BE THE FINAL EXAM, WE'D BETTER FIND AN EXIT!
LOOK! COULD BE A BACK DOOR OVER--
--THERE?
WHRRRR
MORE DREADNOUGHTS!
WHOA--!
HE'S MINE!

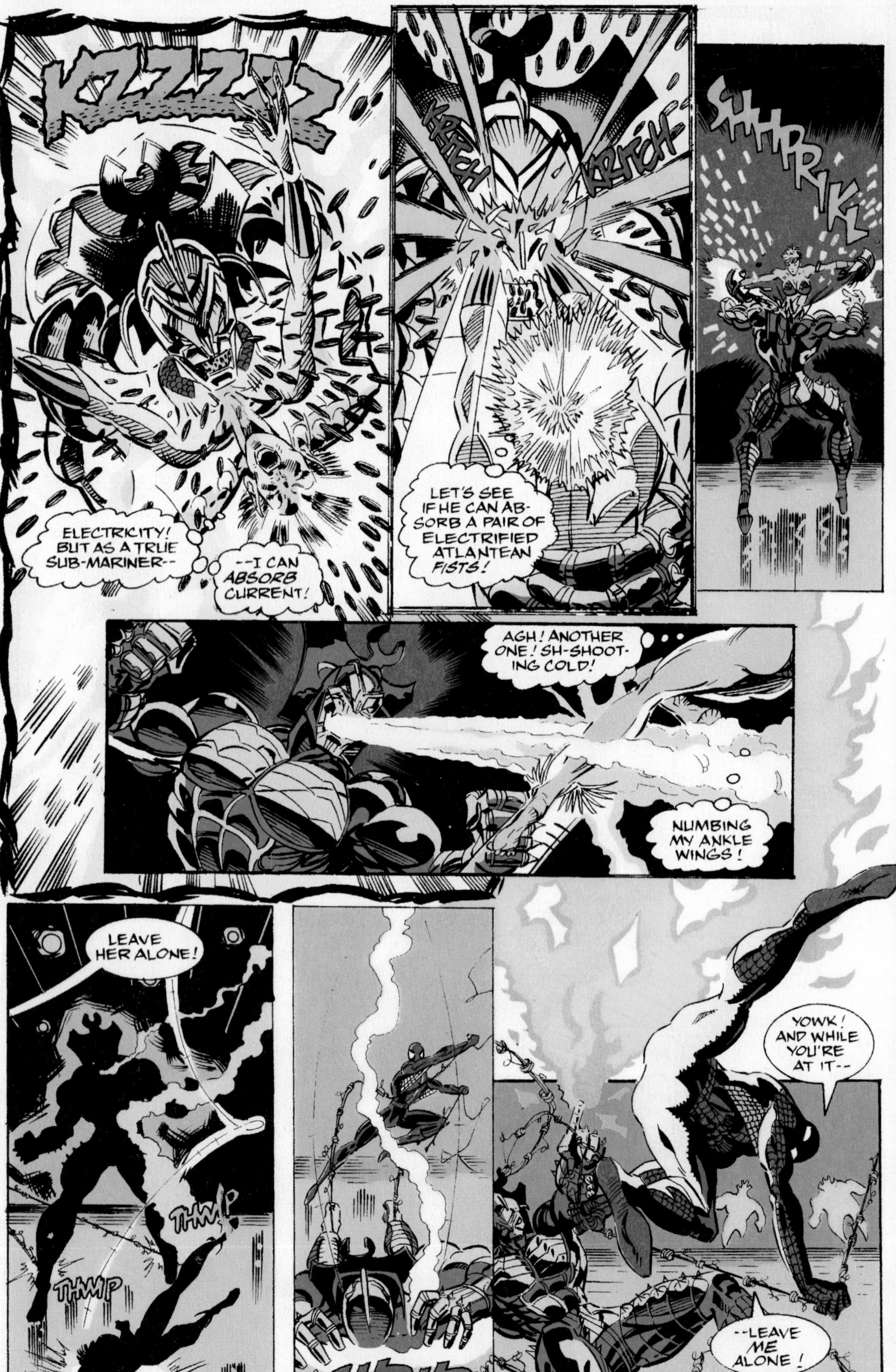
KZZZZZZ
ELECTRICITY! BUT AS A TRUE SUB-MARINER--
--I CAN ABSORB CURRENT!
KRITCH
KRITCH
LET'S SEE IF HE CAN ABSORB A PAIR OF ELECTRIFIED ATLANTEAN FISTS!
SHHPRIKK
AGH! ANOTHER ONE! SH-SHOOTING COLD!
NUMBING MY ANKLE WINGS!
LEAVE HER ALONE!
THWIP
THWIP
CHRUD
YOWK! AND WHILE YOU'RE AT IT--
--LEAVE ME ALONE!

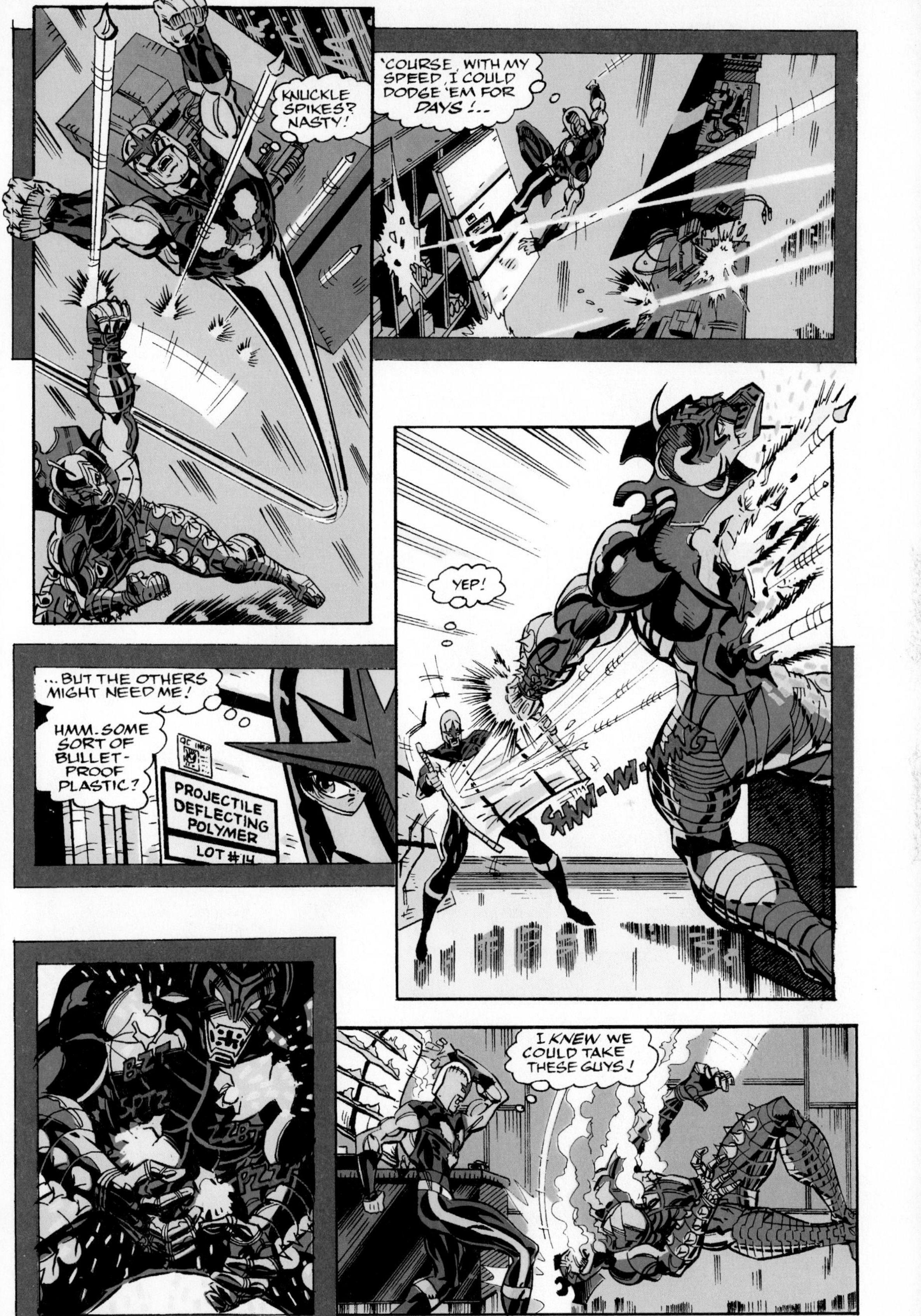
KNUCKLE SPIKES? NASTY!
'COURSE, WITH MY SPEED, I COULD DODGE 'EM FOR DAYS!..
YEP!
...BUT THE OTHERS MIGHT NEED ME!
HMM. SOME SORT OF BULLET-PROOF PLASTIC?
PROJECTILE DEFLECTING POLYMER
LOT #14
SHWI-WI-WING
B-ZZT
SPTZ
ZZZZT
PZZZ
I KNEW WE COULD TAKE THESE GUYS!

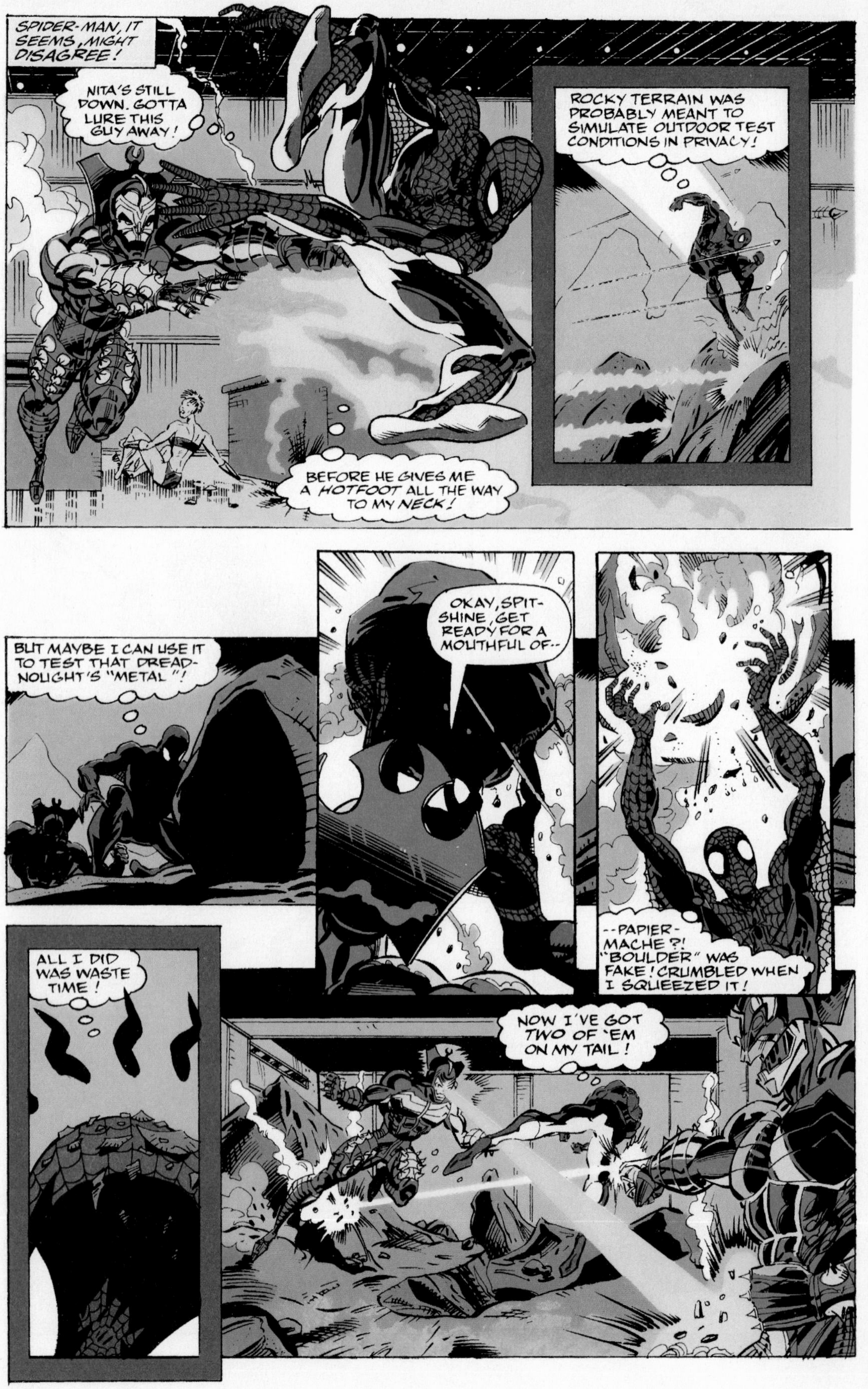
SPIDER-MAN, IT SEEMS, MIGHT DISAGREE!
NITA'S STILL DOWN. GOTTA LURE THIS GUY AWAY!
BEFORE HE GIVES ME A HOTFOOT ALL THE WAY TO MY NECK!
ROCKY TERRAIN WAS PROBABLY MEANT TO SIMULATE OUTDOOR TEST CONDITIONS IN PRIVACY!
BUT MAYBE I CAN USE IT TO TEST THAT DREAD-NOUGHT'S "METAL"!
OKAY, SPIT-SHINE, GET READY FOR A MOUTHFUL OF--
--PAPIER-MACHE?! "BOULDER" WAS FAKE! CRUMBLED WHEN I SQUEEZED IT!
ALL I DID WAS WASTE TIME!
NOW I'VE GOT TWO OF 'EM ON MY TAIL!

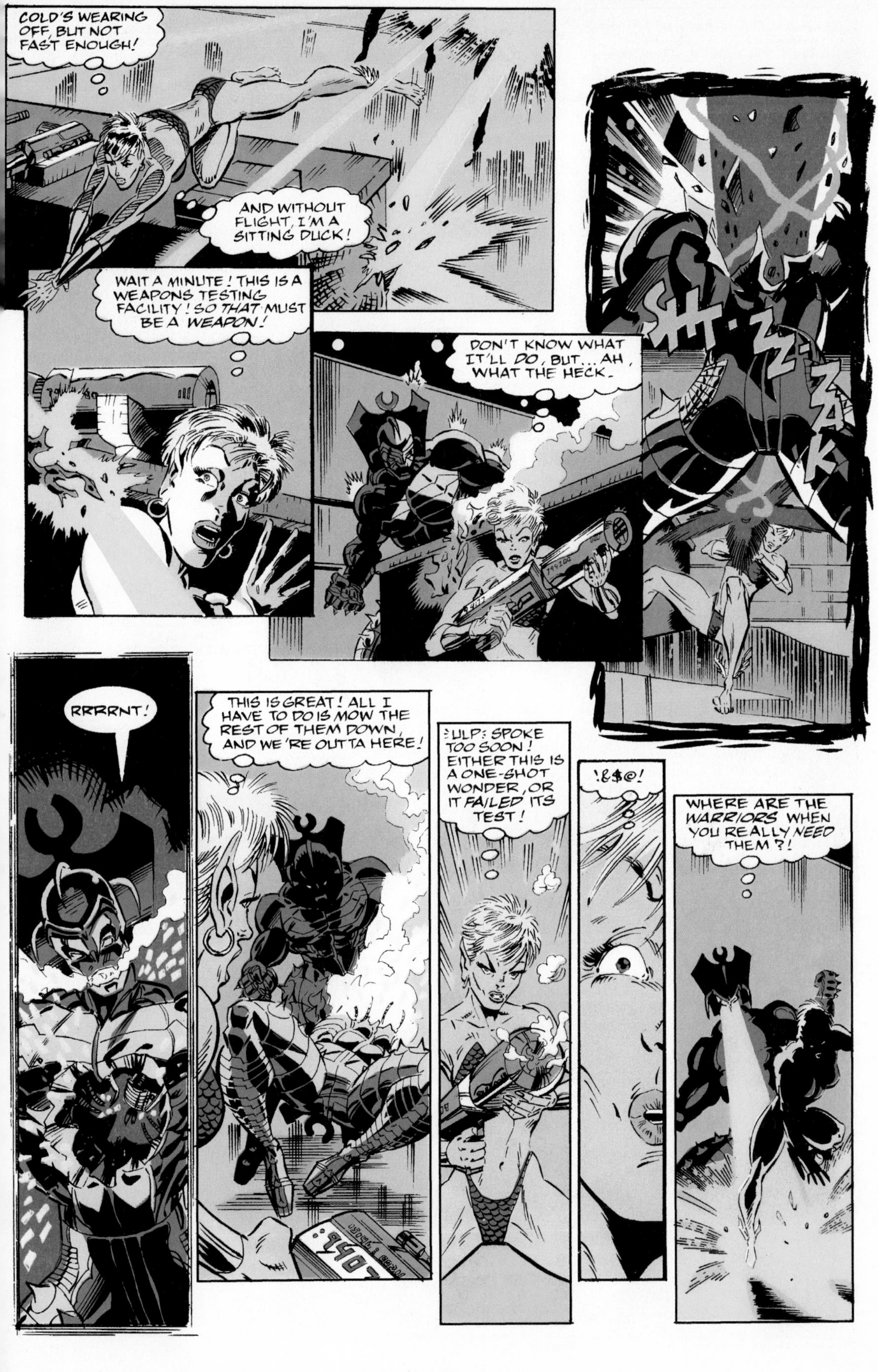
COLD'S WEARING OFF, BUT NOT FAST ENOUGH!
AND WITHOUT FLIGHT, I'M A SITTING DUCK!
WAIT A MINUTE! THIS IS A WEAPONS TESTING FACILITY! SO THAT MUST BE A WEAPON!
DON'T KNOW WHAT IT'LL DO, BUT... AH, WHAT THE HECK.
SHH-ZZ-ZAK
RRRRNT!
THIS IS GREAT! ALL I HAVE TO DO IS MOW THE REST OF THEM DOWN, AND WE'RE OUTTA HERE!
ULP: SPOKE TOO SOON! EITHER THIS IS A ONE-SHOT WONDER, OR IT FAILED ITS TEST!
!&$@!
WHERE ARE THE WARRIORS WHEN YOU REALLY NEED THEM?!

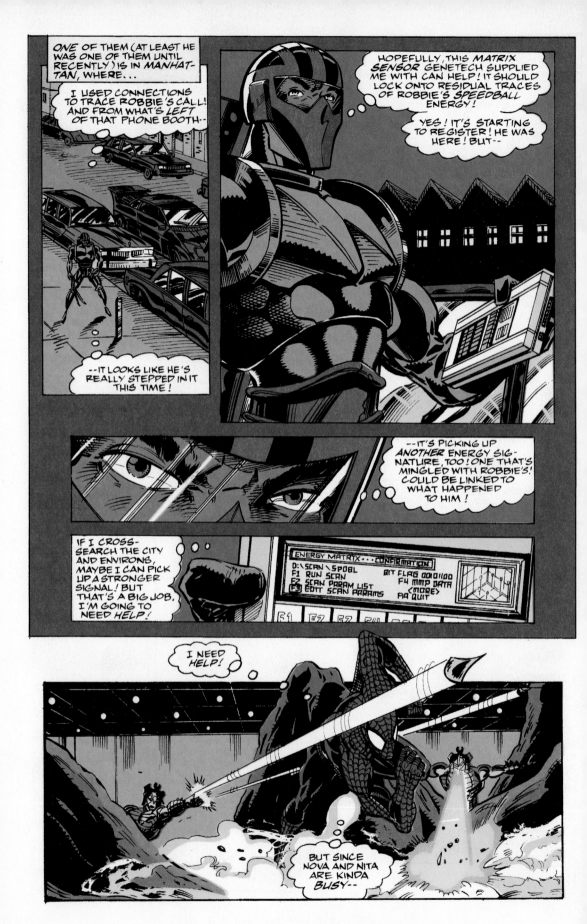

ONE OF THEM (AT LEAST HE WAS ONE OF THEM UNTIL RECENTLY) IS IN MANHATTAN, WHERE...

I USED CONNECTIONS TO TRACE ROBBIE'S CALL! AND FROM WHAT'S *LEFT* OF THAT PHONE BOOTH--

--IT LOOKS LIKE HE'S REALLY STEPPED IN IT THIS TIME!

HOPEFULLY, THIS *MATRIX SENSOR* GENETECH SUPPLIED ME WITH CAN HELP! IT SHOULD LOCK ONTO RESIDUAL TRACES OF ROBBIE'S *SPEEDBALL* ENERGY!

YES! IT'S STARTING TO REGISTER! HE WAS HERE! BUT--

--IT'S PICKING UP *ANOTHER* ENERGY SIGNATURE, TOO! ONE THAT'S MINGLED WITH ROBBIE'S! COULD BE LINKED TO WHAT HAPPENED TO HIM!

IF I CROSS-SEARCH THE CITY AND ENVIRONS, MAYBE I CAN PICK UP A STRONGER SIGNAL! BUT THAT'S A BIG JOB, I'M GOING TO NEED *HELP*!

ENERGY MATRIX...CONFIRMATION

D:\SCAN \ SPOBL   BIT FLAG 00101100
F1 RUN SCAN   F4 MMP DATA
F2 SCAN PARAM LIST   <MORE>
F3 EDIT SCAN PARAMS   F10 QUIT

I NEED HELP!

BUT SINCE NOVA AND NITA ARE KINDA *BUSY*--

30

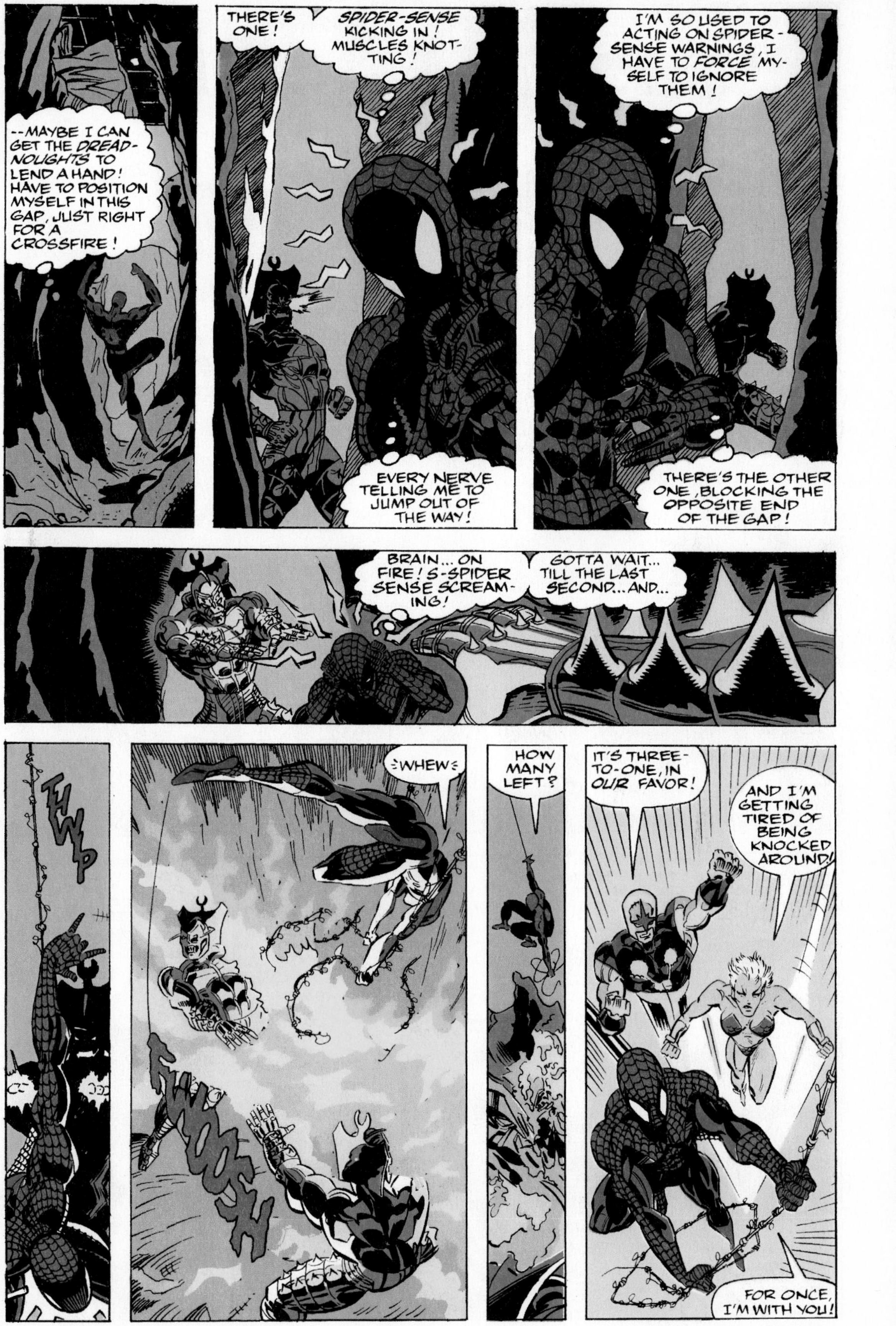
--MAYBE I CAN GET THE DREAD-NOUGHTS TO LEND A HAND! HAVE TO POSITION MYSELF IN THIS GAP, JUST RIGHT FOR A CROSSFIRE!
THERE'S ONE!
SPIDER-SENSE KICKING IN! MUSCLES KNOTTING!
EVERY NERVE TELLING ME TO JUMP OUT OF THE WAY!
I'M SO USED TO ACTING ON SPIDER-SENSE WARNINGS, I HAVE TO FORCE MYSELF TO IGNORE THEM!
THERE'S THE OTHER ONE, BLOCKING THE OPPOSITE END OF THE GAP!
BRAIN... ON FIRE! S-SPIDER SENSE SCREAMING!
GOTTA WAIT... TILL THE LAST SECOND... AND...
THWP
WHEW
FWOOSH
HOW MANY LEFT?
IT'S THREE-TO-ONE, IN OUR FAVOR!
AND I'M GETTING TIRED OF BEING KNOCKED AROUND!
FOR ONCE, I'M WITH YOU!

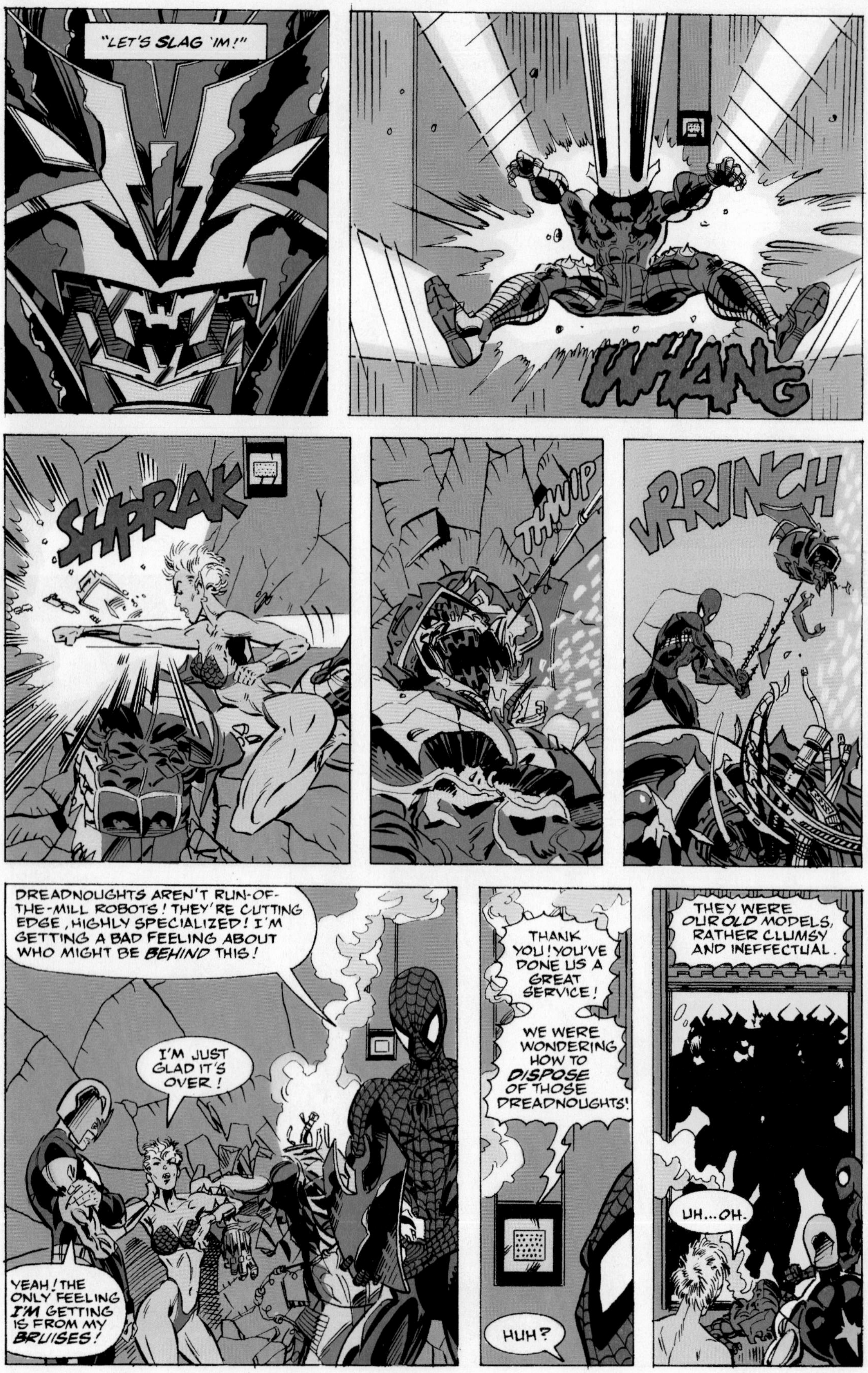
"LET'S SLAG 'IM!"
WHANG
SHPRAK
THWIP
VRRINCH
DREADNOUGHTS AREN'T RUN-OF-THE-MILL ROBOTS! THEY'RE CUTTING EDGE, HIGHLY SPECIALIZED! I'M GETTING A BAD FEELING ABOUT WHO MIGHT BE BEHIND THIS!
I'M JUST GLAD IT'S OVER!
YEAH! THE ONLY FEELING I'M GETTING IS FROM MY BRUISES!
THANK YOU! YOU'VE DONE US A GREAT SERVICE!
WE WERE WONDERING HOW TO DISPOSE OF THOSE DREADNOUGHTS!
HUH?
THEY WERE OUR OLD MODELS, RATHER CLUMSY AND INEFFECTUAL.
UH...OH.

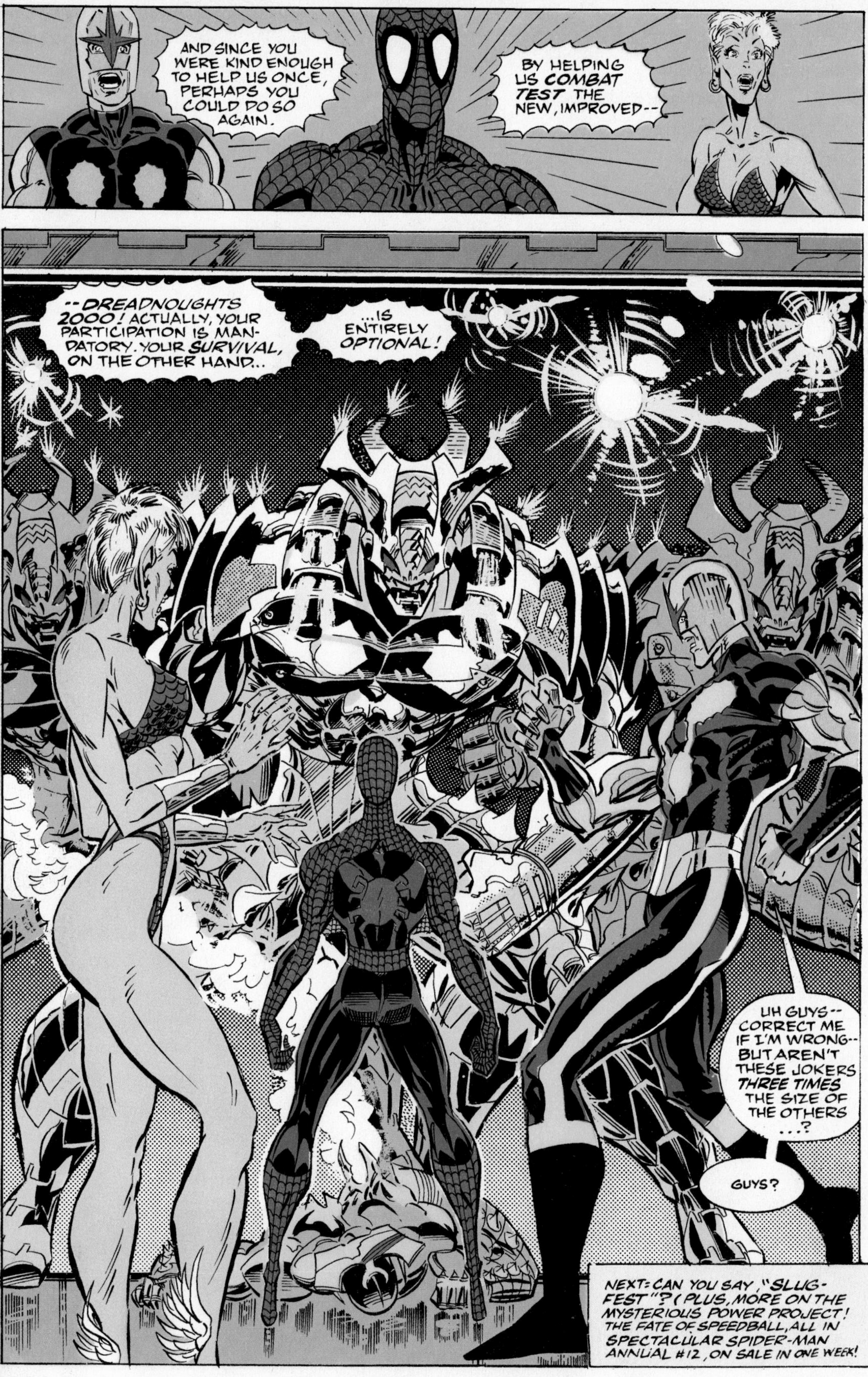
AND SINCE YOU WERE KIND ENOUGH TO HELP US ONCE, PERHAPS YOU COULD DO SO AGAIN.
BY HELPING US COMBAT TEST THE NEW, IMPROVED--
--DREADNOUGHTS 2000! ACTUALLY, YOUR PARTICIPATION IS MANDATORY. YOUR SURVIVAL, ON THE OTHER HAND...
...IS ENTIRELY OPTIONAL!
UH GUYS--CORRECT ME IF I'M WRONG--BUT AREN'T THESE JOKERS THREE TIMES THE SIZE OF THE OTHERS...?
GUYS?
NEXT: CAN YOU SAY, "SLUG-FEST"? (PLUS, MORE ON THE MYSTERIOUS POWER PROJECT! THE FATE OF SPEEDBALL, ALL IN SPECTACULAR SPIDER-MAN ANNUAL #12, ON SALE IN ONE WEEK!

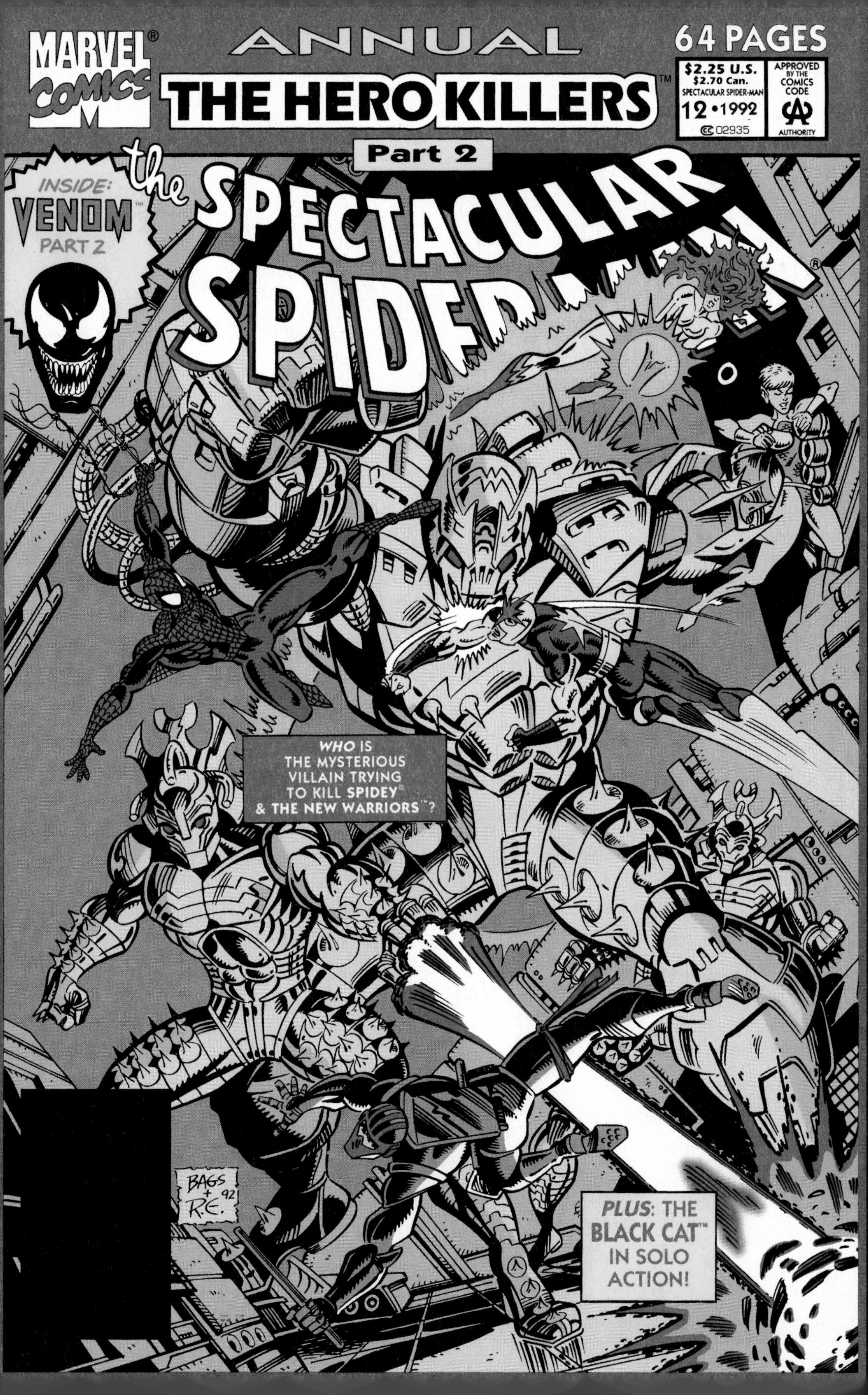
MARVEL® COMICS
ANNUAL
64 PAGES
$2.25 U.S.
$2.70 Can.
SPECTACULAR SPIDER-MAN
12 • 1992
02935
APPROVED BY THE COMICS CODE AUTHORITY
THE HERO KILLERS™
Part 2
INSIDE: VENOM™ PART 2
the SPECTACULAR SPIDER-MAN®
WHO IS THE MYSTERIOUS VILLAIN TRYING TO KILL SPIDEY® & THE NEW WARRIORS™?
BAGS + R.E. '92
PLUS: THE BLACK CAT™ IN SOLO ACTION!

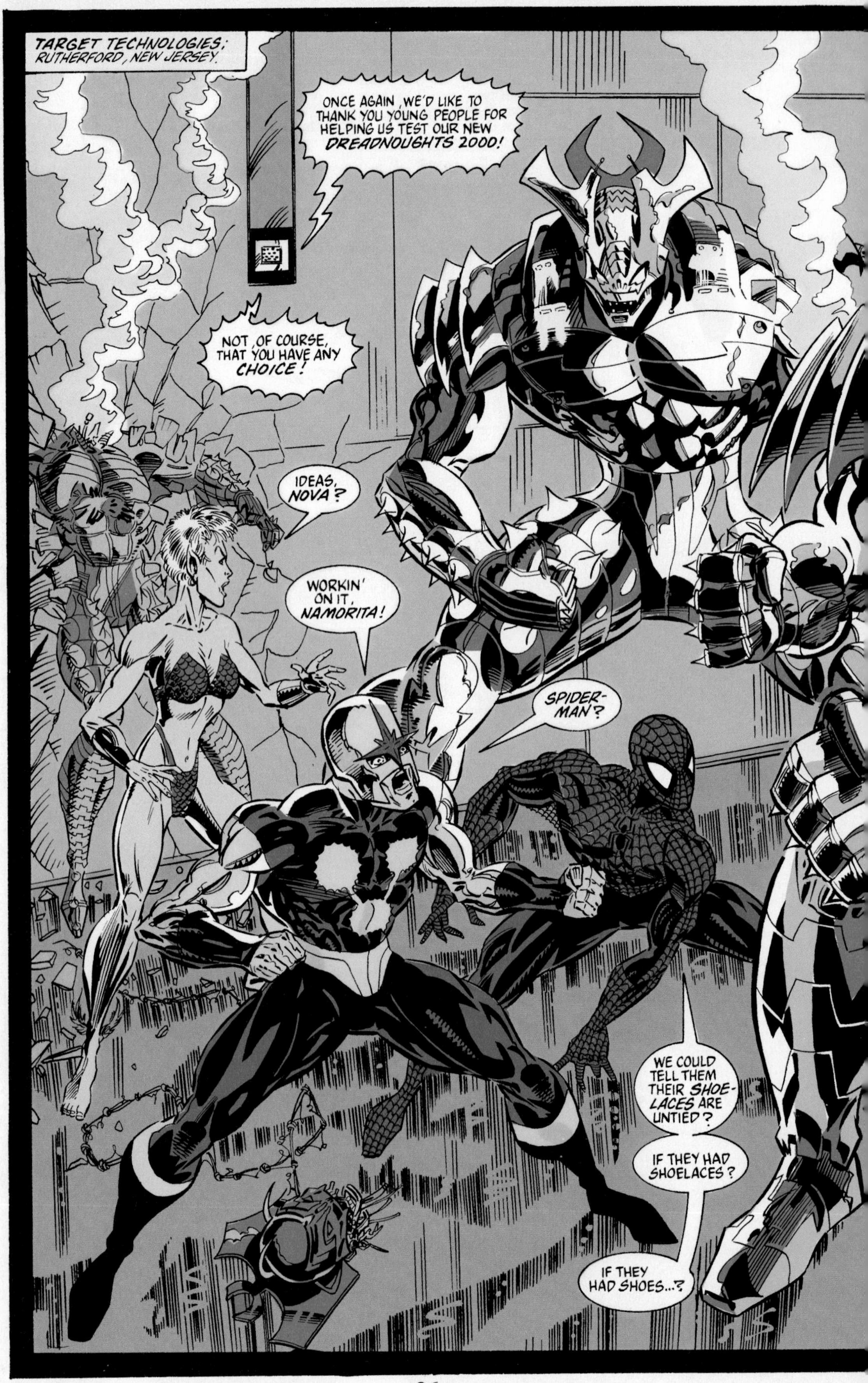
TARGET TECHNOLOGIES:
RUTHERFORD, NEW JERSEY.
ONCE AGAIN, WE'D LIKE TO THANK YOU YOUNG PEOPLE FOR HELPING US TEST OUR NEW DREADNOUGHTS 2000!
NOT, OF COURSE, THAT YOU HAVE ANY CHOICE!
IDEAS, NOVA?
WORKIN' ON IT, NAMORITA!
SPIDER-MAN?
WE COULD TELL THEM THEIR SHOE-LACES ARE UNTIED?
IF THEY HAD SHOELACES?
IF THEY HAD SHOES...?

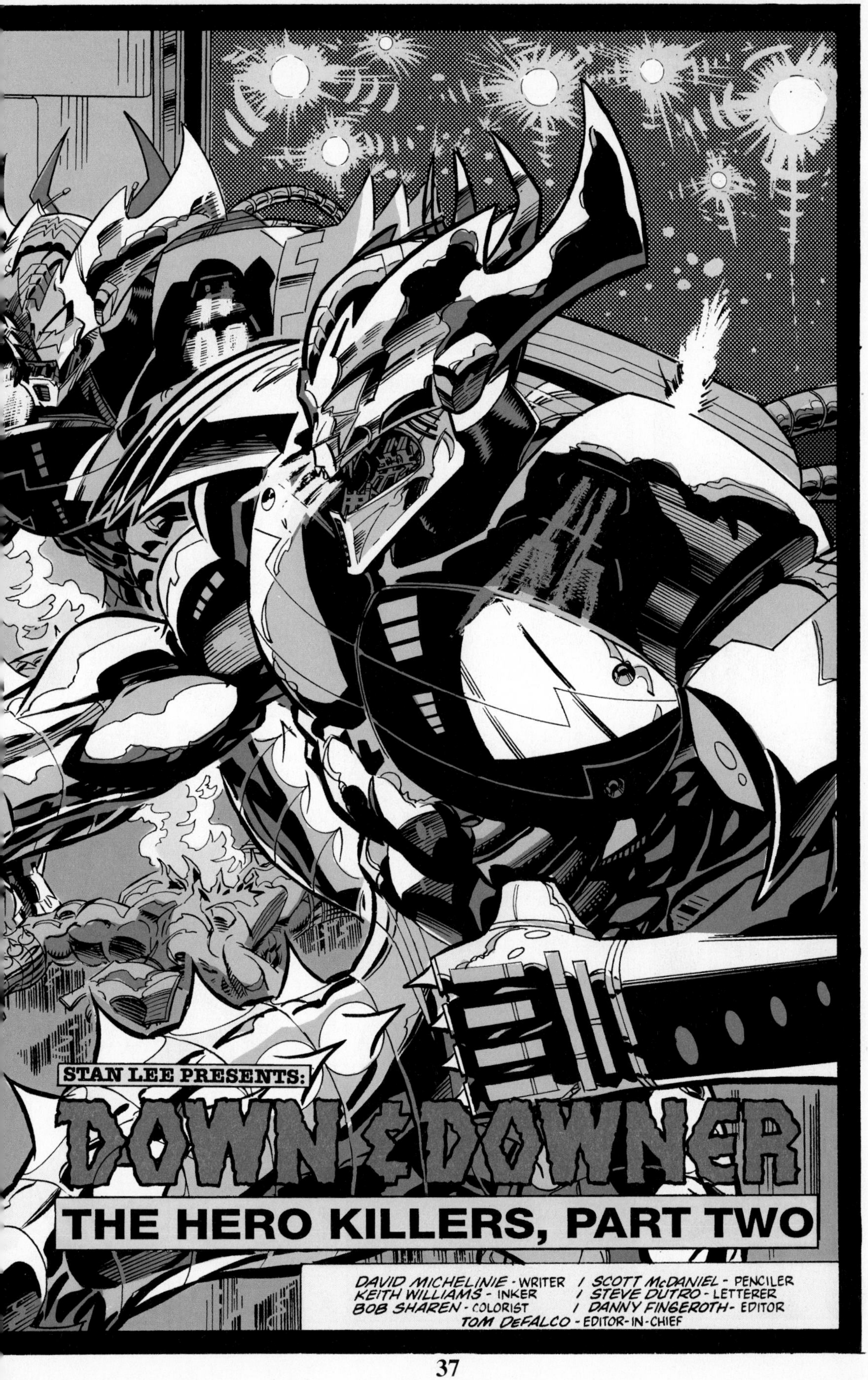
STAN LEE PRESENTS:
DOWN & DOWNER
THE HERO KILLERS, PART TWO
DAVID MICHELINIE - WRITER / SCOTT McDANIEL - PENCILER
KEITH WILLIAMS - INKER / STEVE DUTRO - LETTERER
BOB SHAREN - COLORIST / DANNY FINGEROTH - EDITOR
TOM DeFALCO - EDITOR-IN-CHIEF

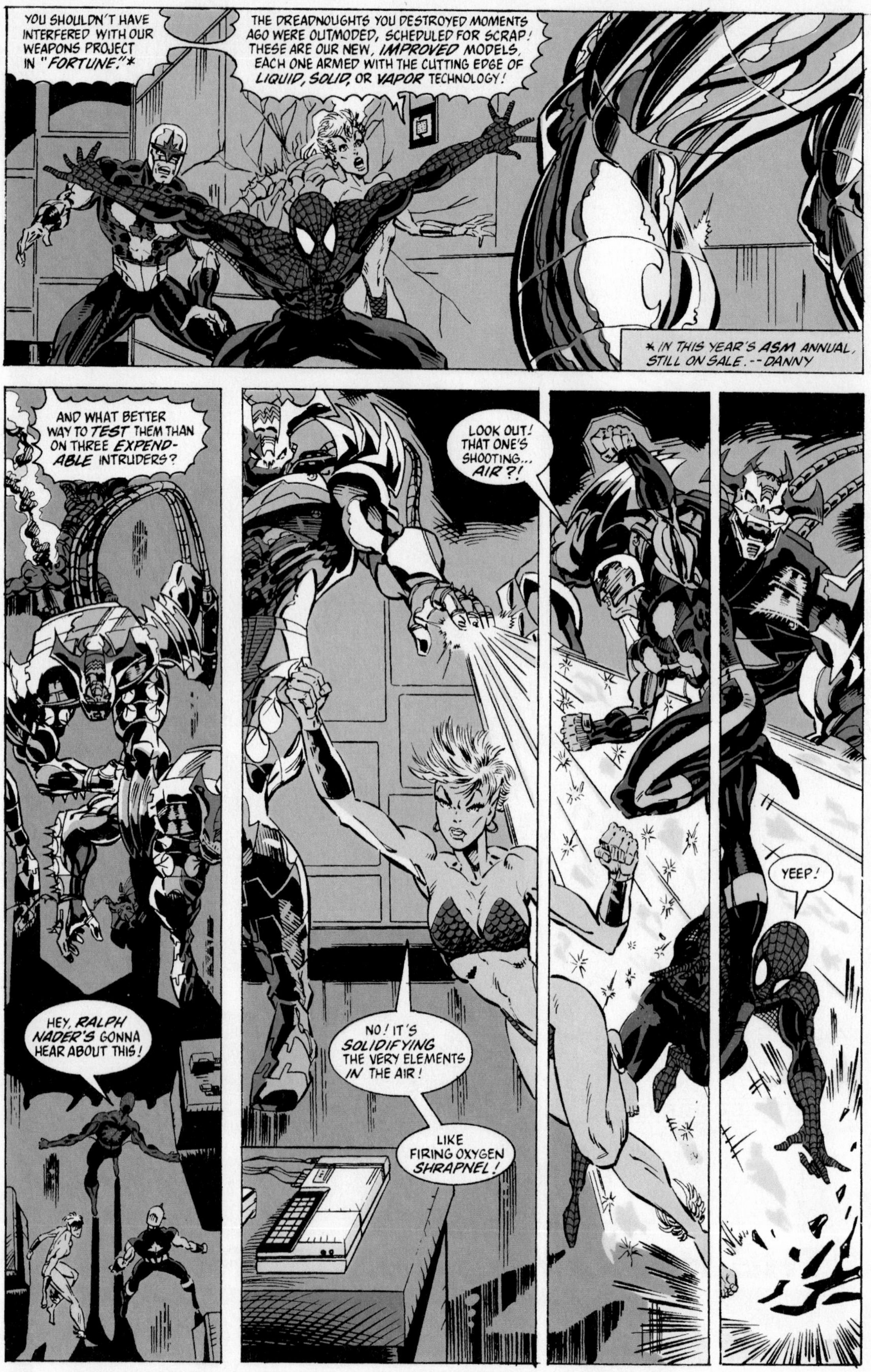

YOU SHOULDN'T HAVE INTERFERED WITH OUR WEAPONS PROJECT IN "FORTUNE."*
THE DREADNOUGHTS YOU DESTROYED MOMENTS AGO WERE OUTMODED, SCHEDULED FOR SCRAP! THESE ARE OUR NEW, IMPROVED MODELS, EACH ONE ARMED WITH THE CUTTING EDGE OF LIQUID, SOLID, OR VAPOR TECHNOLOGY!
* IN THIS YEAR'S ASM ANNUAL, STILL ON SALE. -- DANNY
AND WHAT BETTER WAY TO TEST THEM THAN ON THREE EXPEND-ABLE INTRUDERS?
HEY, RALPH NADER'S GONNA HEAR ABOUT THIS!
LOOK OUT! THAT ONE'S SHOOTING... AIR?!
NO! IT'S SOLIDIFYING THE VERY ELEMENTS IN THE AIR!
LIKE FIRING OXYGEN SHRAPNEL!
YEEP!

?!

SHOOTING HIS BEAM AT MY WEBLINE!

"--BRITTLE?"

SNAP

"TURNING IT SOLID! AND--"

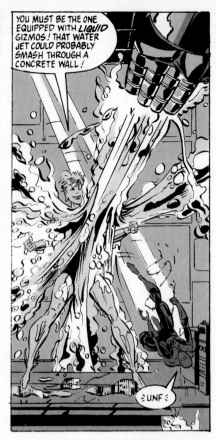

YOU MUST BE THE ONE EQUIPPED WITH *LIQUID* GIZMOS! THAT WATER JET COULD PROBABLY SMASH THROUGH A CONCRETE WALL!

≶UNF≷

NOT GOOD ENOUGH.

I'M A SUB-MARINER!

DIFFERENT BEAM?

L-LIQUEFYING THE STEEL TABLE!

BACK OFF!

THRAK

39

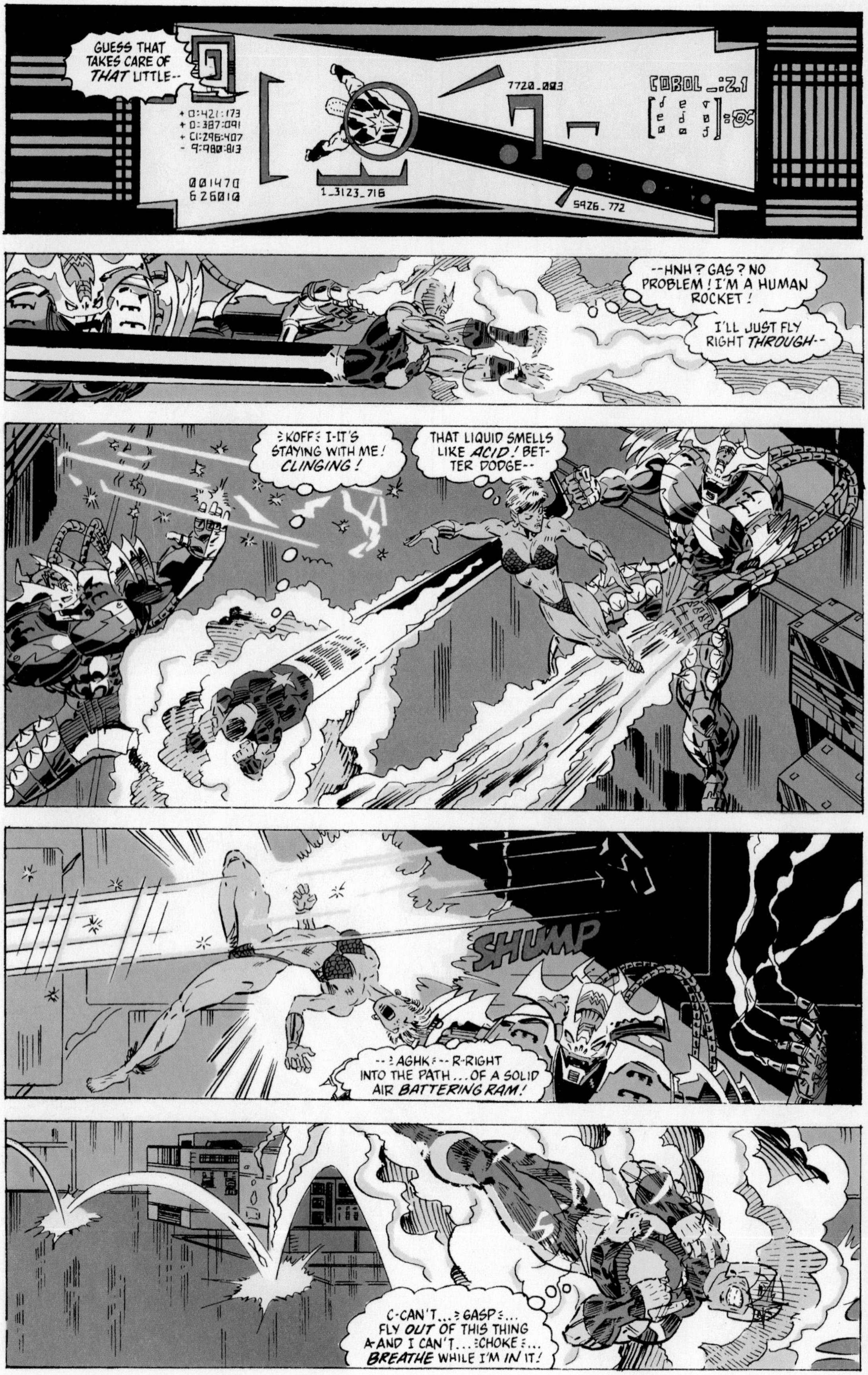
GUESS THAT TAKES CARE OF *THAT* LITTLE--
7720_003
COBOL _:2.1
001470
626010
1_3123_716
5926_772
--HNH? GAS? NO PROBLEM! I'M A HUMAN ROCKET!
I'LL JUST FLY RIGHT *THROUGH*--
≈KOFF≈ I-IT'S STAYING WITH ME! *CLINGING!*
THAT LIQUID SMELLS LIKE *ACID!* BETTER DODGE--
SHUMP
--≈AGHK≈--R-RIGHT INTO THE PATH...OF A SOLID AIR *BATTERING RAM!*
C-CAN'T...≈GASP≈... FLY *OUT* OF THIS THING A-AND I CAN'T...≈CHOKE≈... *BREATHE* WHILE I'M *IN* IT!

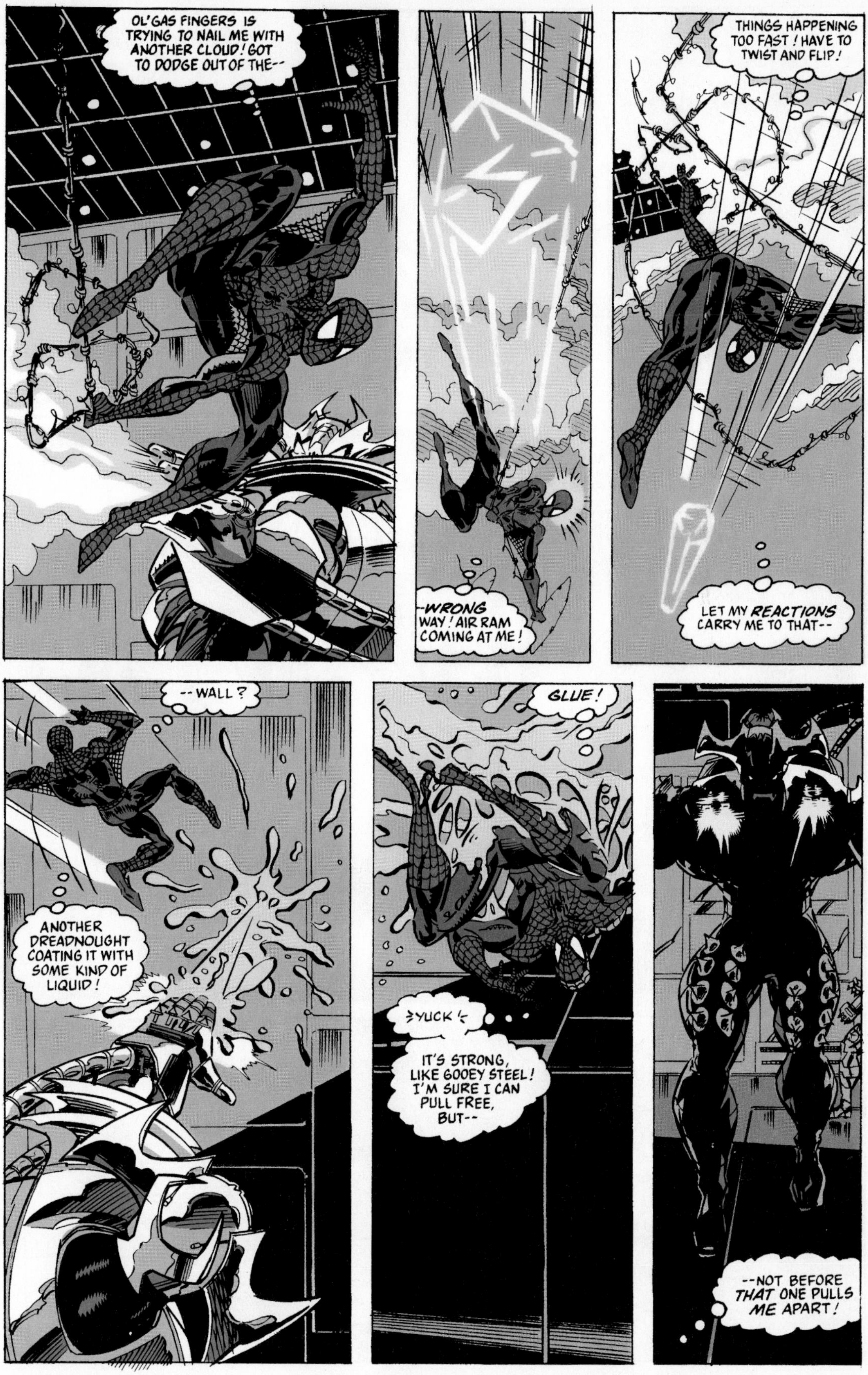
OL' GAS FINGERS IS TRYING TO NAIL ME WITH ANOTHER CLOUD! GOT TO DODGE OUT OF THE--
--WRONG WAY! AIR RAM COMING AT ME!
THINGS HAPPENING TOO FAST! HAVE TO TWIST AND FLIP!
LET MY REACTIONS CARRY ME TO THAT--
--WALL?
ANOTHER DREADNOUGHT COATING IT WITH SOME KIND OF LIQUID!
GLUE!
YUCK
IT'S STRONG, LIKE GOOEY STEEL! I'M SURE I CAN PULL FREE, BUT--
--NOT BEFORE THAT ONE PULLS ME APART!

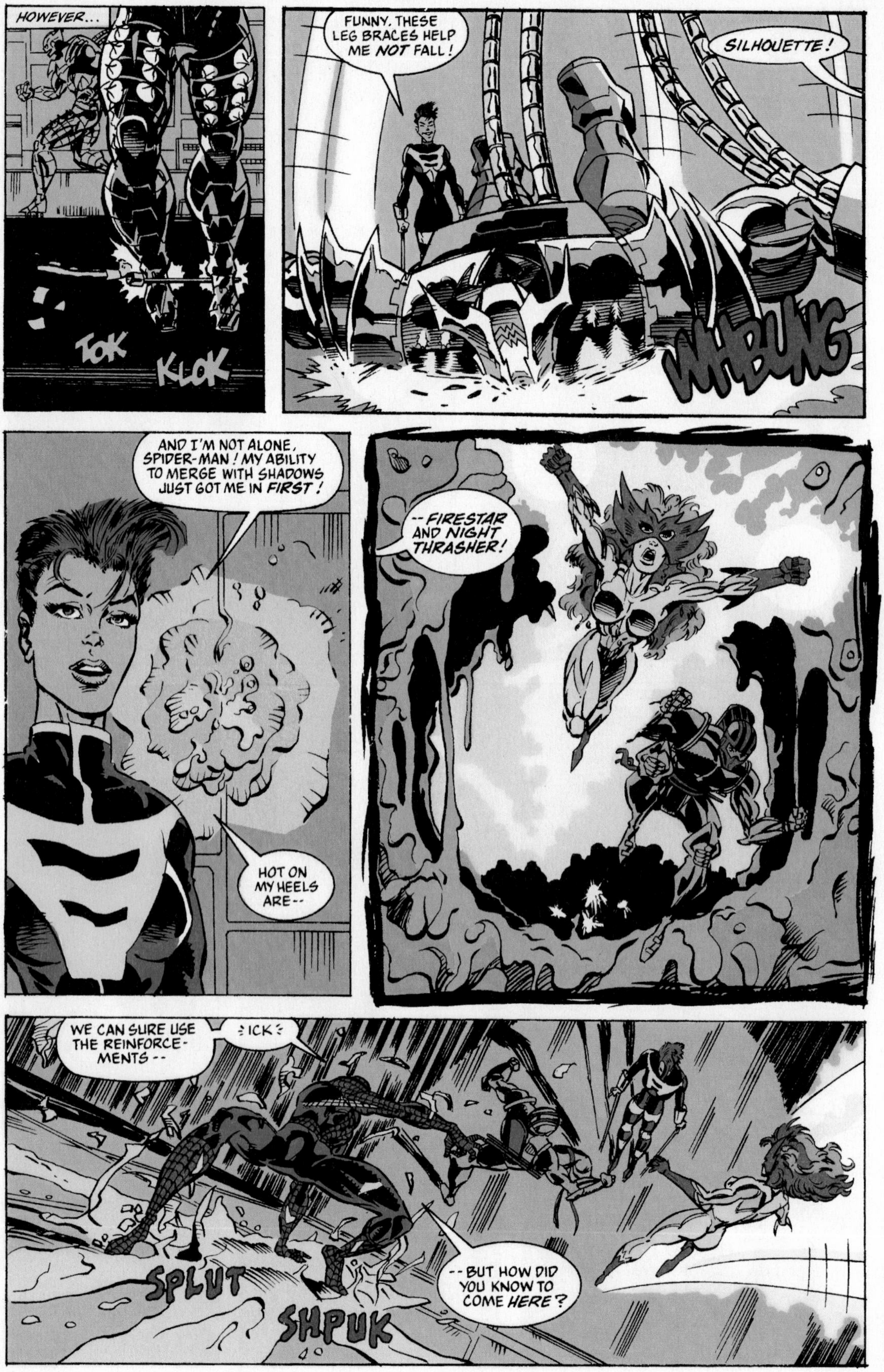
HOWEVER...
TOK
KLOK
FUNNY. THESE LEG BRACES HELP ME NOT FALL!
SILHOUETTE!
WHBUNG
AND I'M NOT ALONE, SPIDER-MAN! MY ABILITY TO MERGE WITH SHADOWS JUST GOT ME IN FIRST!
HOT ON MY HEELS ARE--
--FIRESTAR AND NIGHT THRASHER!
WE CAN SURE USE THE REINFORCE-MENTS--
ICK
--BUT HOW DID YOU KNOW TO COME HERE?
SPLUT
SHPUK

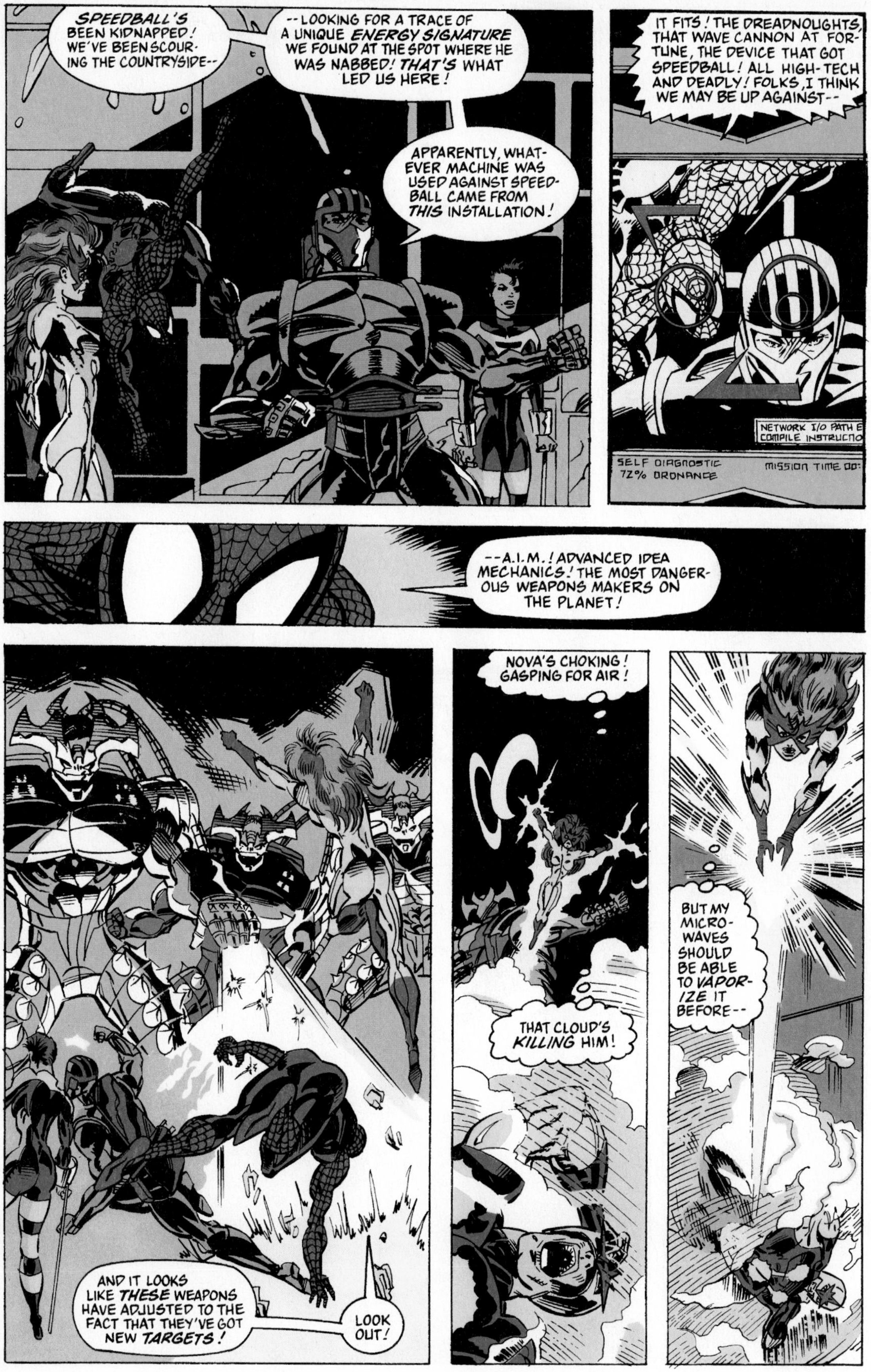

SPEEDBALL'S BEEN KIDNAPPED! WE'VE BEEN SCOURING THE COUNTRYSIDE--
--LOOKING FOR A TRACE OF A UNIQUE ENERGY SIGNATURE WE FOUND AT THE SPOT WHERE HE WAS NABBED! THAT'S WHAT LED US HERE!
APPARENTLY, WHATEVER MACHINE WAS USED AGAINST SPEEDBALL CAME FROM THIS INSTALLATION!
IT FITS! THE DREADNOUGHTS, THAT WAVE CANNON AT FORTUNE, THE DEVICE THAT GOT SPEEDBALL! ALL HIGH-TECH AND DEADLY! FOLKS, I THINK WE MAY BE UP AGAINST--
NETWORK I/O PATH E
COMPILE INSTRUCTIO
SELF DIAGNOSTIC
72% ORDNANCE
MISSION TIME 00:
--A.I.M.! ADVANCED IDEA MECHANICS! THE MOST DANGEROUS WEAPONS MAKERS ON THE PLANET!
AND IT LOOKS LIKE THESE WEAPONS HAVE ADJUSTED TO THE FACT THAT THEY'VE GOT NEW TARGETS!
LOOK OUT!
NOVA'S CHOKING! GASPING FOR AIR!
THAT CLOUD'S KILLING HIM!
BUT MY MICROWAVES SHOULD BE ABLE TO VAPORIZE IT BEFORE--

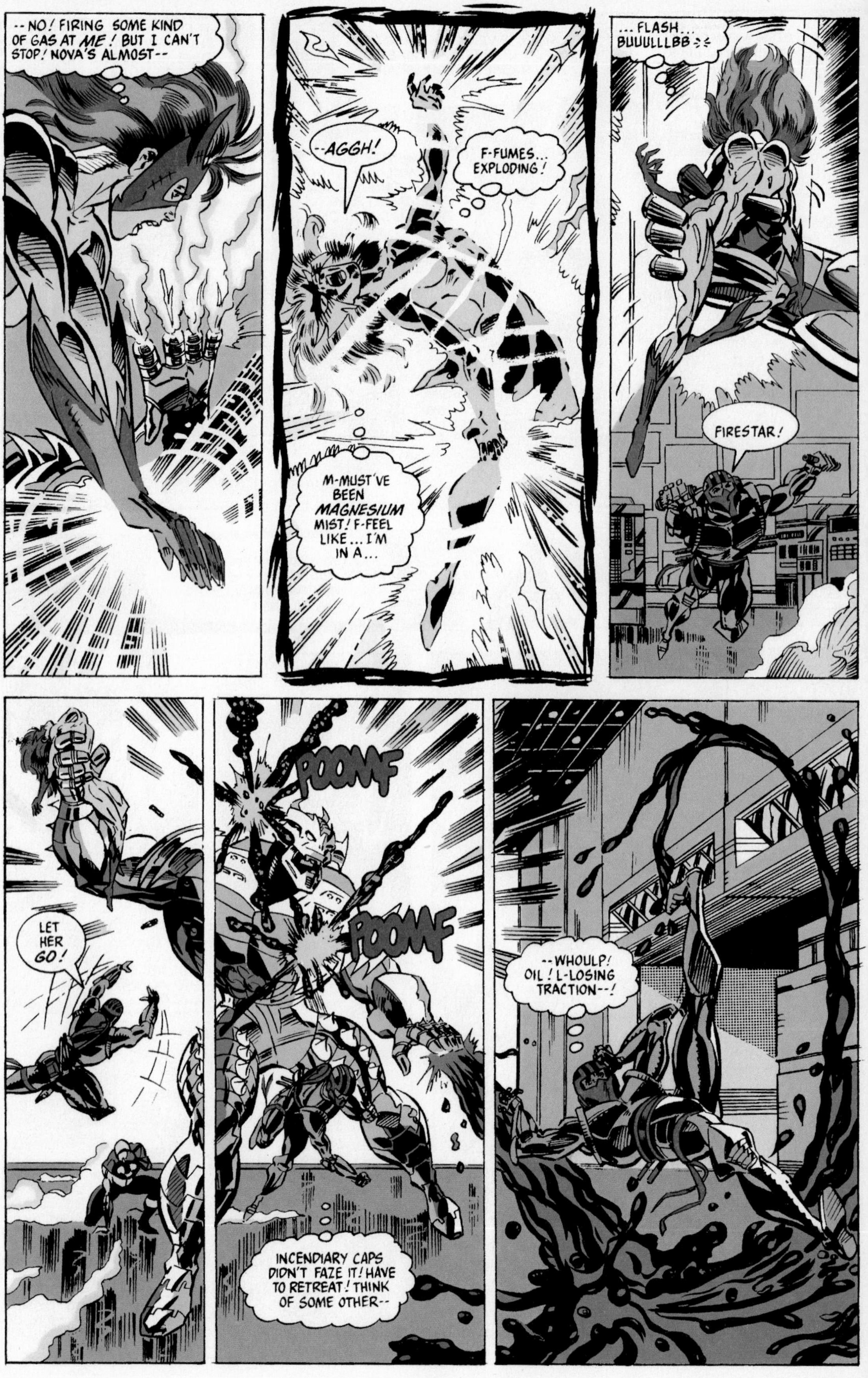
--NO! FIRING SOME KIND OF GAS AT *ME*! BUT I CAN'T STOP! NOVA'S ALMOST--
--AGGH!
F-FUMES... EXPLODING!
M-MUST'VE BEEN *MAGNESIUM* MIST! F-FEEL LIKE... I'M IN A...
...FLASH... BUUULLLBB
FIRESTAR!
LET HER *GO*!
POOMF
POOMF
INCENDIARY CAPS DIDN'T FAZE IT! HAVE TO RETREAT! THINK OF SOME OTHER--
--WHOULP! OIL! L-LOSING TRACTION--!

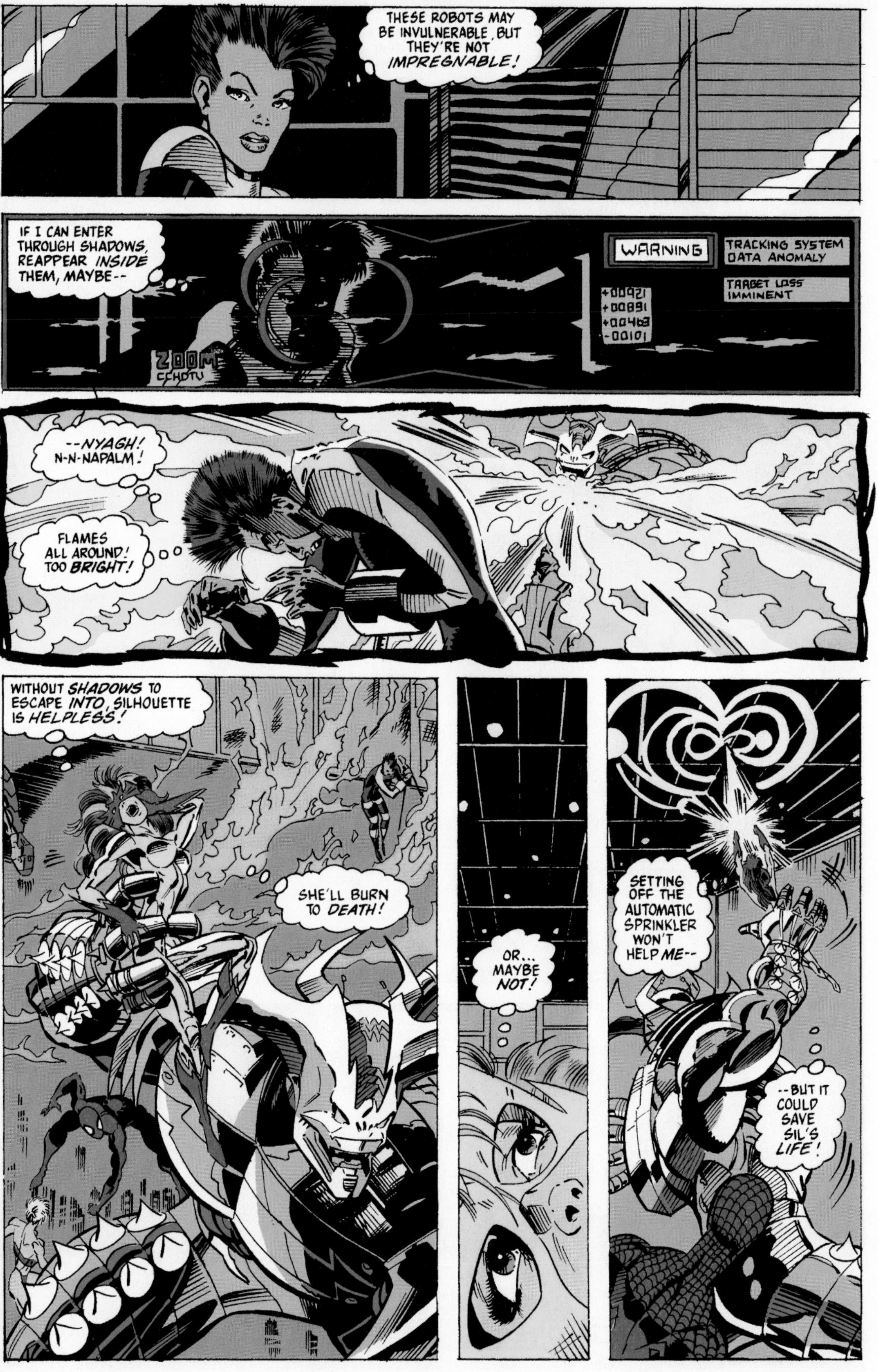
THESE ROBOTS MAY BE INVULNERABLE, BUT THEY'RE NOT IMPREGNABLE!
IF I CAN ENTER THROUGH SHADOWS, REAPPEAR INSIDE THEM, MAYBE--
WARNING
TRACKING SYSTEM DATA ANOMALY
TARGET LOSS IMMINENT
+00921
+00891
+00463
-00101
ZOOM
CCHDTV
--NYAGH! N-N-NAPALM!
FLAMES ALL AROUND! TOO BRIGHT!
WITHOUT SHADOWS TO ESCAPE INTO, SILHOUETTE IS HELPLESS!
SHE'LL BURN TO DEATH!
OR... MAYBE NOT!
SETTING OFF THE AUTOMATIC SPRINKLER WON'T HELP ME--
--BUT IT COULD SAVE SIL'S LIFE!

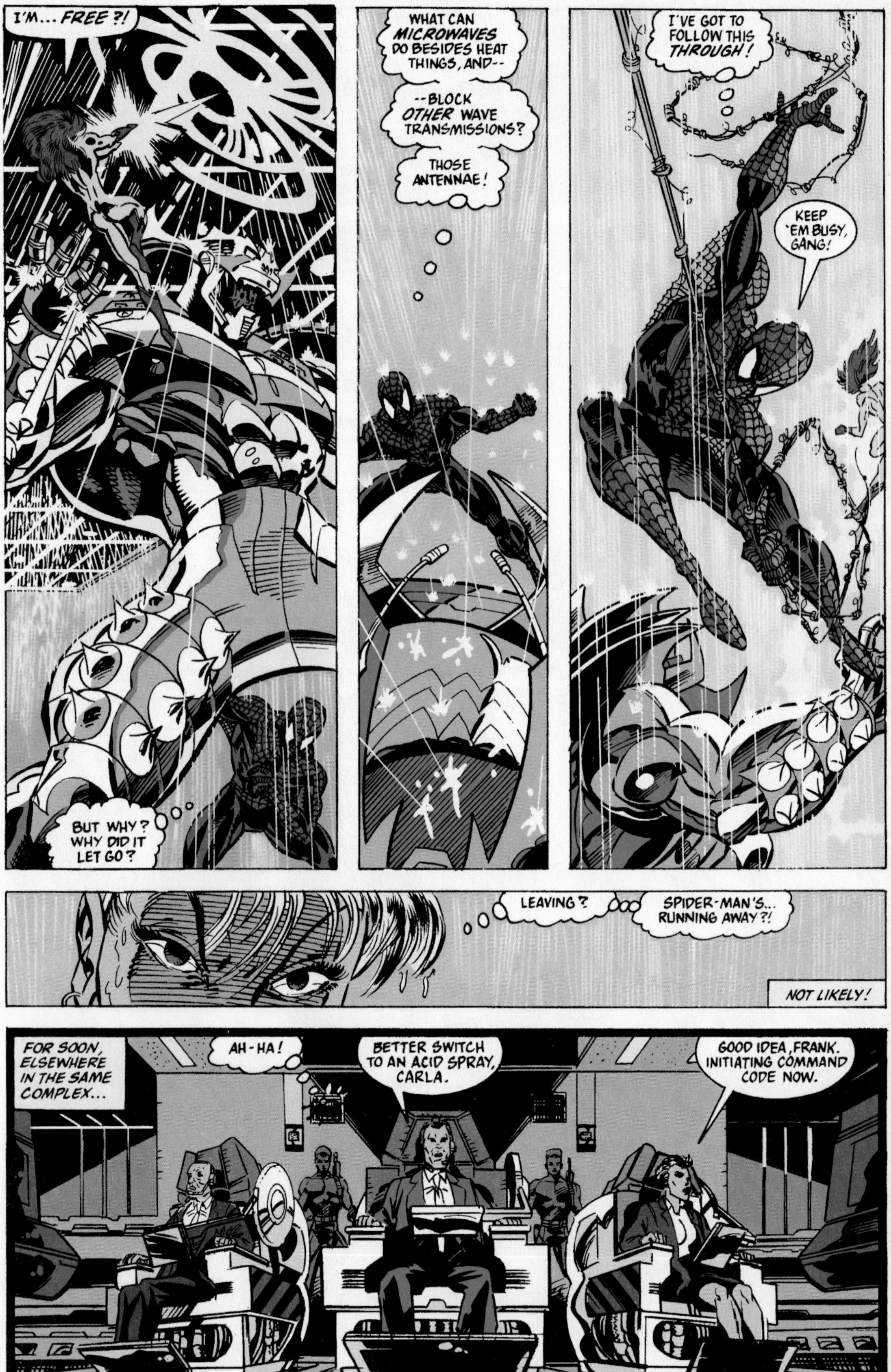
I'M... FREE?!
BUT WHY? WHY DID IT LET GO?
WHAT CAN MICROWAVES DO BESIDES HEAT THINGS, AND--
--BLOCK OTHER WAVE TRANSMISSIONS?
THOSE ANTENNAE!
I'VE GOT TO FOLLOW THIS THROUGH!
KEEP 'EM BUSY, GANG!
LEAVING?
SPIDER-MAN'S... RUNNING AWAY?!
NOT LIKELY!
FOR SOON, ELSEWHERE IN THE SAME COMPLEX...
AH-HA!
BETTER SWITCH TO AN ACID SPRAY, CARLA.
GOOD IDEA, FRANK. INITIATING COMMAND CODE NOW.

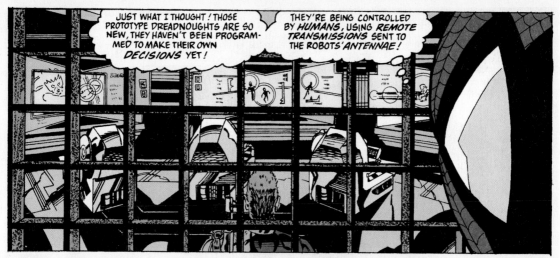

JUST WHAT I THOUGHT! THOSE PROTOTYPE DREADNOUGHTS ARE SO NEW, THEY HAVEN'T BEEN PROGRAMMED TO MAKE THEIR OWN *DECISIONS* YET!

THEY'RE BEING CONTROLLED BY *HUMANS*, USING *REMOTE TRANSMISSIONS* SENT TO THE ROBOTS' *ANTENNAE*!

AND *HUMANS* I CAN *HANDLE!*

THRAK

STOP HIM!

WHAT THE--?

OH, SOMEONE'S GONNA BE *STOPPED*, ALL RIGHT!

ALTER PROGRAMMING! BRING THE DREADNOUGHTS *HERE* BEFORE--

NAH! I'D RATHER SEE HOW THE BIG BRUISERS DO--

--ON THEIR *OWN!*

47

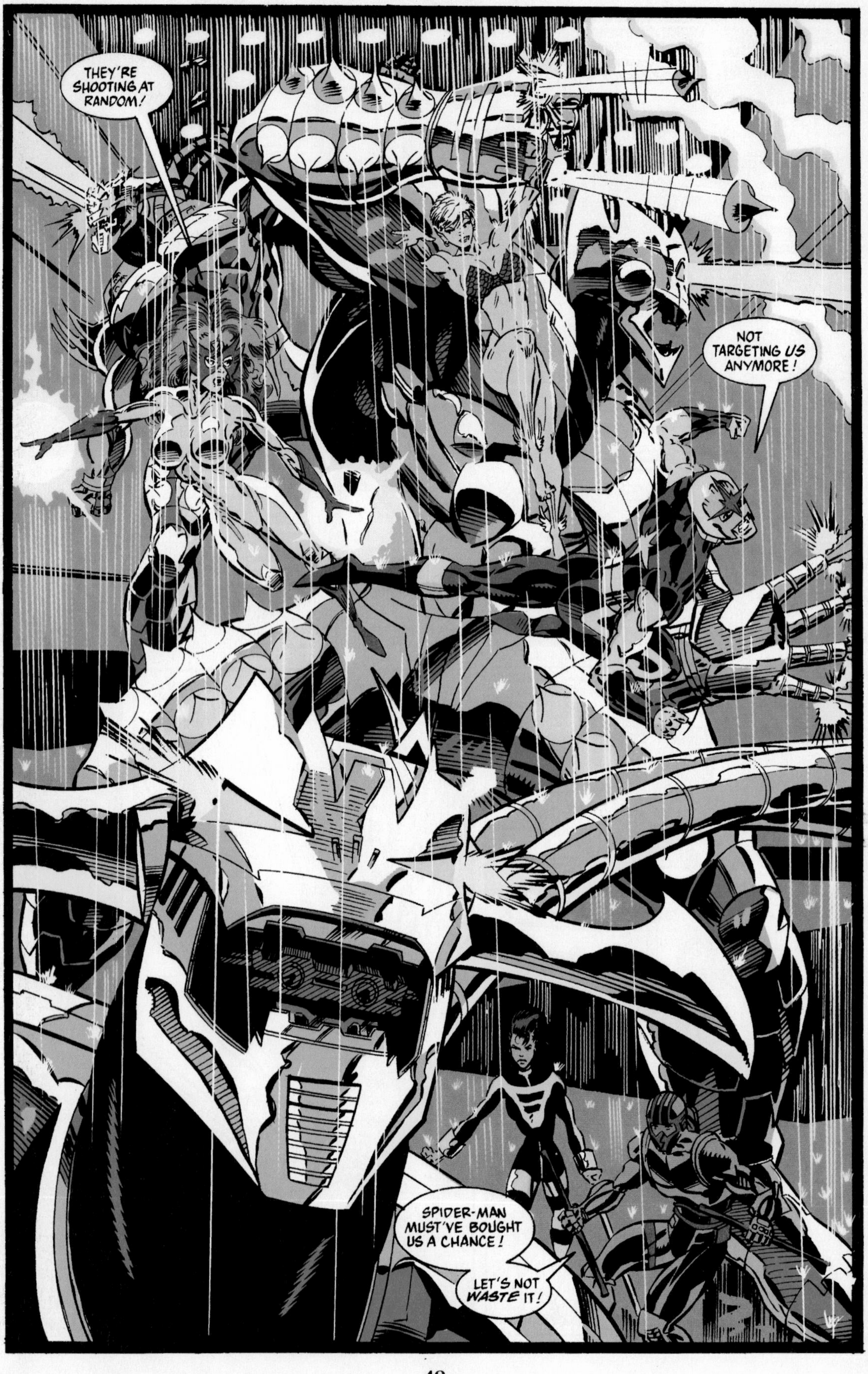
THEY'RE SHOOTING AT RANDOM!
NOT TARGETING US ANYMORE!
SPIDER-MAN MUST'VE BOUGHT US A CHANCE!
LET'S NOT WASTE IT!

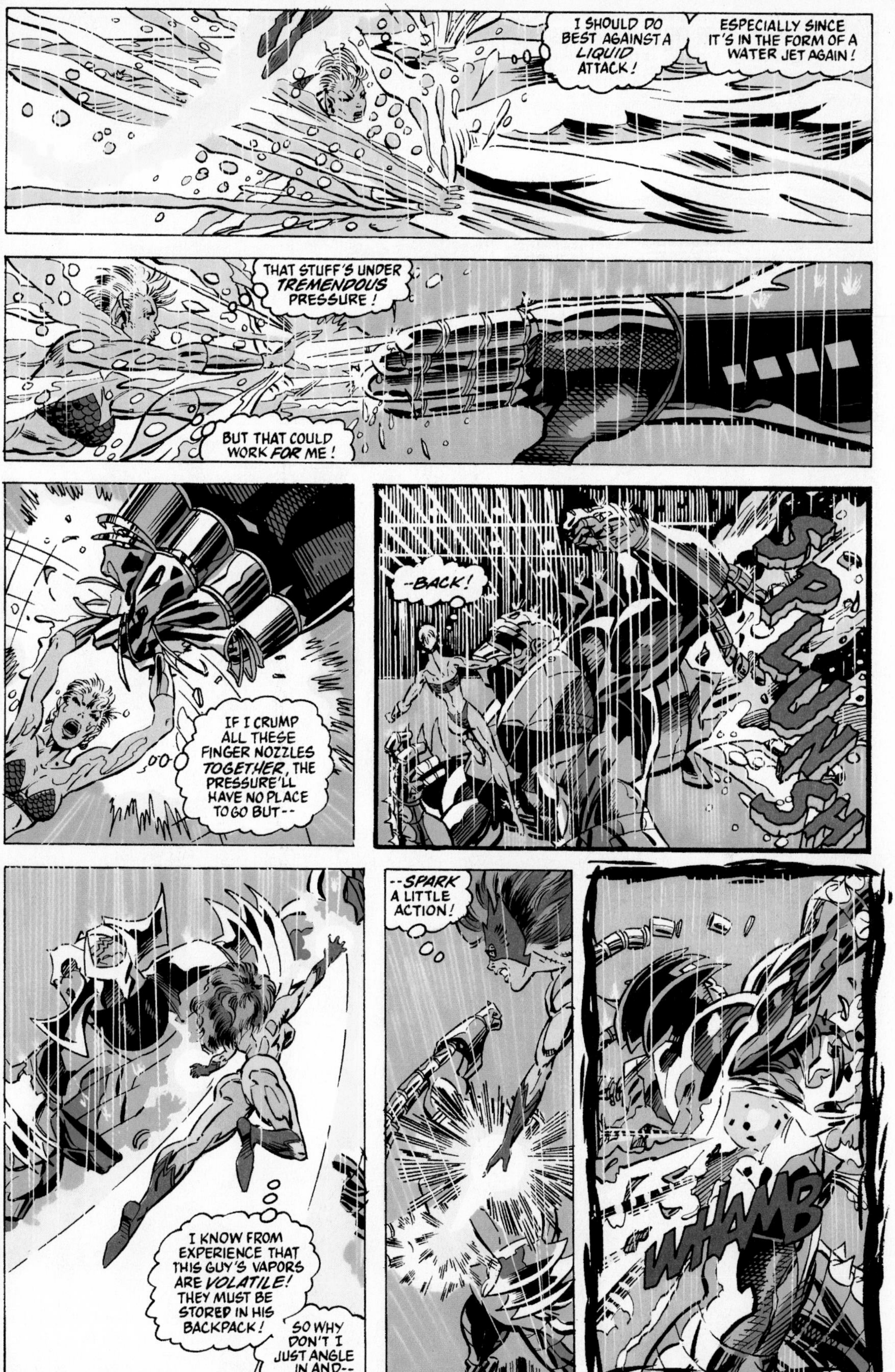
I SHOULD DO BEST AGAINST A *LIQUID* ATTACK!
ESPECIALLY SINCE IT'S IN THE FORM OF A WATER JET AGAIN!
THAT STUFF'S UNDER *TREMENDOUS* PRESSURE!
BUT THAT COULD WORK *FOR* ME!
IF I CRUMP ALL THESE FINGER NOZZLES *TOGETHER*, THE PRESSURE'LL HAVE NO PLACE TO GO BUT--
--*BACK*!
SPLUNSH
I KNOW FROM EXPERIENCE THAT THIS GUY'S VAPORS ARE *VOLATILE*! THEY MUST BE STORED IN HIS BACKPACK!
SO WHY DON'T I JUST ANGLE IN AND--
--*SPARK* A LITTLE ACTION!
WHAMB

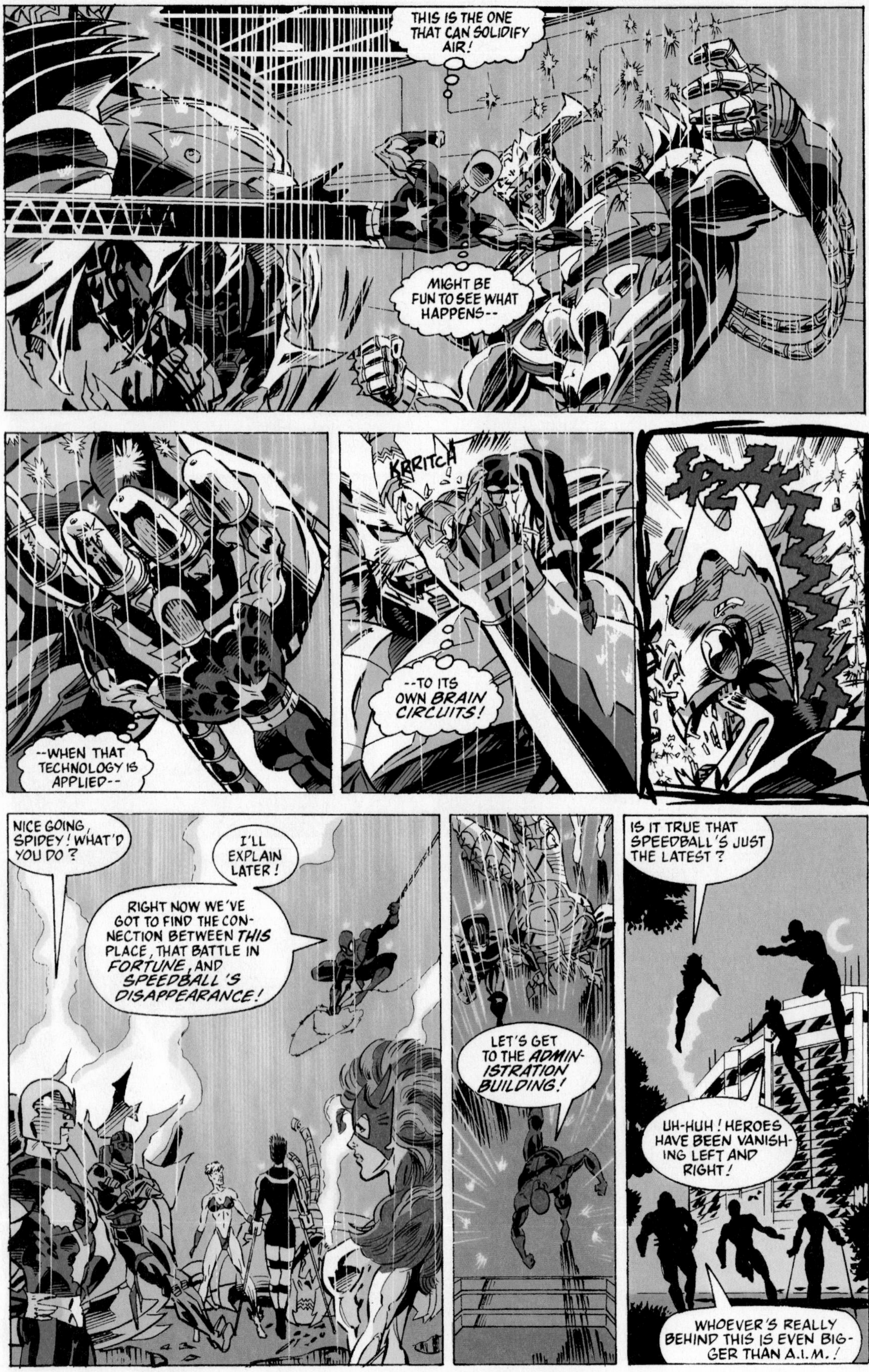
THIS IS THE ONE THAT CAN SOLIDIFY AIR!
MIGHT BE FUN TO SEE WHAT HAPPENS--
--WHEN THAT TECHNOLOGY IS APPLIED--
KRRITCH
--TO ITS OWN BRAIN CIRCUITS!
NICE GOING, SPIDEY! WHAT'D YOU DO?
I'LL EXPLAIN LATER!
RIGHT NOW WE'VE GOT TO FIND THE CONNECTION BETWEEN THIS PLACE, THAT BATTLE IN FORTUNE, AND SPEEDBALL'S DISAPPEARANCE!
LET'S GET TO THE ADMINISTRATION BUILDING!
IS IT TRUE THAT SPEEDBALL'S JUST THE LATEST?
UH-HUH! HEROES HAVE BEEN VANISHING LEFT AND RIGHT!
WHOEVER'S REALLY BEHIND THIS IS EVEN BIGGER THAN A.I.M.!

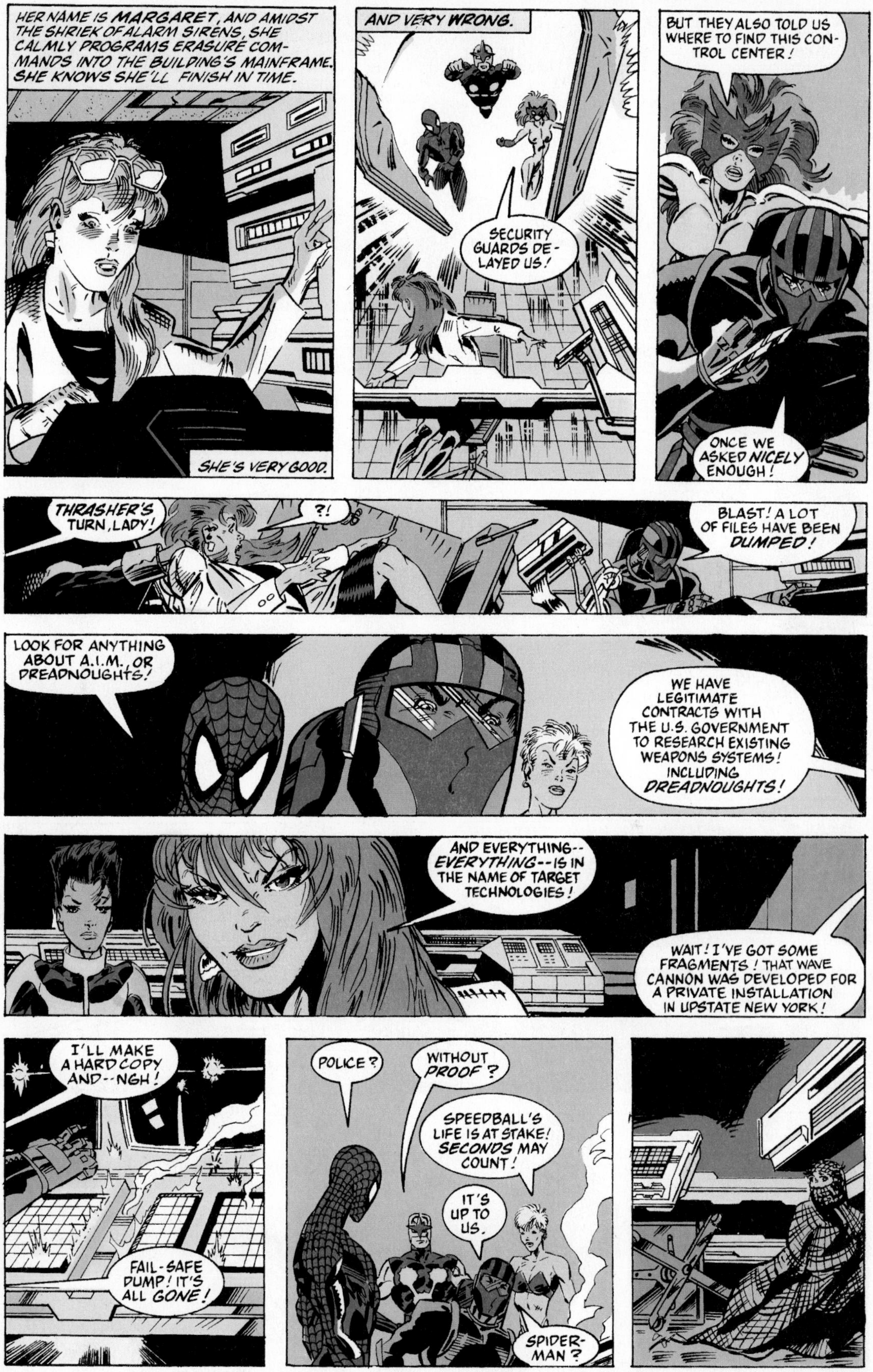
HER NAME IS MARGARET, AND AMIDST THE SHRIEK OF ALARM SIRENS, SHE CALMLY PROGRAMS ERASURE COMMANDS INTO THE BUILDING'S MAINFRAME. SHE KNOWS SHE'LL FINISH IN TIME.
SHE'S VERY GOOD.
AND VERY WRONG.
SECURITY GUARDS DELAYED US!
BUT THEY ALSO TOLD US WHERE TO FIND THIS CONTROL CENTER!
ONCE WE ASKED NICELY ENOUGH!
THRASHER'S TURN, LADY!
?!
BLAST! A LOT OF FILES HAVE BEEN DUMPED!
LOOK FOR ANYTHING ABOUT A.I.M., OR DREADNOUGHTS!
WE HAVE LEGITIMATE CONTRACTS WITH THE U.S. GOVERNMENT TO RESEARCH EXISTING WEAPONS SYSTEMS! INCLUDING DREADNOUGHTS!
AND EVERYTHING--EVERYTHING--IS IN THE NAME OF TARGET TECHNOLOGIES!
WAIT! I'VE GOT SOME FRAGMENTS! THAT WAVE CANNON WAS DEVELOPED FOR A PRIVATE INSTALLATION IN UPSTATE NEW YORK!
I'LL MAKE A HARD COPY AND--NGH!
FAIL-SAFE DUMP! IT'S ALL GONE!
POLICE?
WITHOUT PROOF?
SPEEDBALL'S LIFE IS AT STAKE! SECONDS MAY COUNT!
IT'S UP TO US.
SPIDER-MAN?

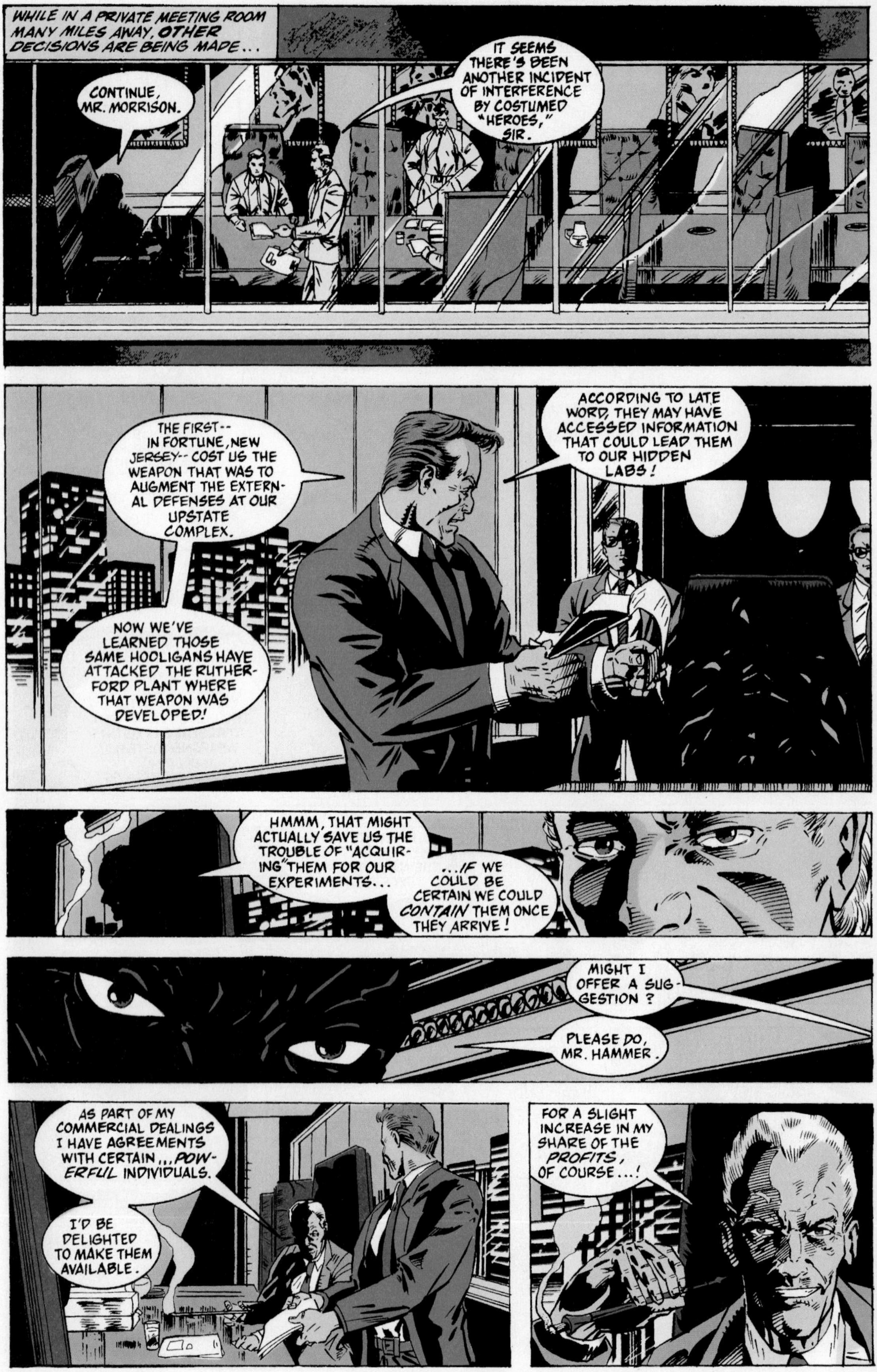
WHILE IN A PRIVATE MEETING ROOM MANY MILES AWAY, OTHER DECISIONS ARE BEING MADE...
CONTINUE, MR. MORRISON.
IT SEEMS THERE'S BEEN ANOTHER INCIDENT OF INTERFERENCE BY COSTUMED "HEROES," SIR.
THE FIRST--IN FORTUNE, NEW JERSEY--COST US THE WEAPON THAT WAS TO AUGMENT THE EXTERNAL DEFENSES AT OUR UPSTATE COMPLEX.
NOW WE'VE LEARNED THOSE SAME HOOLIGANS HAVE ATTACKED THE RUTHERFORD PLANT WHERE THAT WEAPON WAS DEVELOPED!
ACCORDING TO LATE WORD, THEY MAY HAVE ACCESSED INFORMATION THAT COULD LEAD THEM TO OUR HIDDEN LABS!
HMMM, THAT MIGHT ACTUALLY SAVE US THE TROUBLE OF "ACQUIRING" THEM FOR OUR EXPERIMENTS...
...IF WE COULD BE CERTAIN WE COULD CONTAIN THEM ONCE THEY ARRIVE!
MIGHT I OFFER A SUGGESTION?
PLEASE DO, MR. HAMMER.
AS PART OF MY COMMERCIAL DEALINGS I HAVE AGREEMENTS WITH CERTAIN... POWERFUL INDIVIDUALS.
I'D BE DELIGHTED TO MAKE THEM AVAILABLE.
FOR A SLIGHT INCREASE IN MY SHARE OF THE PROFITS, OF COURSE...!

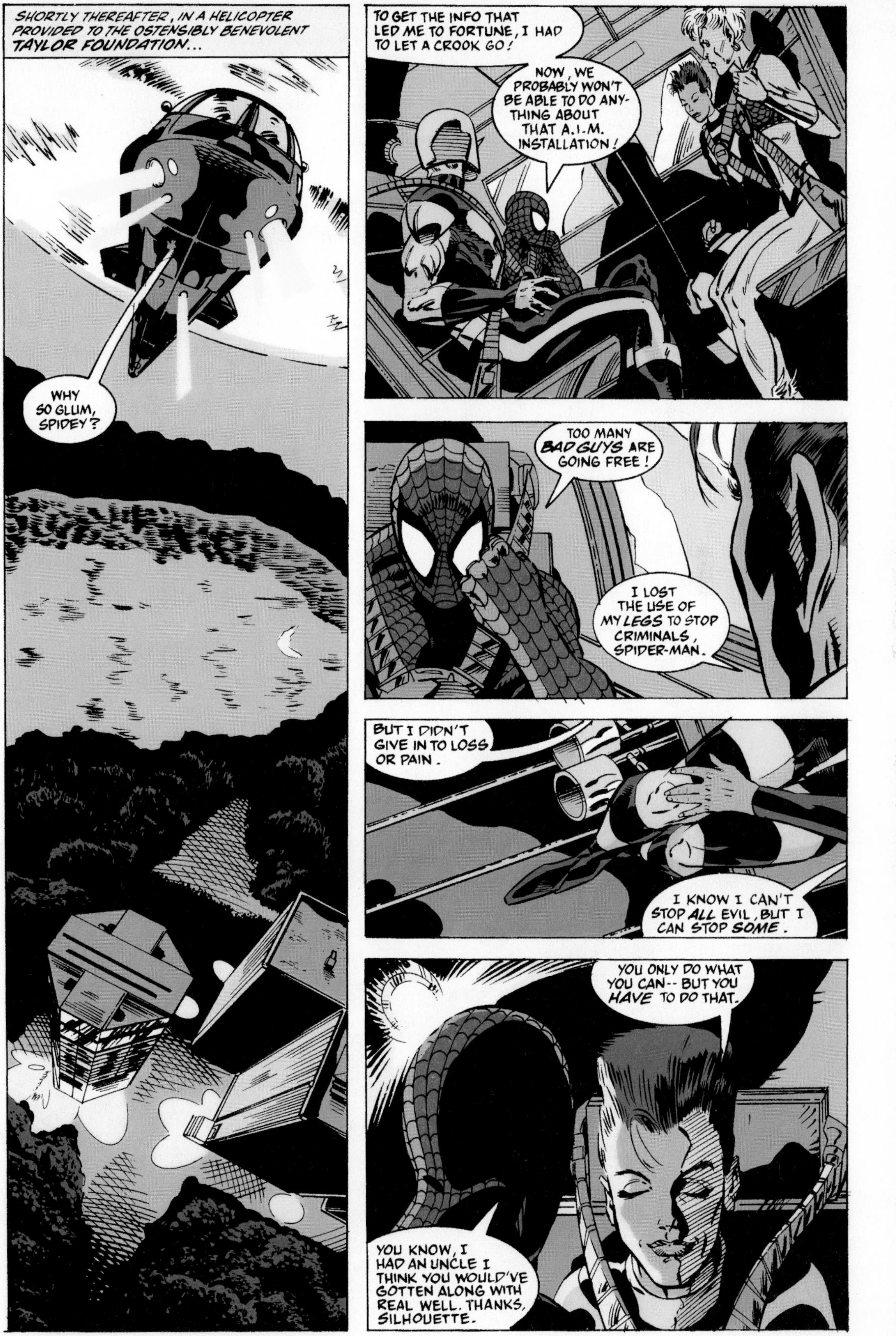
SHORTLY THEREAFTER, IN A HELICOPTER PROVIDED TO THE OSTENSIBLY BENEVOLENT TAYLOR FOUNDATION...
WHY SO GLUM, SPIDEY?
TO GET THE INFO THAT LED ME TO FORTUNE, I HAD TO LET A CROOK GO!
NOW, WE PROBABLY WON'T BE ABLE TO DO ANYTHING ABOUT THAT A.I.M. INSTALLATION!
TOO MANY BAD GUYS ARE GOING FREE!
I LOST THE USE OF MY LEGS TO STOP CRIMINALS, SPIDER-MAN.
BUT I DIDN'T GIVE IN TO LOSS OR PAIN.
I KNOW I CAN'T STOP ALL EVIL, BUT I CAN STOP SOME.
YOU ONLY DO WHAT YOU CAN-- BUT YOU HAVE TO DO THAT.
YOU KNOW, I HAD AN UNCLE I THINK YOU WOULD'VE GOTTEN ALONG WITH REAL WELL. THANKS, SILHOUETTE.

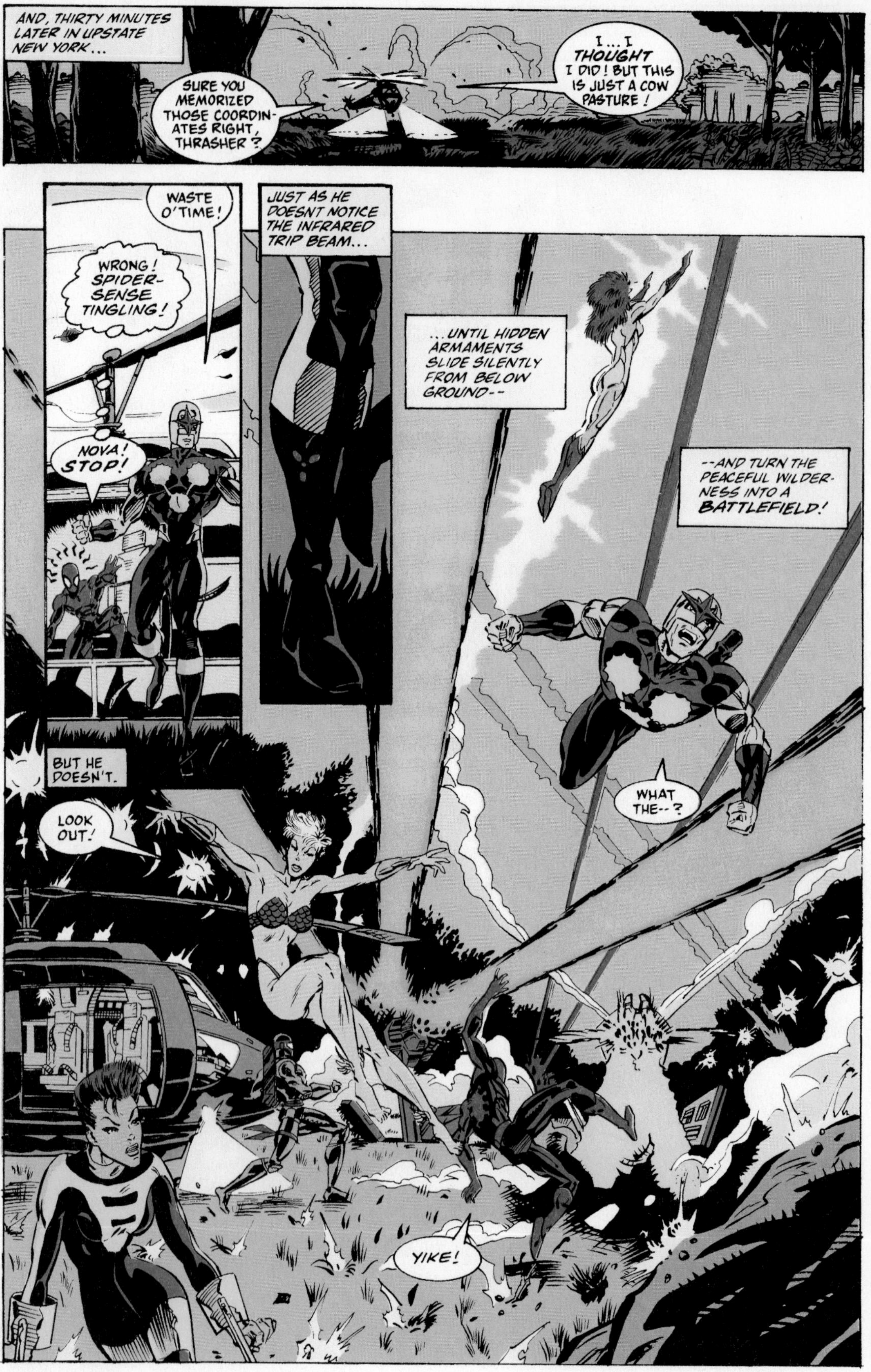
AND, THIRTY MINUTES LATER IN UPSTATE NEW YORK...
SURE YOU MEMORIZED THOSE COORDINATES RIGHT, THRASHER?
I... I THOUGHT I DID! BUT THIS IS JUST A COW PASTURE!
WASTE O'TIME!
WRONG! SPIDER-SENSE TINGLING!
NOVA! STOP!
JUST AS HE DOESN'T NOTICE THE INFRARED TRIP BEAM...
BUT HE DOESN'T.
...UNTIL HIDDEN ARMAMENTS SLIDE SILENTLY FROM BELOW GROUND--
--AND TURN THE PEACEFUL WILDERNESS INTO A BATTLEFIELD!
WHAT THE--?
LOOK OUT!
YIKE!

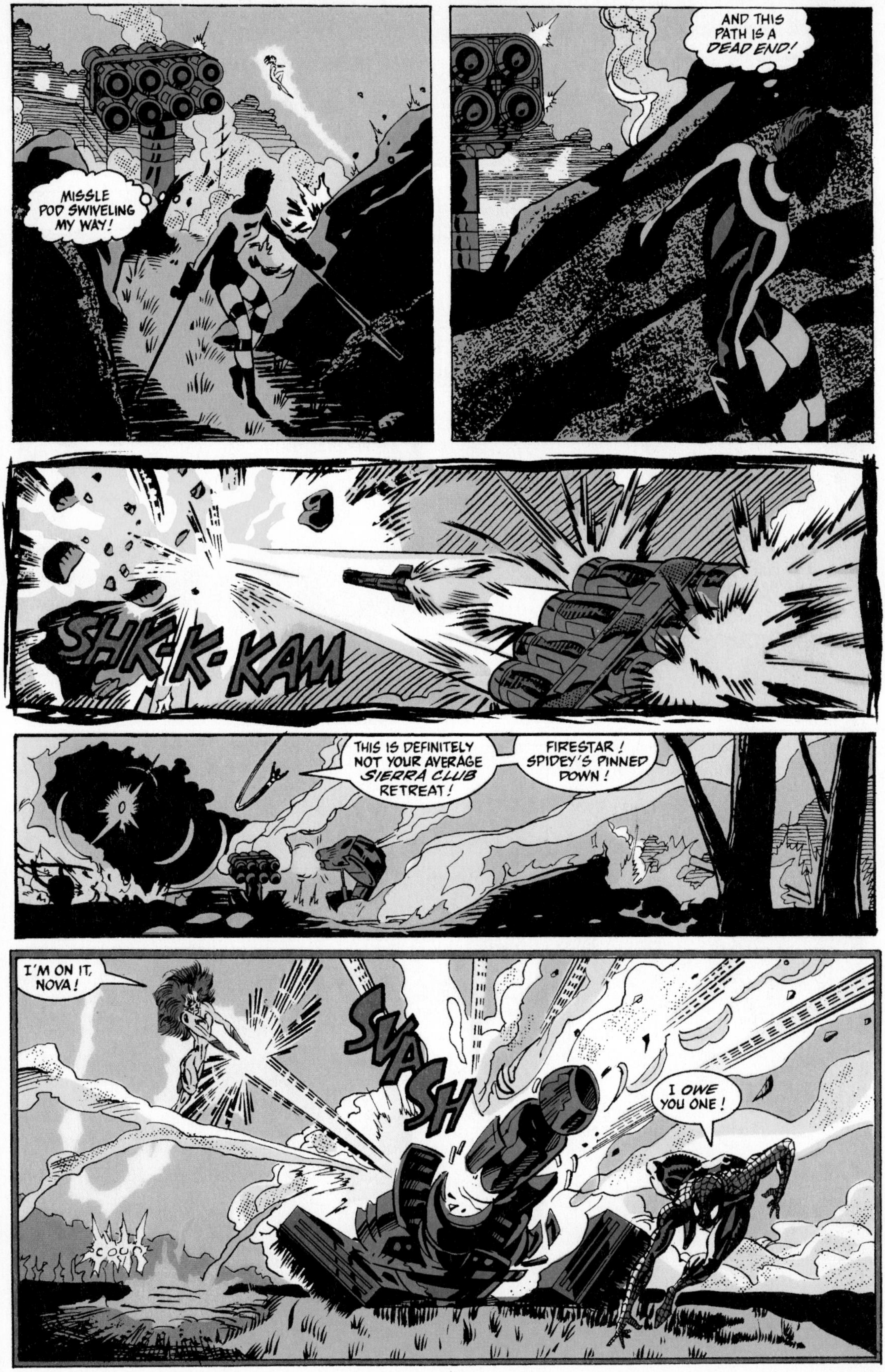
MISSLE POD SWIVELING MY WAY!
AND THIS PATH IS A DEAD END!
SHK-K-KAM
THIS IS DEFINITELY NOT YOUR AVERAGE SIERRA CLUB RETREAT!
FIRESTAR! SPIDEY'S PINNED DOWN!
I'M ON IT, NOVA!
SVASH
I OWE YOU ONE!

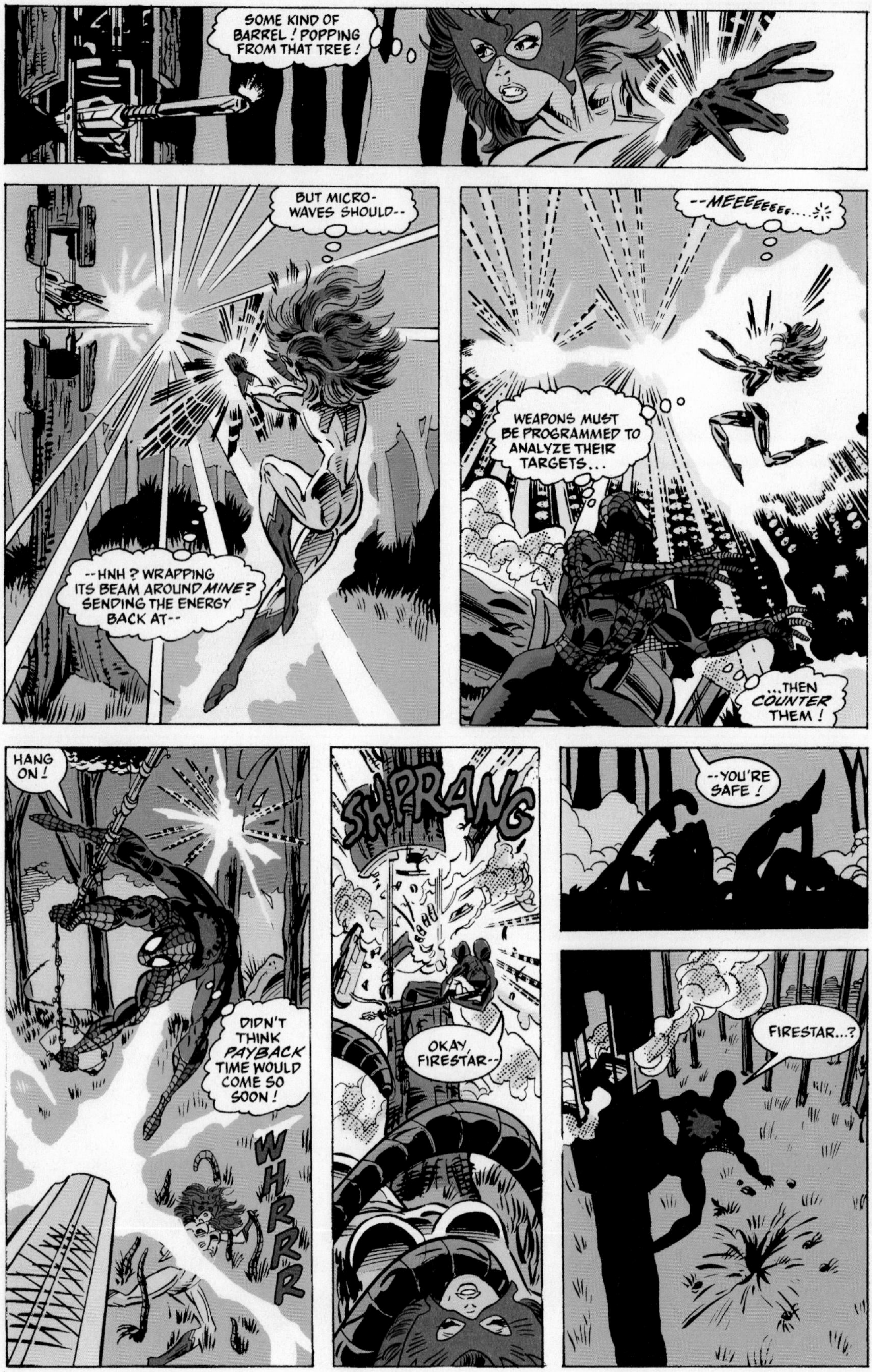
SOME KIND OF BARREL! POPPING FROM THAT TREE!
BUT MICRO-WAVES SHOULD--
--HNH? WRAPPING ITS BEAM AROUND MINE? SENDING THE ENERGY BACK AT--
--MEEEeeeee....
WEAPONS MUST BE PROGRAMMED TO ANALYZE THEIR TARGETS...
...THEN COUNTER THEM!
HANG ON!
DIDN'T THINK PAYBACK TIME WOULD COME SO SOON!
WHRRR
SHPRANG
OKAY, FIRESTAR--
--YOU'RE SAFE!
FIRESTAR...?

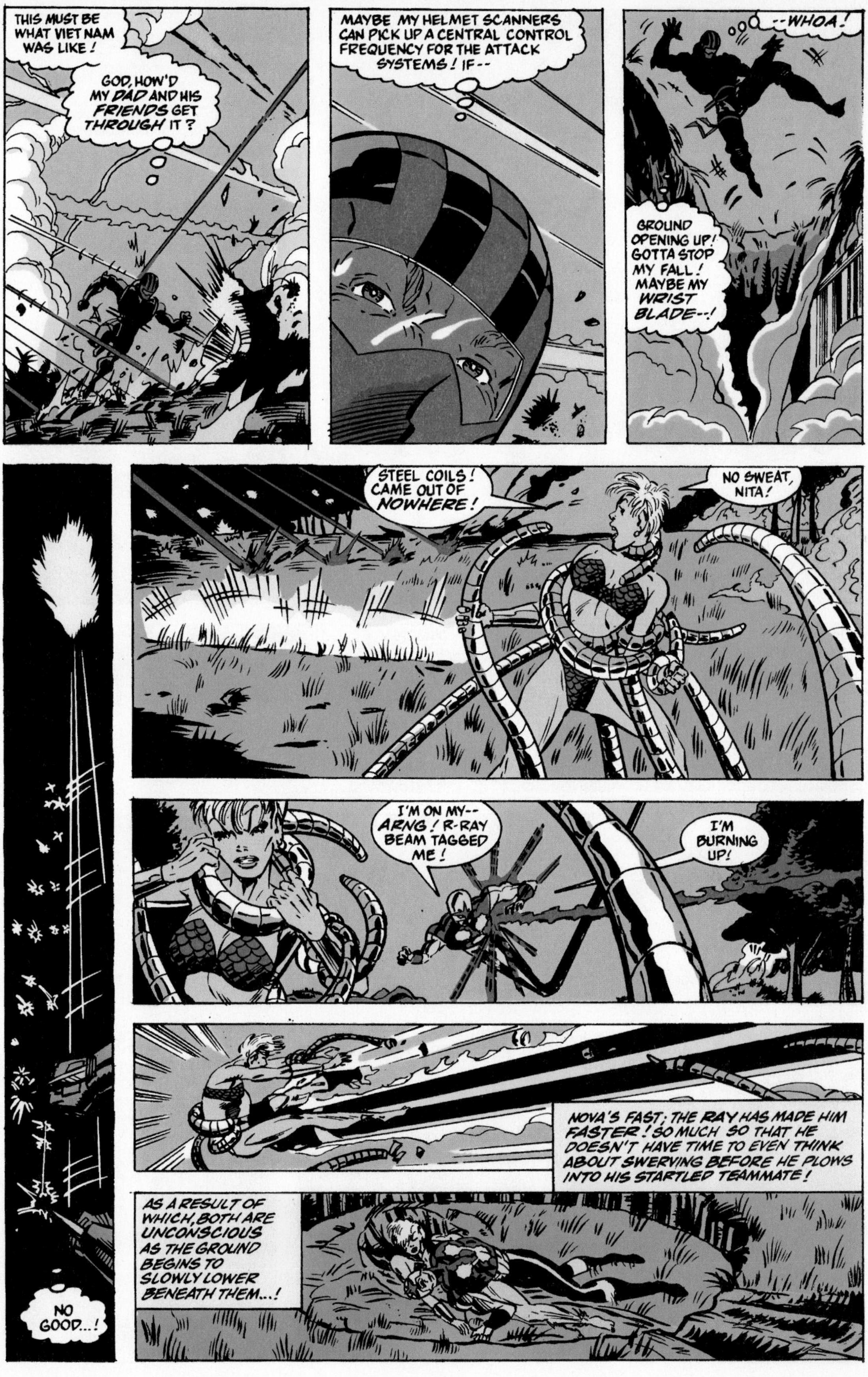
THIS MUST BE WHAT VIET NAM WAS LIKE!
GOD, HOW'D MY DAD AND HIS FRIENDS GET THROUGH IT?
MAYBE MY HELMET SCANNERS CAN PICK UP A CENTRAL CONTROL FREQUENCY FOR THE ATTACK SYSTEMS! IF--
--WHOA!
GROUND OPENING UP! GOTTA STOP MY FALL! MAYBE MY WRIST BLADE--!
STEEL COILS! CAME OUT OF NOWHERE!
NO SWEAT, NITA!
I'M ON MY-- ARNG! R-RAY BEAM TAGGED ME!
I'M BURNING UP!
NOVA'S FAST; THE RAY HAS MADE HIM FASTER! SO MUCH SO THAT HE DOESN'T HAVE TIME TO EVEN THINK ABOUT SWERVING BEFORE HE PLOWS INTO HIS STARTLED TEAMMATE!
AS A RESULT OF WHICH, BOTH ARE UNCONSCIOUS AS THE GROUND BEGINS TO SLOWLY LOWER BENEATH THEM...!
NO GOOD...!

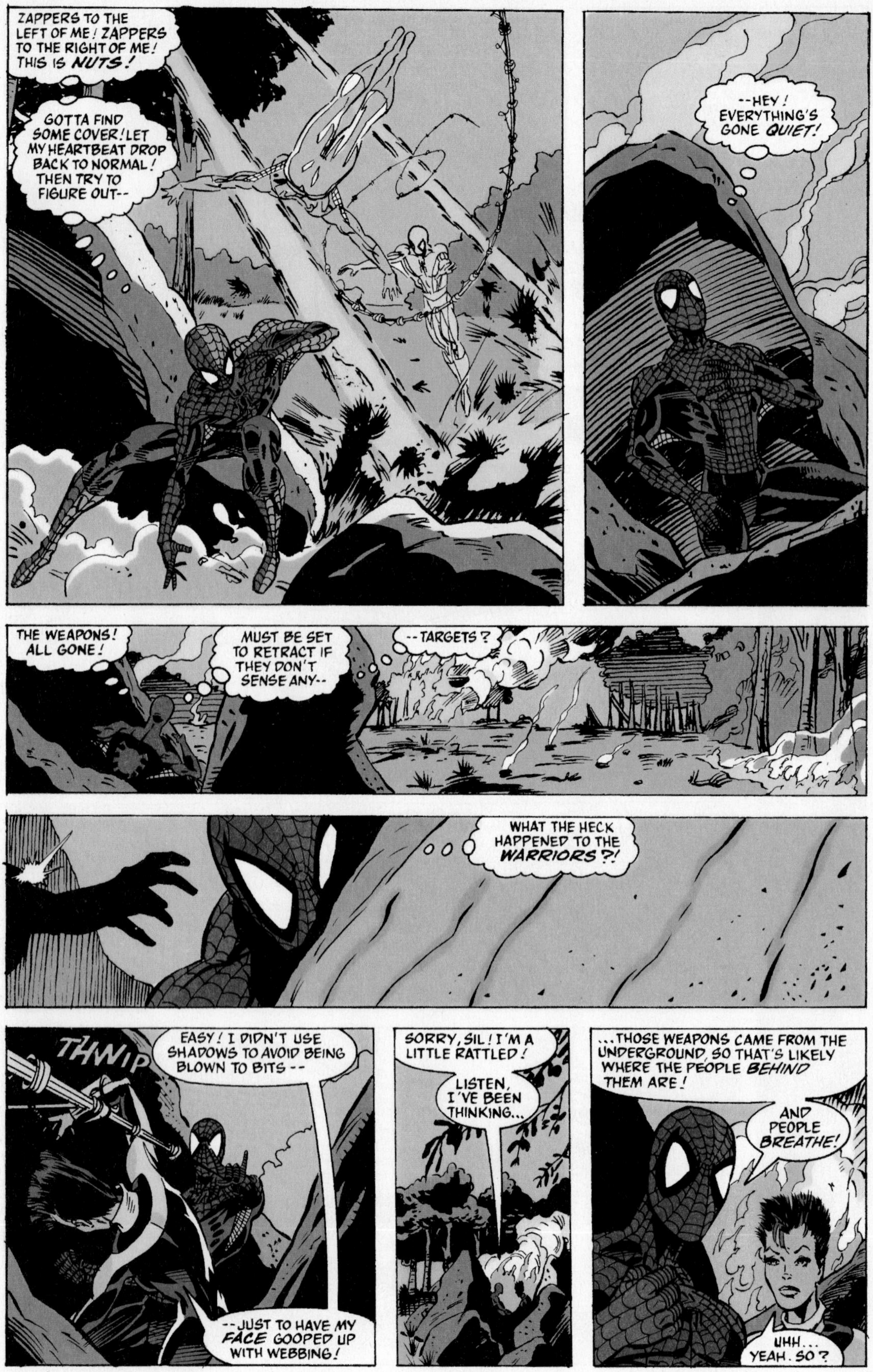
ZAPPERS TO THE LEFT OF ME! ZAPPERS TO THE RIGHT OF ME! THIS IS NUTS!
GOTTA FIND SOME COVER! LET MY HEARTBEAT DROP BACK TO NORMAL! THEN TRY TO FIGURE OUT--
--HEY! EVERYTHING'S GONE QUIET!
THE WEAPONS! ALL GONE!
MUST BE SET TO RETRACT IF THEY DON'T SENSE ANY--
--TARGETS?
WHAT THE HECK HAPPENED TO THE WARRIORS?!
THWIP
EASY! I DIDN'T USE SHADOWS TO AVOID BEING BLOWN TO BITS--
--JUST TO HAVE MY FACE GOOPED UP WITH WEBBING!
SORRY, SIL! I'M A LITTLE RATTLED!
LISTEN, I'VE BEEN THINKING...
...THOSE WEAPONS CAME FROM THE UNDERGROUND, SO THAT'S LIKELY WHERE THE PEOPLE BEHIND THEM ARE!
AND PEOPLE BREATHE!
UHH... YEAH. SO?

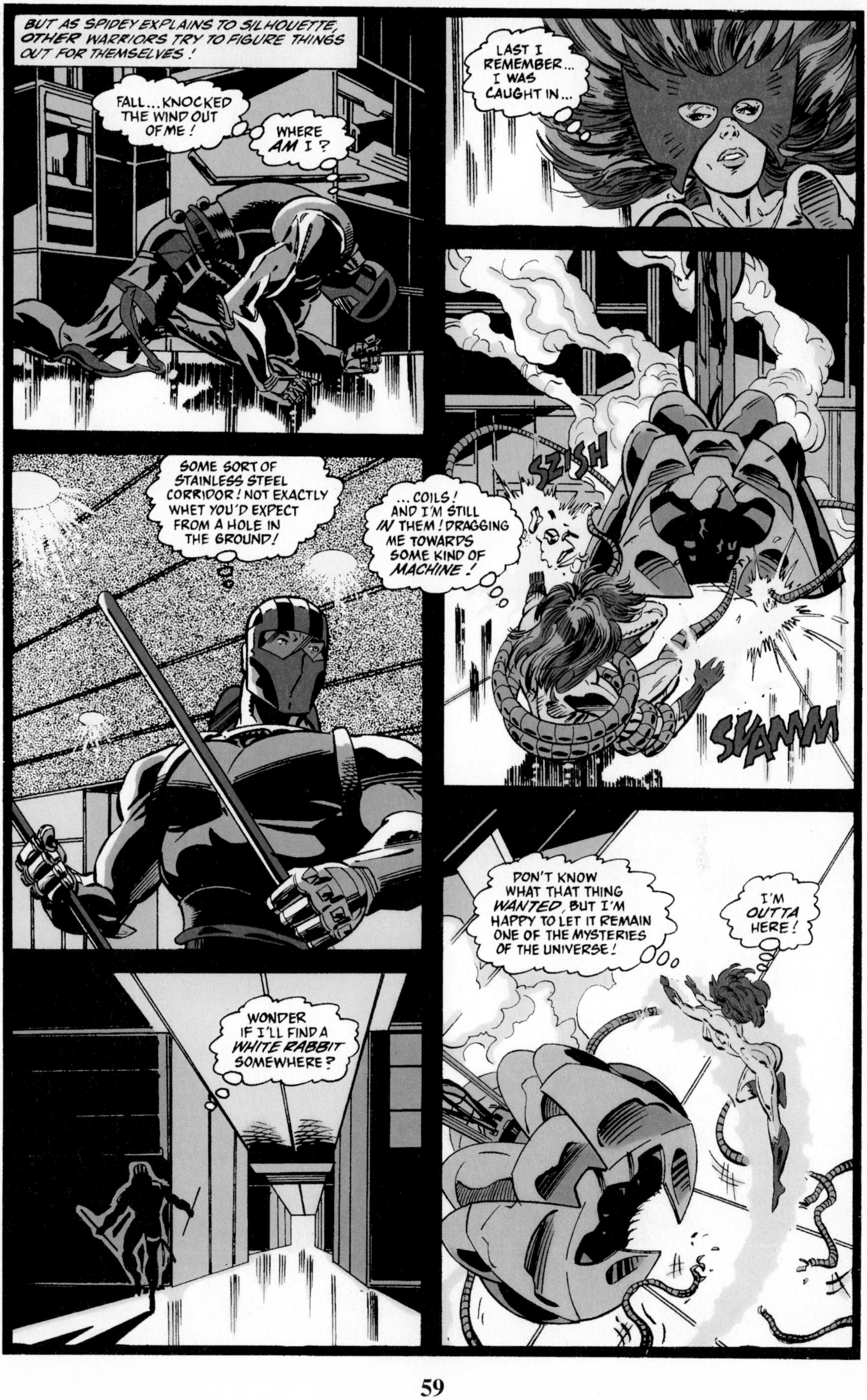
BUT AS SPIDEY EXPLAINS TO SILHOUETTE, OTHER WARRIORS TRY TO FIGURE THINGS OUT FOR THEMSELVES!
FALL...KNOCKED THE WIND OUT OF ME!
WHERE AM I?
LAST I REMEMBER... I WAS CAUGHT IN...
SOME SORT OF STAINLESS STEEL CORRIDOR! NOT EXACTLY WHET YOU'D EXPECT FROM A HOLE IN THE GROUND!
SZISH
...COILS! AND I'M STILL IN THEM! DRAGGING ME TOWARDS SOME KIND OF MACHINE!
SLAMM
WONDER IF I'LL FIND A WHITE RABBIT SOMEWHERE?
DON'T KNOW WHAT THAT THING WANTED, BUT I'M HAPPY TO LET IT REMAIN ONE OF THE MYSTERIES OF THE UNIVERSE!
I'M OUTTA HERE!

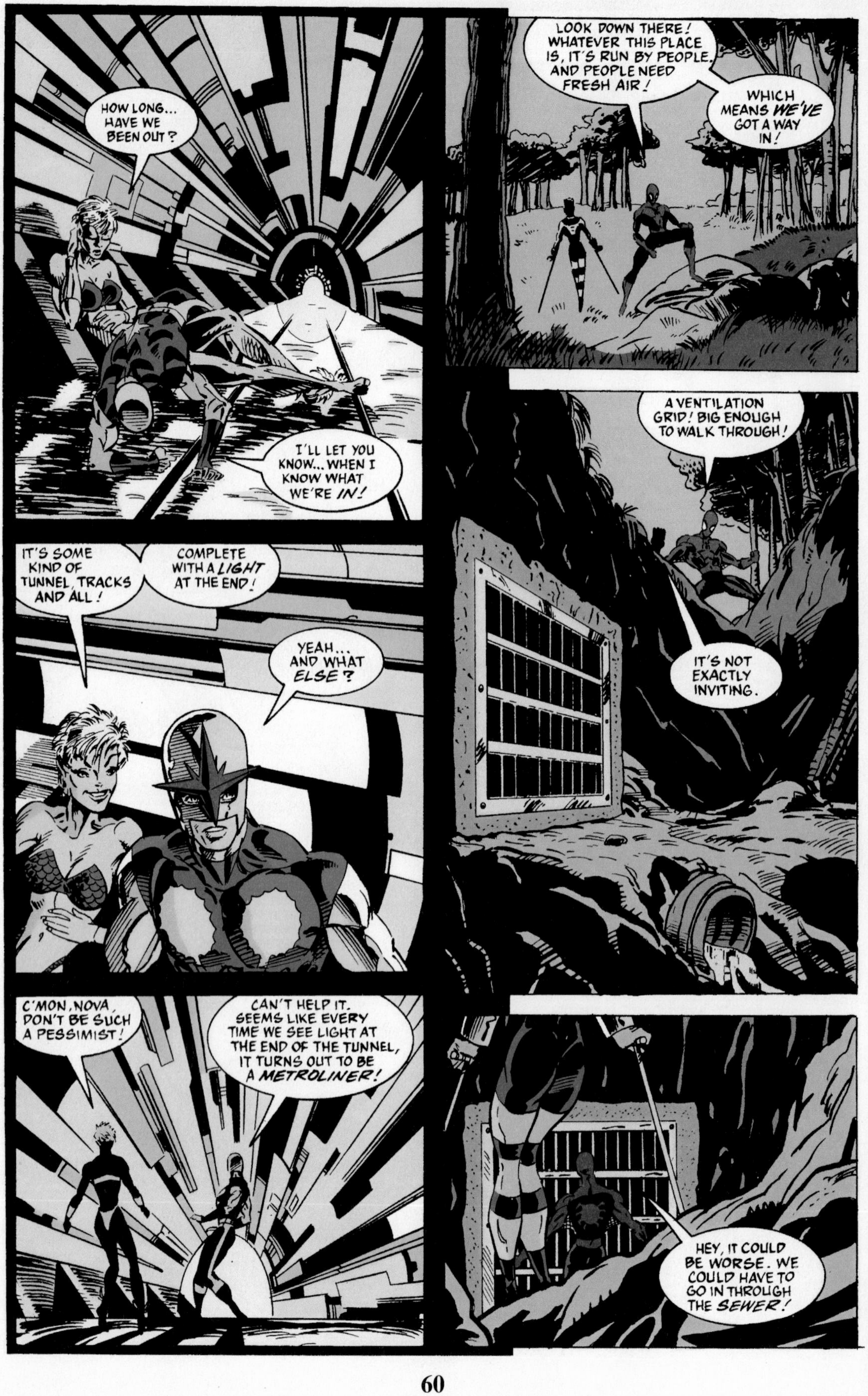
HOW LONG... HAVE WE BEEN OUT?
I'LL LET YOU KNOW... WHEN I KNOW WHAT WE'RE IN!
IT'S SOME KIND OF TUNNEL, TRACKS AND ALL!
COMPLETE WITH A LIGHT AT THE END!
YEAH... AND WHAT ELSE?
C'MON, NOVA, DON'T BE SUCH A PESSIMIST!
CAN'T HELP IT. SEEMS LIKE EVERY TIME WE SEE LIGHT AT THE END OF THE TUNNEL, IT TURNS OUT TO BE A METROLINER!
LOOK DOWN THERE! WHATEVER THIS PLACE IS, IT'S RUN BY PEOPLE, AND PEOPLE NEED FRESH AIR!
WHICH MEANS WE'VE GOT A WAY IN!
A VENTILATION GRID! BIG ENOUGH TO WALK THROUGH!
IT'S NOT EXACTLY INVITING.
HEY, IT COULD BE WORSE. WE COULD HAVE TO GO IN THROUGH THE SEWER!

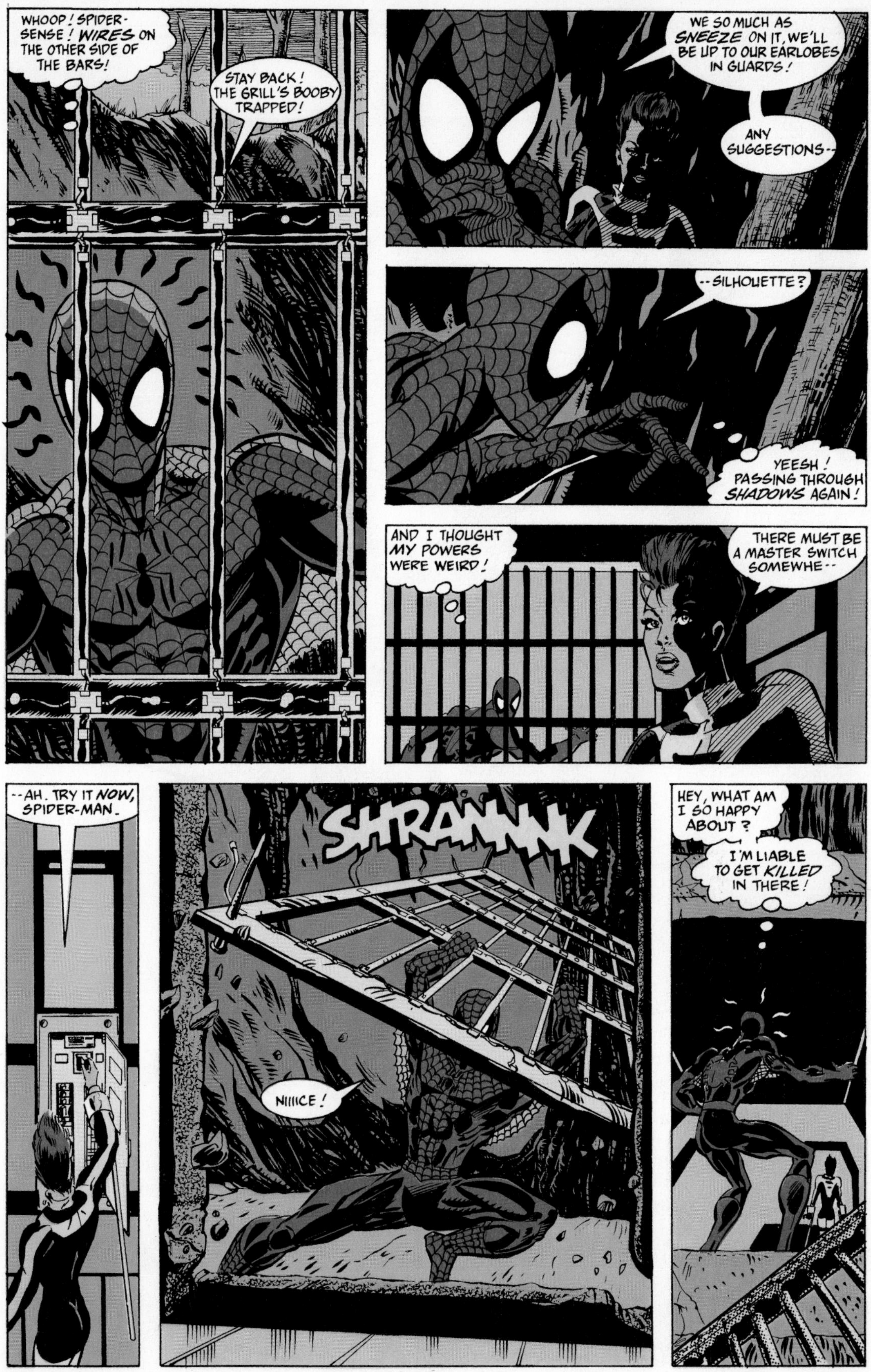
WHOOP! SPIDER-SENSE! WIRES ON THE OTHER SIDE OF THE BARS!
STAY BACK! THE GRILL'S BOOBY TRAPPED!
WE SO MUCH AS SNEEZE ON IT, WE'LL BE UP TO OUR EARLOBES IN GUARDS!
ANY SUGGESTIONS--
--SILHOUETTE?
YEESH! PASSING THROUGH SHADOWS AGAIN!
AND I THOUGHT MY POWERS WERE WEIRD!
THERE MUST BE A MASTER SWITCH SOMEWHE--
--AH. TRY IT NOW, SPIDER-MAN.
SHRANNNK
NIIIICE!
HEY, WHAT AM I SO HAPPY ABOUT?
I'M LIABLE TO GET KILLED IN THERE!

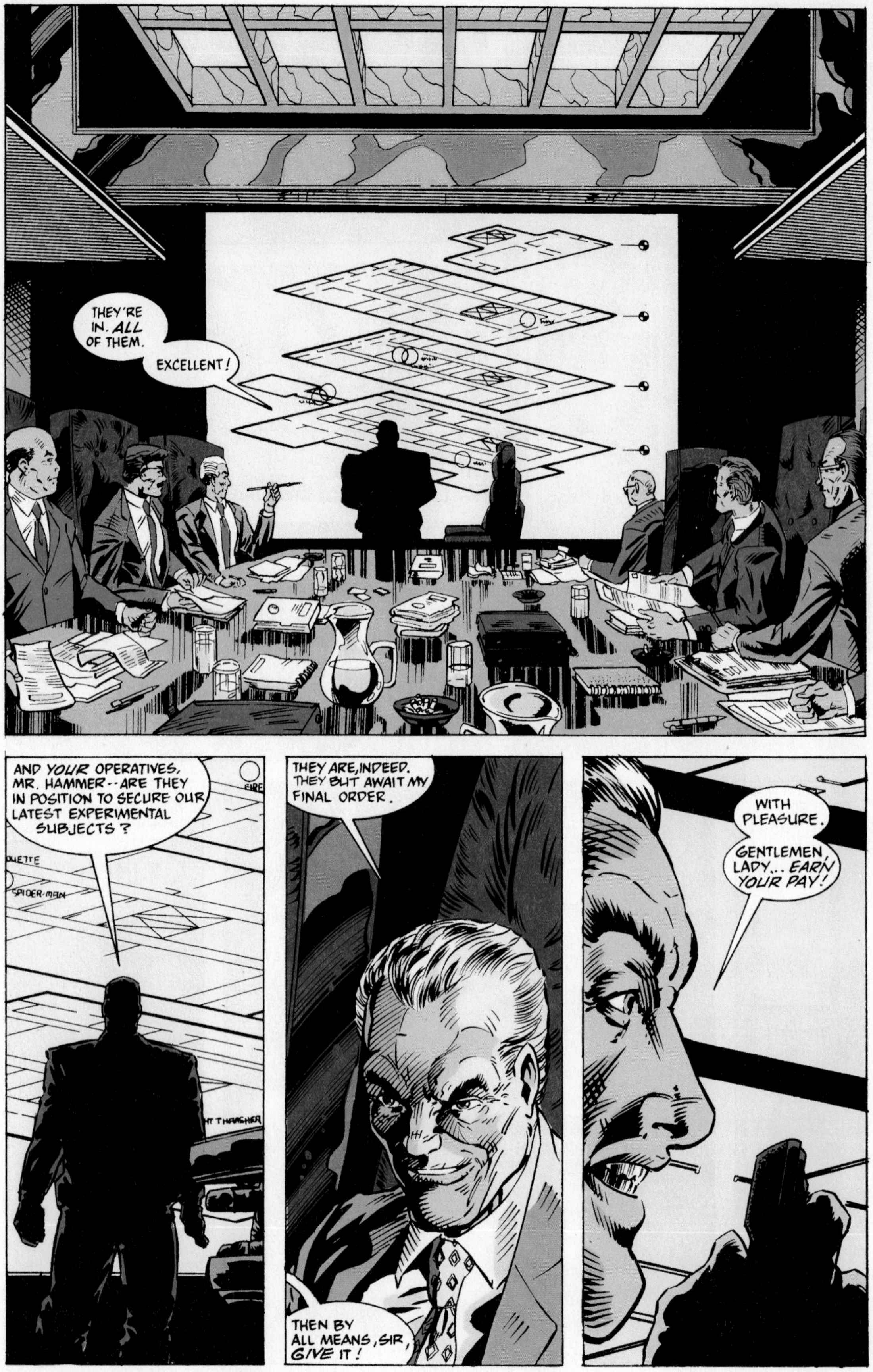
THEY'RE IN. ALL OF THEM.
EXCELLENT!
AND YOUR OPERATIVES, MR. HAMMER--ARE THEY IN POSITION TO SECURE OUR LATEST EXPERIMENTAL SUBJECTS?
SPIDER-MAN
THEY ARE, INDEED. THEY BUT AWAIT MY FINAL ORDER.
THEN BY ALL MEANS, SIR, GIVE IT!
WITH PLEASURE.
GENTLEMEN, LADY... EARN YOUR PAY!

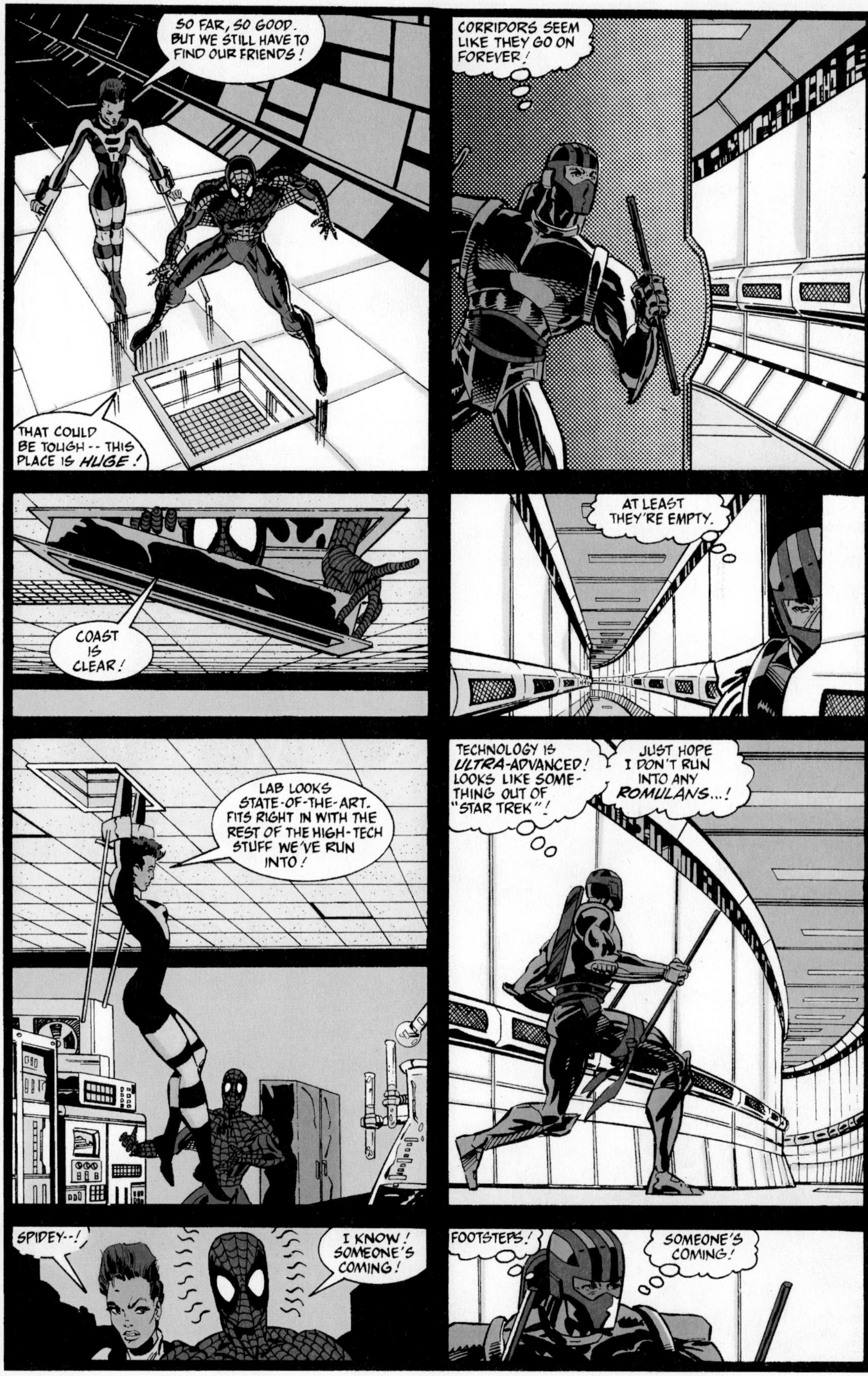
SO FAR, SO GOOD. BUT WE STILL HAVE TO FIND OUR FRIENDS!
THAT COULD BE TOUGH -- THIS PLACE IS *HUGE*!
CORRIDORS SEEM LIKE THEY GO ON FOREVER!
COAST IS CLEAR!
AT LEAST THEY'RE EMPTY.
LAB LOOKS STATE-OF-THE-ART. FITS RIGHT IN WITH THE REST OF THE HIGH-TECH STUFF WE'VE RUN INTO!
TECHNOLOGY IS *ULTRA*-ADVANCED! LOOKS LIKE SOMETHING OUT OF "STAR TREK"!
JUST HOPE I DON'T RUN INTO ANY *ROMULANS*...!
SPIDEY--!
I KNOW! SOMEONE'S COMING!
FOOTSTEPS!
SOMEONE'S COMING!

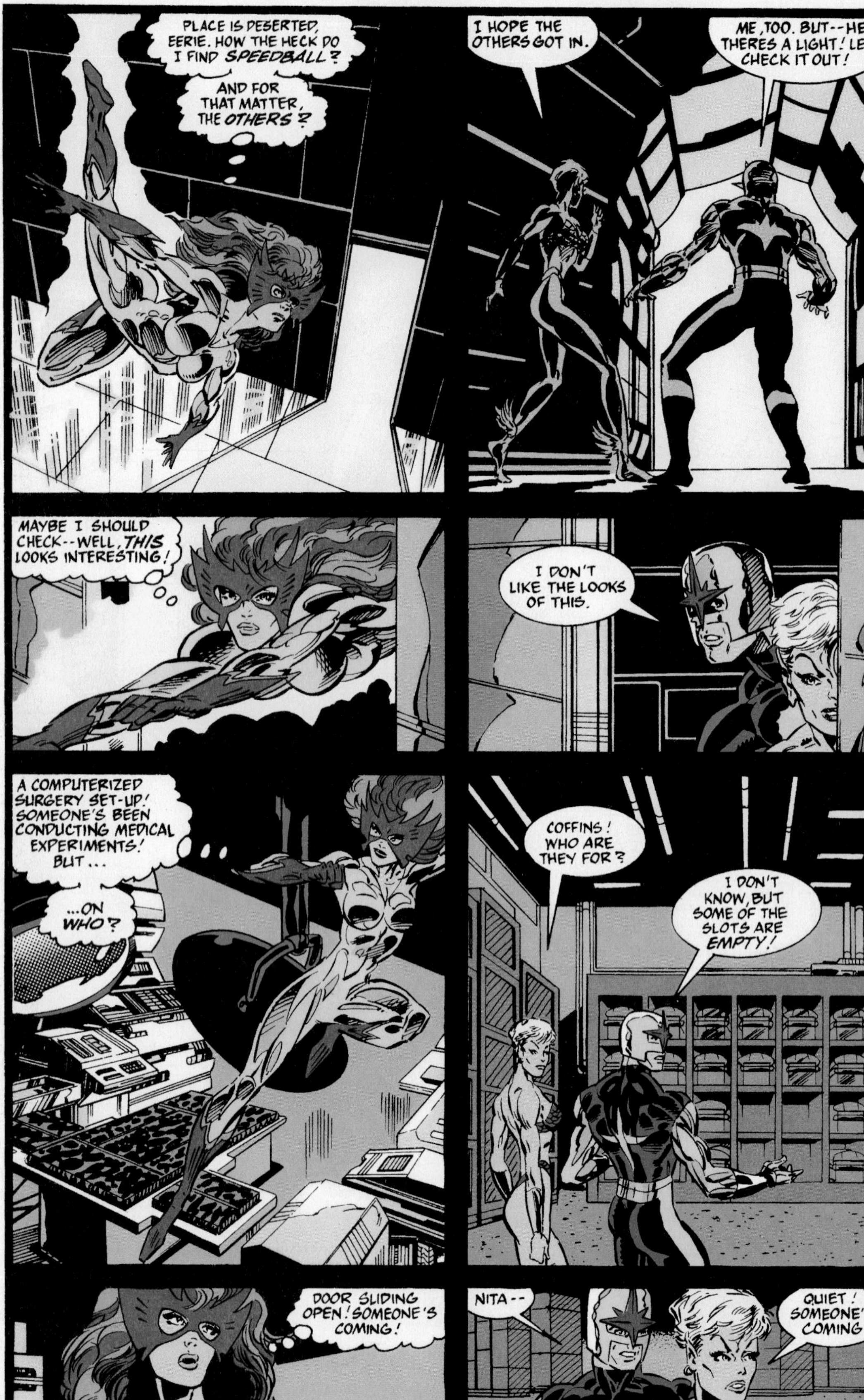
PLACE IS DESERTED, EERIE. HOW THE HECK DO I FIND SPEEDBALL?
AND FOR THAT MATTER, THE OTHERS?
I HOPE THE OTHERS GOT IN.
ME, TOO. BUT--HEY, THERES A LIGHT! LET'S CHECK IT OUT!
MAYBE I SHOULD CHECK--WELL, THIS LOOKS INTERESTING!
I DON'T LIKE THE LOOKS OF THIS.
A COMPUTERIZED SURGERY SET-UP! SOMEONE'S BEEN CONDUCTING MEDICAL EXPERIMENTS! BUT...
...ON WHO?
COFFINS! WHO ARE THEY FOR?
I DON'T KNOW, BUT SOME OF THE SLOTS ARE EMPTY!
DOOR SLIDING OPEN! SOMEONE'S COMING!
NITA--
QUIET! SOMEONE'S COMING

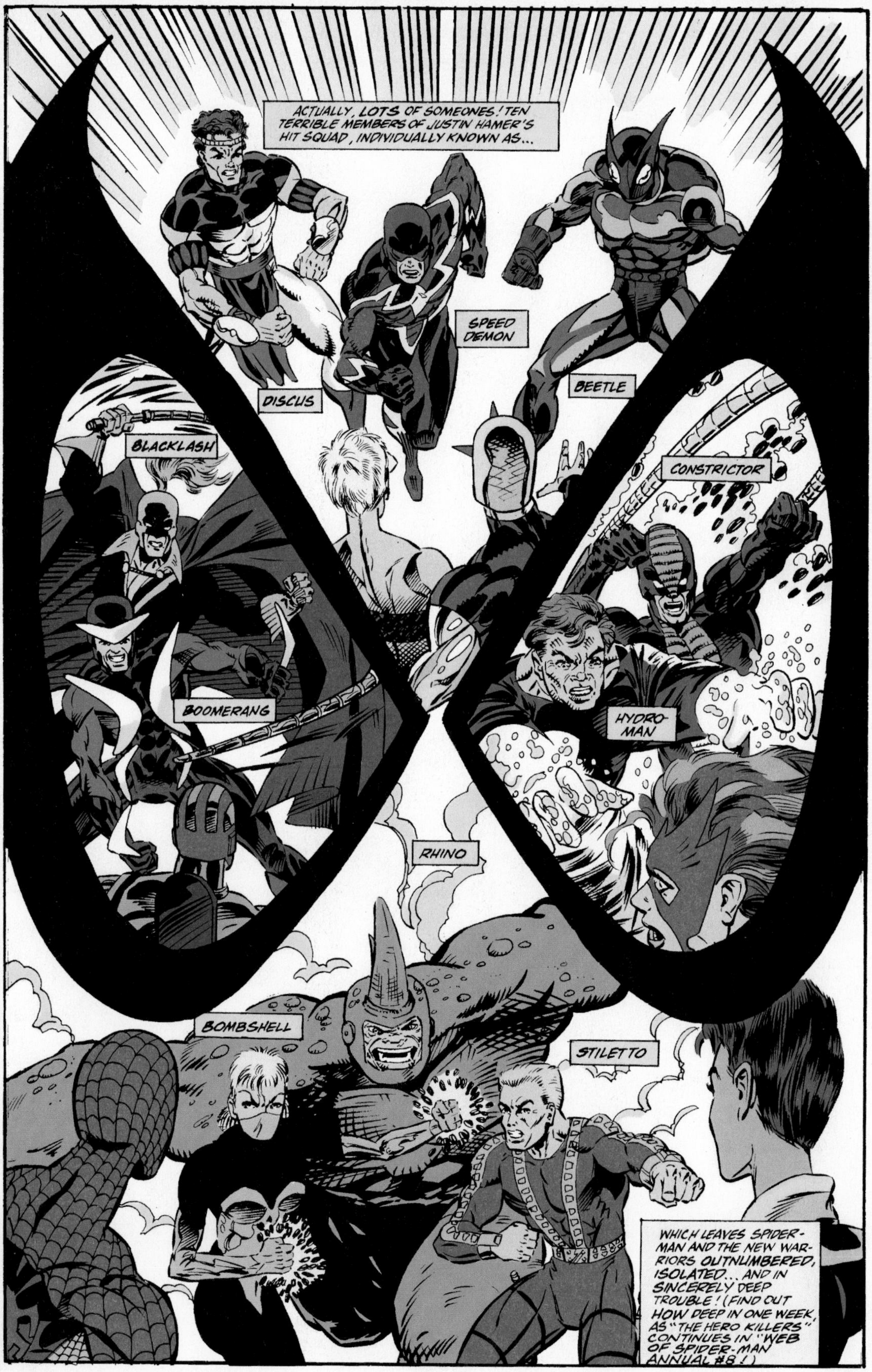
ACTUALLY, LOTS OF SOMEONES! TEN TERRIBLE MEMBERS OF JUSTIN HAMER'S HIT SQUAD, INDIVIDUALLY KNOWN AS...
SPEED DEMON
DISCUS
BEETLE
BLACKLASH
CONSTRICTOR
BOOMERANG
HYDRO-MAN
RHINO
BOMBSHELL
STILETTO
WHICH LEAVES SPIDER-MAN AND THE NEW WARRIORS OUTNUMBERED, ISOLATED... AND IN SINCERELY DEEP TROUBLE! (FIND OUT HOW DEEP IN ONE WEEK, AS "THE HERO KILLERS" CONTINUES IN "WEB OF SPIDER-MAN ANNUAL #8!)

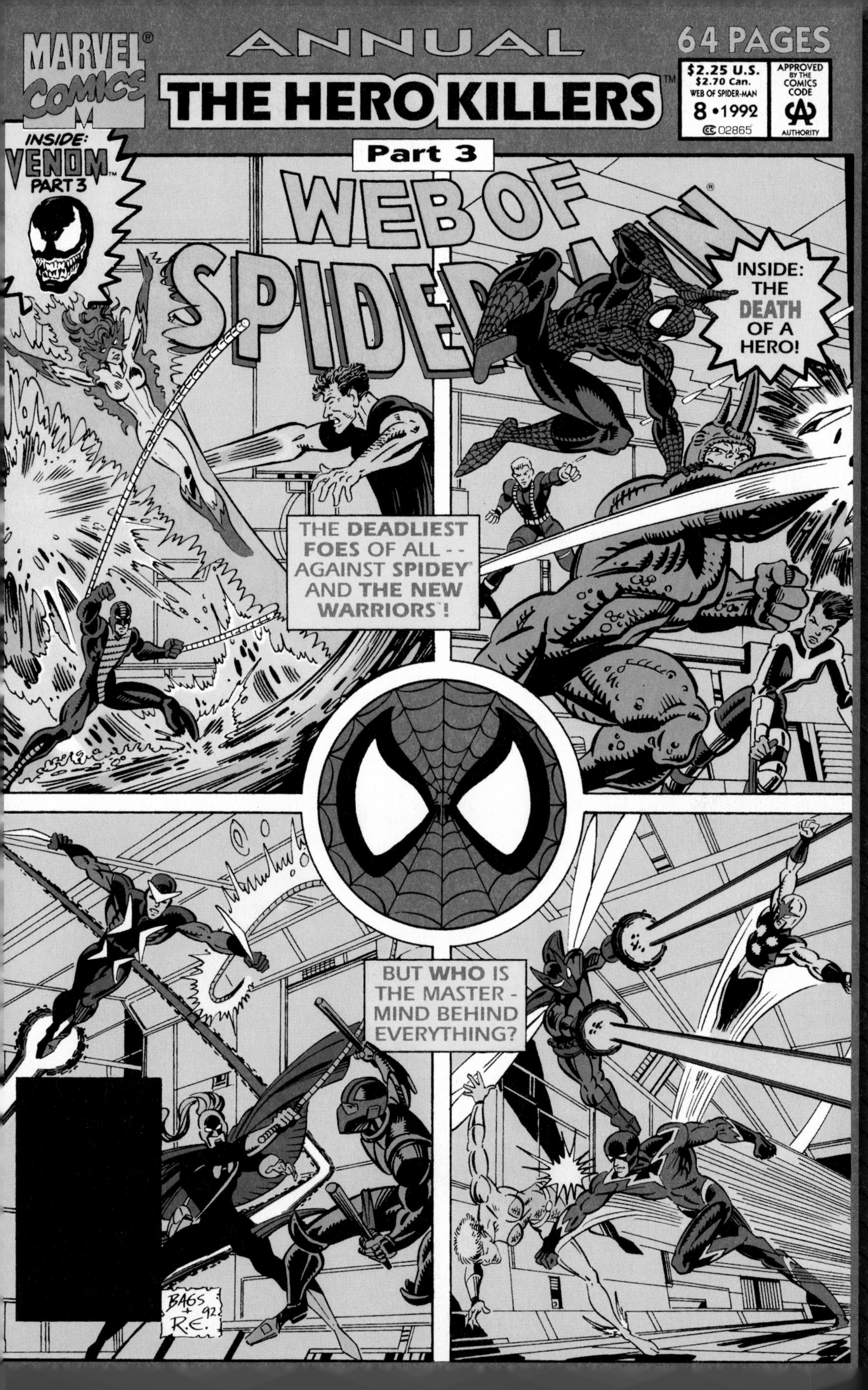
MARVEL® COMICS
ANNUAL
64 PAGES
THE HERO KILLERS™
$2.25 U.S.
$2.70 Can.
WEB OF SPIDER-MAN
8 •1992
02865
APPROVED BY THE COMICS CODE AUTHORITY
INSIDE: VENOM™ PART 3
Part 3
WEB OF SPIDER-MAN®
INSIDE: THE DEATH OF A HERO!
THE DEADLIEST FOES OF ALL - - AGAINST SPIDEY® AND THE NEW WARRIORS™!
BUT WHO IS THE MASTER - MIND BEHIND EVERYTHING?
BAGS + '92 R.E.

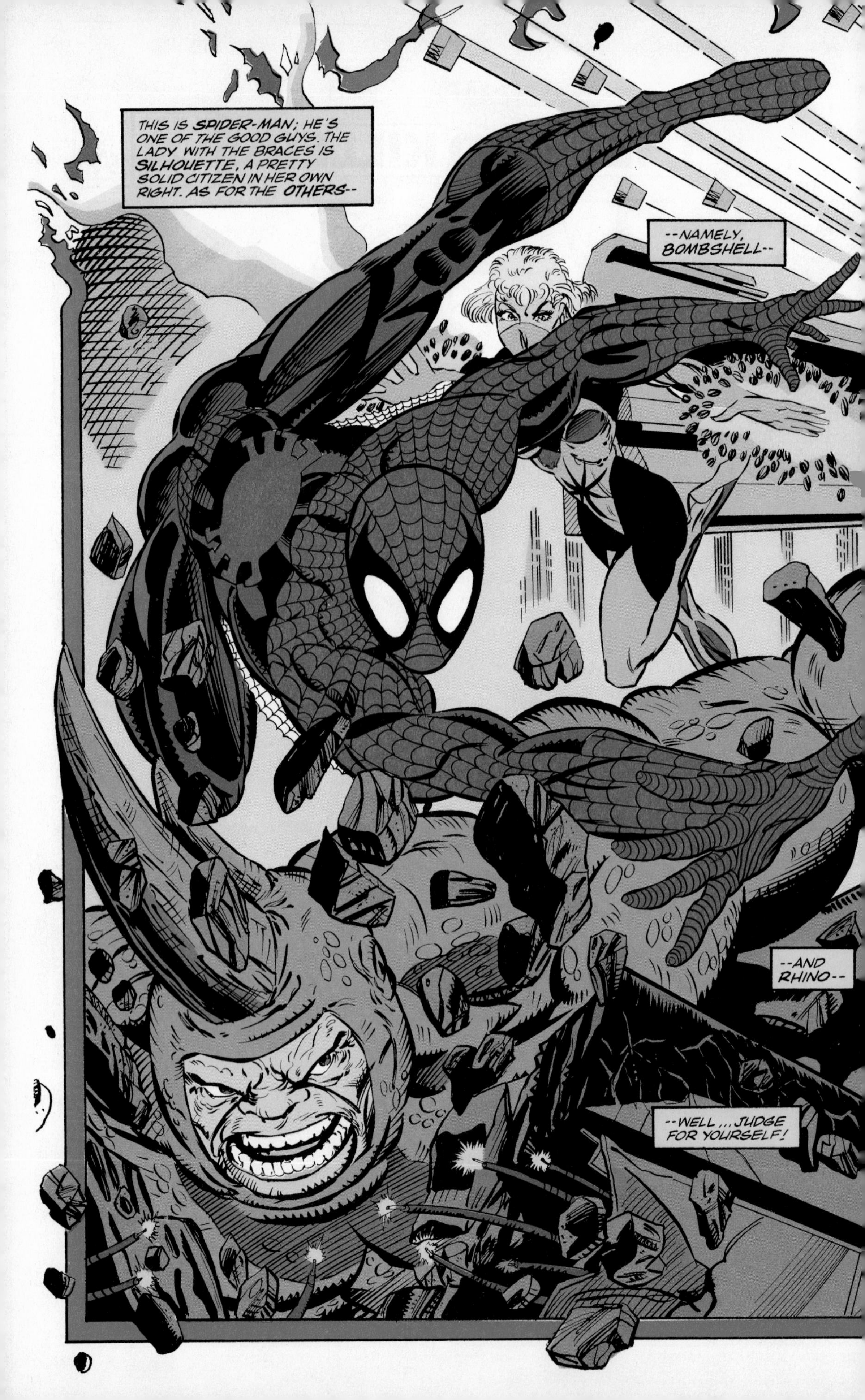
THIS IS SPIDER-MAN; HE'S ONE OF THE GOOD GUYS. THE LADY WITH THE BRACES IS SILHOUETTE, A PRETTY SOLID CITIZEN IN HER OWN RIGHT. AS FOR THE OTHERS--
--NAMELY, BOMBSHELL--
--AND RHINO--
--WELL,...JUDGE FOR YOURSELF!

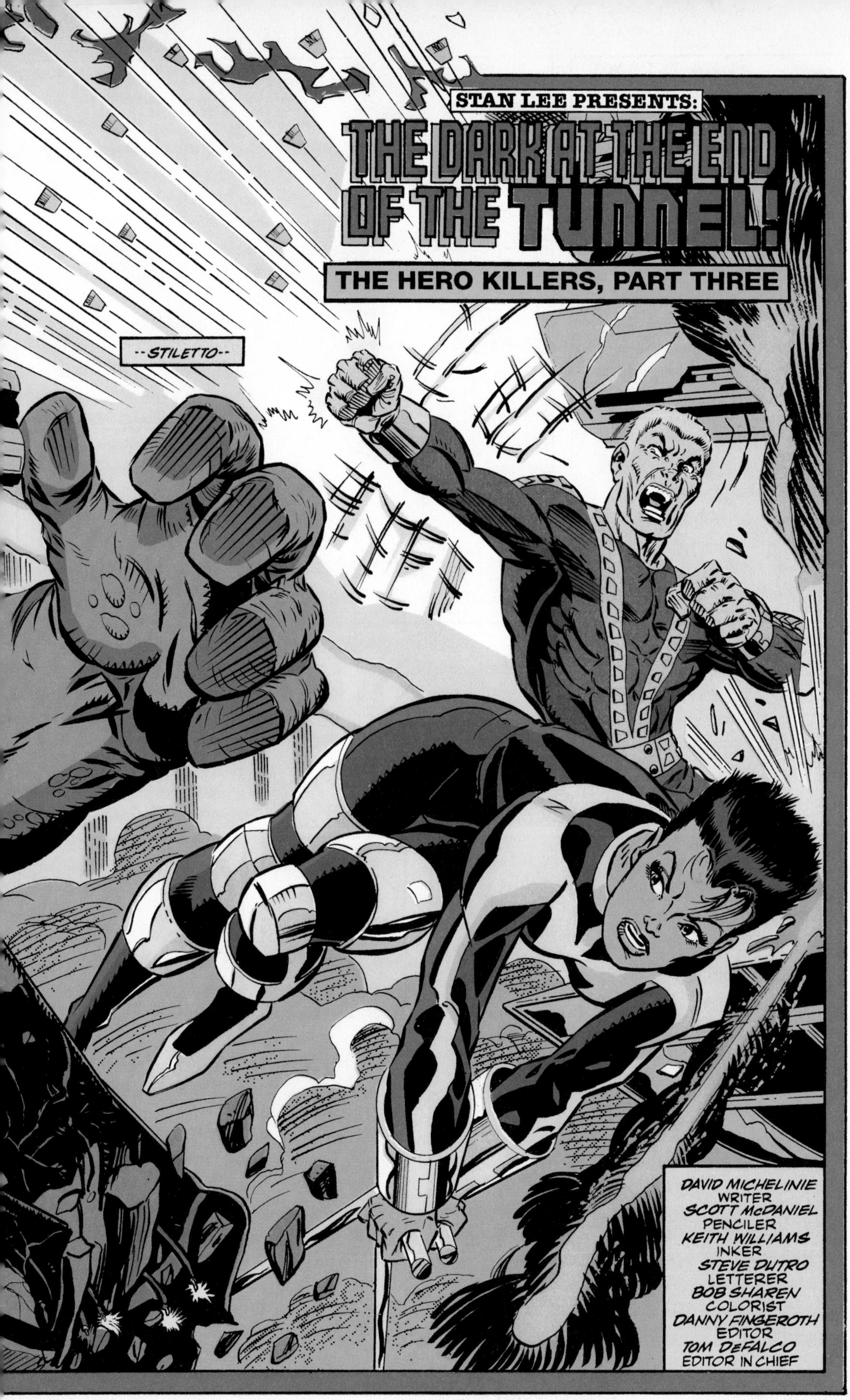
STAN LEE PRESENTS:
THE DARK AT THE END OF THE TUNNEL!
THE HERO KILLERS, PART THREE
--STILETTO--
DAVID MICHELINIE
WRITER
SCOTT McDANIEL
PENCILER
KEITH WILLIAMS
INKER
STEVE DUTRO
LETTERER
BOB SHAREN
COLORIST
DANNY FINGEROTH
EDITOR
TOM DeFALCO
EDITOR IN CHIEF

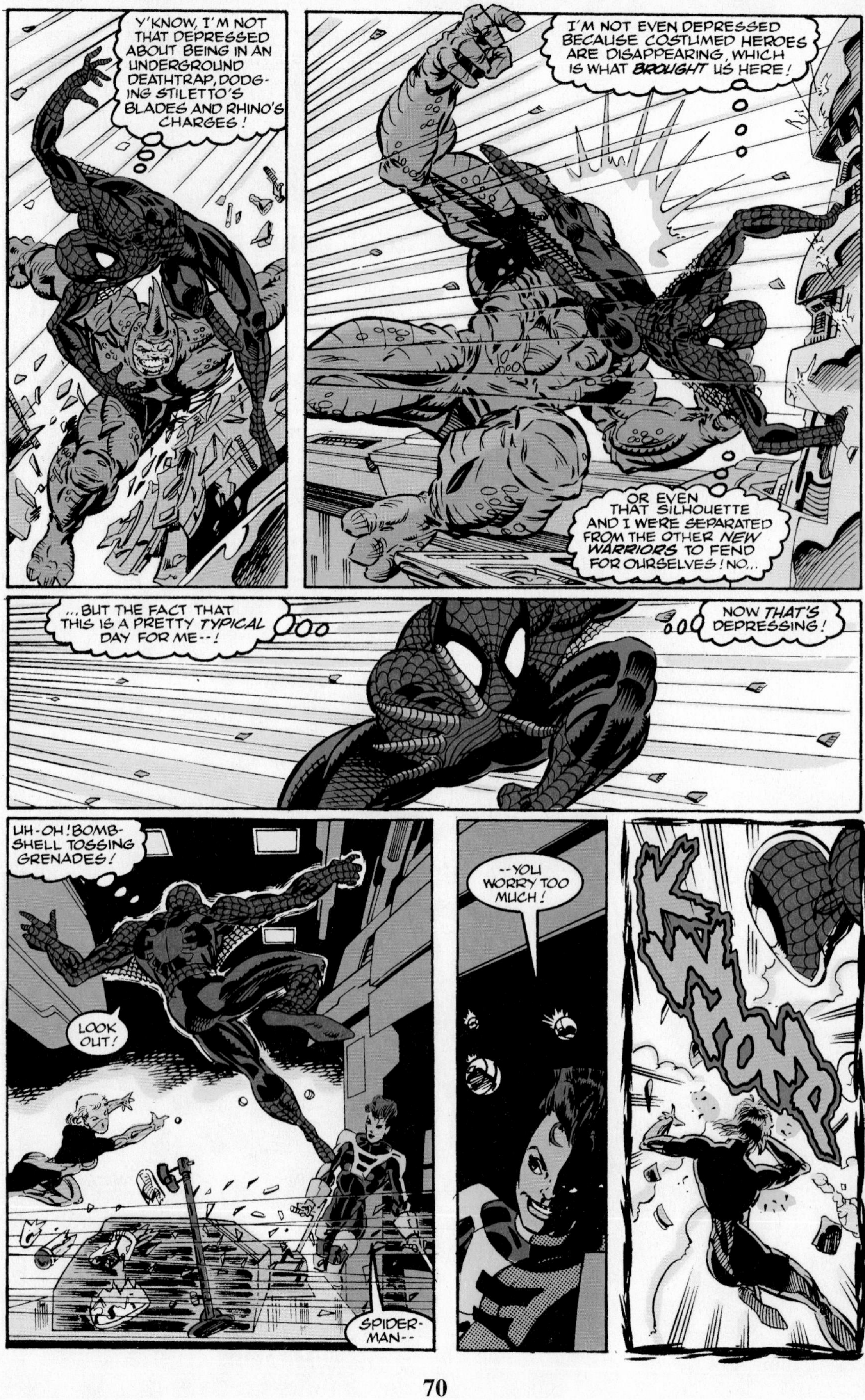

Y'KNOW, I'M NOT THAT DEPRESSED ABOUT BEING IN AN UNDERGROUND DEATHTRAP, DODGING STILETTO'S BLADES AND RHINO'S CHARGES!
I'M NOT EVEN DEPRESSED BECAUSE COSTUMED HEROES ARE DISAPPEARING, WHICH IS WHAT BROUGHT US HERE!
OR EVEN THAT SILHOUETTE AND I WERE SEPARATED FROM THE OTHER NEW WARRIORS TO FEND FOR OURSELVES! NO...
...BUT THE FACT THAT THIS IS A PRETTY TYPICAL DAY FOR ME--!
NOW THAT'S DEPRESSING!
UH-OH! BOMBSHELL TOSSING GRENADES!
LOOK OUT!
SPIDER-MAN--
--YOU WORRY TOO MUCH!

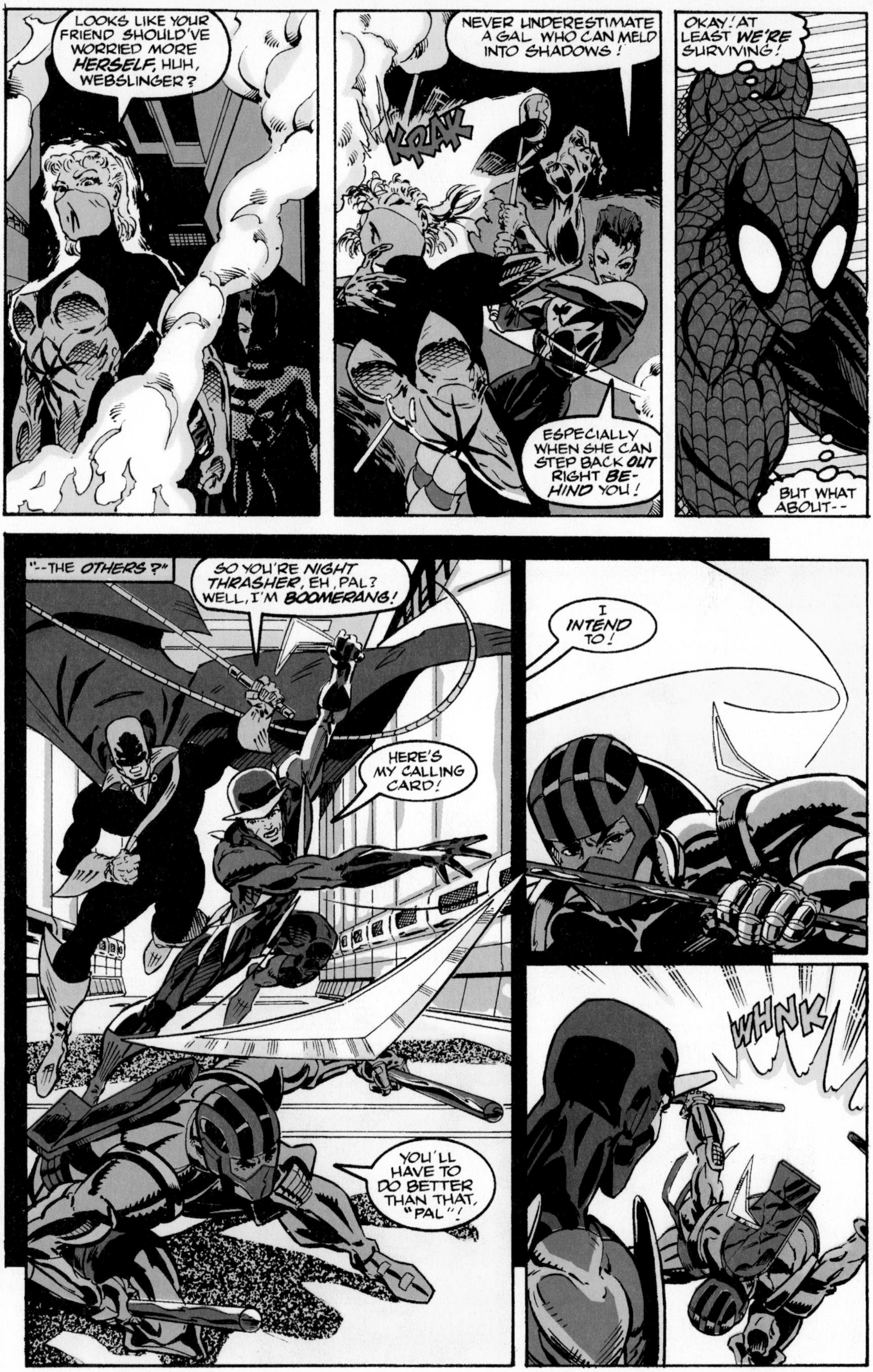
LOOKS LIKE YOUR FRIEND SHOULD'VE WORRIED MORE HERSELF, HUH, WEBSLINGER?
NEVER UNDERESTIMATE A GAL WHO CAN MELD INTO SHADOWS!
KRAK
ESPECIALLY WHEN SHE CAN STEP BACK OUT RIGHT BE-HIND YOU!
OKAY! AT LEAST WE'RE SURVIVING!
BUT WHAT ABOUT--
"--THE OTHERS?"
SO YOU'RE NIGHT THRASHER, EH, PAL? WELL, I'M BOOMERANG!
HERE'S MY CALLING CARD!
YOU'LL HAVE TO DO BETTER THAN THAT, "PAL"!
I INTEND TO!
WHNK

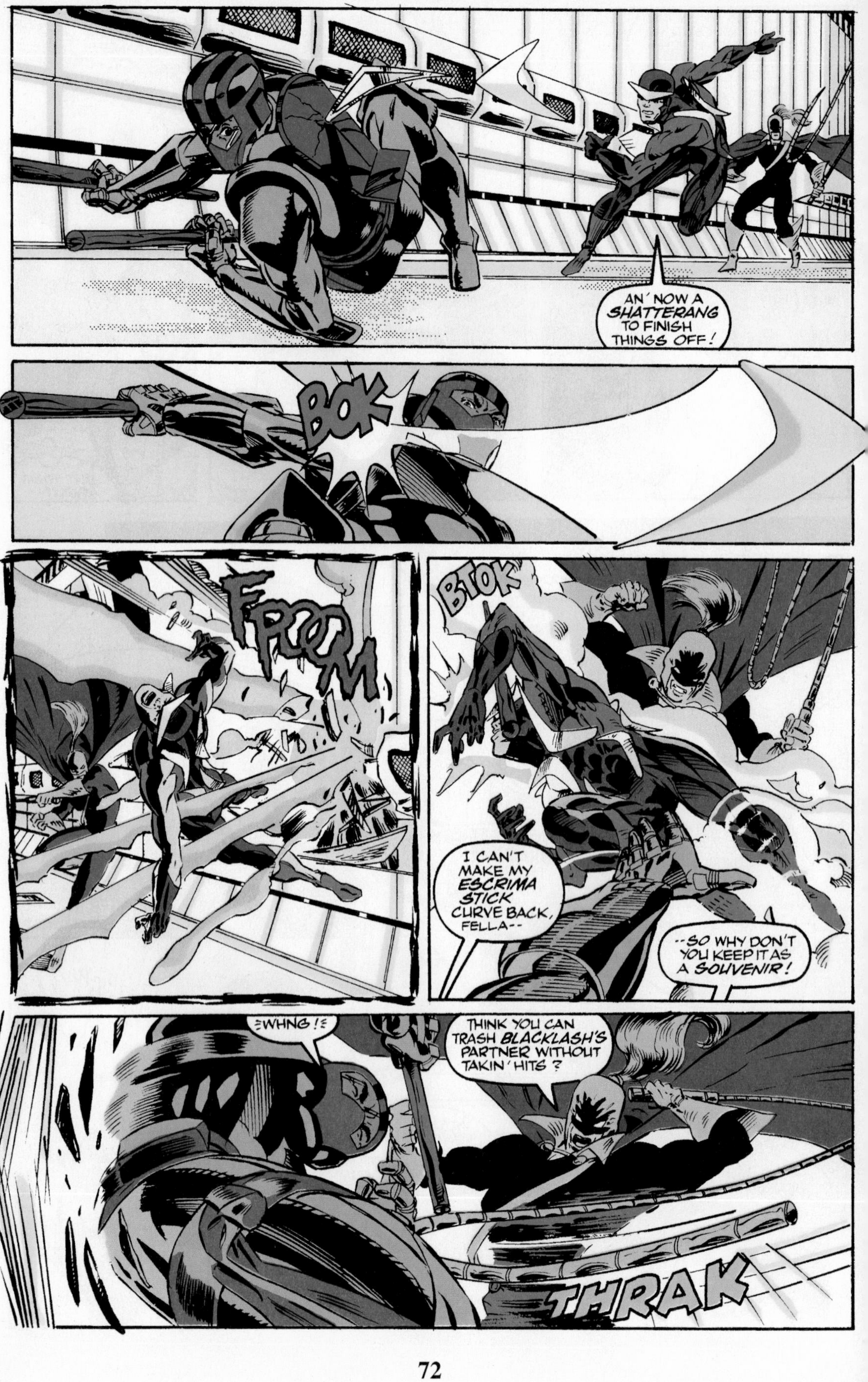
AN' NOW A SHATTERANG TO FINISH THINGS OFF!
BOK
FROOM
BTOK
I CAN'T MAKE MY ESCRIMA STICK CURVE BACK, FELLA--
--SO WHY DON'T YOU KEEP IT AS A SOUVENIR!
=WHNG!=
THINK YOU CAN TRASH BLACKLASH'S PARTNER WITHOUT TAKIN' HITS?
THRAK

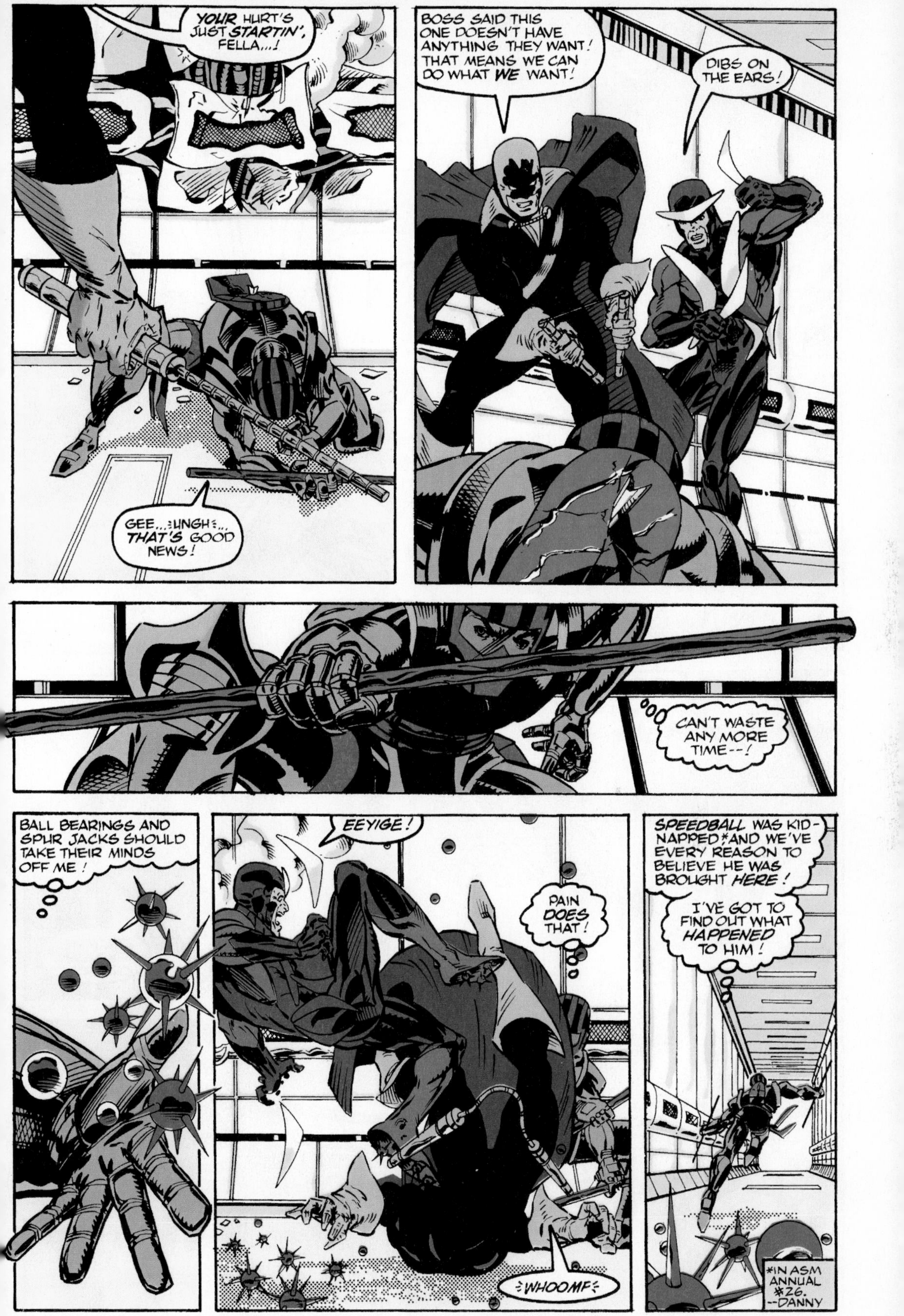
YOUR HURT'S JUST STARTIN', FELLA...!
GEE... UNGH... THAT'S GOOD NEWS!
BOSS SAID THIS ONE DOESN'T HAVE ANYTHING THEY WANT! THAT MEANS WE CAN DO WHAT WE WANT!
DIBS ON THE EARS!
CAN'T WASTE ANY MORE TIME--!
BALL BEARINGS AND SPUR JACKS SHOULD TAKE THEIR MINDS OFF ME!
EEYIGE!
PAIN DOES THAT!
WHOOMF
SPEEDBALL WAS KID-NAPPED* AND WE'VE EVERY REASON TO BELIEVE HE WAS BROUGHT HERE!
I'VE GOT TO FIND OUT WHAT HAPPENED TO HIM!
*IN ASM ANNUAL #26. --DANNY

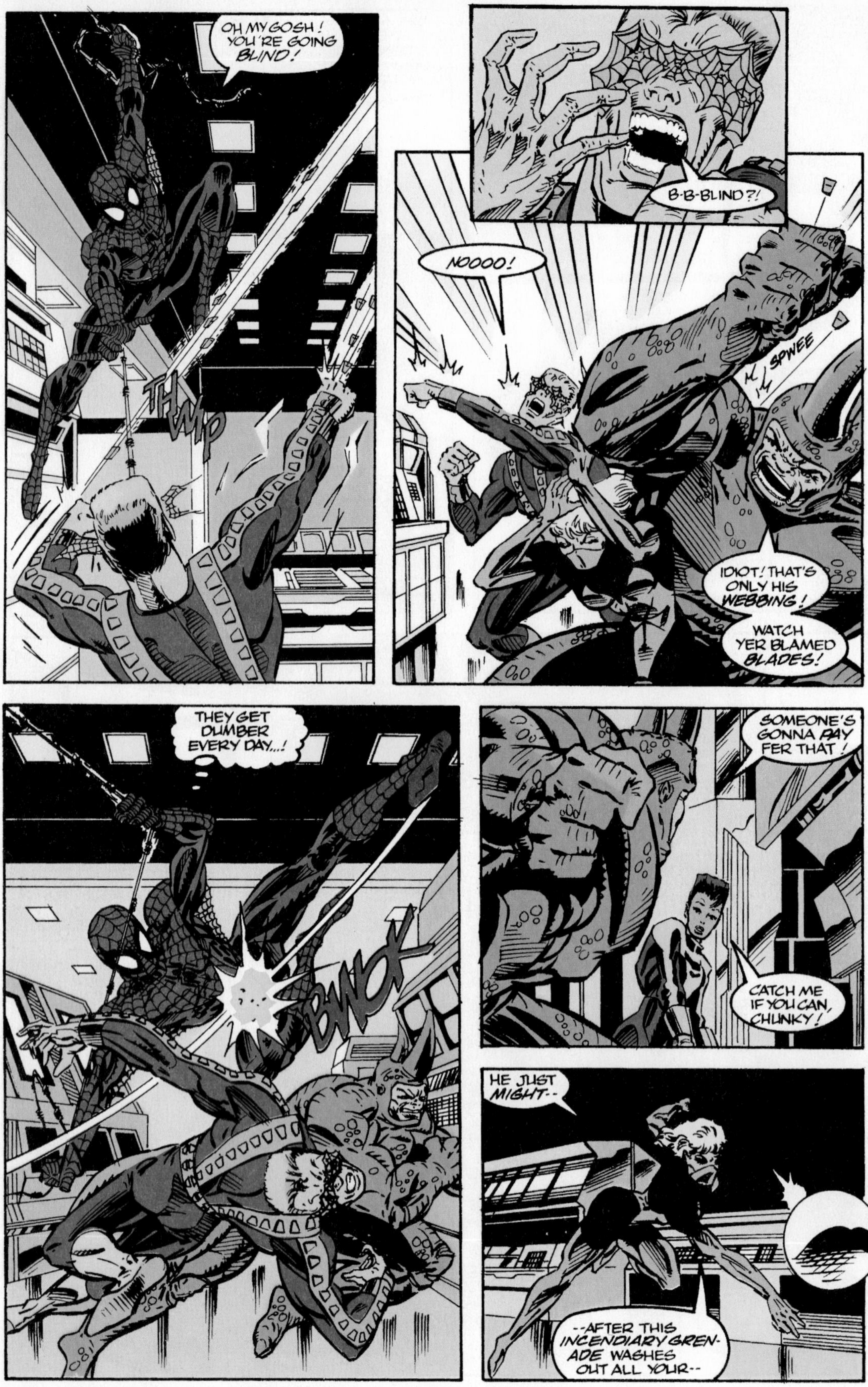

OH MY GOSH! YOU'RE GOING BLIND!
THWIP
B-B-BLIND?!
NOOOO!
SPWEE
IDIOT! THAT'S ONLY HIS WEBBING!
WATCH YER BLAMED BLADES!
THEY GET DUMBER EVERY DAY...!
BWOK
SOMEONE'S GONNA PAY FER THAT!
CATCH ME IF YOU CAN, CHUNKY!
HE JUST MIGHT--
--AFTER THIS INCENDIARY GRENADE WASHES OUT ALL YOUR--

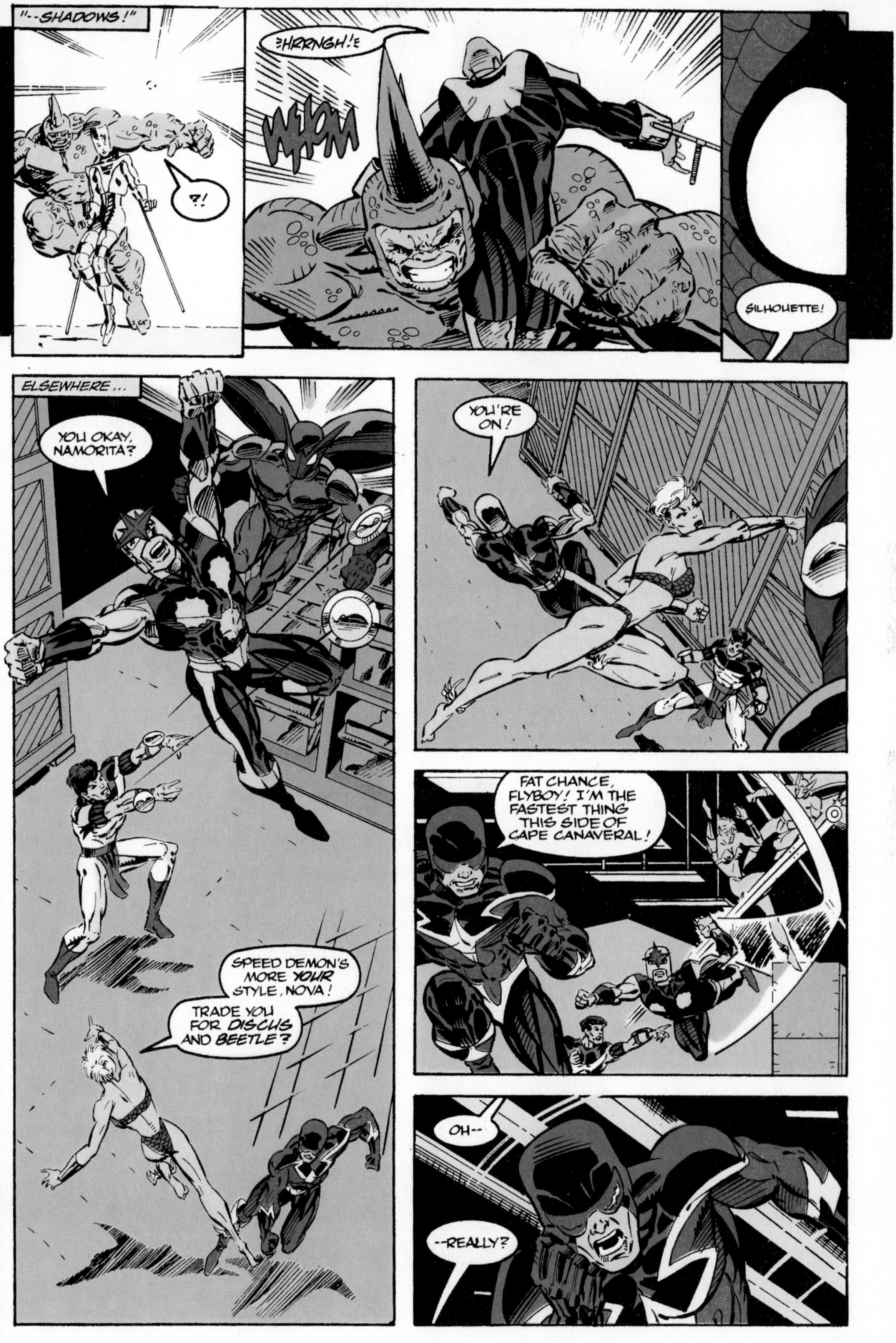
"--SHADOWS!"
?!
HRRNGH!
WHOM
SILHOUETTE!
ELSEWHERE...
YOU OKAY, NAMORITA?
SPEED DEMON'S MORE YOUR STYLE, NOVA!
TRADE YOU FOR DISCUS AND BEETLE?
YOU'RE ON!
FAT CHANCE, FLYBOY! I'M THE FASTEST THING THIS SIDE OF CAPE CANAVERAL!
OH--
--REALLY?

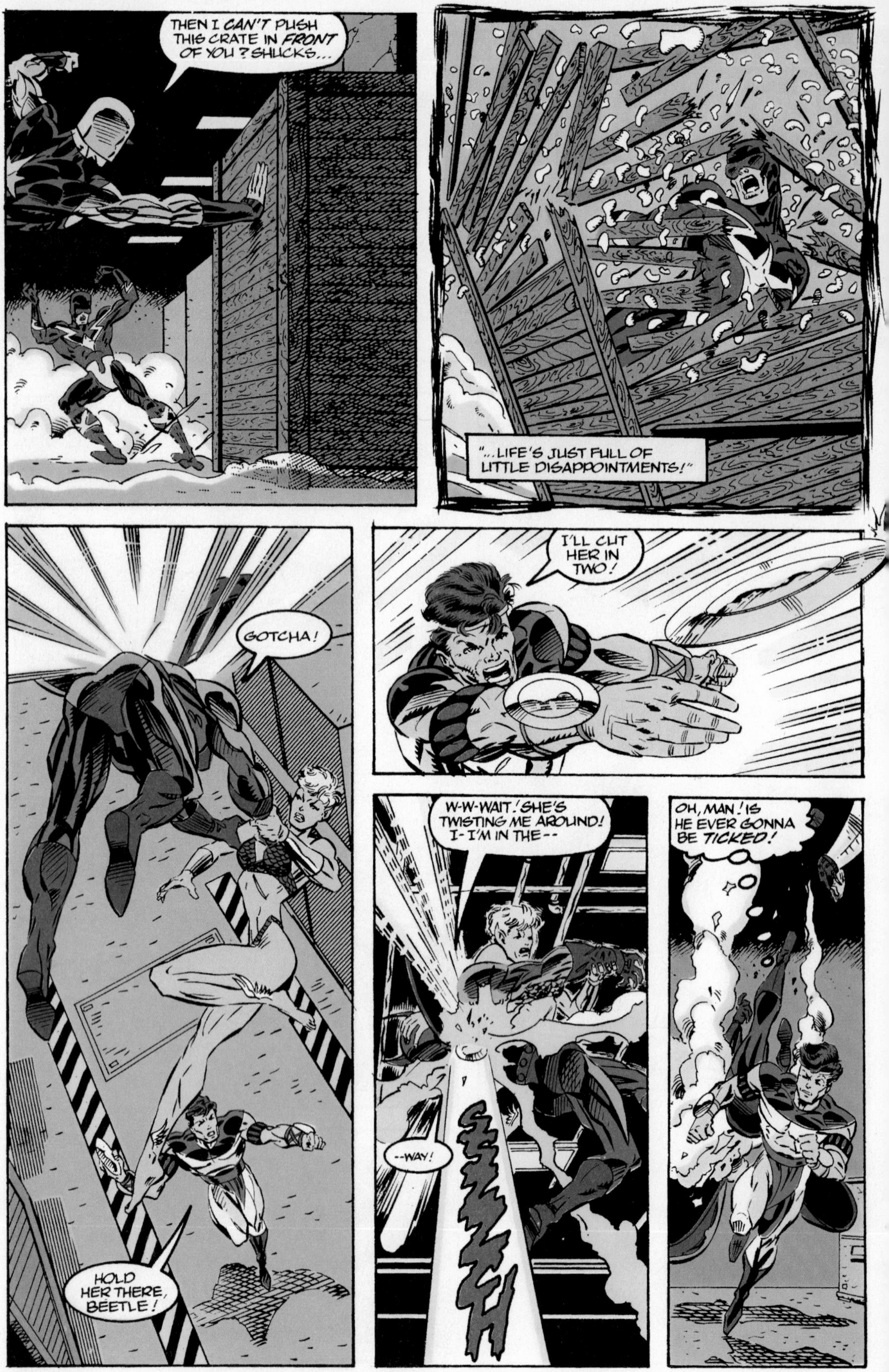
THEN I CAN'T PUSH THIS CRATE IN FRONT OF YOU? SHUCKS...
"...LIFE'S JUST FULL OF LITTLE DISAPPOINTMENTS!"
GOTCHA!
HOLD HER THERE, BEETLE!
I'LL CUT HER IN TWO!
W-W-WAIT! SHE'S TWISTING ME AROUND! I- I'M IN THE--
--WAY!
SHNNCH
OH, MAN! IS HE EVER GONNA BE TICKED!

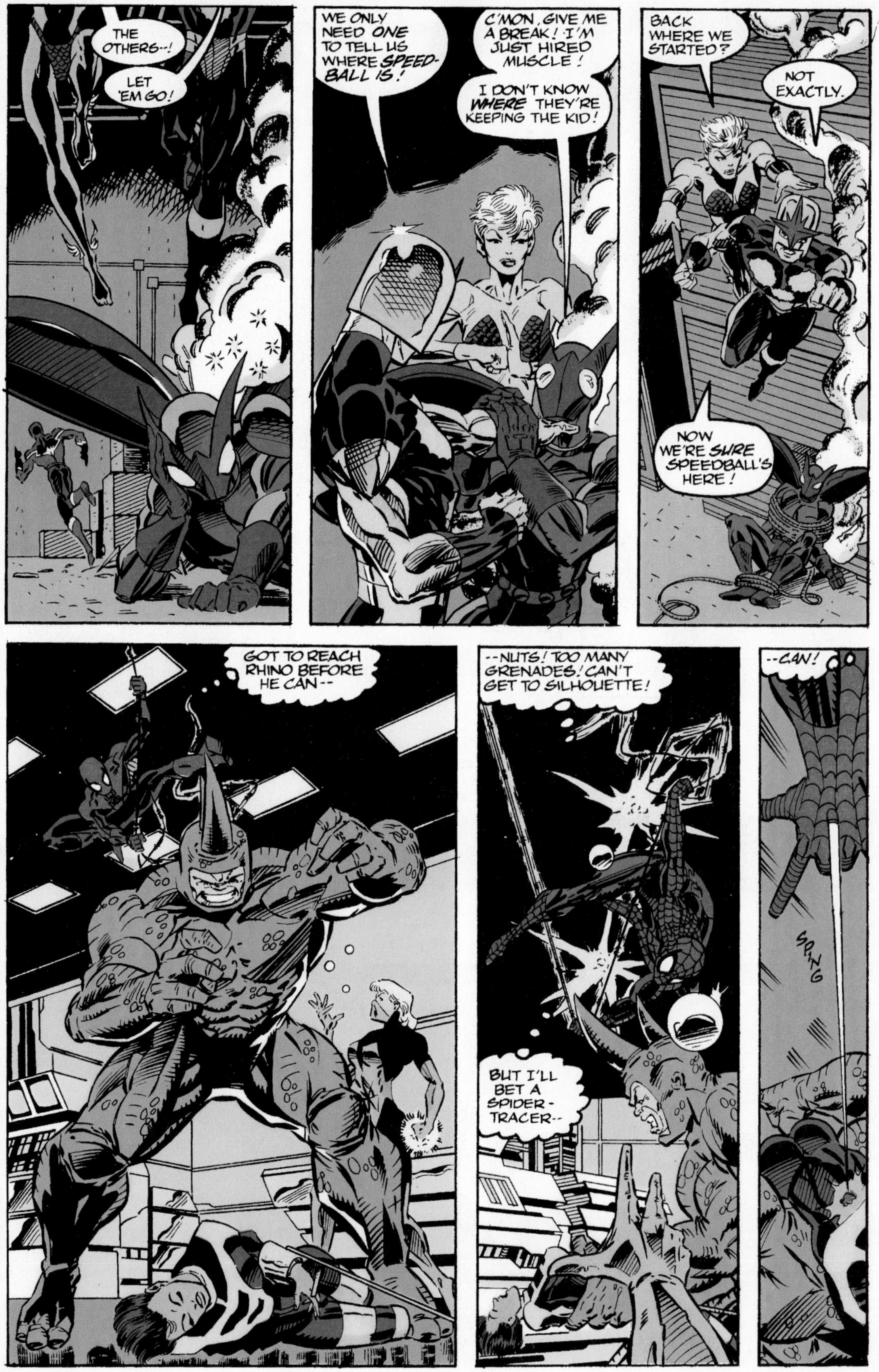
THE OTHERS--!
LET 'EM GO!
WE ONLY NEED ONE TO TELL US WHERE SPEEDBALL IS!
C'MON, GIVE ME A BREAK! I'M JUST HIRED MUSCLE!
I DON'T KNOW WHERE THEY'RE KEEPING THE KID!
BACK WHERE WE STARTED?
NOT EXACTLY.
NOW WE'RE SURE SPEEDBALL'S HERE!
GOT TO REACH RHINO BEFORE HE CAN--
--NUTS! TOO MANY GRENADES! CAN'T GET TO SILHOUETTE!
BUT I'LL BET A SPIDER-TRACER--
--CAN!
SPUNG

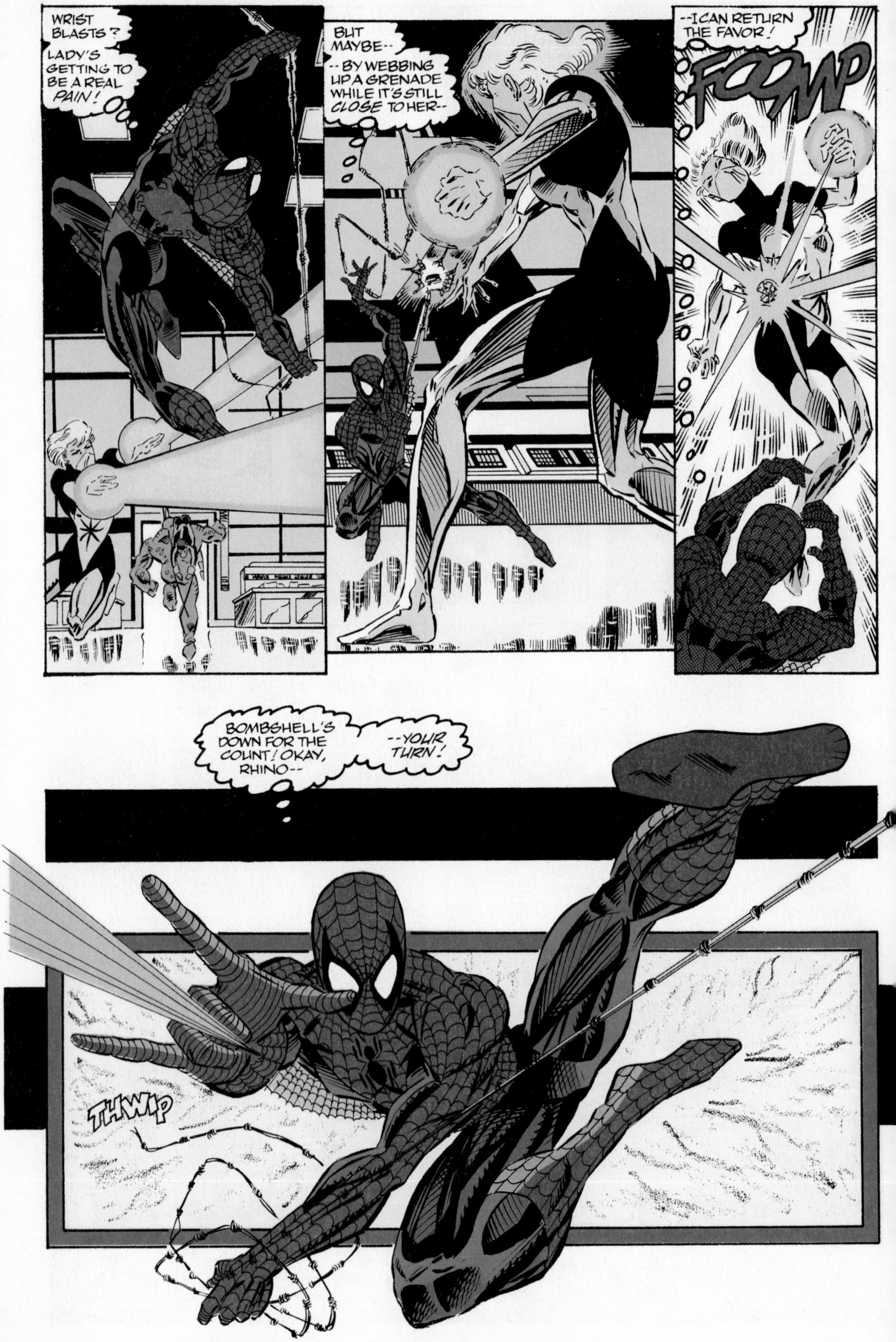
WRIST BLASTS? LADY'S GETTING TO BE A REAL PAIN!
BUT MAYBE--
--BY WEBBING UP A GRENADE WHILE IT'S STILL CLOSE TO HER--
--I CAN RETURN THE FAVOR!
FOOMP
BOMBSHELL'S DOWN FOR THE COUNT! OKAY, RHINO--
--YOUR TURN!
THWIP

FIRESTAR'S A FLYER, HYDRO-MAN! SPLASH 'ER BEFORE SHE GETS AIRBORNE!

DON'T TELL ME MY JOB, CONSTRICTOR!

HOW ELSE WILL YOU LEARN NOT TO USE WATER ON A LADY WITH MICRO-WAVE POWERS?

HAVE A STEAM BATH, WET STUFF!

SOMEBODY'S GOT TO!

YOU'RE GONNA BE A LOT THINNER YOUR-SELF, SWEETHEART!

MY ADAMANTIUM COILS SQUEEZE AT 115 POUNDS PER INCH!

ADAMANTIUM, HUH? TOUGH STUFF! EVEN I CAN'T MELT IT!

BUT FROM WHAT I UNDERSTAND, IT DOES MAKE A DARN GOOD--

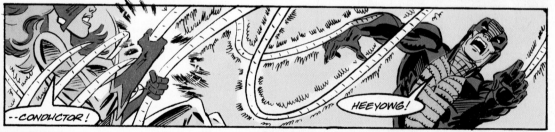

--CONDUCTOR!

HEEYOWG!

GET THE WITCH!

LIKE YA HADDA TELL ME!

THOSE GENTLE-MEN ARE NOT HAPPY CAMPERS!

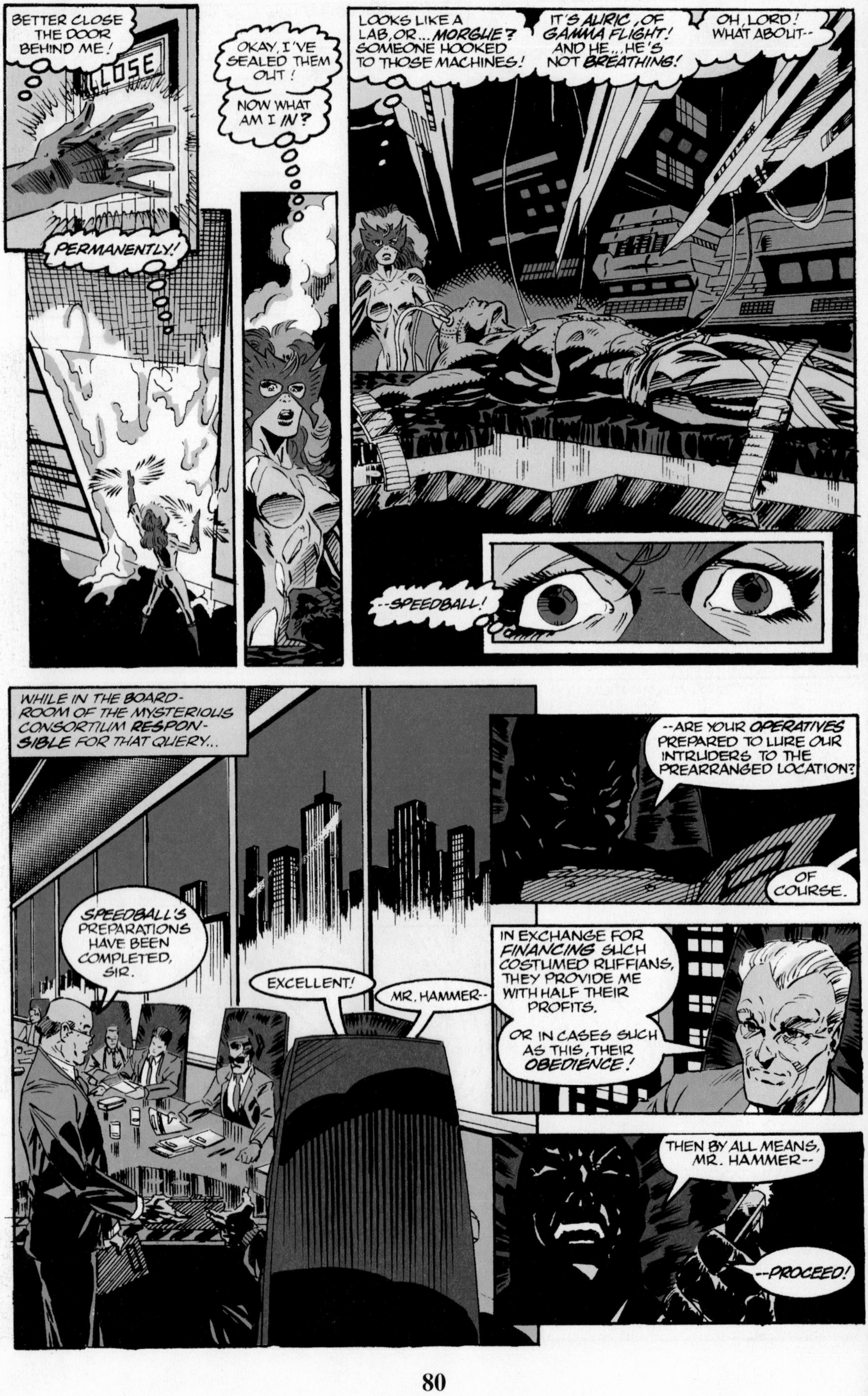
BETTER CLOSE THE DOOR BEHIND ME!
CLOSE
PERMANENTLY!
OKAY, I'VE SEALED THEM OUT!
NOW WHAT AM I IN?
LOOKS LIKE A LAB, OR... MORGUE? SOMEONE HOOKED TO THOSE MACHINES!
IT'S AURIC, OF GAMMA FLIGHT! AND HE... HE'S NOT BREATHING!
OH, LORD! WHAT ABOUT--
--SPEEDBALL!
WHILE IN THE BOARD-ROOM OF THE MYSTERIOUS CONSORTIUM RESPONSIBLE FOR THAT QUERY...
SPEEDBALL'S PREPARATIONS HAVE BEEN COMPLETED, SIR.
EXCELLENT!
MR. HAMMER--
--ARE YOUR OPERATIVES PREPARED TO LURE OUR INTRUDERS TO THE PREARRANGED LOCATION?
OF COURSE.
IN EXCHANGE FOR FINANCING SUCH COSTUMED RUFFIANS, THEY PROVIDE ME WITH HALF THEIR PROFITS.
OR IN CASES SUCH AS THIS, THEIR OBEDIENCE!
THEN BY ALL MEANS, MR. HAMMER--
--PROCEED!

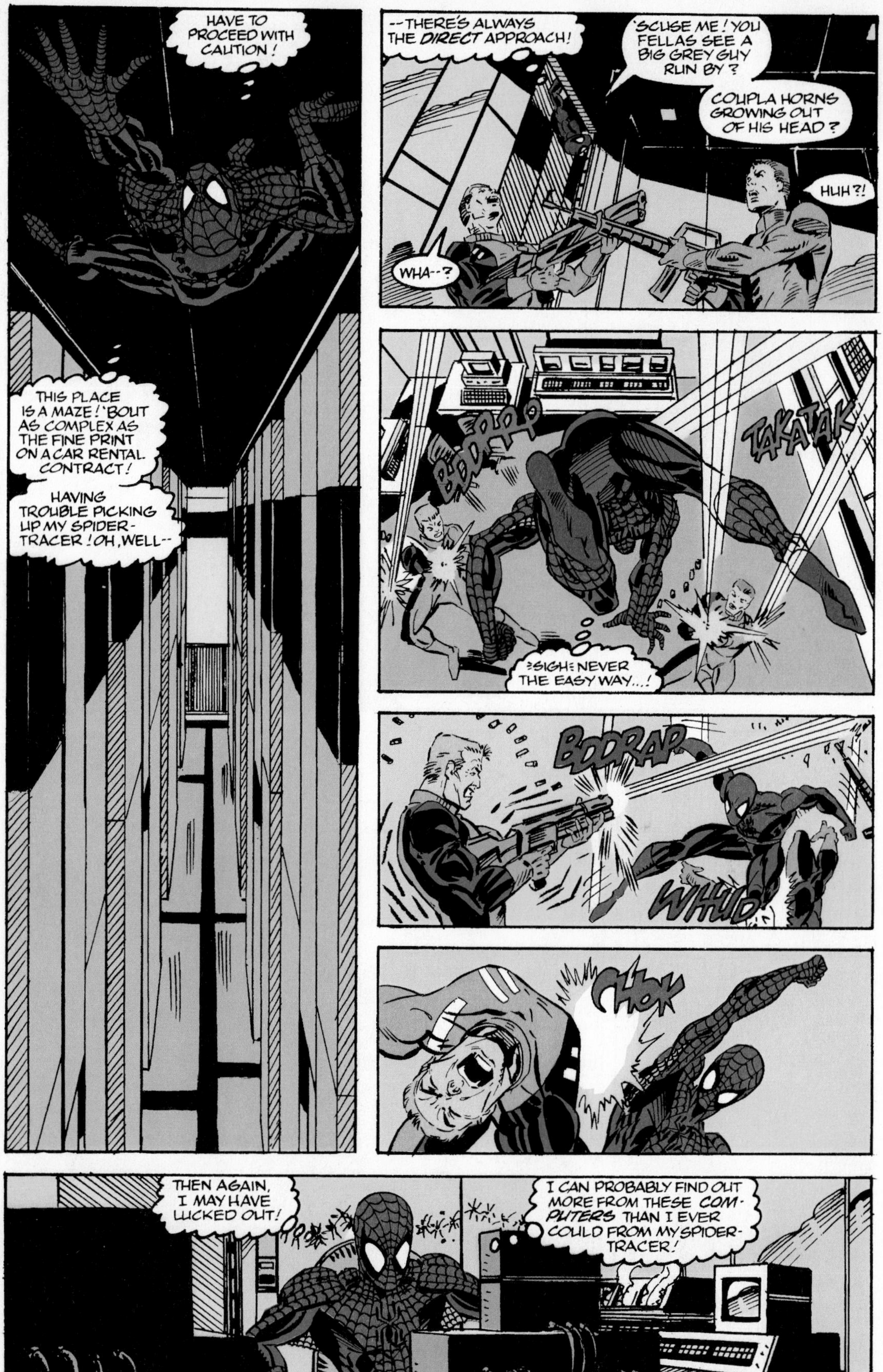
HAVE TO PROCEED WITH CAUTION!
THIS PLACE IS A MAZE! 'BOUT AS COMPLEX AS THE FINE PRINT ON A CAR RENTAL CONTRACT!
HAVING TROUBLE PICKING UP MY SPIDER-TRACER! OH, WELL--
--THERE'S ALWAYS THE DIRECT APPROACH!
'SCUSE ME! YOU FELLAS SEE A BIG GREY GUY RUN BY?
COUPLA HORNS GROWING OUT OF HIS HEAD?
HUH?!
WHA--?
BDDRRRP
TAKATAK
SIGH NEVER THE EASY WAY...!
BDDRAP
WHUD
CHOK
THEN AGAIN, I MAY HAVE LUCKED OUT!
I CAN PROBABLY FIND OUT MORE FROM THESE COMPUTERS THAN I EVER COULD FROM MY SPIDER-TRACER!

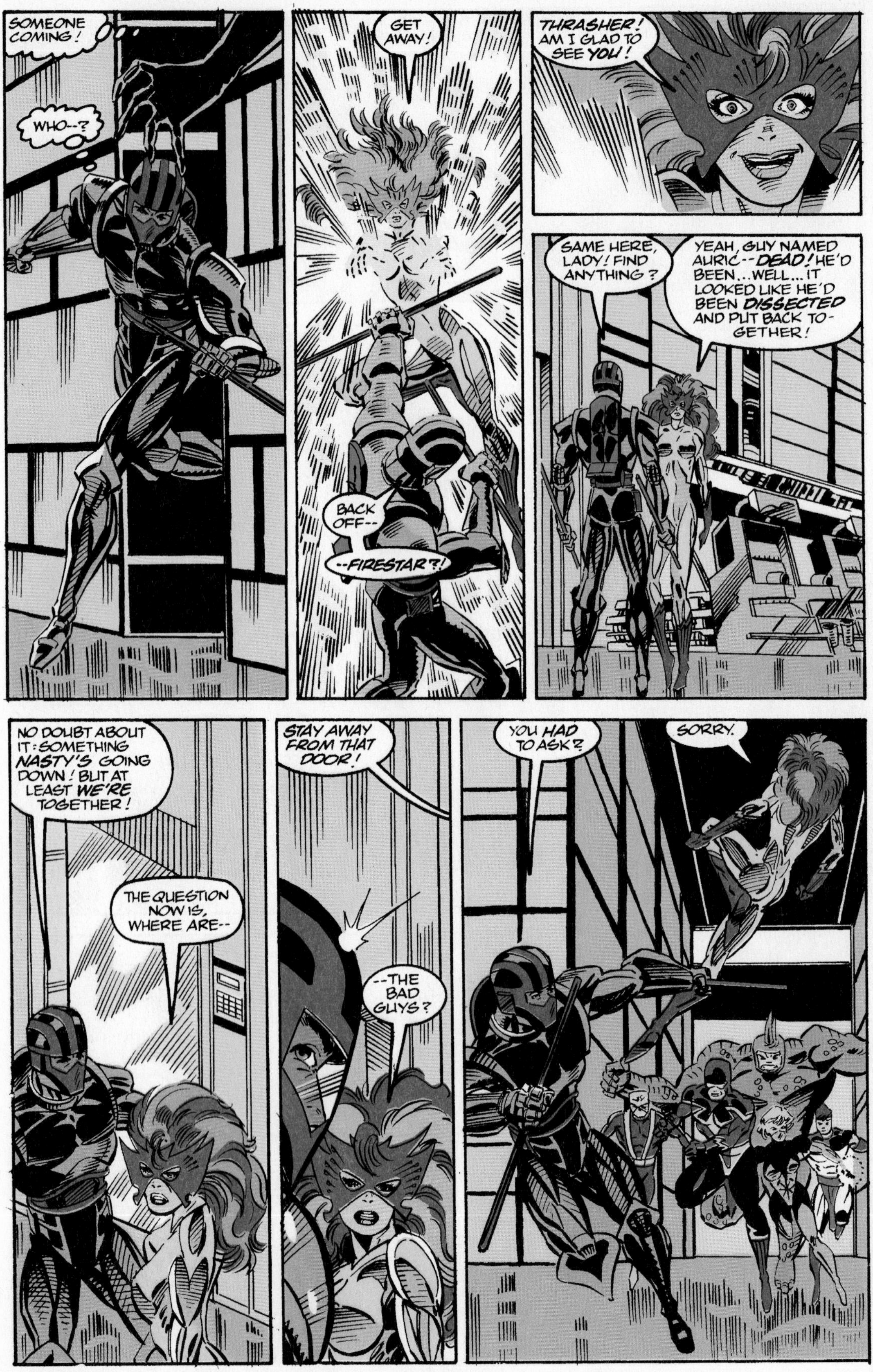
SOMEONE COMING!
WHO--?
GET AWAY!
BACK OFF--
--FIRESTAR?!
THRASHER! AM I GLAD TO SEE YOU!
SAME HERE, LADY! FIND ANYTHING?
YEAH, GUY NAMED AURIC--DEAD! HE'D BEEN...WELL...IT LOOKED LIKE HE'D BEEN DISSECTED AND PUT BACK TO-GETHER!
NO DOUBT ABOUT IT: SOMETHING NASTY'S GOING DOWN! BUT AT LEAST WE'RE TOGETHER!
THE QUESTION NOW IS, WHERE ARE--
STAY AWAY FROM THAT DOOR!
--THE BAD GUYS?
YOU HAD TO ASK?
SORRY.

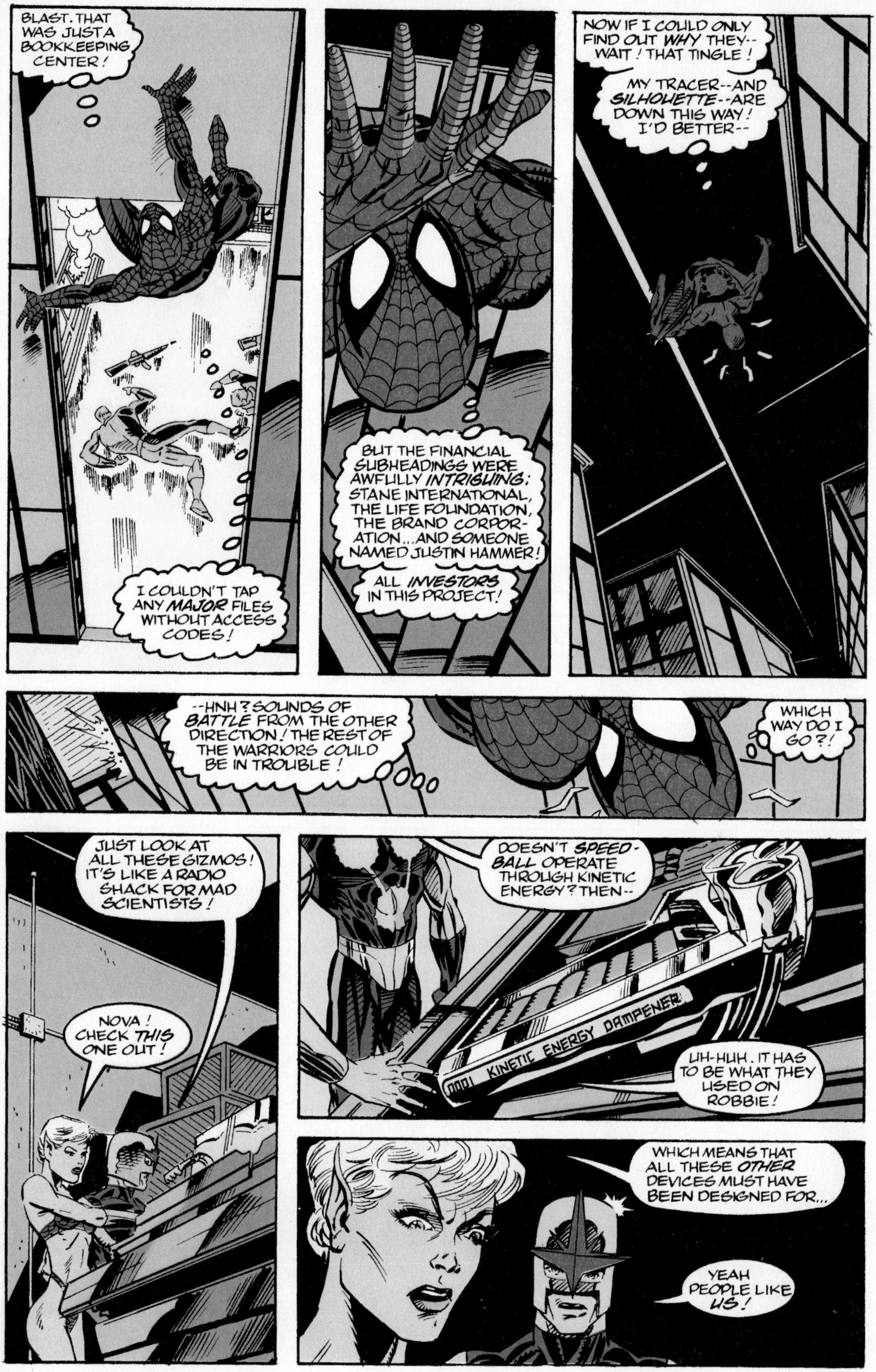
BLAST. THAT WAS JUST A BOOKKEEPING CENTER!
I COULDN'T TAP ANY MAJOR FILES WITHOUT ACCESS CODES!
BUT THE FINANCIAL SUBHEADINGS WERE AWFULLY INTRIGUING: STANE INTERNATIONAL, THE LIFE FOUNDATION, THE BRAND CORPORATION...AND SOMEONE NAMED JUSTIN HAMMER!
ALL INVESTORS IN THIS PROJECT!
NOW IF I COULD ONLY FIND OUT WHY THEY-- WAIT! THAT TINGLE!
MY TRACER--AND SILHOUETTE--ARE DOWN THIS WAY! I'D BETTER--
--HNH? SOUNDS OF BATTLE FROM THE OTHER DIRECTION! THE REST OF THE WARRIORS COULD BE IN TROUBLE!
WHICH WAY DO I GO?!
JUST LOOK AT ALL THESE GIZMOS! IT'S LIKE A RADIO SHACK FOR MAD SCIENTISTS!
NOVA! CHECK THIS ONE OUT!
DOESN'T SPEEDBALL OPERATE THROUGH KINETIC ENERGY? THEN--
KINETIC ENERGY DAMPENER
UH-HUH. IT HAS TO BE WHAT THEY USED ON ROBBIE!
WHICH MEANS THAT ALL THESE OTHER DEVICES MUST HAVE BEEN DESIGNED FOR...
YEAH PEOPLE LIKE US!

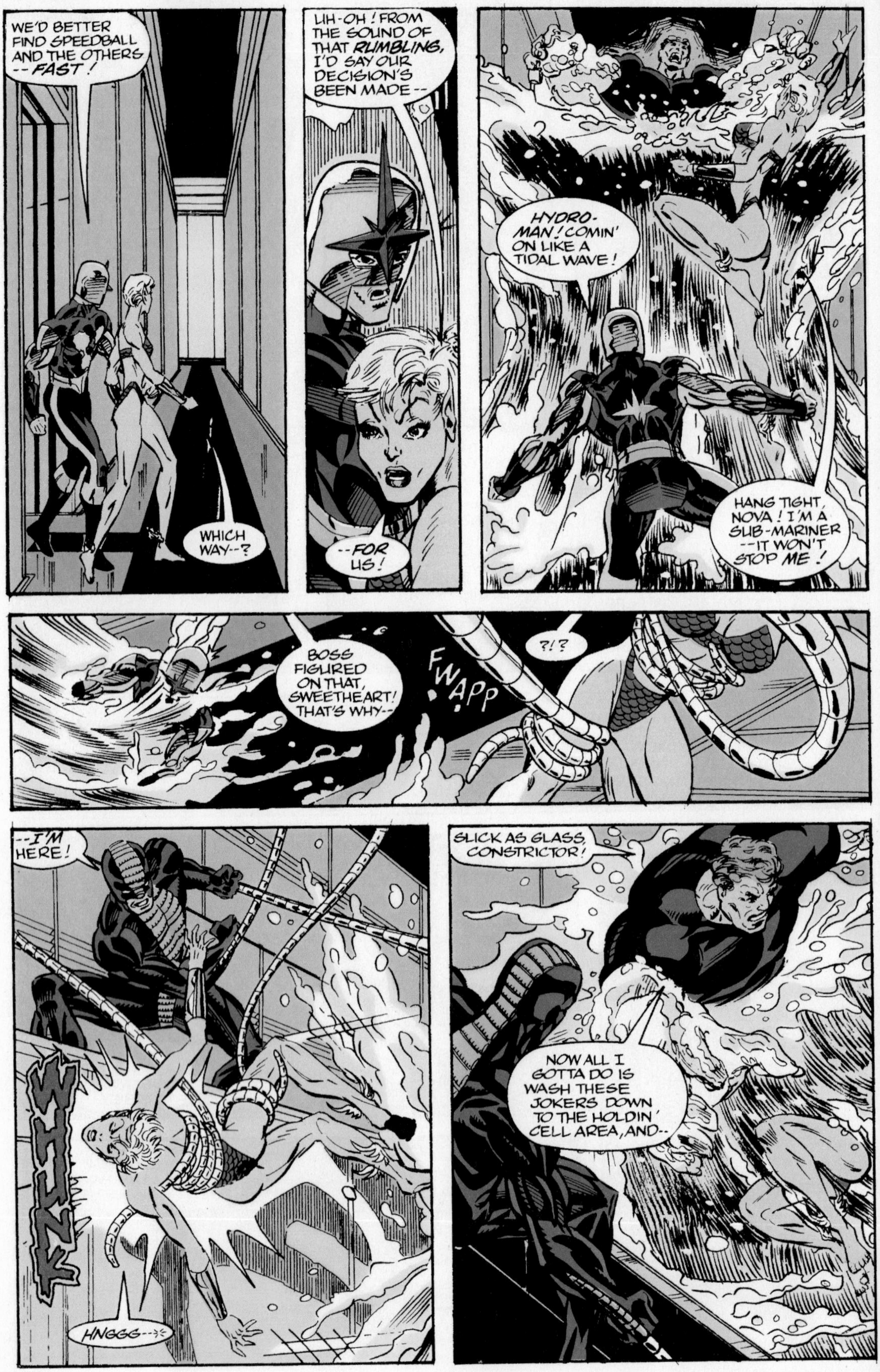
WE'D BETTER FIND SPEEDBALL AND THE OTHERS --FAST!
WHICH WAY--?
UH-OH! FROM THE SOUND OF THAT RUMBLING, I'D SAY OUR DECISION'S BEEN MADE--
--FOR US!
HYDRO-MAN! COMIN' ON LIKE A TIDAL WAVE!
HANG TIGHT, NOVA! I'M A SUB-MARINER --IT WON'T STOP ME!
BOSS FIGURED ON THAT, SWEETHEART! THAT'S WHY--
FWAPP
?!?
--I'M HERE!
WHUK
HNGGG--
SLICK AS GLASS, CONSTRICTOR!
NOW ALL I GOTTA DO IS WASH THESE JOKERS DOWN TO THE HOLDIN' CELL AREA, AND--

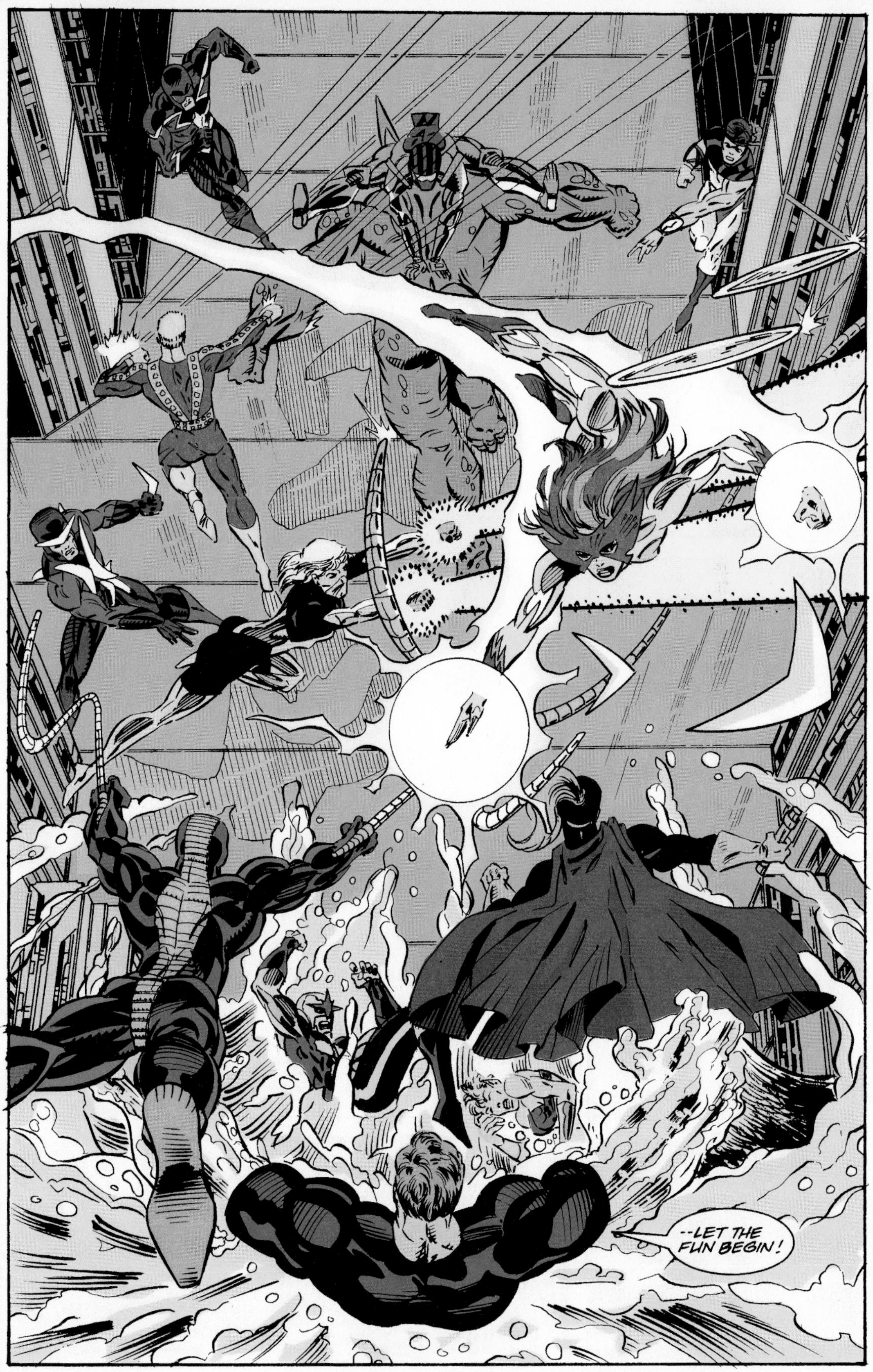
--LET THE FUN BEGIN!

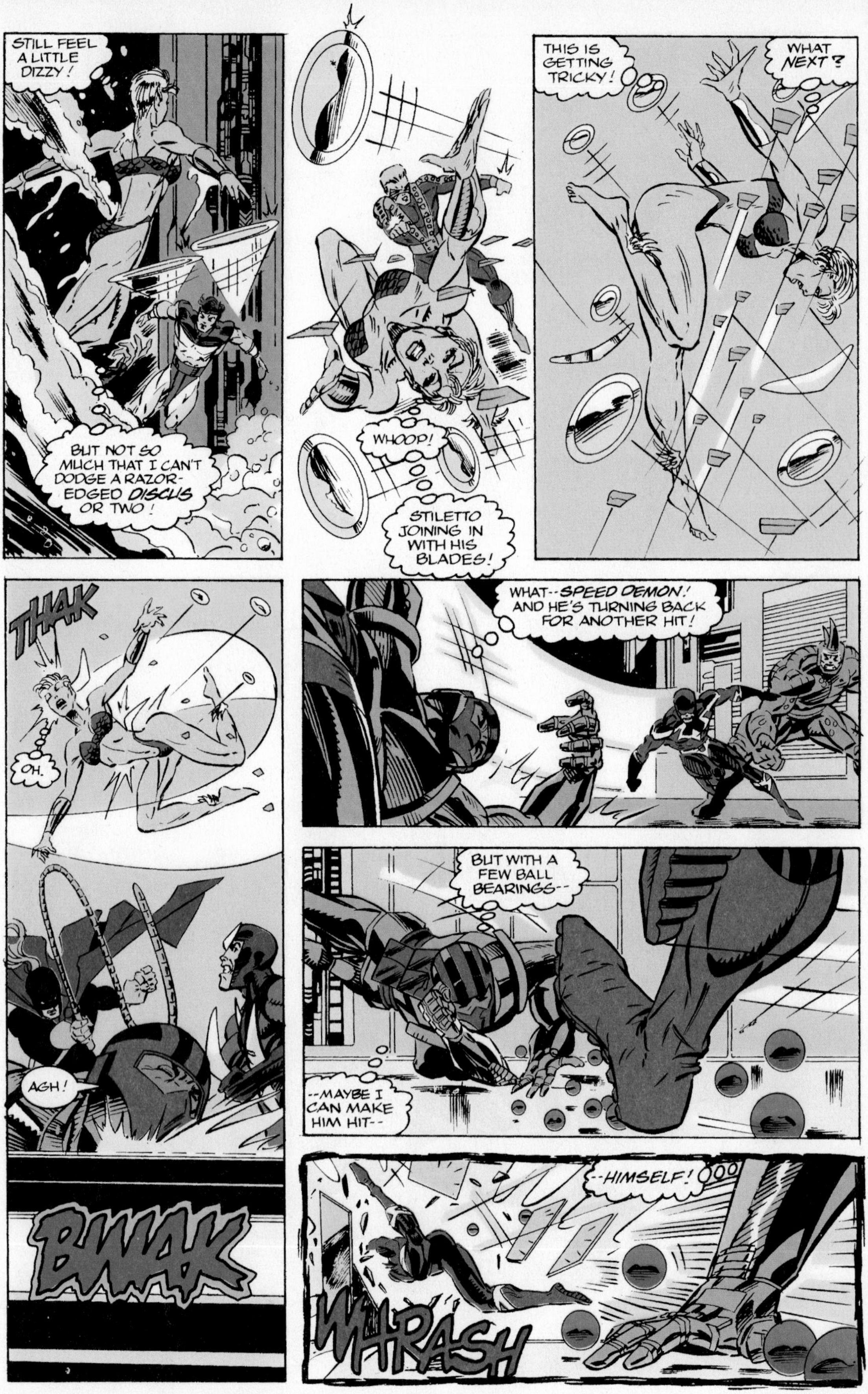
STILL FEEL A LITTLE DIZZY!
BUT NOT SO MUCH THAT I CAN'T DODGE A RAZOR-EDGED DISCUS OR TWO!
WHOOP!
STILETTO JOINING IN WITH HIS BLADES!
THIS IS GETTING TRICKY!
WHAT NEXT?
THAK
OH.
WHAT--SPEED DEMON! AND HE'S TURNING BACK FOR ANOTHER HIT!
AGH!
BWAK
BUT WITH A FEW BALL BEARINGS--
--MAYBE I CAN MAKE HIM HIT--
--HIMSELF!
WHRASH

HYDRO-MAN CREATING A SERIES OF *WAVE BARRIERS!*

BUT BY SMASHING *THROUGH* THEM, I'LL CATCH UP TO HIS HEAD AT THE END!

ONLY PROBLEM IS, I CAN'T SEE WHAT'S ON THE *OTHER SIDE* OF EACH WAVE UNTIL I--

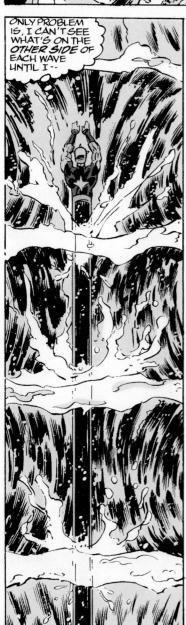

--GET THERE?

I DOUBT I COULD'VE TAGGED YOU ON MY OWN, ROCKET MAN!

GUESS THE KEY WORD HERE IS--

THROM

--SURPRISE!

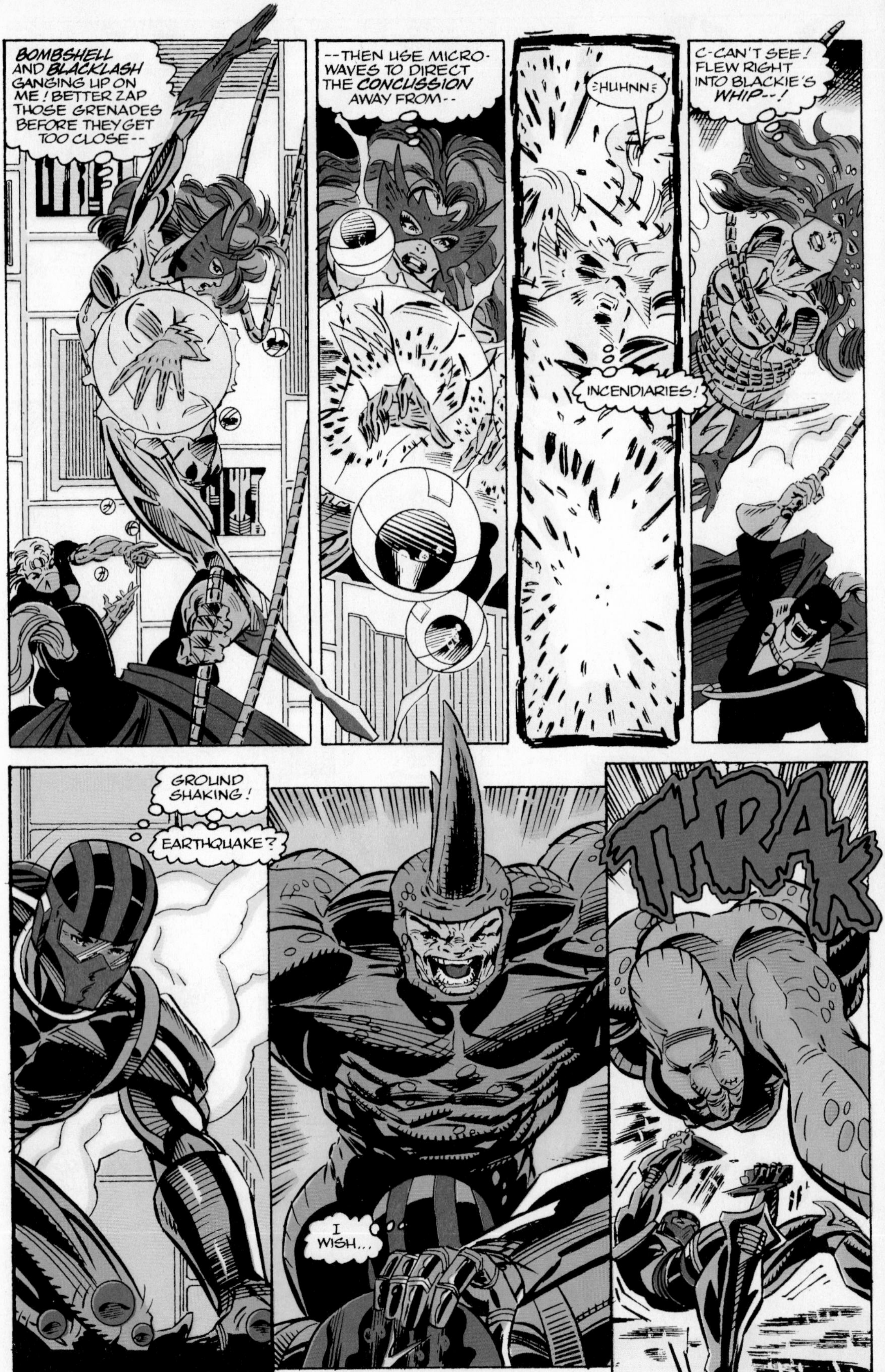
BOMBSHELL AND BLACKLASH GANGING UP ON ME! BETTER ZAP THOSE GRENADES BEFORE THEY GET TOO CLOSE--
--THEN USE MICRO-WAVES TO DIRECT THE CONCUSSION AWAY FROM--
HUHNN
INCENDIARIES!
C-CAN'T SEE! FLEW RIGHT INTO BLACKIE'S WHIP--!
GROUND SHAKING!
EARTHQUAKE?
I WISH...
THRAK

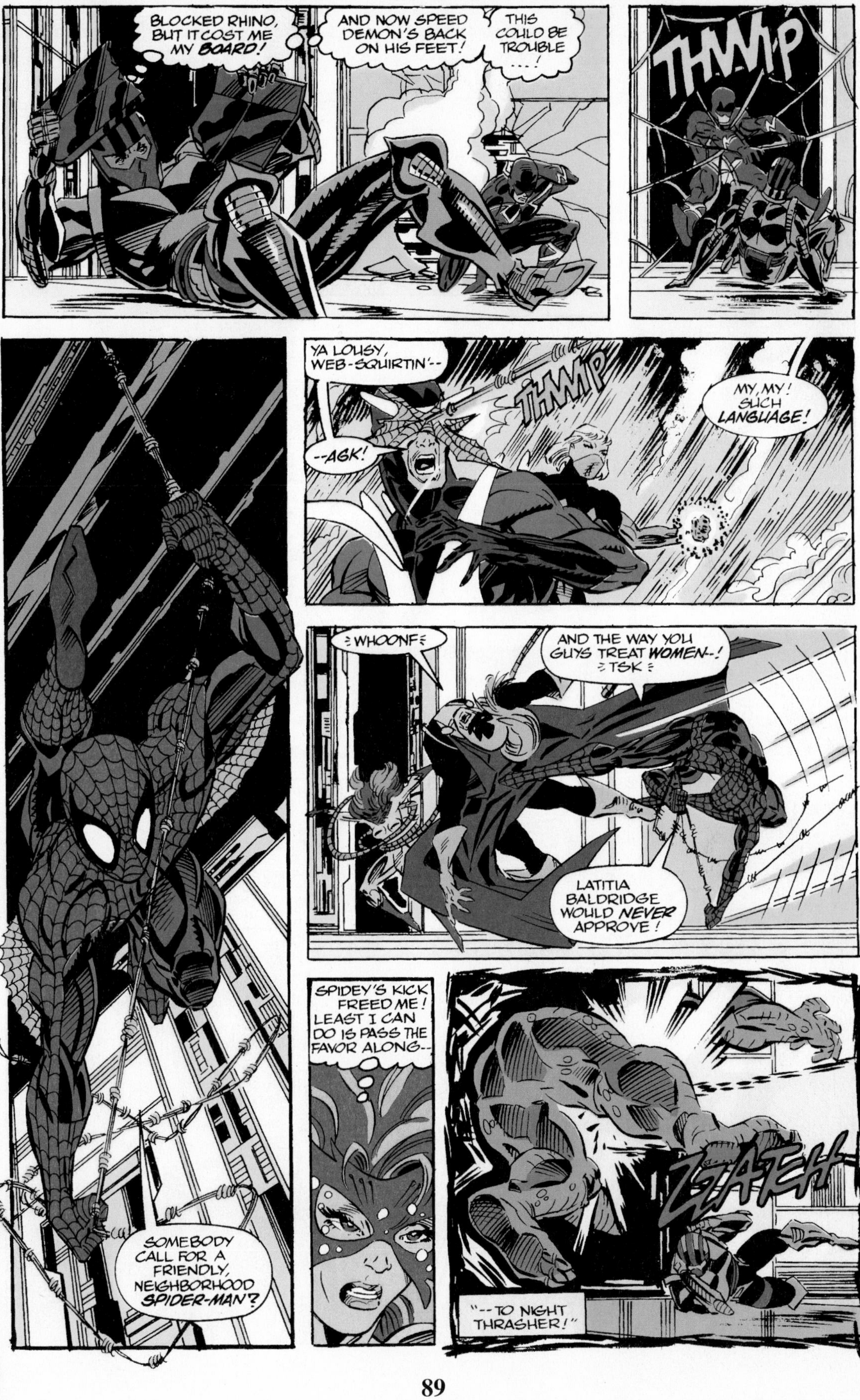
BLOCKED RHINO, BUT IT COST ME MY BOARD!
AND NOW SPEED DEMON'S BACK ON HIS FEET!
THIS COULD BE TROUBLE ...!
THWIP
YA LOUSY, WEB-SQUIRTIN'--
THWIP
--AGK!
MY, MY! SUCH LANGUAGE!
WHOONF
AND THE WAY YOU GUYS TREAT WOMEN--! TSK
LATITIA BALDRIDGE WOULD NEVER APPROVE!
SOMEBODY CALL FOR A FRIENDLY, NEIGHBORHOOD SPIDER-MAN?
SPIDEY'S KICK FREED ME! LEAST I CAN DO IS PASS THE FAVOR ALONG--
ZZATCH
"--TO NIGHT THRASHER!"

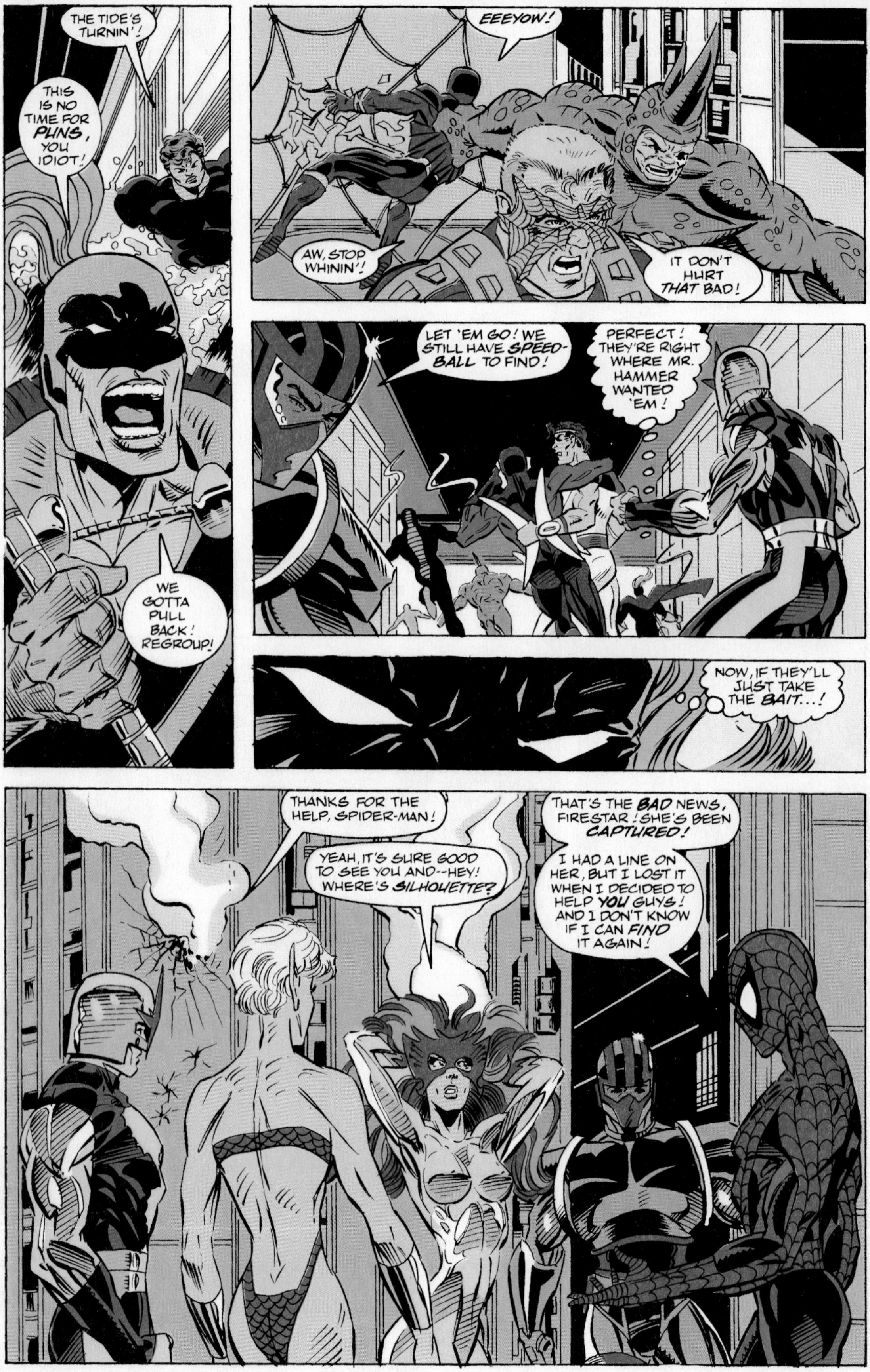
THE TIDE'S TURNIN'!
THIS IS NO TIME FOR PUNS, YOU IDIOT!
WE GOTTA PULL BACK! REGROUP!
EEEYOW!
AW, STOP WHININ'!
IT DON'T HURT THAT BAD!
LET 'EM GO! WE STILL HAVE SPEEDBALL TO FIND!
PERFECT! THEY'RE RIGHT WHERE MR. HAMMER WANTED 'EM!
NOW, IF THEY'LL JUST TAKE THE BAIT...!
THANKS FOR THE HELP, SPIDER-MAN!
YEAH, IT'S SURE GOOD TO SEE YOU AND--HEY! WHERE'S SILHOUETTE?
THAT'S THE BAD NEWS, FIRESTAR! SHE'S BEEN CAPTURED!
I HAD A LINE ON HER, BUT I LOST IT WHEN I DECIDED TO HELP YOU GUYS! AND I DON'T KNOW IF I CAN FIND IT AGAIN!

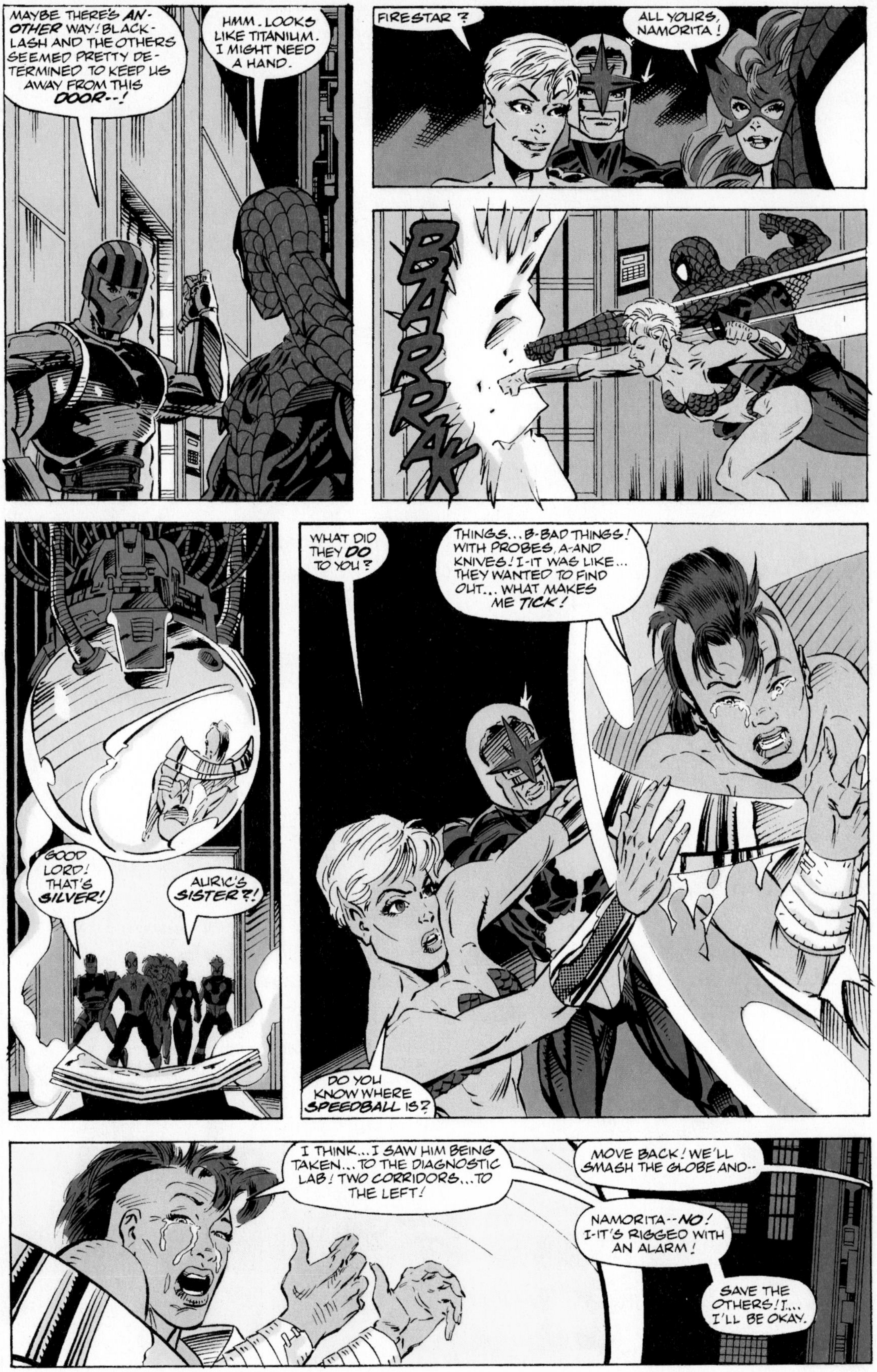

MAYBE THERE'S ANOTHER WAY! BLACKLASH AND THE OTHERS SEEMED PRETTY DETERMINED TO KEEP US AWAY FROM THIS DOOR--!
HMM. LOOKS LIKE TITANIUM. I MIGHT NEED A HAND.
FIRESTAR?
ALL YOURS, NAMORITA!
BARRRAK
GOOD LORD! THAT'S SILVER!
AURIC'S SISTER?!
WHAT DID THEY DO TO YOU?
THINGS... B-BAD THINGS! WITH PROBES, A-AND KNIVES! I-IT WAS LIKE... THEY WANTED TO FIND OUT... WHAT MAKES ME TICK!
DO YOU KNOW WHERE SPEEDBALL IS?
I THINK... I SAW HIM BEING TAKEN... TO THE DIAGNOSTIC LAB! TWO CORRIDORS... TO THE LEFT!
MOVE BACK! WE'LL SMASH THE GLOBE AND--
NAMORITA--NO! I-IT'S RIGGED WITH AN ALARM!
SAVE THE OTHERS! I... I'LL BE OKAY.

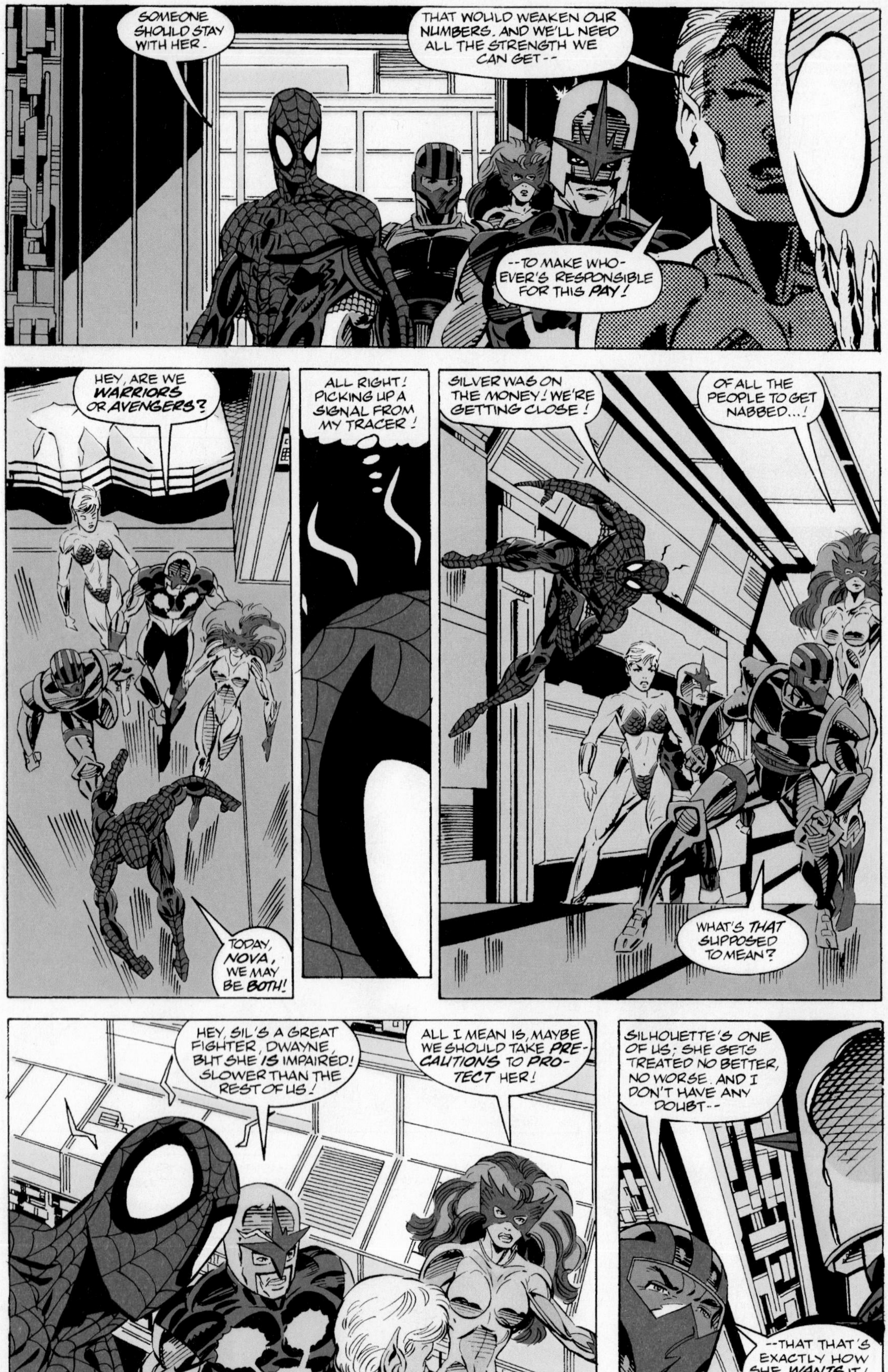
SOMEONE SHOULD STAY WITH HER.
THAT WOULD WEAKEN OUR NUMBERS. AND WE'LL NEED ALL THE STRENGTH WE CAN GET--
--TO MAKE WHO-EVER'S RESPONSIBLE FOR THIS PAY!
HEY, ARE WE WARRIORS OR AVENGERS?
TODAY, NOVA, WE MAY BE BOTH!
ALL RIGHT! PICKING UP A SIGNAL FROM MY TRACER!
SILVER WAS ON THE MONEY! WE'RE GETTING CLOSE!
OF ALL THE PEOPLE TO GET NABBED...!
WHAT'S THAT SUPPOSED TO MEAN?
HEY, SIL'S A GREAT FIGHTER, DWAYNE, BUT SHE IS IMPAIRED! SLOWER THAN THE REST OF US!
ALL I MEAN IS, MAYBE WE SHOULD TAKE PRE-CAUTIONS TO PRO-TECT HER!
SILHOUETTE'S ONE OF US; SHE GETS TREATED NO BETTER, NO WORSE. AND I DON'T HAVE ANY DOUBT--
--THAT THAT'S EXACTLY HOW SHE WANTS IT!

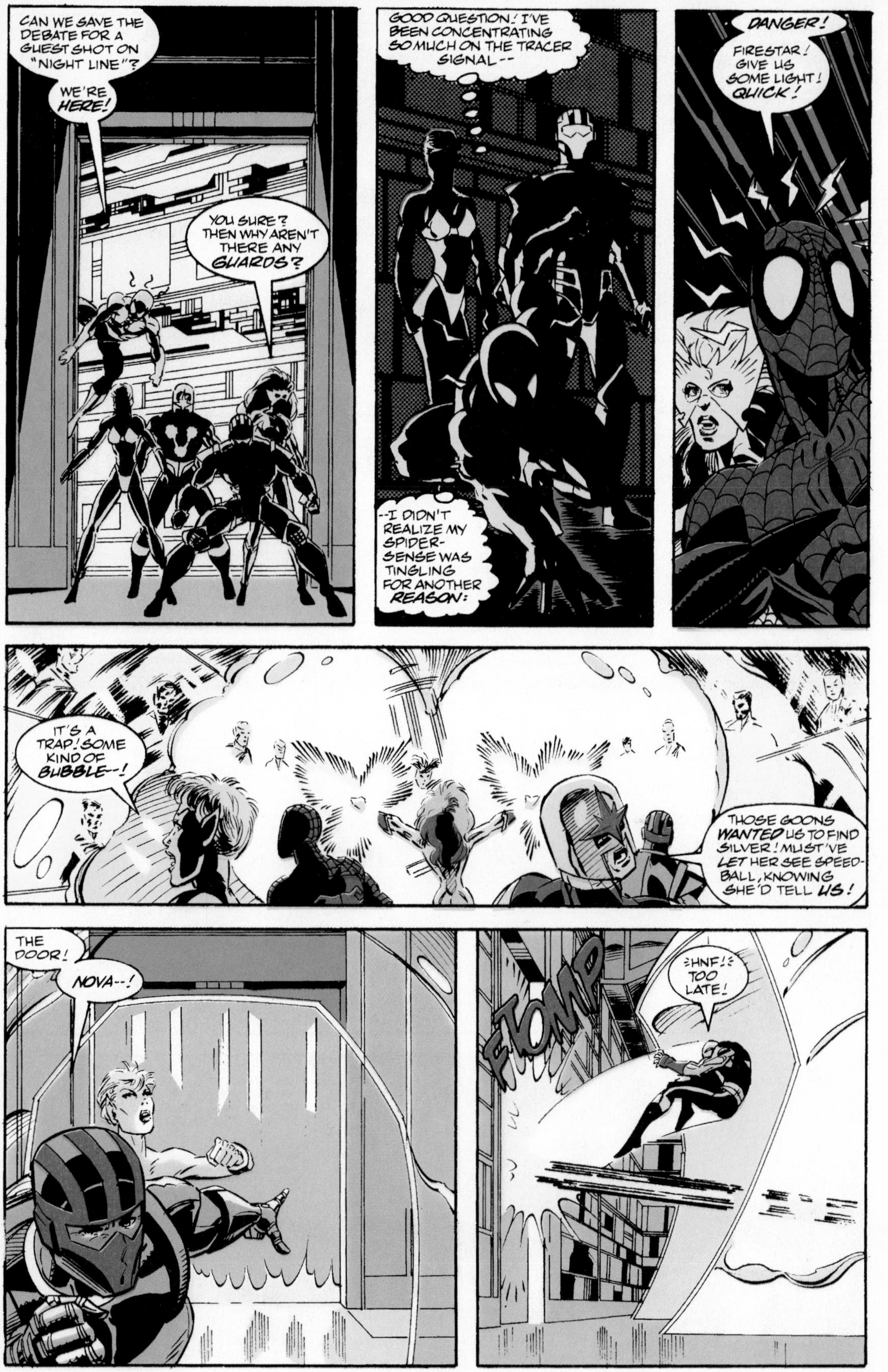

CAN WE SAVE THE DEBATE FOR A GUEST SHOT ON "NIGHT LINE"?
WE'RE HERE!
YOU SURE? THEN WHY AREN'T THERE ANY GUARDS?
GOOD QUESTION! I'VE BEEN CONCENTRATING SO MUCH ON THE TRACER SIGNAL--
--I DIDN'T REALIZE MY SPIDER-SENSE WAS TINGLING FOR ANOTHER REASON:
DANGER!
FIRESTAR! GIVE US SOME LIGHT! QUICK!
IT'S A TRAP! SOME KIND OF BUBBLE--!
THOSE GOONS WANTED US TO FIND SILVER! MUST'VE LET HER SEE SPEED-BALL, KNOWING SHE'D TELL US!
THE DOOR!
NOVA--!
FTOMP
HNF! TOO LATE!

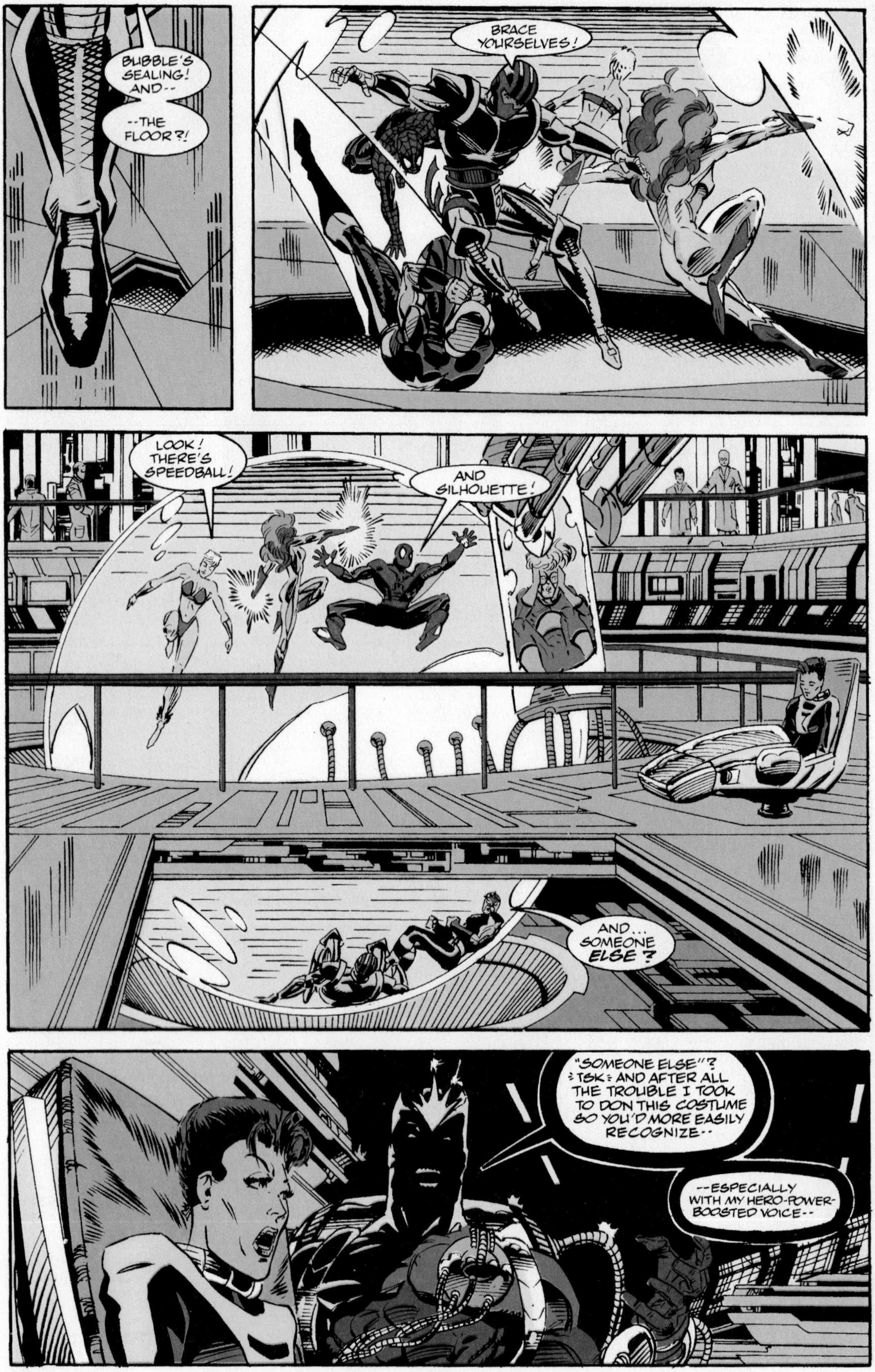

BUBBLE'S SEALING! AND--
--THE FLOOR?!
BRACE YOURSELVES!
LOOK! THERE'S SPEEDBALL!
AND SILHOUETTE!
AND... SOMEONE ELSE?
"SOMEONE ELSE"? ≈TSK≈ AND AFTER ALL THE TROUBLE I TOOK TO DON THIS COSTUME SO YOU'D MORE EASILY RECOGNIZE--
--ESPECIALLY WITH MY HERO-POWER-BOOSTED VOICE--

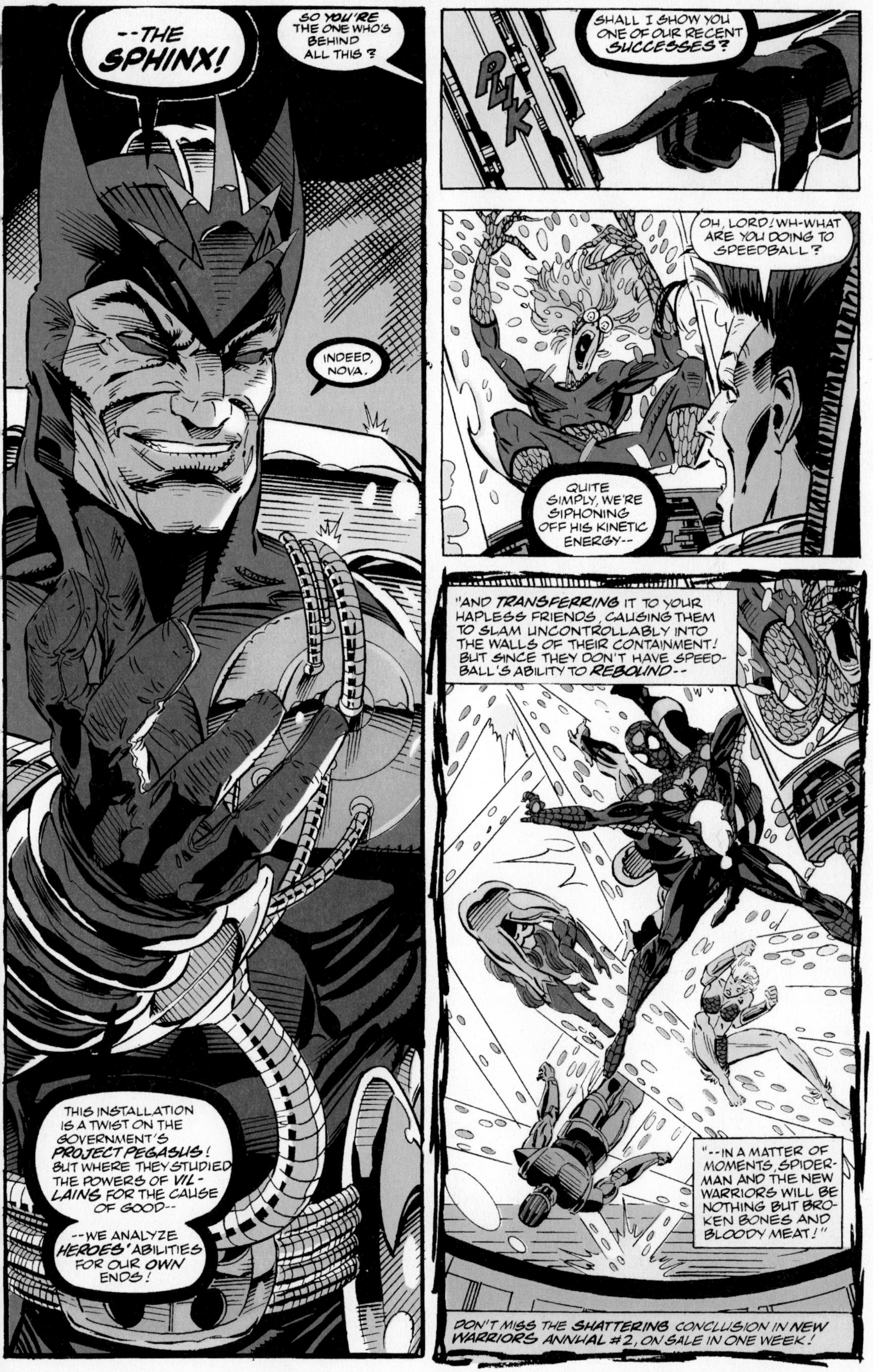
--THE SPHINX!
SO YOU'RE THE ONE WHO'S BEHIND ALL THIS?
INDEED, NOVA.
THIS INSTALLATION IS A TWIST ON THE GOVERNMENT'S PROJECT PEGASUS! BUT WHERE THEY STUDIED THE POWERS OF VILLAINS FOR THE CAUSE OF GOOD--
--WE ANALYZE HEROES' ABILITIES FOR OUR OWN ENDS!
SHALL I SHOW YOU ONE OF OUR RECENT SUCCESSES?
PLIK
OH, LORD! WH-WHAT ARE YOU DOING TO SPEEDBALL?
QUITE SIMPLY, WE'RE SIPHONING OFF HIS KINETIC ENERGY--
"AND TRANSFERRING IT TO YOUR HAPLESS FRIENDS, CAUSING THEM TO SLAM UNCONTROLLABLY INTO THE WALLS OF THEIR CONTAINMENT! BUT SINCE THEY DON'T HAVE SPEEDBALL'S ABILITY TO REBOUND--
"--IN A MATTER OF MOMENTS, SPIDER-MAN AND THE NEW WARRIORS WILL BE NOTHING BUT BROKEN BONES AND BLOODY MEAT!"
DON'T MISS THE SHATTERING CONCLUSION IN NEW WARRIORS ANNUAL #2, ON SALE IN ONE WEEK!

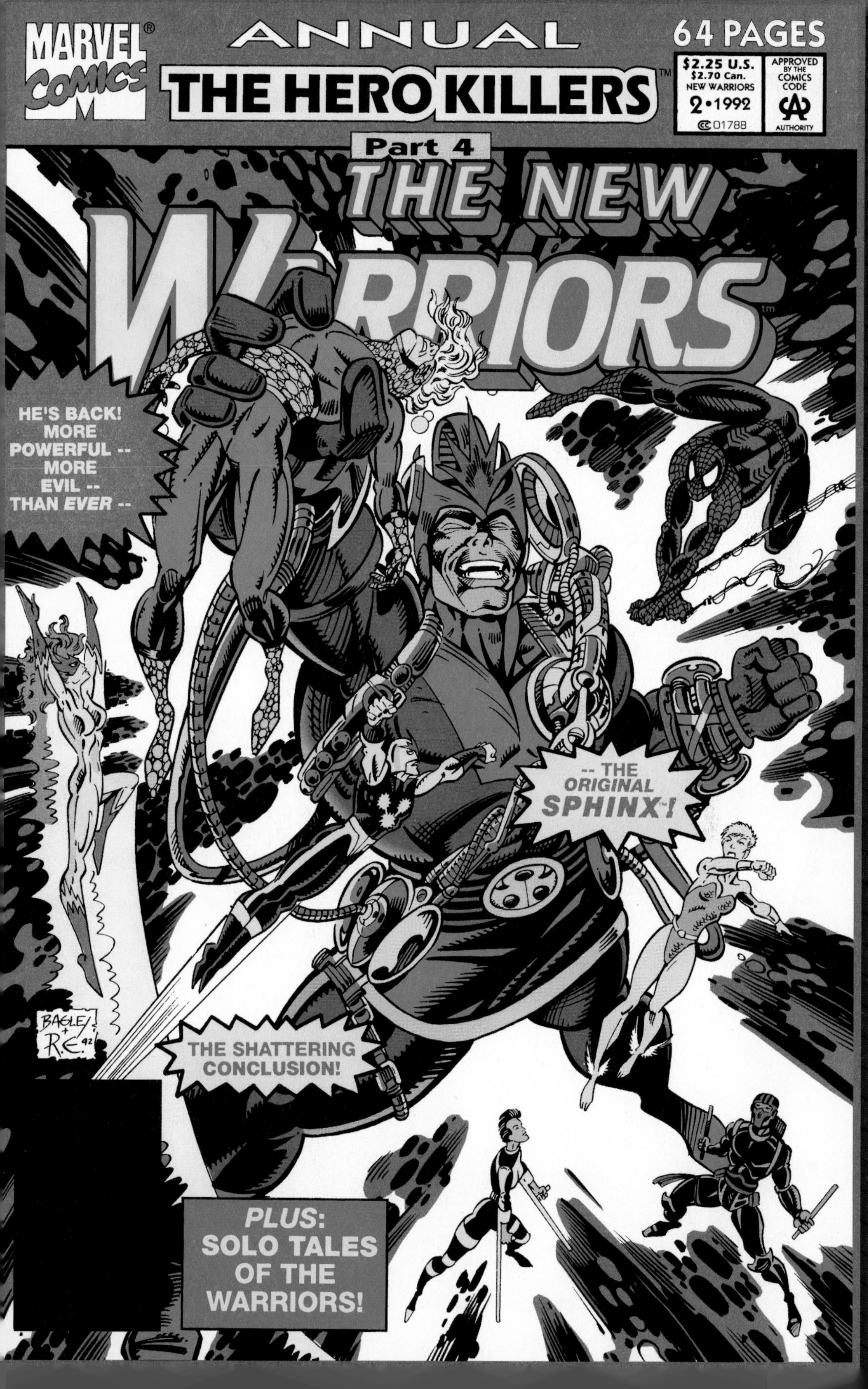
MARVEL® COMICS
ANNUAL
64 PAGES
THE HERO KILLERS™
$2.25 U.S.
$2.70 Can.
NEW WARRIORS
2•1992
01788
APPROVED BY THE COMICS CODE AUTHORITY
Part 4
THE NEW WARRIORS™
HE'S BACK! MORE POWERFUL -- MORE EVIL -- THAN EVER --
-- THE ORIGINAL SPHINX™!
BAGLEY + R.E. '92
THE SHATTERING CONCLUSION!
PLUS: SOLO TALES OF THE WARRIORS!

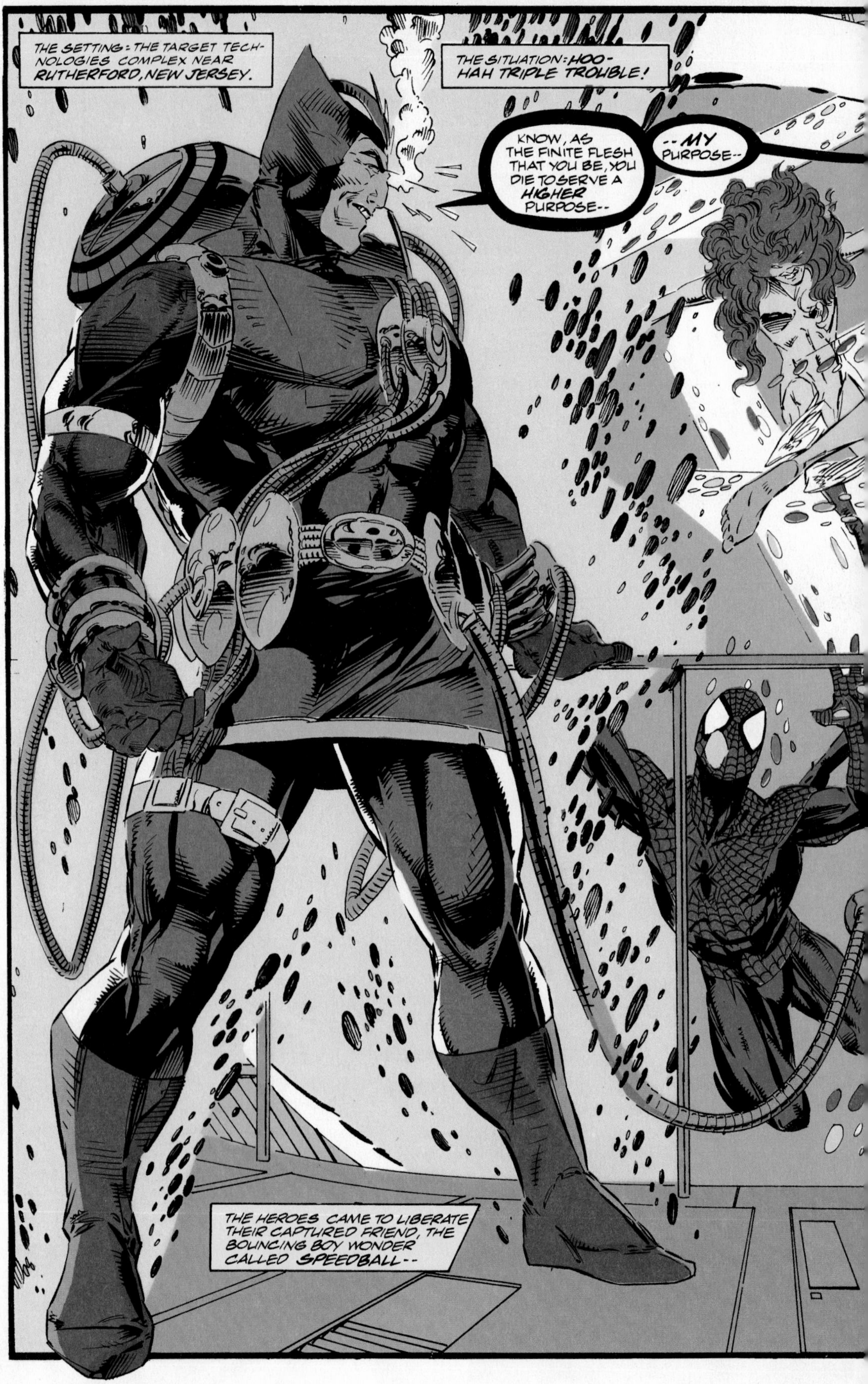
THE SETTING: THE TARGET TECHNOLOGIES COMPLEX NEAR RUTHERFORD, NEW JERSEY.
THE SITUATION: HOO-HAH TRIPLE TROUBLE!
KNOW, AS THE FINITE FLESH THAT YOU BE, YOU DIE TO SERVE A HIGHER PURPOSE--
--MY PURPOSE--
THE HEROES CAME TO LIBERATE THEIR CAPTURED FRIEND, THE BOUNCING BOY WONDER CALLED SPEEDBALL--

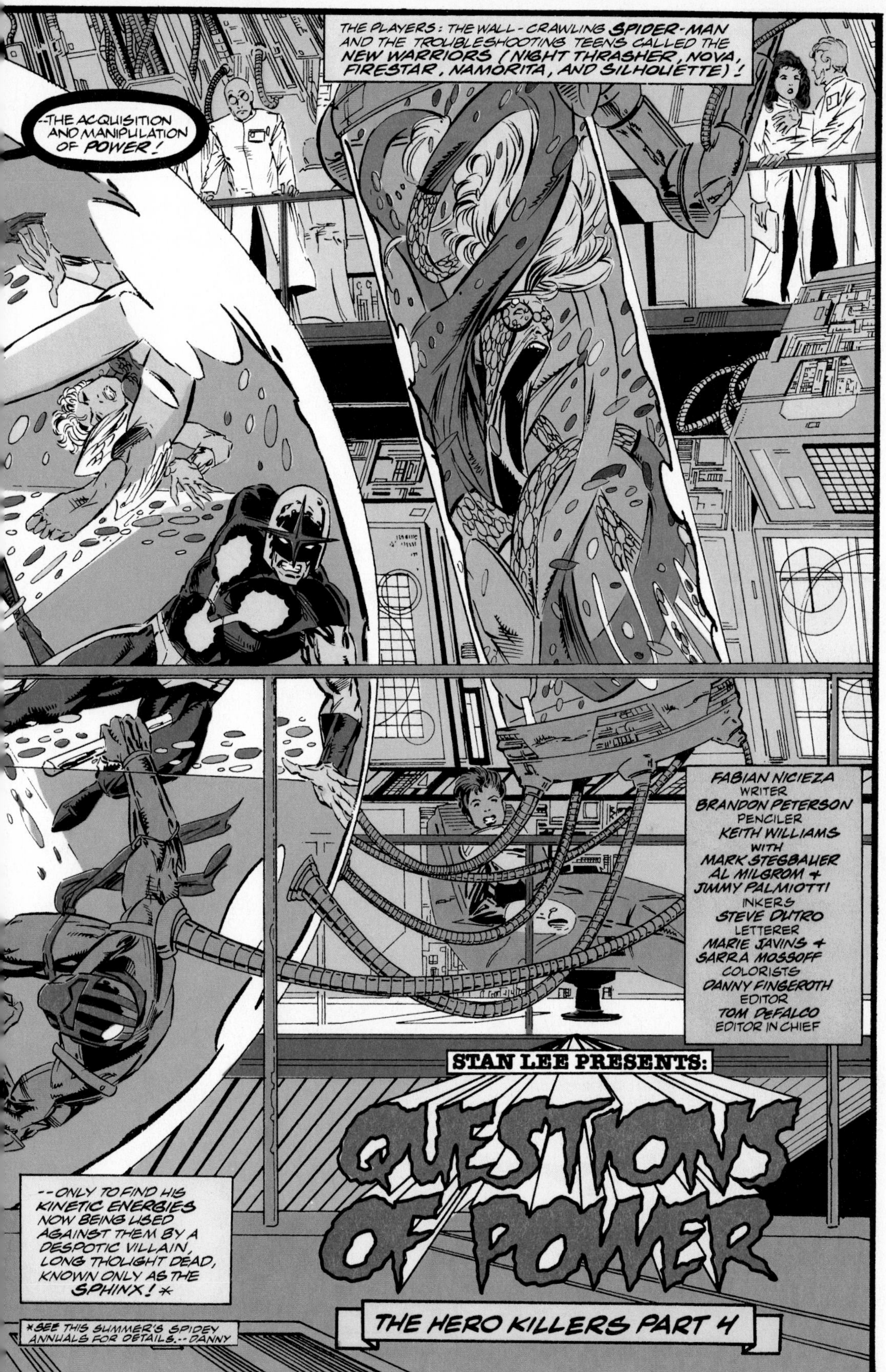
THE PLAYERS: THE WALL-CRAWLING SPIDER-MAN AND THE TROUBLESHOOTING TEENS CALLED THE NEW WARRIORS (NIGHT THRASHER, NOVA, FIRESTAR, NAMORITA, AND SILHOUETTE)!
--THE ACQUISITION AND MANIPULATION OF POWER!
FABIAN NICIEZA WRITER BRANDON PETERSON PENCILER KEITH WILLIAMS WITH MARK STEGBAUER AL MILGROM & JIMMY PALMIOTTI INKERS STEVE DUTRO LETTERER MARIE JAVINS & SARRA MOSSOFF COLORISTS DANNY FINGEROTH EDITOR TOM DeFALCO EDITOR IN CHIEF
STAN LEE PRESENTS:
QUESTIONS OF POWER
--ONLY TO FIND HIS KINETIC ENERGIES NOW BEING USED AGAINST THEM BY A DESPOTIC VILLAIN, LONG THOUGHT DEAD, KNOWN ONLY AS THE SPHINX! *
THE HERO KILLERS PART 4
*SEE THIS SUMMER'S SPIDEY ANNUALS FOR DETAILS.--DANNY

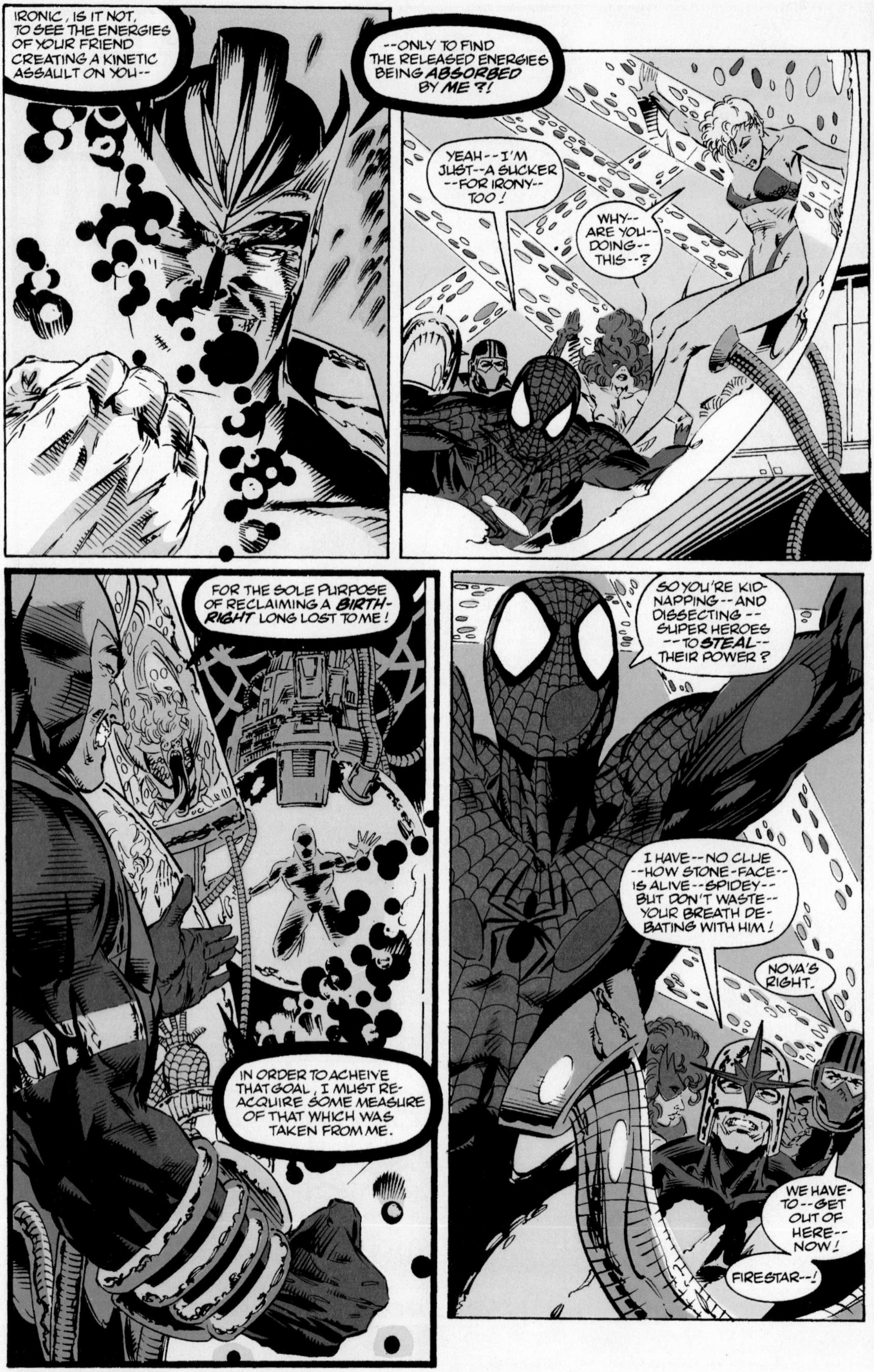
IRONIC, IS IT NOT, TO SEE THE ENERGIES OF YOUR FRIEND CREATING A KINETIC ASSAULT ON YOU--
--ONLY TO FIND THE RELEASED ENERGIES BEING ABSORBED BY ME ?!
YEAH--I'M JUST--A SUCKER --FOR IRONY-- TOO!
WHY-- ARE YOU-- DOING-- THIS--?
FOR THE SOLE PURPOSE OF RECLAIMING A BIRTH-RIGHT LONG LOST TO ME!
IN ORDER TO ACHEIVE THAT GOAL, I MUST RE-ACQUIRE SOME MEASURE OF THAT WHICH WAS TAKEN FROM ME.
SO YOU'RE KID-NAPPING--AND DISSECTING-- SUPER HEROES --TO STEAL-- THEIR POWER?
I HAVE--NO CLUE --HOW STONE-FACE-- IS ALIVE--SPIDEY-- BUT DON'T WASTE-- YOUR BREATH DE-BATING WITH HIM!
NOVA'S RIGHT.
WE HAVE-TO--GET OUT OF HERE-- NOW!
FIRESTAR--!

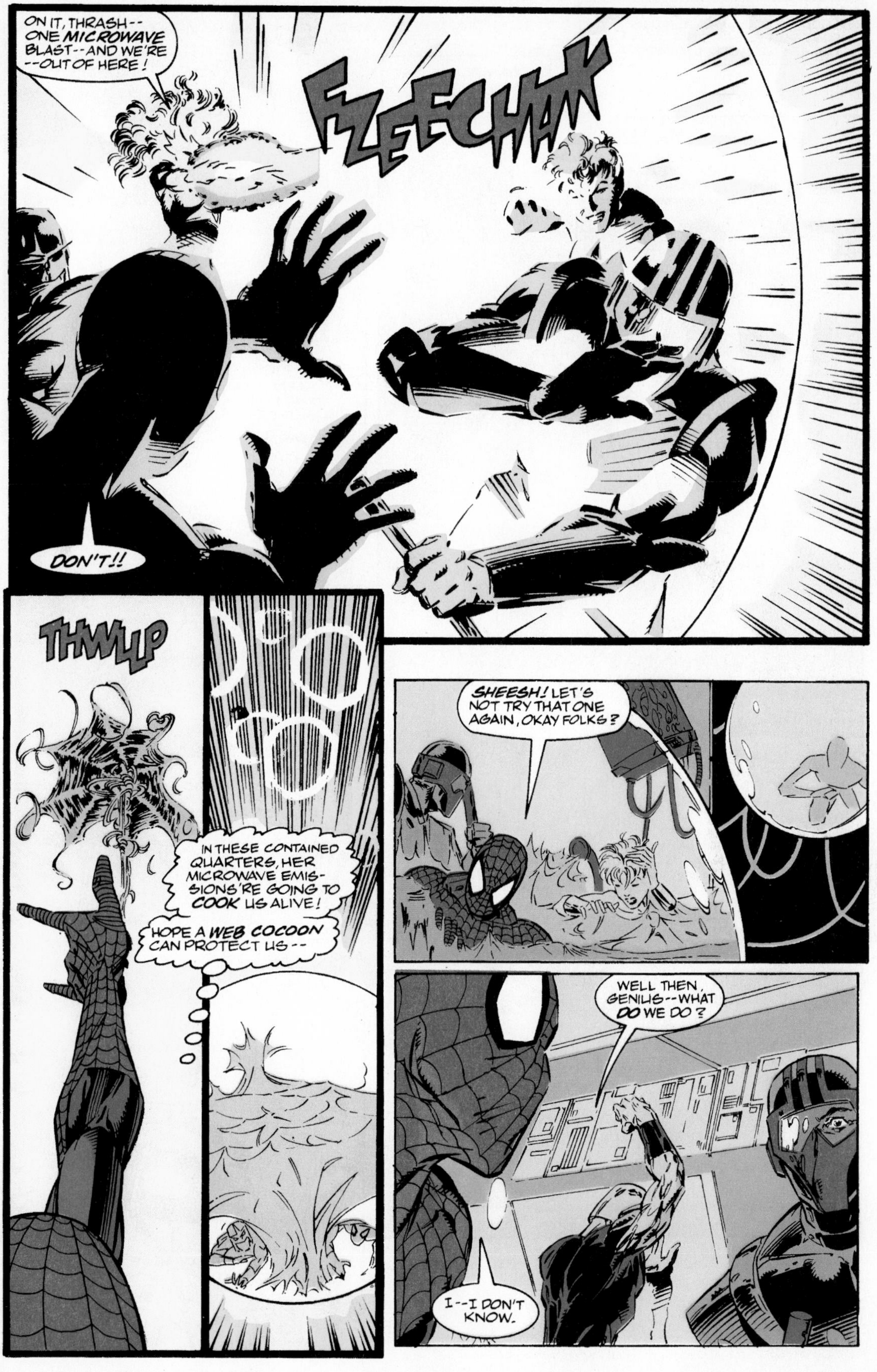
ON IT, THRASH--
ONE MICROWAVE
BLAST--AND WE'RE
--OUT OF HERE!
FZEEFCHAK
DON'T!!
THWUP
IN THESE CONTAINED QUARTERS, HER MICROWAVE EMISSIONS'RE GOING TO COOK US ALIVE!
HOPE A WEB COCOON CAN PROTECT US--
SHEESH! LET'S NOT TRY THAT ONE AGAIN, OKAY FOLKS?
WELL THEN, GENIUS--WHAT DO WE DO?
I--I DON'T KNOW.

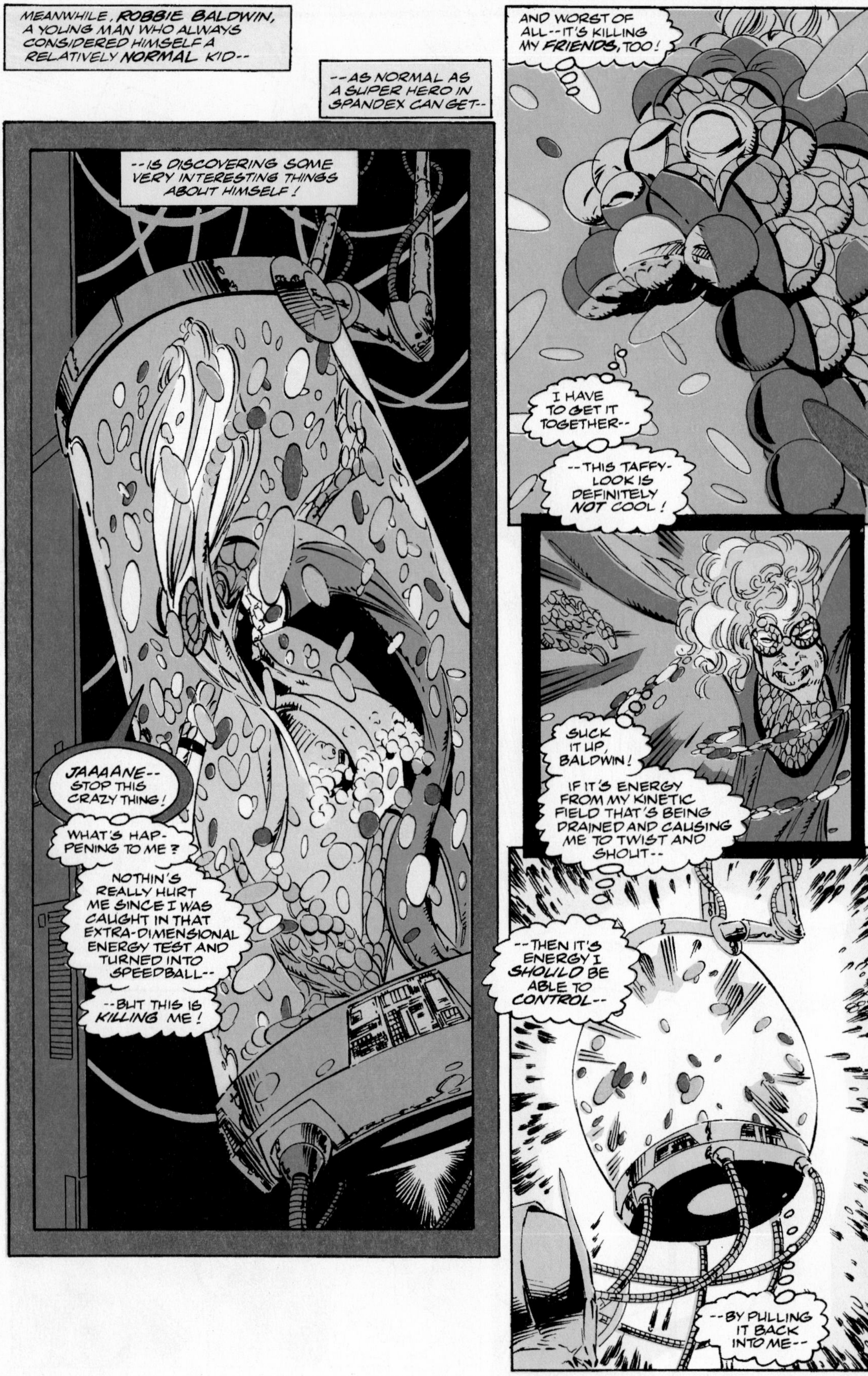

MEANWHILE, ROBBIE BALDWIN, A YOUNG MAN WHO ALWAYS CONSIDERED HIMSELF A RELATIVELY NORMAL KID--
--AS NORMAL AS A SUPER HERO IN SPANDEX CAN GET--
--IS DISCOVERING SOME VERY INTERESTING THINGS ABOUT HIMSELF!
JAAAANE-- STOP THIS CRAZY THING!
WHAT'S HAP-PENING TO ME?
NOTHIN'S REALLY HURT ME SINCE I WAS CAUGHT IN THAT EXTRA-DIMENSIONAL ENERGY TEST AND TURNED INTO SPEEDBALL--
--BUT THIS IS KILLING ME!
AND WORST OF ALL--IT'S KILLING MY FRIENDS, TOO!
I HAVE TO GET IT TOGETHER--
--THIS TAFFY-LOOK IS DEFINITELY NOT COOL!
SUCK IT UP, BALDWIN!
IF IT'S ENERGY FROM MY KINETIC FIELD THAT'S BEING DRAINED AND CAUSING ME TO TWIST AND SHOUT--
--THEN IT'S ENERGY I SHOULD BE ABLE TO CONTROL--
--BY PULLING IT BACK INTO ME--

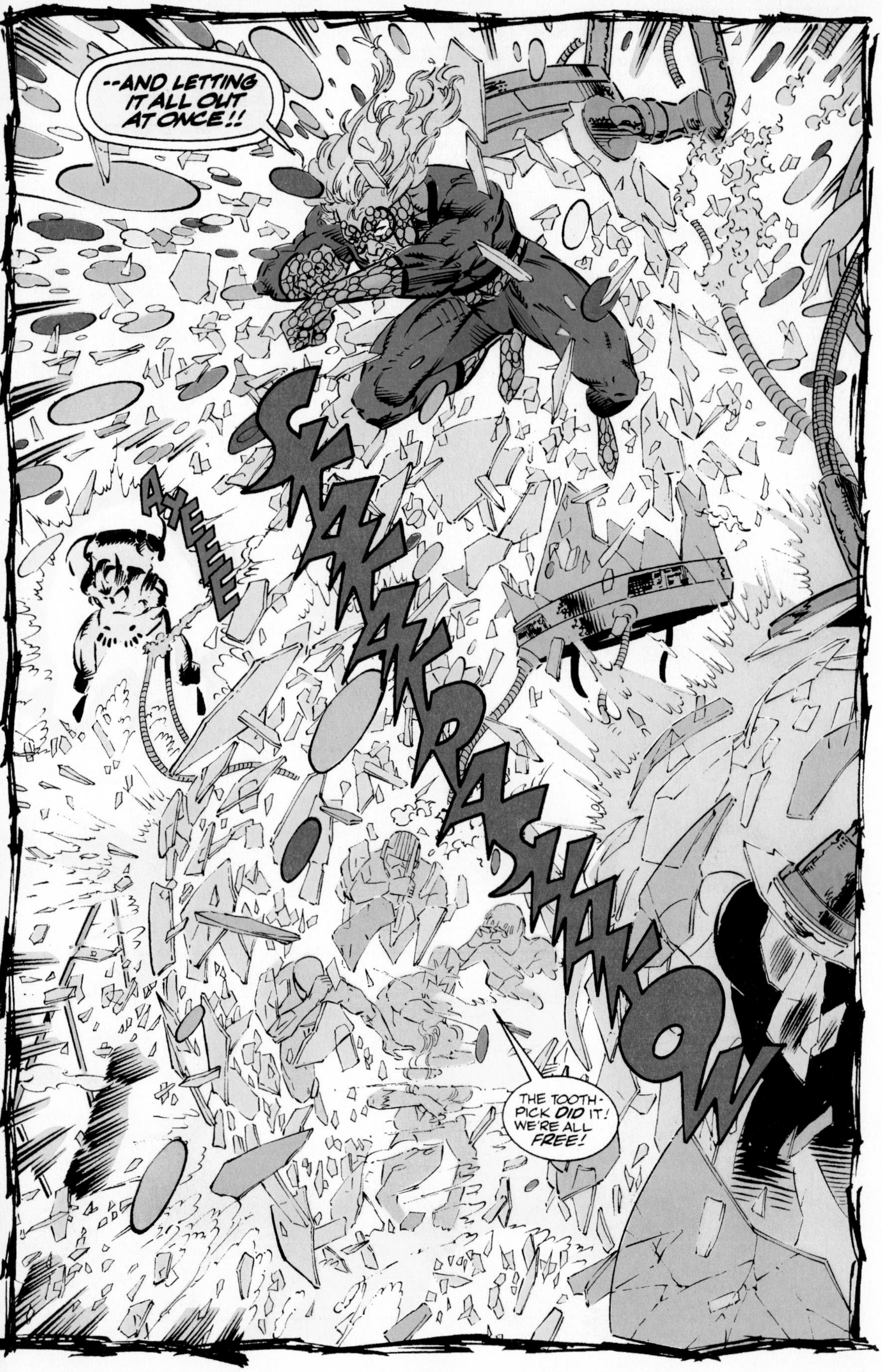
--AND LETTING IT ALL OUT AT ONCE!!
AYEEEE
SKAKAKRASHAKOW
THE TOOTH-PICK DID IT! WE'RE ALL FREE!

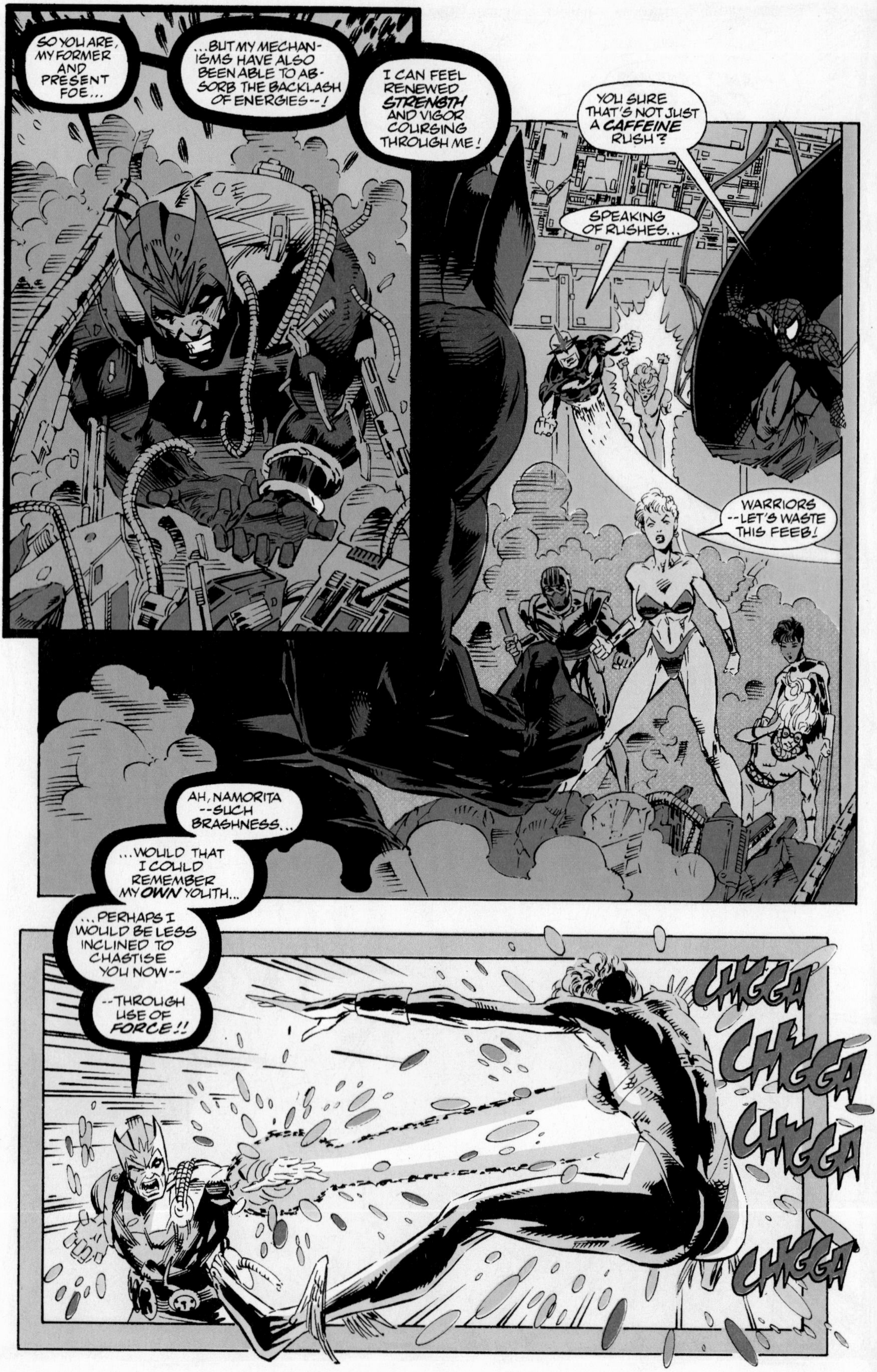
SO YOU ARE, MY FORMER AND PRESENT FOE...
...BUT MY MECHANISMS HAVE ALSO BEEN ABLE TO ABSORB THE BACKLASH OF ENERGIES--!
I CAN FEEL RENEWED STRENGTH AND VIGOR COURSING THROUGH ME!
YOU SURE THAT'S NOT JUST A CAFFEINE RUSH?
SPEAKING OF RUSHES...
WARRIORS --LET'S WASTE THIS FEEB!
AH, NAMORITA --SUCH BRASHNESS...
...WOULD THAT I COULD REMEMBER MY OWN YOUTH...
...PERHAPS I WOULD BE LESS INCLINED TO CHASTISE YOU NOW--
--THROUGH USE OF FORCE!!
CHGGA
CHGGA
CHGGA
CHGGA

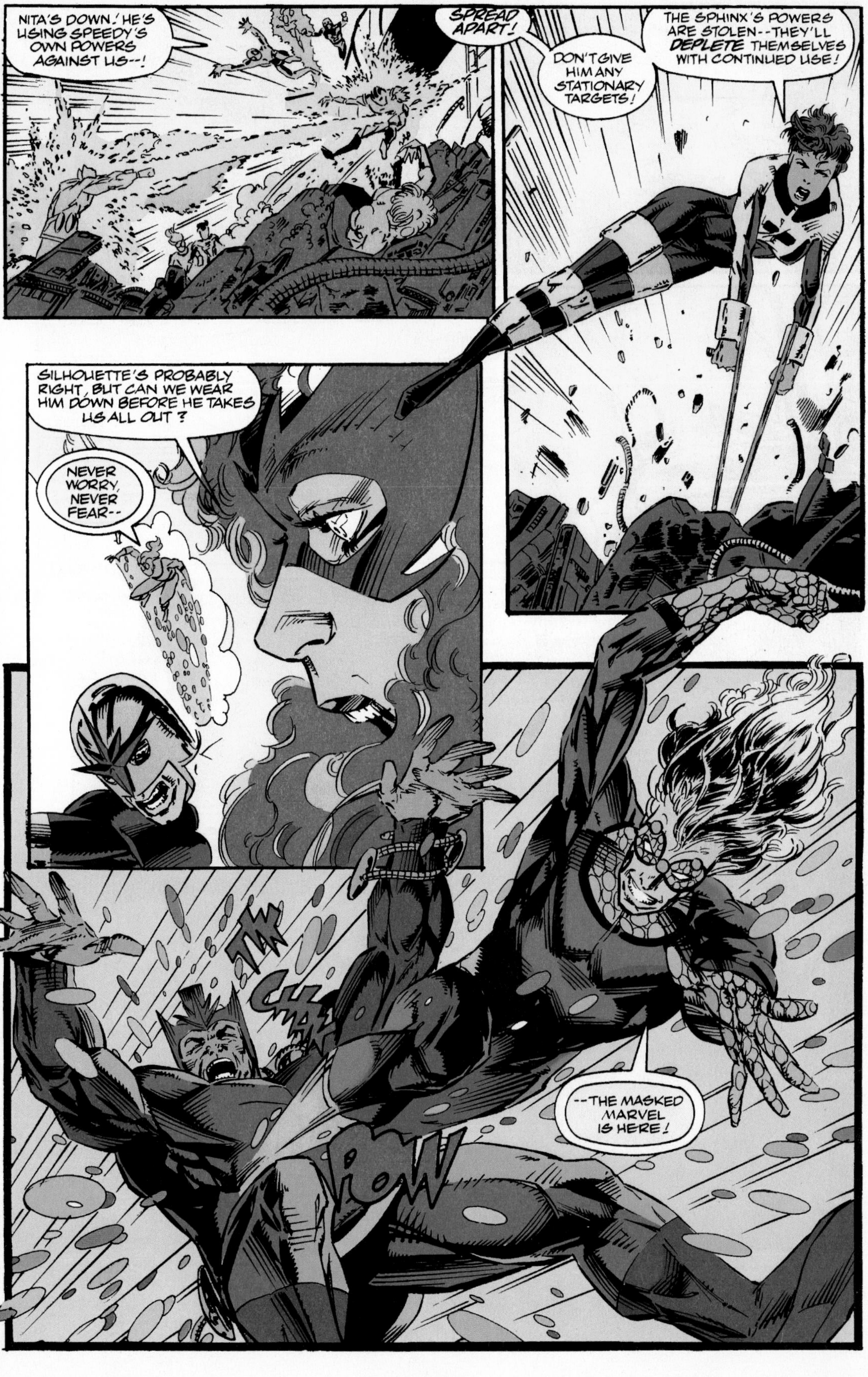
NITA'S DOWN! HE'S USING SPEEDY'S OWN POWERS AGAINST US--!
SPREAD APART!
DON'T GIVE HIM ANY STATIONARY TARGETS!
THE SPHINX'S POWERS ARE STOLEN--THEY'LL DEPLETE THEMSELVES WITH CONTINUED USE!
SILHOUETTE'S PROBABLY RIGHT, BUT CAN WE WEAR HIM DOWN BEFORE HE TAKES US ALL OUT?
NEVER WORRY, NEVER FEAR--
--THE MASKED MARVEL IS HERE!
POW

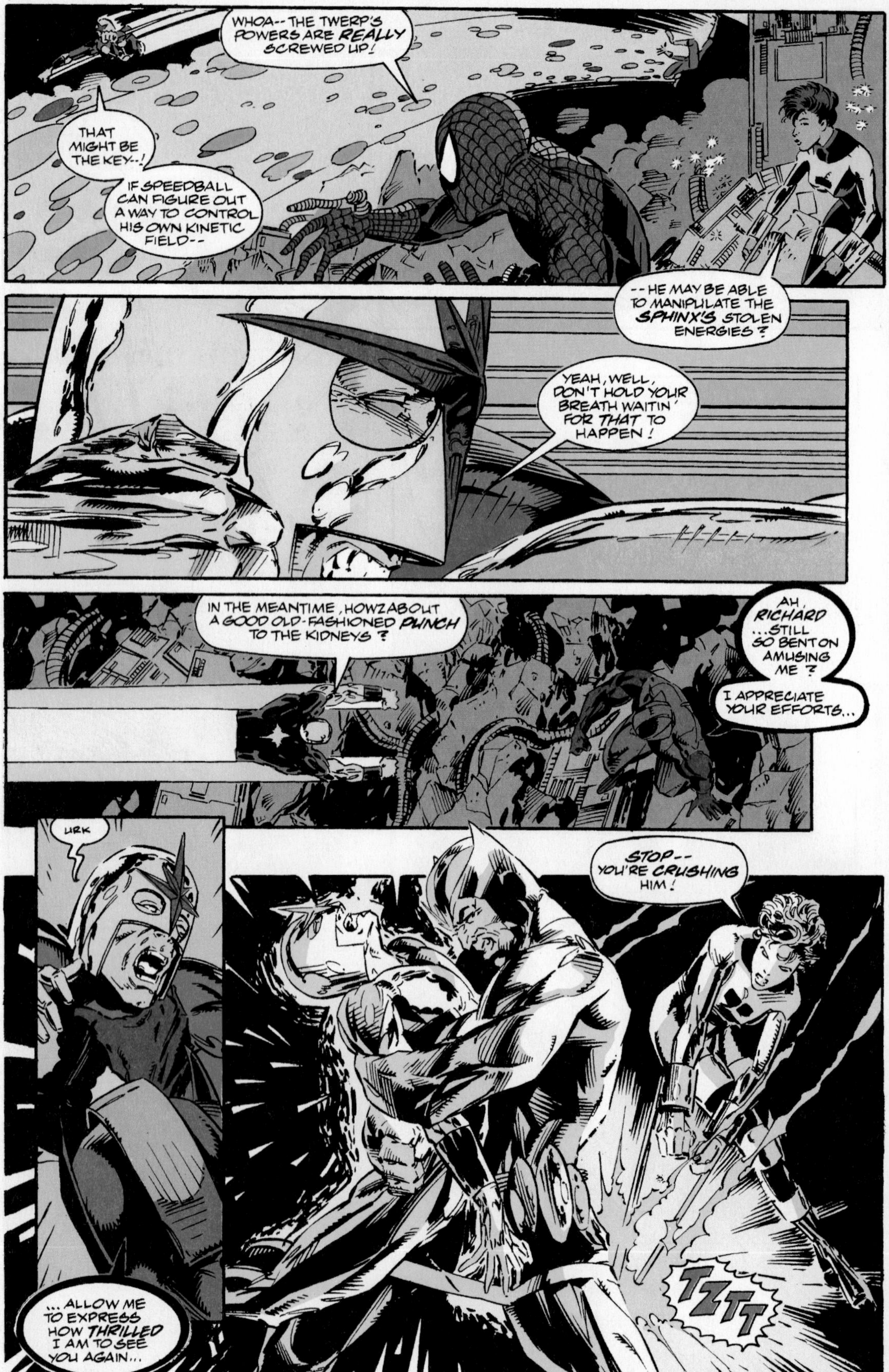
WHOA-- THE TWERP'S POWERS ARE REALLY SCREWED UP!
THAT MIGHT BE THE KEY--!
IF SPEEDBALL CAN FIGURE OUT A WAY TO CONTROL HIS OWN KINETIC FIELD--
--HE MAY BE ABLE TO MANIPULATE THE SPHINX'S STOLEN ENERGIES?
YEAH, WELL, DON'T HOLD YOUR BREATH WAITIN' FOR THAT TO HAPPEN!
IN THE MEANTIME, HOWZABOUT A GOOD OLD-FASHIONED PUNCH TO THE KIDNEYS?
AH, RICHARD ...STILL SO BENT ON AMUSING ME?
I APPRECIATE YOUR EFFORTS...
URK
...ALLOW ME TO EXPRESS HOW THRILLED I AM TO SEE YOU AGAIN...
STOP-- YOU'RE CRUSHING HIM!
TZTT

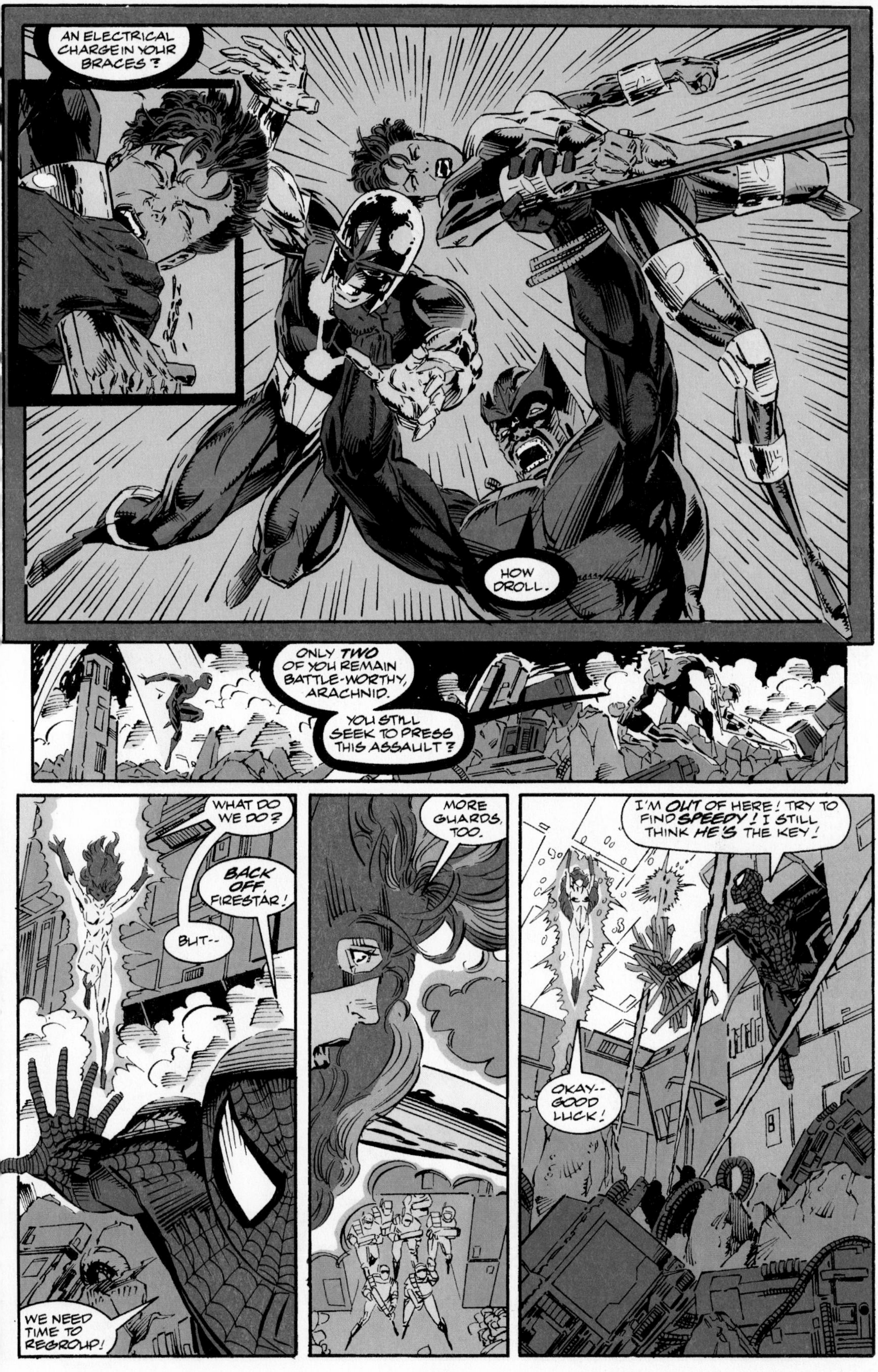
AN ELECTRICAL CHARGE IN YOUR BRACES?
HOW DROLL.
ONLY TWO OF YOU REMAIN BATTLE-WORTHY, ARACHNID.
YOU STILL SEEK TO PRESS THIS ASSAULT?
WHAT DO WE DO?
BACK OFF, FIRESTAR!
BUT--
WE NEED TIME TO REGROUP!
MORE GUARDS, TOO.
I'M OUT OF HERE! TRY TO FIND SPEEDY! I STILL THINK HE'S THE KEY!
OKAY-- GOOD LUCK!

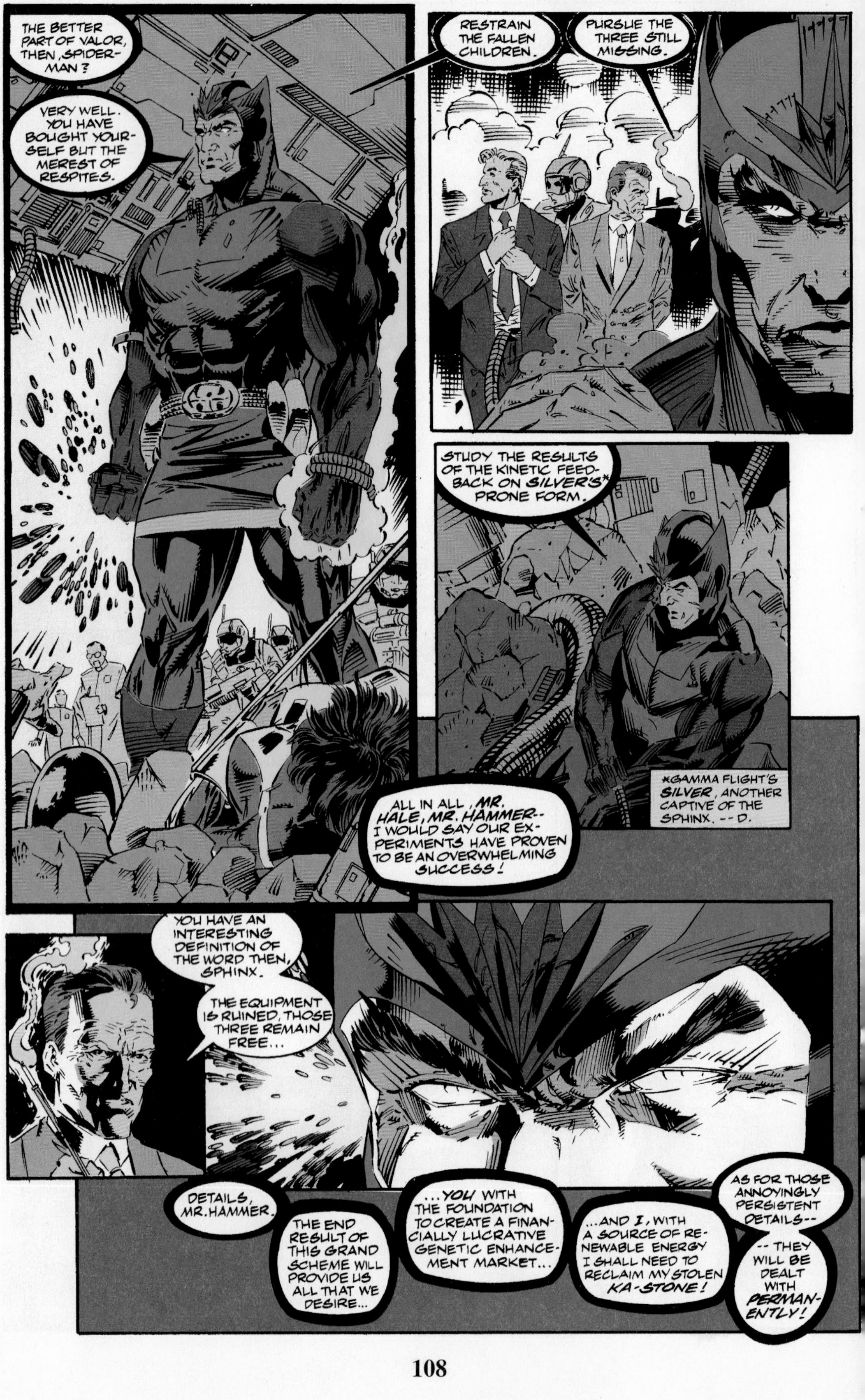
THE BETTER PART OF VALOR, THEN, SPIDER-MAN?
VERY WELL. YOU HAVE BOUGHT YOURSELF BUT THE MEREST OF RESPITES.
RESTRAIN THE FALLEN CHILDREN.
PURSUE THE THREE STILL MISSING.
STUDY THE RESULTS OF THE KINETIC FEED-BACK ON SILVER'S* PRONE FORM.
*GAMMA FLIGHT'S SILVER, ANOTHER CAPTIVE OF THE SPHINX. --D.
ALL IN ALL, MR. HALE, MR. HAMMER-- I WOULD SAY OUR EXPERIMENTS HAVE PROVEN TO BE AN OVERWHELMING SUCCESS!
YOU HAVE AN INTERESTING DEFINITION OF THE WORD THEN, SPHINX.
THE EQUIPMENT IS RUINED, THOSE THREE REMAIN FREE...
DETAILS, MR. HAMMER.
THE END RESULT OF THIS GRAND SCHEME WILL PROVIDE US ALL THAT WE DESIRE...
...YOU WITH THE FOUNDATION TO CREATE A FINANCIALLY LUCRATIVE GENETIC ENHANCEMENT MARKET...
...AND I, WITH A SOURCE OF RENEWABLE ENERGY I SHALL NEED TO RECLAIM MY STOLEN KA-STONE!
AS FOR THOSE ANNOYINGLY PERSISTENT DETAILS--
-- THEY WILL BE DEALT WITH PERMANENTLY!

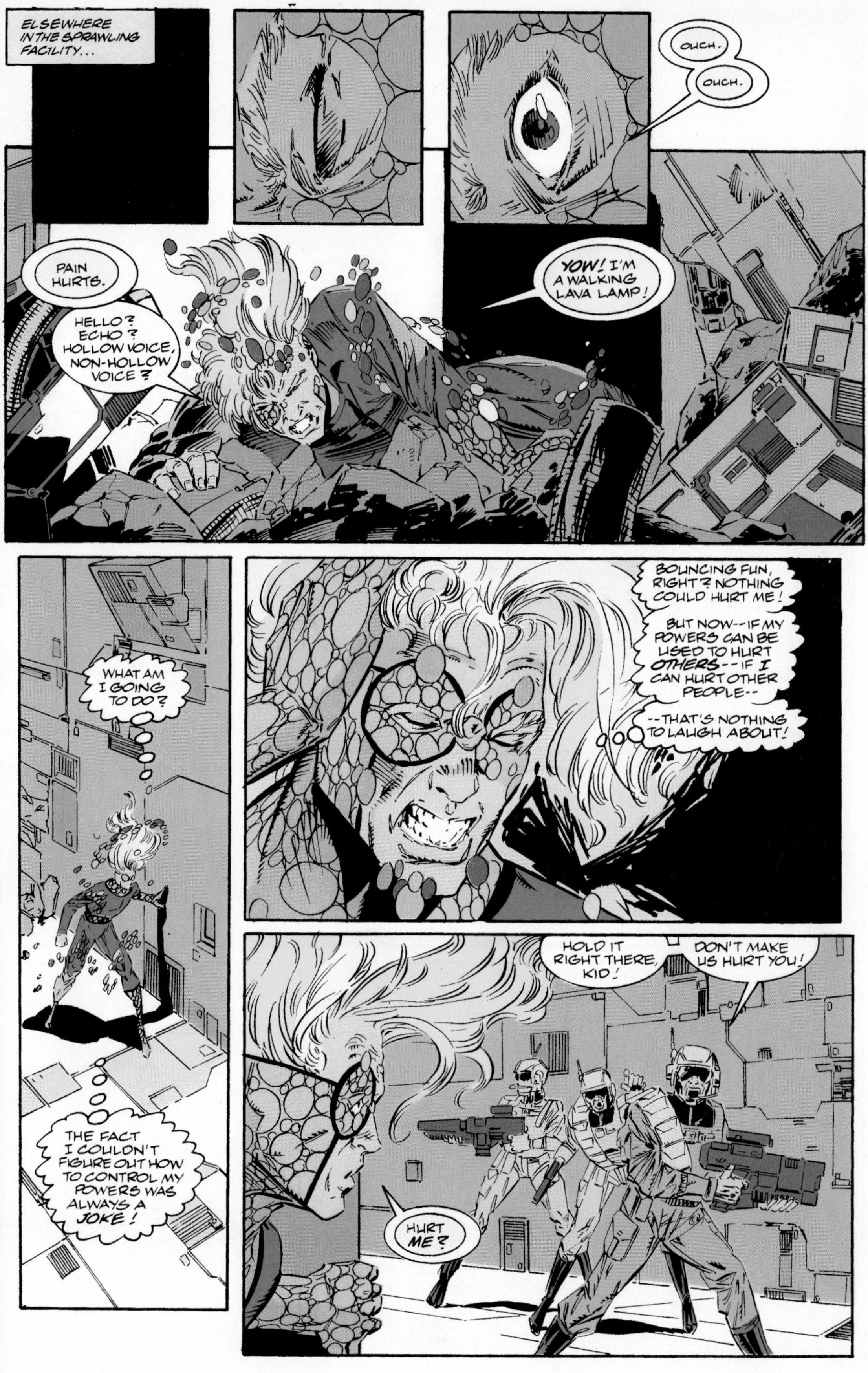
ELSEWHERE IN THE SPRAWLING FACILITY...
OUCH.
OUCH.
PAIN HURTS.
HELLO? ECHO? HOLLOW VOICE, NON-HOLLOW VOICE?
YOW! I'M A WALKING LAVA LAMP!
WHAT AM I GOING TO DO?
THE FACT I COULDN'T FIGURE OUT HOW TO CONTROL MY POWERS WAS ALWAYS A JOKE!
BOUNCING FUN, RIGHT? NOTHING COULD HURT ME!
BUT NOW--IF MY POWERS CAN BE USED TO HURT OTHERS--IF I CAN HURT OTHER PEOPLE--
--THAT'S NOTHING TO LAUGH ABOUT!
HOLD IT RIGHT THERE, KID!
DON'T MAKE US HURT YOU!
HURT ME?

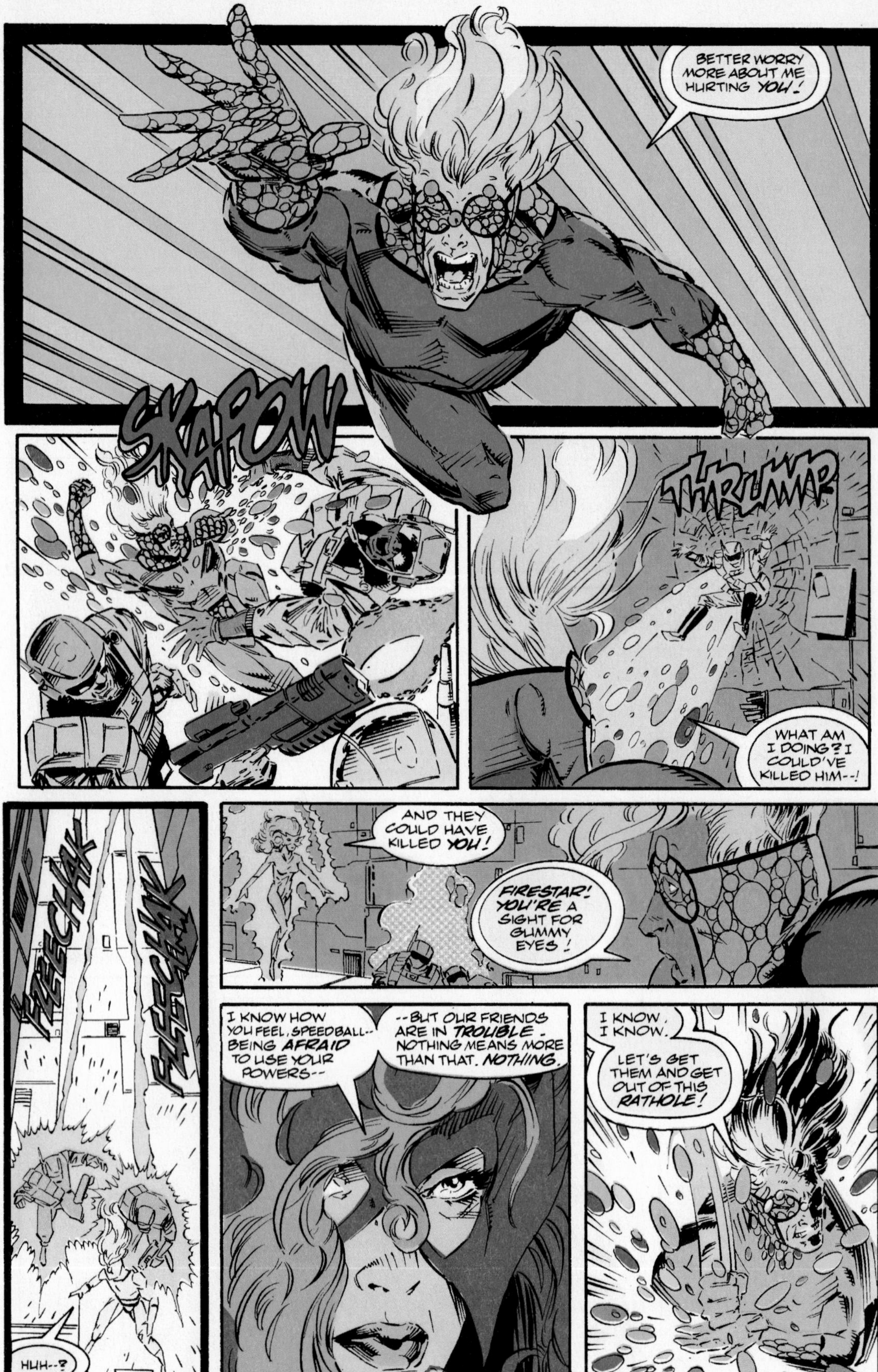
BETTER WORRY MORE ABOUT ME HURTING YOU!
SKAPOW
THRUMP
WHAT AM I DOING? I COULD'VE KILLED HIM--!
FEECHAK
FEECHAK
HUH--?
AND THEY COULD HAVE KILLED YOU!
FIRESTAR! YOU'RE A SIGHT FOR GUMMY EYES!
I KNOW HOW YOU FEEL, SPEEDBALL-- BEING AFRAID TO USE YOUR POWERS--
--BUT OUR FRIENDS ARE IN TROUBLE. NOTHING MEANS MORE THAN THAT. NOTHING.
I KNOW. I KNOW.
LET'S GET THEM AND GET OUT OF THIS RATHOLE!

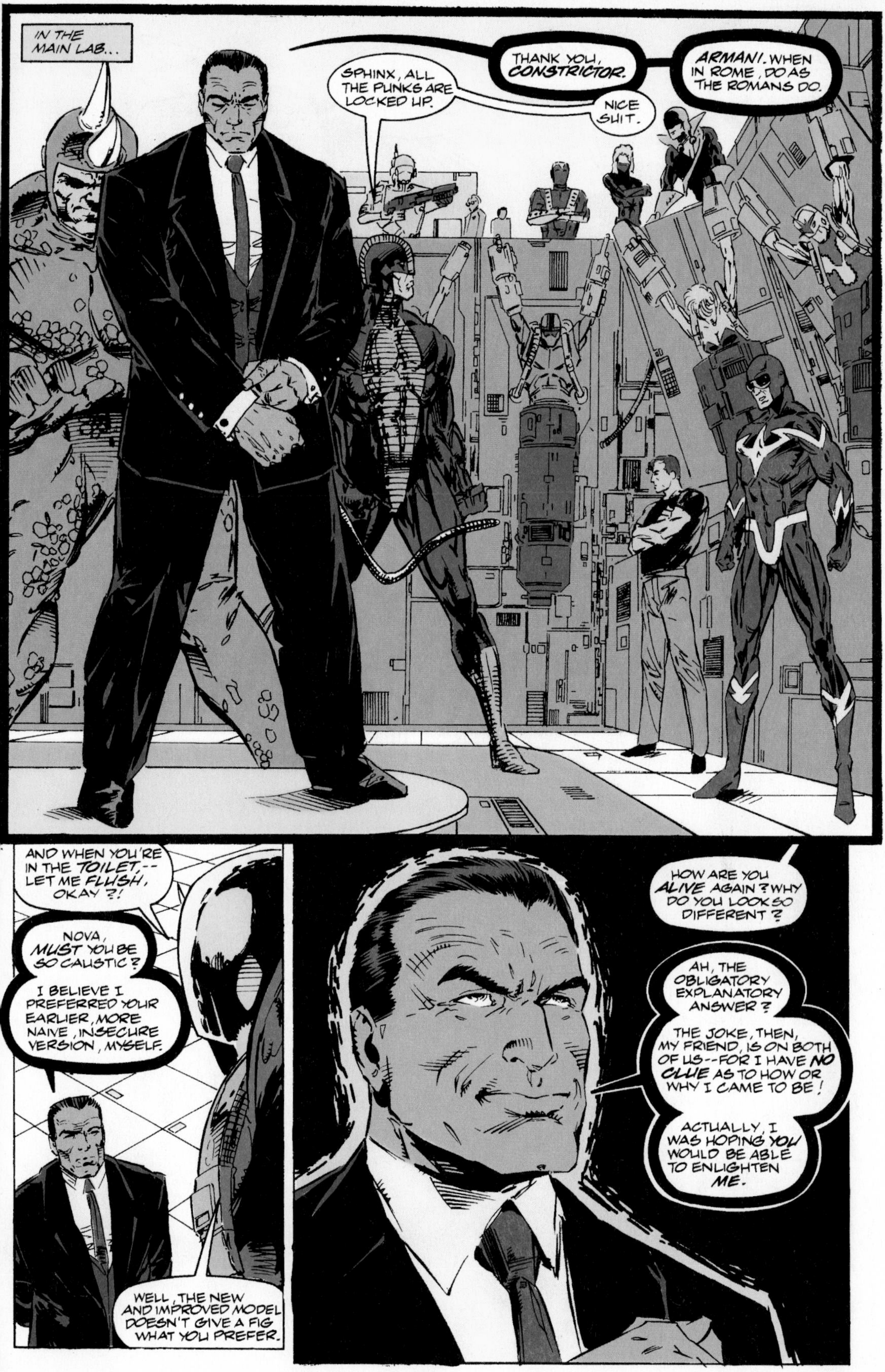
IN THE MAIN LAB...
SPHINX, ALL THE PUNKS ARE LOCKED UP.
NICE SUIT.
THANK YOU, CONSTRICTOR.
ARMANI. WHEN IN ROME, DO AS THE ROMANS DO.
AND WHEN YOU'RE IN THE TOILET,-- LET ME FLUSH, OKAY ?!
NOVA, MUST YOU BE SO CAUSTIC?
I BELIEVE I PREFERRED YOUR EARLIER, MORE NAIVE, INSECURE VERSION, MYSELF.
WELL, THE NEW AND IMPROVED MODEL DOESN'T GIVE A FIG WHAT YOU PREFER.
HOW ARE YOU ALIVE AGAIN? WHY DO YOU LOOK SO DIFFERENT?
AH, THE OBLIGATORY EXPLANATORY ANSWER?
THE JOKE, THEN, MY FRIEND, IS ON BOTH OF US--FOR I HAVE NO CLUE AS TO HOW OR WHY I CAME TO BE!
ACTUALLY, I WAS HOPING YOU WOULD BE ABLE TO ENLIGHTEN ME.

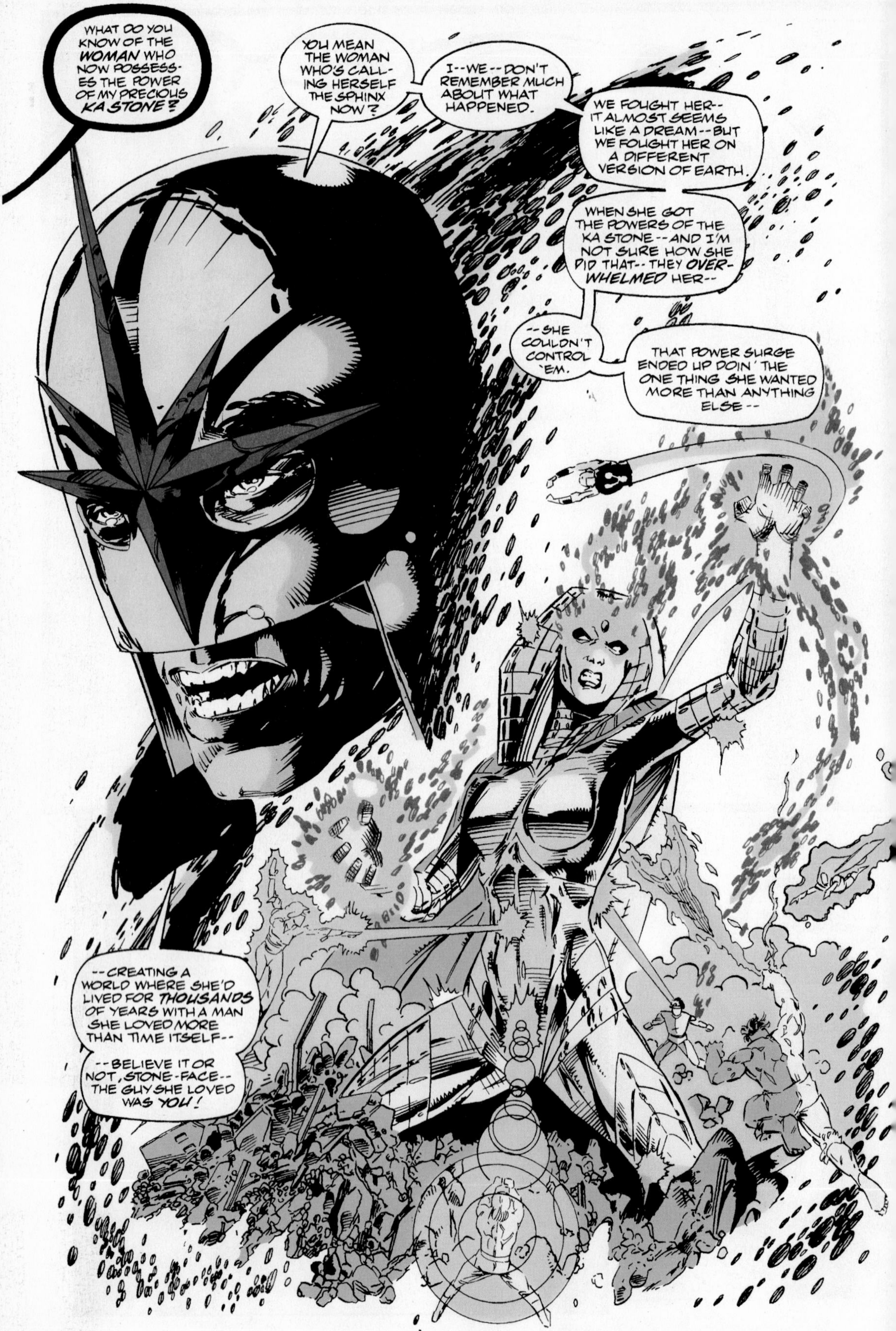
WHAT DO YOU KNOW OF THE WOMAN WHO NOW POSSESS-ES THE POWER OF MY PRECIOUS KA STONE?
YOU MEAN THE WOMAN WHO'S CALL-ING HERSELF THE SPHINX NOW?
I--WE--DON'T REMEMBER MUCH ABOUT WHAT HAPPENED.
WE FOUGHT HER--IT ALMOST SEEMS LIKE A DREAM--BUT WE FOUGHT HER ON A DIFFERENT VERSION OF EARTH.
WHEN SHE GOT THE POWERS OF THE KA STONE--AND I'M NOT SURE HOW SHE DID THAT--THEY OVER-WHELMED HER--
--SHE COULDN'T CONTROL 'EM.
THAT POWER SURGE ENDED UP DOIN' THE ONE THING SHE WANTED MORE THAN ANYTHING ELSE--
--CREATING A WORLD WHERE SHE'D LIVED FOR THOUSANDS OF YEARS WITH A MAN SHE LOVED MORE THAN TIME ITSELF--
--BELIEVE IT OR NOT, STONE-FACE--THE GUY SHE LOVED WAS YOU!

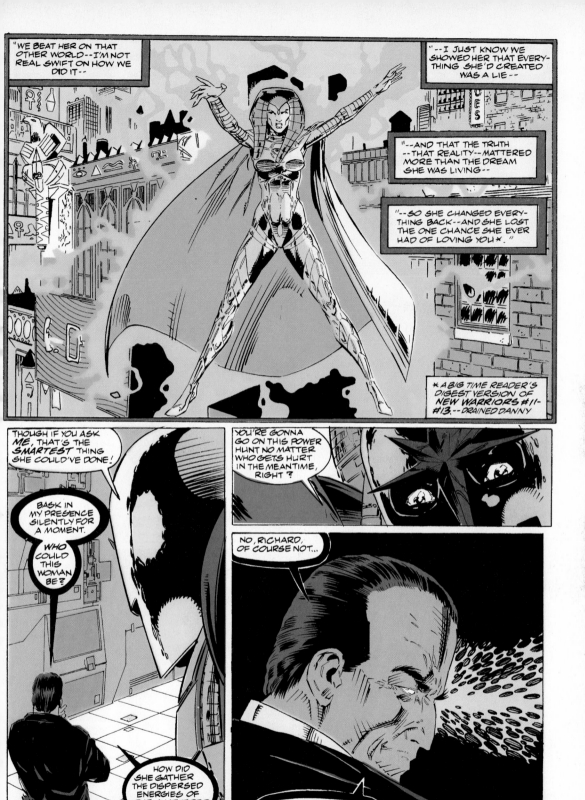

"WE BEAT HER ON THAT OTHER WORLD--I'M NOT REAL SWIFT ON HOW WE DID IT--

"--I JUST KNOW WE SHOWED HER THAT EVERYTHING SHE'D CREATED WAS A LIE--

"--AND THAT THE TRUTH --THAT REALITY--MATTERED MORE THAN THE DREAM SHE WAS LIVING--

"--SO SHE CHANGED EVERYTHING BACK--AND SHE LOST THE ONE CHANCE SHE EVER HAD OF LOVING YOU*."

* A BIG TIME READER'S DIGEST VERSION OF NEW WARRIORS #11-#13.--DRAINED DANNY

THOUGH IF YOU ASK ME, THAT'S THE SMARTEST THING SHE COULD'VE DONE!

BASK IN MY PRESENCE SILENTLY FOR A MOMENT.

WHO COULD THIS WOMAN BE?

HOW DID SHE GATHER THE DISPERSED ENERGIES OF THE SHATTERED KA STONE?

AND HOW MUCH POWER MUST I GAIN BEFORE I CAN CONFRONT HER AND RECLAIM THAT WHICH IS RIGHTFULLY MINE?

YOU'RE GONNA GO ON THIS POWER HUNT NO MATTER WHO GETS HURT IN THE MEANTIME, RIGHT?

NO, RICHARD, OF COURSE NOT...

...I WILL CONTINUE WITH MY PLANS ESPECIALLY BECAUSE OF WHO GETS HURT IN THE PROCESS!

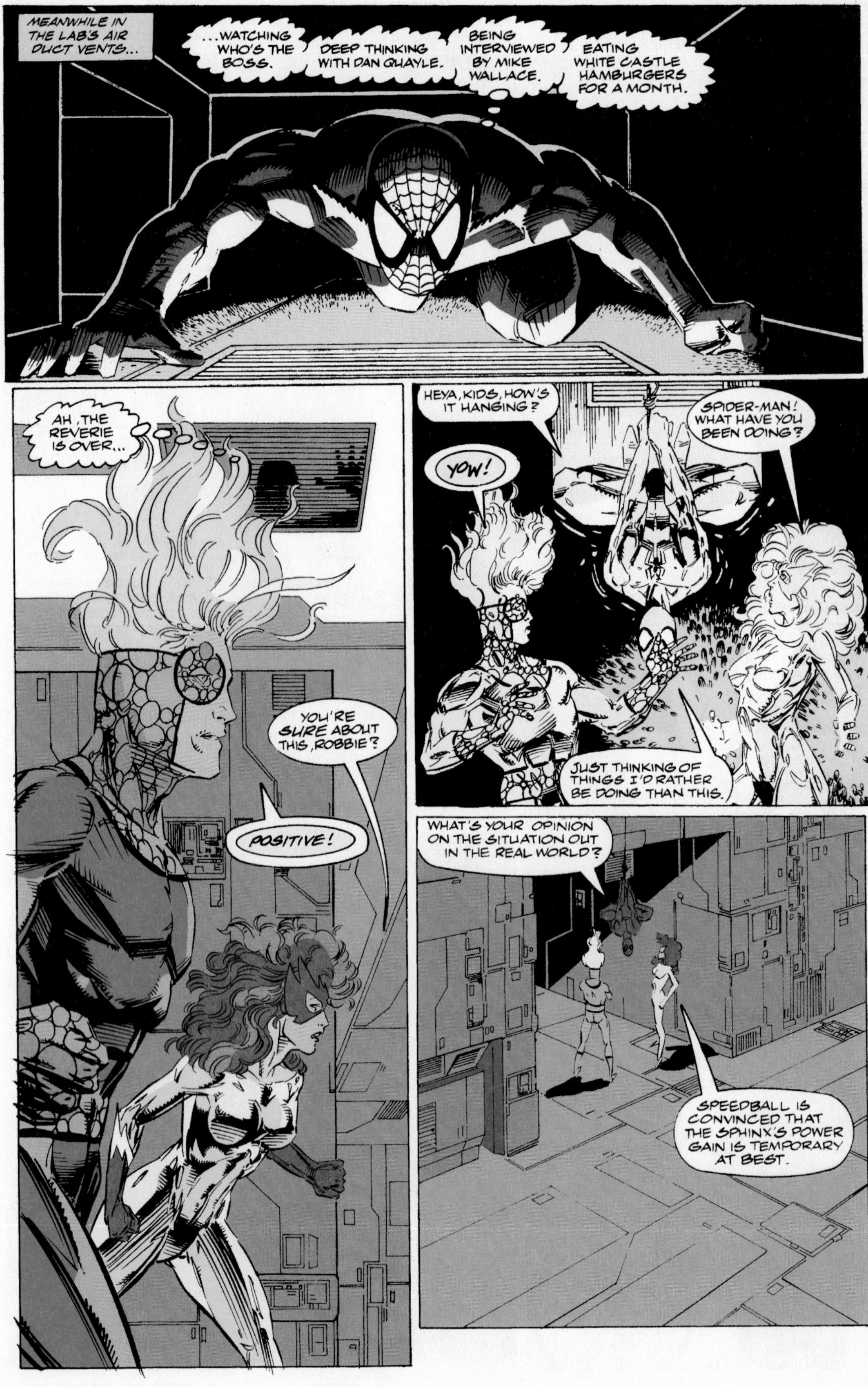
MEANWHILE IN THE LAB'S AIR DUCT VENTS...
...WATCHING WHO'S THE BOSS.
DEEP THINKING WITH DAN QUAYLE.
BEING INTERVIEWED BY MIKE WALLACE.
EATING WHITE CASTLE HAMBURGERS FOR A MONTH.
AH, THE REVERIE IS OVER...
YOU'RE SURE ABOUT THIS, ROBBIE?
POSITIVE!
HEYA, KIDS, HOW'S IT HANGING?
YOW!
SPIDER-MAN! WHAT HAVE YOU BEEN DOING?
JUST THINKING OF THINGS I'D RATHER BE DOING THAN THIS.
WHAT'S YOUR OPINION ON THE SITUATION OUT IN THE REAL WORLD?
SPEEDBALL IS CONVINCED THAT THE SPHINX'S POWER GAIN IS TEMPORARY AT BEST.

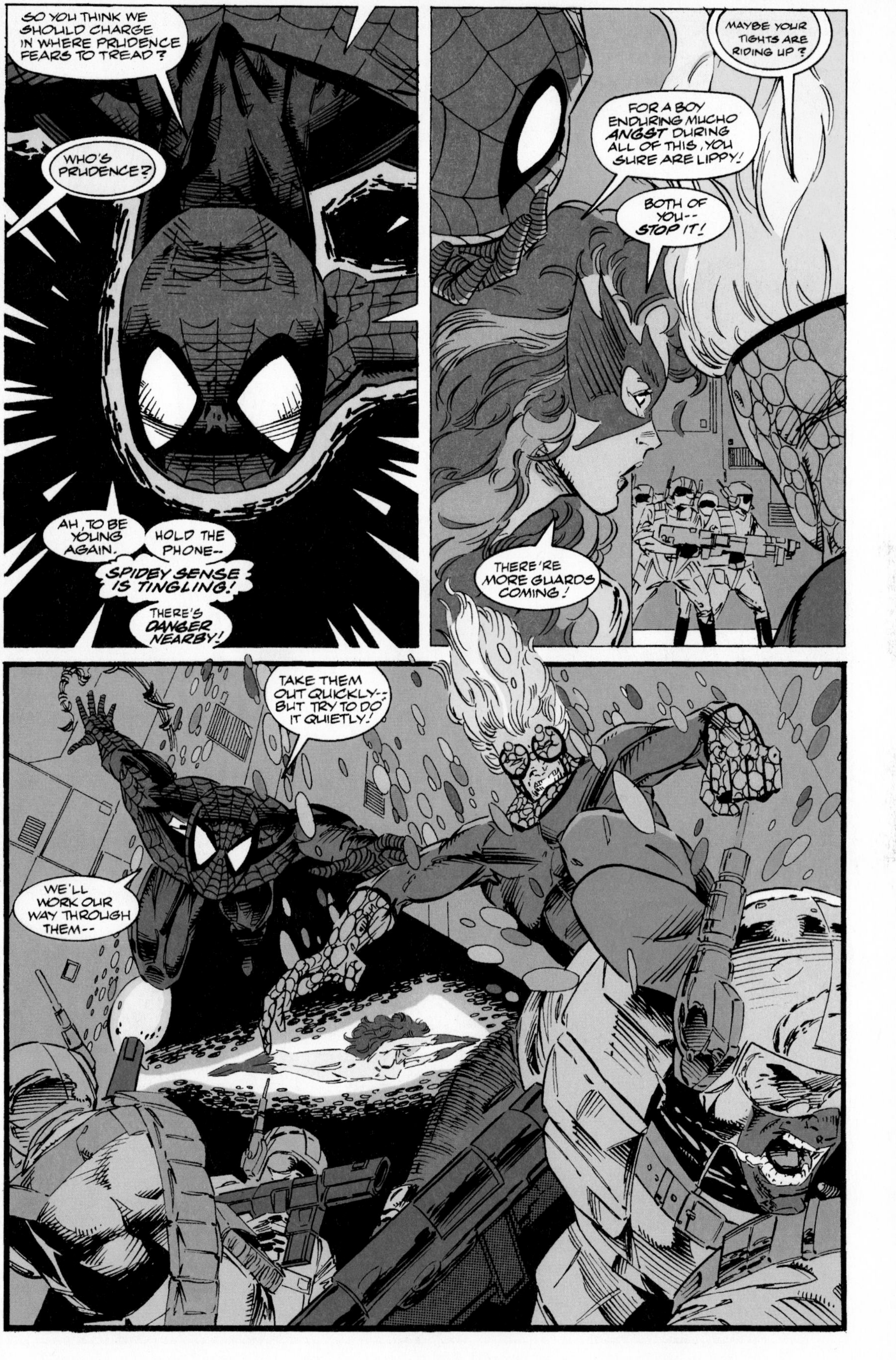
SO YOU THINK WE SHOULD CHARGE IN WHERE PRUDENCE FEARS TO TREAD?
WHO'S PRUDENCE?
AH, TO BE YOUNG AGAIN.
HOLD THE PHONE-- SPIDEY SENSE IS TINGLING!
THERE'S DANGER NEARBY!
MAYBE YOUR TIGHTS ARE RIDING UP?
FOR A BOY ENDURING MUCHO ANGST DURING ALL OF THIS, YOU SURE ARE LIPPY!
BOTH OF YOU-- STOP IT!
THERE'RE MORE GUARDS COMING!
TAKE THEM OUT QUICKLY-- BUT TRY TO DO IT QUIETLY!
WE'LL WORK OUR WAY THROUGH THEM--

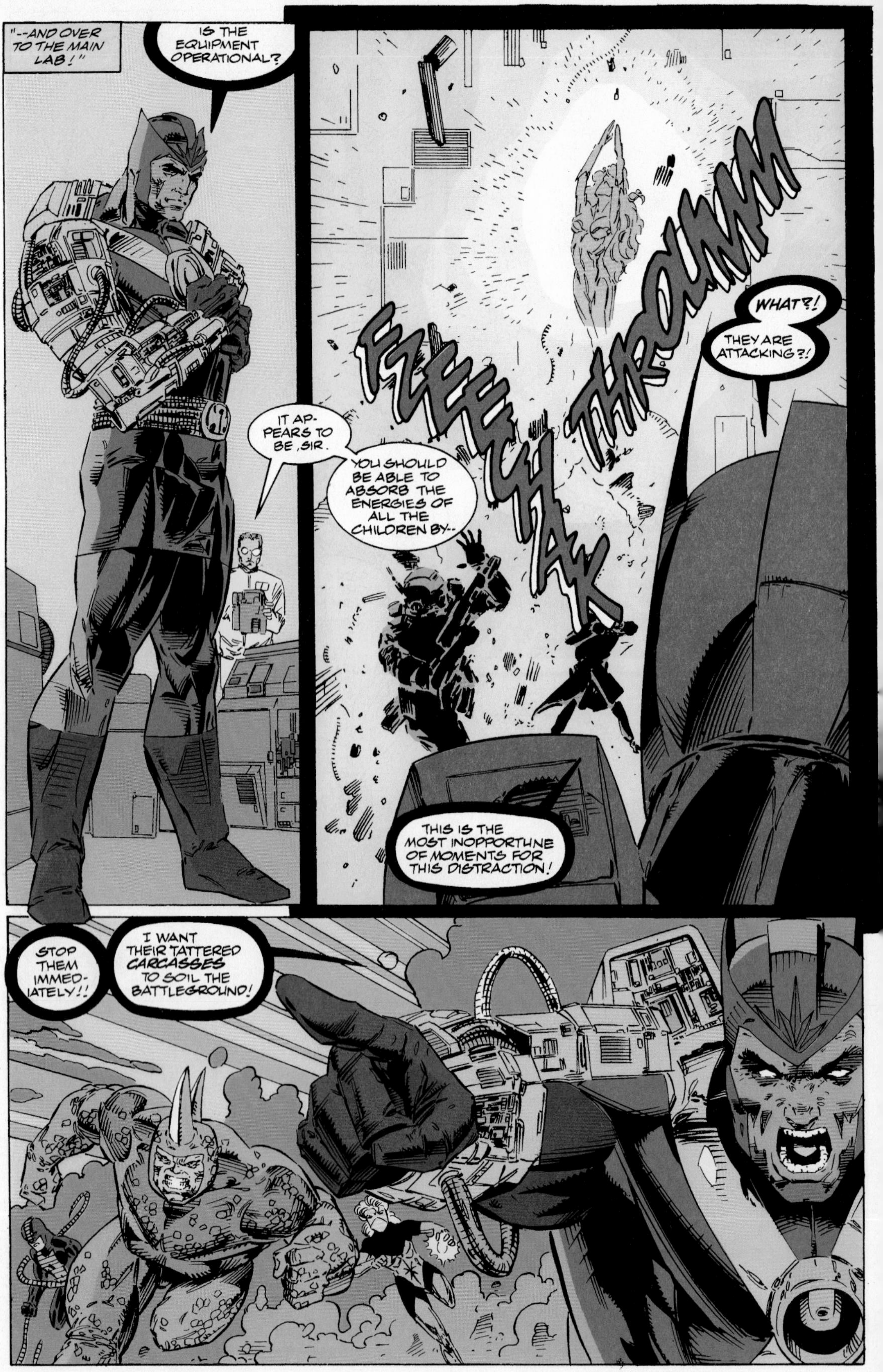
"--AND OVER TO THE MAIN LAB!"
IS THE EQUIPMENT OPERATIONAL?
IT AP-PEARS TO BE, SIR.
YOU SHOULD BE ABLE TO ABSORB THE ENERGIES OF ALL THE CHILDREN BY--
FZEECHAK
THROUMM
WHAT?!
THEY ARE ATTACKING?!
THIS IS THE MOST INOPPORTUNE OF MOMENTS FOR THIS DISTRACTION!
STOP THEM IMMED-IATELY!!
I WANT THEIR TATTERED *CARCASSES* TO SOIL THE BATTLEGROUND!

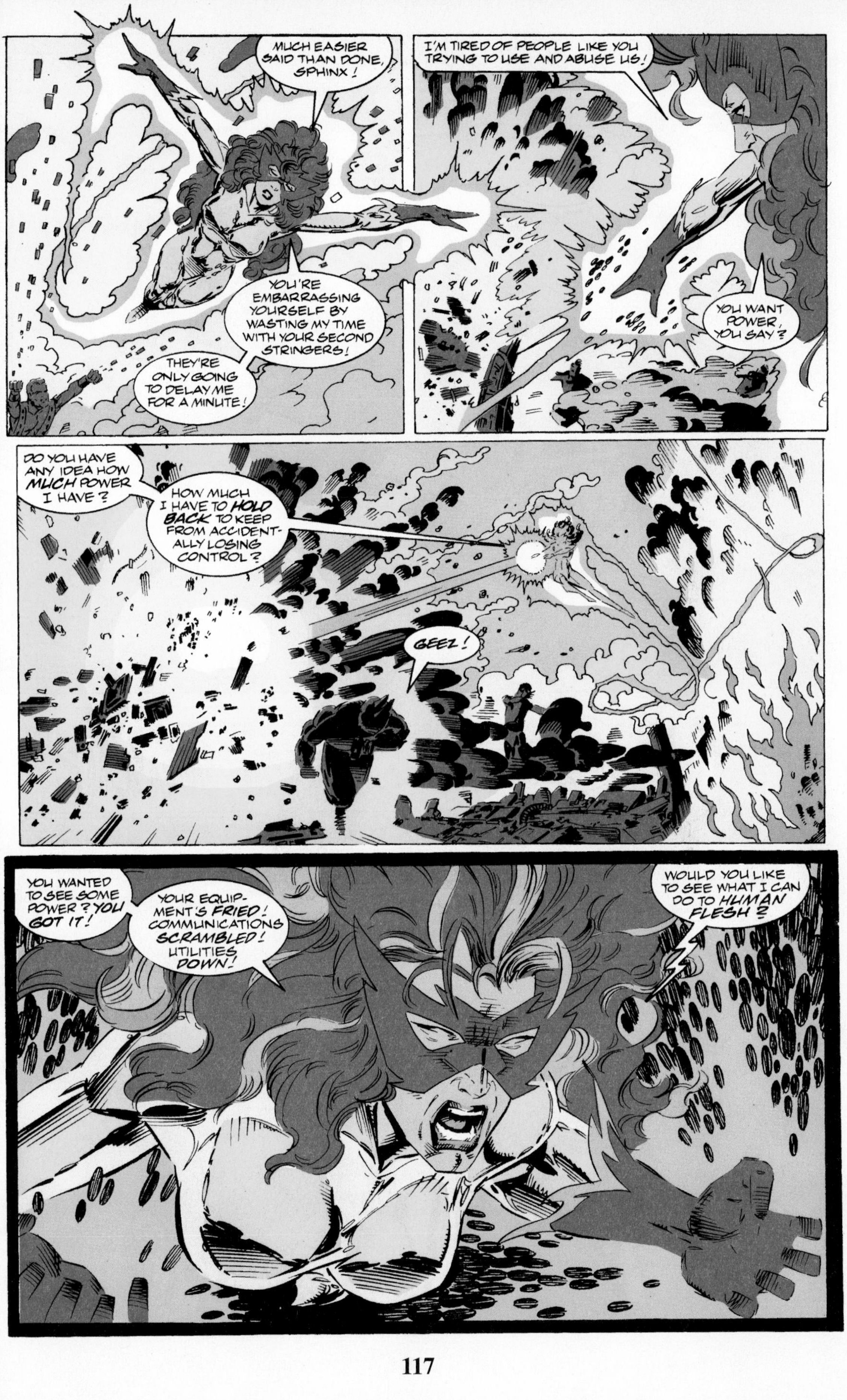
MUCH EASIER SAID THAN DONE, SPHINX!
YOU'RE EMBARRASSING YOURSELF BY WASTING MY TIME WITH YOUR SECOND STRINGERS!
THEY'RE ONLY GOING TO DELAY ME FOR A MINUTE!
I'M TIRED OF PEOPLE LIKE YOU TRYING TO USE AND ABUSE US!
YOU WANT POWER, YOU SAY?
DO YOU HAVE ANY IDEA HOW MUCH POWER I HAVE?
HOW MUCH I HAVE TO HOLD BACK TO KEEP FROM ACCIDENT-ALLY LOSING CONTROL?
GEEZ!
YOU WANTED TO SEE SOME POWER? YOU GOT IT!
YOUR EQUIP-MENT'S FRIED! COMMUNICATIONS SCRAMBLED! UTILITIES DOWN!
WOULD YOU LIKE TO SEE WHAT I CAN DO TO HUMAN FLESH?

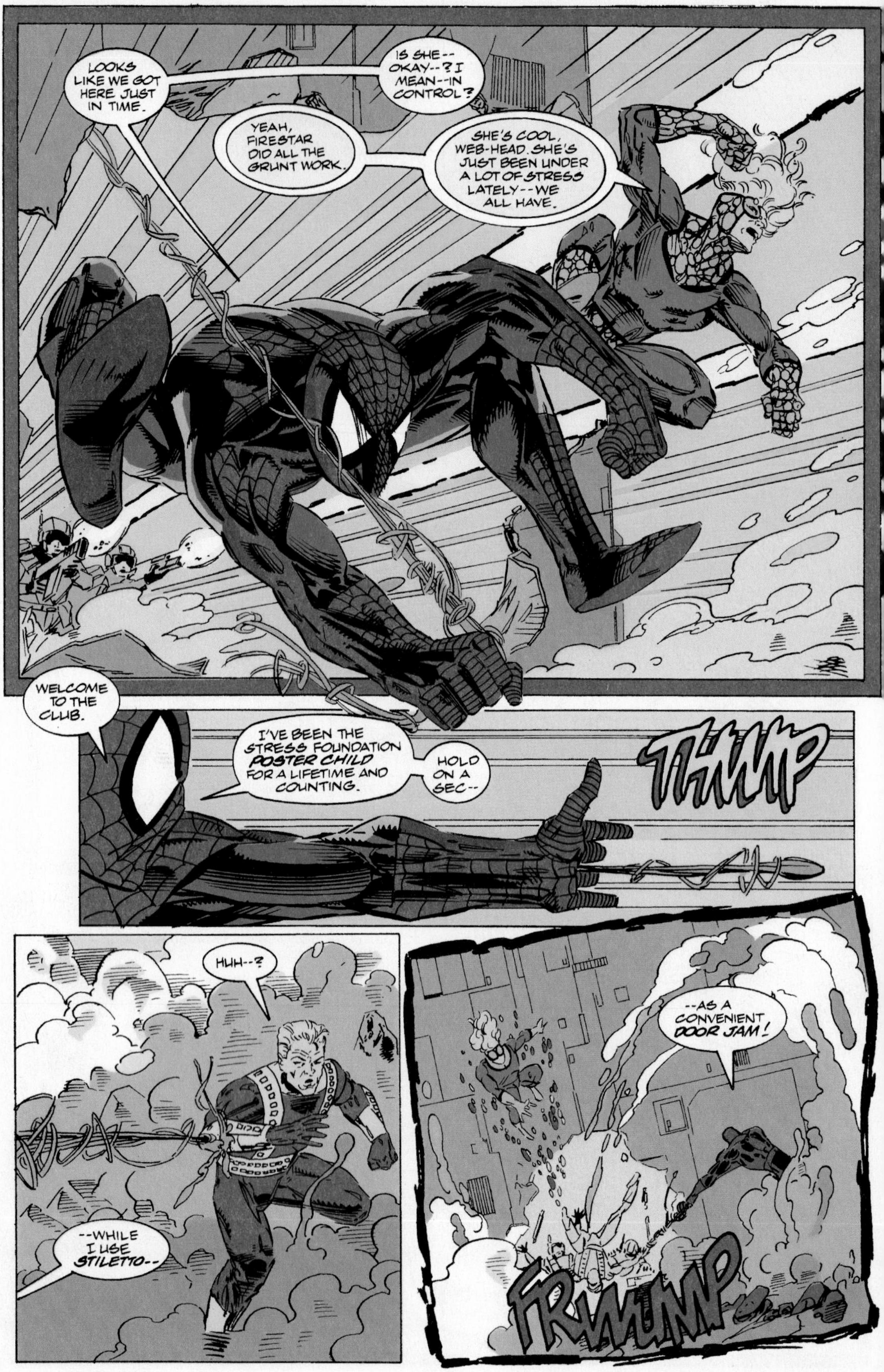

LOOKS LIKE WE GOT HERE JUST IN TIME.
IS SHE-- OKAY--? I MEAN--IN CONTROL?
YEAH, FIRESTAR DID ALL THE GRUNT WORK.
SHE'S COOL, WEB-HEAD. SHE'S JUST BEEN UNDER A LOT OF STRESS LATELY--WE ALL HAVE.
WELCOME TO THE CLUB.
I'VE BEEN THE STRESS FOUNDATION POSTER CHILD FOR A LIFETIME AND COUNTING.
HOLD ON A SEC--
THUMP
HUH--?
--WHILE I USE STILETTO--
--AS A CONVENIENT DOOR JAM!
FRUMMP

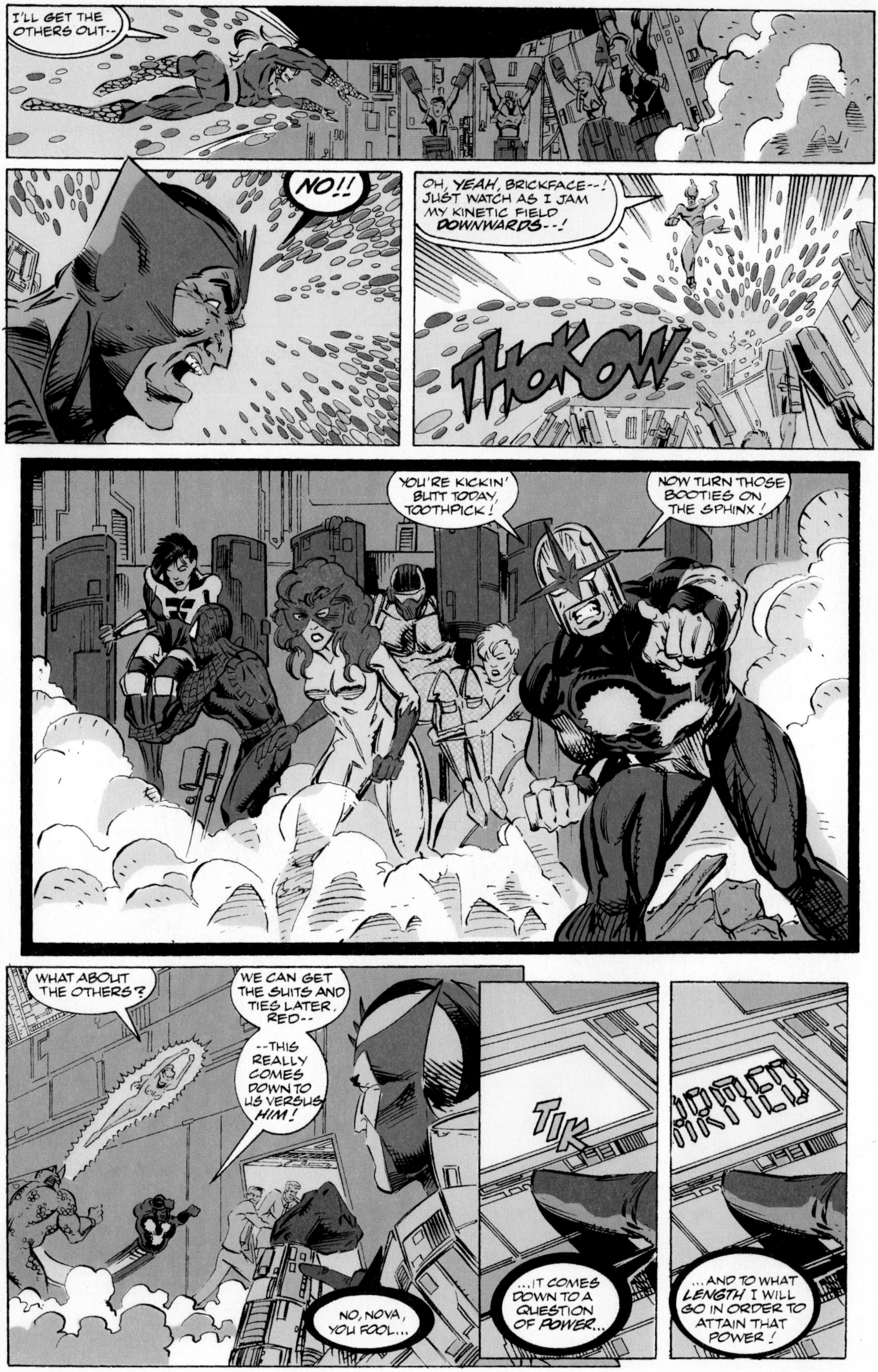
I'LL GET THE OTHERS OUT--
NO!!
OH, YEAH, BRICKFACE--! JUST WATCH AS I JAM MY KINETIC FIELD DOWNWARDS--!
THOKOW
YOU'RE KICKIN' BUTT TODAY, TOOTHPICK!
NOW TURN THOSE BOOTIES ON THE SPHINX!
WHAT ABOUT THE OTHERS?
WE CAN GET THE SUITS AND TIES LATER, RED--
--THIS REALLY COMES DOWN TO US VERSUS HIM!
NO, NOVA, YOU FOOL...
TIK
...IT COMES DOWN TO A QUESTION OF POWER...
...AND TO WHAT LENGTH I WILL GO IN ORDER TO ATTAIN THAT POWER!

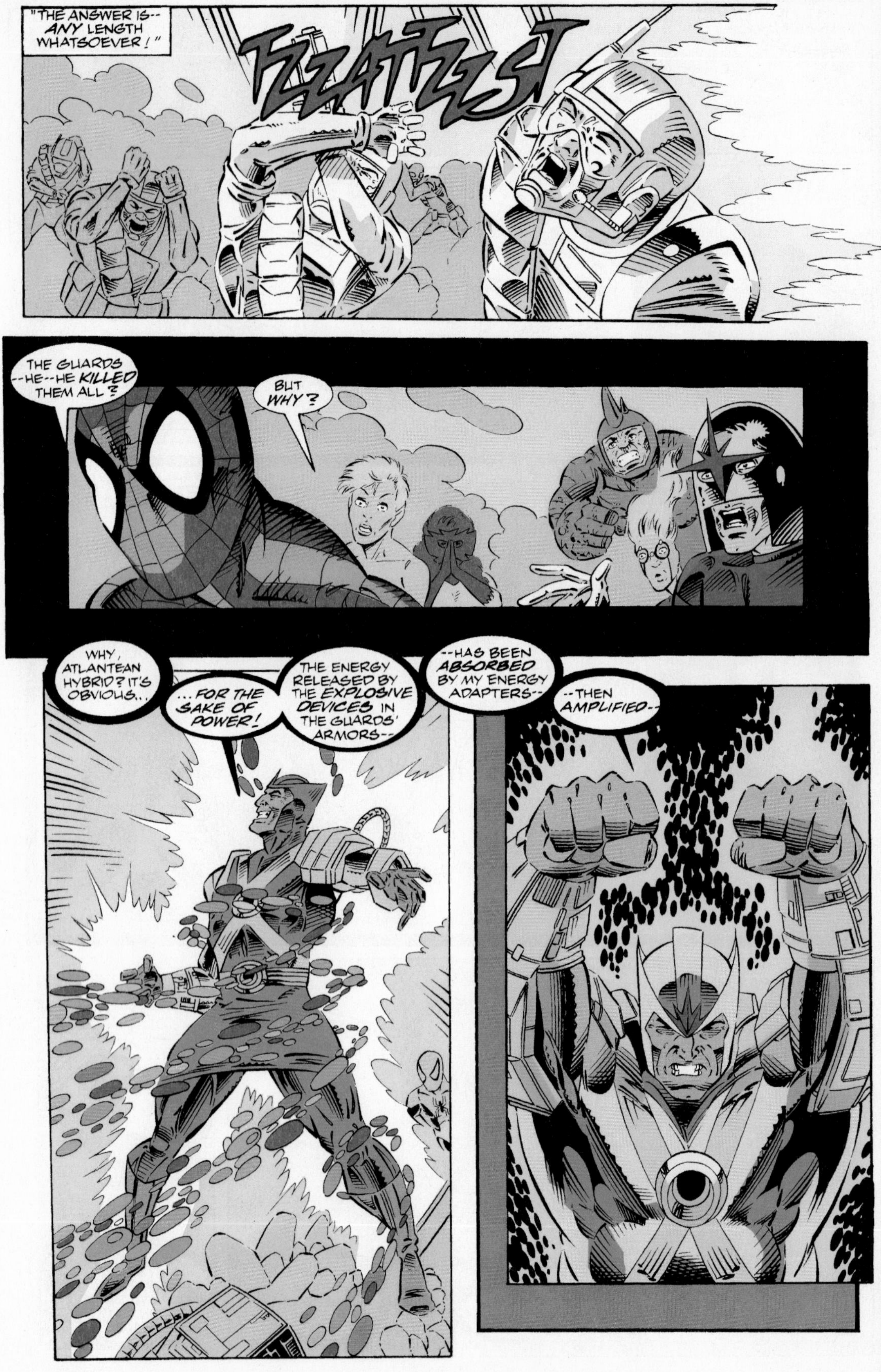
"THE ANSWER IS-- ANY LENGTH WHATSOEVER!"
FZZATZZST
THE GUARDS --HE--HE KILLED THEM ALL?
BUT WHY?
WHY, ATLANTEAN HYBRID? IT'S OBVIOUS...
...FOR THE SAKE OF POWER!
THE ENERGY RELEASED BY THE EXPLOSIVE DEVICES IN THE GUARDS' ARMORS--
--HAS BEEN ABSORBED BY MY ENERGY ADAPTERS--
--THEN AMPLIFIED--

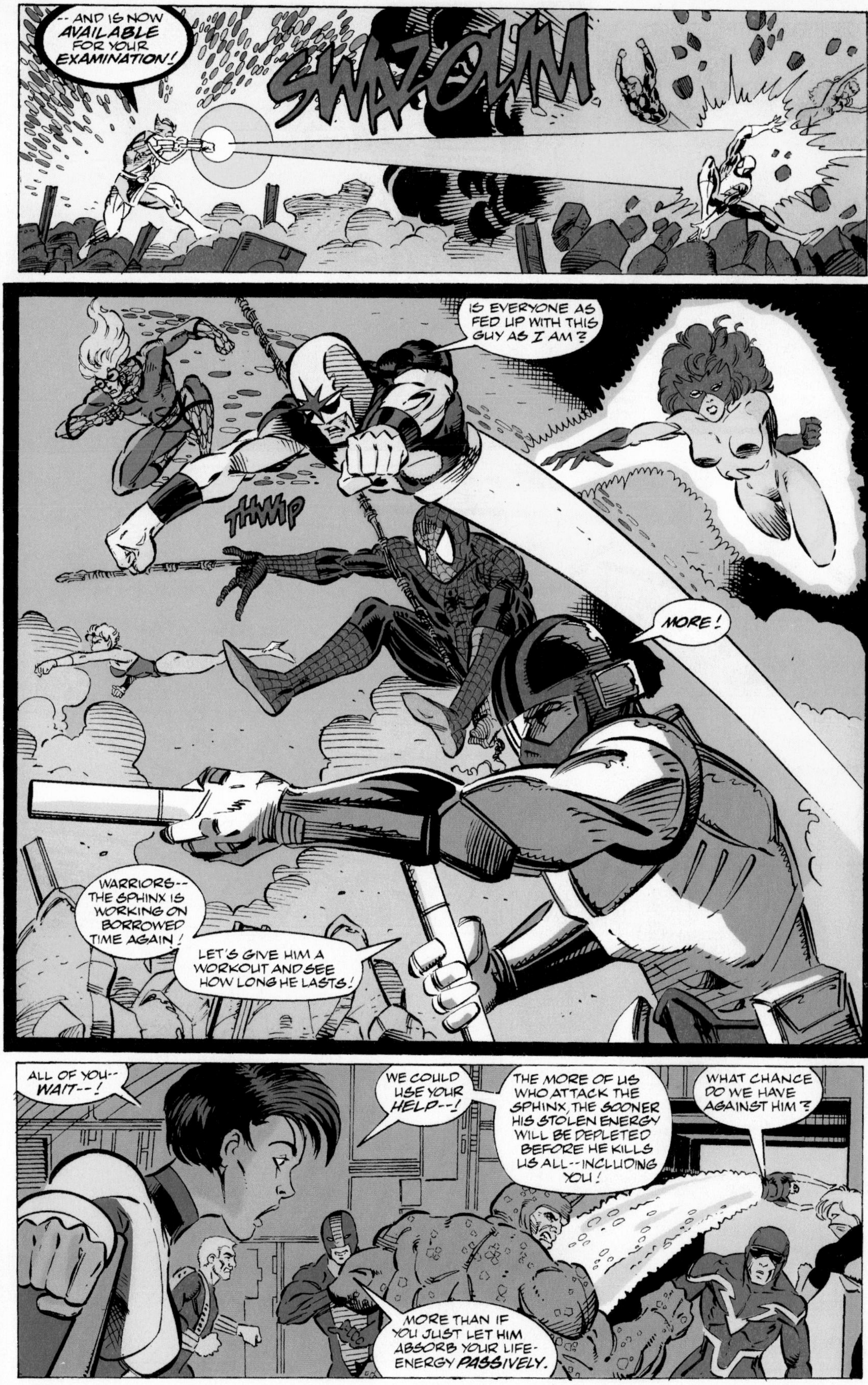
--AND IS NOW AVAILABLE FOR YOUR EXAMINATION!
SWAZOUM
IS EVERYONE AS FED UP WITH THIS GUY AS I AM?
THWIP
MORE!
WARRIORS-- THE SPHINX IS WORKING ON BORROWED TIME AGAIN!
LET'S GIVE HIM A WORKOUT AND SEE HOW LONG HE LASTS!
ALL OF YOU-- WAIT--!
WE COULD USE YOUR HELP--!
THE MORE OF US WHO ATTACK THE SPHINX, THE SOONER HIS STOLEN ENERGY WILL BE DEPLETED BEFORE HE KILLS US ALL--INCLUDING YOU!
WHAT CHANCE DO WE HAVE AGAINST HIM?
MORE THAN IF YOU JUST LET HIM ABSORB YOUR LIFE-ENERGY PASSIVELY.

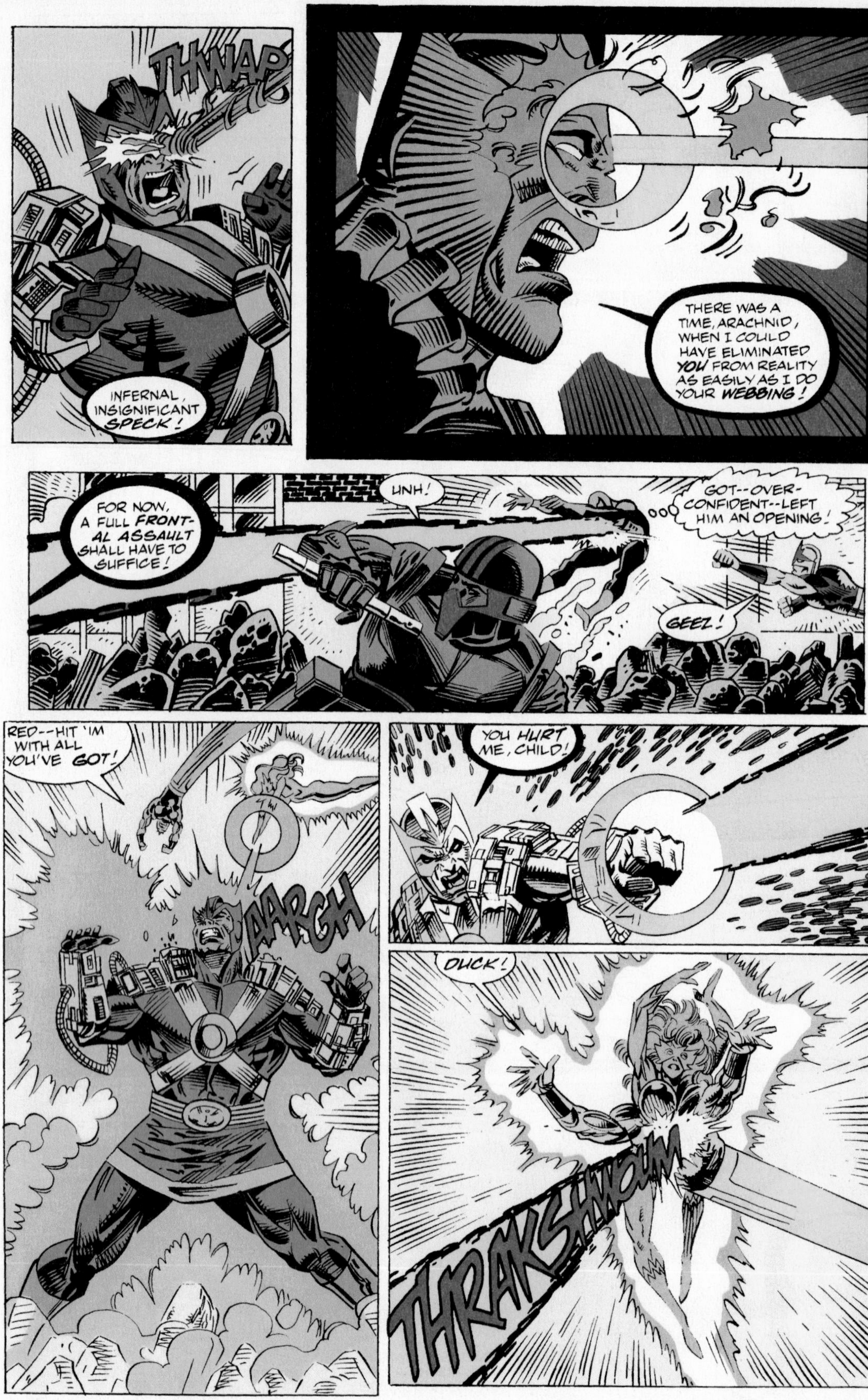
THWAP
INFERNAL, INSIGNIFICANT SPECK!
THERE WAS A TIME, ARACHNID, WHEN I COULD HAVE ELIMINATED YOU FROM REALITY AS EASILY AS I DO YOUR WEBBING!
FOR NOW, A FULL FRONTAL ASSAULT SHALL HAVE TO SUFFICE!
UNH!
GOT--OVER-CONFIDENT--LEFT HIM AN OPENING!
GEEZ!
RED--HIT 'IM WITH ALL YOU'VE GOT!
AARGH
YOU HURT ME, CHILD!
OUCK!
THRAKSHOOM

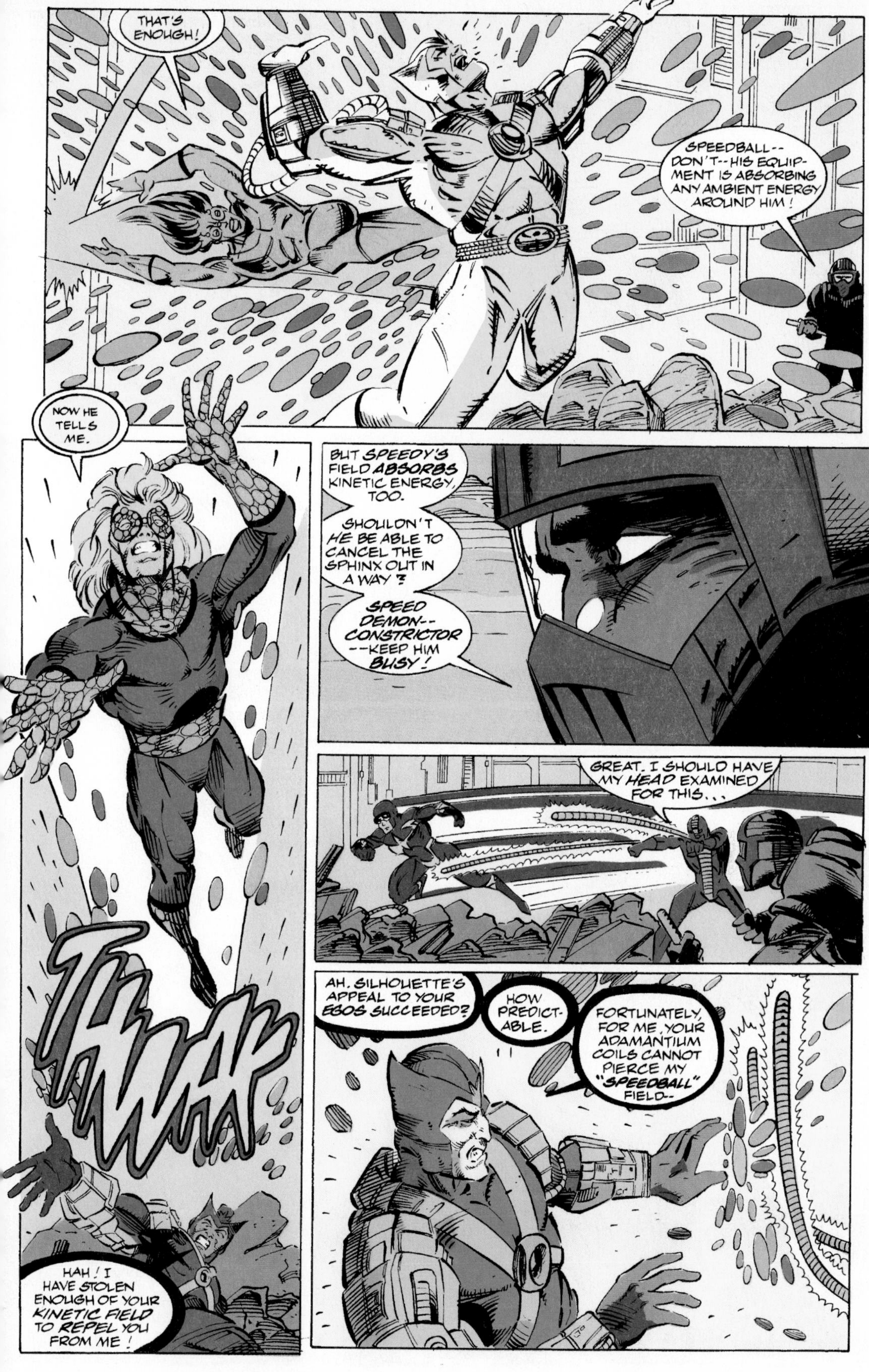
THAT'S ENOUGH!
SPEEDBALL-- DON'T--HIS EQUIPMENT IS ABSORBING ANY AMBIENT ENERGY AROUND HIM!
NOW HE TELLS ME.
BUT SPEEDY'S FIELD ABSORBS KINETIC ENERGY, TOO.
SHOULDN'T HE BE ABLE TO CANCEL THE SPHINX OUT IN A WAY?
SPEED DEMON-- CONSTRICTOR --KEEP HIM BUSY!
GREAT. I SHOULD HAVE MY HEAD EXAMINED FOR THIS...
THWAP
HAH! I HAVE STOLEN ENOUGH OF YOUR KINETIC FIELD TO REPEL YOU FROM ME!
AH. SILHOUETTE'S APPEAL TO YOUR EGOS SUCCEEDED?
HOW PREDICTABLE.
FORTUNATELY, FOR ME, YOUR ADAMANTIUM COILS CANNOT PIERCE MY "SPEEDBALL" FIELD--

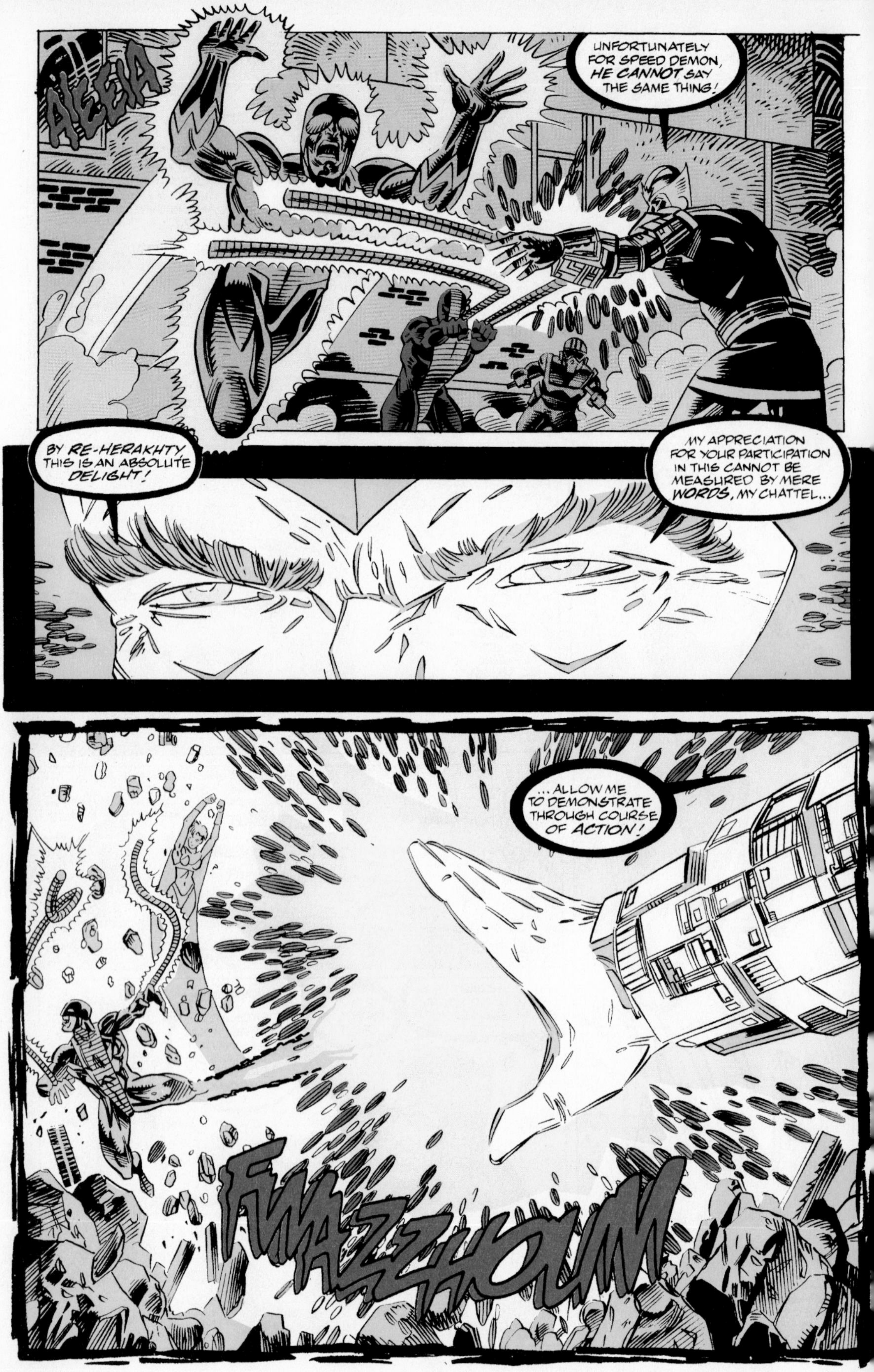
AIEEIA
UNFORTUNATELY FOR SPEED DEMON, HE CANNOT SAY THE SAME THING!
BY RE-HERAKHTY, THIS IS AN ABSOLUTE DELIGHT!
MY APPRECIATION FOR YOUR PARTICIPATION IN THIS CANNOT BE MEASURED BY MERE WORDS, MY CHATTEL...
...ALLOW ME TO DEMONSTRATE THROUGH COURSE OF ACTION!
FWAZZHOUM

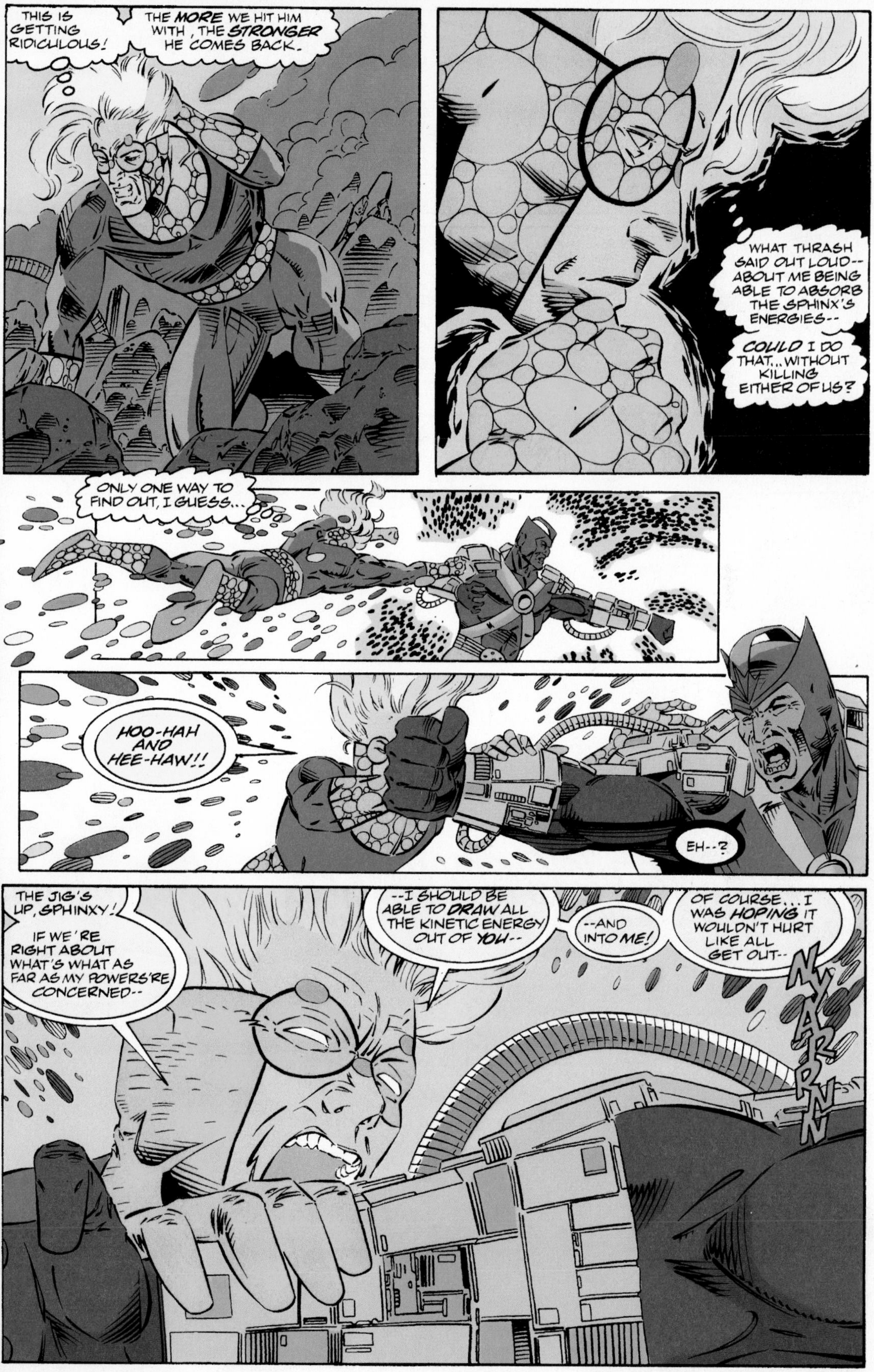

THIS IS GETTING RIDICULOUS!
THE MORE WE HIT HIM WITH, THE STRONGER HE COMES BACK.
WHAT THRASH SAID OUT LOUD-- ABOUT ME BEING ABLE TO ABSORB THE SPHINX'S ENERGIES--
COULD I DO THAT... WITHOUT KILLING EITHER OF US?
ONLY ONE WAY TO FIND OUT, I GUESS...
HOO-HAH AND HEE-HAW!!
EH--?
THE JIG'S UP, SPHINXY!
IF WE'RE RIGHT ABOUT WHAT'S WHAT AS FAR AS MY POWERS'RE CONCERNED--
--I SHOULD BE ABLE TO DRAW ALL THE KINETIC ENERGY OUT OF YOU--
--AND INTO ME!
OF COURSE... I WAS HOPING IT WOULDN'T HURT LIKE ALL GET OUT--
NYARRNN

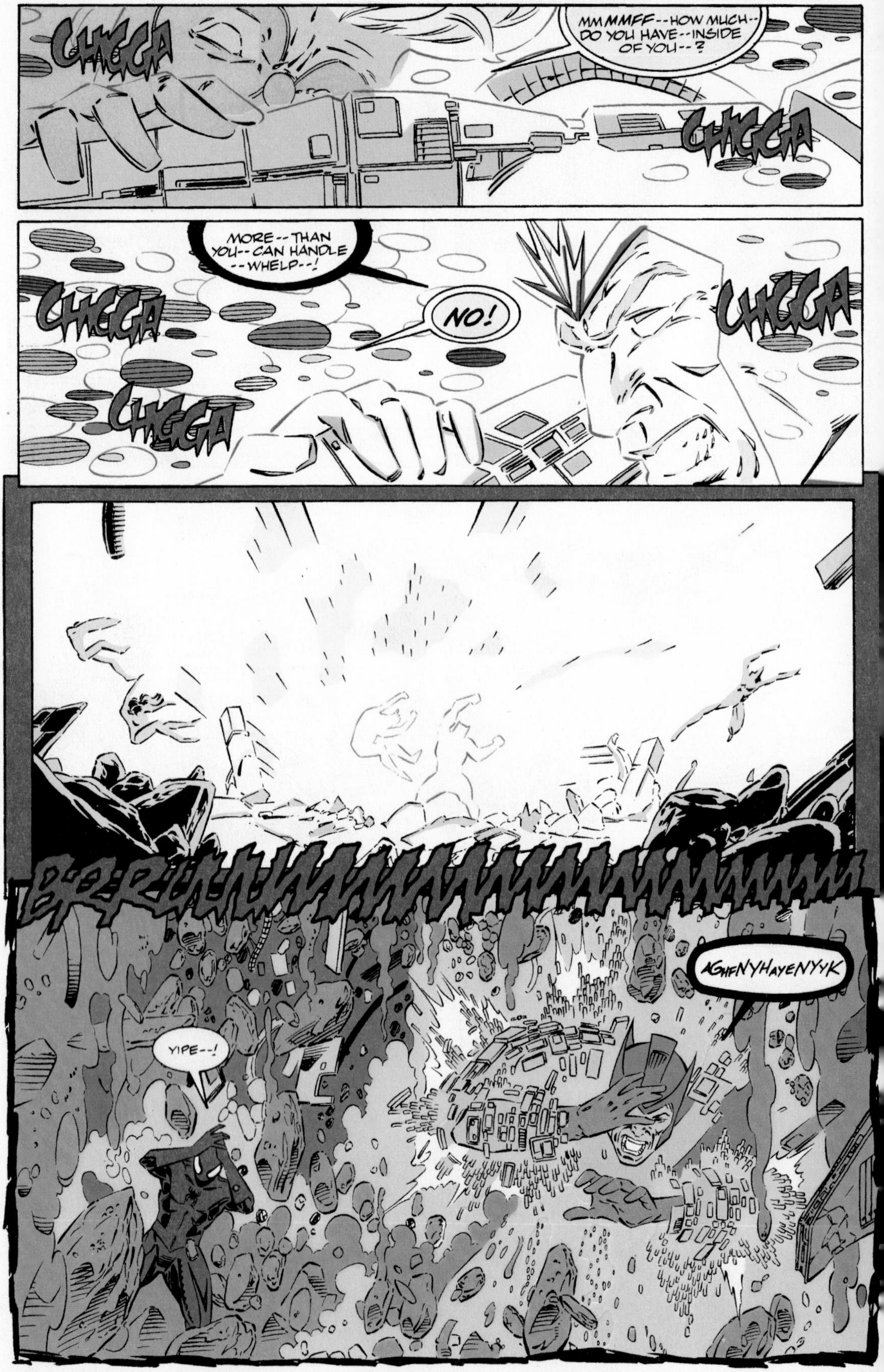

CHGGA
MMMMFF--HOW MUCH--DO YOU HAVE--INSIDE OF YOU--?
CHGGA
MORE--THAN YOU--CAN HANDLE--WHELP--!
CHGGA
NO!
CHGGA
CHGGA
AGHFNYHAYENYYK
YIPE--!

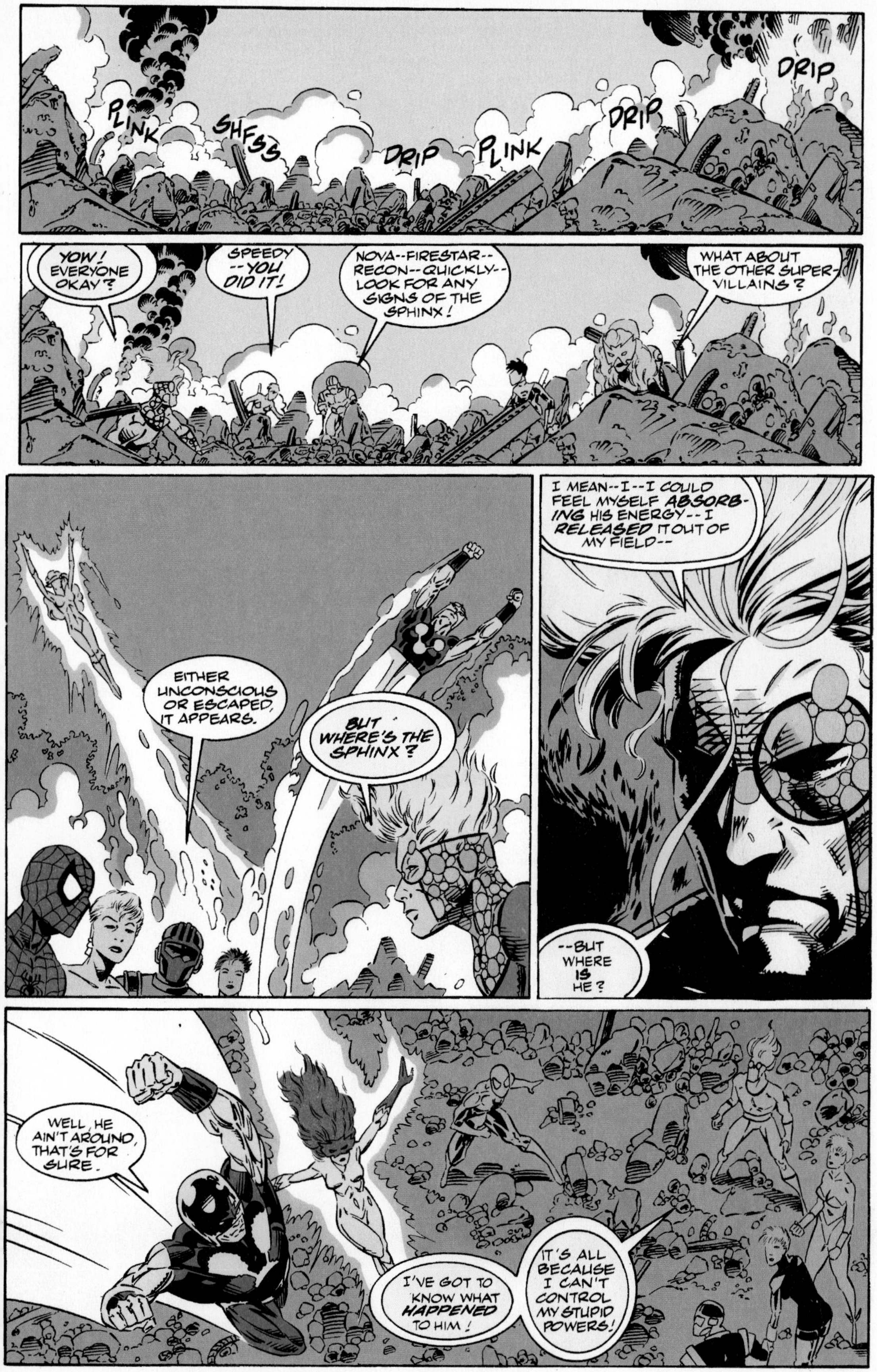
PLINK
SHFSS
DRIP
PLINK
DRIP
DRIP
YOW! EVERYONE OKAY?
SPEEDY --YOU DID IT!
NOVA--FIRESTAR-- RECON--QUICKLY-- LOOK FOR ANY SIGNS OF THE SPHINX!
WHAT ABOUT THE OTHER SUPER-VILLAINS?
EITHER UNCONSCIOUS OR ESCAPED, IT APPEARS.
BUT WHERE'S THE SPHINX?
I MEAN--I--I COULD FEEL MYSELF ABSORB-ING HIS ENERGY--I RELEASED IT OUT OF MY FIELD--
--BUT WHERE IS HE?
WELL, HE AIN'T AROUND, THAT'S FOR SURE.
I'VE GOT TO KNOW WHAT HAPPENED TO HIM!
IT'S ALL BECAUSE I CAN'T CONTROL MY STUPID POWERS!

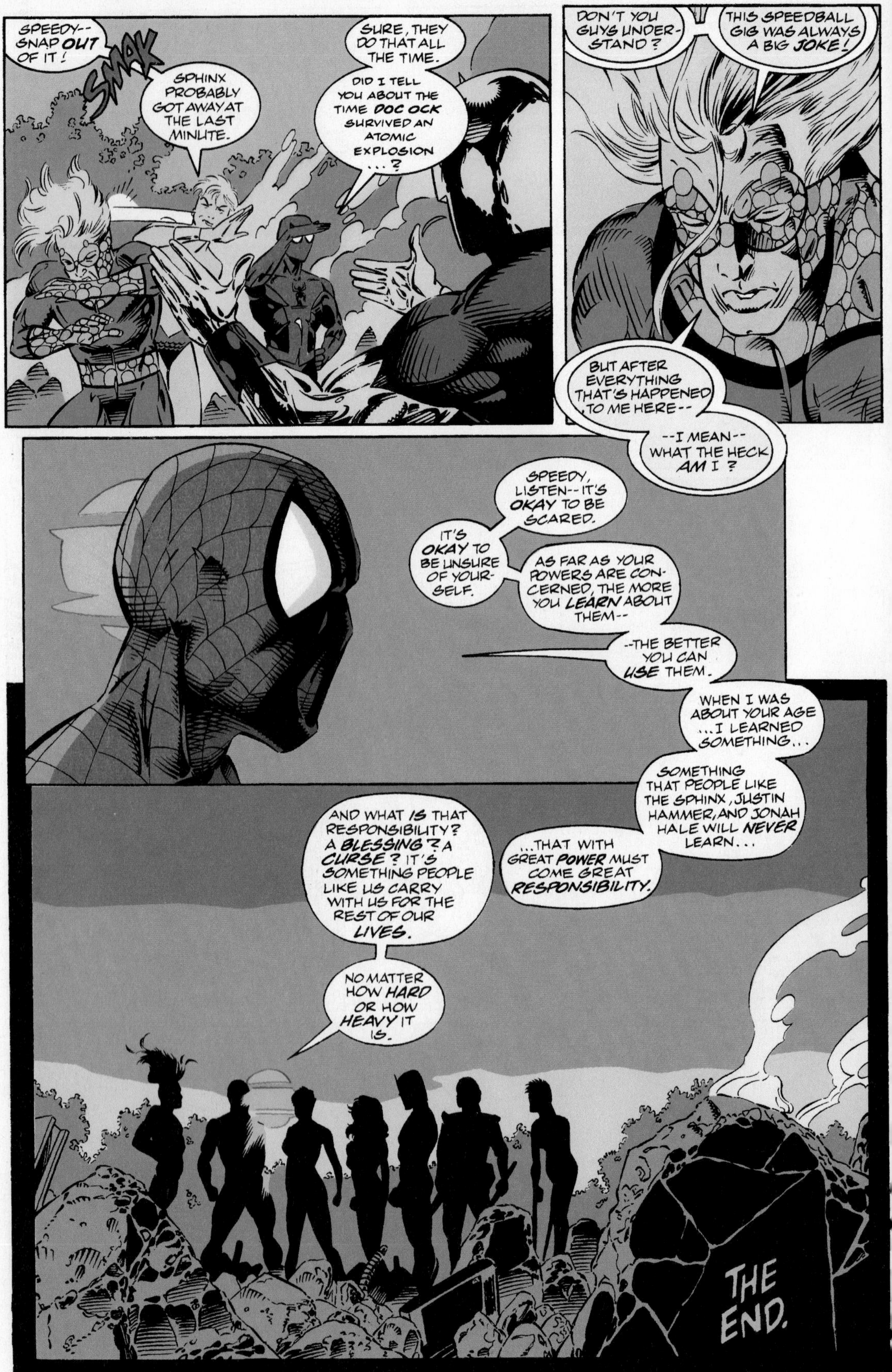
SPEEDY-- SNAP OUT OF IT!
SMAK
SPHINX PROBABLY GOT AWAY AT THE LAST MINUTE.
SURE, THEY DO THAT ALL THE TIME.
DID I TELL YOU ABOUT THE TIME DOC OCK SURVIVED AN ATOMIC EXPLOSION ...?
DON'T YOU GUYS UNDERSTAND?
THIS SPEEDBALL GIG WAS ALWAYS A BIG JOKE!
BUT AFTER EVERYTHING THAT'S HAPPENED TO ME HERE--
--I MEAN-- WHAT THE HECK AM I?
SPEEDY, LISTEN-- IT'S OKAY TO BE SCARED.
IT'S OKAY TO BE UNSURE OF YOURSELF.
AS FAR AS YOUR POWERS ARE CONCERNED, THE MORE YOU LEARN ABOUT THEM--
--THE BETTER YOU CAN USE THEM.
WHEN I WAS ABOUT YOUR AGE ...I LEARNED SOMETHING...
SOMETHING THAT PEOPLE LIKE THE SPHINX, JUSTIN HAMMER, AND JONAH HALE WILL NEVER LEARN...
...THAT WITH GREAT POWER MUST COME GREAT RESPONSIBILITY.
AND WHAT IS THAT RESPONSIBILITY? A BLESSING? A CURSE? IT'S SOMETHING PEOPLE LIKE US CARRY WITH US FOR THE REST OF OUR LIVES.
NO MATTER HOW HARD OR HOW HEAVY IT IS.
THE END.

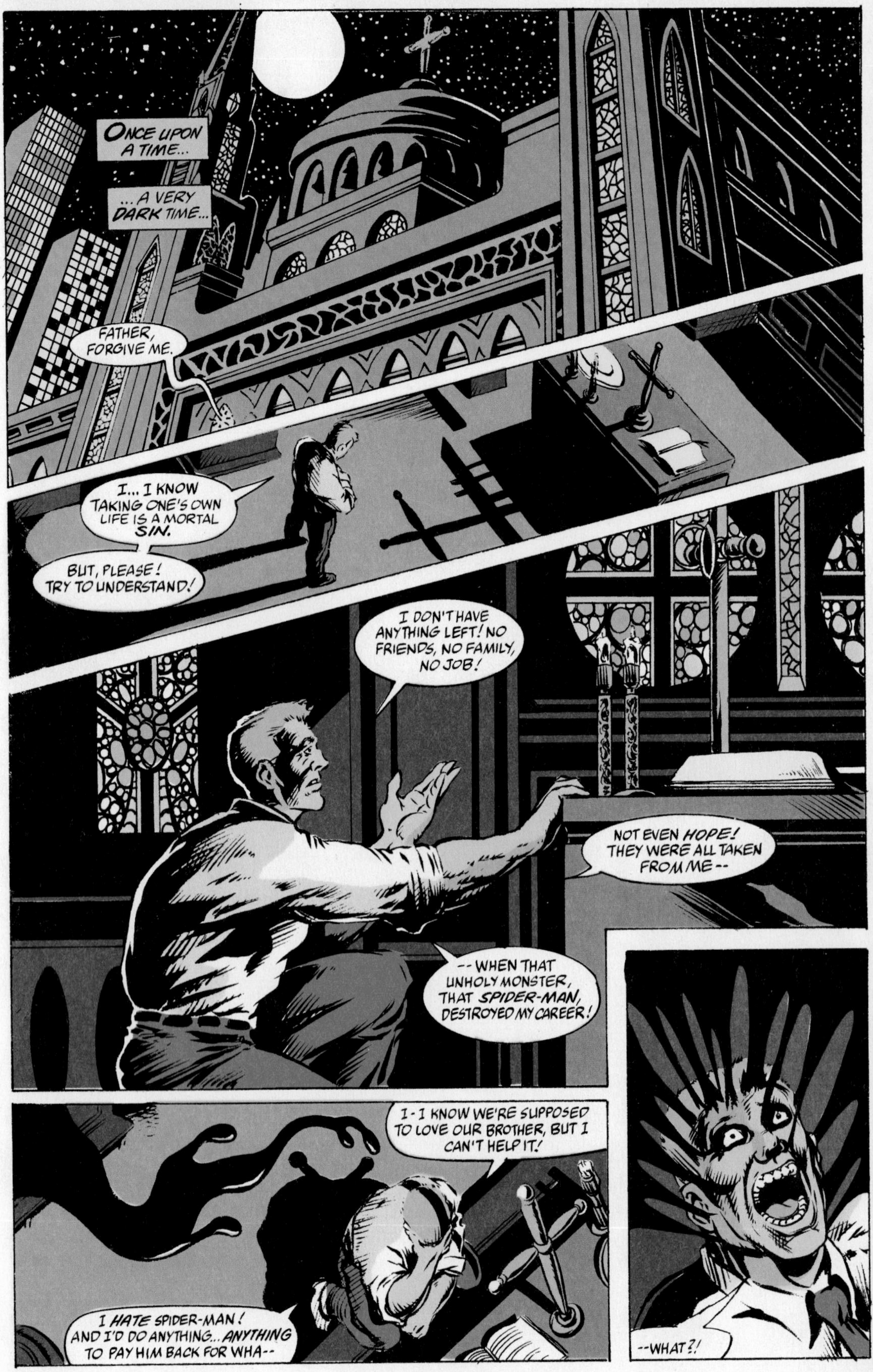

ONCE UPON A TIME...
...A VERY DARK TIME...
FATHER, FORGIVE ME.
I... I KNOW TAKING ONE'S OWN LIFE IS A MORTAL SIN.
BUT, PLEASE! TRY TO UNDERSTAND!
I DON'T HAVE ANYTHING LEFT! NO FRIENDS, NO FAMILY, NO JOB!
NOT EVEN HOPE! THEY WERE ALL TAKEN FROM ME--
--WHEN THAT UNHOLY MONSTER, THAT SPIDER-MAN, DESTROYED MY CAREER!
I-I KNOW WE'RE SUPPOSED TO LOVE OUR BROTHER, BUT I CAN'T HELP IT!
I HATE SPIDER-MAN! AND I'D DO ANYTHING... ANYTHING TO PAY HIM BACK FOR WHA--
--WHAT?!

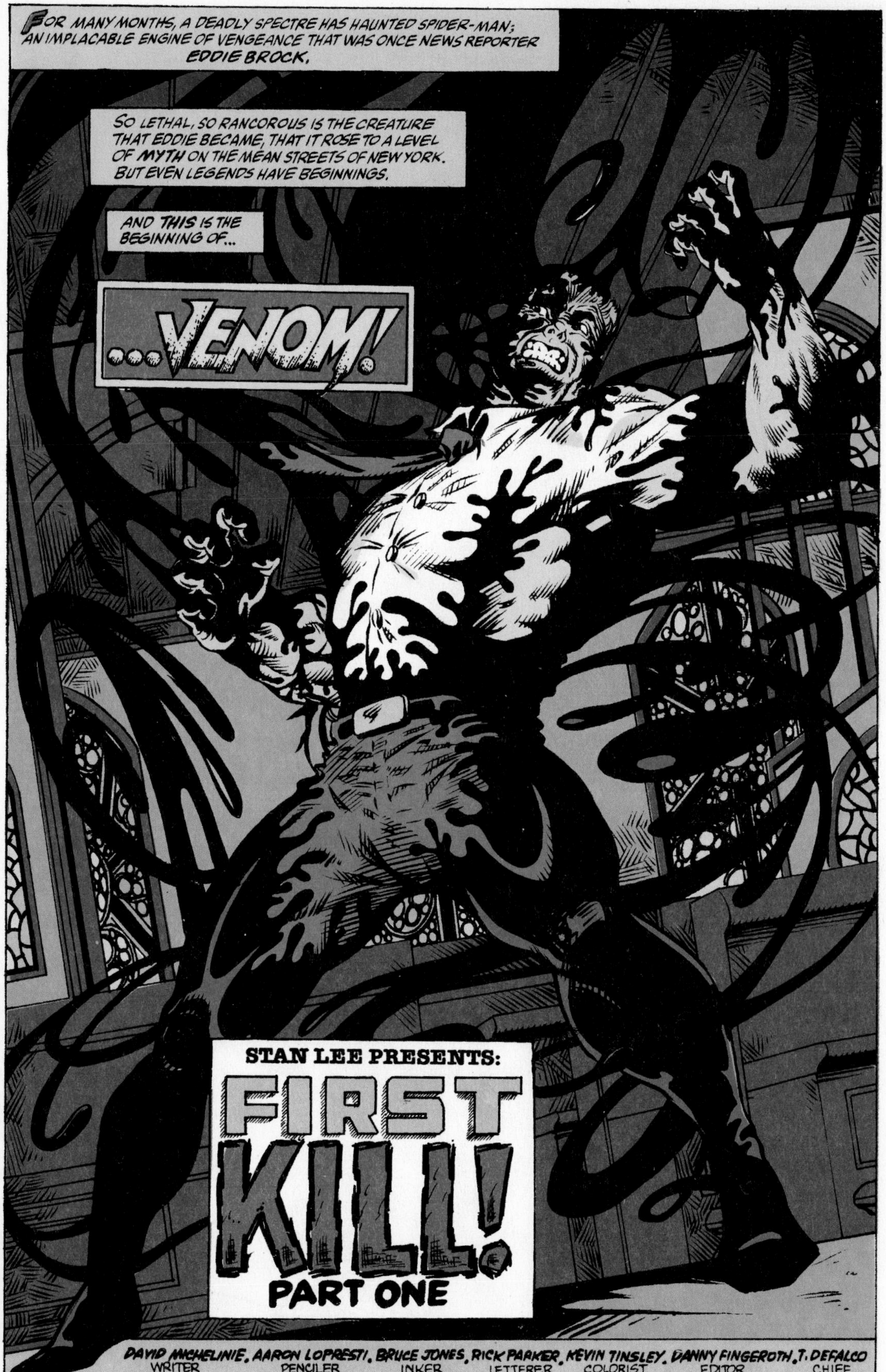

FOR MANY MONTHS, A DEADLY SPECTRE HAS HAUNTED SPIDER-MAN; AN IMPLACABLE ENGINE OF VENGEANCE THAT WAS ONCE NEWS REPORTER EDDIE BROCK.
SO LETHAL, SO RANCOROUS IS THE CREATURE THAT EDDIE BECAME, THAT IT ROSE TO A LEVEL OF MYTH ON THE MEAN STREETS OF NEW YORK. BUT EVEN LEGENDS HAVE BEGINNINGS.
AND THIS IS THE BEGINNING OF...
...VENOM!
STAN LEE PRESENTS:
FIRST KILL!
PART ONE
DAVID MICHELINIE, WRITER. AARON LOPRESTI, PENCILER. BRUCE JONES, INKER. RICK PARKER, LETTERER. KEVIN TINSLEY, COLORIST. DANNY FINGEROTH, EDITOR. T. DEFALCO, CHIEF

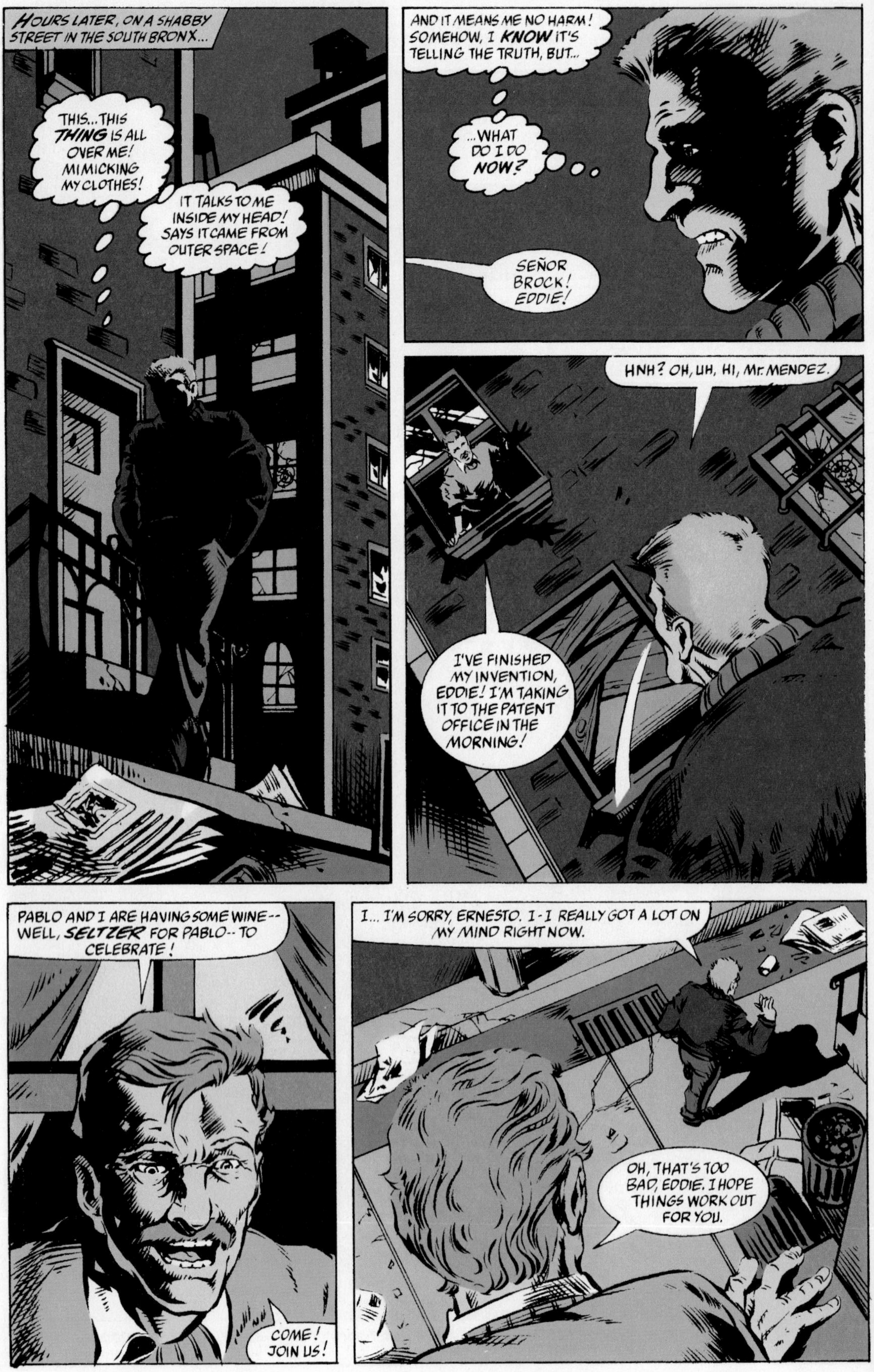
HOURS LATER, ON A SHABBY STREET IN THE SOUTH BRONX...
THIS...THIS THING IS ALL OVER ME! MIMICKING MY CLOTHES!
IT TALKS TO ME INSIDE MY HEAD! SAYS IT CAME FROM OUTER SPACE!
AND IT MEANS ME NO HARM! SOMEHOW, I KNOW IT'S TELLING THE TRUTH, BUT...
...WHAT DO I DO NOW?
SEÑOR BROCK! EDDIE!
HNH? OH, UH, HI, Mr. MENDEZ.
I'VE FINISHED MY INVENTION, EDDIE! I'M TAKING IT TO THE PATENT OFFICE IN THE MORNING!
PABLO AND I ARE HAVING SOME WINE-- WELL, SELTZER FOR PABLO-- TO CELEBRATE!
COME! JOIN US!
I... I'M SORRY, ERNESTO. I-I REALLY GOT A LOT ON MY MIND RIGHT NOW.
OH, THAT'S TOO BAD, EDDIE. I HOPE THINGS WORK OUT FOR YOU.

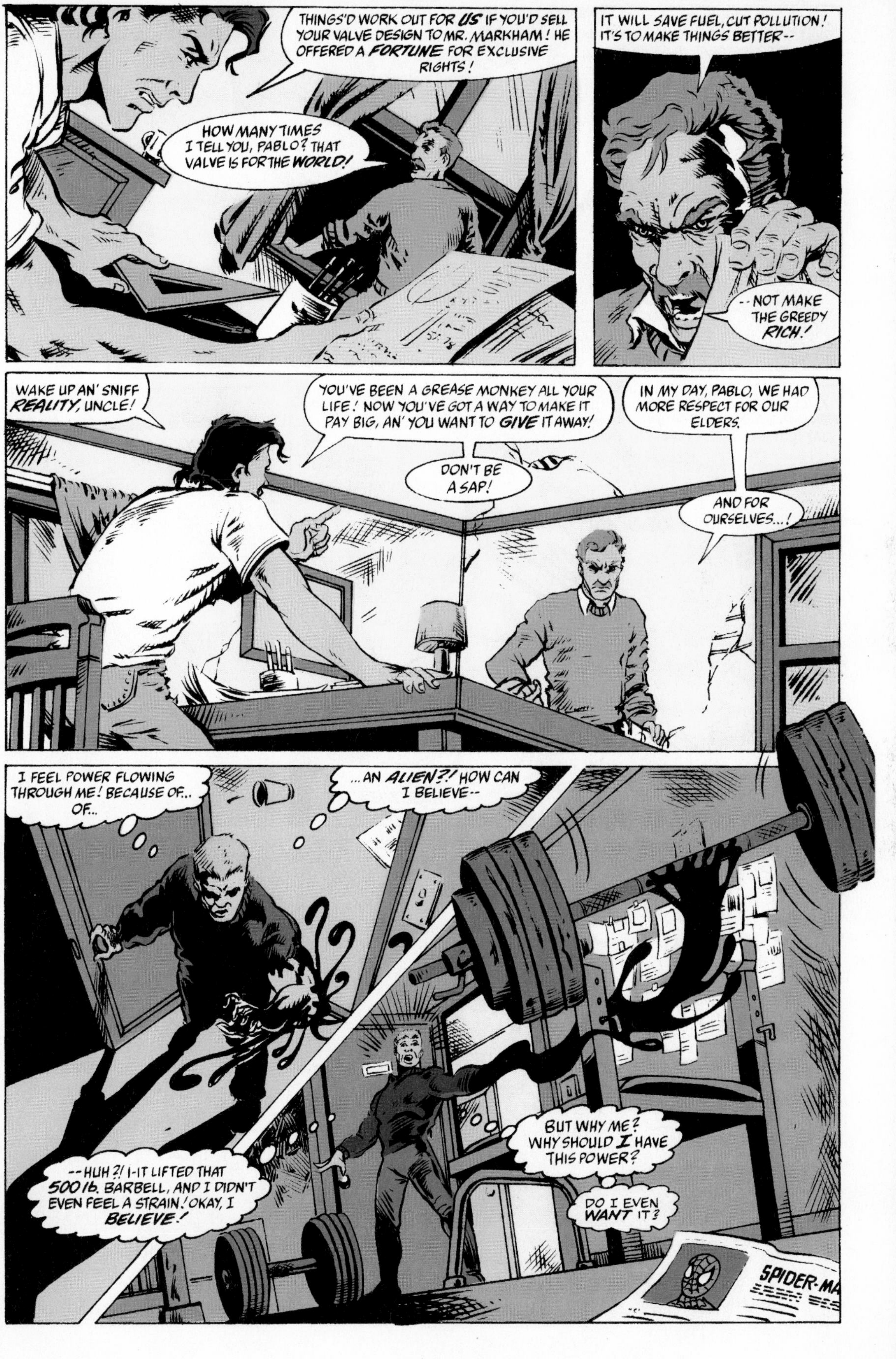
THINGS'D WORK OUT FOR US IF YOU'D SELL YOUR VALVE DESIGN TO MR. MARKHAM! HE OFFERED A FORTUNE FOR EXCLUSIVE RIGHTS!
HOW MANY TIMES I TELL YOU, PABLO? THAT VALVE IS FOR THE WORLD!
IT WILL SAVE FUEL, CUT POLLUTION! IT'S TO MAKE THINGS BETTER--
--NOT MAKE THE GREEDY RICH!
WAKE UP AN' SNIFF REALITY, UNCLE!
YOU'VE BEEN A GREASE MONKEY ALL YOUR LIFE! NOW YOU'VE GOT A WAY TO MAKE IT PAY BIG, AN' YOU WANT TO GIVE IT AWAY!
DON'T BE A SAP!
IN MY DAY, PABLO, WE HAD MORE RESPECT FOR OUR ELDERS.
AND FOR OURSELVES...!
I FEEL POWER FLOWING THROUGH ME! BECAUSE OF... OF...
...AN ALIEN?! HOW CAN I BELIEVE--
--HUH?! I-IT LIFTED THAT 500 lb. BARBELL, AND I DIDN'T EVEN FEEL A STRAIN! OKAY, I BELIEVE!
BUT WHY ME? WHY SHOULD I HAVE THIS POWER?
DO I EVEN WANT IT?
SPIDER-MA

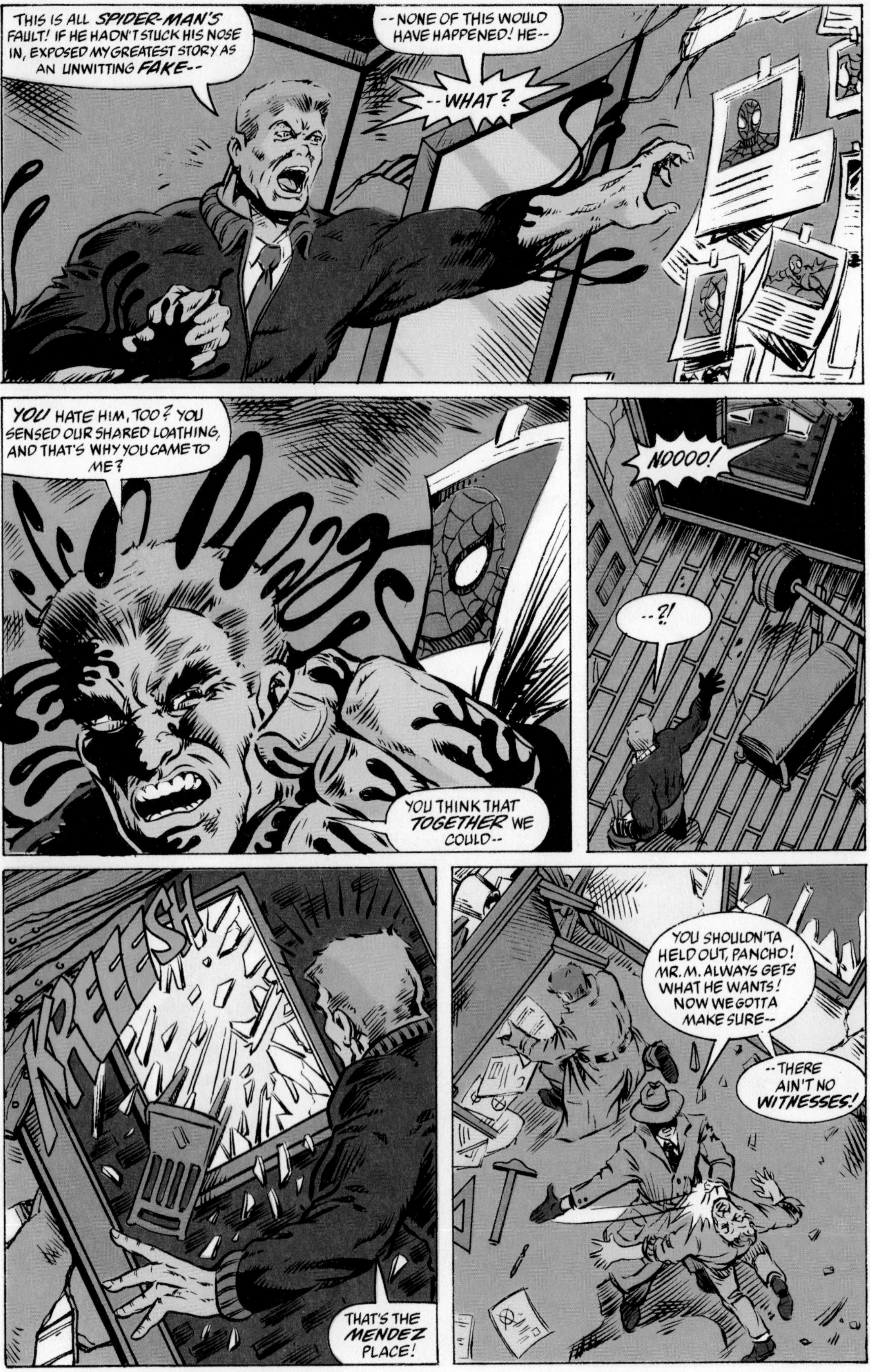

THIS IS ALL SPIDER-MAN'S FAULT! IF HE HADN'T STUCK HIS NOSE IN, EXPOSED MY GREATEST STORY AS AN UNWITTING FAKE--
--NONE OF THIS WOULD HAVE HAPPENED! HE--
--WHAT?
YOU HATE HIM, TOO? YOU SENSED OUR SHARED LOATHING, AND THAT'S WHY YOU CAME TO ME?
YOU THINK THAT TOGETHER WE COULD--
NOOOO!
--?!
KREEESH
THAT'S THE MENDEZ PLACE!
YOU SHOULDN'TA HELD OUT, PANCHO! MR. M. ALWAYS GETS WHAT HE WANTS! NOW WE GOTTA MAKE SURE--
--THERE AIN'T NO WITNESSES!

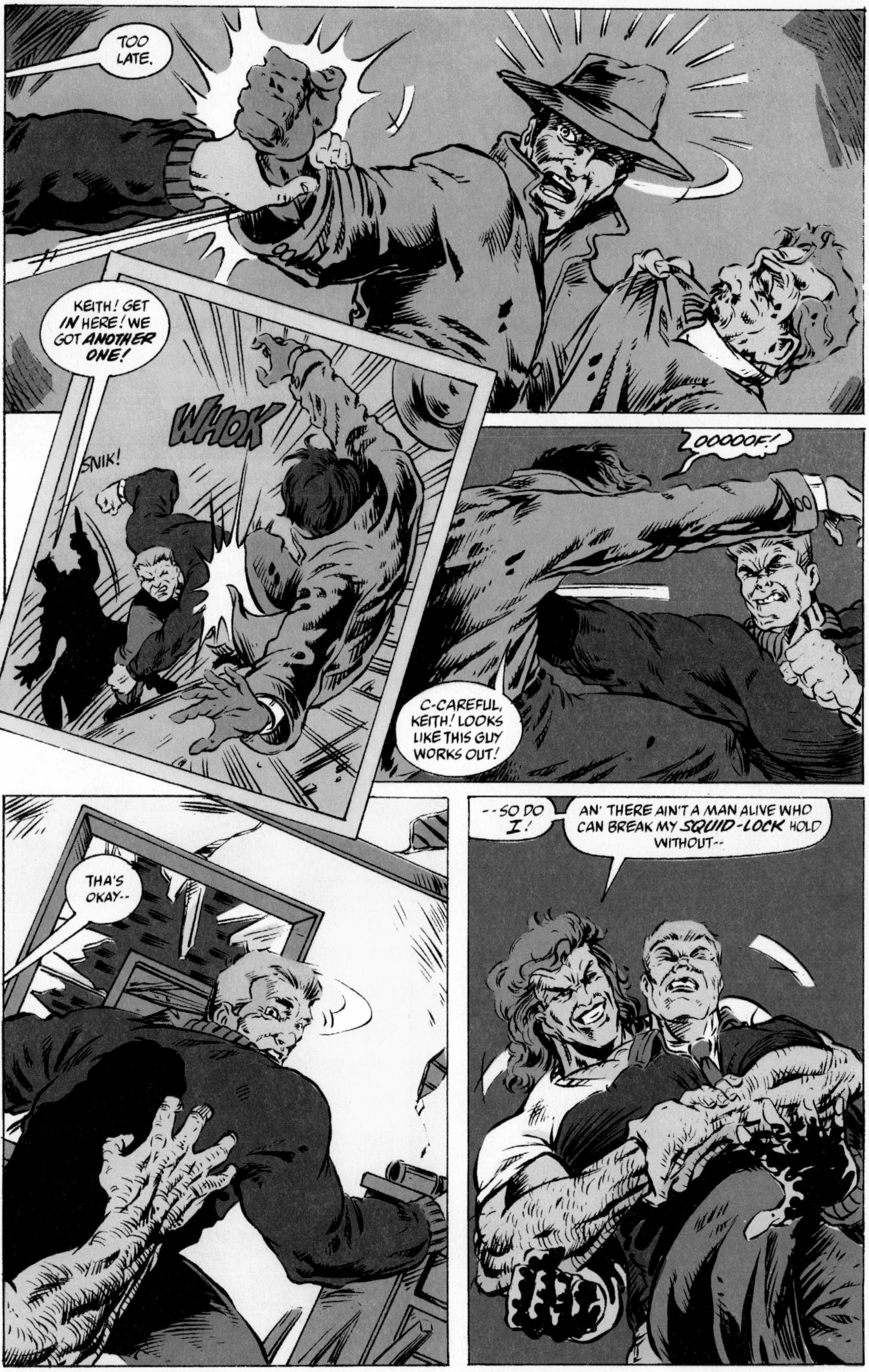
TOO LATE.
KEITH! GET IN HERE! WE GOT ANOTHER ONE!
WHOK
SNIK!
OOOOOF!
C-CAREFUL, KEITH! LOOKS LIKE THIS GUY WORKS OUT!
THA'S OKAY--
--SO DO I!
AN' THERE AIN'T A MAN ALIVE WHO CAN BREAK MY SQUID-LOCK HOLD WITHOUT--

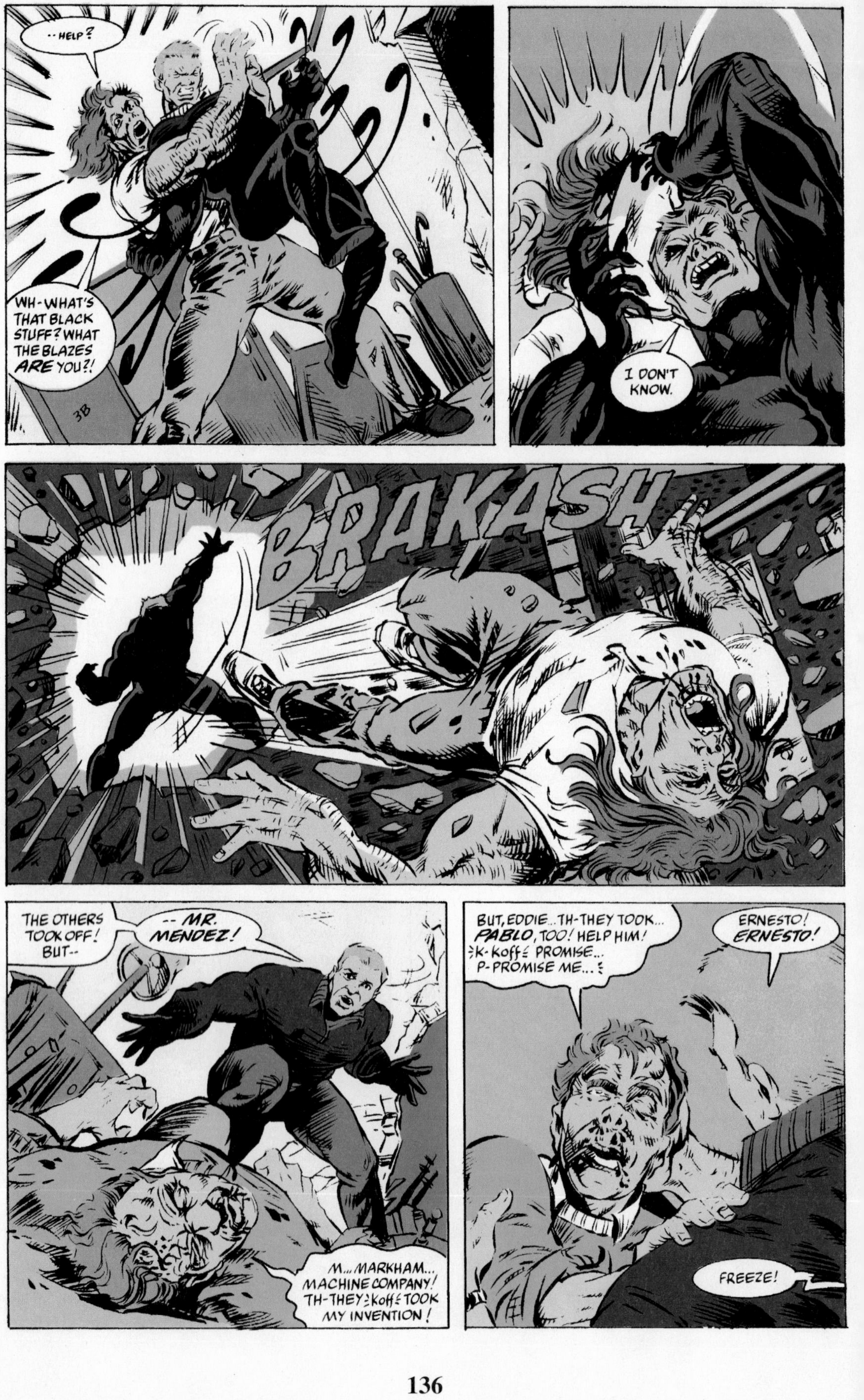
-- HELP?
WH-WHAT'S THAT BLACK STUFF? WHAT THE BLAZES *ARE* YOU?!
I DON'T KNOW.
BRAKASH
THE OTHERS TOOK OFF! BUT--
-- *MR. MENDEZ!*
M... MARKHAM... MACHINE COMPANY! TH-THEY ~koff~ TOOK MY INVENTION!
BUT, EDDIE... TH-THEY TOOK... *PABLO*, TOO! HELP HIM! ~K-KOFF~ PROMISE... P-PROMISE ME... ~
ERNESTO! *ERNESTO!*
FREEZE!

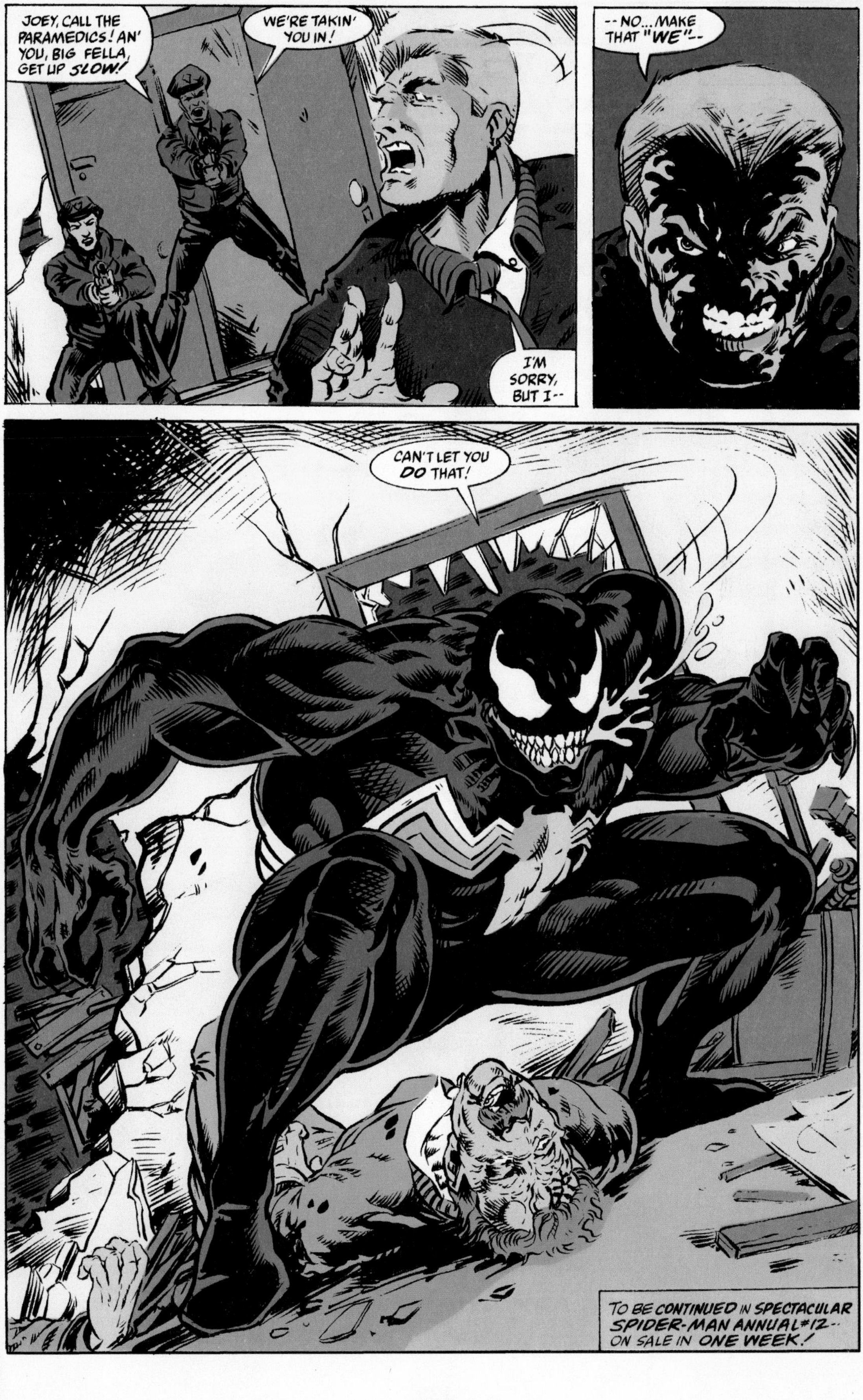
JOEY, CALL THE PARAMEDICS! AN' YOU, BIG FELLA, GET UP SLOW!
WE'RE TAKIN' YOU IN!
I'M SORRY, BUT I--
--NO...MAKE THAT "WE"--
CAN'T LET YOU DO THAT!
TO BE CONTINUED IN SPECTACULAR SPIDER-MAN ANNUAL #12--ON SALE IN ONE WEEK!

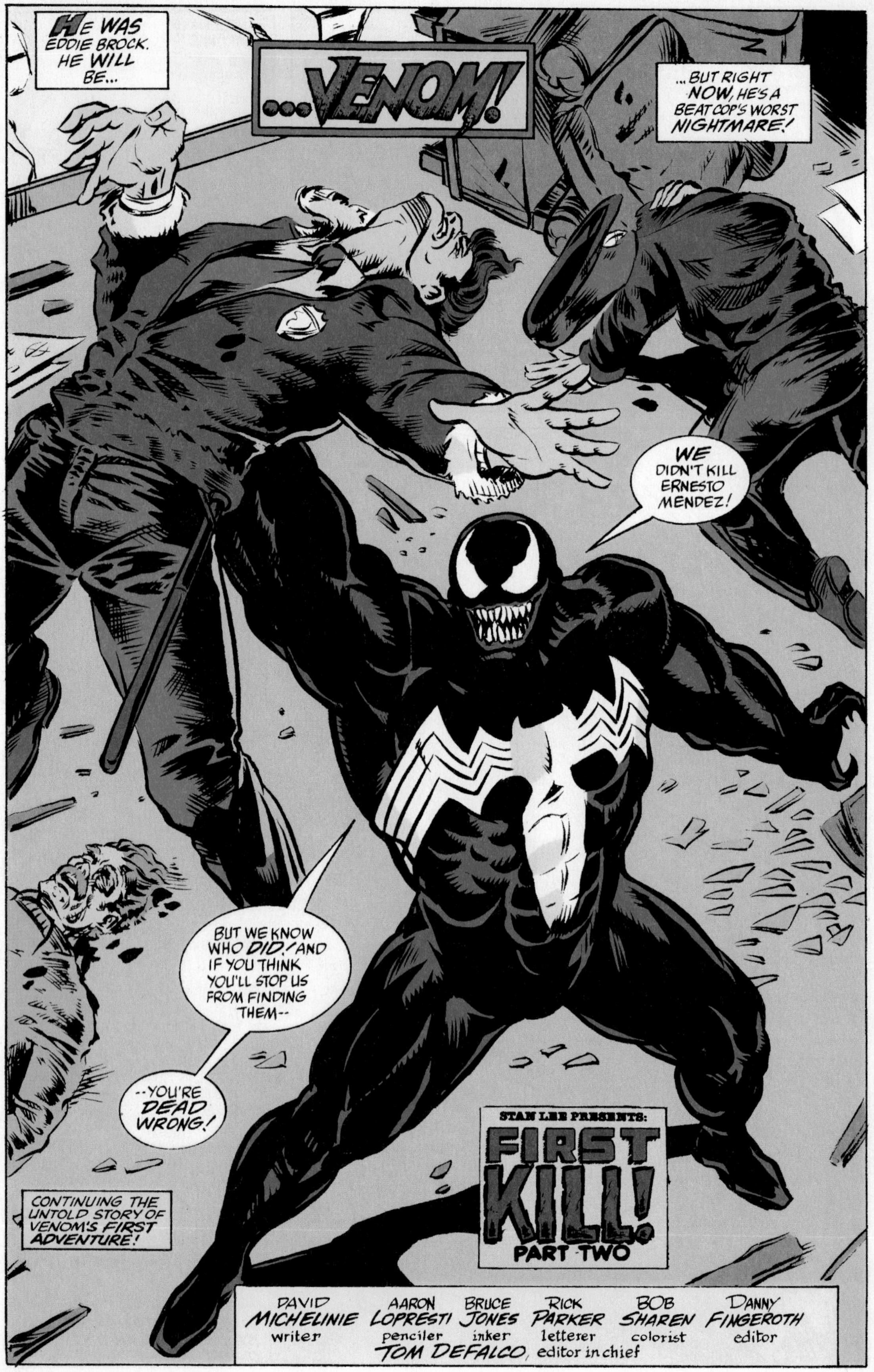
HE WAS EDDIE BROCK. HE WILL BE...
...VENOM!
...BUT RIGHT NOW, HE'S A BEAT COP'S WORST NIGHTMARE!
WE DIDN'T KILL ERNESTO MENDEZ!
BUT WE KNOW WHO DID! AND IF YOU THINK YOU'LL STOP US FROM FINDING THEM--
--YOU'RE DEAD WRONG!
CONTINUING THE UNTOLD STORY OF VENOM'S FIRST ADVENTURE!
STAN LEE PRESENTS:
FIRST KILL!
PART TWO
DAVID MICHELINIE writer
AARON LOPRESTI penciler
BRUCE JONES inker
RICK PARKER letterer
BOB SHAREN colorist
DANNY FINGEROTH editor
TOM DEFALCO, editor in chief

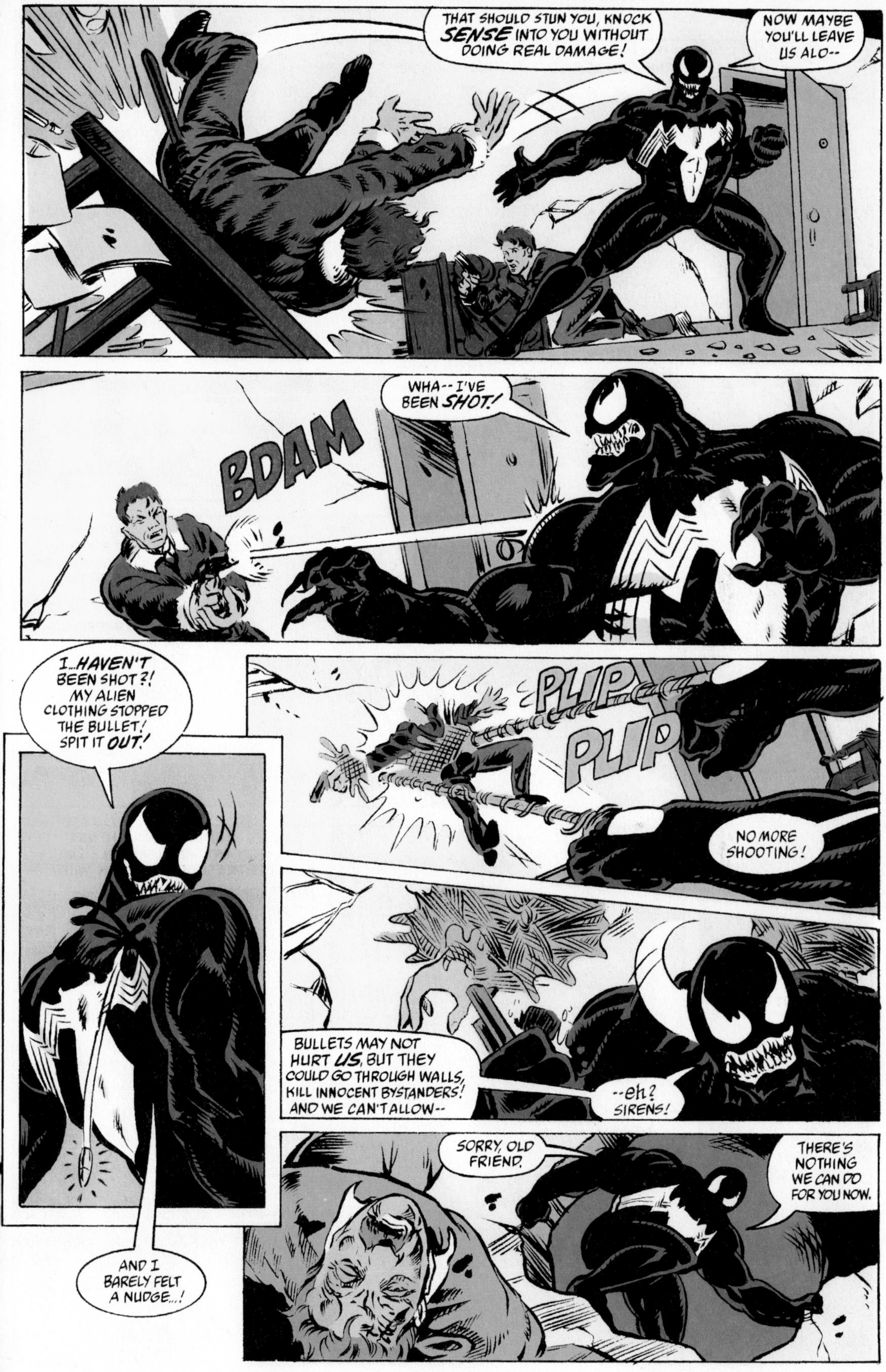
THAT SHOULD STUN YOU, KNOCK SENSE INTO YOU WITHOUT DOING REAL DAMAGE!
NOW MAYBE YOU'LL LEAVE US ALO--
WHA-- I'VE BEEN SHOT!
BDAM
I...HAVEN'T BEEN SHOT?! MY ALIEN CLOTHING STOPPED THE BULLET! SPIT IT OUT!
AND I BARELY FELT A NUDGE...!
PLIP
PLIP
NO MORE SHOOTING!
BULLETS MAY NOT HURT US, BUT THEY COULD GO THROUGH WALLS, KILL INNOCENT BYSTANDERS! AND WE CAN'T ALLOW--
--eh? SIRENS!
SORRY, OLD FRIEND.
THERE'S NOTHING WE CAN DO FOR YOU NOW.

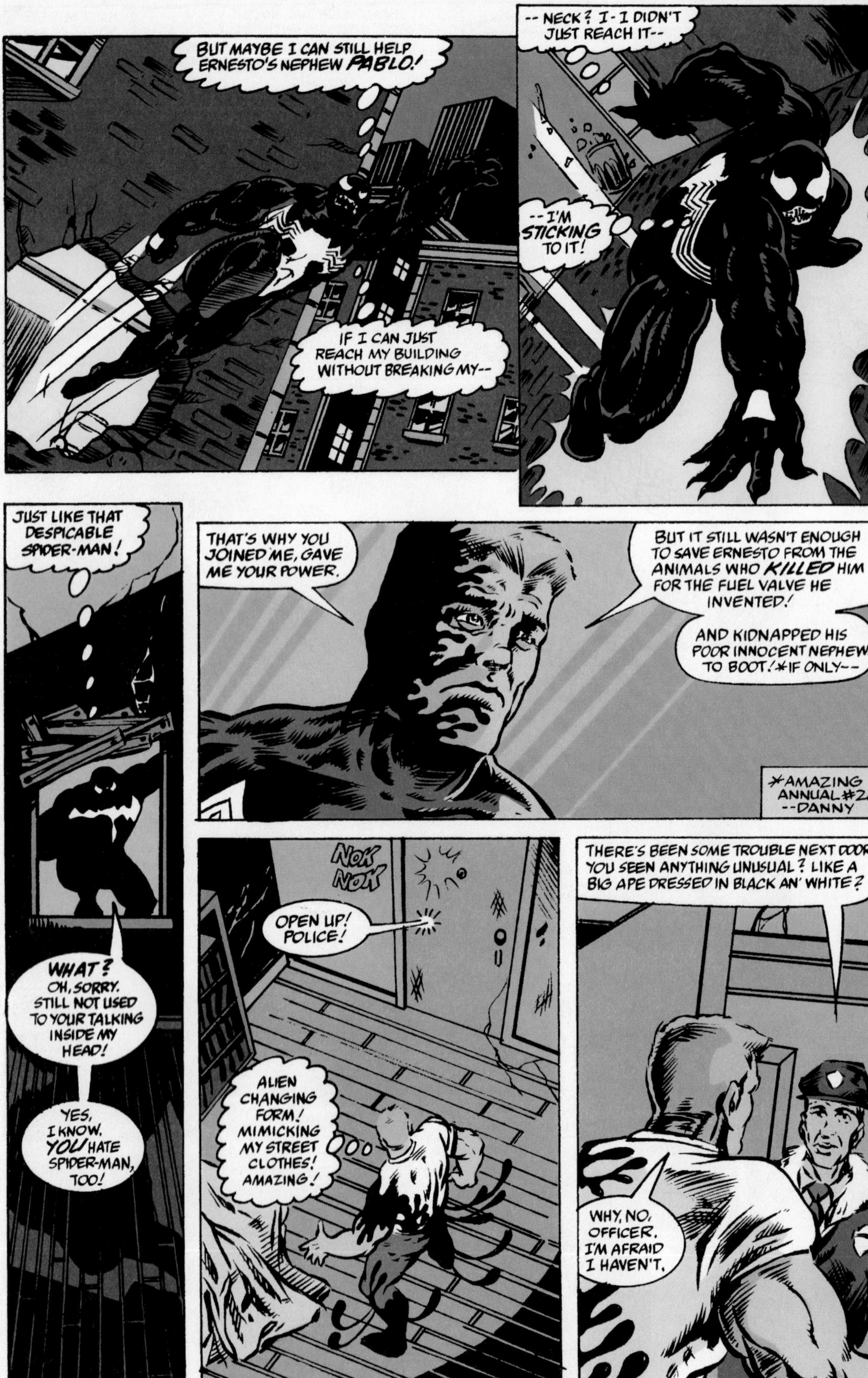
BUT MAYBE I CAN STILL HELP ERNESTO'S NEPHEW PABLO!
IF I CAN JUST REACH MY BUILDING WITHOUT BREAKING MY--
-- NECK? I-I DIDN'T JUST REACH IT--
--I'M STICKING TO IT!
JUST LIKE THAT DESPICABLE SPIDER-MAN!
THAT'S WHY YOU JOINED ME, GAVE ME YOUR POWER.
BUT IT STILL WASN'T ENOUGH TO SAVE ERNESTO FROM THE ANIMALS WHO KILLED HIM FOR THE FUEL VALVE HE INVENTED!
AND KIDNAPPED HIS POOR INNOCENT NEPHEW. TO BOOT! *IF ONLY--
*AMAZING ANNUAL #26. --DANNY
WHAT? OH, SORRY. STILL NOT USED TO YOUR TALKING INSIDE MY HEAD!
YES, I KNOW. YOU HATE SPIDER-MAN, TOO!
NOK NOK
OPEN UP! POLICE!
ALIEN CHANGING FORM! MIMICKING MY STREET CLOTHES! AMAZING!
THERE'S BEEN SOME TROUBLE NEXT DOOR. YOU SEEN ANYTHING UNUSUAL? LIKE A BIG APE DRESSED IN BLACK AN' WHITE?
WHY, NO, OFFICER. I'M AFRAID I HAVEN'T.

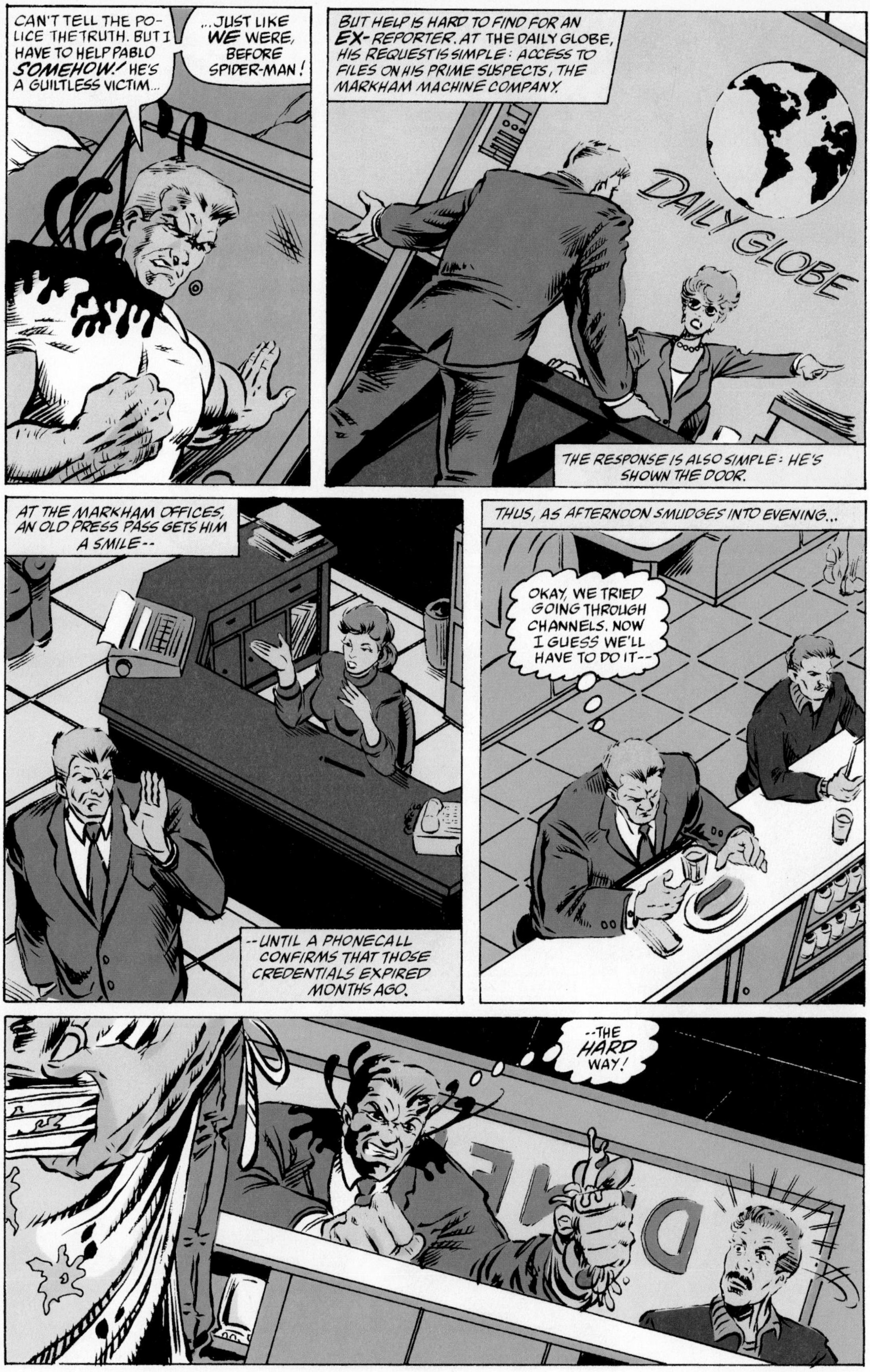
CAN'T TELL THE POLICE THE TRUTH. BUT I HAVE TO HELP PABLO SOMEHOW! HE'S A GUILTLESS VICTIM...
...JUST LIKE WE WERE, BEFORE SPIDER-MAN!
BUT HELP IS HARD TO FIND FOR AN EX-REPORTER. AT THE DAILY GLOBE, HIS REQUEST IS SIMPLE: ACCESS TO FILES ON HIS PRIME SUSPECTS, THE MARKHAM MACHINE COMPANY.
DAILY GLOBE
THE RESPONSE IS ALSO SIMPLE: HE'S SHOWN THE DOOR.
AT THE MARKHAM OFFICES, AN OLD PRESS PASS GETS HIM A SMILE--
--UNTIL A PHONECALL CONFIRMS THAT THOSE CREDENTIALS EXPIRED MONTHS AGO.
THUS, AS AFTERNOON SMUDGES INTO EVENING...
OKAY, WE TRIED GOING THROUGH CHANNELS. NOW I GUESS WE'LL HAVE TO DO IT--
--THE HARD WAY!

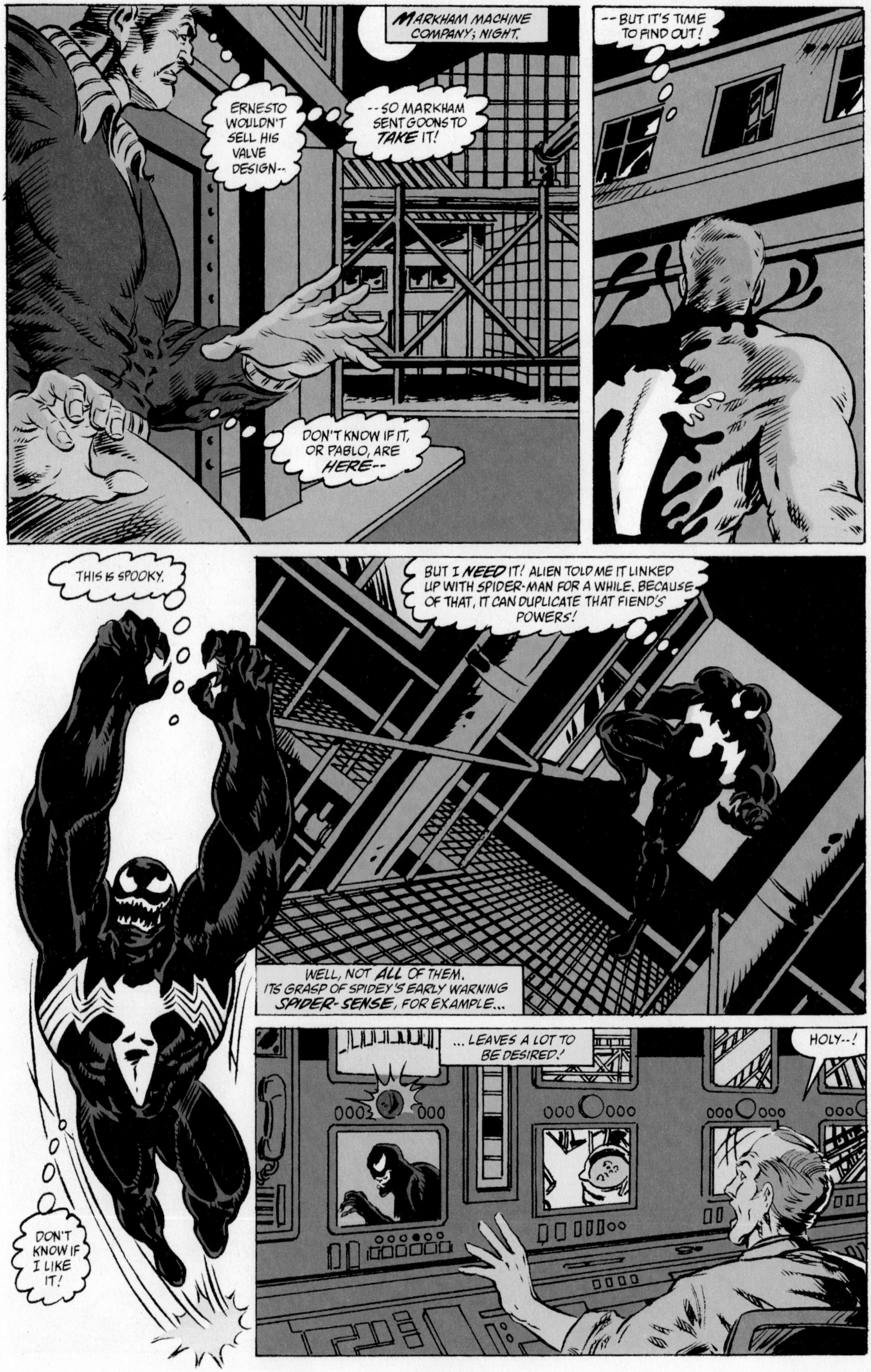
MARKHAM MACHINE COMPANY; NIGHT.
ERNESTO WOULDN'T SELL HIS VALVE DESIGN--
--SO MARKHAM SENT GOONS TO TAKE IT!
DON'T KNOW IF IT, OR PABLO, ARE HERE--
--BUT IT'S TIME TO FIND OUT!
THIS IS SPOOKY.
BUT I NEED IT! ALIEN TOLD ME IT LINKED UP WITH SPIDER-MAN FOR A WHILE. BECAUSE OF THAT, IT CAN DUPLICATE THAT FIEND'S POWERS!
WELL, NOT ALL OF THEM. ITS GRASP OF SPIDEY'S EARLY WARNING SPIDER-SENSE, FOR EXAMPLE...
DON'T KNOW IF I LIKE IT!
... LEAVES A LOT TO BE DESIRED!
HOLY--!

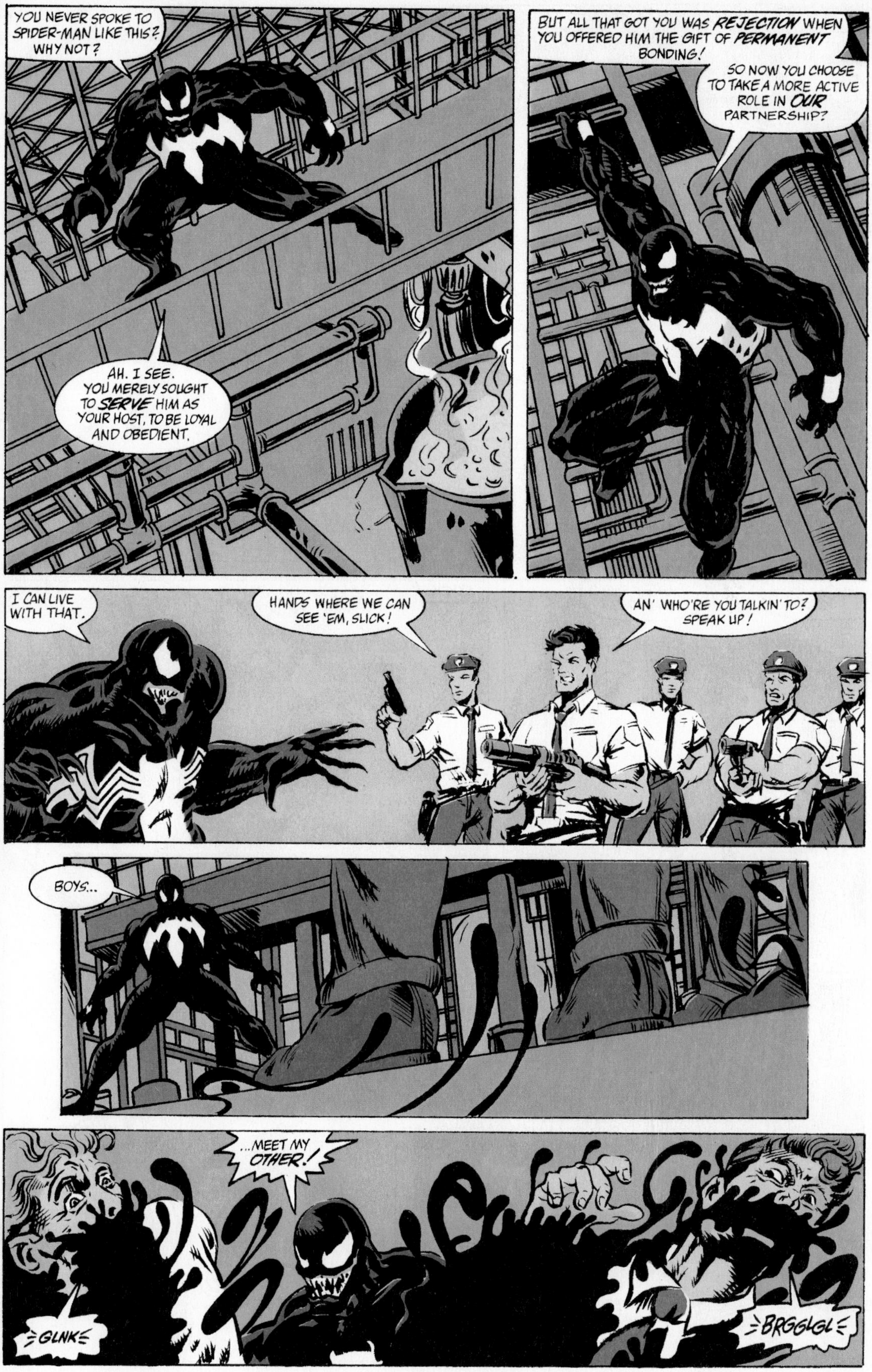
YOU NEVER SPOKE TO SPIDER-MAN LIKE THIS? WHY NOT?
AH. I SEE. YOU MERELY SOUGHT TO SERVE HIM AS YOUR HOST, TO BE LOYAL AND OBEDIENT.
BUT ALL THAT GOT YOU WAS REJECTION WHEN YOU OFFERED HIM THE GIFT OF PERMANENT BONDING!
SO NOW YOU CHOOSE TO TAKE A MORE ACTIVE ROLE IN OUR PARTNERSHIP?
I CAN LIVE WITH THAT.
HANDS WHERE WE CAN SEE 'EM, SLICK!
AN' WHO'RE YOU TALKIN' TO? SPEAK UP!
BOYS...
...MEET MY OTHER!
GLNK
BRGGLGL

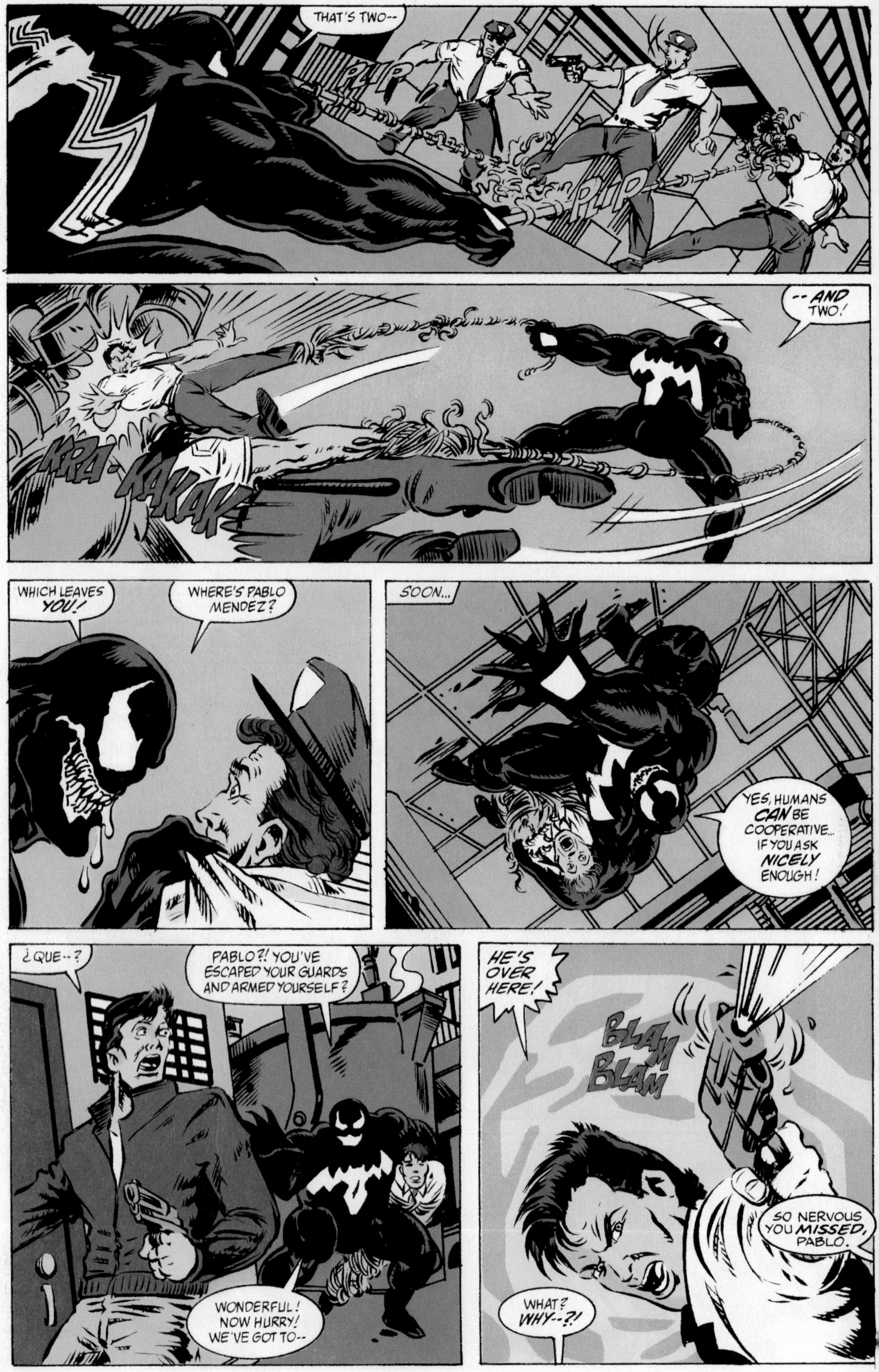
THAT'S TWO--
PLIP
PLIP
--AND TWO!
KRA-KAKAK
WHICH LEAVES YOU!
WHERE'S PABLO MENDEZ?
SOON...
YES, HUMANS CAN BE COOPERATIVE... IF YOU ASK NICELY ENOUGH!
¿QUE--?
PABLO?! YOU'VE ESCAPED YOUR GUARDS AND ARMED YOURSELF?
WONDERFUL! NOW HURRY! WE'VE GOT TO--
HE'S OVER HERE!
BLAM BLAM
SO NERVOUS YOU MISSED, PABLO.
WHAT? WHY--?!

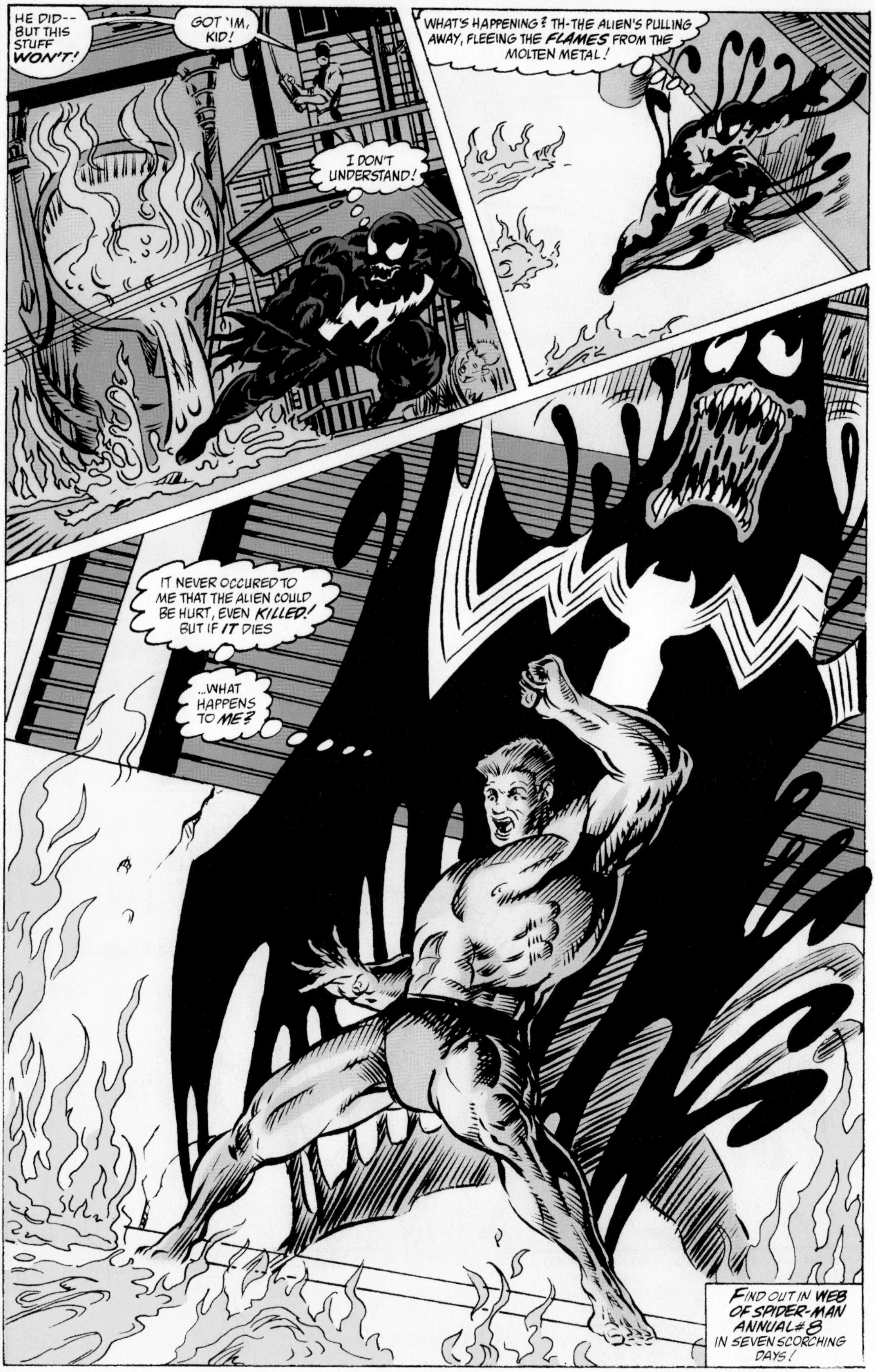
GOT 'IM, KID!
HE DID-- BUT THIS STUFF WON'T!
I DON'T UNDERSTAND!
WHAT'S HAPPENING? TH-THE ALIEN'S PULLING AWAY, FLEEING THE FLAMES FROM THE MOLTEN METAL!
IT NEVER OCCURED TO ME THAT THE ALIEN COULD BE HURT, EVEN KILLED! BUT IF IT DIES
...WHAT HAPPENS TO ME?
FIND OUT IN WEB OF SPIDER-MAN ANNUAL #8 IN SEVEN SCORCHING DAYS!

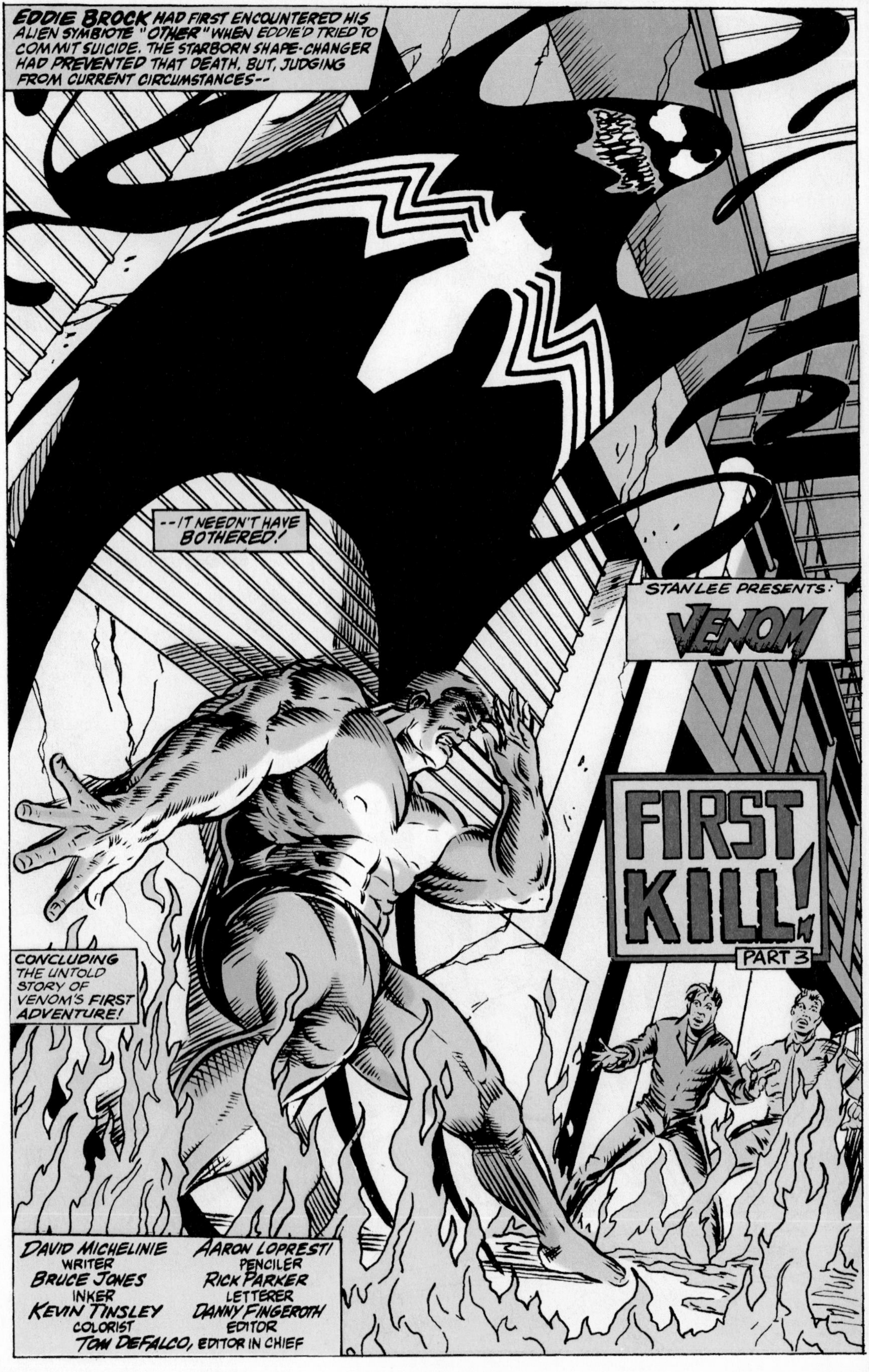

EDDIE BROCK HAD FIRST ENCOUNTERED HIS ALIEN SYMBIOTE "OTHER" WHEN EDDIE'D TRIED TO COMMIT SUICIDE. THE STARBORN SHAPE-CHANGER HAD PREVENTED THAT DEATH. BUT, JUDGING FROM CURRENT CIRCUMSTANCES--
--IT NEEDN'T HAVE BOTHERED!
STAN LEE PRESENTS:
VENOM
FIRST KILL!
PART 3
CONCLUDING THE UNTOLD STORY OF VENOM'S FIRST ADVENTURE!
DAVID MICHELINIE WRITER
AARON LOPRESTI PENCILER
BRUCE JONES INKER
RICK PARKER LETTERER
KEVIN TINSLEY COLORIST
DANNY FINGEROTH EDITOR
TOM DEFALCO, EDITOR IN CHIEF

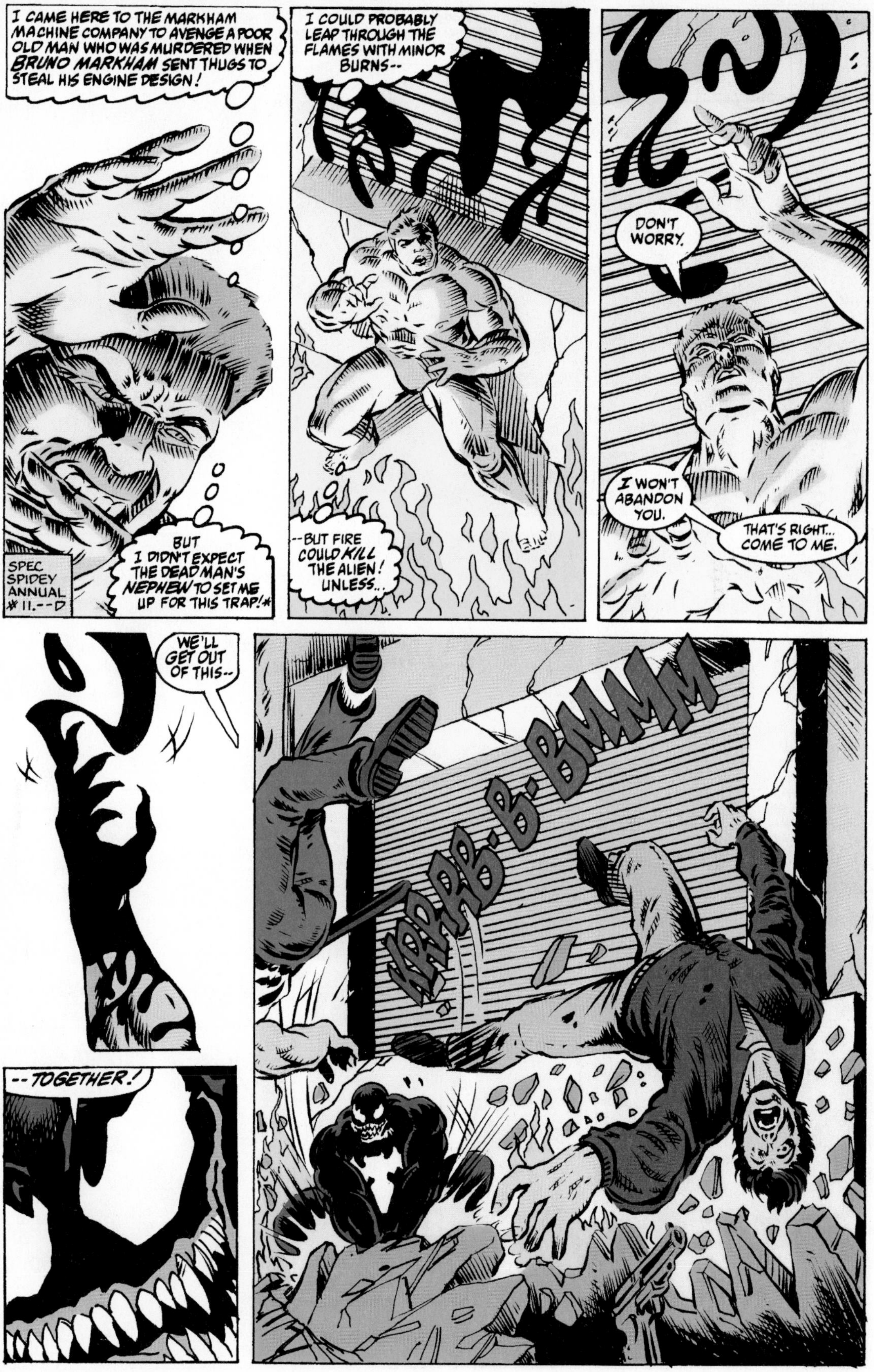

I CAME HERE TO THE MARKHAM MACHINE COMPANY TO AVENGE A POOR OLD MAN WHO WAS MURDERED WHEN BRUNO MARKHAM SENT THUGS TO STEAL HIS ENGINE DESIGN!
BUT I DIDN'T EXPECT THE DEAD MAN'S NEPHEW TO SET ME UP FOR THIS TRAP!*
SPEC SPIDEY ANNUAL #11.--D
I COULD PROBABLY LEAP THROUGH THE FLAMES WITH MINOR BURNS--
--BUT FIRE COULD KILL THE ALIEN! UNLESS..
DON'T WORRY.
I WON'T ABANDON YOU.
THAT'S RIGHT... COME TO ME.
WE'LL GET OUT OF THIS--
--TOGETHER!
KRRRB-B-BMMMM

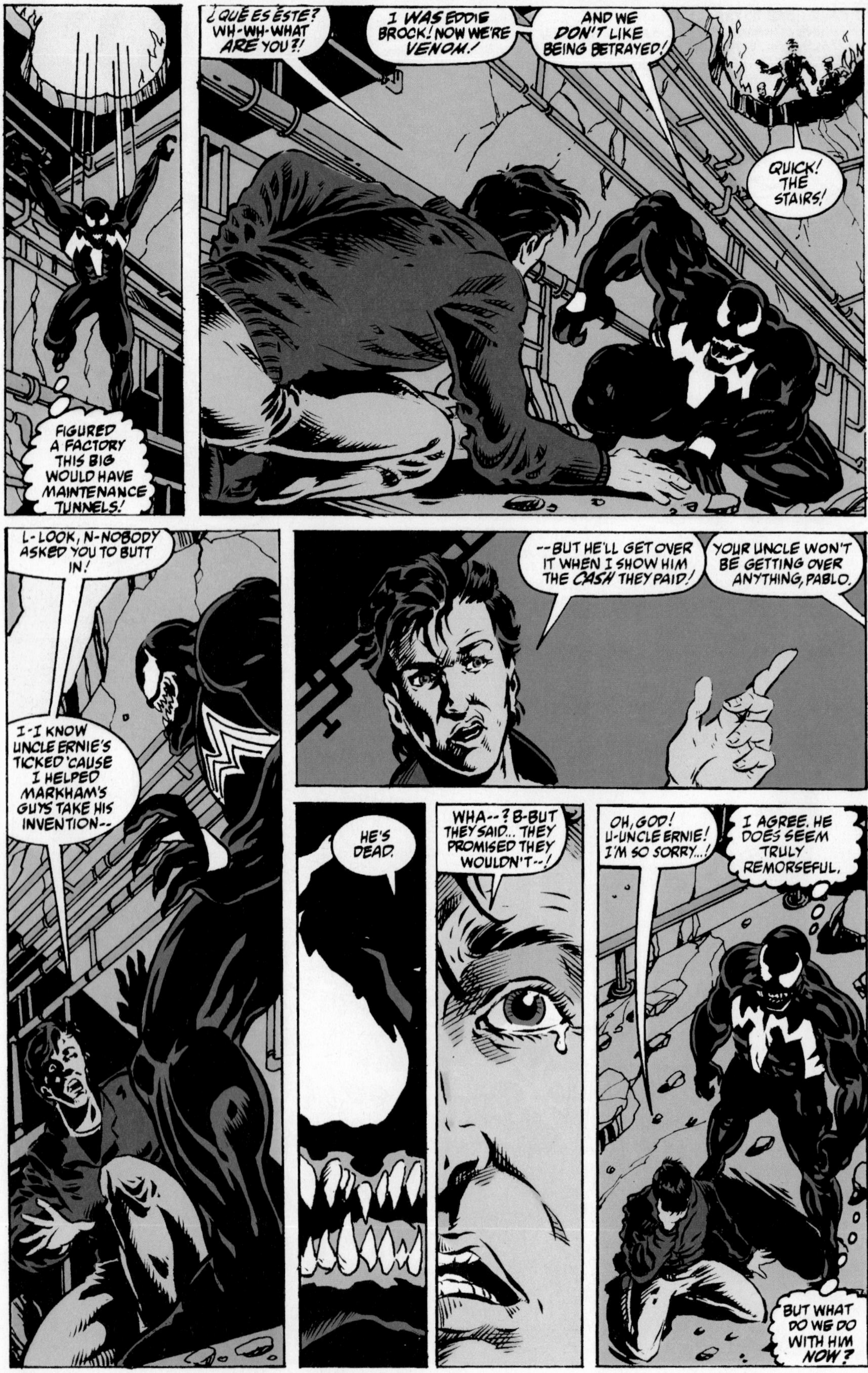
FIGURED A FACTORY THIS BIG WOULD HAVE MAINTENANCE TUNNELS!
¿QUÉ ES ÉSTE? WH-WH-WHAT ARE YOU?!
I WAS EDDIE BROCK! NOW WE'RE VENOM!
AND WE DON'T LIKE BEING BETRAYED!
QUICK! THE STAIRS!
L-LOOK, N-NOBODY ASKED YOU TO BUTT IN!
I-I KNOW UNCLE ERNIE'S TICKED 'CAUSE I HELPED MARKHAM'S GUYS TAKE HIS INVENTION--
--BUT HE'LL GET OVER IT WHEN I SHOW HIM THE CASH THEY PAID!
YOUR UNCLE WON'T BE GETTING OVER ANYTHING, PABLO.
HE'S DEAD.
WHA--? B-BUT THEY SAID... THEY PROMISED THEY WOULDN'T--!
OH, GOD! U-UNCLE ERNIE! I'M SO SORRY...!
I AGREE. HE DOES SEEM TRULY REMORSEFUL.
BUT WHAT DO WE DO WITH HIM NOW?

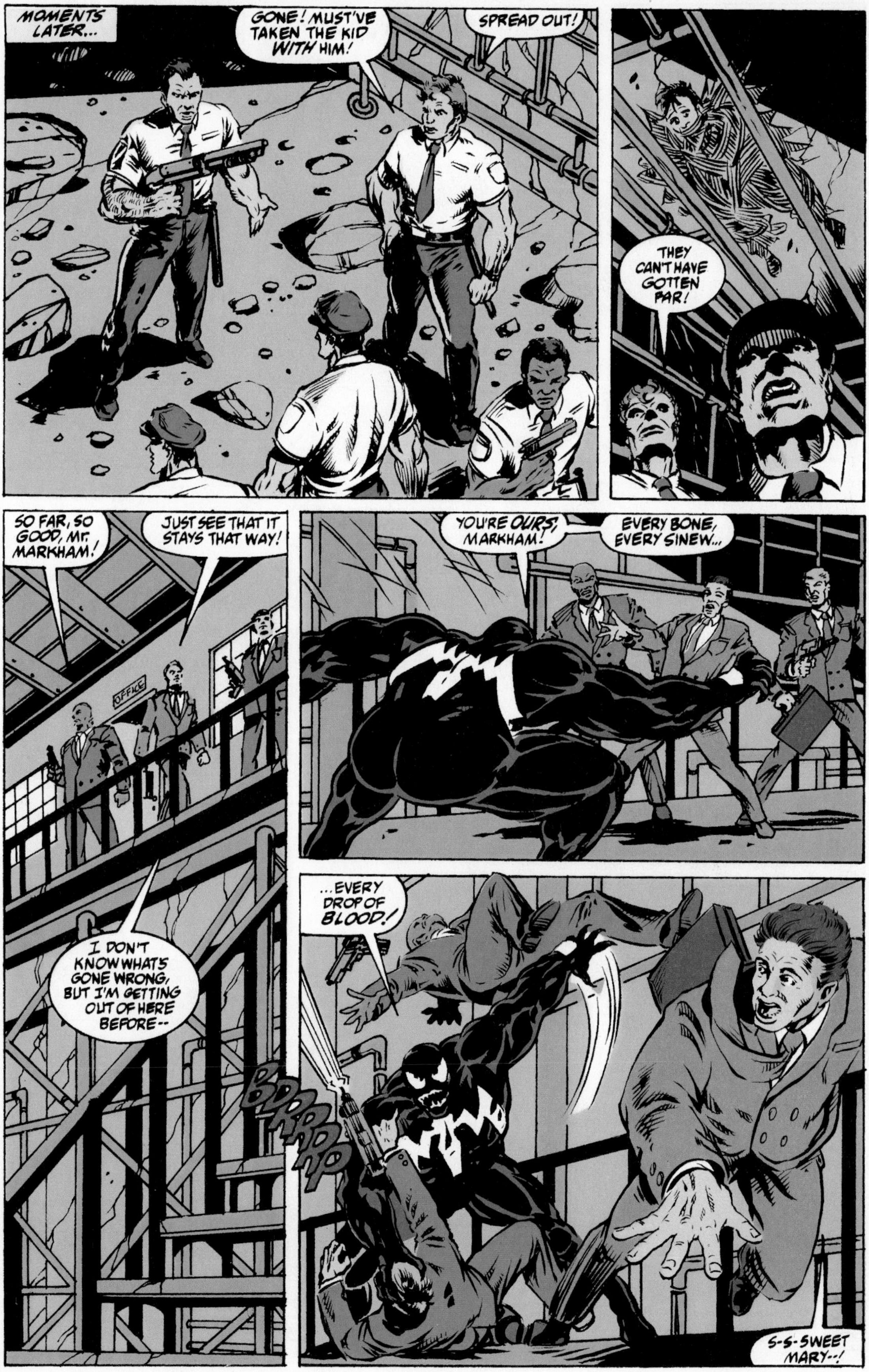
MOMENTS LATER...
GONE! MUST'VE TAKEN THE KID WITH HIM!
SPREAD OUT!
THEY CAN'T HAVE GOTTEN FAR!
SO FAR, SO GOOD, Mr. MARKHAM!
JUST SEE THAT IT STAYS THAT WAY!
OFFICE
I DON'T KNOW WHAT'S GONE WRONG, BUT I'M GETTING OUT OF HERE BEFORE--
YOU'RE OURS, MARKHAM!
EVERY BONE, EVERY SINEW...
...EVERY DROP OF BLOOD!
BDRRRP
S-S-SWEET MARY--!

YOUR LACKEYS KILLED ERNESTO MENDEZ-- BUT *YOU'RE* THE MAN RESPONSIBLE!

MENDEZ? TH-THEN YOU'RE SOME KIND OF... WHAT... *COP?*

S-SOME SORTA SUPER- *S.W.A.T.* GUY?!

TOUGH LUCK, PAL!

SEE THIS BLUEPRINT?

IT'S THE ONLY COPY OF THE OLD GUY'S DESIGN! ONCE IT'S ASHES, THERE'S NOTHING TO LINK ME TO THE CRIME!

YOU'RE NOT TAKIN' *ME* TO JAIL!

YOU'RE RIGHT.

A MAN'S LIFE IS MEASURED IN MOMENTS.

AND *THIS* IS A MOMENT THAT WILL CHANGE *EDDIE BROCK'S* LIFE FOREVER.

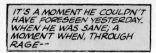

IT'S A MOMENT HE COULDN'T HAVE FORESEEN YESTERDAY. WHEN HE WAS SANE; A MOMENT WHEN, THROUGH RAGE--

--AND ALIEN ENCOUR- AGEMENT.

SKRRRK

150

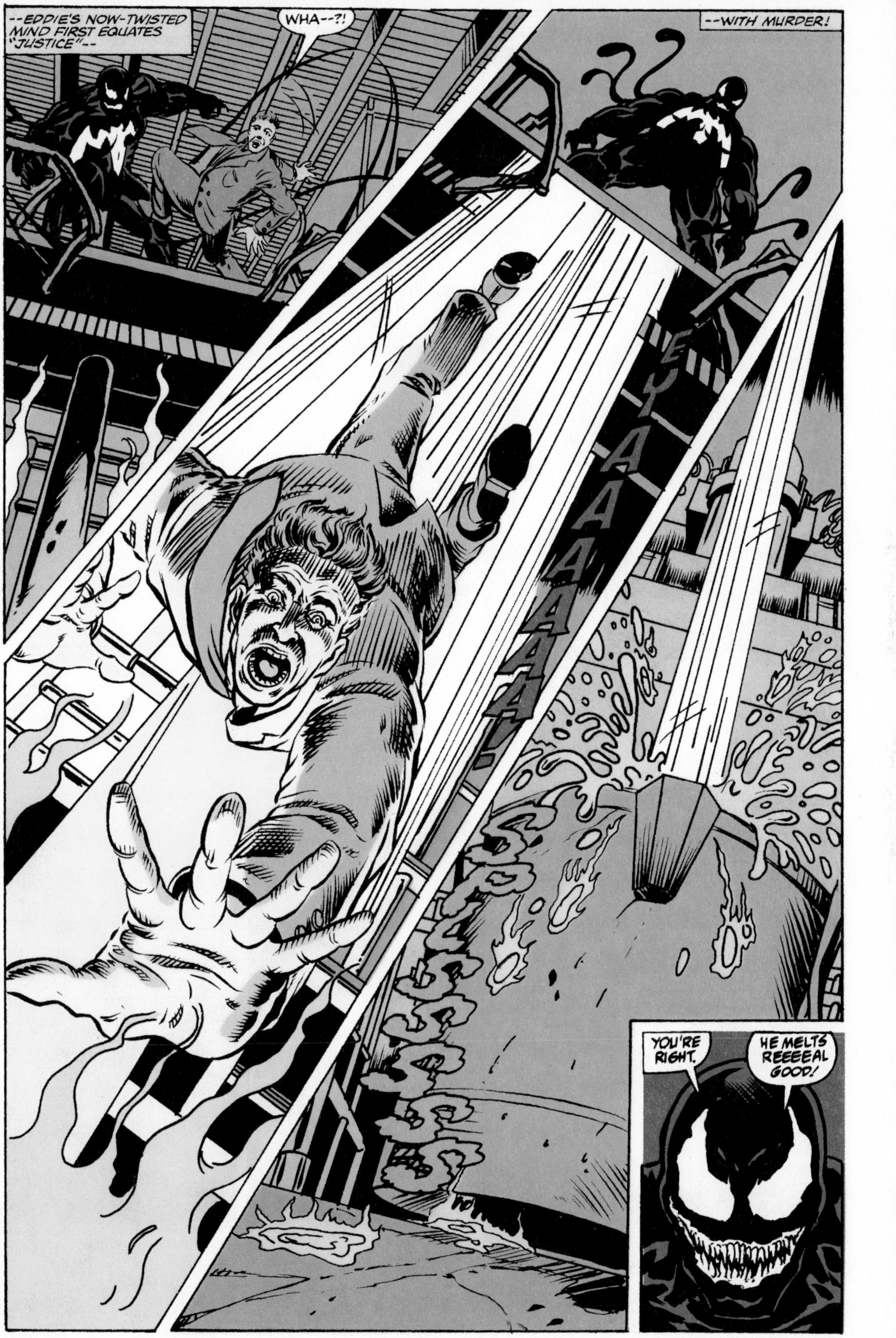
--EDDIE'S NOW-TWISTED MIND FIRST EQUATES "JUSTICE"--
WHA--?!
--WITH MURDER!
EEYAAAAAAAA!
SPLUSSSSSSS
YOU'RE RIGHT.
HE MELTS REEEEAL GOOD!

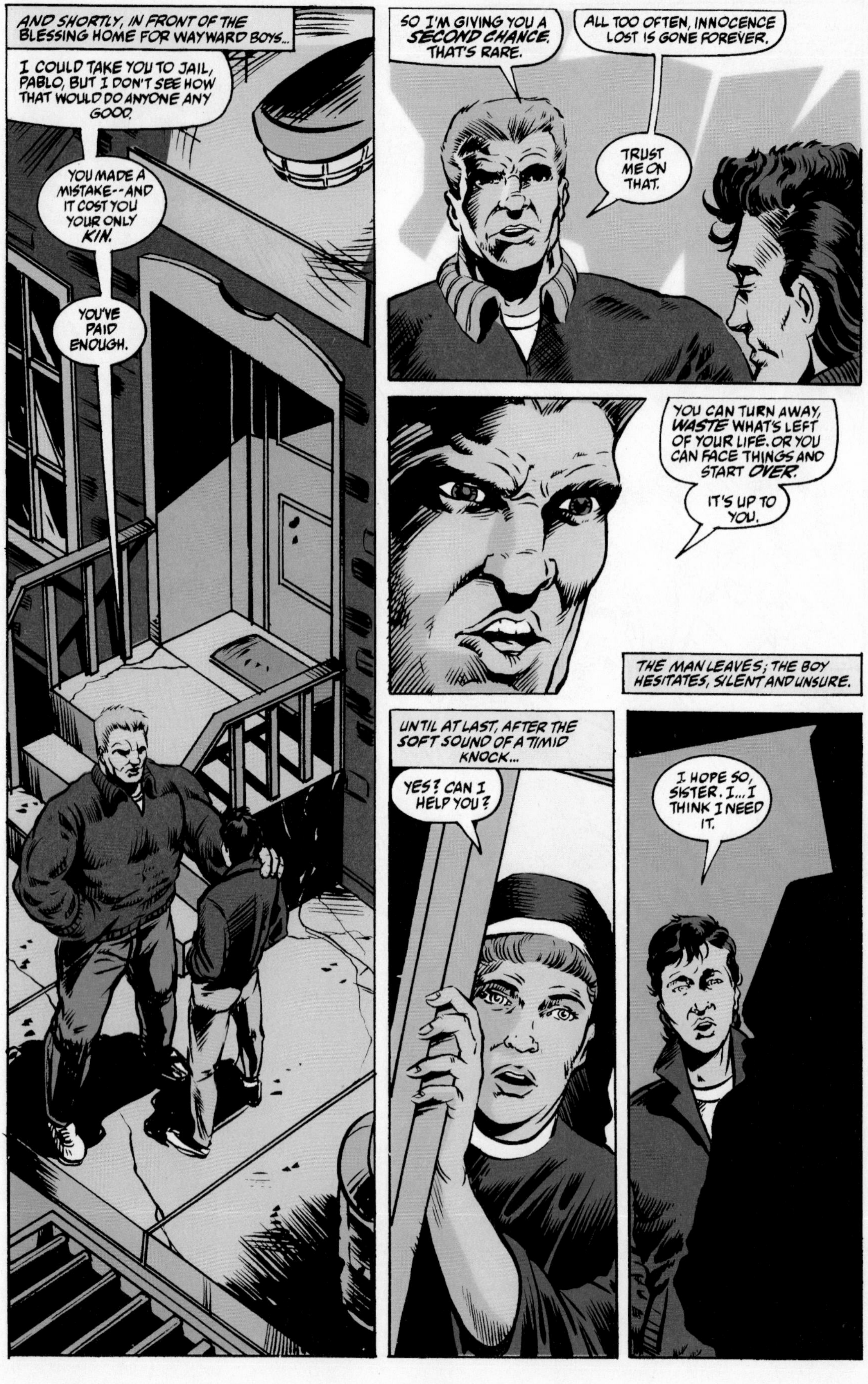
AND SHORTLY, IN FRONT OF THE BLESSING HOME FOR WAYWARD BOYS...
I COULD TAKE YOU TO JAIL, PABLO, BUT I DON'T SEE HOW THAT WOULD DO ANYONE ANY GOOD.
YOU MADE A MISTAKE--AND IT COST YOU YOUR ONLY KIN.
YOU'VE PAID ENOUGH.
SO I'M GIVING YOU A SECOND CHANCE. THAT'S RARE.
ALL TOO OFTEN, INNOCENCE LOST IS GONE FOREVER.
TRUST ME ON THAT.
YOU CAN TURN AWAY, WASTE WHAT'S LEFT OF YOUR LIFE. OR YOU CAN FACE THINGS AND START OVER.
IT'S UP TO YOU.
THE MAN LEAVES; THE BOY HESITATES, SILENT AND UNSURE.
UNTIL AT LAST, AFTER THE SOFT SOUND OF A TIMID KNOCK...
YES? CAN I HELP YOU?
I HOPE SO, SISTER. I...I THINK I NEED IT.

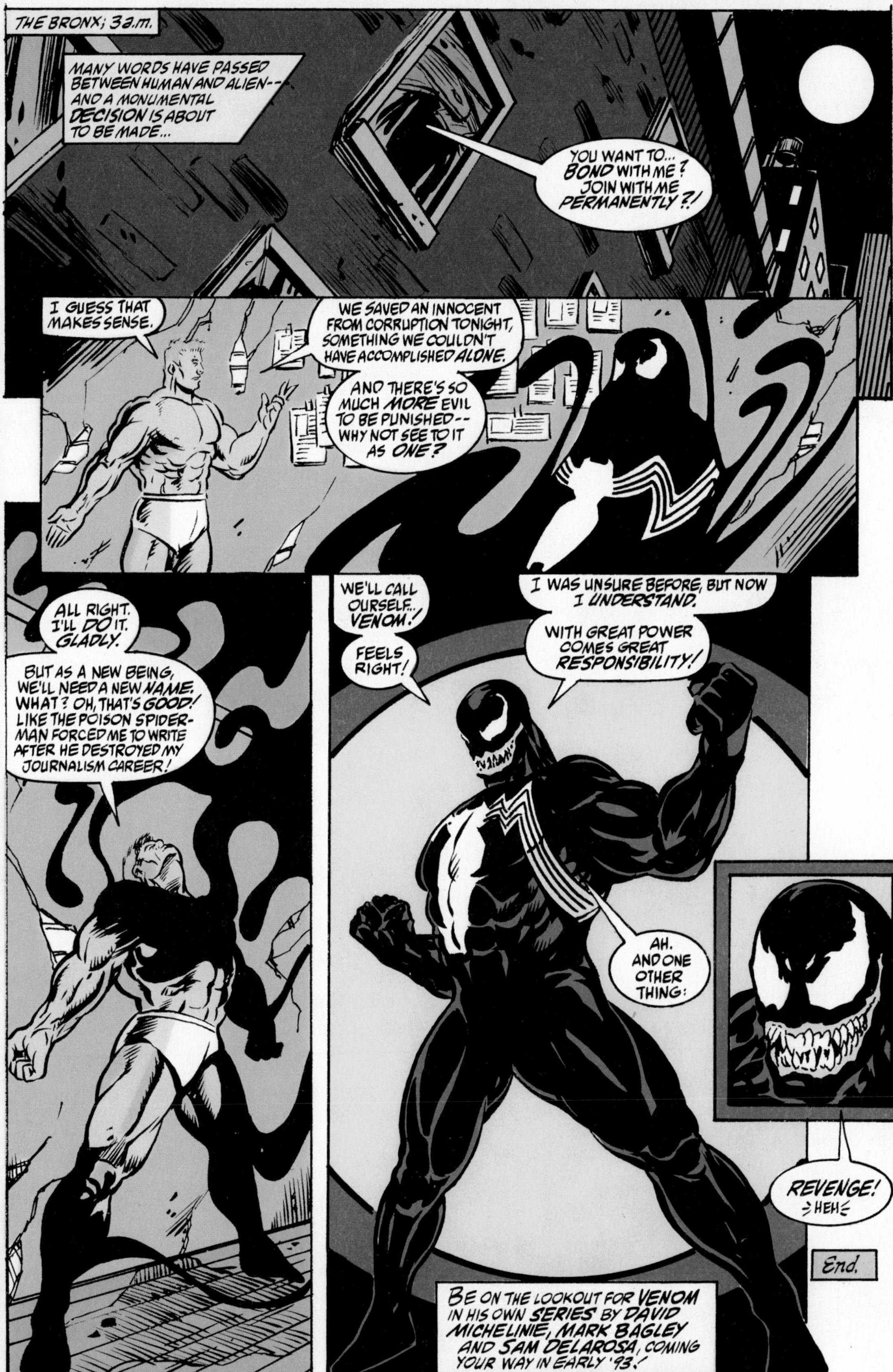
THE BRONX; 3 a.m.
MANY WORDS HAVE PASSED BETWEEN HUMAN AND ALIEN-- AND A MONUMENTAL DECISION IS ABOUT TO BE MADE...
YOU WANT TO... BOND WITH ME? JOIN WITH ME PERMANENTLY?!
I GUESS THAT MAKES SENSE.
WE SAVED AN INNOCENT FROM CORRUPTION TONIGHT, SOMETHING WE COULDN'T HAVE ACCOMPLISHED ALONE.
AND THERE'S SO MUCH MORE EVIL TO BE PUNISHED-- WHY NOT SEE TO IT AS ONE?
ALL RIGHT. I'LL DO IT. GLADLY.
BUT AS A NEW BEING, WE'LL NEED A NEW NAME. WHAT? OH, THAT'S GOOD! LIKE THE POISON SPIDER-MAN FORCED ME TO WRITE AFTER HE DESTROYED MY JOURNALISM CAREER!
WE'LL CALL OURSELF... VENOM!
FEELS RIGHT!
I WAS UNSURE BEFORE, BUT NOW I UNDERSTAND.
WITH GREAT POWER COMES GREAT RESPONSIBILITY!
AH. AND ONE OTHER THING:
REVENGE! HEH
End.
BE ON THE LOOKOUT FOR VENOM IN HIS OWN SERIES BY DAVID MICHELINIE, MARK BAGLEY AND SAM DELAROSA, COMING YOUR WAY IN EARLY '93!

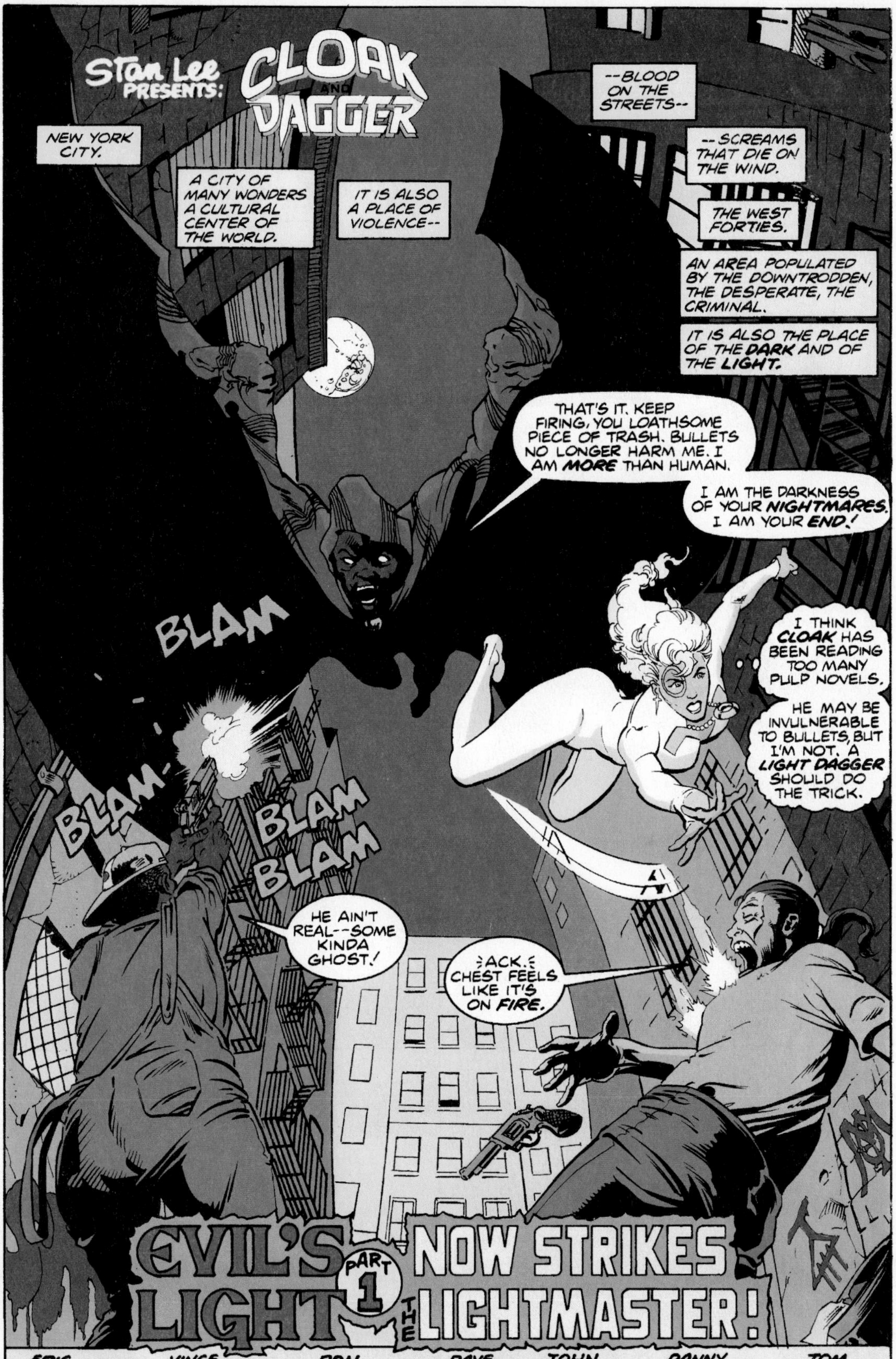

Stan Lee PRESENTS: CLOAK AND DAGGER
NEW YORK CITY.
A CITY OF MANY WONDERS A CULTURAL CENTER OF THE WORLD.
IT IS ALSO A PLACE OF VIOLENCE--
--BLOOD ON THE STREETS--
--SCREAMS THAT DIE ON THE WIND.
THE WEST FORTIES.
AN AREA POPULATED BY THE DOWNTRODDEN, THE DESPERATE, THE CRIMINAL.
IT IS ALSO THE PLACE OF THE DARK AND OF THE LIGHT.
THAT'S IT. KEEP FIRING, YOU LOATHSOME PIECE OF TRASH. BULLETS NO LONGER HARM ME. I AM MORE THAN HUMAN.
I AM THE DARKNESS OF YOUR NIGHTMARES. I AM YOUR END!
BLAM
BLAM
BLAM
BLAM
I THINK CLOAK HAS BEEN READING TOO MANY PULP NOVELS.
HE MAY BE INVULNERABLE TO BULLETS, BUT I'M NOT. A LIGHT DAGGER SHOULD DO THE TRICK.
HE AIN'T REAL--SOME KINDA GHOST!
ACK. CHEST FEELS LIKE IT'S ON FIRE.
EVIL'S LIGHT PART 1 NOW STRIKES THE LIGHTMASTER!
ERIC FEIN WRITER
VINCE EVANS PENCILER
DON HUDSON INKER
DAVE SHARPE LETTERER
JOHN KALISZ COLORIST
DANNY FINGEROTH EDITOR
TOM DeFALCO CHIEF

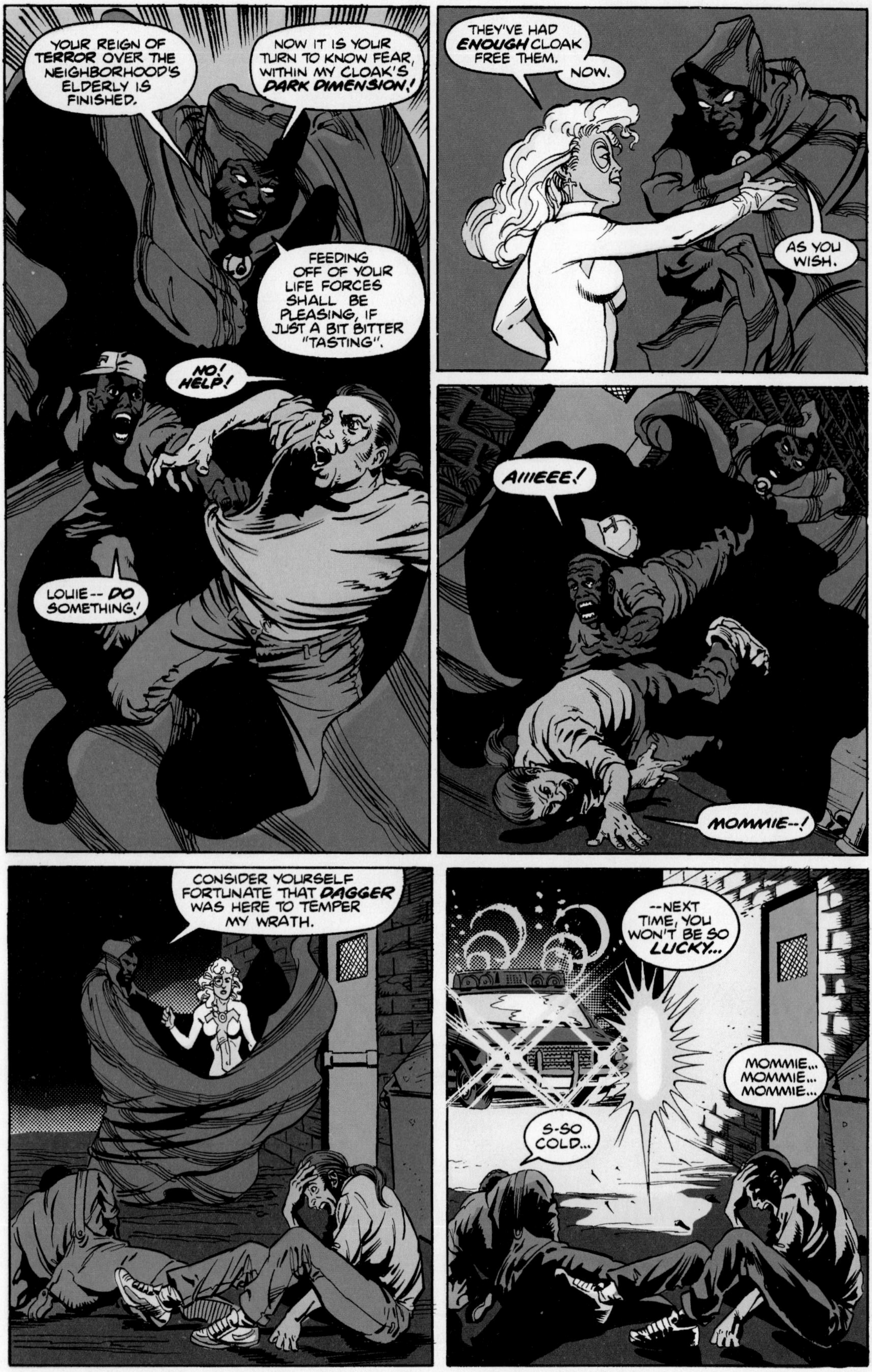
YOUR REIGN OF TERROR OVER THE NEIGHBORHOOD'S ELDERLY IS FINISHED.
NOW IT IS YOUR TURN TO KNOW FEAR, WITHIN MY CLOAK'S DARK DIMENSION!
FEEDING OFF OF YOUR LIFE FORCES SHALL BE PLEASING, IF JUST A BIT BITTER "TASTING".
NO! HELP!
LOUIE-- DO SOMETHING!
THEY'VE HAD ENOUGH CLOAK FREE THEM.
NOW.
AS YOU WISH.
AIIIEEE!
MOMMIE--!
CONSIDER YOURSELF FORTUNATE THAT DAGGER WAS HERE TO TEMPER MY WRATH.
--NEXT TIME, YOU WON'T BE SO LUCKY...
MOMMIE... MOMMIE... MOMMIE...
S-SO COLD...

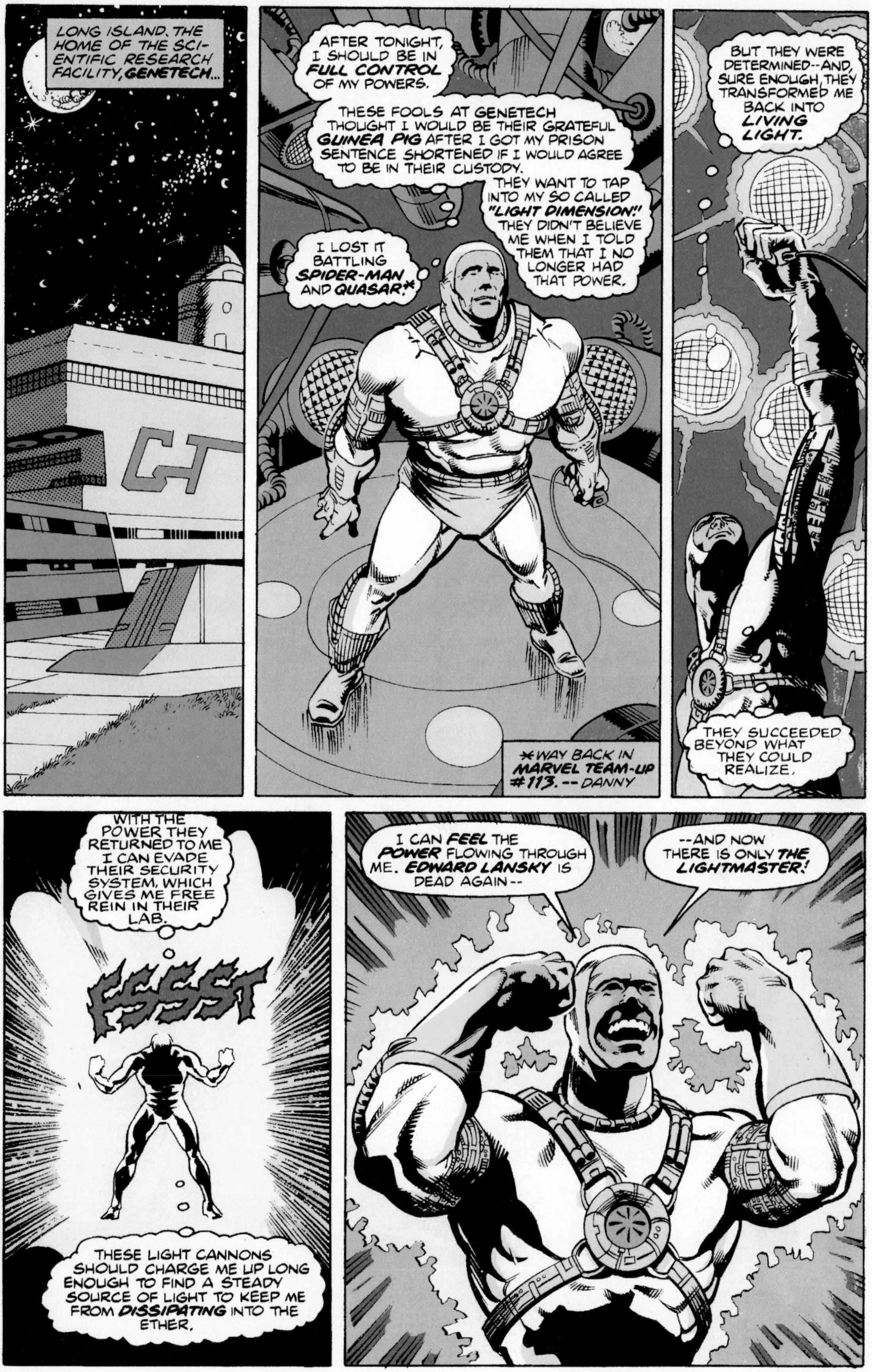
LONG ISLAND. THE HOME OF THE SCIENTIFIC RESEARCH FACILITY, GENETECH...
AFTER TONIGHT, I SHOULD BE IN FULL CONTROL OF MY POWERS.
THESE FOOLS AT GENETECH THOUGHT I WOULD BE THEIR GRATEFUL GUINEA PIG AFTER I GOT MY PRISON SENTENCE SHORTENED IF I WOULD AGREE TO BE IN THEIR CUSTODY.
THEY WANT TO TAP INTO MY SO CALLED "LIGHT DIMENSION!" THEY DIDN'T BELIEVE ME WHEN I TOLD THEM THAT I NO LONGER HAD THAT POWER.
I LOST IT BATTLING SPIDER-MAN AND QUASAR!*
*WAY BACK IN MARVEL TEAM-UP #113. -- DANNY
BUT THEY WERE DETERMINED--AND, SURE ENOUGH, THEY TRANSFORMED ME BACK INTO LIVING LIGHT.
THEY SUCCEEDED BEYOND WHAT THEY COULD REALIZE.
WITH THE POWER THEY RETURNED TO ME I CAN EVADE THEIR SECURITY SYSTEM, WHICH GIVES ME FREE REIN IN THEIR LAB.
FSSST
THESE LIGHT CANNONS SHOULD CHARGE ME UP LONG ENOUGH TO FIND A STEADY SOURCE OF LIGHT TO KEEP ME FROM DISSIPATING INTO THE ETHER.
I CAN FEEL THE POWER FLOWING THROUGH ME. EDWARD LANSKY IS DEAD AGAIN --
--AND NOW THERE IS ONLY THE LIGHTMASTER!

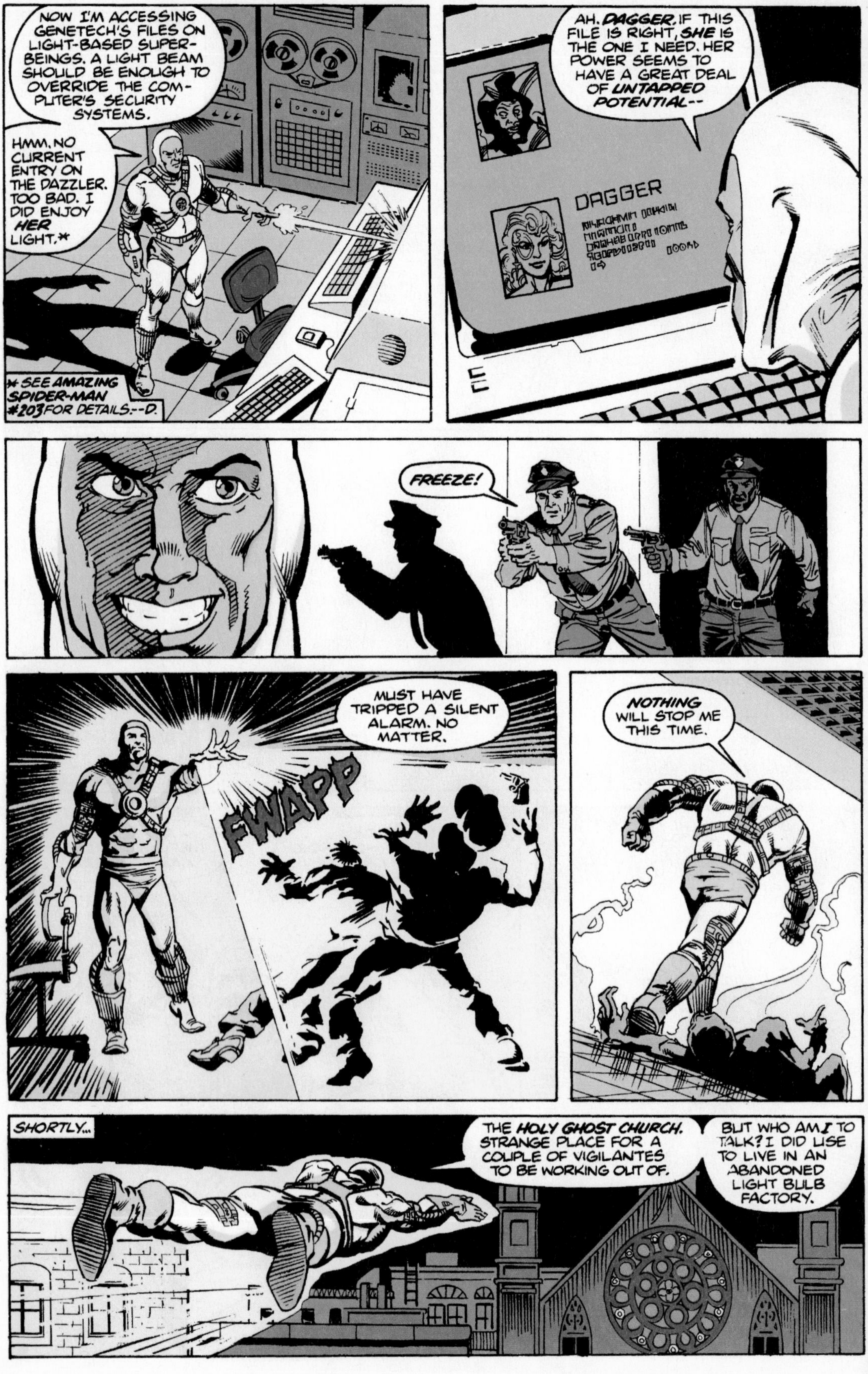
NOW I'M ACCESSING GENETECH'S FILES ON LIGHT-BASED SUPER-BEINGS. A LIGHT BEAM SHOULD BE ENOUGH TO OVERRIDE THE COM-PUTER'S SECURITY SYSTEMS.
HMM. NO CURRENT ENTRY ON THE DAZZLER. TOO BAD. I DID ENJOY HER LIGHT.*
* SEE AMAZING SPIDER-MAN #203 FOR DETAILS.--D.
AH. DAGGER. IF THIS FILE IS RIGHT, SHE IS THE ONE I NEED. HER POWER SEEMS TO HAVE A GREAT DEAL OF UNTAPPED POTENTIAL--
DAGGER
FREEZE!
MUST HAVE TRIPPED A SILENT ALARM. NO MATTER.
FWAPP
NOTHING WILL STOP ME THIS TIME.
SHORTLY...
THE HOLY GHOST CHURCH. STRANGE PLACE FOR A COUPLE OF VIGILANTES TO BE WORKING OUT OF.
BUT WHO AM I TO TALK? I DID USE TO LIVE IN AN ABANDONED LIGHT BULB FACTORY.

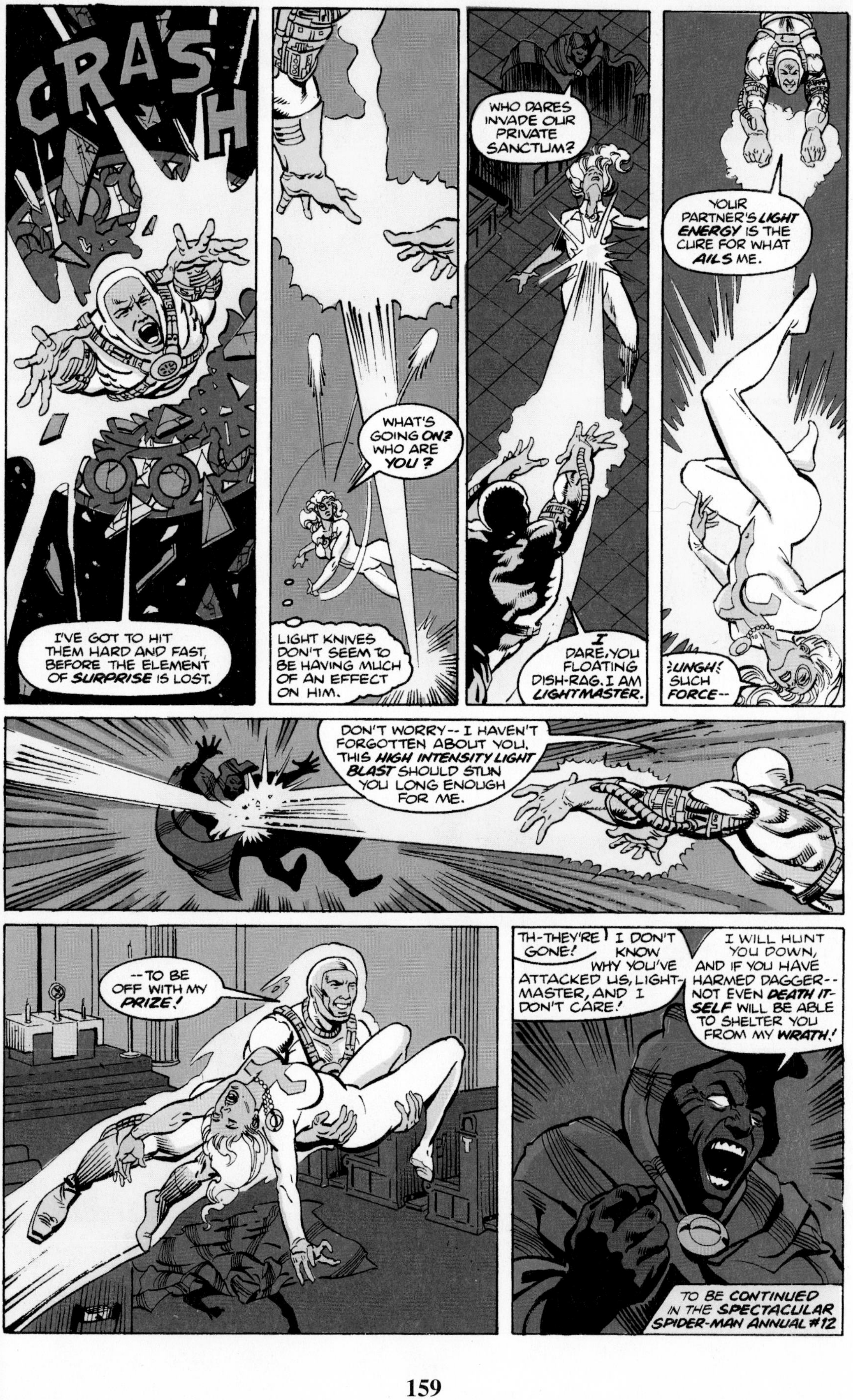
CRASH
I'VE GOT TO HIT THEM HARD AND FAST, BEFORE THE ELEMENT OF SURPRISE IS LOST.
WHAT'S GOING ON? WHO ARE YOU?
LIGHT KNIVES DON'T SEEM TO BE HAVING MUCH OF AN EFFECT ON HIM.
WHO DARES INVADE OUR PRIVATE SANCTUM?
I DARE, YOU FLOATING DISH-RAG. I AM LIGHTMASTER.
YOUR PARTNER'S LIGHT ENERGY IS THE CURE FOR WHAT AILS ME.
UNGH! SUCH FORCE--
DON'T WORRY-- I HAVEN'T FORGOTTEN ABOUT YOU. THIS HIGH INTENSITY LIGHT BLAST SHOULD STUN YOU LONG ENOUGH FOR ME.
--TO BE OFF WITH MY PRIZE!
TH-THEY'RE GONE!
I DON'T KNOW WHY YOU'VE ATTACKED US, LIGHTMASTER, AND I DON'T CARE!
I WILL HUNT YOU DOWN, AND IF YOU HAVE HARMED DAGGER-- NOT EVEN DEATH ITSELF WILL BE ABLE TO SHELTER YOU FROM MY WRATH!
TO BE CONTINUED IN THE SPECTACULAR SPIDER-MAN ANNUAL #12

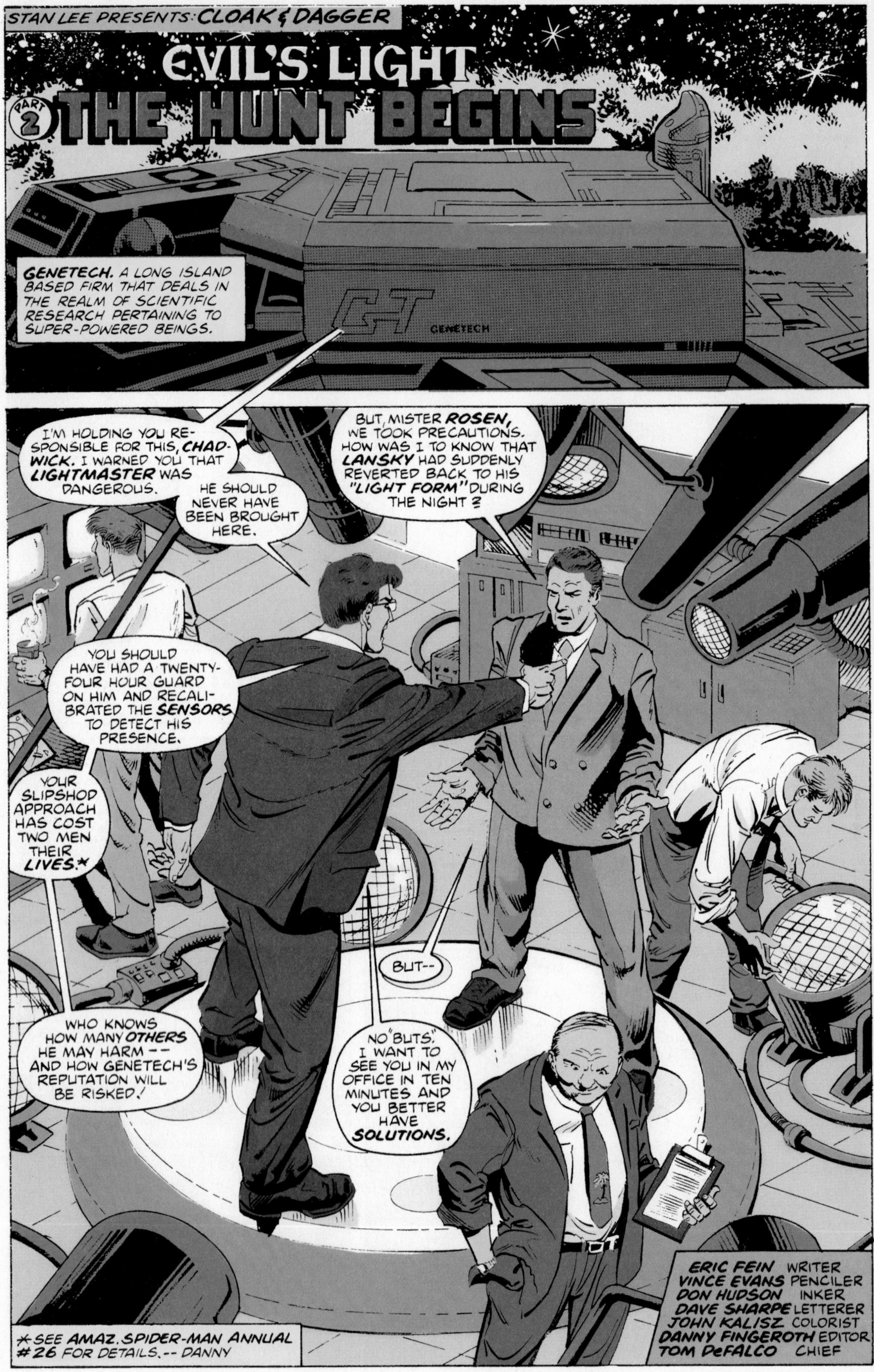
STAN LEE PRESENTS: CLOAK & DAGGER
EVIL'S LIGHT
PART 2 THE HUNT BEGINS
GENETECH. A LONG ISLAND BASED FIRM THAT DEALS IN THE REALM OF SCIENTIFIC RESEARCH PERTAINING TO SUPER-POWERED BEINGS.
GENETECH
I'M HOLDING YOU RESPONSIBLE FOR THIS, CHADWICK. I WARNED YOU THAT LIGHTMASTER WAS DANGEROUS.
HE SHOULD NEVER HAVE BEEN BROUGHT HERE.
BUT, MISTER ROSEN, WE TOOK PRECAUTIONS. HOW WAS I TO KNOW THAT LANSKY HAD SUDDENLY REVERTED BACK TO HIS "LIGHT FORM" DURING THE NIGHT?
YOU SHOULD HAVE HAD A TWENTY-FOUR HOUR GUARD ON HIM AND RECALIBRATED THE SENSORS TO DETECT HIS PRESENCE.
YOUR SLIPSHOD APPROACH HAS COST TWO MEN THEIR LIVES.*
BUT--
WHO KNOWS HOW MANY OTHERS HE MAY HARM -- AND HOW GENETECH'S REPUTATION WILL BE RISKED!
NO "BUTS." I WANT TO SEE YOU IN MY OFFICE IN TEN MINUTES AND YOU BETTER HAVE SOLUTIONS.
*SEE AMAZ. SPIDER-MAN ANNUAL #26 FOR DETAILS. -- DANNY
ERIC FEIN WRITER
VINCE EVANS PENCILER
DON HUDSON INKER
DAVE SHARPE LETTERER
JOHN KALISZ COLORIST
DANNY FINGEROTH EDITOR
TOM DeFALCO CHIEF

MEANWHILE...

AN ABANDONED HYDRO-ELECTRIC PLANT IN LOWER MANHATTAN.

THE SUB-SUB-BASEMENT.

AH, YOU'RE AWAKE. GOOD.

WE CAN BEGIN SHORTLY.

UNNH.

WHAT ARE YOU TALKING ABOUT? WHO ARE YOU?

MY NAME IS EDWARD LANSKY. I'M CALLED THE LIGHTMASTER.

WHO?

SOON, EVERYONE WILL CRINGE IN FEAR AT MY POWER.

STARTING WITH GENE-TECH!

WHAT DO YOU WANT FROM ME?

YOUR LIGHT. I NEED TO AB-SORB IT TO KEEP MYSELF FROM DISSIPATING.

AND I'M GOING TO TAKE IT...

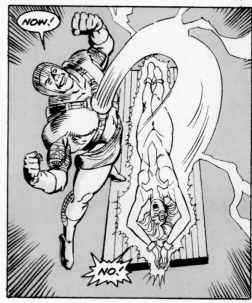

NOW!

NO!

161

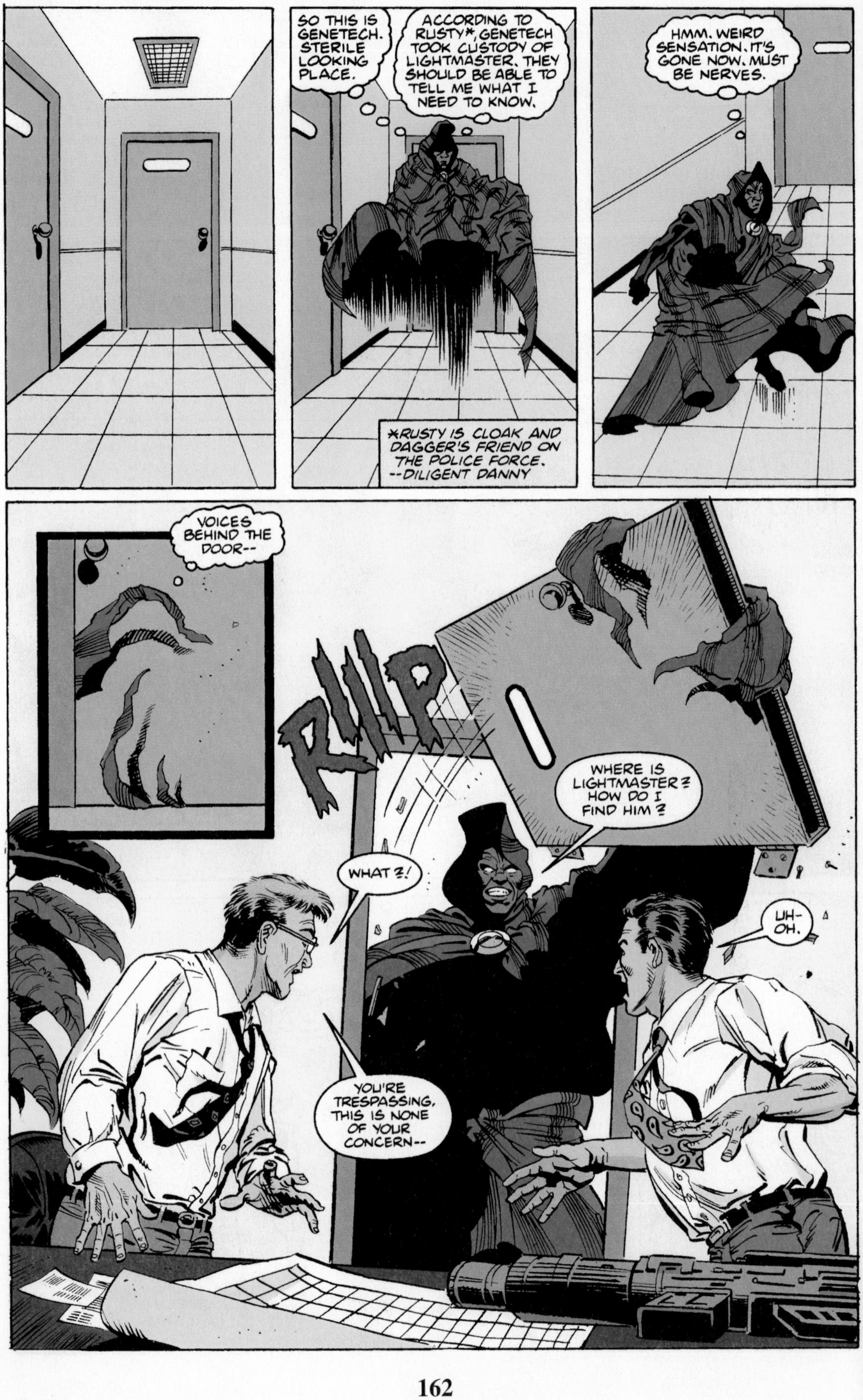
SO THIS IS GENETECH. STERILE LOOKING PLACE.
ACCORDING TO RUSTY*, GENETECH TOOK CUSTODY OF LIGHTMASTER. THEY SHOULD BE ABLE TO TELL ME WHAT I NEED TO KNOW.
*RUSTY IS CLOAK AND DAGGER'S FRIEND ON THE POLICE FORCE. --DILIGENT DANNY
HMM. WEIRD SENSATION. IT'S GONE NOW. MUST BE NERVES.
VOICES BEHIND THE DOOR--
RIIIP
WHERE IS LIGHTMASTER?! HOW DO I FIND HIM?
WHAT?!
UH-OH.
YOU'RE TRESPASSING. THIS IS NONE OF YOUR CONCERN--

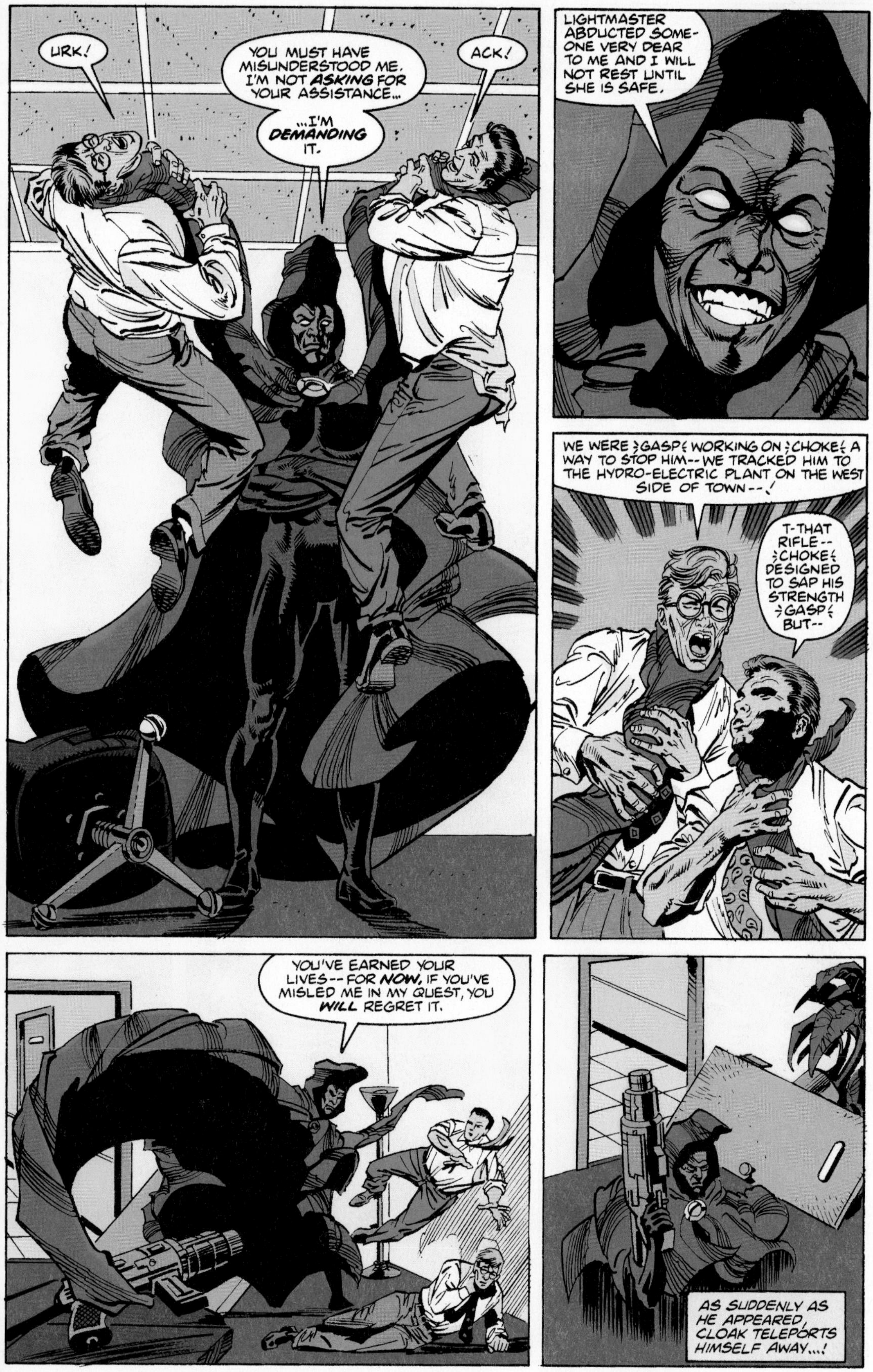
URK!
YOU MUST HAVE MISUNDERSTOOD ME. I'M NOT ASKING FOR YOUR ASSISTANCE...
...I'M DEMANDING IT.
ACK!
LIGHTMASTER ABDUCTED SOME-ONE VERY DEAR TO ME AND I WILL NOT REST UNTIL SHE IS SAFE.
WE WERE GASP WORKING ON CHOKE A WAY TO STOP HIM-- WE TRACKED HIM TO THE HYDRO-ELECTRIC PLANT ON THE WEST SIDE OF TOWN--!
T-THAT RIFLE-- CHOKE DESIGNED TO SAP HIS STRENGTH GASP BUT--
YOU'VE EARNED YOUR LIVES-- FOR NOW. IF YOU'VE MISLED ME IN MY QUEST, YOU WILL REGRET IT.
AS SUDDENLY AS HE APPEARED, CLOAK TELEPORTS HIMSELF AWAY...!

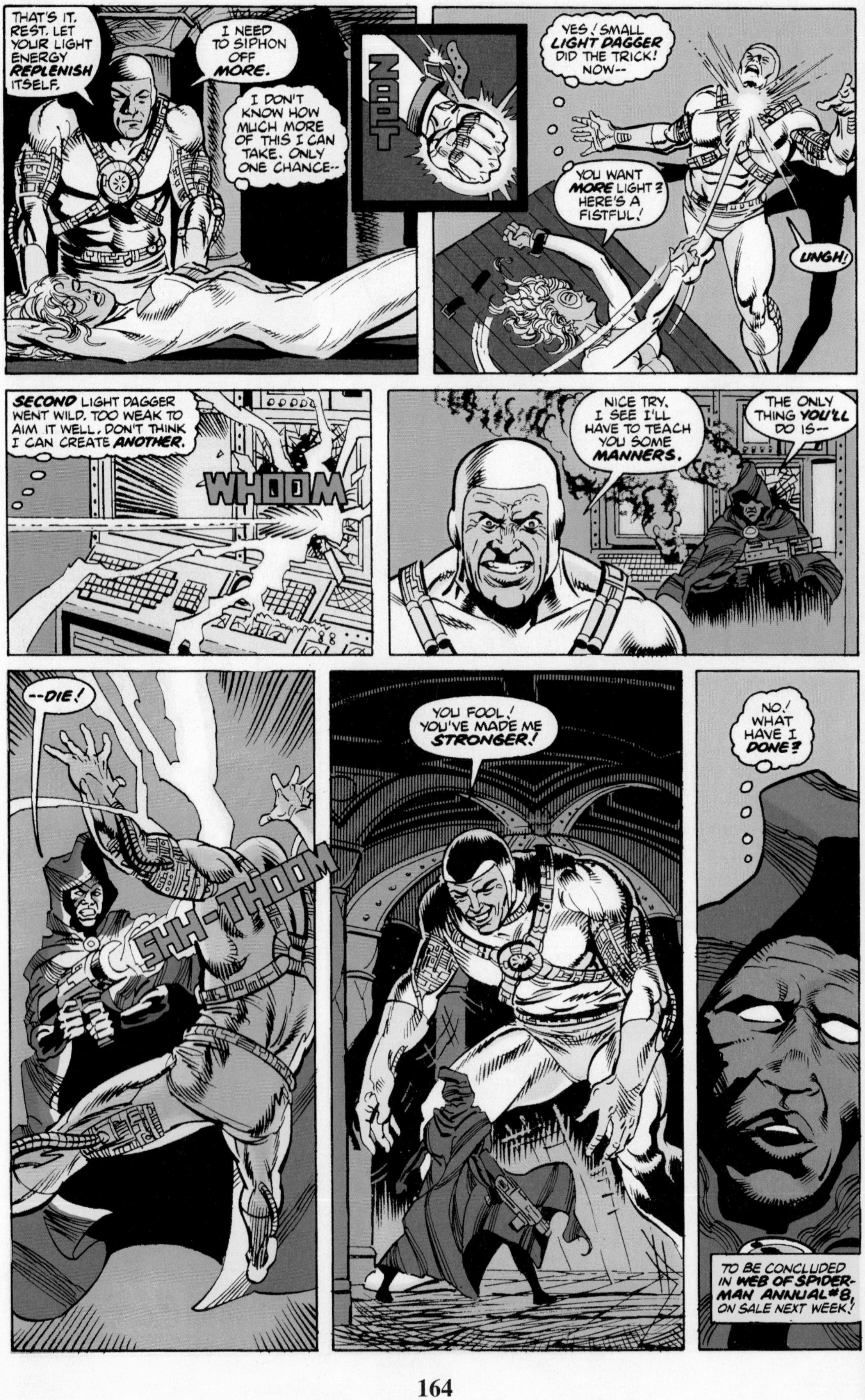
THAT'S IT. REST. LET YOUR LIGHT ENERGY REPLENISH ITSELF.
I NEED TO SIPHON OFF MORE.
I DON'T KNOW HOW MUCH MORE OF THIS I CAN TAKE. ONLY ONE CHANCE--
ZAPT
YES! SMALL LIGHT DAGGER DID THE TRICK! NOW--
YOU WANT MORE LIGHT? HERE'S A FISTFUL!
UNGH!
SECOND LIGHT DAGGER WENT WILD. TOO WEAK TO AIM IT WELL. DON'T THINK I CAN CREATE ANOTHER.
WHOOM
NICE TRY. I SEE I'LL HAVE TO TEACH YOU SOME MANNERS.
THE ONLY THING YOU'LL DO IS--
--DIE!
SHH-THOOM
YOU FOOL! YOU'VE MADE ME STRONGER!
NO! WHAT HAVE I DONE?
TO BE CONCLUDED IN WEB OF SPIDER-MAN ANNUAL #8, ON SALE NEXT WEEK!

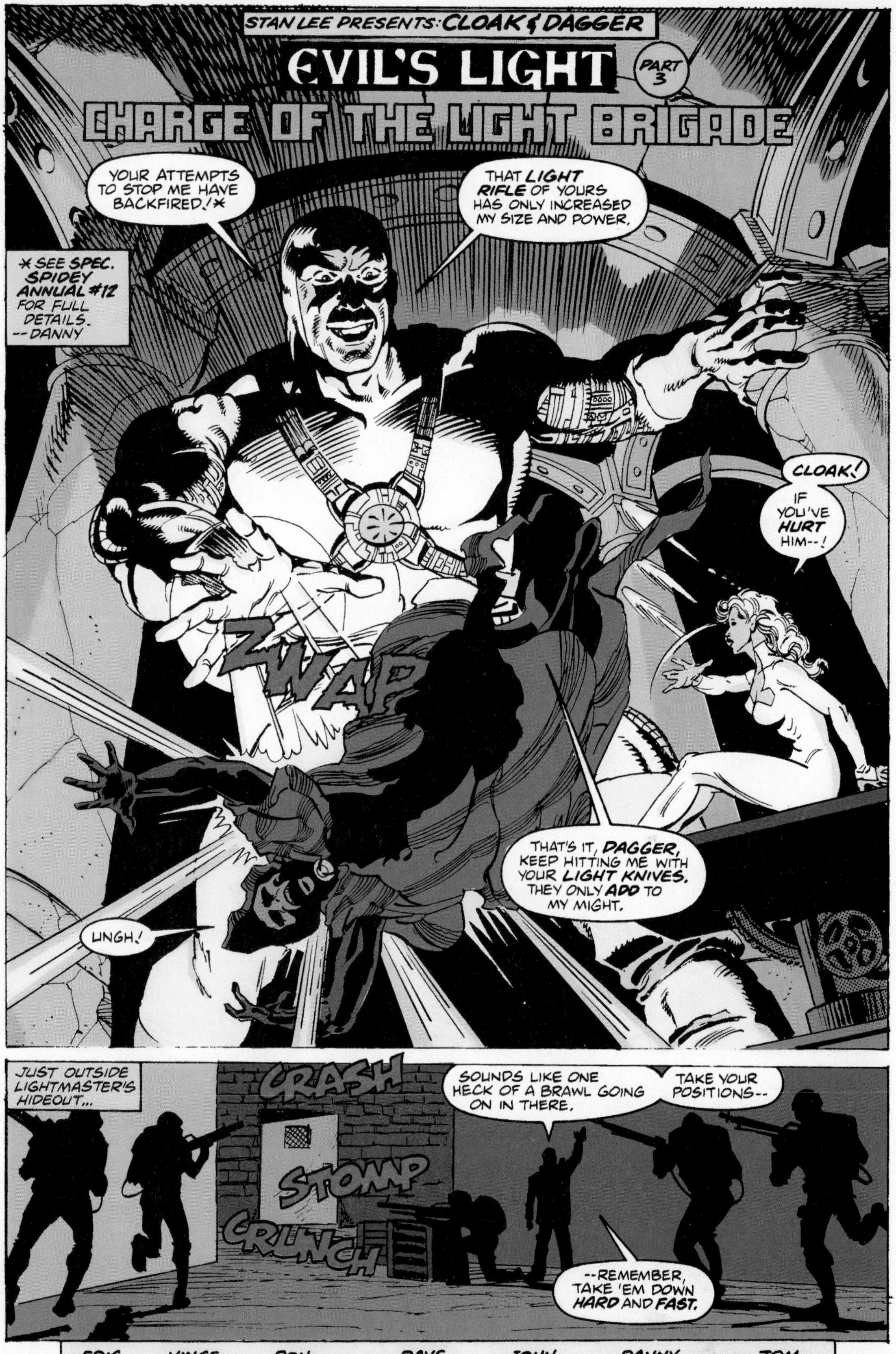
STAN LEE PRESENTS: CLOAK & DAGGER
EVIL'S LIGHT PART 3
CHARGE OF THE LIGHT BRIGADE
YOUR ATTEMPTS TO STOP ME HAVE BACKFIRED!*
THAT LIGHT RIFLE OF YOURS HAS ONLY INCREASED MY SIZE AND POWER.
*SEE SPEC. SPIDEY ANNUAL #12 FOR FULL DETAILS. --DANNY
CLOAK!
IF YOU'VE HURT HIM--!
ZWAP
THAT'S IT, DAGGER, KEEP HITTING ME WITH YOUR LIGHT KNIVES. THEY ONLY ADD TO MY MIGHT.
UNGH!
JUST OUTSIDE LIGHTMASTER'S HIDEOUT...
CRASH
SOUNDS LIKE ONE HECK OF A BRAWL GOING ON IN THERE.
TAKE YOUR POSITIONS--
STOMP
CRUNCH
--REMEMBER, TAKE 'EM DOWN HARD AND FAST.

ERIC FEIN	VINCE EVANS	DON HUDSON	DAVE SHARPE	JOHN KALISZ	DANNY FINGEROTH	TOM DeFALCO
WRITER	PENCILS	INKS	LETTERS	COLORS	EDITOR	CHIEF

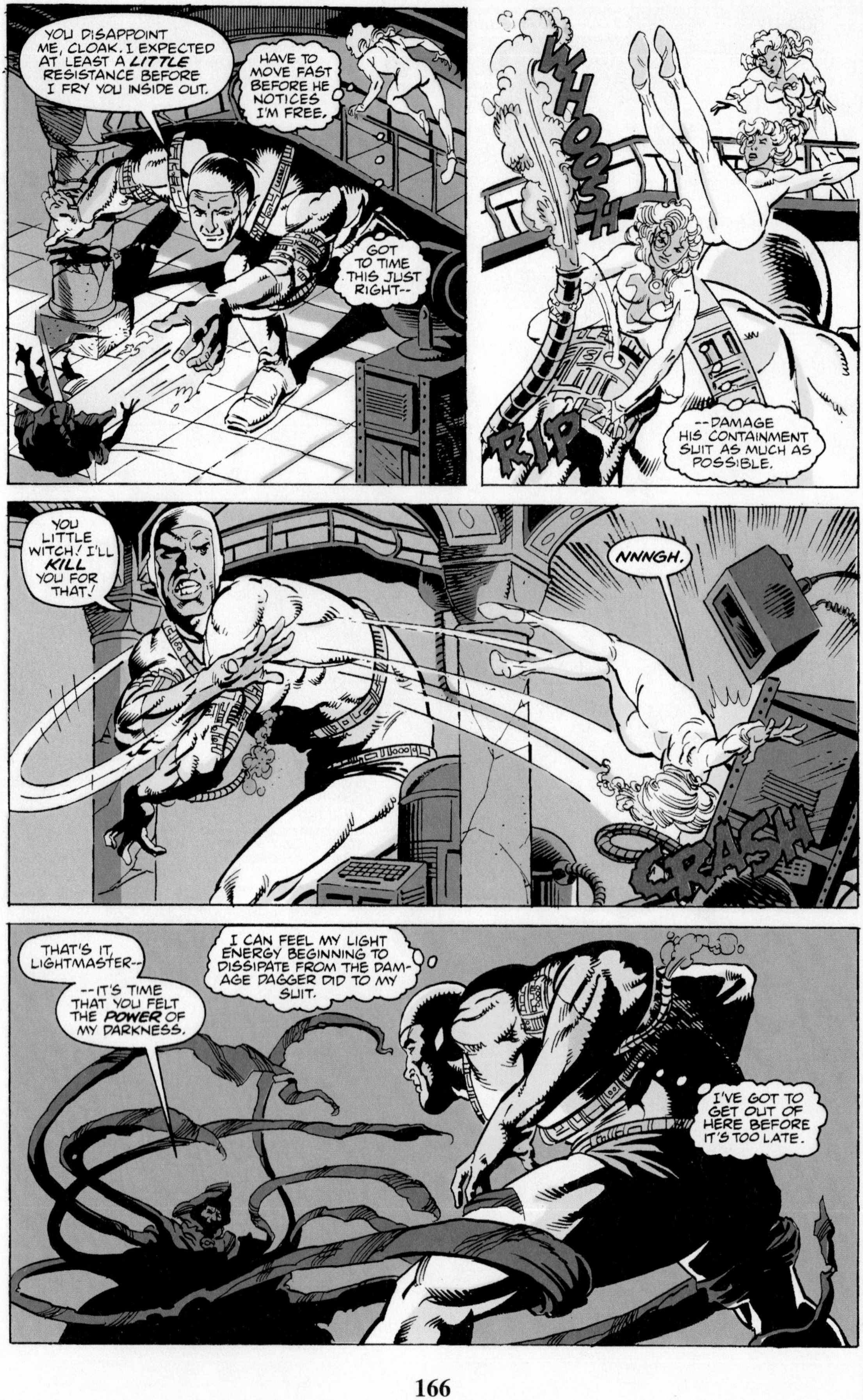
YOU DISAPPOINT ME, CLOAK. I EXPECTED AT LEAST A LITTLE RESISTANCE BEFORE I FRY YOU INSIDE OUT.
HAVE TO MOVE FAST BEFORE HE NOTICES I'M FREE.
GOT TO TIME THIS JUST RIGHT--
WHOOOSH
RIP
--DAMAGE HIS CONTAINMENT SUIT AS MUCH AS POSSIBLE.
YOU LITTLE WITCH! I'LL KILL YOU FOR THAT!
NNNGH.
CRASH
THAT'S IT, LIGHTMASTER--
--IT'S TIME THAT YOU FELT THE POWER OF MY DARKNESS.
I CAN FEEL MY LIGHT ENERGY BEGINNING TO DISSIPATE FROM THE DAMAGE DAGGER DID TO MY SUIT.
I'VE GOT TO GET OUT OF HERE BEFORE IT'S TOO LATE.

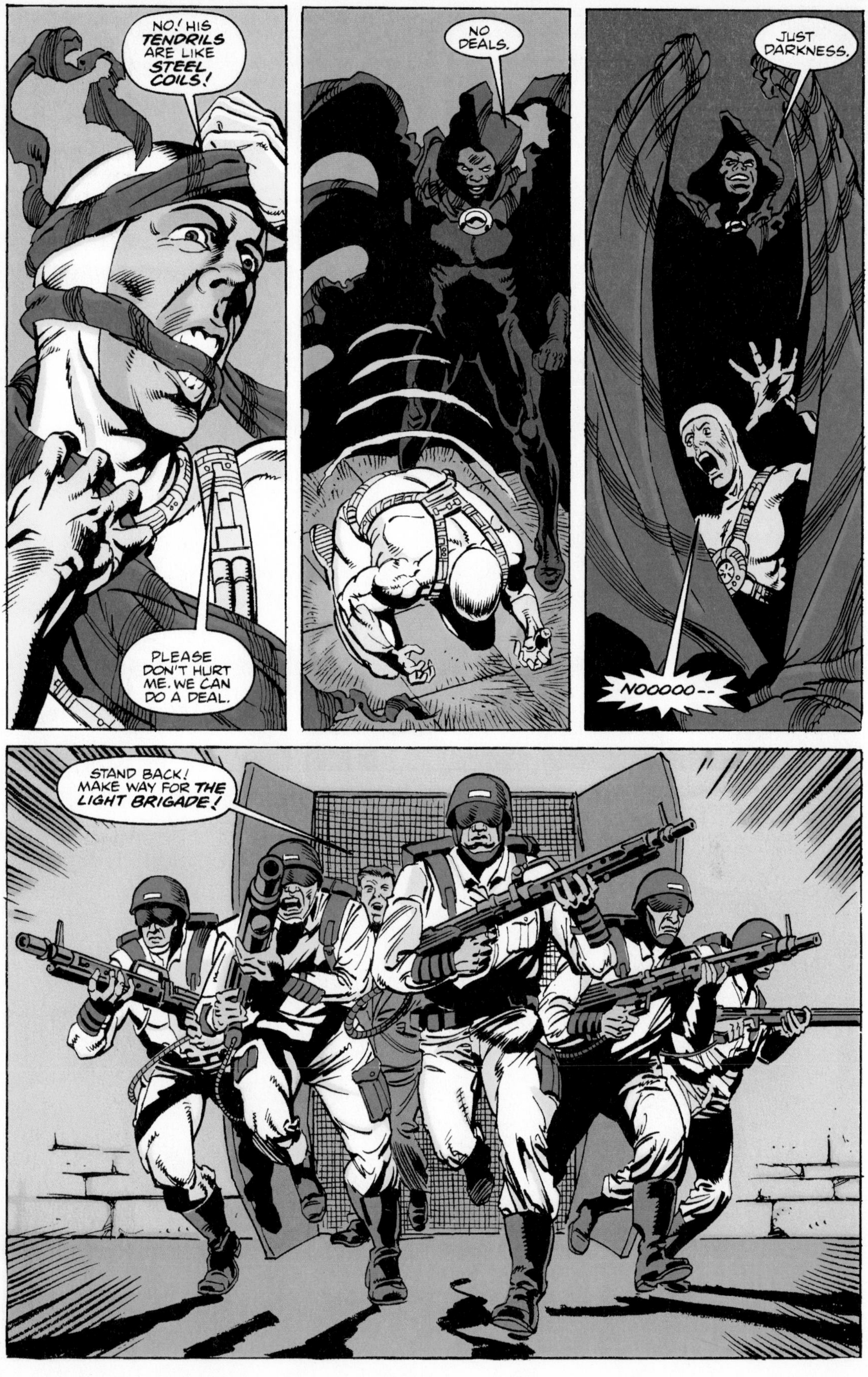
NO! HIS TENDRILS ARE LIKE STEEL COILS!
PLEASE DON'T HURT ME. WE CAN DO A DEAL.
NO DEALS.
JUST DARKNESS.
NOOOOO--
STAND BACK! MAKE WAY FOR THE LIGHT BRIGADE!

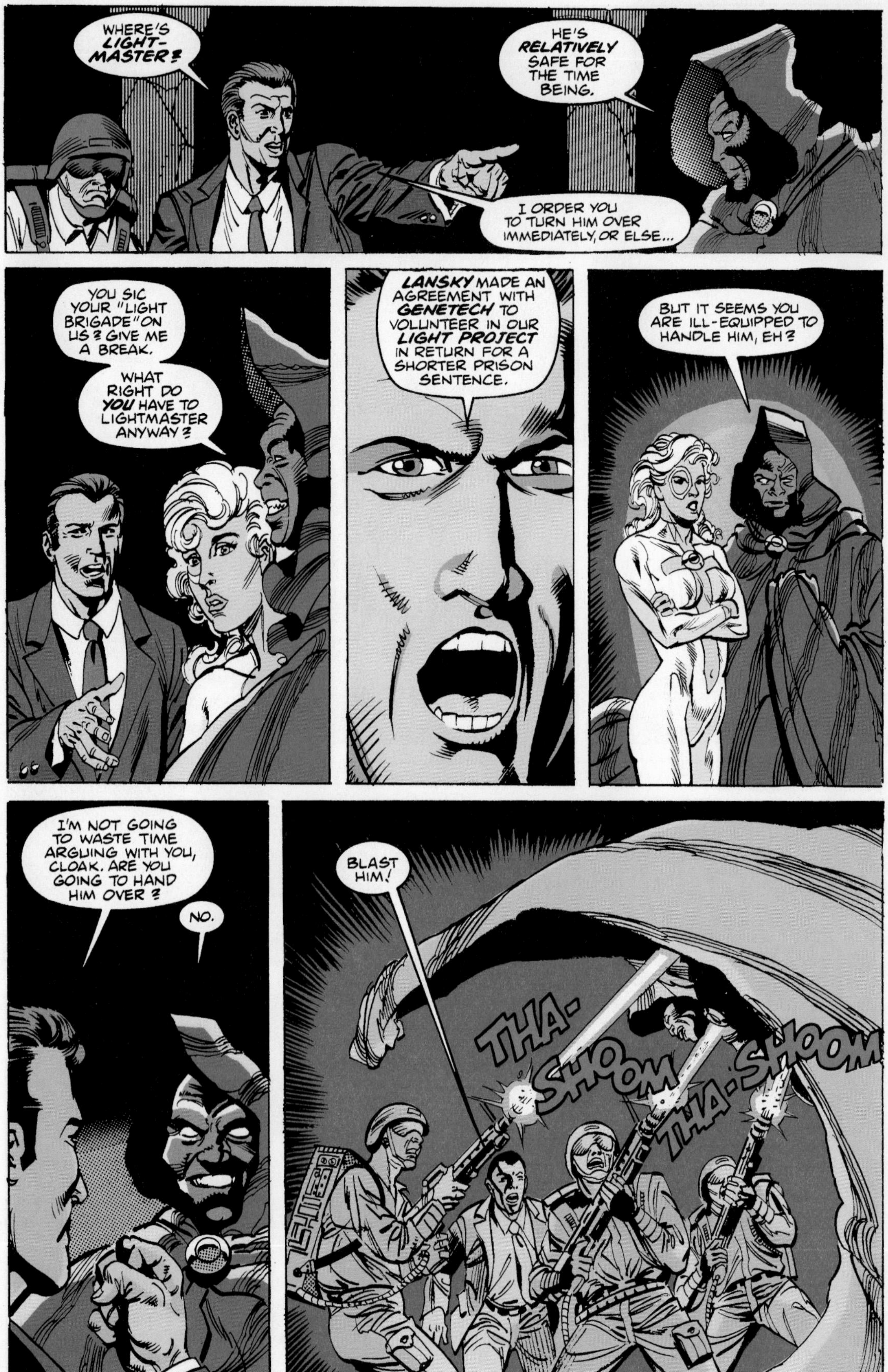
WHERE'S LIGHT-MASTER?
HE'S RELATIVELY SAFE FOR THE TIME BEING.
I ORDER YOU TO TURN HIM OVER IMMEDIATELY, OR ELSE...
YOU SIC YOUR "LIGHT BRIGADE" ON US? GIVE ME A BREAK.
WHAT RIGHT DO YOU HAVE TO LIGHTMASTER ANYWAY?
LANSKY MADE AN AGREEMENT WITH GENETECH TO VOLUNTEER IN OUR LIGHT PROJECT IN RETURN FOR A SHORTER PRISON SENTENCE.
BUT IT SEEMS YOU ARE ILL-EQUIPPED TO HANDLE HIM, EH?
I'M NOT GOING TO WASTE TIME ARGUING WITH YOU, CLOAK. ARE YOU GOING TO HAND HIM OVER?
NO.
BLAST HIM!
THA-SHOOM
THA-SHOOM

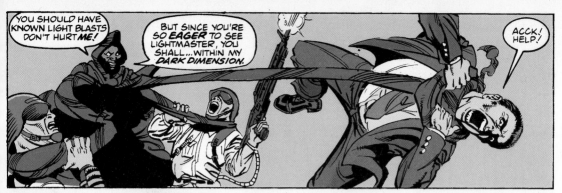

YOU SHOULD HAVE KNOWN LIGHT BLASTS DON'T HURT *ME!*

BUT SINCE YOU'RE SO *EAGER* TO SEE LIGHTMASTER, YOU SHALL...WITHIN MY *DARK DIMENSION.*

ACCK! HELP!

CLOAK--DON'T PULL THEM IN! THERE'S BEEN *ENOUGH* VIOLENCE TODAY.

VERY WELL....

GASP.

HERE, CHADWICK. I HOPE YOU KEEP A TIGHTER REIN ON HIM THIS TIME--

--WHAT'S LEFT OF HIM.

HURRY UP WITH THAT *LIGHT MOLECULAR RECOMBINATOR.* MY SENSORS SHOW THERE ARE STILL *TRACES* OF LIGHTMAS-TER'S LIGHT ENERGY.

WE MAY BE ABLE TO RE-GENERATE HIS CONSCIOUSNESS AND LIGHT FORM BACK AT GENETECH.

I SHOULD HAVE THE TWO OF YOU ARRESTED FOR YOUR INTERFERENCE--!

BUT YOU WON'T. *YOU'RE* NOT OPERATING FULLY WITHIN THE LAW, EITHER, ARE YOU?

WE'LL BE AROUND, CHADWICK. *REMEMBER* THAT.

THE END

WANT MORE *CLOAK AND DAGGER*? SEE UPCOMING ISSUES OF *THE NEW WARRIORS!*

THE HERO KILLERS™
Part 1

FEATURING:

the AMAZING SPIDER-MAN®

"FORTUNE AND STEEL" (THE HERO KILLERS PART 1) .... PAGE 2

WRITER - DAVID MICHELINIE
PENCILER - SCOTT McDANIEL
INKER - KEITH WILLIAMS
LETTERER - STEVE DUTRO
COLORIST - BOB SHAREN

"FIRST KILL, PART ONE" .... PAGE 36

WRITER - DAVID MICHELINIE
ARTIST - AARON LOPRESTI
LETTERER - RICK PARKER
COLORIST - KEVIN TINSLEY

"THE WRONGED MAN" .... PAGE 44

WRITER - ERIC FEIN
PENCILER - SCOTT KOLINS
INKER - SAM DeLaROSA
LETTERER - CHRIS ELIOPOULOS
COLORIST - JOHN KALISZ

"MAKING THE GRADE" .... PAGE 55

WRITERS - TOM BREVOORT
          & MIKE KANTEROVICH
ARTIST - AARON LOPRESTI
LETTERER - DAVE SHARPE
COLORIST - SARRA MOSSOFF

"EVIL'S LIGHT PART ONE, NOW STRIKES THE LIGHTMASTER" .... PAGE 59

WRITER - ERIC FEIN
PENCILER - VINCE EVANS
INKER - DON HUDSON
LETTERER - DAVE SHARPE
COLORIST - JOHN KALISZ

ASSISTANT EDITOR- ERIC FEIN   EDITOR - DANNY FINGEROTH   EDITOR IN CHIEF - TOM DeFALCO

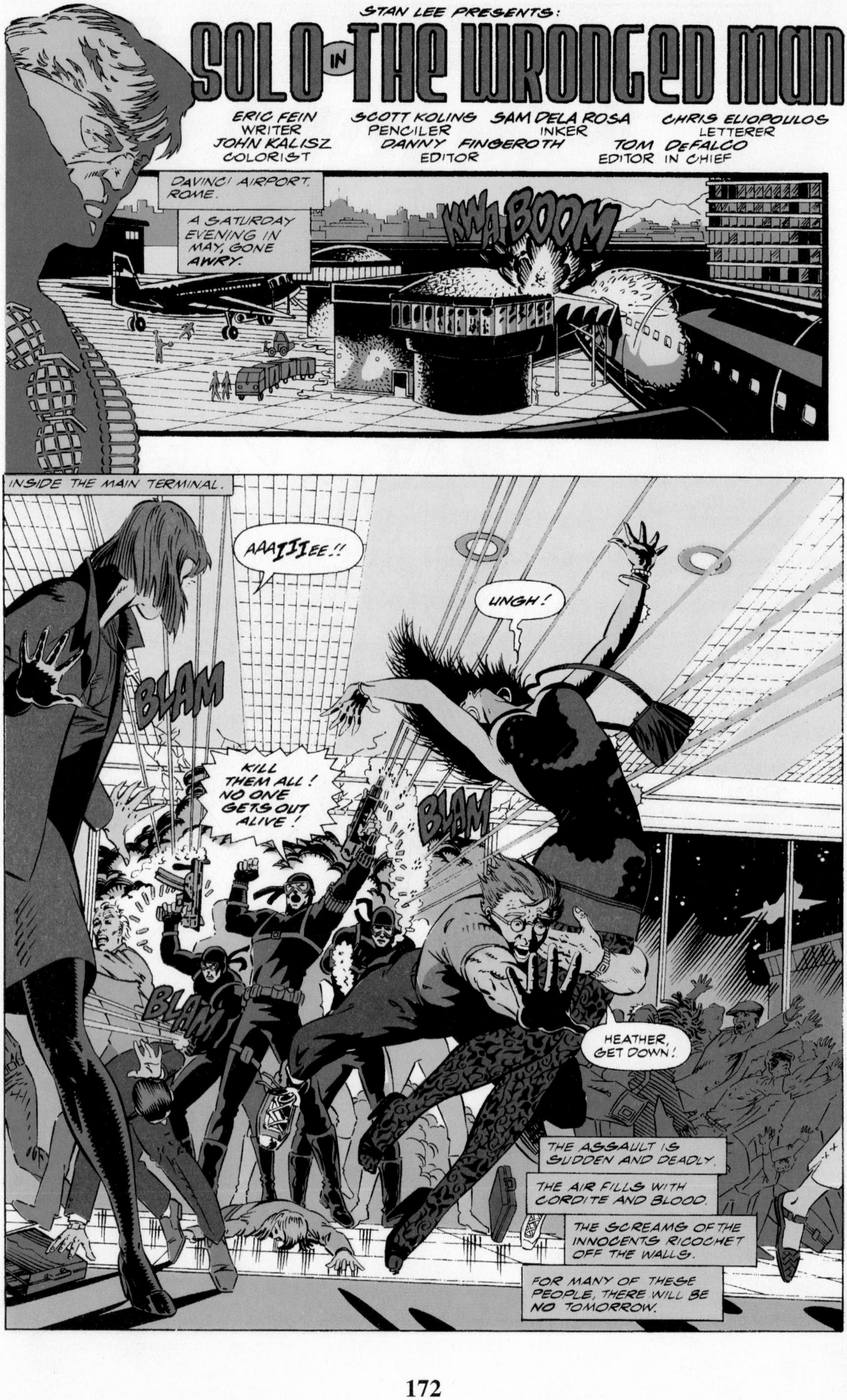
STAN LEE PRESENTS:
SOLO IN THE WRONGED MAN
ERIC FEIN WRITER
SCOTT KOLING PENCILER
SAM DELA ROSA INKER
CHRIS ELIOPOULOS LETTERER
JOHN KALISZ COLORIST
DANNY FINGEROTH EDITOR
TOM DEFALCO EDITOR IN CHIEF
DAVINCI AIRPORT, ROME.
A SATURDAY EVENING IN MAY, GONE AWRY.
KWA BOOM
INSIDE THE MAIN TERMINAL.
AAAIIIEE!!
UNGH!
BLAM
KILL THEM ALL! NO ONE GETS OUT ALIVE!
BLAM
BLAM
HEATHER, GET DOWN!
THE ASSAULT IS SUDDEN AND DEADLY.
THE AIR FILLS WITH CORDITE AND BLOOD.
THE SCREAMS OF THE INNOCENTS RICOCHET OFF THE WALLS.
FOR MANY OF THESE PEOPLE, THERE WILL BE NO TOMORROW.

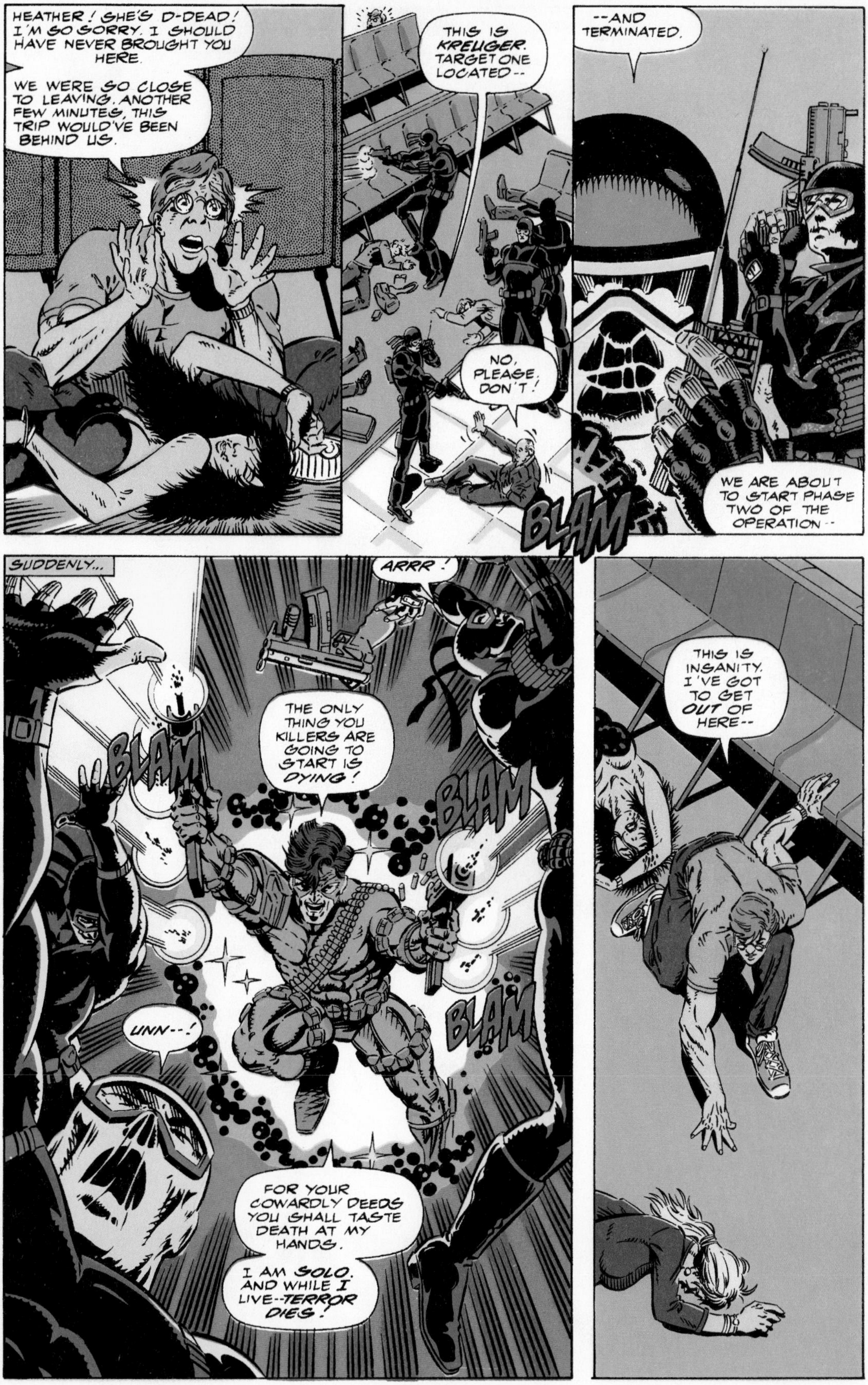

HEATHER! SHE'S D-DEAD! I'M SO SORRY. I SHOULD HAVE NEVER BROUGHT YOU HERE.
WE WERE SO CLOSE TO LEAVING. ANOTHER FEW MINUTES, THIS TRIP WOULD'VE BEEN BEHIND US.
THIS IS KREUGER. TARGET ONE LOCATED--
NO, PLEASE, DON'T!
--AND TERMINATED.
WE ARE ABOUT TO START PHASE TWO OF THE OPERATION--
BLAM
SUDDENLY...
ARRR!
THE ONLY THING YOU KILLERS ARE GOING TO START IS DYING!
BLAM
BLAM
BLAM
UNN--!
FOR YOUR COWARDLY DEEDS YOU SHALL TASTE DEATH AT MY HANDS.
I AM SOLO. AND WHILE I LIVE--TERROR DIES!
THIS IS INSANITY. I'VE GOT TO GET OUT OF HERE--

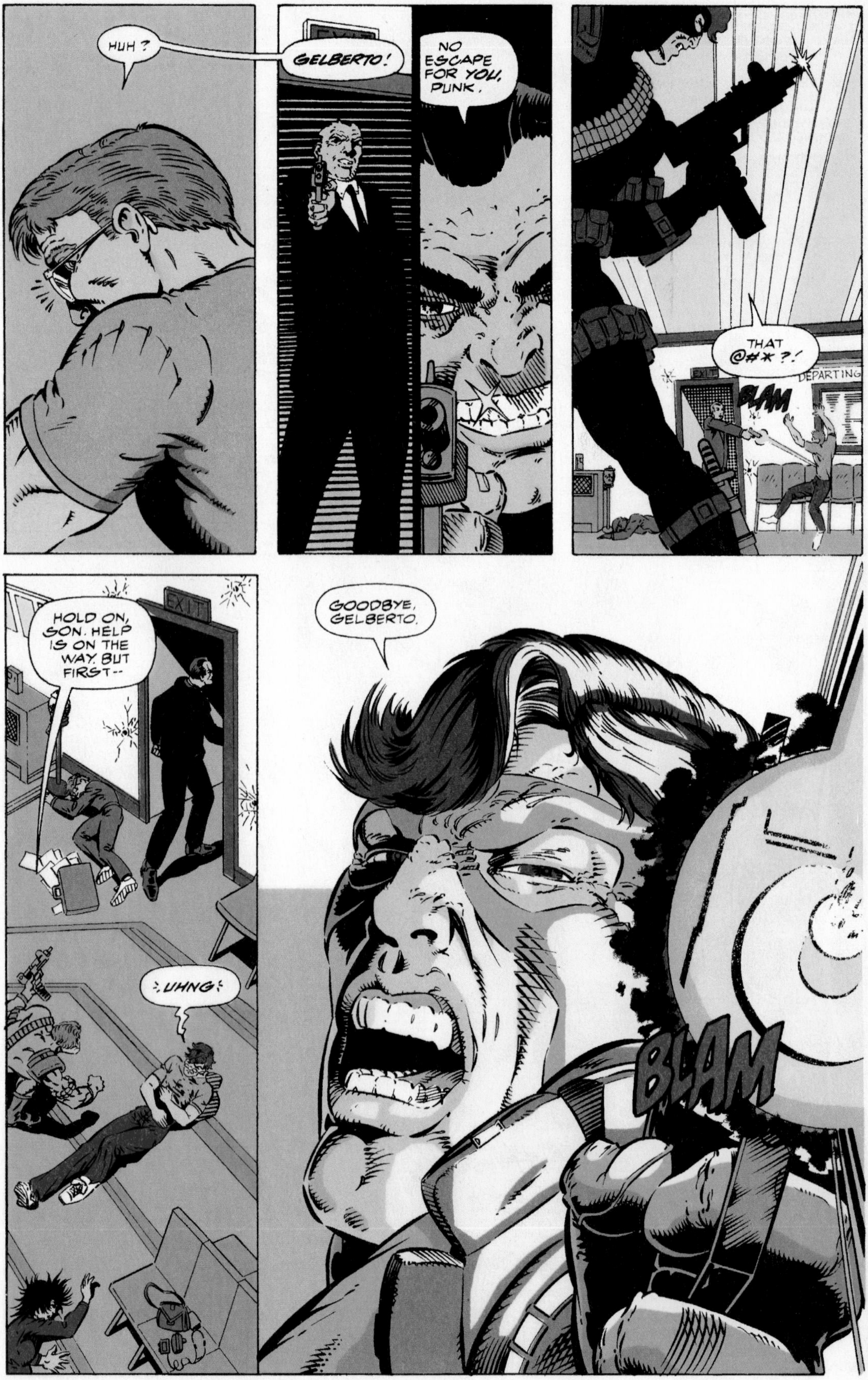
HUH ?
GELBERTO!
NO ESCAPE FOR YOU, PUNK.
THAT @#*?!
EXIT
DEPARTING
BLAM
EXIT
HOLD ON, SON. HELP IS ON THE WAY. BUT FIRST--
UHNG
GOODBYE, GELBERTO.
BLAM

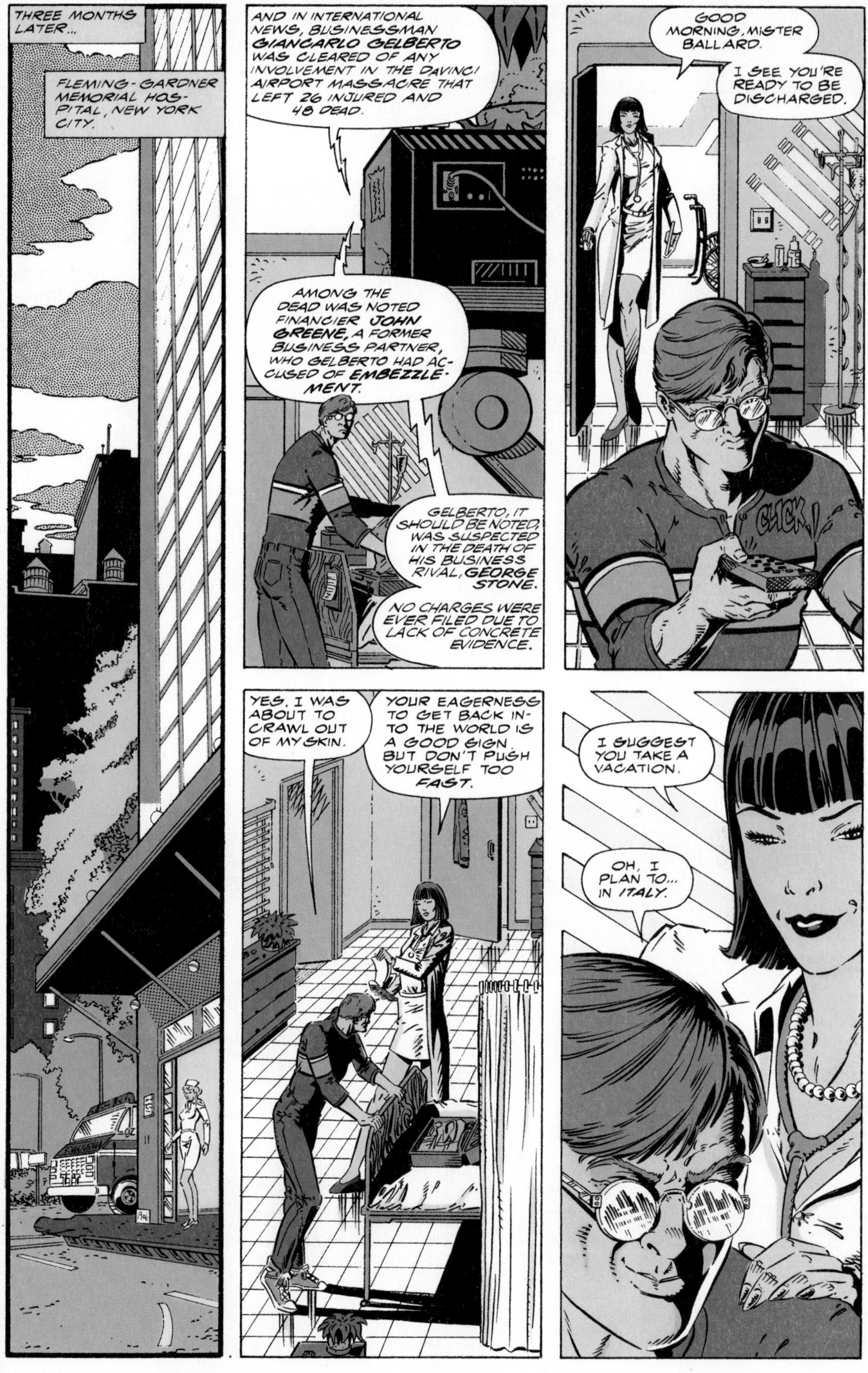

THREE MONTHS LATER...
FLEMING-GARDNER MEMORIAL HOSPITAL, NEW YORK CITY.
AND IN INTERNATIONAL NEWS, BUSINESSMAN GIANCARLO GELBERTO WAS CLEARED OF ANY INVOLVEMENT IN THE DAVINCI AIRPORT MASSACRE THAT LEFT 26 INJURED AND 48 DEAD.
AMONG THE DEAD WAS NOTED FINANCIER JOHN GREENE, A FORMER BUSINESS PARTNER, WHO GELBERTO HAD ACCUSED OF EMBEZZLEMENT.
GELBERTO, IT SHOULD BE NOTED, WAS SUSPECTED IN THE DEATH OF HIS BUSINESS RIVAL, GEORGE STONE.
NO CHARGES WERE EVER FILED DUE TO LACK OF CONCRETE EVIDENCE.
GOOD MORNING, MISTER BALLARD.
I SEE YOU'RE READY TO BE DISCHARGED.
CLICK!
YES. I WAS ABOUT TO CRAWL OUT OF MY SKIN.
YOUR EAGERNESS TO GET BACK INTO THE WORLD IS A GOOD SIGN BUT DON'T PUSH YOURSELF TOO FAST.
I SUGGEST YOU TAKE A VACATION.
OH, I PLAN TO... IN ITALY.

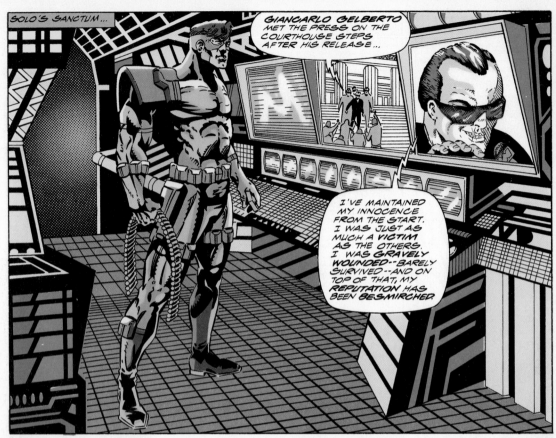

SOLO'S SANCTUM...

GIANCARLO GELBERTO MET THE PRESS ON THE COURTHOUSE STEPS AFTER HIS RELEASE...

I'VE MAINTAINED MY INNOCENCE FROM THE START. I WAS JUST AS MUCH A VICTIM AS THE OTHERS. I WAS GRAVELY WOUNDED--BARELY SURVIVED--AND ON TOP OF THAT, MY REPUTATION HAS BEEN BESMIRCHED.

I HAVE SUFFERED TERRIBLE WRONGS.

I SHOULD HAVE KNOWN THAT SLIME LIKE HIM WOULD HAVE TAKEN PRECAUTIONS-- BULLET PROOF VEST MOST LIKELY.

IF I DIDN'T HAVE TO TAKE BALLARD TO THE HOSPITAL...

AND LET ME TAKE THIS OPPORTUNITY TO ONCE AGAIN STATE THAT I AM INNOCENT. I WOULD NEVER KNOWINGLY HARM ANOTHER PERSON--

CLICK

THERE IS SOMETHING VERY STRANGE GOING ON HERE AND I PLAN TO FIND OUT WHAT IT IS.

AND WITH A MERE THOUGHT, SOLO TELEPORTS HIM- SELF AWAY...

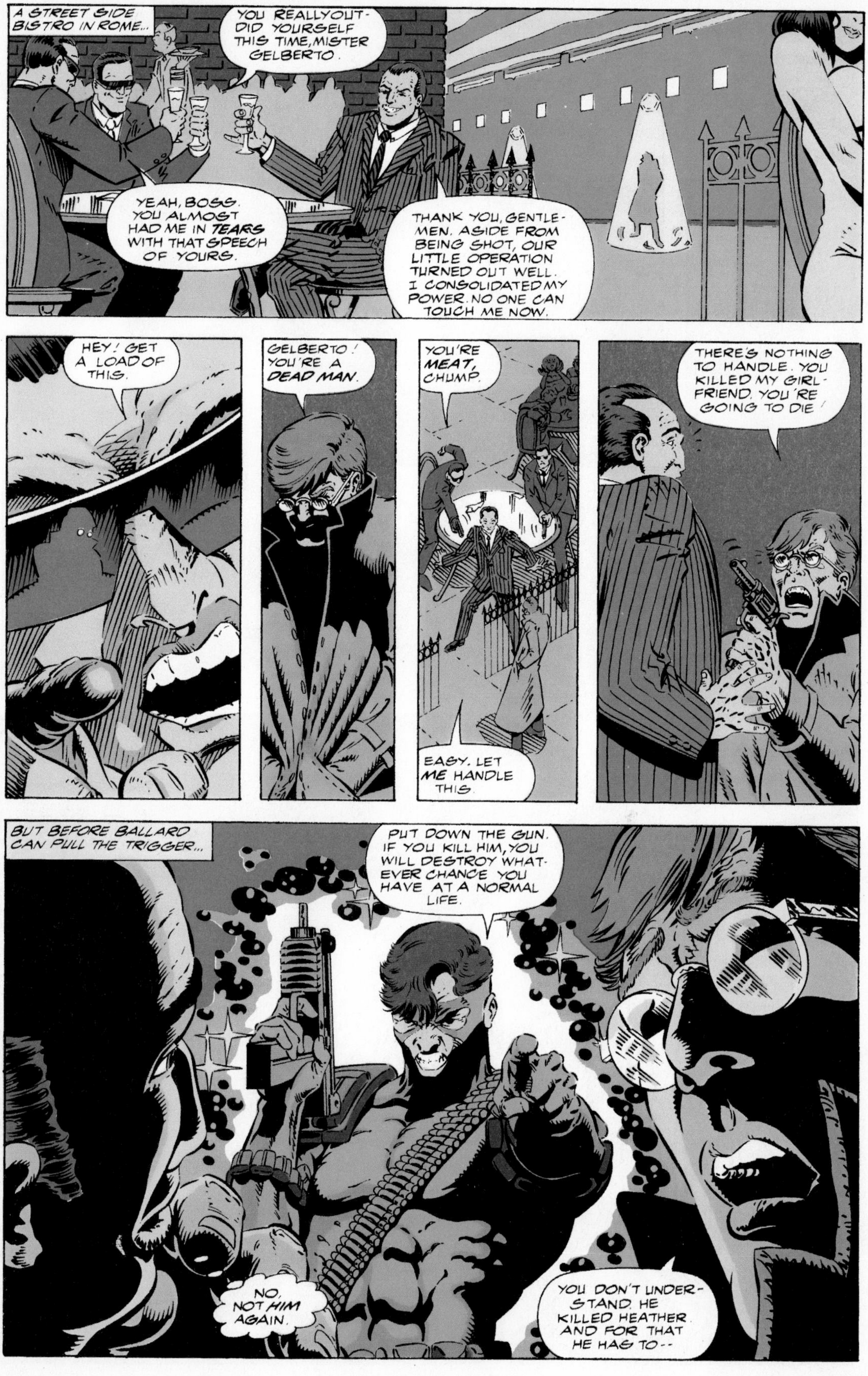

A STREET SIDE BISTRO IN ROME...
YOU REALLY OUT-DID YOURSELF THIS TIME, MISTER GELBERTO.
YEAH, BOSS. YOU ALMOST HAD ME IN TEARS WITH THAT SPEECH OF YOURS.
THANK YOU, GENTLEMEN. ASIDE FROM BEING SHOT, OUR LITTLE OPERATION TURNED OUT WELL. I CONSOLIDATED MY POWER. NO ONE CAN TOUCH ME NOW.
HEY! GET A LOAD OF THIS.
GELBERTO! YOU'RE A DEAD MAN.
YOU'RE MEAT, CHUMP.
EASY. LET ME HANDLE THIS.
THERE'S NOTHING TO HANDLE. YOU KILLED MY GIRLFRIEND. YOU'RE GOING TO DIE!
BUT BEFORE BALLARD CAN PULL THE TRIGGER...
PUT DOWN THE GUN. IF YOU KILL HIM, YOU WILL DESTROY WHATEVER CHANCE YOU HAVE AT A NORMAL LIFE.
NO, NOT HIM AGAIN.
YOU DON'T UNDERSTAND. HE KILLED HEATHER. AND FOR THAT HE HAS TO--

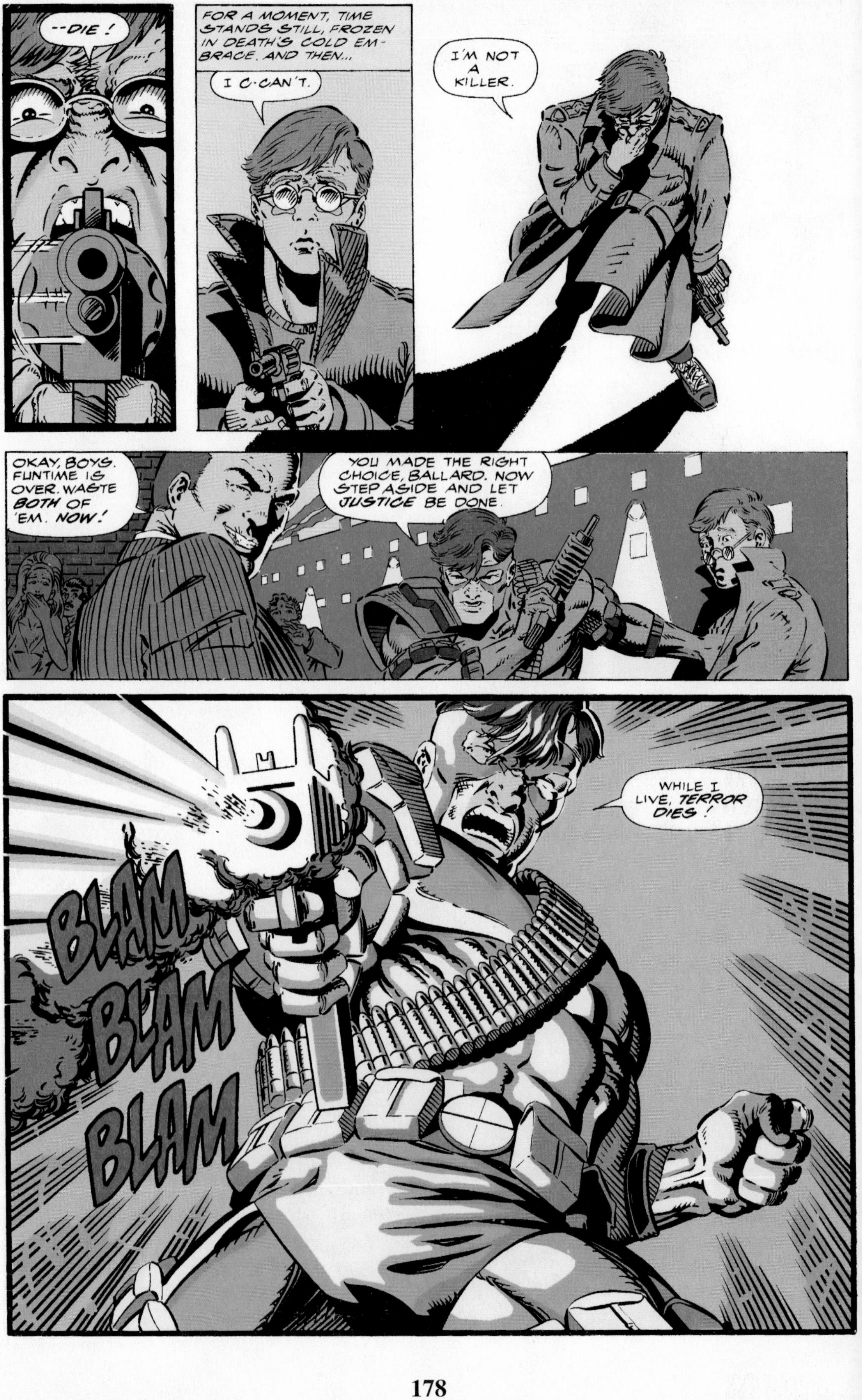
--DIE!
FOR A MOMENT, TIME STANDS STILL, FROZEN IN DEATH'S COLD EMBRACE. AND THEN...
I C-CAN'T.
I'M NOT A KILLER.
OKAY, BOYS. FUNTIME IS OVER. WASTE BOTH OF 'EM. NOW!
YOU MADE THE RIGHT CHOICE, BALLARD. NOW STEP ASIDE AND LET JUSTICE BE DONE.
WHILE I LIVE, TERROR DIES!
BLAM
BLAM
BLAM

YOU-- YOU *KILLED THEM ALL.*

THEY WERE GOING TO DO THE SAME TO *US.* THESE MEN WERE *EVIL.* THEY RESORTED TO *TERRORISM* TO ACHIEVE THEIR BUSINESS GOALS.

THEY *DESERVED* DEATH.

BUT *YOU'RE* NOT INNOCENT, EITHER. ARE YOU?

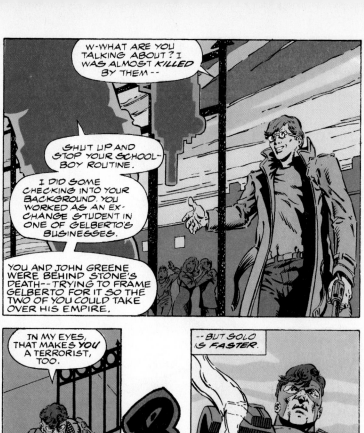

W-WHAT ARE YOU TALKING ABOUT? I WAS ALMOST *KILLED* BY THEM--

SHUT UP AND STOP YOUR SCHOOL-BOY ROUTINE.

I DID SOME CHECKING INTO YOUR BACKGROUND. YOU WORKED AS AN EXCHANGE STUDENT IN ONE OF *GELBERTO'S* BUSINESSES.

YOU AND JOHN GREENE WERE BEHIND STONE'S DEATH-- TRYING TO FRAME GELBERTO FOR IT SO THE TWO OF YOU COULD TAKE OVER HIS EMPIRE.

IN MY EYES, THAT MAKES *YOU* A TERRORIST, TOO.

NO.

BALLARD IS FAST--

BLAMM

-- BUT SOLO IS *FASTER.*

SOLO LOOKS INTO THE DYING MAN'S EYES. THERE IS NO REGRET. JUST COLD, HARD ANGER.

IT IS SOMETHING HE HAS SEEN BEFORE. AND KNOWS HE WILL SEE AGAIN.

-- THE END.

179

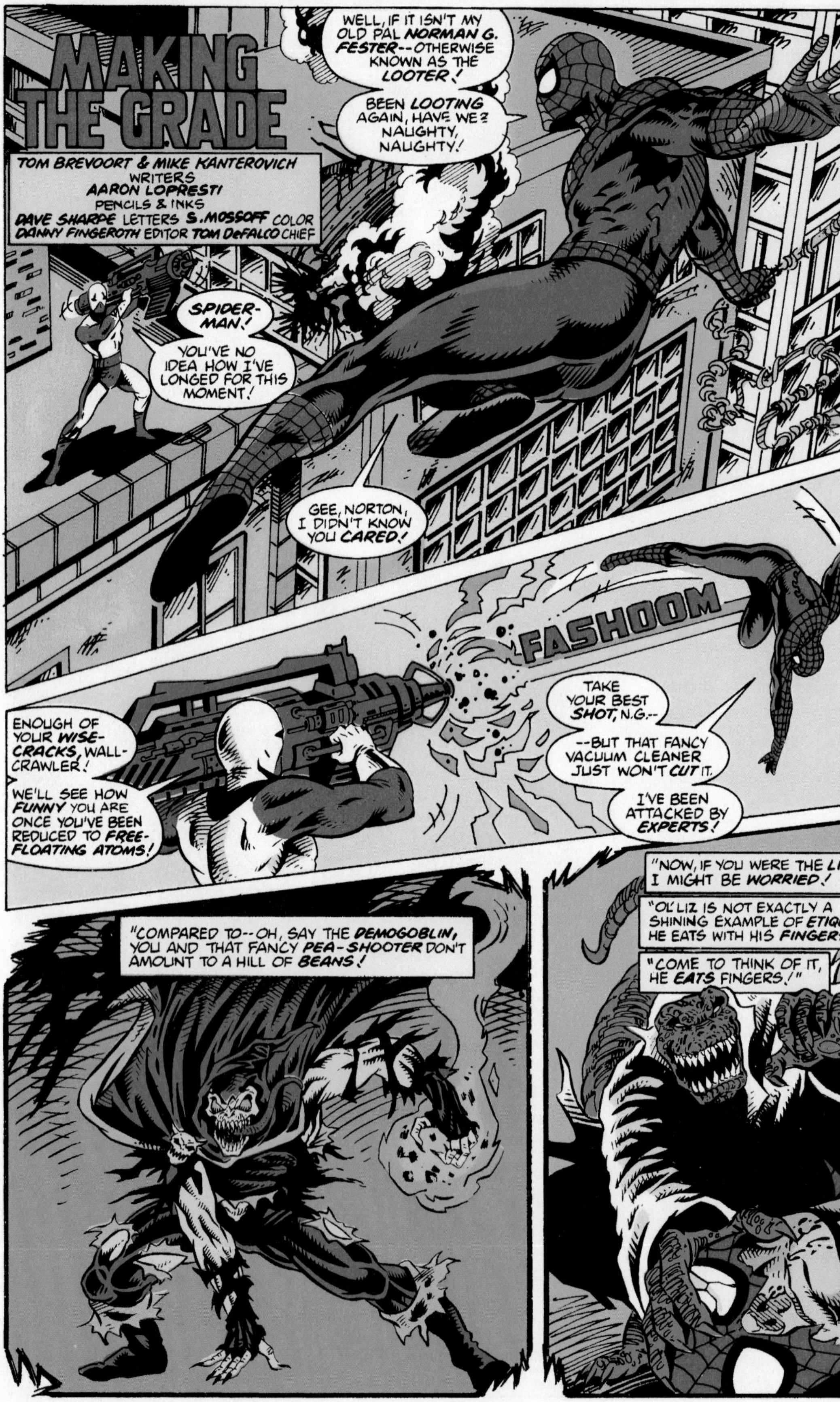
MAKING THE GRADE
TOM BREVOORT & MIKE KANTEROVICH WRITERS
AARON LOPRESTI PENCILS & INKS
DAVE SHARPE LETTERS S. MOSSOFF COLOR
DANNY FINGEROTH EDITOR TOM DeFALCO CHIEF
WELL, IF IT ISN'T MY OLD PAL NORMAN G. FESTER--OTHERWISE KNOWN AS THE LOOTER!
BEEN LOOTING AGAIN, HAVE WE? NAUGHTY, NAUGHTY!
SPIDER-MAN!
YOU'VE NO IDEA HOW I'VE LONGED FOR THIS MOMENT!
GEE, NORTON, I DIDN'T KNOW YOU CARED!
FASHOOM
ENOUGH OF YOUR WISE-CRACKS, WALL-CRAWLER!
WE'LL SEE HOW FUNNY YOU ARE ONCE YOU'VE BEEN REDUCED TO FREE-FLOATING ATOMS!
TAKE YOUR BEST SHOT, N.G.--
--BUT THAT FANCY VACUUM CLEANER JUST WON'T CUT IT.
I'VE BEEN ATTACKED BY EXPERTS!
"COMPARED TO--OH, SAY THE DEMOGOBLIN, YOU AND THAT FANCY PEA-SHOOTER DON'T AMOUNT TO A HILL OF BEANS!
"NOW, IF YOU WERE THE LIZARD, I MIGHT BE WORRIED!
"OL' LIZ IS NOT EXACTLY A SHINING EXAMPLE OF ETIQUETTE. HE EATS WITH HIS FINGERS!
"COME TO THINK OF IT, HE EATS FINGERS!"

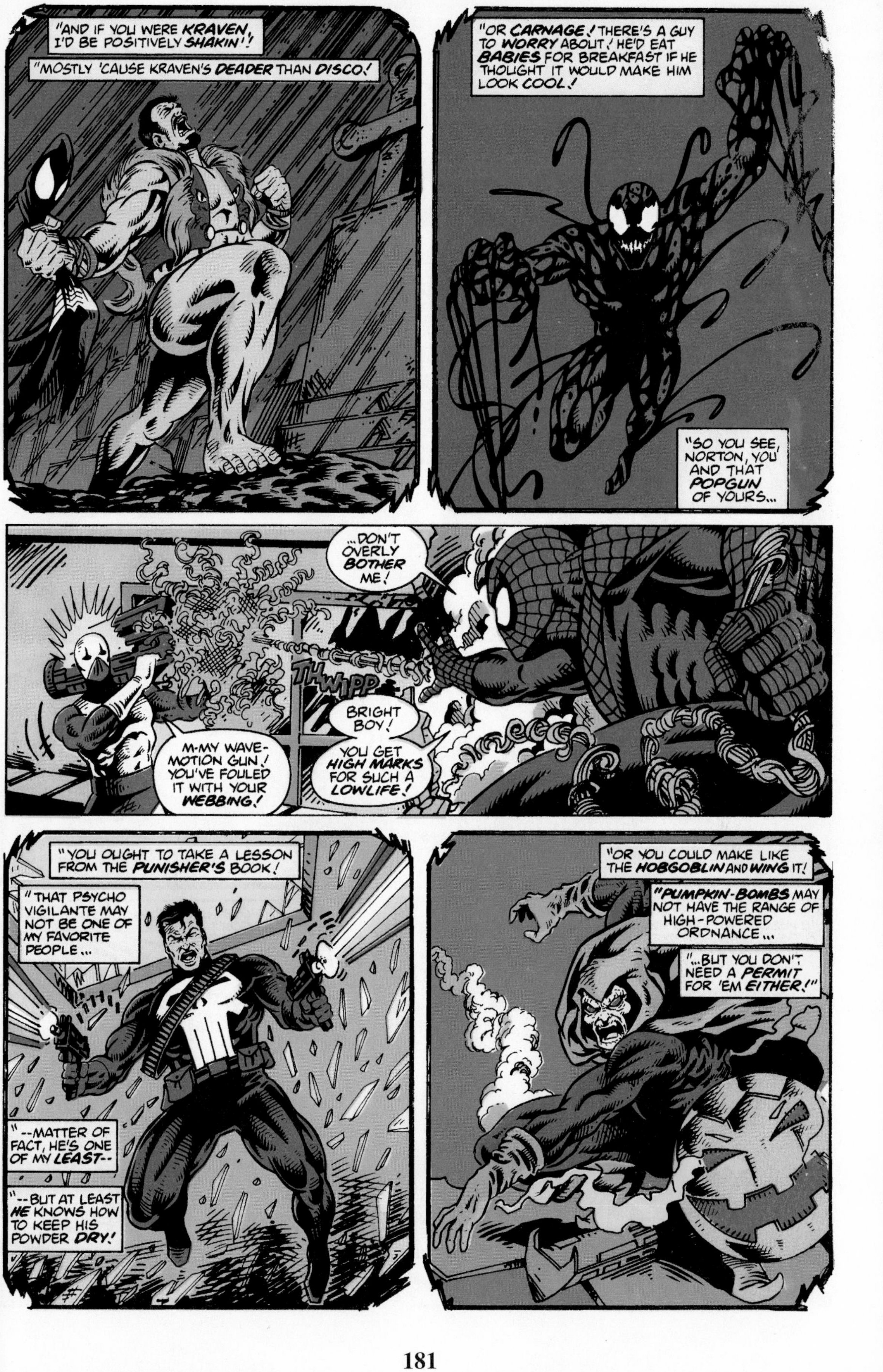
"AND IF YOU WERE KRAVEN, I'D BE POSITIVELY SHAKIN'!
"MOSTLY 'CAUSE KRAVEN'S DEADER THAN DISCO!
"OR CARNAGE! THERE'S A GUY TO WORRY ABOUT! HE'D EAT BABIES FOR BREAKFAST IF HE THOUGHT IT WOULD MAKE HIM LOOK COOL!
"SO YOU SEE, NORTON, YOU AND THAT POPGUN OF YOURS...
...DON'T OVERLY BOTHER ME!
THWIPP
M-MY WAVE-MOTION GUN! YOU'VE FOULED IT WITH YOUR WEBBING!
BRIGHT BOY!
YOU GET HIGH MARKS FOR SUCH A LOWLIFE!
"YOU OUGHT TO TAKE A LESSON FROM THE PUNISHER'S BOOK!
"THAT PSYCHO VIGILANTE MAY NOT BE ONE OF MY FAVORITE PEOPLE...
"--MATTER OF FACT, HE'S ONE OF MY LEAST--
"--BUT AT LEAST HE KNOWS HOW TO KEEP HIS POWDER DRY!
"OR YOU COULD MAKE LIKE THE HOBGOBLIN AND WING IT!
"PUMPKIN-BOMBS MAY NOT HAVE THE RANGE OF HIGH-POWERED ORDNANCE...
"...BUT YOU DON'T NEED A PERMIT FOR 'EM EITHER!"

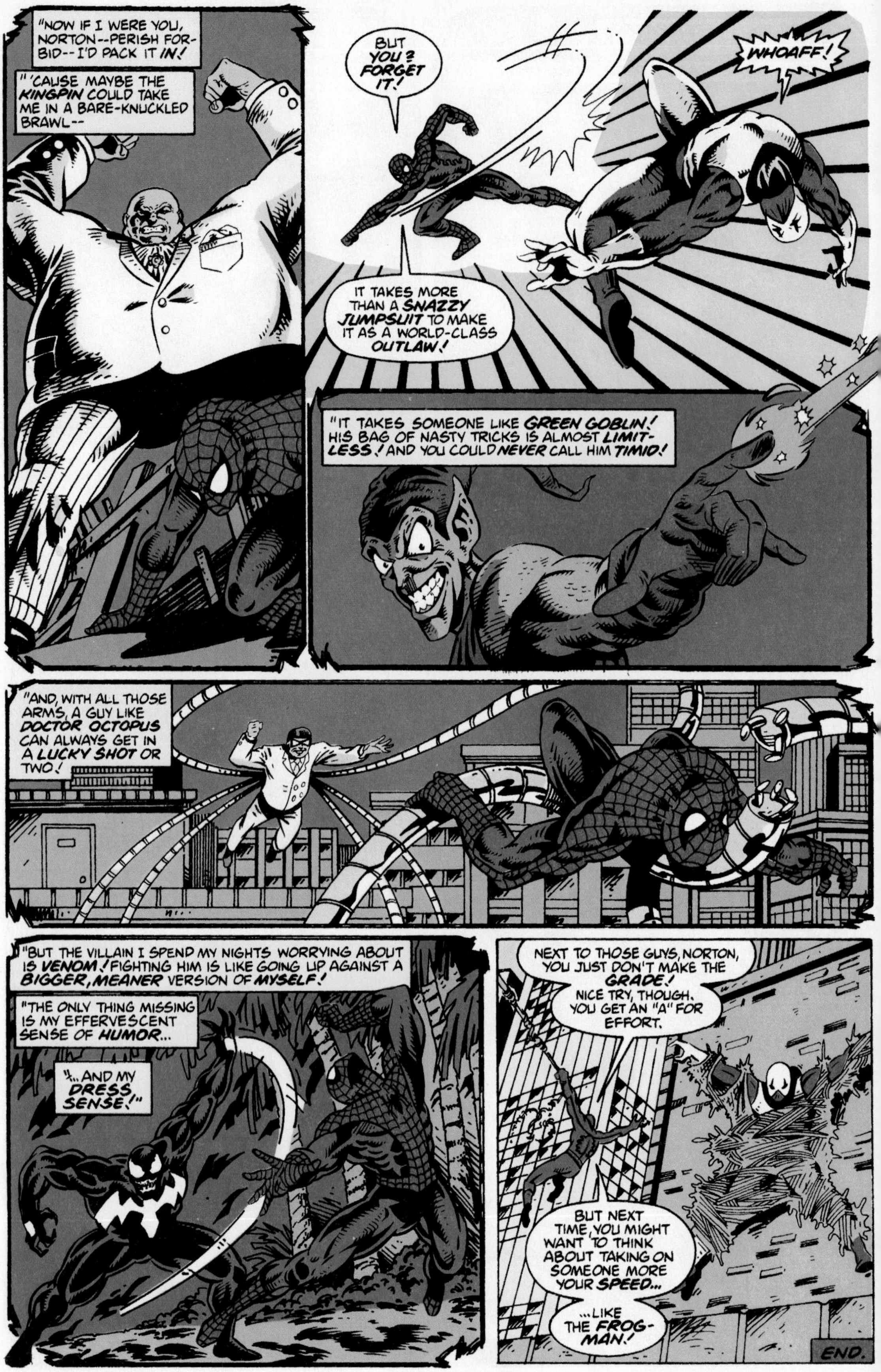
"NOW IF I WERE YOU, NORTON--PERISH FORBID--I'D PACK IT IN!
"'CAUSE MAYBE THE KINGPIN COULD TAKE ME IN A BARE-KNUCKLED BRAWL--
BUT YOU? FORGET IT!
WHOAFF!
IT TAKES MORE THAN A SNAZZY JUMPSUIT TO MAKE IT AS A WORLD-CLASS OUTLAW!
"IT TAKES SOMEONE LIKE GREEN GOBLIN! HIS BAG OF NASTY TRICKS IS ALMOST LIMITLESS! AND YOU COULD NEVER CALL HIM TIMID!
"AND, WITH ALL THOSE ARMS, A GUY LIKE DOCTOR OCTOPUS CAN ALWAYS GET IN A LUCKY SHOT OR TWO!
"BUT THE VILLAIN I SPEND MY NIGHTS WORRYING ABOUT IS VENOM! FIGHTING HIM IS LIKE GOING UP AGAINST A BIGGER, MEANER VERSION OF MYSELF!
"THE ONLY THING MISSING IS MY EFFERVESCENT SENSE OF HUMOR...
"...AND MY DRESS SENSE!"
NEXT TO THOSE GUYS, NORTON, YOU JUST DON'T MAKE THE GRADE! NICE TRY, THOUGH. YOU GET AN "A" FOR EFFORT.
BUT NEXT TIME, YOU MIGHT WANT TO THINK ABOUT TAKING ON SOMEONE MORE YOUR SPEED...
...LIKE THE FROG-MAN!
END.

THE HERO KILLERS ™
Part 2

FEATURING:

the SPECTACULAR SPIDER-MAN ®

"DOWN AND DOWNER" (THE HERO KILLERS PART 2) .... PAGE 2

WRITER - DAVID MICHELINIE
PENCILER - SCOTT McDANIEL
INKER - KEITH WILLIAMS
LETTERER - STEVE DUTRO
COLORIST - BOB SHAREN

"FIRST KILL, PART TWO" .... PAGE 36

WRITER - DAVID MICHELINIE
PENCILER - AARON LOPRESTI
INKER - BRUCE JONES
LETTEREER - RICK PARKER
COLORIST - KEVIN TINSLEY

"SONS OF THE TIGER" .... PAGE 44

WRITER - GLENN HERDLING
PENCILER - TOD SMITH
INKER - DON HUDSON
LETTERER - JON BABCOCK
COLORIST - MARIE JAVINS

"TEN MOST EMBARRASSING MOMENTS" .... PAGE 55

WRITERS - TOM BREVOORT
          & MIKE KANTEROVICH
ARTIST - AARON LOPRESTI
LETTERER - DAVID SHARPE
COLORIST - SARRA MOSSOFF

"EVIL'S LIGHT PART ONE THE HUNT BEGINS" .... PAGE 59

WRITER - ERIC FEIN
PENCILER - VINCE EVANS
INKER - DON HUDSON
LETTERER - DAVID SHARPE
COLORIST - JOHN KALISZ

ASSISTANT EDITOR - ERIC FEIN   EDITOR - DANNY FINGEROTH   EDITOR IN CHIEF - TOM DeFALCO

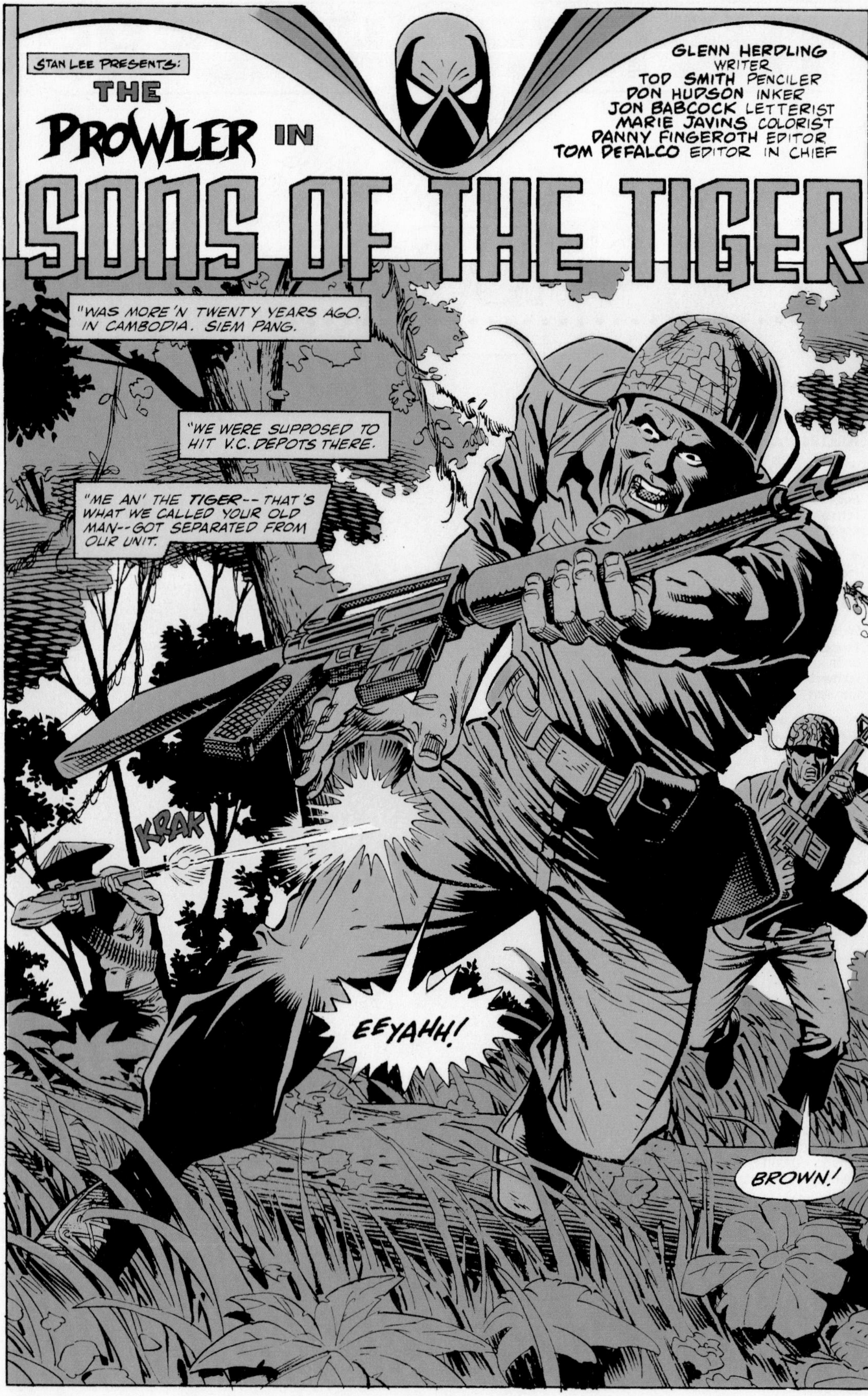
STAN LEE PRESENTS:
THE PROWLER IN
SONS OF THE TIGER
GLENN HERDLING WRITER
TOD SMITH PENCILER
DON HUDSON INKER
JON BABCOCK LETTERIST
MARIE JAVINS COLORIST
DANNY FINGEROTH EDITOR
TOM DEFALCO EDITOR IN CHIEF
"WAS MORE'N TWENTY YEARS AGO. IN CAMBODIA. SIEM PANG.
"WE WERE SUPPOSED TO HIT V.C. DEPOTS THERE.
"ME AN' THE TIGER-- THAT'S WHAT WE CALLED YOUR OLD MAN--GOT SEPARATED FROM OUR UNIT.
KRAK
EEYAHH!
BROWN!

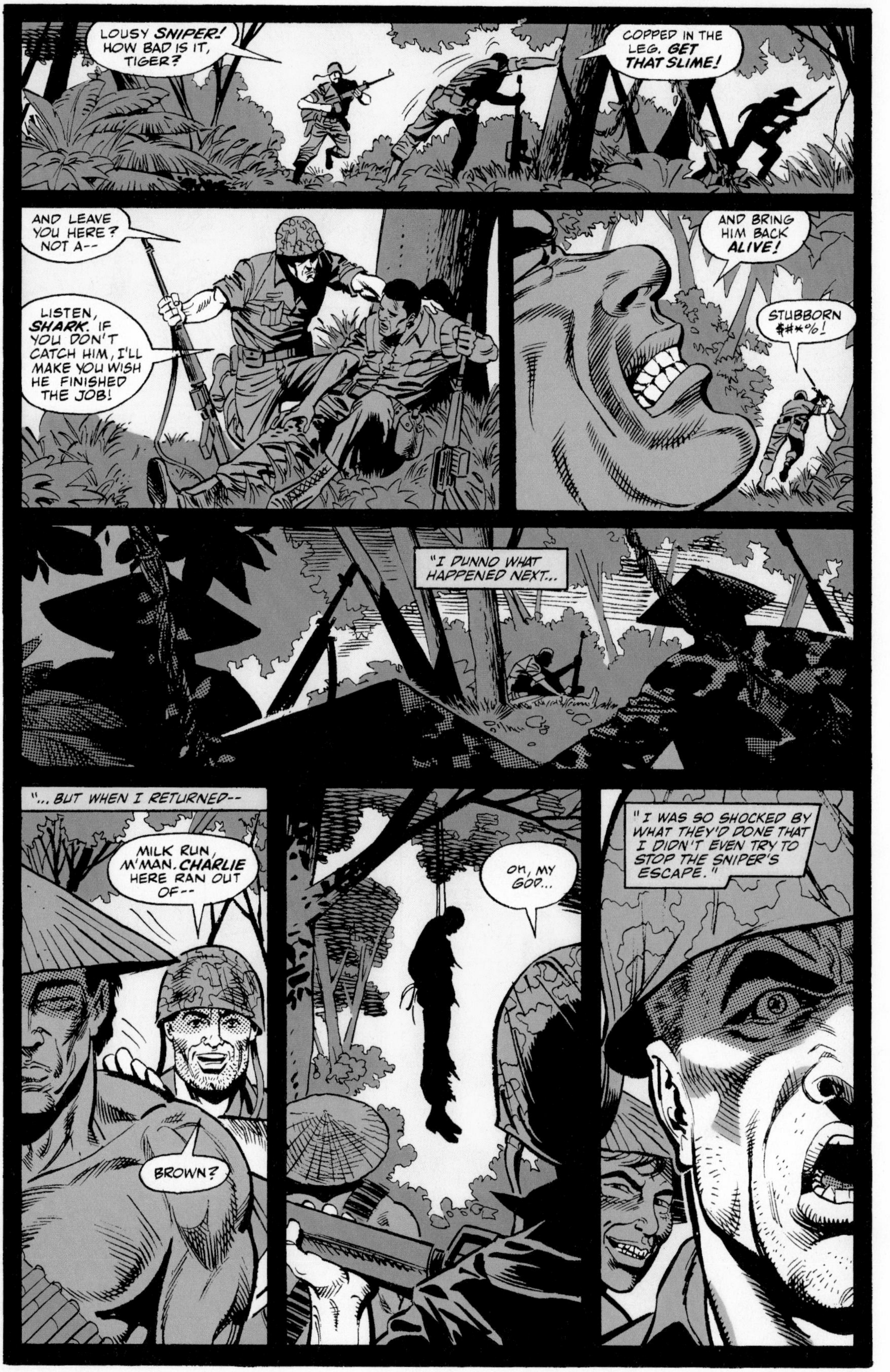
LOUSY SNIPER! HOW BAD IS IT, TIGER?
COPPED IN THE LEG. GET THAT SLIME!
AND LEAVE YOU HERE? NOT A--
LISTEN, SHARK. IF YOU DON'T CATCH HIM, I'LL MAKE YOU WISH HE FINISHED THE JOB!
AND BRING HIM BACK ALIVE!
STUBBORN $#*%!
"I DUNNO WHAT HAPPENED NEXT...
"... BUT WHEN I RETURNED--
MILK RUN, M'MAN. CHARLIE HERE RAN OUT OF--
BROWN?
OH, MY GOD...
"I WAS SO SHOCKED BY WHAT THEY'D DONE THAT I DIDN'T EVEN TRY TO STOP THE SNIPER'S ESCAPE."

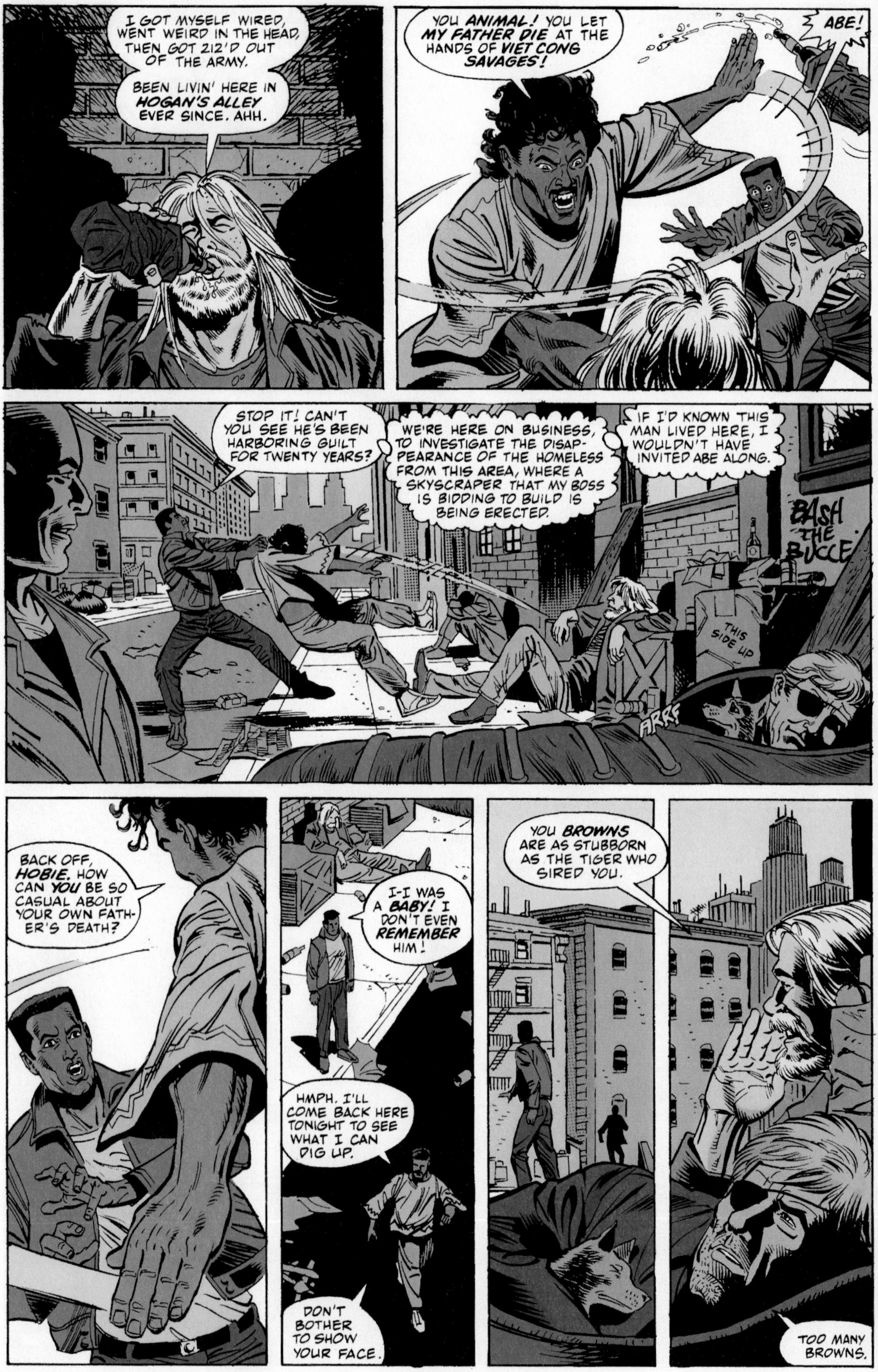
I GOT MYSELF WIRED, WENT WEIRD IN THE HEAD, THEN GOT 212'D OUT OF THE ARMY.
BEEN LIVIN' HERE IN HOGAN'S ALLEY EVER SINCE. AHH.
YOU ANIMAL! YOU LET MY FATHER DIE AT THE HANDS OF VIET CONG SAVAGES!
ABE!
STOP IT! CAN'T YOU SEE HE'S BEEN HARBORING GUILT FOR TWENTY YEARS?
WE'RE HERE ON BUSINESS, TO INVESTIGATE THE DISAPPEARANCE OF THE HOMELESS FROM THIS AREA, WHERE A SKYSCRAPER THAT MY BOSS IS BIDDING TO BUILD IS BEING ERECTED.
IF I'D KNOWN THIS MAN LIVED HERE, I WOULDN'T HAVE INVITED ABE ALONG.
BASH THE BUCCE
THIS SIDE UP
ARRF
BACK OFF, HOBIE. HOW CAN YOU BE SO CASUAL ABOUT YOUR OWN FATHER'S DEATH?
I-I WAS A BABY! I DON'T EVEN REMEMBER HIM!
HMPH. I'LL COME BACK HERE TONIGHT TO SEE WHAT I CAN DIG UP.
DON'T BOTHER TO SHOW YOUR FACE.
YOU BROWNS ARE AS STUBBORN AS THE TIGER WHO SIRED YOU.
TOO MANY BROWNS.

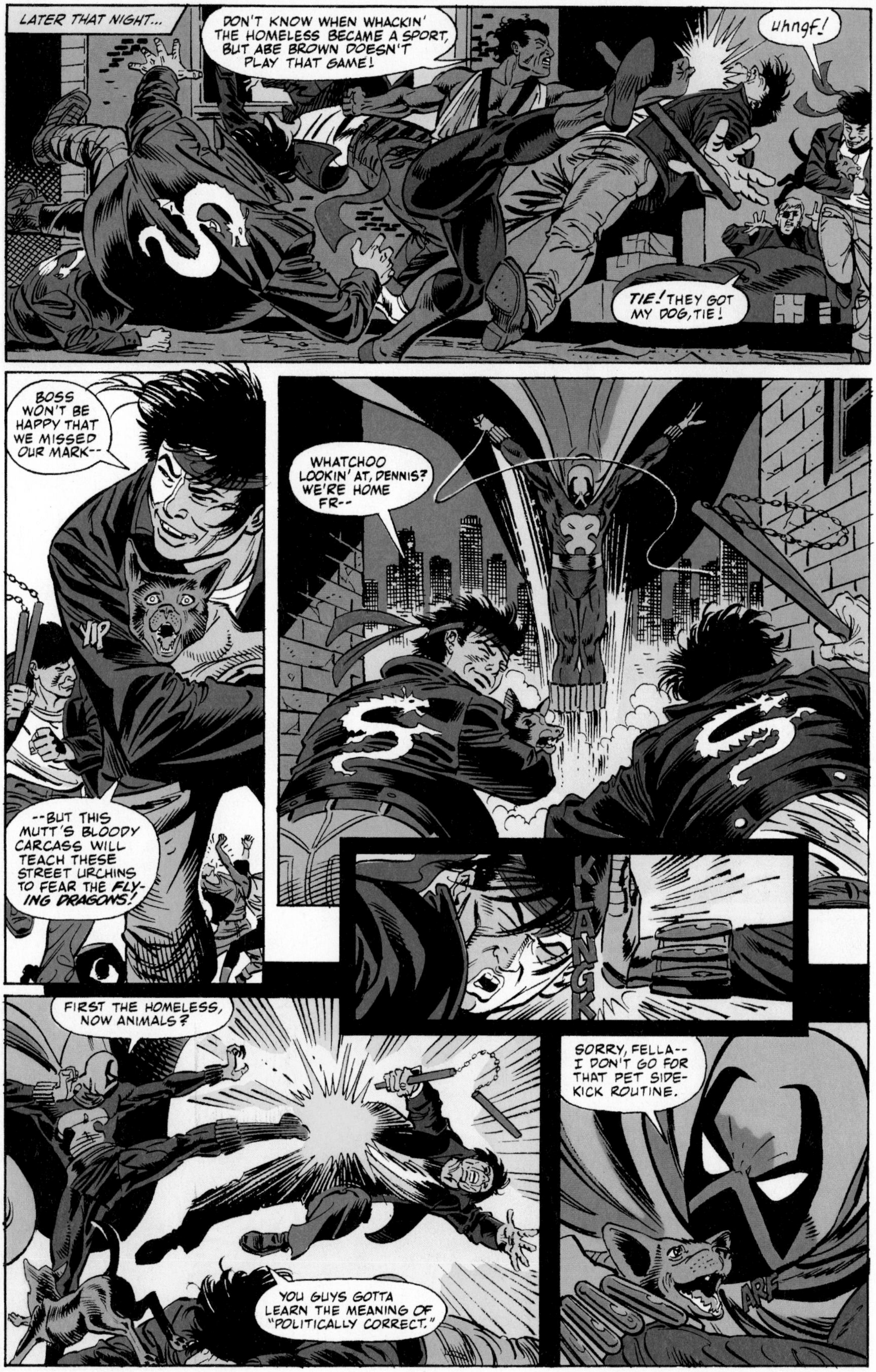

LATER THAT NIGHT...
DON'T KNOW WHEN WHACKIN' THE HOMELESS BECAME A SPORT, BUT ABE BROWN DOESN'T PLAY THAT GAME!
uhngf!
TIE! THEY GOT MY DOG, TIE!
BOSS WON'T BE HAPPY THAT WE MISSED OUR MARK--
YIP
--BUT THIS MUTT'S BLOODY CARCASS WILL TEACH THESE STREET URCHINS TO FEAR THE FLYING DRAGONS!
WHATCHOO LOOKIN' AT, DENNIS? WE'RE HOME FR--
KLANGK
FIRST THE HOMELESS, NOW ANIMALS?
YOU GUYS GOTTA LEARN THE MEANING OF "POLITICALLY CORRECT."
SORRY, FELLA-- I DON'T GO FOR THAT PET SIDE-KICK ROUTINE.
ARF

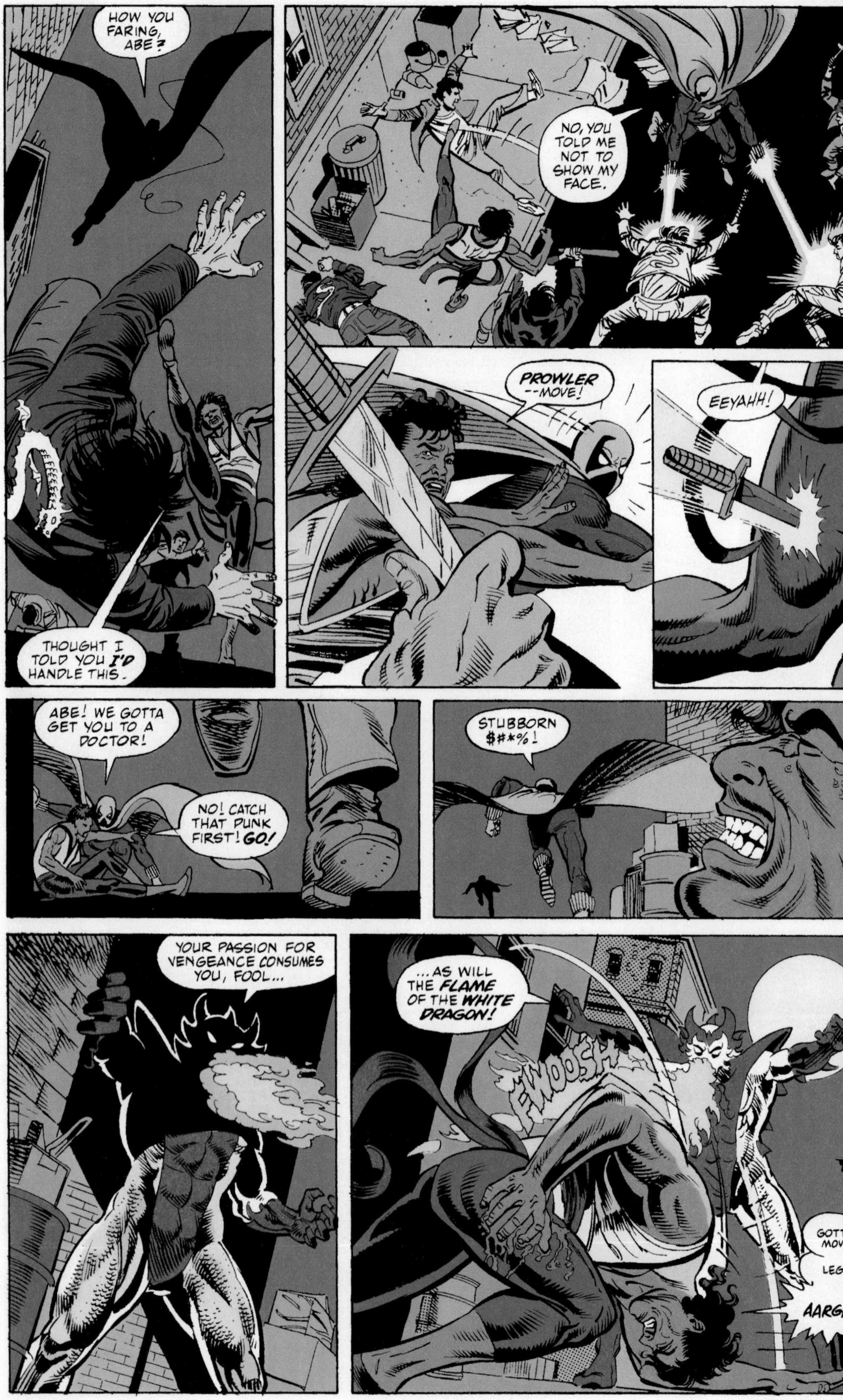

HOW YOU FARING, ABE?
THOUGHT I TOLD YOU I'D HANDLE THIS.
NO, YOU TOLD ME NOT TO SHOW MY FACE.
PROWLER --MOVE!
EEYAHH!
ABE! WE GOTTA GET YOU TO A DOCTOR!
NO! CATCH THAT PUNK FIRST! GO!
STUBBORN $#*%!
YOUR PASSION FOR VENGEANCE CONSUMES YOU, FOOL...
...AS WILL THE FLAME OF THE WHITE DRAGON!
FWOOSH
GOTTA MOVE.
LEG--
AARGH!

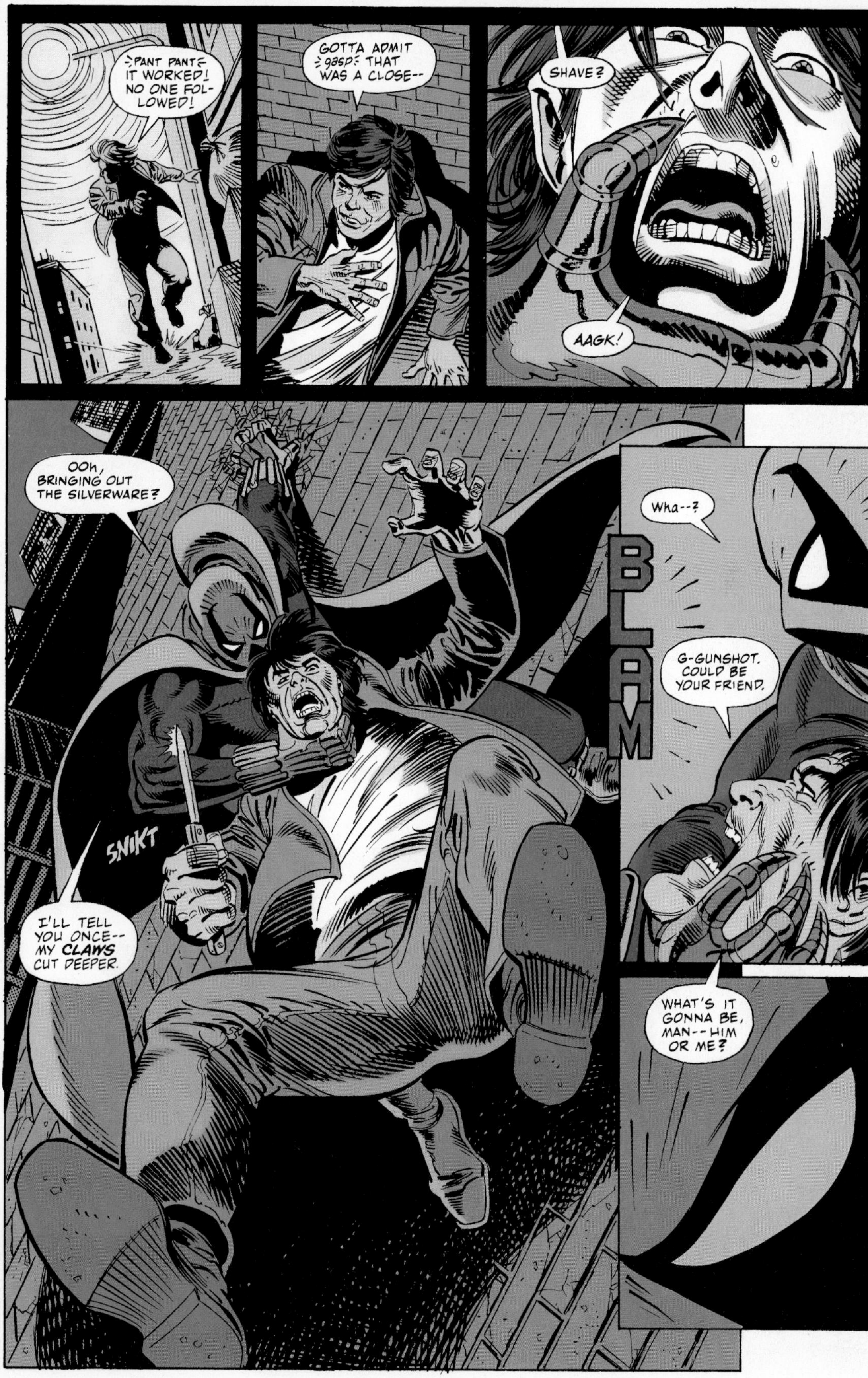
PANT PANT
IT WORKED! NO ONE FOLLOWED!
GOTTA ADMIT gasp THAT WAS A CLOSE--
SHAVE?
AAGK!
OOh, BRINGING OUT THE SILVERWARE?
SNIKT
I'LL TELL YOU ONCE-- MY CLAWS CUT DEEPER.
Wha--?
BLAM
G-GUNSHOT. COULD BE YOUR FRIEND.
WHAT'S IT GONNA BE, MAN-- HIM OR ME?

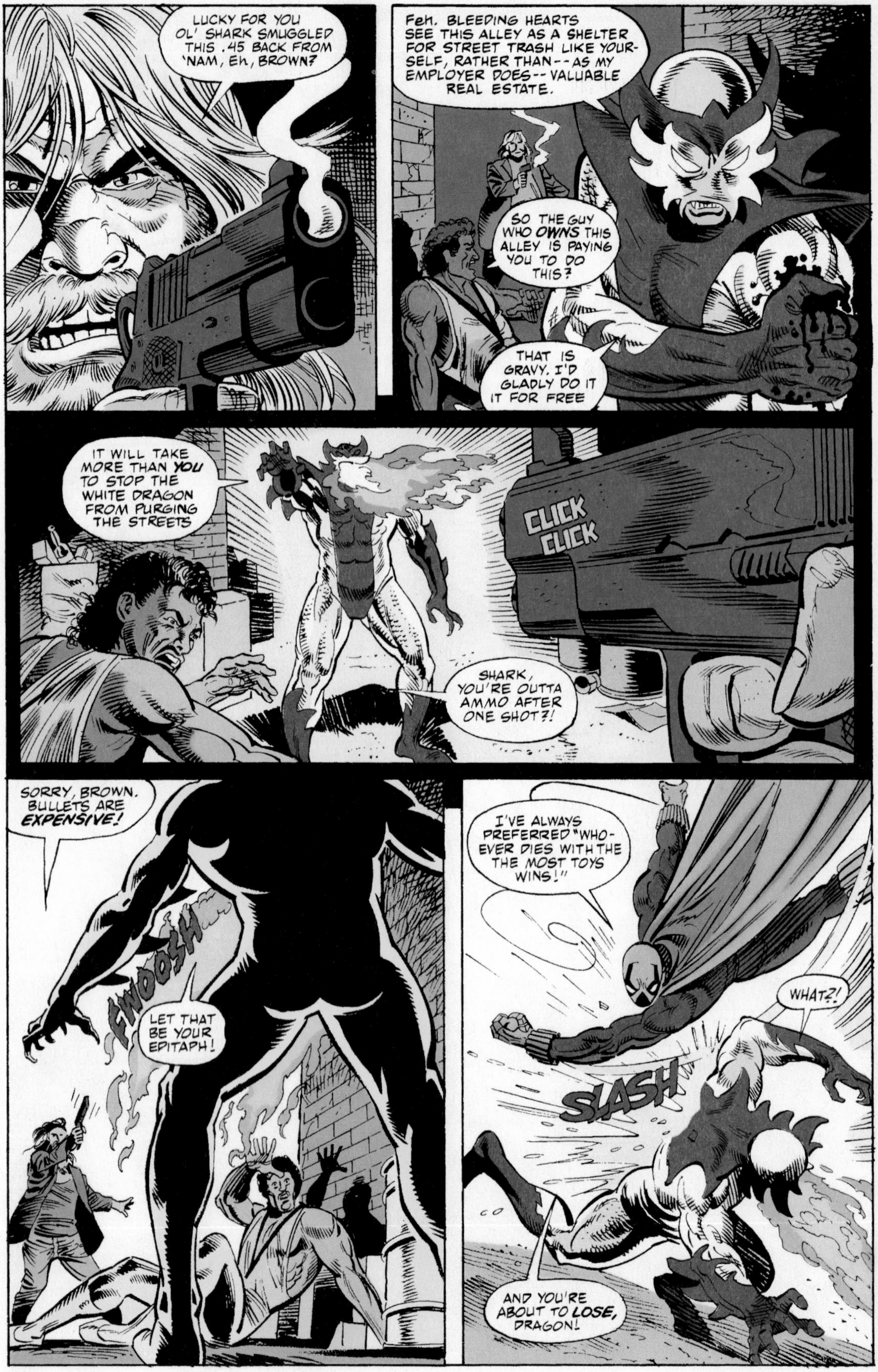

LUCKY FOR YOU OL' SHARK SMUGGLED THIS .45 BACK FROM 'NAM, Eh, BROWN?
Feh. BLEEDING HEARTS SEE THIS ALLEY AS A SHELTER FOR STREET TRASH LIKE YOURSELF, RATHER THAN-- AS MY EMPLOYER DOES-- VALUABLE REAL ESTATE.
SO THE GUY WHO OWNS THIS ALLEY IS PAYING YOU TO DO THIS?
THAT IS GRAVY. I'D GLADLY DO IT IT FOR FREE
IT WILL TAKE MORE THAN YOU TO STOP THE WHITE DRAGON FROM PURGING THE STREETS
CLICK CLICK
SHARK, YOU'RE OUTTA AMMO AFTER ONE SHOT?!
SORRY, BROWN. BULLETS ARE EXPENSIVE!
FWOOSH
LET THAT BE YOUR EPITAPH!
I'VE ALWAYS PREFERRED "WHO-EVER DIES WITH THE THE MOST TOYS WINS!"
WHAT?!
SLASH
AND YOU'RE ABOUT TO LOSE, DRAGON!

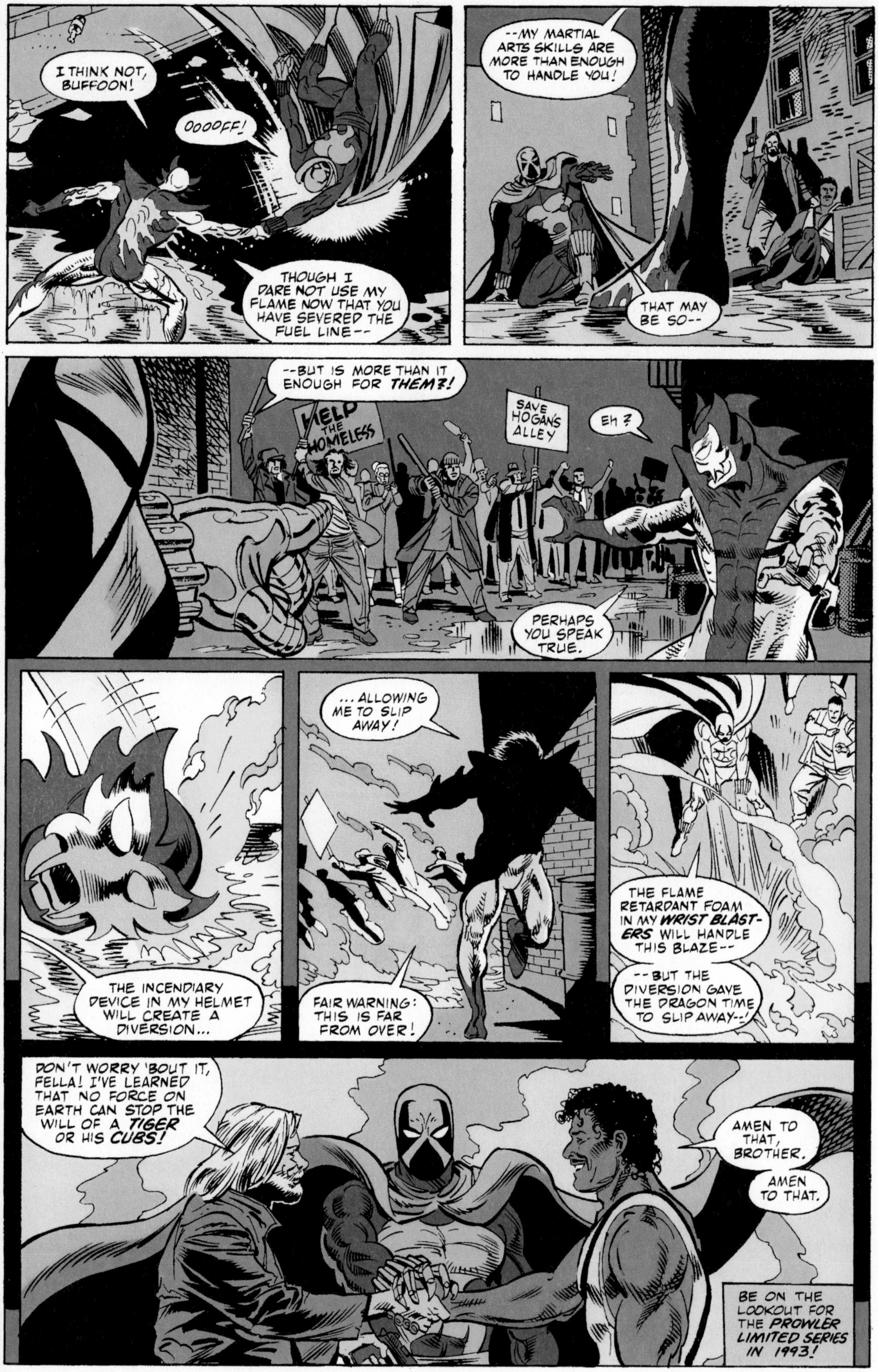
I THINK NOT, BUFFOON!
OOOOFF!
THOUGH I DARE NOT USE MY FLAME NOW THAT YOU HAVE SEVERED THE FUEL LINE--
--MY MARTIAL ARTS SKILLS ARE MORE THAN ENOUGH TO HANDLE YOU!
THAT MAY BE SO--
--BUT IS MORE THAN IT ENOUGH FOR THEM?!
HELP THE HOMELESS
SAVE HOGAN'S ALLEY
Eh?
PERHAPS YOU SPEAK TRUE.
THE INCENDIARY DEVICE IN MY HELMET WILL CREATE A DIVERSION...
...ALLOWING ME TO SLIP AWAY!
FAIR WARNING: THIS IS FAR FROM OVER!
THE FLAME RETARDANT FOAM IN MY WRIST BLASTERS WILL HANDLE THIS BLAZE--
--BUT THE DIVERSION GAVE THE DRAGON TIME TO SLIP AWAY--!
DON'T WORRY 'BOUT IT, FELLA! I'VE LEARNED THAT NO FORCE ON EARTH CAN STOP THE WILL OF A TIGER OR HIS CUBS!
AMEN TO THAT, BROTHER.
AMEN TO THAT.
BE ON THE LOOKOUT FOR THE PROWLER LIMITED SERIES IN 1993!

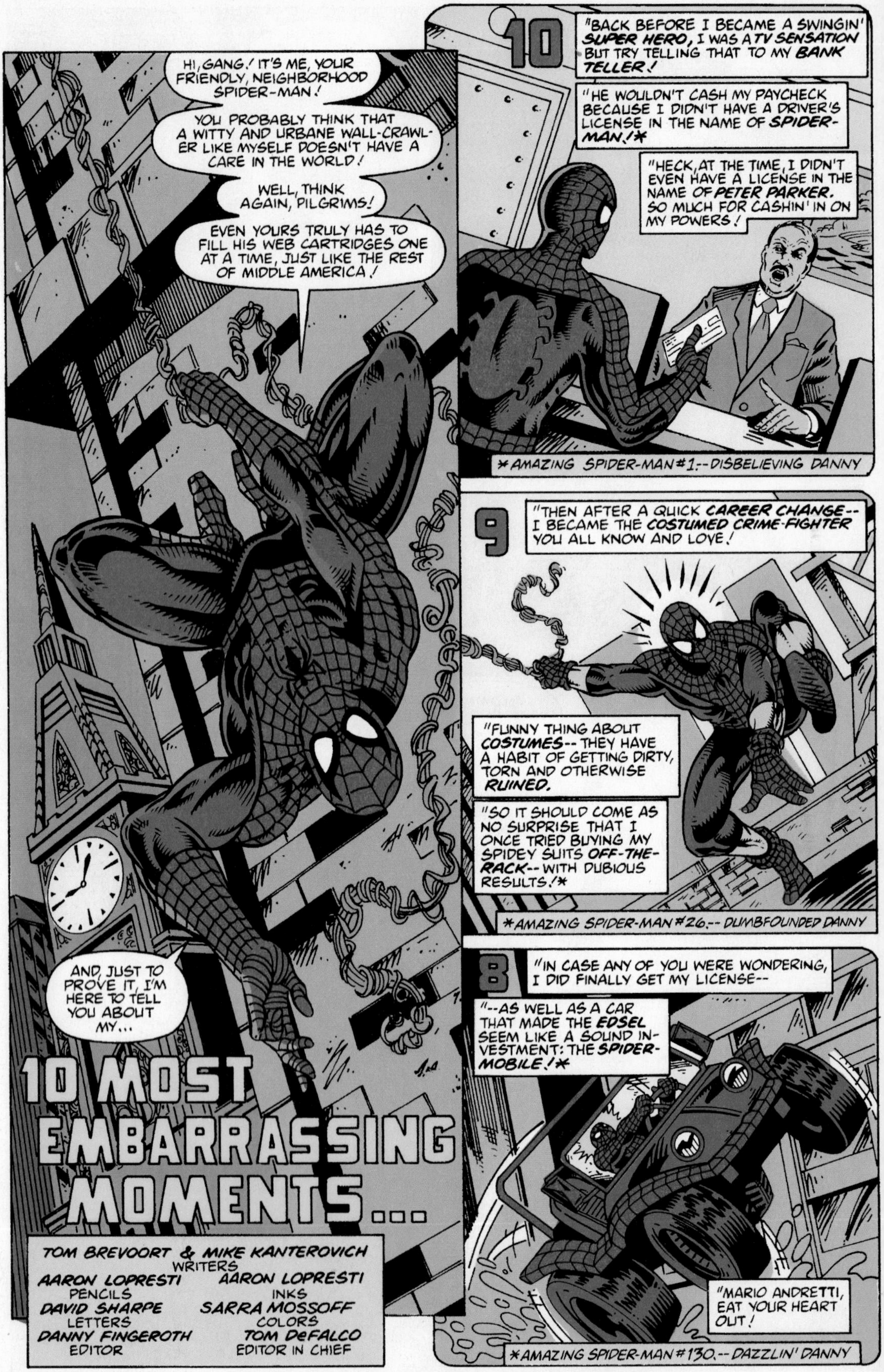

HI, GANG! IT'S ME, YOUR FRIENDLY, NEIGHBORHOOD SPIDER-MAN!
YOU PROBABLY THINK THAT A WITTY AND URBANE WALL-CRAWLER LIKE MYSELF DOESN'T HAVE A CARE IN THE WORLD!
WELL, THINK AGAIN, PILGRIMS!
EVEN YOURS TRULY HAS TO FILL HIS WEB CARTRIDGES ONE AT A TIME, JUST LIKE THE REST OF MIDDLE AMERICA!
AND, JUST TO PROVE IT, I'M HERE TO TELL YOU ABOUT MY...
10 MOST EMBARRASSING MOMENTS...
TOM BREVOORT & MIKE KANTEROVICH WRITERS
AARON LOPRESTI PENCILS
AARON LOPRESTI INKS
DAVID SHARPE LETTERS
SARRA MOSSOFF COLORS
DANNY FINGEROTH EDITOR
TOM DeFALCO EDITOR IN CHIEF
10
"BACK BEFORE I BECAME A SWINGIN' SUPER HERO, I WAS A TV SENSATION BUT TRY TELLING THAT TO MY BANK TELLER!
"HE WOULDN'T CASH MY PAYCHECK BECAUSE I DIDN'T HAVE A DRIVER'S LICENSE IN THE NAME OF SPIDER-MAN!*
"HECK, AT THE TIME, I DIDN'T EVEN HAVE A LICENSE IN THE NAME OF PETER PARKER. SO MUCH FOR CASHIN' IN ON MY POWERS!
*AMAZING SPIDER-MAN #1.--DISBELIEVING DANNY
9
"THEN AFTER A QUICK CAREER CHANGE--I BECAME THE COSTUMED CRIME-FIGHTER YOU ALL KNOW AND LOVE!
"FUNNY THING ABOUT COSTUMES-- THEY HAVE A HABIT OF GETTING DIRTY, TORN AND OTHERWISE RUINED.
"SO IT SHOULD COME AS NO SURPRISE THAT I ONCE TRIED BUYING MY SPIDEY SUITS OFF-THE-RACK-- WITH DUBIOUS RESULTS!*
*AMAZING SPIDER-MAN #26.-- DUMBFOUNDED DANNY
8
"IN CASE ANY OF YOU WERE WONDERING, I DID FINALLY GET MY LICENSE--
"--AS WELL AS A CAR THAT MADE THE EDSEL SEEM LIKE A SOUND INVESTMENT: THE SPIDER-MOBILE!*
"MARIO ANDRETTI, EAT YOUR HEART OUT!
*AMAZING SPIDER-MAN #130.-- DAZZLIN' DANNY

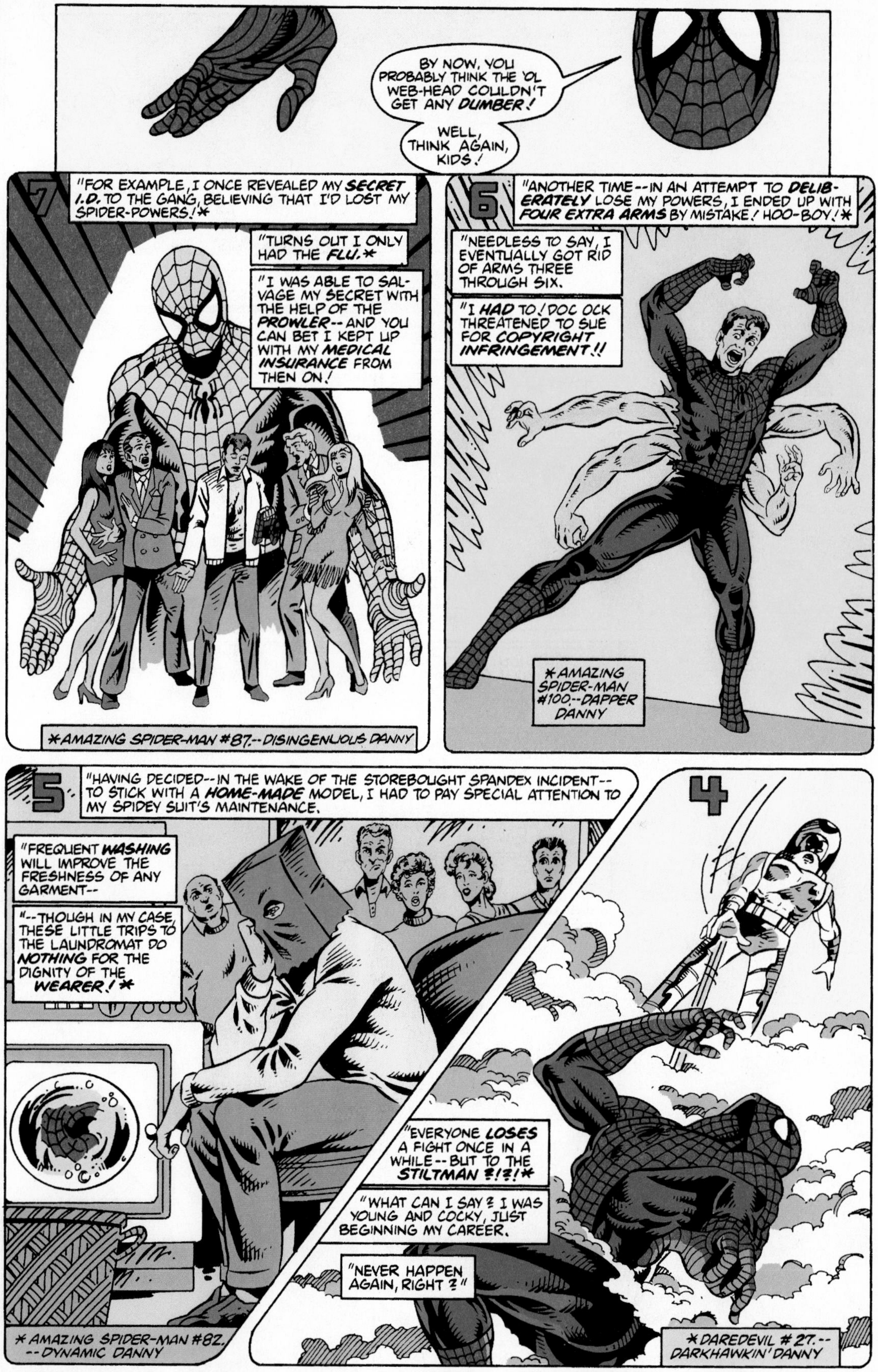
BY NOW, YOU PROBABLY THINK THE 'OL WEB-HEAD COULDN'T GET ANY DUMBER!
WELL, THINK AGAIN, KIDS!
7
"FOR EXAMPLE, I ONCE REVEALED MY SECRET I.D. TO THE GANG, BELIEVING THAT I'D LOST MY SPIDER-POWERS!*
"TURNS OUT I ONLY HAD THE FLU.*
"I WAS ABLE TO SALVAGE MY SECRET WITH THE HELP OF THE PROWLER--AND YOU CAN BET I KEPT UP WITH MY MEDICAL INSURANCE FROM THEN ON!
*AMAZING SPIDER-MAN #87.--DISINGENUOUS DANNY
6
"ANOTHER TIME--IN AN ATTEMPT TO DELIBERATELY LOSE MY POWERS, I ENDED UP WITH FOUR EXTRA ARMS BY MISTAKE! HOO-BOY!*
"NEEDLESS TO SAY, I EVENTUALLY GOT RID OF ARMS THREE THROUGH SIX.
"I HAD TO! DOC OCK THREATENED TO SUE FOR COPYRIGHT INFRINGEMENT!!
*AMAZING SPIDER-MAN #100.--DAPPER DANNY
5
"HAVING DECIDED--IN THE WAKE OF THE STOREBOUGHT SPANDEX INCIDENT--TO STICK WITH A HOME-MADE MODEL, I HAD TO PAY SPECIAL ATTENTION TO MY SPIDEY SUIT'S MAINTENANCE.
"FREQUENT WASHING WILL IMPROVE THE FRESHNESS OF ANY GARMENT--
"--THOUGH IN MY CASE, THESE LITTLE TRIPS TO THE LAUNDROMAT DO NOTHING FOR THE DIGNITY OF THE WEARER!*
*AMAZING SPIDER-MAN #82. --DYNAMIC DANNY
4
"EVERYONE LOSES A FIGHT ONCE IN A WHILE--BUT TO THE STILTMAN ?!?!*
"WHAT CAN I SAY? I WAS YOUNG AND COCKY, JUST BEGINNING MY CAREER.
"NEVER HAPPEN AGAIN, RIGHT?"
*DAREDEVIL #27.--DARKHAWKIN' DANNY

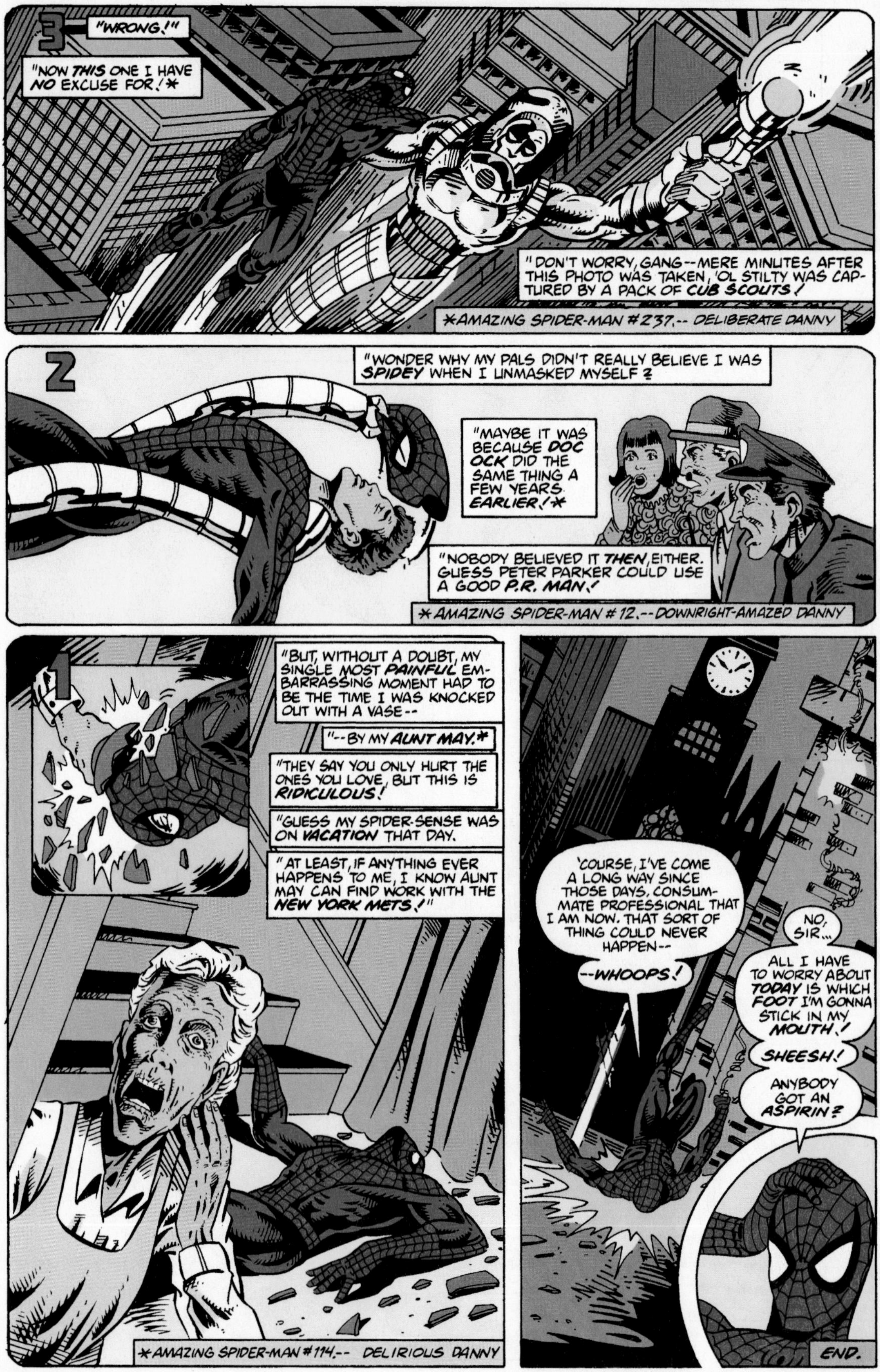
3
"WRONG!"
"NOW THIS ONE I HAVE NO EXCUSE FOR!*
"DON'T WORRY, GANG--MERE MINUTES AFTER THIS PHOTO WAS TAKEN, 'OL STILTY WAS CAPTURED BY A PACK OF CUB SCOUTS!
*AMAZING SPIDER-MAN #237.-- DELIBERATE DANNY
2
"WONDER WHY MY PALS DIDN'T REALLY BELIEVE I WAS SPIDEY WHEN I UNMASKED MYSELF?
"MAYBE IT WAS BECAUSE DOC OCK DID THE SAME THING A FEW YEARS EARLIER!*
"NOBODY BELIEVED IT THEN, EITHER. GUESS PETER PARKER COULD USE A GOOD P.R. MAN!
*AMAZING SPIDER-MAN #12.--DOWNRIGHT-AMAZED DANNY
1
"BUT, WITHOUT A DOUBT, MY SINGLE MOST PAINFUL EMBARRASSING MOMENT HAD TO BE THE TIME I WAS KNOCKED OUT WITH A VASE--
"--BY MY AUNT MAY.*
"THEY SAY YOU ONLY HURT THE ONES YOU LOVE, BUT THIS IS RIDICULOUS!
"GUESS MY SPIDER-SENSE WAS ON VACATION THAT DAY.
"AT LEAST, IF ANYTHING EVER HAPPENS TO ME, I KNOW AUNT MAY CAN FIND WORK WITH THE NEW YORK METS!"
*AMAZING SPIDER-MAN #114.-- DELIRIOUS DANNY
'COURSE, I'VE COME A LONG WAY SINCE THOSE DAYS. CONSUMMATE PROFESSIONAL THAT I AM NOW. THAT SORT OF THING COULD NEVER HAPPEN--
--WHOOPS!
NO, SIR...
ALL I HAVE TO WORRY ABOUT TODAY IS WHICH FOOT I'M GONNA STICK IN MY MOUTH!
SHEESH!
ANYBODY GOT AN ASPIRIN?
END.

THE HERO KILLERS™
Part 3
WEB OF SPIDER-MAN®

"THE DARK AT THE END OF THE TUNNEL" (THE HERO KILLERS, PART 3).... PAGE 2

WRITER - DAVID MICHELINIE
PENCILER - SCOTT McDANIEL
INKER - KEITH WILLIAMS
LETTERER - STEVE DUTRO
COLORIST - BOB SHAREN

VENOM IN "FIRST KILL, PART THREE" .... PAGE 34

WRITER - DAVID MICHELINIE
PENCILER - AARON LOPRESTI
INKER - BRUCE JONES
LETTEREER - RICK PARKER
COLORIST - KEVIN TINSLEY

THE BLACK CAT IN "THE SECURITY GAUNTLET" ... PAGE 42

WRITER - G. ALAN BARNUM
PENCILER - TOD SMITH
INKER - DON HUDSON
LETTERER - DAVE SHARPE
COLORIST - SARRA MOSSOFF

"DOWN MEMORY LANE" .... PAGE 52

WRITERS - TOM BREVOORT
& MIKE KANTEROVICH
ARTIST - AARON LOPRESTI
LETTERER - STEVE DUTRO
COLORIST - SARRA MOSSOFF

CLOAK & DAGGER IN "EVIL'S LIGHT, PART THREE: CHARGE OF THE LIGHT BRIGADE" ..... PAGE 57

WRITER - ERIC FEIN
PENCILER - VINCE EVANS
INKER - DON HUDSON
LETTERER - DAVID SHARPE
COLORIST - JOHN KALISZ

ASSISTANT EDITOR - ERIC FEIN   EDITOR - DANNY FINGEROTH   EDITOR IN CHIEF - TOM DeFALCO

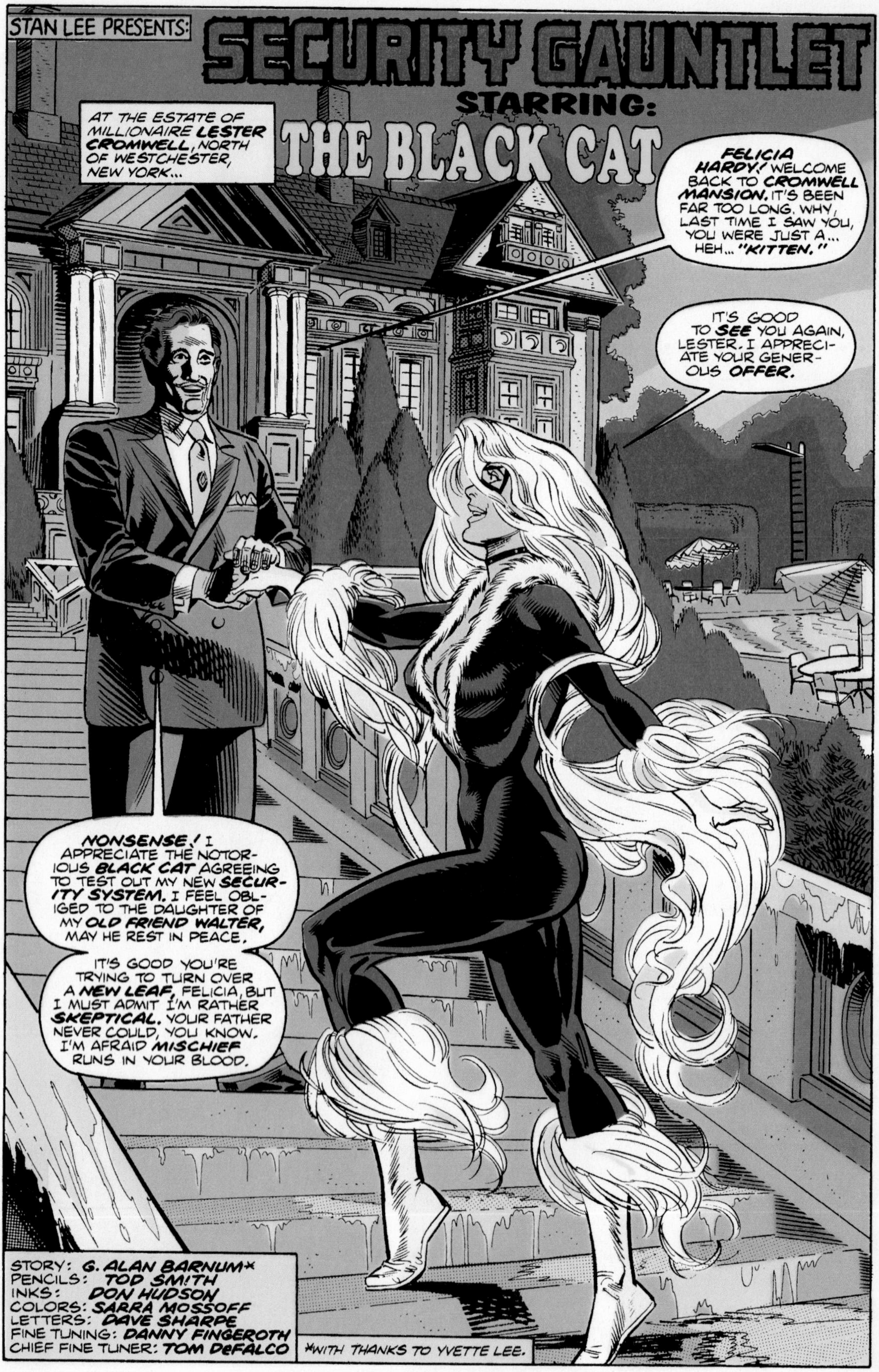
STAN LEE PRESENTS:
SECURITY GAUNTLET
STARRING:
THE BLACK CAT
AT THE ESTATE OF MILLIONAIRE LESTER CROMWELL, NORTH OF WESTCHESTER, NEW YORK...
FELICIA HARDY! WELCOME BACK TO CROMWELL MANSION. IT'S BEEN FAR TOO LONG. WHY, LAST TIME I SAW YOU, YOU WERE JUST A... HEH... "KITTEN."
IT'S GOOD TO SEE YOU AGAIN, LESTER. I APPRECIATE YOUR GENEROUS OFFER.
NONSENSE! I APPRECIATE THE NOTORIOUS BLACK CAT AGREEING TO TEST OUT MY NEW SECURITY SYSTEM. I FEEL OBLIGED TO THE DAUGHTER OF MY OLD FRIEND WALTER, MAY HE REST IN PEACE.
IT'S GOOD YOU'RE TRYING TO TURN OVER A NEW LEAF, FELICIA, BUT I MUST ADMIT I'M RATHER SKEPTICAL. YOUR FATHER NEVER COULD, YOU KNOW. I'M AFRAID MISCHIEF RUNS IN YOUR BLOOD.
STORY: G. ALAN BARNUM*
PENCILS: TOD SMITH
INKS: DON HUDSON
COLORS: SARRA MOSSOFF
LETTERS: DAVE SHARPE
FINE TUNING: DANNY FINGEROTH
CHIEF FINE TUNER: TOM DeFALCO
*WITH THANKS TO YVETTE LEE.

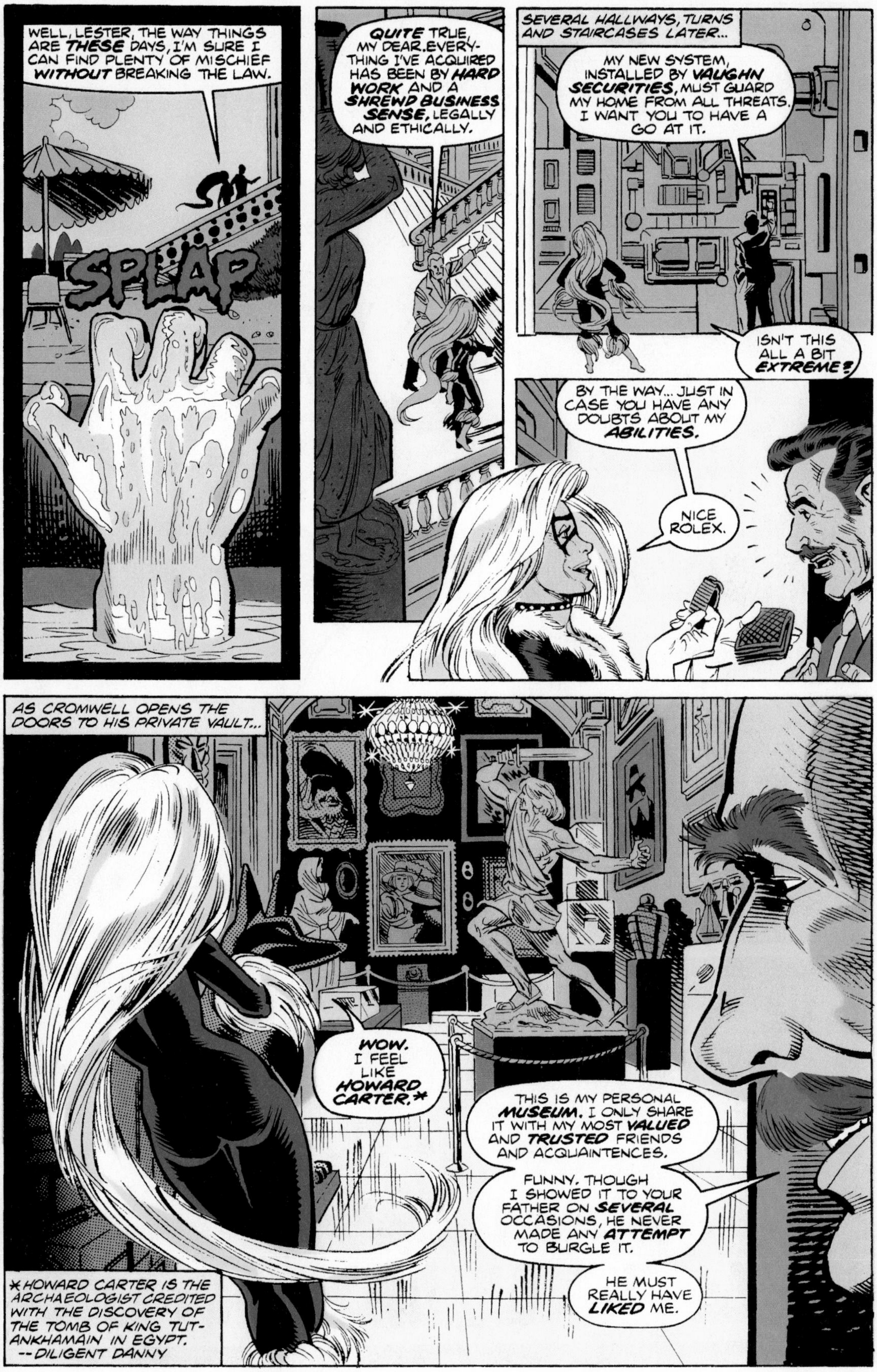
WELL, LESTER, THE WAY THINGS ARE THESE DAYS, I'M SURE I CAN FIND PLENTY OF MISCHIEF WITHOUT BREAKING THE LAW.
SPLAP
QUITE TRUE, MY DEAR. EVERYTHING I'VE ACQUIRED HAS BEEN BY HARD WORK AND A SHREWD BUSINESS SENSE, LEGALLY AND ETHICALLY.
SEVERAL HALLWAYS, TURNS AND STAIRCASES LATER...
MY NEW SYSTEM, INSTALLED BY VAUGHN SECURITIES, MUST GUARD MY HOME FROM ALL THREATS. I WANT YOU TO HAVE A GO AT IT.
ISN'T THIS ALL A BIT EXTREME?
BY THE WAY... JUST IN CASE YOU HAVE ANY DOUBTS ABOUT MY ABILITIES.
NICE ROLEX.
AS CROMWELL OPENS THE DOORS TO HIS PRIVATE VAULT...
WOW. I FEEL LIKE HOWARD CARTER.*
THIS IS MY PERSONAL MUSEUM. I ONLY SHARE IT WITH MY MOST VALUED AND TRUSTED FRIENDS AND ACQUAINTENCES.
FUNNY. THOUGH I SHOWED IT TO YOUR FATHER ON SEVERAL OCCASIONS, HE NEVER MADE ANY ATTEMPT TO BURGLE IT.
HE MUST REALLY HAVE LIKED ME.
*HOWARD CARTER IS THE ARCHAEOLOGIST CREDITED WITH THE DISCOVERY OF THE TOMB OF KING TUT-ANKHAMAIN IN EGYPT. --DILIGENT DANNY

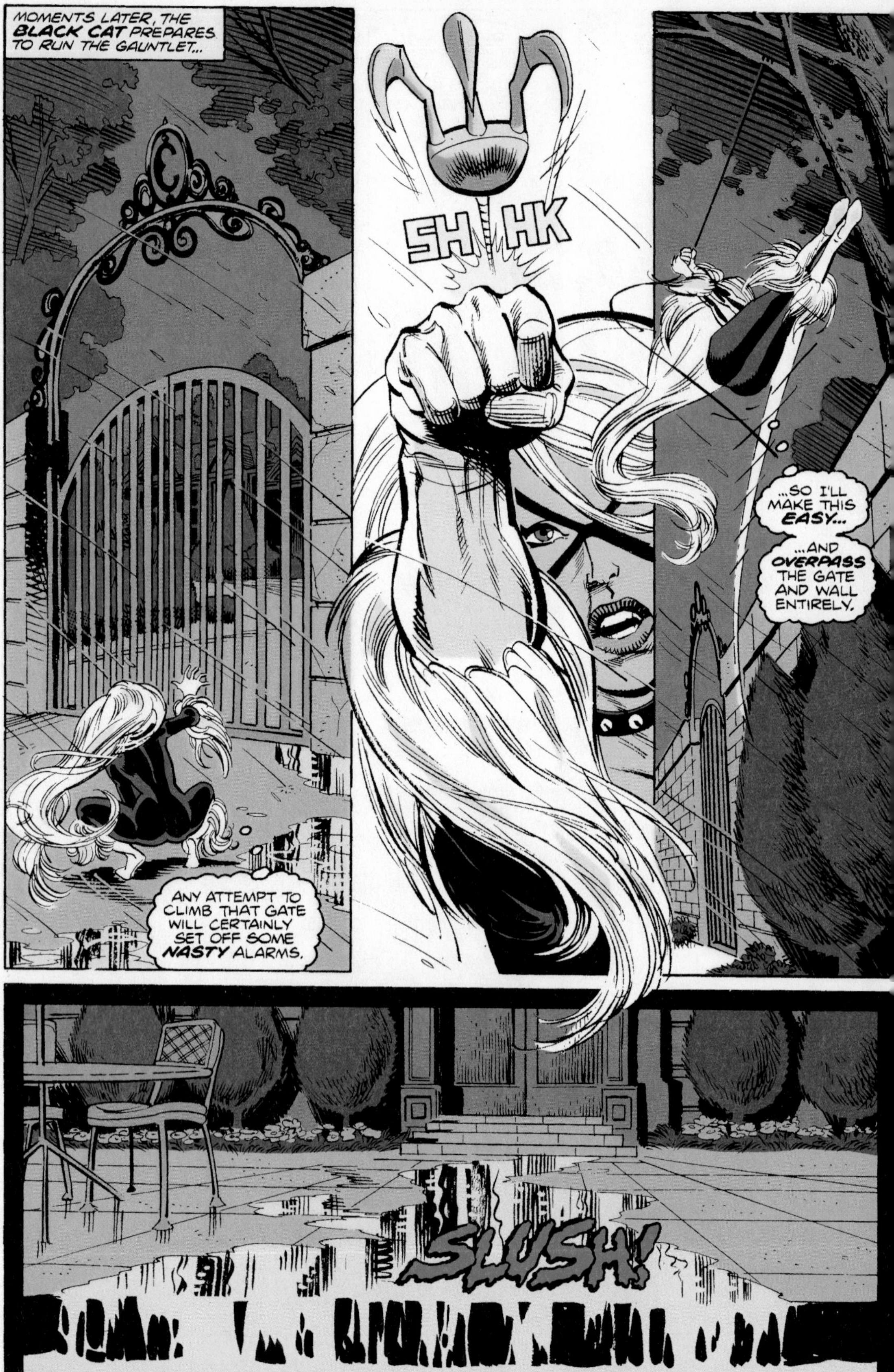

MOMENTS LATER, THE BLACK CAT PREPARES TO RUN THE GAUNTLET...
ANY ATTEMPT TO CLIMB THAT GATE WILL CERTAINLY SET OFF SOME NASTY ALARMS.
SH HK
...SO I'LL MAKE THIS EASY...
...AND OVERPASS THE GATE AND WALL ENTIRELY.
SLUSH!

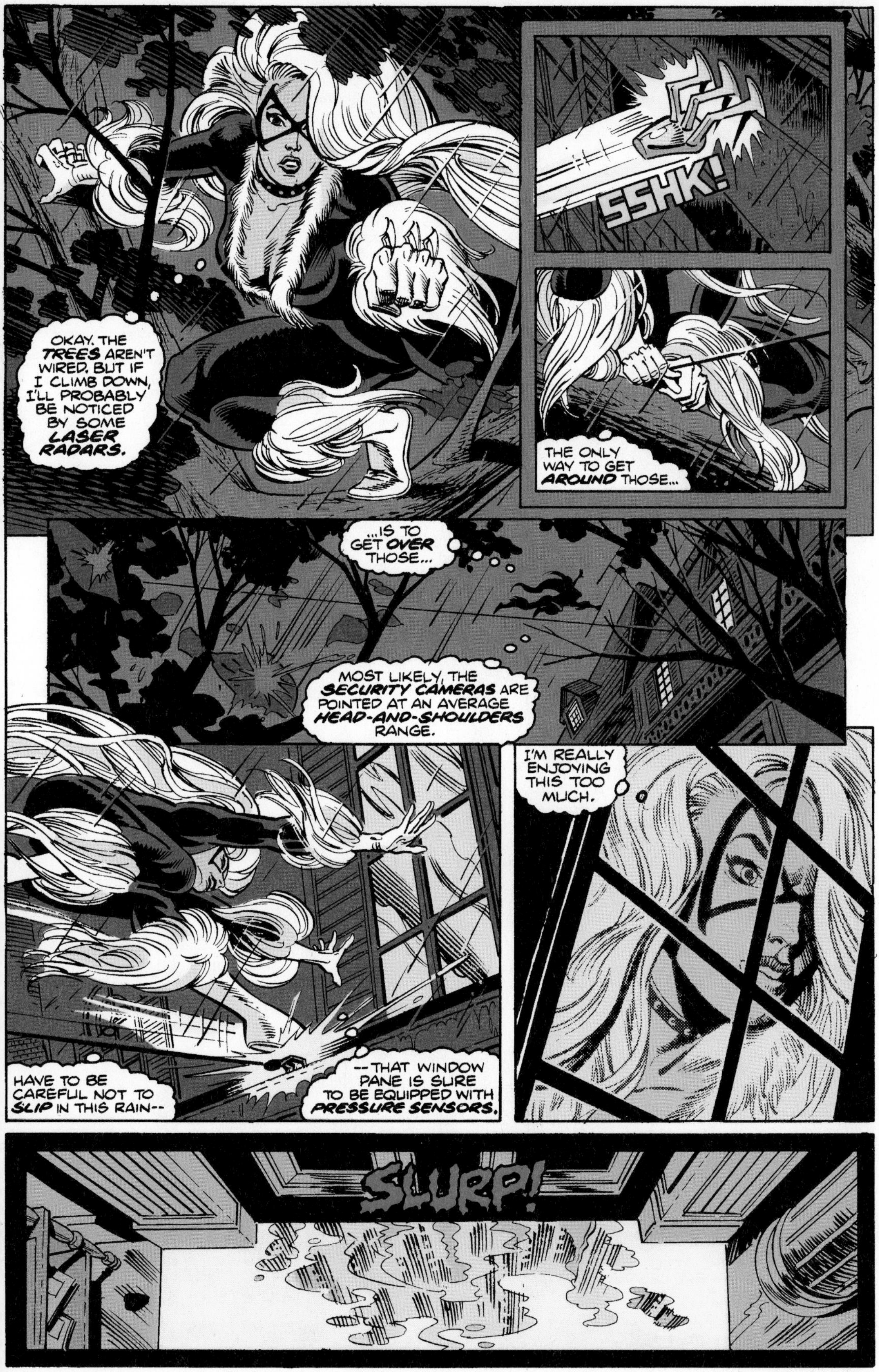

OKAY. THE TREES AREN'T WIRED. BUT IF I CLIMB DOWN, I'LL PROBABLY BE NOTICED BY SOME LASER RADARS.
SSHK!
THE ONLY WAY TO GET AROUND THOSE...
...IS TO GET OVER THOSE...
MOST LIKELY, THE SECURITY CAMERAS ARE POINTED AT AN AVERAGE HEAD-AND-SHOULDERS RANGE.
HAVE TO BE CAREFUL NOT TO SLIP IN THIS RAIN--
--THAT WINDOW PANE IS SURE TO BE EQUIPPED WITH PRESSURE SENSORS.
I'M REALLY ENJOYING THIS TOO MUCH.
SLURP!

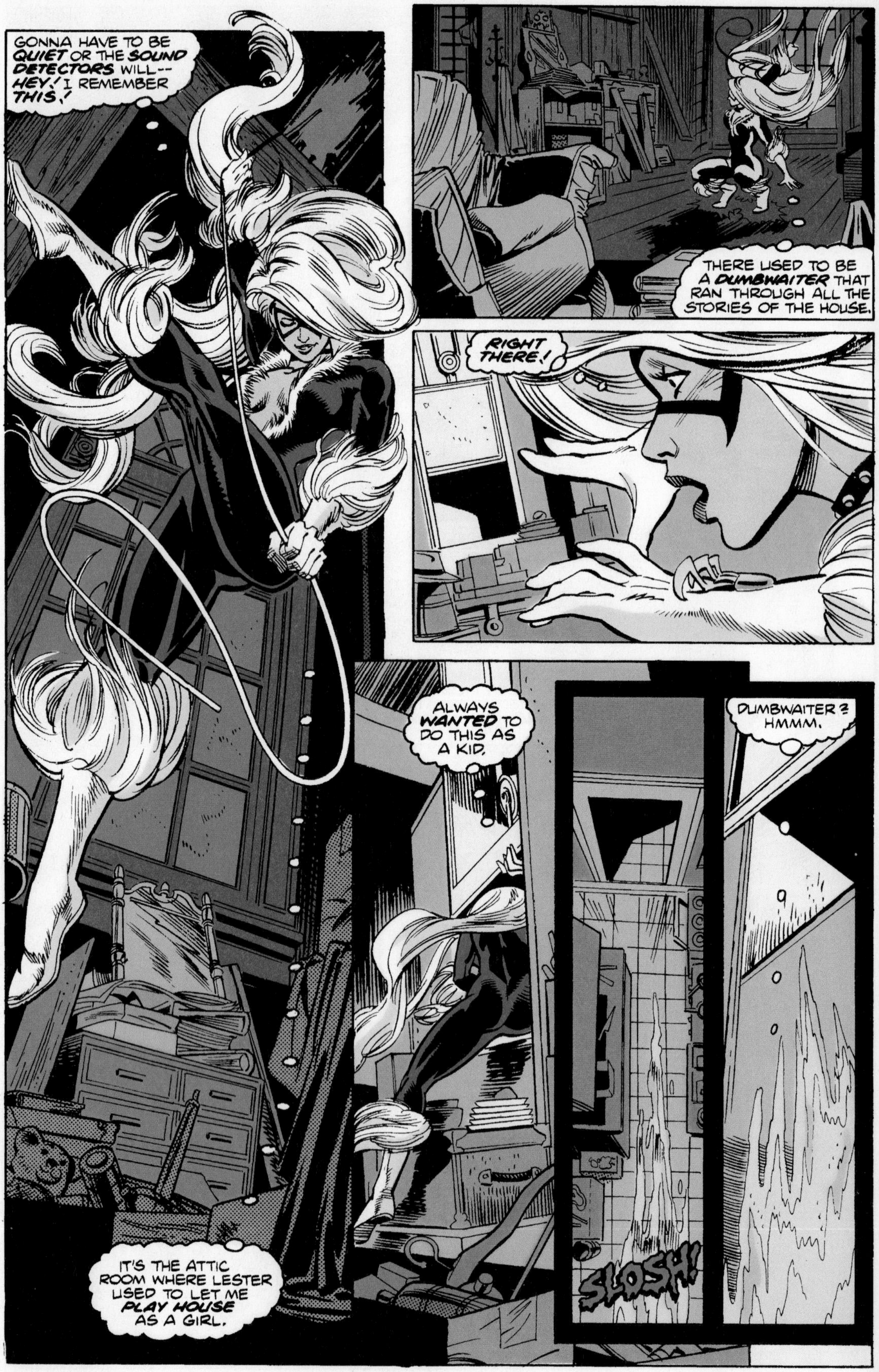

GONNA HAVE TO BE QUIET OR THE SOUND DETECTORS WILL-- HEY! I REMEMBER THIS!
IT'S THE ATTIC ROOM WHERE LESTER USED TO LET ME PLAY HOUSE AS A GIRL.
THERE USED TO BE A DUMBWAITER THAT RAN THROUGH ALL THE STORIES OF THE HOUSE.
RIGHT THERE!
ALWAYS WANTED TO DO THIS AS A KID.
DUMBWAITER? HMMM.
SLOSH!

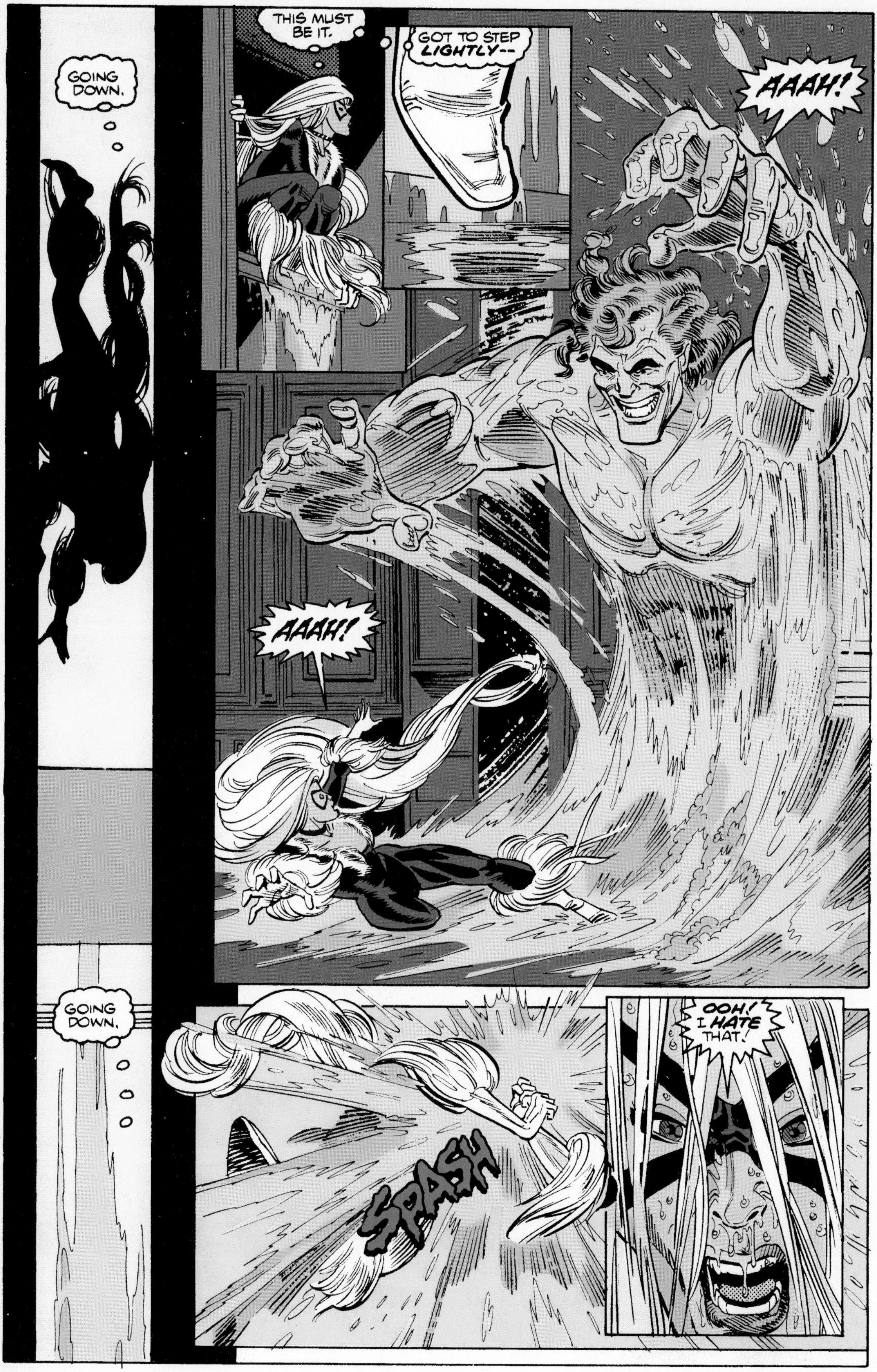
GOING DOWN.
THIS MUST BE IT.
GOT TO STEP LIGHTLY--
AAAH!
AAAH!
GOING DOWN.
SPASH
OOH! I HATE THAT!

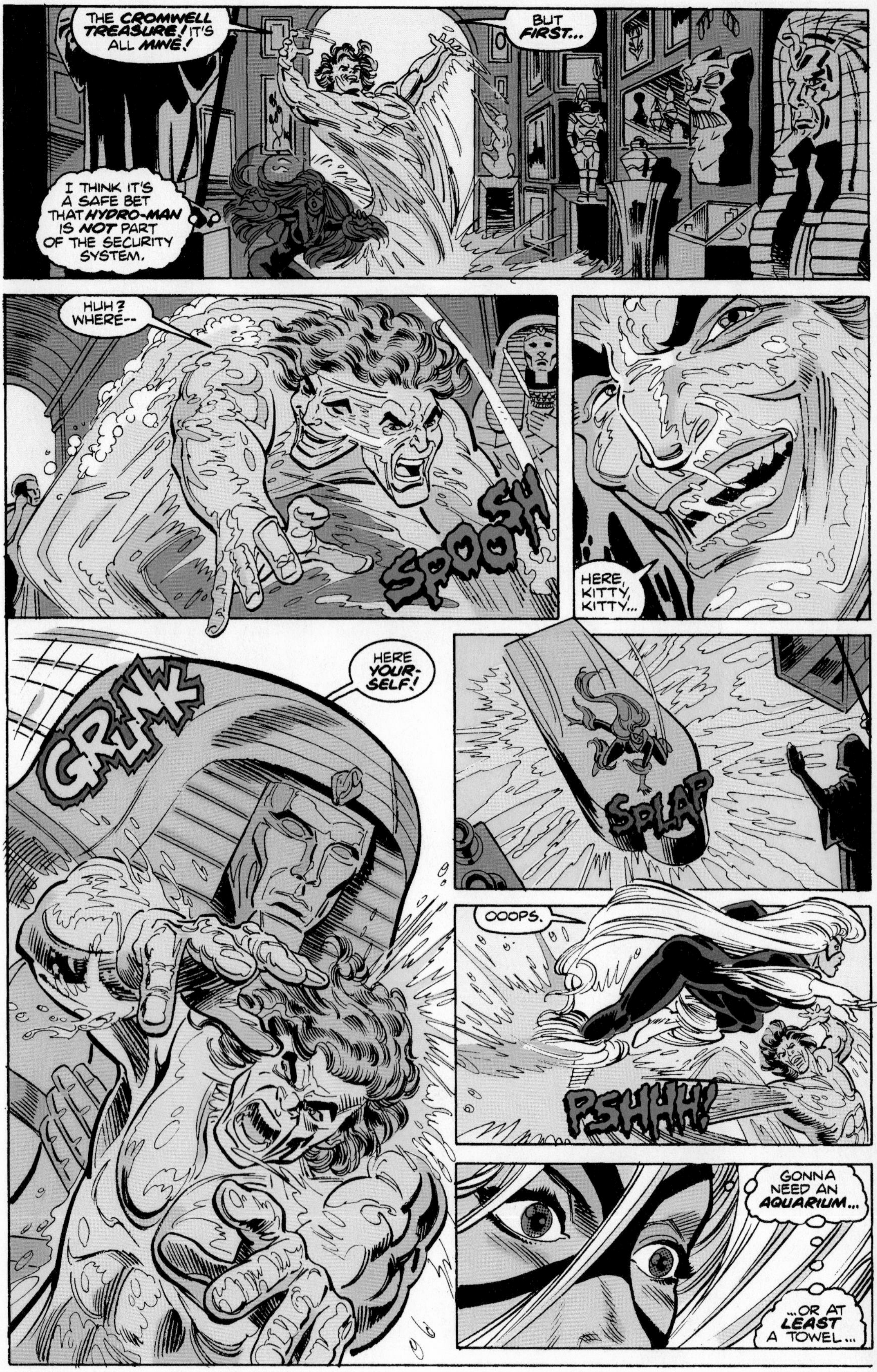
THE CROMWELL TREASURE! IT'S ALL MINE!
BUT FIRST...
I THINK IT'S A SAFE BET THAT HYDRO-MAN IS NOT PART OF THE SECURITY SYSTEM.
HUH? WHERE--
SPOOSH
HERE, KITTY, KITTY...
HERE YOURSELF!
GRUNK
SPLAP
OOOPS.
PSHHH!
GONNA NEED AN AQUARIUM...
...OR AT LEAST A TOWEL...

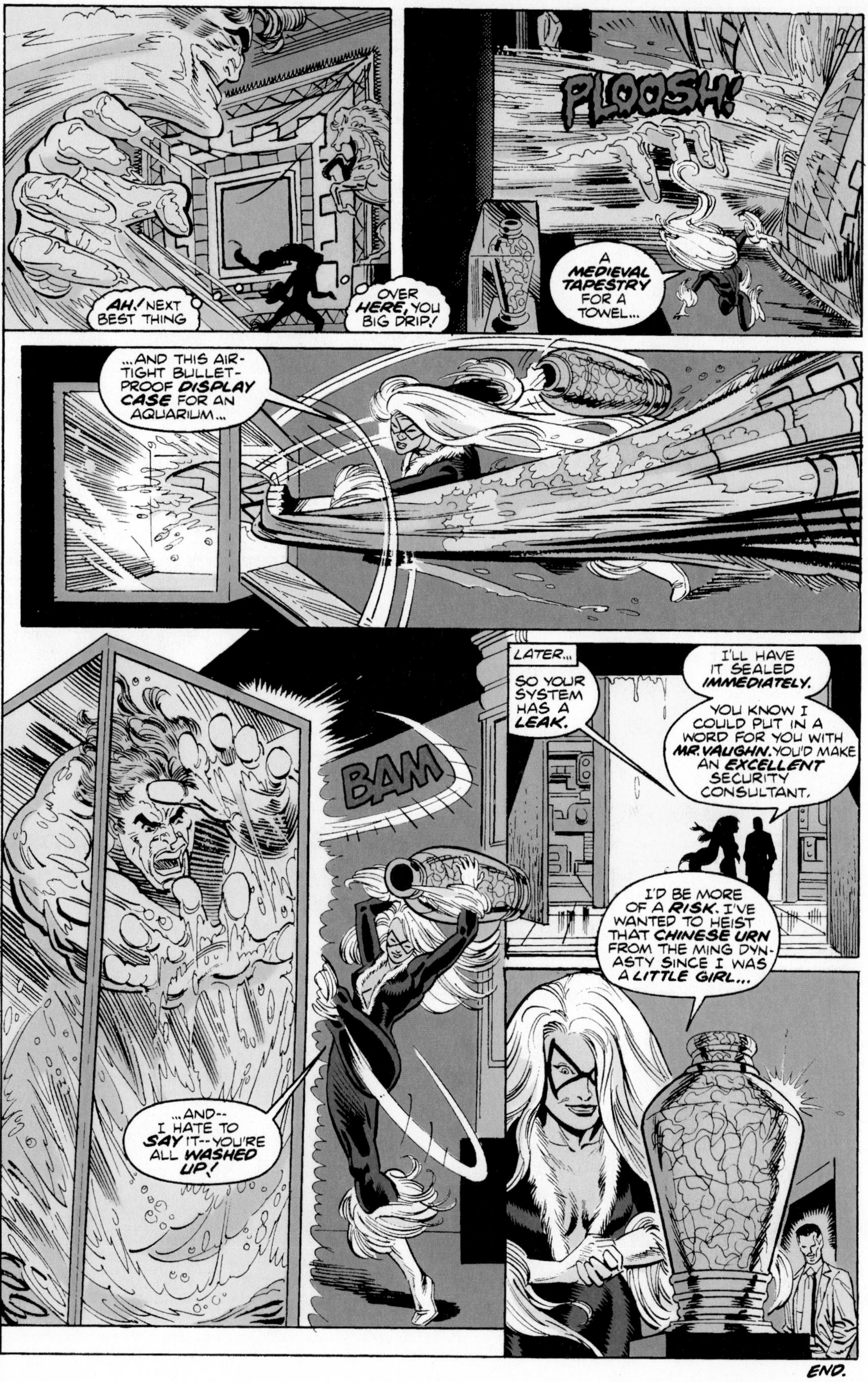
AH! NEXT BEST THING
OVER HERE, YOU BIG DRIP!
PLOOSH!
A MEDIEVAL TAPESTRY FOR A TOWEL...
...AND THIS AIR-TIGHT BULLET-PROOF DISPLAY CASE FOR AN AQUARIUM...
BAM
...AND-- I HATE TO SAY IT--YOU'RE ALL WASHED UP!
LATER...
SO YOUR SYSTEM HAS A LEAK.
I'LL HAVE IT SEALED IMMEDIATELY.
YOU KNOW I COULD PUT IN A WORD FOR YOU WITH MR. VAUGHN. YOU'D MAKE AN EXCELLENT SECURITY CONSULTANT.
I'D BE MORE OF A RISK. I'VE WANTED TO HEIST THAT CHINESE URN FROM THE MING DYNASTY SINCE I WAS A LITTLE GIRL...
END.

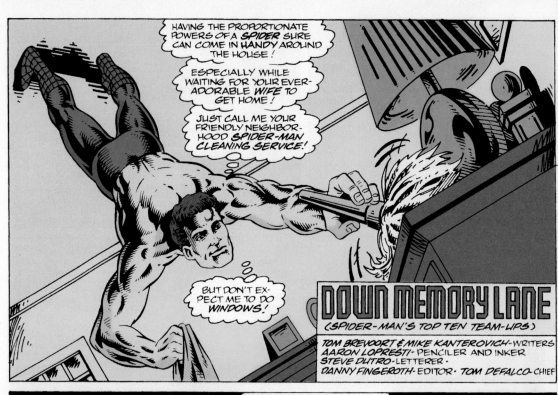

HAVING THE PROPORTIONATE POWERS OF A *SPIDER* SURE CAN COME IN *HANDY* AROUND THE HOUSE!

ESPECIALLY WHILE WAITING FOR YOUR EVER-ADORABLE *WIFE* TO GET HOME!

JUST CALL ME YOUR FRIENDLY NEIGHBORHOOD *SPIDER-MAN* CLEANING SERVICE!

BUT DON'T EXPECT ME TO DO *WINDOWS!*

DOWN MEMORY LANE
(SPIDER-MAN'S TOP TEN TEAM-UPS)

TOM BREVOORT & MIKE KANTEROVICH-WRITERS
AARON LOPRESTI- PENCILER AND INKER
STEVE DUTRO- LETTERER -
DANNY FINGEROTH- EDITOR · TOM DEFALCO-CHIEF

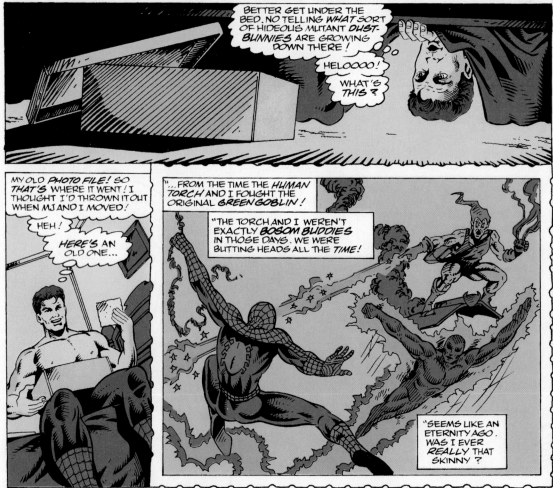

BETTER GET UNDER THE BED. NO TELLING *WHAT* SORT OF HIDEOUS MUTANT *DUST-BUNNIES* ARE GROWING DOWN THERE!

HELOOOO!

WHAT'S THIS?

MY OLD *PHOTO FILE!* SO *THAT'S* WHERE IT WENT! I THOUGHT I'D THROWN IT OUT WHEN MJ AND I MOVED!

HEH!

HERE'S AN OLD ONE...

"...FROM THE TIME THE *HUMAN TORCH* AND I FOUGHT THE ORIGINAL *GREEN GOBLIN!*

"THE TORCH AND I WEREN'T EXACTLY *BOSOM BUDDIES* IN THOSE DAYS. WE WERE BUTTING HEADS ALL THE *TIME!*

"SEEMS LIKE AN ETERNITY AGO. WAS I EVER *REALLY* THAT SKINNY?

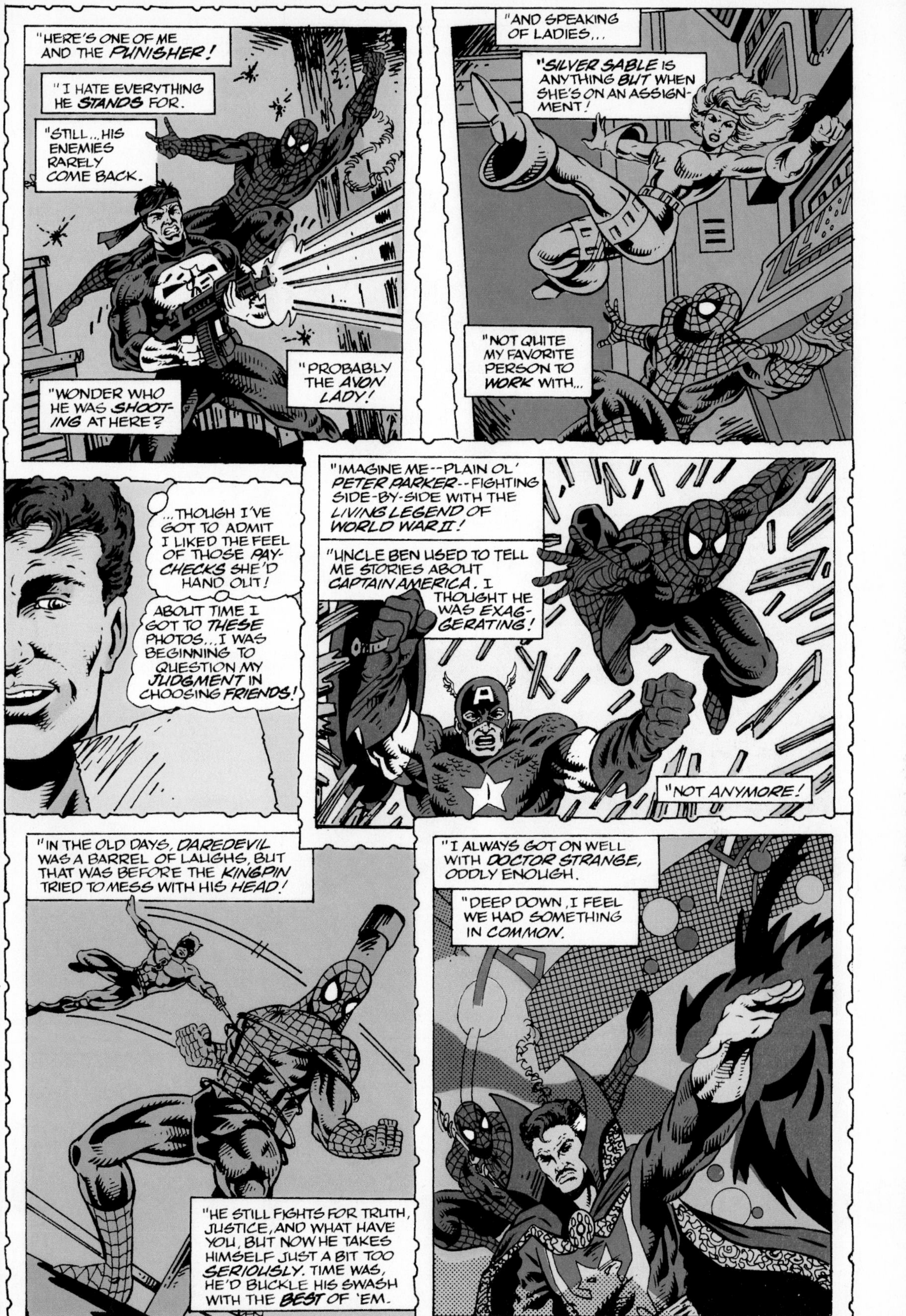
"HERE'S ONE OF ME AND THE PUNISHER!
"I HATE EVERYTHING HE STANDS FOR.
"STILL...HIS ENEMIES RARELY COME BACK.
"WONDER WHO HE WAS SHOOTING AT HERE?
"PROBABLY THE AVON LADY!
"AND SPEAKING OF LADIES...
"SILVER SABLE IS ANYTHING BUT WHEN SHE'S ON AN ASSIGNMENT!
"NOT QUITE MY FAVORITE PERSON TO WORK WITH...
...THOUGH I'VE GOT TO ADMIT I LIKED THE FEEL OF THOSE PAYCHECKS SHE'D HAND OUT!
ABOUT TIME I GOT TO THESE PHOTOS...I WAS BEGINNING TO QUESTION MY JUDGMENT IN CHOOSING FRIENDS!
"IMAGINE ME--PLAIN OL' PETER PARKER--FIGHTING SIDE-BY-SIDE WITH THE LIVING LEGEND OF WORLD WAR II!
"UNCLE BEN USED TO TELL ME STORIES ABOUT CAPTAIN AMERICA. I THOUGHT HE WAS EXAGGERATING!
"NOT ANYMORE!
"IN THE OLD DAYS, DAREDEVIL WAS A BARREL OF LAUGHS, BUT THAT WAS BEFORE THE KINGPIN TRIED TO MESS WITH HIS HEAD!
"HE STILL FIGHTS FOR TRUTH, JUSTICE, AND WHAT HAVE YOU, BUT NOW HE TAKES HIMSELF JUST A BIT TOO SERIOUSLY. TIME WAS, HE'D BUCKLE HIS SWASH WITH THE BEST OF 'EM.
"I ALWAYS GOT ON WELL WITH DOCTOR STRANGE, ODDLY ENOUGH.
"DEEP DOWN, I FEEL WE HAD SOMETHING IN COMMON.

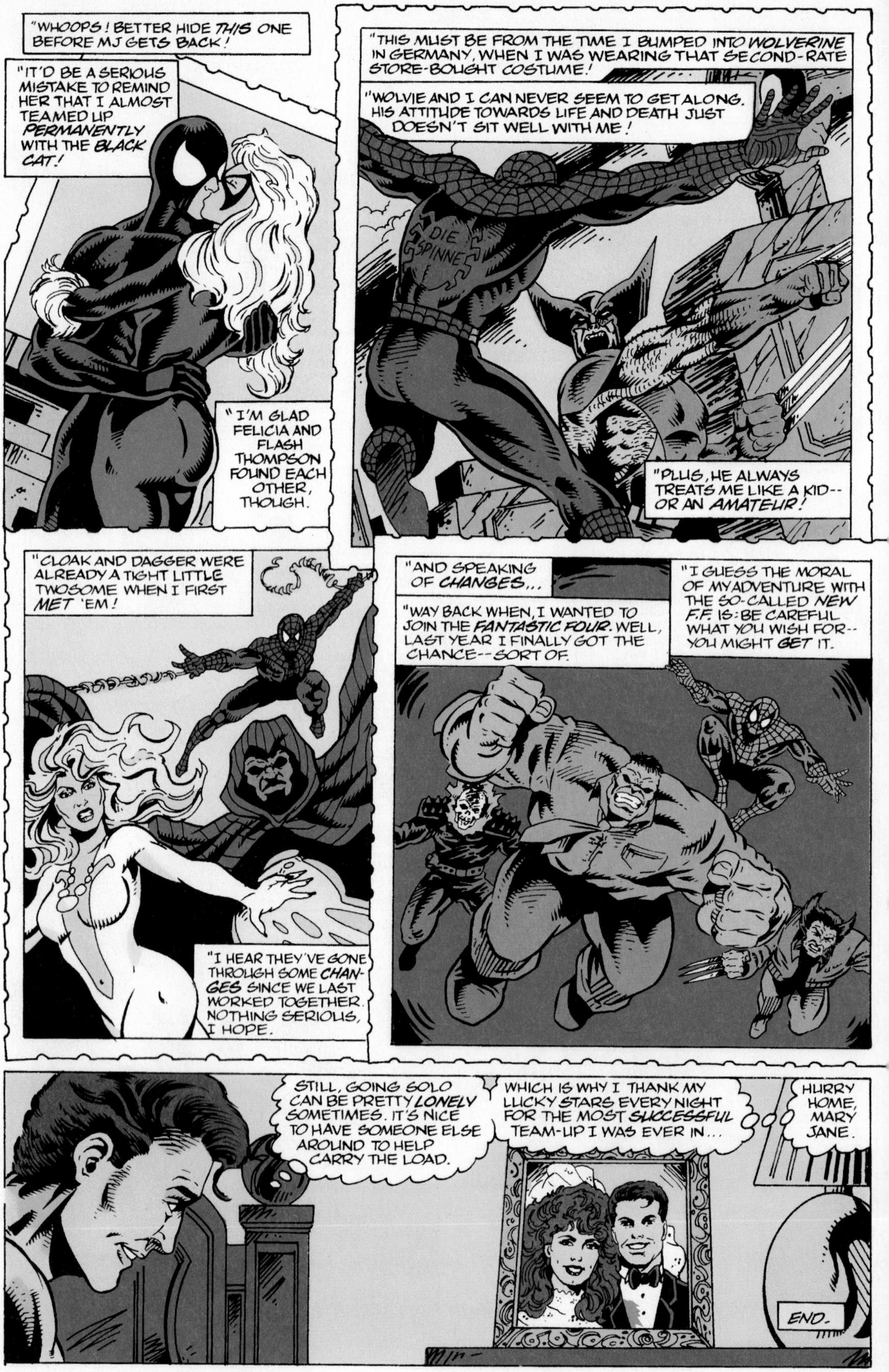
"WHOOPS! BETTER HIDE THIS ONE BEFORE MJ GETS BACK!
"IT'D BE A SERIOUS MISTAKE TO REMIND HER THAT I ALMOST TEAMED UP PERMANENTLY WITH THE BLACK CAT!
"I'M GLAD FELICIA AND FLASH THOMPSON FOUND EACH OTHER, THOUGH.
"THIS MUST BE FROM THE TIME I BUMPED INTO WOLVERINE IN GERMANY, WHEN I WAS WEARING THAT SECOND-RATE STORE-BOUGHT COSTUME!
"WOLVIE AND I CAN NEVER SEEM TO GET ALONG. HIS ATTITUDE TOWARDS LIFE AND DEATH JUST DOESN'T SIT WELL WITH ME!
DIE SPINNE
"PLUS, HE ALWAYS TREATS ME LIKE A KID-- OR AN AMATEUR!
"CLOAK AND DAGGER WERE ALREADY A TIGHT LITTLE TWOSOME WHEN I FIRST MET 'EM!
"I HEAR THEY'VE GONE THROUGH SOME CHANGES SINCE WE LAST WORKED TOGETHER. NOTHING SERIOUS, I HOPE.
"AND SPEAKING OF CHANGES...
"WAY BACK WHEN, I WANTED TO JOIN THE FANTASTIC FOUR. WELL, LAST YEAR I FINALLY GOT THE CHANCE-- SORT OF.
"I GUESS THE MORAL OF MY ADVENTURE WITH THE SO-CALLED NEW F.F. IS: BE CAREFUL WHAT YOU WISH FOR-- YOU MIGHT GET IT.
STILL, GOING SOLO CAN BE PRETTY LONELY SOMETIMES. IT'S NICE TO HAVE SOMEONE ELSE AROUND TO HELP CARRY THE LOAD.
WHICH IS WHY I THANK MY LUCKY STARS EVERY NIGHT FOR THE MOST SUCCESSFUL TEAM-UP I WAS EVER IN...
HURRY HOME, MARY JANE.
END.

THE HERO KILLERS ™

Part 4

THE NEW WARRIORS ™

"QUESTIONS OF POWER" (THE HERO KILLERS PART 4) .... PAGE 2

WRITER - FABIAN NICIEZA
PENCILER - BRANDON PETERSON
INKERS - KEITH WILLIAMS WITH
        MARK STEGBAUER, AL MILGROM
        & JIMMY PALMIOTTI
LETTERER - STEVE DUTRO
COLORISTS - MARIE JAVINS &
        SARRA MOSSOFF

SPEEDBALL'S TOP TEN LIST OF VILLAINS, NE'ER-DO-WELLS, AND GEEKS .... PAGE 41

WRITER - FABIAN NICIEZA
ARTIST - AARON LOPRESTI
LETTERER - DAVE SHARPE
COLORIST - SARRA MOSSOFF

DAYS AND NIGHTS:

PART ONE
FIRESTAR .... PAGE 43

PART TWO
NOVA .... PAGE 47

PART THREE
SILHOUETTE .... PAGE 51

PART FOUR
SPEEDBALL .... PAGE 55

PART FIVE
NAMORITA .... PAGE 59

WRITER - FABIAN NICIEZA
ARTIST/COLORIST - STEVE BUCCELLATTO
LETTERER - CHRIS ELIOPOULOS

ASSISTANT EDITOR - ERIC FEIN   EDITOR - DANNY FINGEROTH   EDITOR IN CHIEF - TOM DEFALCO

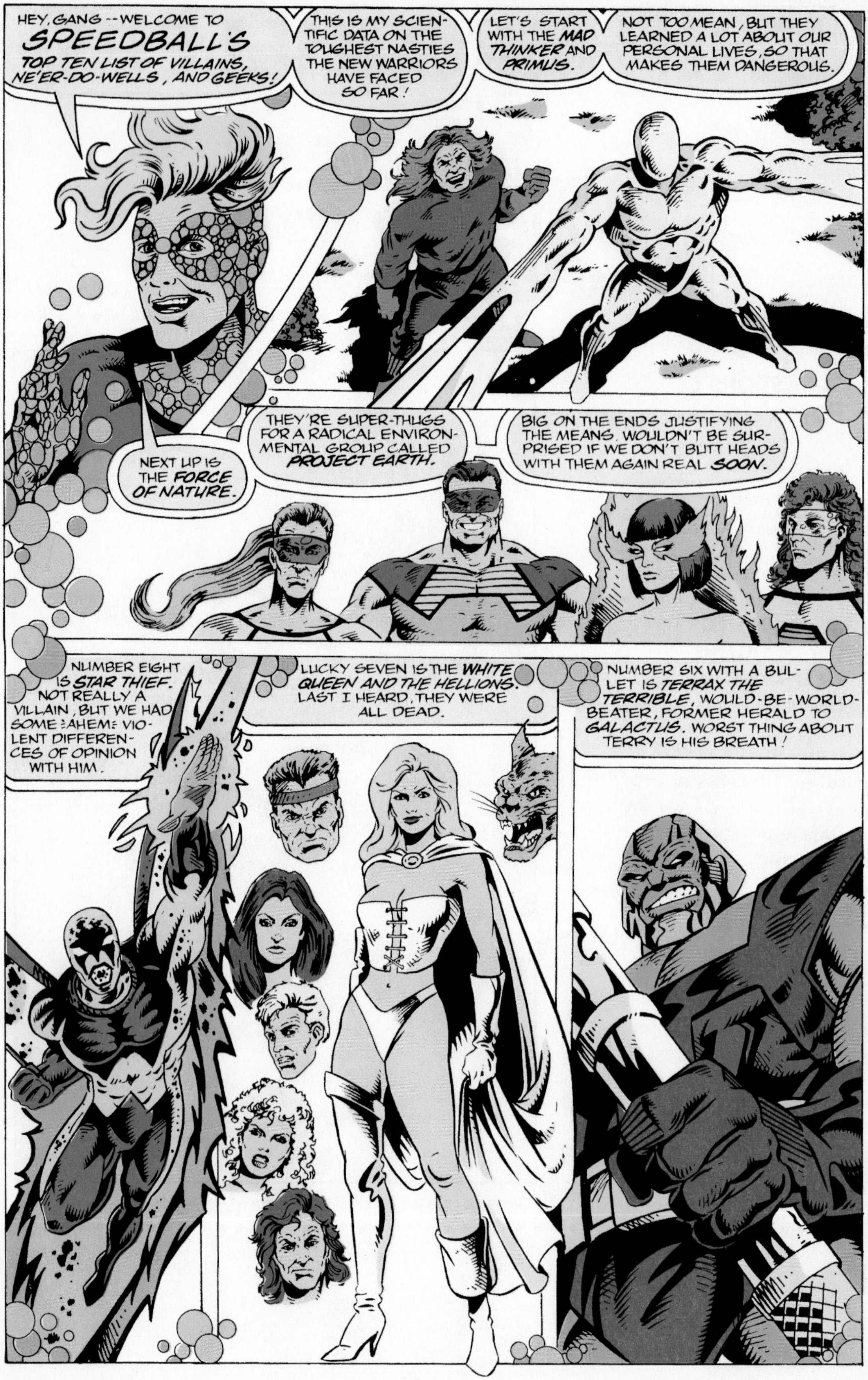
HEY, GANG --WELCOME TO SPEEDBALL'S TOP TEN LIST OF VILLAINS, NE'ER-DO-WELLS, AND GEEKS!
THIS IS MY SCIENTIFIC DATA ON THE TOUGHEST NASTIES THE NEW WARRIORS HAVE FACED SO FAR!
LET'S START WITH THE MAD THINKER AND PRIMUS.
NOT TOO MEAN, BUT THEY LEARNED A LOT ABOUT OUR PERSONAL LIVES, SO THAT MAKES THEM DANGEROUS.
NEXT UP IS THE FORCE OF NATURE.
THEY'RE SUPER-THUGS FOR A RADICAL ENVIRONMENTAL GROUP CALLED PROJECT EARTH.
BIG ON THE ENDS JUSTIFYING THE MEANS. WOULDN'T BE SURPRISED IF WE DON'T BUTT HEADS WITH THEM AGAIN REAL SOON.
NUMBER EIGHT IS STAR THIEF. NOT REALLY A VILLAIN, BUT WE HAD SOME :AHEM: VIOLENT DIFFERENCES OF OPINION WITH HIM.
LUCKY SEVEN IS THE WHITE QUEEN AND THE HELLIONS. LAST I HEARD, THEY WERE ALL DEAD.
NUMBER SIX WITH A BULLET IS TERRAX THE TERRIBLE, WOULD-BE-WORLD-BEATER, FORMER HERALD TO GALACTUS. WORST THING ABOUT TERRY IS HIS BREATH!

THE SHADOW COUNTS THEM DOWN--NUMERO CINCO--THE *SPHINXES!*

THE FINAL FOUR STARTS WITH *PSIONEX*-- PSYCHO-TEENS WITH A CHIP ON THEIR SHOULDER AND A WIGGLE IN THEIR WALK!

STAR-CROSSED LOVERS WITH TIME-ALTERING POWERS--AND THE WARRIORS ALWAYS GET STUCK IN THE MIDDLE!

COMING INTO THE HOME-STRETCH, AT NUMBER THREE--THE *FOLDING CIRCLE!* MOODY, MYSTERIOUS, TIES TO OUR PAST, FUNKY NAMES-- WHAT MORE COULD YOU ASK FOR?!

THEY'RE FUN TO FIGHT 'CAUSE I ALWAYS LIKE GOING ONE ON ONE WITH *PRETTY PER-SUASIONS.*

NUMBER TWO, SO SHE TRIES HARDER, IS *TAI*, THE KILLER HOUSEKEEPER.

AND THE *NUMBER ONE*, BIG ENCHILADA, MY MOST FRIGTENING FOE-- *MR. HINKERSON,* MY ALGEBRA-TRIG TEACHER!

HEY I DID SAY IT WAS MY LIST, DIDN'T I?

$a^2 + b^2 = c^2$

$\sin \theta =$

$\cos \theta =$

$\tan \theta =$

WHADDYOU WANT FROM ME? WHAT CAN I SAY-- I HATE MATH, OKAY?

SHE HELPED CREATE THE WARRIORS JUST SO SHE COULD KILL US! BRRR! BAD SKIN, TO BOOT!

C'EST FINI!

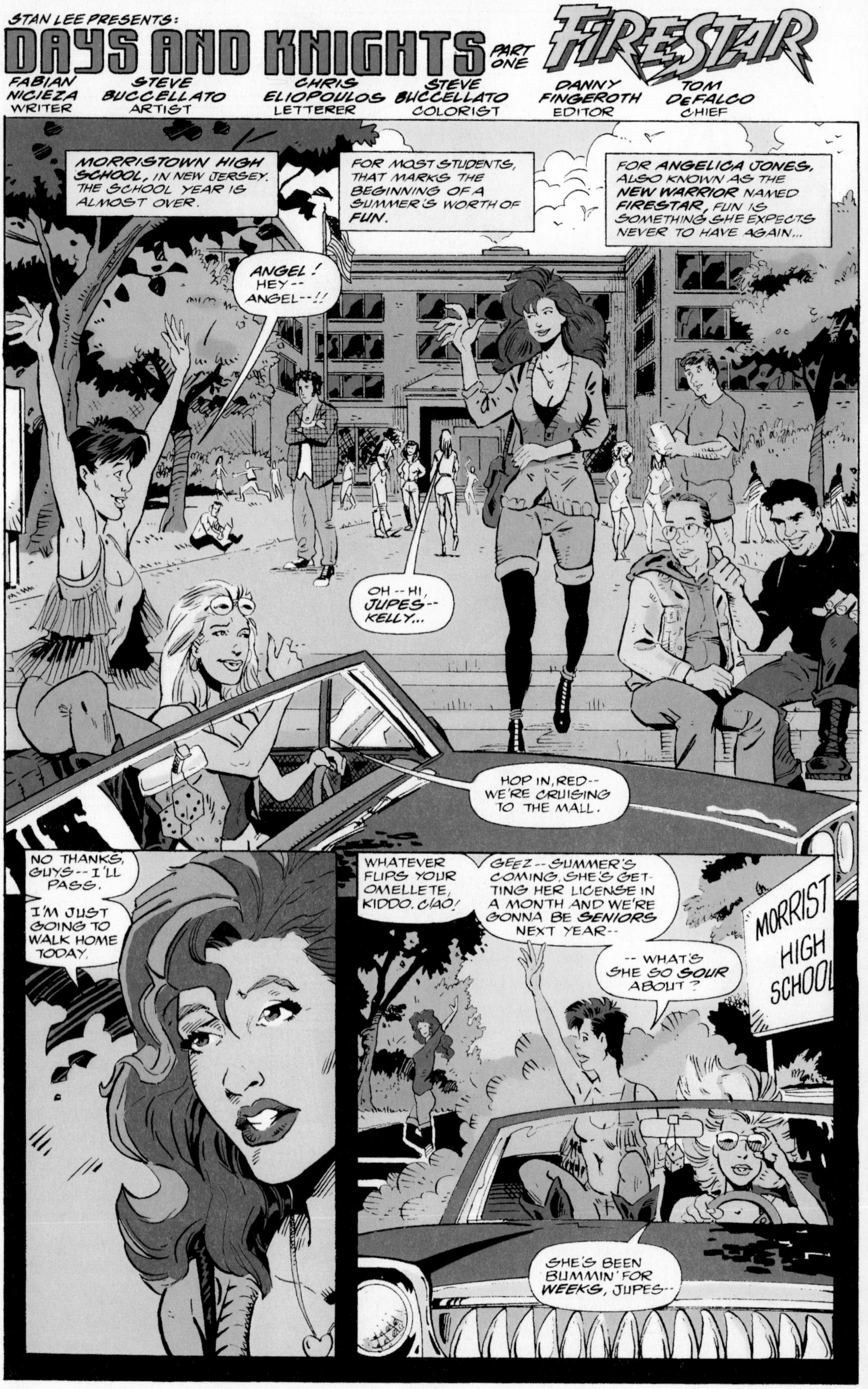
STAN LEE PRESENTS:
DAYS AND KNIGHTS PART ONE
FIRESTAR
FABIAN NICIEZA WRITER
STEVE BUCCELLATO ARTIST
CHRIS ELIOPOULOS LETTERER
STEVE BUCCELLATO COLORIST
DANNY FINGEROTH EDITOR
TOM DEFALCO CHIEF
MORRISTOWN HIGH SCHOOL, IN NEW JERSEY. THE SCHOOL YEAR IS ALMOST OVER.
FOR MOST STUDENTS, THAT MARKS THE BEGINNING OF A SUMMER'S WORTH OF FUN.
FOR ANGELICA JONES, ALSO KNOWN AS THE NEW WARRIOR NAMED FIRESTAR, FUN IS SOMETHING SHE EXPECTS NEVER TO HAVE AGAIN...
ANGEL! HEY-- ANGEL--!!
OH--HI, JUPES-- KELLY...
HOP IN, RED-- WE'RE CRUISING TO THE MALL.
NO THANKS, GUYS--I'LL PASS.
I'M JUST GOING TO WALK HOME TODAY.
WHATEVER FLIPS YOUR OMELLETE, KIDDO. CIAO!
GEEZ--SUMMER'S COMING, SHE'S GETTING HER LICENSE IN A MONTH AND WE'RE GONNA BE SENIORS NEXT YEAR--
--WHAT'S SHE SO SOUR ABOUT?
MORRIST HIGH SCHOOL
SHE'S BEEN BUMMIN' FOR WEEKS, JUPES--

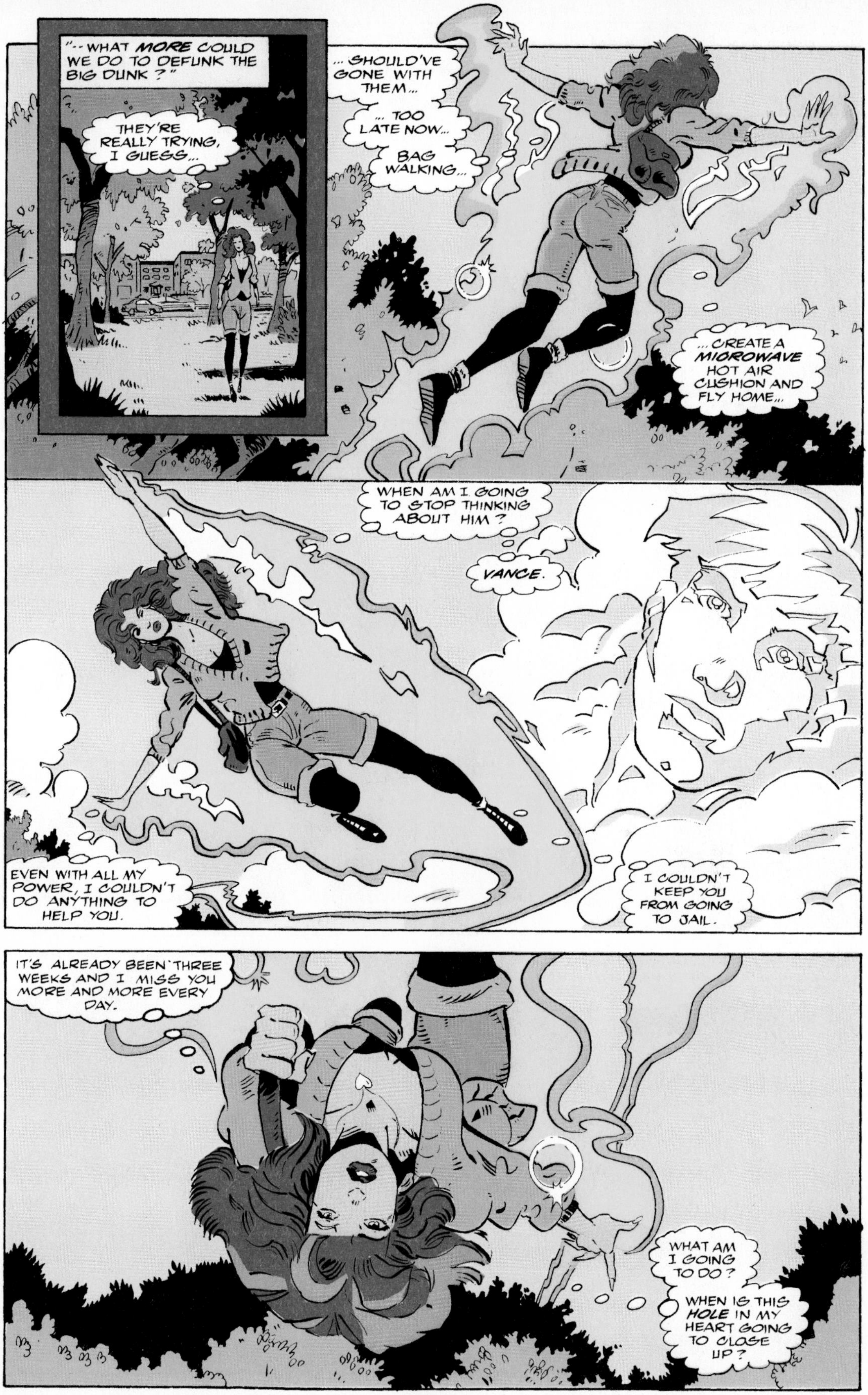
"--WHAT MORE COULD WE DO TO DEFUNK THE BIG DUNK?"
THEY'RE REALLY TRYING, I GUESS...
...SHOULD'VE GONE WITH THEM...
...TOO LATE NOW...
BAG WALKING...
...CREATE A MICROWAVE HOT AIR CUSHION AND FLY HOME...
WHEN AM I GOING TO STOP THINKING ABOUT HIM?
VANCE.
EVEN WITH ALL MY POWER, I COULDN'T DO ANYTHING TO HELP YOU.
I COULDN'T KEEP YOU FROM GOING TO JAIL.
IT'S ALREADY BEEN THREE WEEKS AND I MISS YOU MORE AND MORE EVERY DAY.
WHAT AM I GOING TO DO?
WHEN IS THIS HOLE IN MY HEART GOING TO CLOSE UP?

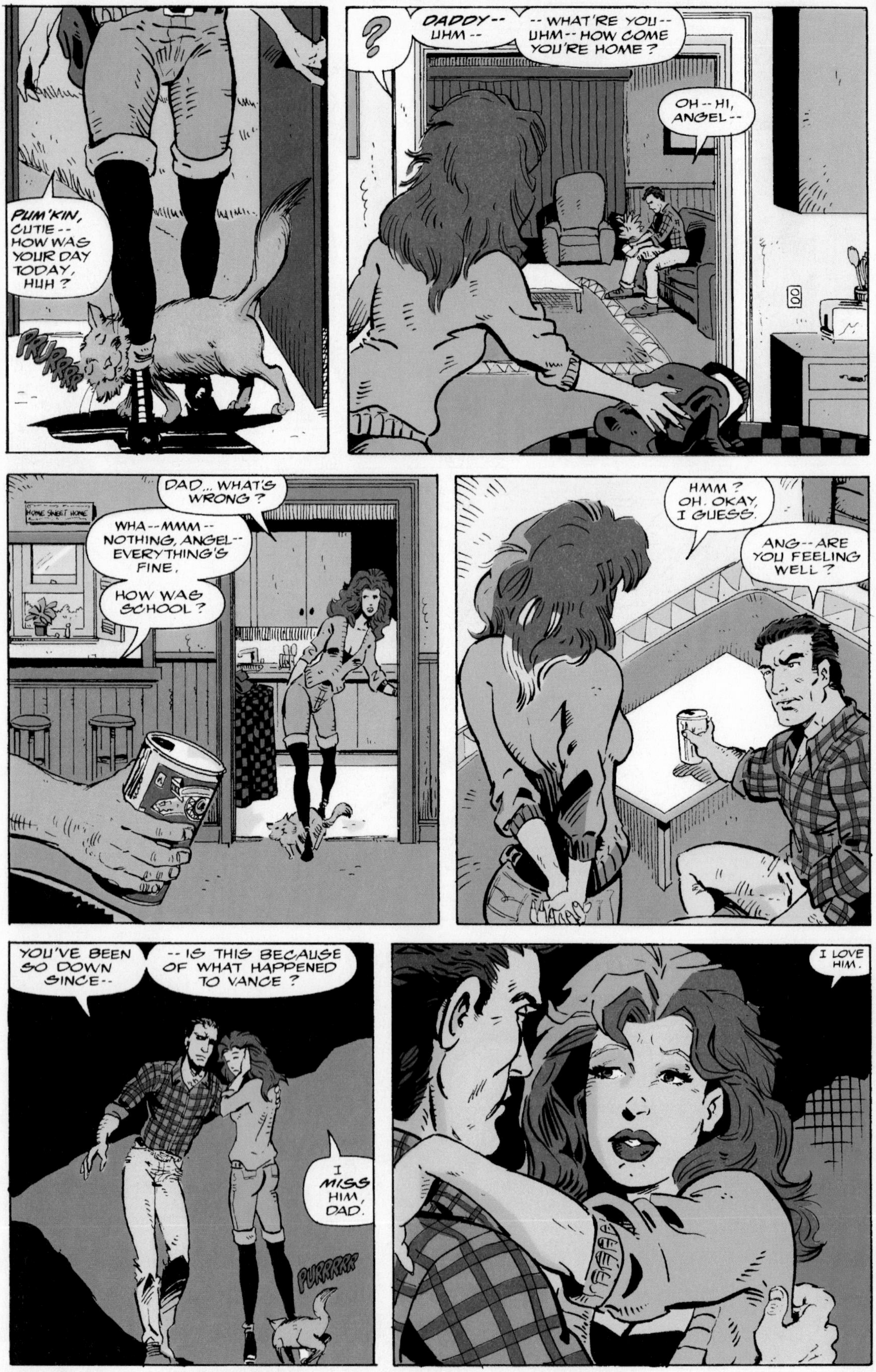
PUM'KIN, CUTIE -- HOW WAS YOUR DAY TODAY, HUH ?
PRURRRR
?
DADDY -- UHM --
-- WHAT'RE YOU -- UHM -- HOW COME YOU'RE HOME ?
OH -- HI, ANGEL --
HOME SWEET HOME
DAD... WHAT'S WRONG ?
WHA -- MMM -- NOTHING, ANGEL -- EVERYTHING'S FINE.
HOW WAS SCHOOL ?
HMM ? OH. OKAY, I GUESS.
ANG -- ARE YOU FEELING WELL ?
YOU'VE BEEN SO DOWN SINCE --
-- IS THIS BECAUSE OF WHAT HAPPENED TO VANCE ?
I MISS HIM, DAD.
PURRRRR
I LOVE HIM.

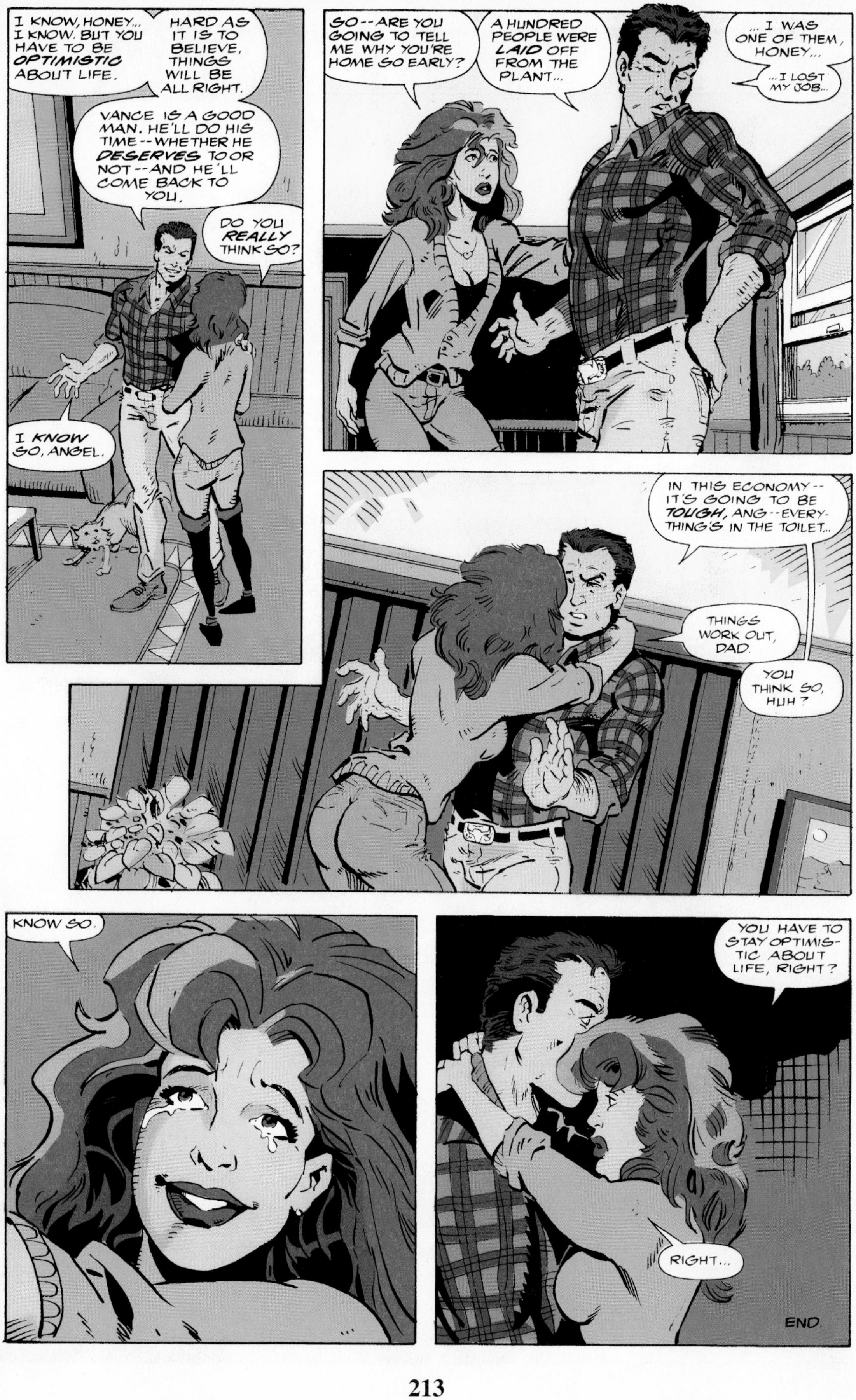
I KNOW, HONEY... I KNOW. BUT YOU HAVE TO BE OPTIMISTIC ABOUT LIFE.
HARD AS IT IS TO BELIEVE, THINGS WILL BE ALL RIGHT.
VANCE IS A GOOD MAN. HE'LL DO HIS TIME -- WHETHER HE DESERVES TO OR NOT -- AND HE'LL COME BACK TO YOU.
DO YOU REALLY THINK SO?
I KNOW SO, ANGEL.
SO -- ARE YOU GOING TO TELL ME WHY YOU'RE HOME SO EARLY?
A HUNDRED PEOPLE WERE LAID OFF FROM THE PLANT...
... I WAS ONE OF THEM, HONEY...
... I LOST MY JOB...
IN THIS ECONOMY -- IT'S GOING TO BE TOUGH, ANG -- EVERYTHING'S IN THE TOILET...
THINGS WORK OUT, DAD.
YOU THINK SO, HUH?
KNOW SO.
YOU HAVE TO STAY OPTIMISTIC ABOUT LIFE, RIGHT?
RIGHT...
END.

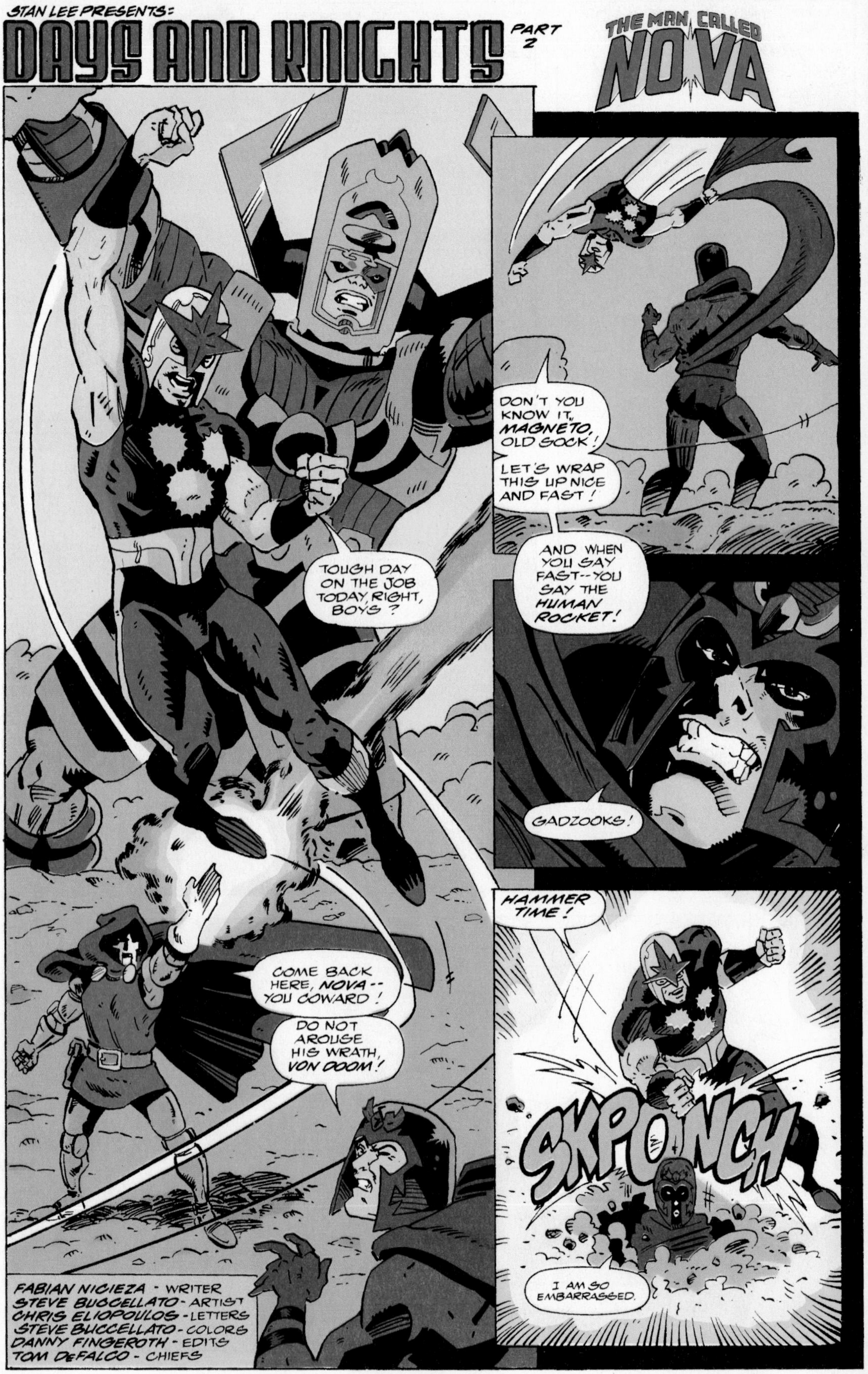
STAN LEE PRESENTS:
DAYS AND KNIGHTS PART 2
THE MAN CALLED NOVA
TOUGH DAY ON THE JOB TODAY, RIGHT, BOYS?
COME BACK HERE, NOVA-- YOU COWARD!
DO NOT AROUSE HIS WRATH, VON DOOM!
DON'T YOU KNOW IT, MAGNETO, OLD SOCK!
LET'S WRAP THIS UP NICE AND FAST!
AND WHEN YOU SAY FAST--YOU SAY THE HUMAN ROCKET!
GADZOOKS!
HAMMER TIME!
SKPONCH
I AM SO EMBARRASSED.
FABIAN NICIEZA - WRITER
STEVE BUCCELLATO - ARTIST
CHRIS ELIOPOULOS - LETTERS
STEVE BUCCELLATO - COLORS
DANNY FINGEROTH - EDITS
TOM DEFALCO - CHIEFS

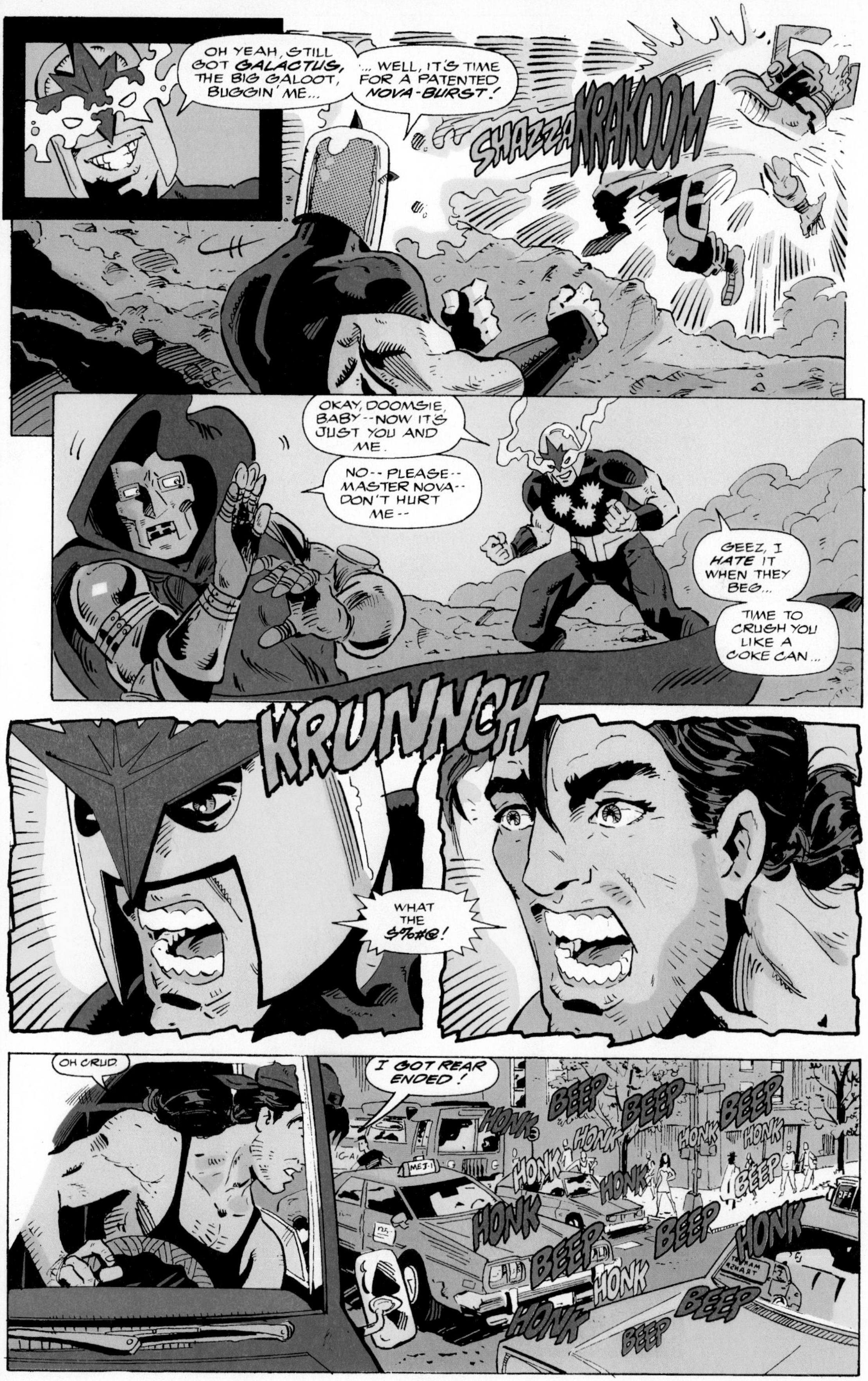
OH YEAH, STILL GOT GALACTUS, THE BIG GALOOT, BUGGIN' ME...
... WELL, IT'S TIME FOR A PATENTED NOVA-BURST!
SHAZZAKRAKOOM
OKAY, DOOMSIE, BABY--NOW IT'S JUST YOU AND ME.
NO--PLEASE--MASTER NOVA--DON'T HURT ME--
GEEZ, I HATE IT WHEN THEY BEG...
TIME TO CRUSH YOU LIKE A COKE CAN...
KRUNNCH
WHAT THE $%#@!
OH CRUD.
I GOT REAR ENDED!
HONK
BEEP
BEEP
HONK
BEEP
HONK
HONK
BEEP
HONK
HONK
BEEP
HONK
BEEP
HONK
HONK
BEEP
HONK
BEEP
BEEP

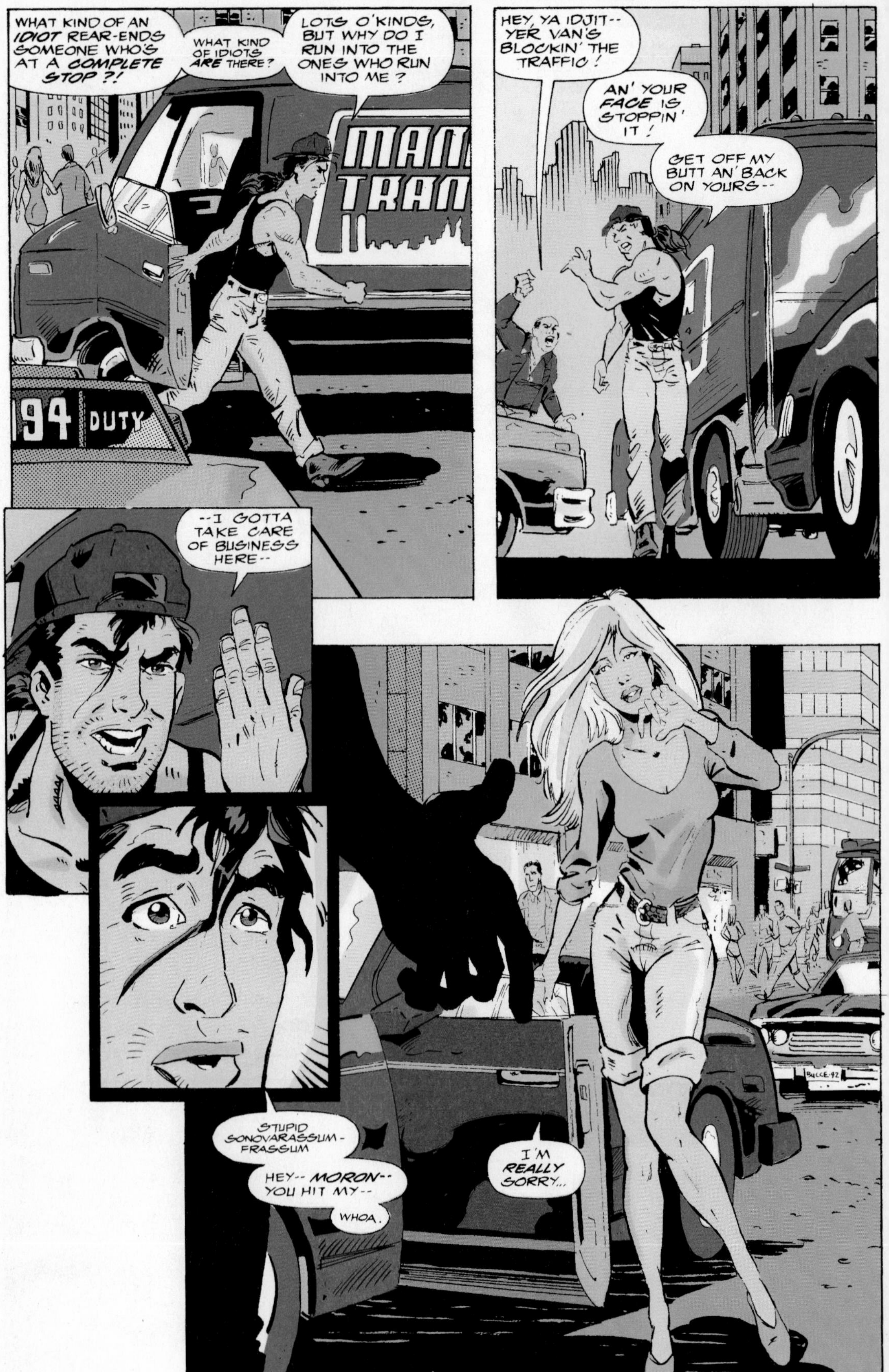
WHAT KIND OF AN IDIOT REAR-ENDS SOMEONE WHO'S AT A COMPLETE STOP ?!
WHAT KIND OF IDIOTS ARE THERE?
LOTS O'KINDS, BUT WHY DO I RUN INTO THE ONES WHO RUN INTO ME?
194 DUTY
HEY, YA IDJIT-- YER VAN'S BLOCKIN' THE TRAFFIC!
AN' YOUR FACE IS STOPPIN' IT!
GET OFF MY BUTT AN' BACK ON YOURS--
--I GOTTA TAKE CARE OF BUSINESS HERE--
STUPID SONOVARASSUM-FRASSUM
HEY-- MORON-- YOU HIT MY--
WHOA.
I'M REALLY SORRY...

I'M SORRY-- IT WAS ALL MY FAULT.--

NO-- NO-- IT COULDA-- COULD HAVE-- BEEN MINE.

I WAS DAY-DREAMING. TOTAL REM CYCLE.

BEE BEEEP

BEEEP

HONK

HONK HO HONK HONK

GET OUT THE H YOU

HEY, MOVE THA PIE O

YOU WERE? REALLY? SO WAS I!

I CAN'T TELL MY BOSS MOTHER ABOUT THIS!

HA HA HA HA

YO, ROMEO-- YOU GONNA MOVE THAT TRUCK OR WHAT?

SHUT UP!

HA HA HA HA HA

LISTEN-- THIS IS MY HOME NUMBER-- CALL ME AND WE'LL STRAIGHTEN THIS OUT.

YEAH? COOL.

203 AREA CODE? YOU LIVE IN CONNECTI-CUT...?

YEAH-- I'M HOME FROM SCHOOL FOR THE SUMMER.

WHICH COLLEGE YOU GO TO?

YALE.

OH.

CALL ME, OKAY-- UHM--

RICH

MY NAME'S LAURA. UHM... MAYBE WE CAN STRAIGHTEN THIS OUT OVER A BITE TO EAT? CALL ME...

YEAH, SURE, MS. YALE-GIRL.

ON MY BUDGET, A BITE IS ALL I'LL BE ABLE TO AFFORD.

END.

217

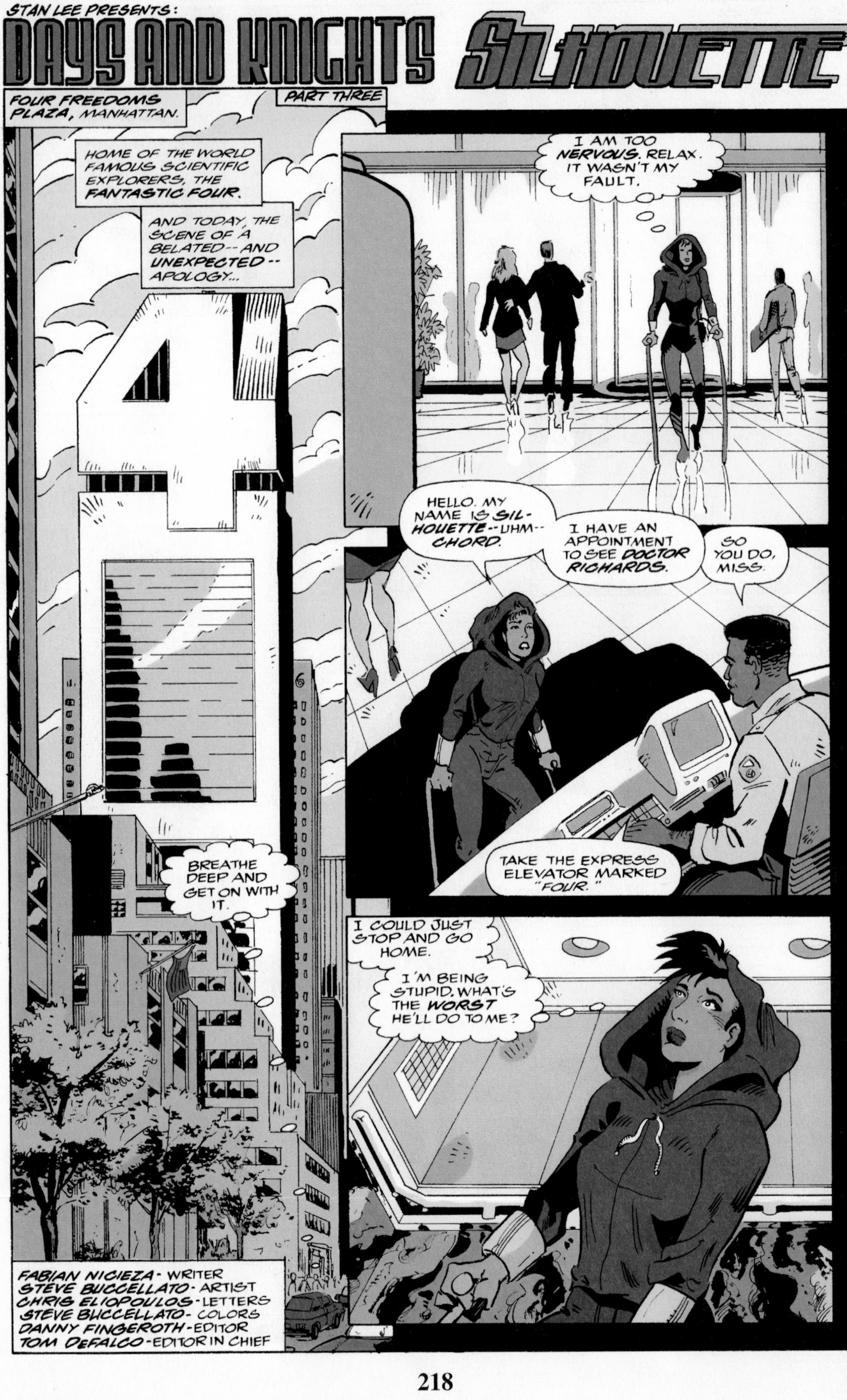
STAN LEE PRESENTS:
DAYS AND KNIGHTS
SILHOUETTE
FOUR FREEDOMS PLAZA, MANHATTAN.
PART THREE
HOME OF THE WORLD FAMOUS SCIENTIFIC EXPLORERS, THE FANTASTIC FOUR.
AND TODAY, THE SCENE OF A BELATED-- AND UNEXPECTED-- APOLOGY...
BREATHE DEEP AND GET ON WITH IT.
I AM TOO NERVOUS. RELAX. IT WASN'T MY FAULT.
HELLO. MY NAME IS SIL-HOUETTE--UHM--CHORD.
I HAVE AN APPOINTMENT TO SEE DOCTOR RICHARDS.
SO YOU DO, MISS.
TAKE THE EXPRESS ELEVATOR MARKED "FOUR."
I COULD JUST STOP AND GO HOME.
I'M BEING STUPID. WHAT'S THE WORST HE'LL DO TO ME?
FABIAN NICIEZA- WRITER
STEVE BUCCELLATO- ARTIST
CHRIS ELIOPOULOS- LETTERS
STEVE BUCCELLATO- COLORS
DANNY FINGEROTH- EDITOR
TOM DEFALCO- EDITOR IN CHIEF

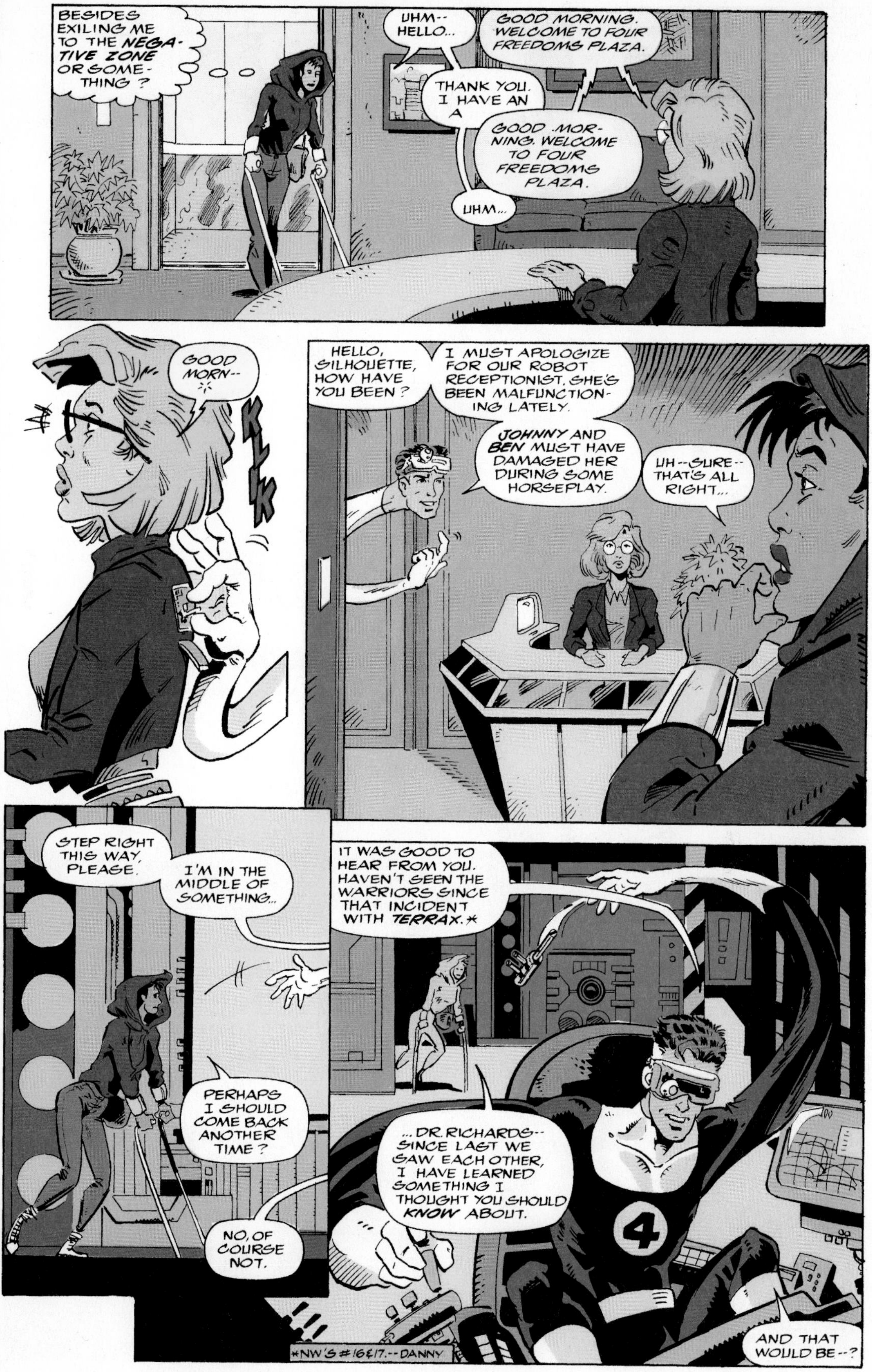
BESIDES EXILING ME TO THE NEGATIVE ZONE OR SOMETHING ?
UHM-- HELLO...
GOOD MORNING. WELCOME TO FOUR FREEDOMS PLAZA.
THANK YOU. I HAVE AN A
GOOD MORNING. WELCOME TO FOUR FREEDOMS PLAZA.
UHM...
GOOD MORN--
KLIK
HELLO, SILHOUETTE, HOW HAVE YOU BEEN ?
I MUST APOLOGIZE FOR OUR ROBOT RECEPTIONIST. SHE'S BEEN MALFUNCTIONING LATELY.
JOHNNY AND BEN MUST HAVE DAMAGED HER DURING SOME HORSEPLAY.
UH--SURE-- THAT'S ALL RIGHT...
STEP RIGHT THIS WAY, PLEASE.
I'M IN THE MIDDLE OF SOMETHING...
PERHAPS I SHOULD COME BACK ANOTHER TIME ?
NO, OF COURSE NOT.
IT WAS GOOD TO HEAR FROM YOU. HAVEN'T SEEN THE WARRIORS SINCE THAT INCIDENT WITH TERRAX.*
...DR. RICHARDS-- SINCE LAST WE SAW EACH OTHER, I HAVE LEARNED SOMETHING I THOUGHT YOU SHOULD KNOW ABOUT.
*NW'S #16&17.--DANNY
AND THAT WOULD BE--?

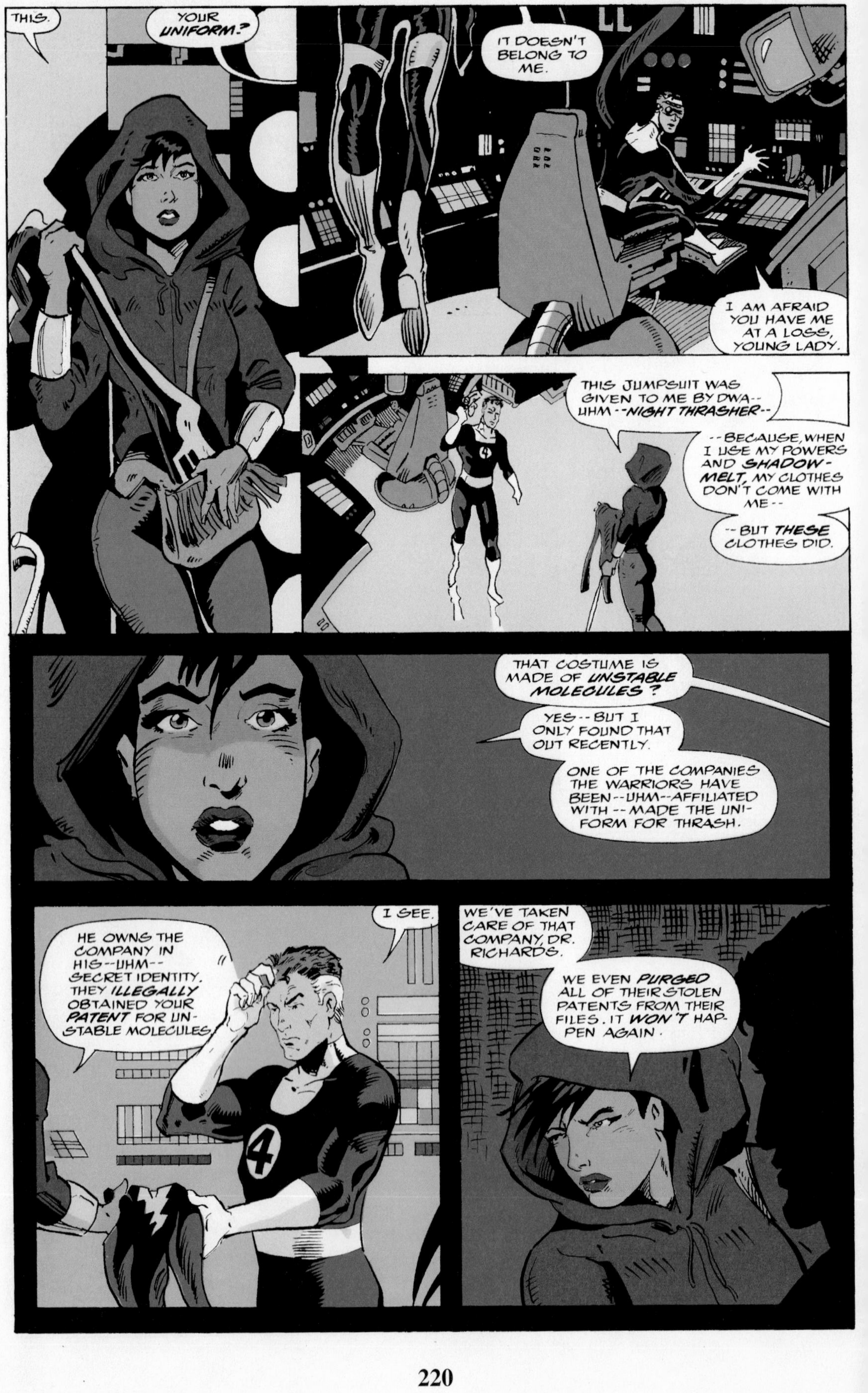
THIS.
YOUR UNIFORM?
IT DOESN'T BELONG TO ME.
I AM AFRAID YOU HAVE ME AT A LOSS, YOUNG LADY.
THIS JUMPSUIT WAS GIVEN TO ME BY DWA-- UHM --NIGHT THRASHER--
--BECAUSE, WHEN I USE MY POWERS AND SHADOW-MELT, MY CLOTHES DON'T COME WITH ME--
--BUT THESE CLOTHES DID.
THAT COSTUME IS MADE OF UNSTABLE MOLECULES?
YES--BUT I ONLY FOUND THAT OUT RECENTLY.
ONE OF THE COMPANIES THE WARRIORS HAVE BEEN--UHM--AFFILIATED WITH --MADE THE UNIFORM FOR THRASH.
I SEE.
HE OWNS THE COMPANY IN HIS--UHM-- SECRET IDENTITY. THEY ILLEGALLY OBTAINED YOUR PATENT FOR UNSTABLE MOLECULES.
WE'VE TAKEN CARE OF THAT COMPANY, DR. RICHARDS.
WE EVEN PURGED ALL OF THEIR STOLEN PATENTS FROM THEIR FILES. IT WON'T HAPPEN AGAIN.

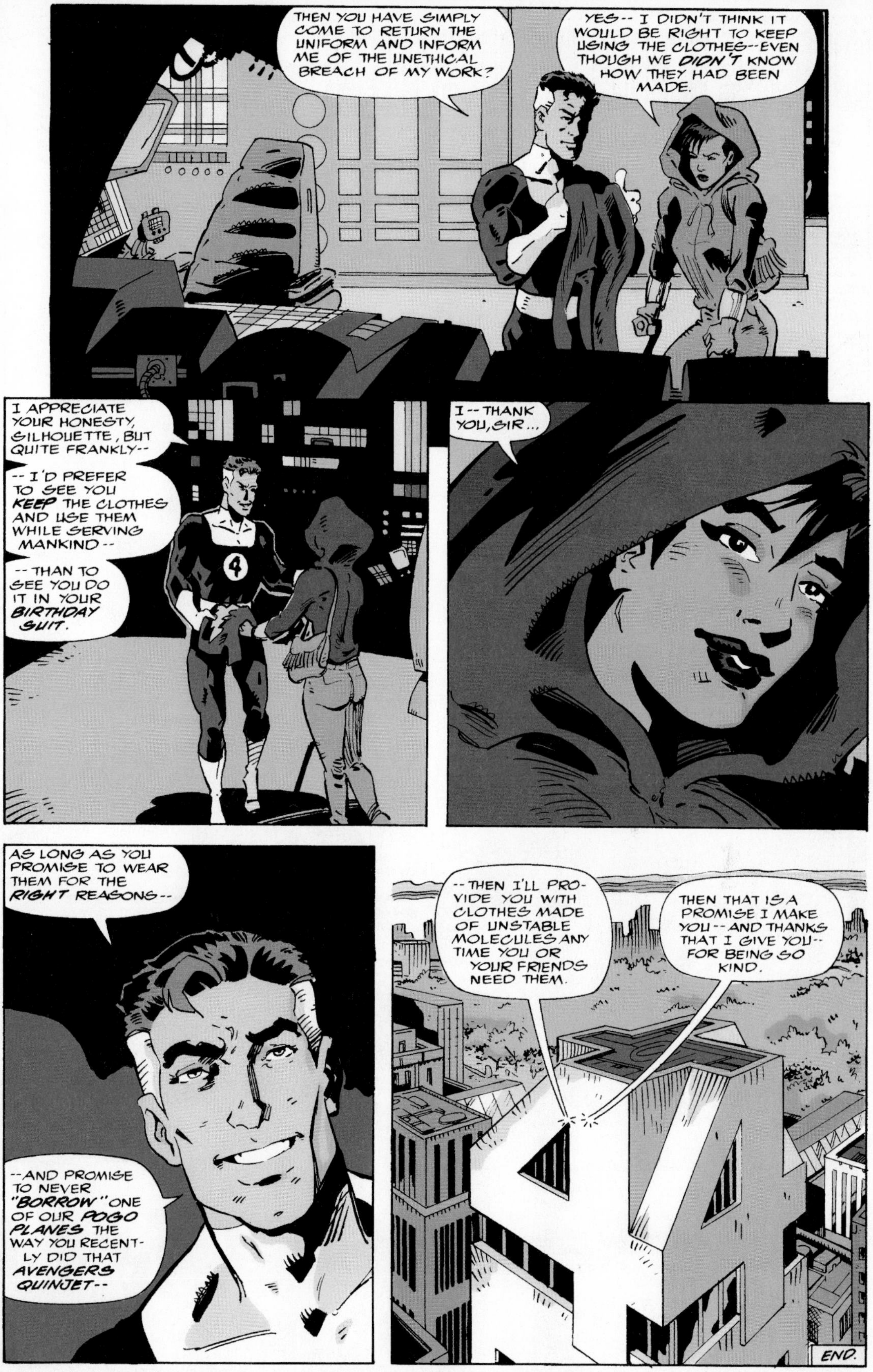
THEN YOU HAVE SIMPLY COME TO RETURN THE UNIFORM AND INFORM ME OF THE UNETHICAL BREACH OF MY WORK?
YES-- I DIDN'T THINK IT WOULD BE RIGHT TO KEEP USING THE CLOTHES--EVEN THOUGH WE DIDN'T KNOW HOW THEY HAD BEEN MADE.
I APPRECIATE YOUR HONESTY, SILHOUETTE, BUT QUITE FRANKLY--
-- I'D PREFER TO SEE YOU KEEP THE CLOTHES AND USE THEM WHILE SERVING MANKIND--
-- THAN TO SEE YOU DO IT IN YOUR BIRTHDAY SUIT.
I -- THANK YOU, SIR...
AS LONG AS YOU PROMISE TO WEAR THEM FOR THE RIGHT REASONS--
--AND PROMISE TO NEVER "BORROW" ONE OF OUR POGO PLANES THE WAY YOU RECENTLY DID THAT AVENGERS QUINJET--
-- THEN I'LL PROVIDE YOU WITH CLOTHES MADE OF UNSTABLE MOLECULES ANY TIME YOU OR YOUR FRIENDS NEED THEM.
THEN THAT IS A PROMISE I MAKE YOU -- AND THANKS THAT I GIVE YOU-- FOR BEING SO KIND.
END.

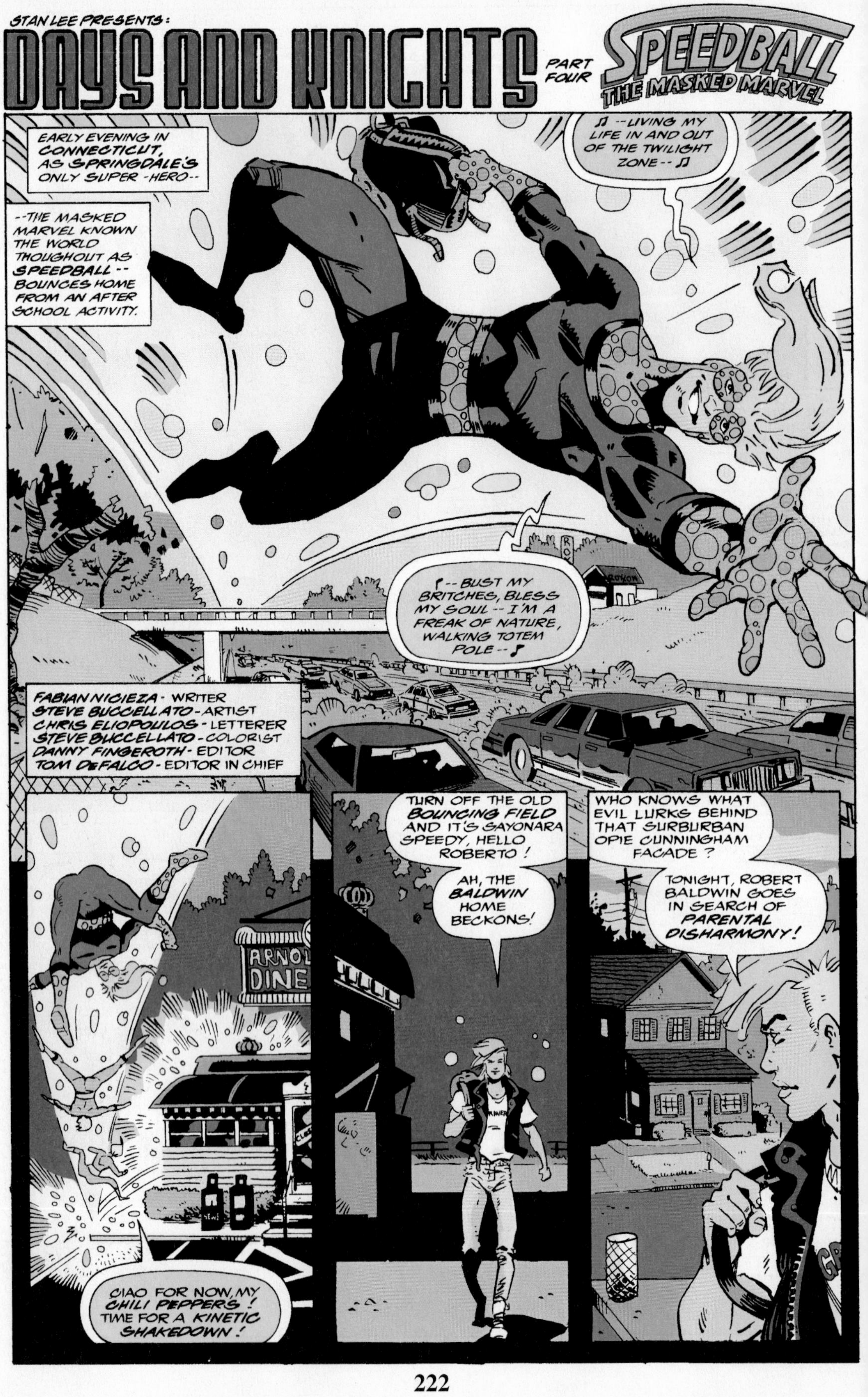
STAN LEE PRESENTS:
DAYS AND KNIGHTS
PART FOUR
SPEEDBALL
THE MASKED MARVEL
EARLY EVENING IN CONNECTICUT, AS SPRINGDALE'S ONLY SUPER-HERO--
♫ --LIVING MY LIFE IN AND OUT OF THE TWILIGHT ZONE-- ♫
--THE MASKED MARVEL KNOWN THE WORLD THOUGHOUT AS SPEEDBALL-- BOUNCES HOME FROM AN AFTER SCHOOL ACTIVITY.
♪ --BUST MY BRITCHES, BLESS MY SOUL--I'M A FREAK OF NATURE, WALKING TOTEM POLE-- ♪
FABIAN NICIEZA - WRITER
STEVE BUCCELLATO - ARTIST
CHRIS ELIOPOULOS - LETTERER
STEVE BUCCELLATO - COLORIST
DANNY FINGEROTH - EDITOR
TOM DEFALCO - EDITOR IN CHIEF
ARNOL
DINE
CIAO FOR NOW, MY CHILI PEPPERS! TIME FOR A KINETIC SHAKEDOWN!
TURN OFF THE OLD BOUNCING FIELD AND IT'S SAYONARA SPEEDY, HELLO ROBERTO!
AH, THE BALDWIN HOME BECKONS!
WHO KNOWS WHAT EVIL LURKS BEHIND THAT SURBURBAN OPIE CUNNINGHAM FACADE?
TONIGHT, ROBERT BALDWIN GOES IN SEARCH OF PARENTAL DISHARMONY!

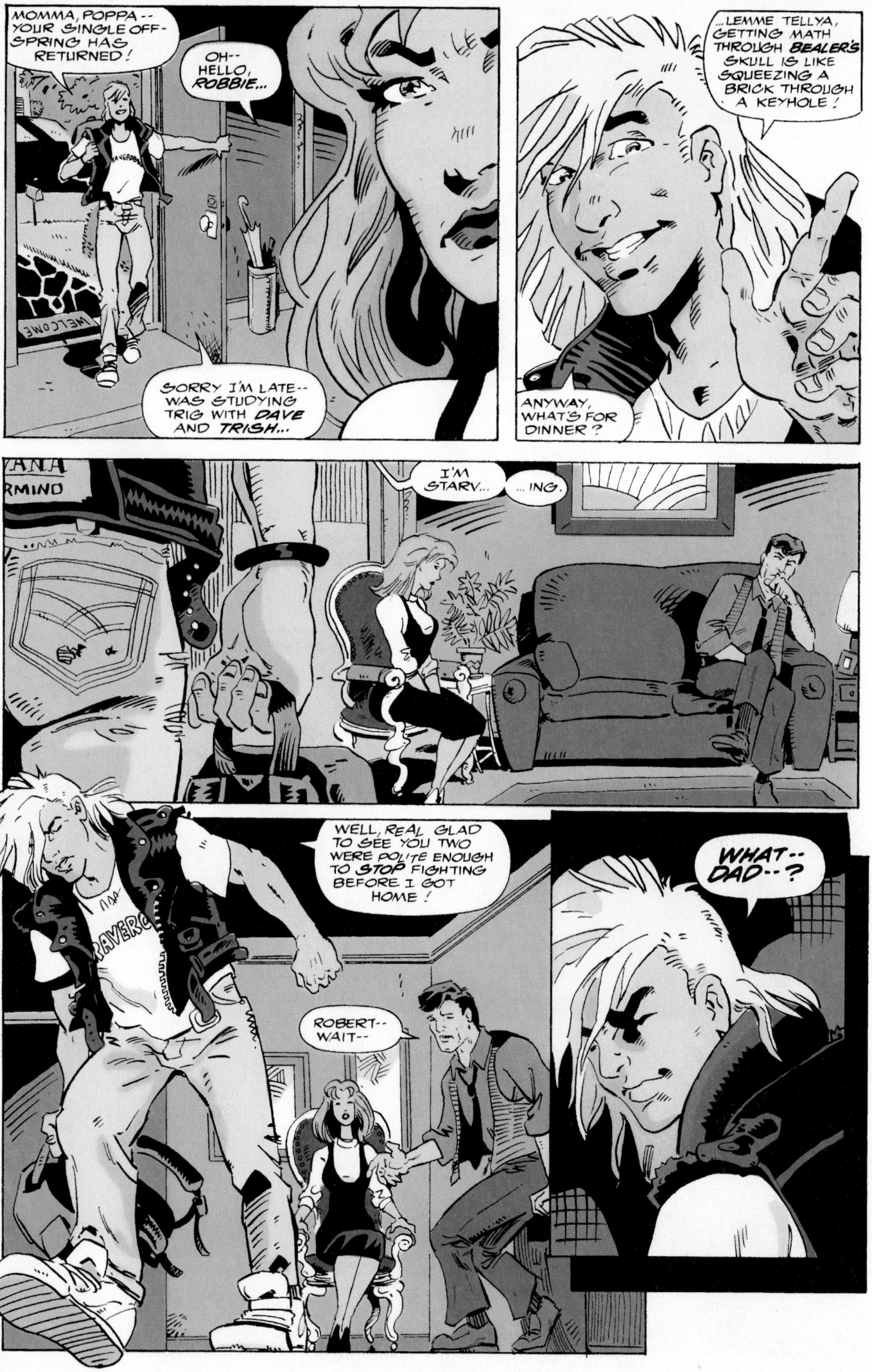
MOMMA, POPPA -- YOUR SINGLE OFF-SPRING HAS RETURNED!
OH-- HELLO, ROBBIE...
SORRY I'M LATE-- WAS STUDYING TRIG WITH DAVE AND TRISH...
...LEMME TELLYA, GETTING MATH THROUGH BEALER'S SKULL IS LIKE SQUEEZING A BRICK THROUGH A KEYHOLE!
ANYWAY, WHAT'S FOR DINNER?
I'M STARV...
...ING.
WELL, REAL GLAD TO SEE YOU TWO WERE POLITE ENOUGH TO STOP FIGHTING BEFORE I GOT HOME!
ROBERT-- WAIT--
WHAT-- DAD--?

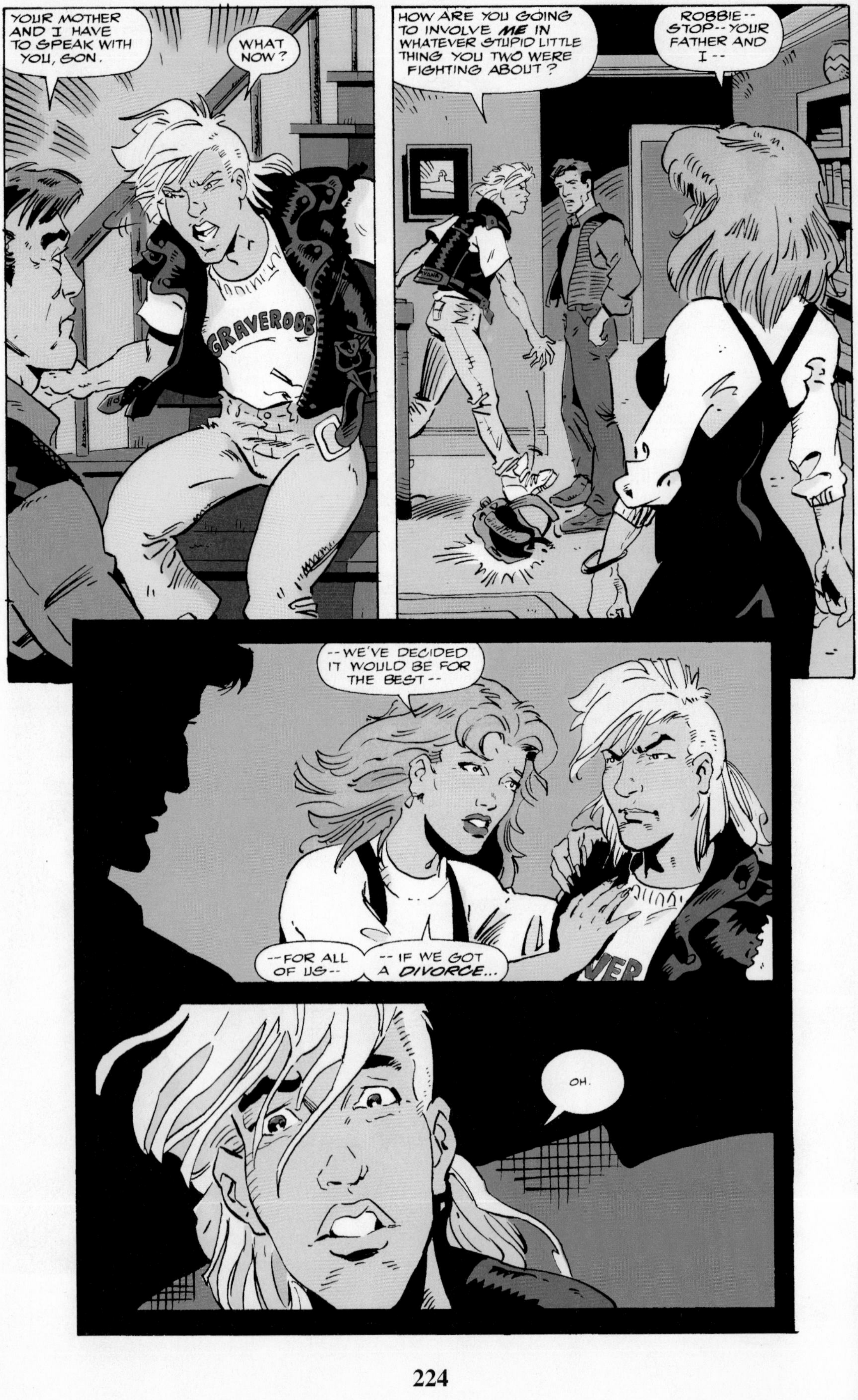
YOUR MOTHER AND I HAVE TO SPEAK WITH YOU, SON.
WHAT NOW?
GRAVEROBB
HOW ARE YOU GOING TO INVOLVE ME IN WHATEVER STUPID LITTLE THING YOU TWO WERE FIGHTING ABOUT?
ROBBIE-- STOP-- YOUR FATHER AND I--
--WE'VE DECIDED IT WOULD BE FOR THE BEST--
--FOR ALL OF US--
--IF WE GOT A DIVORCE...
OH.

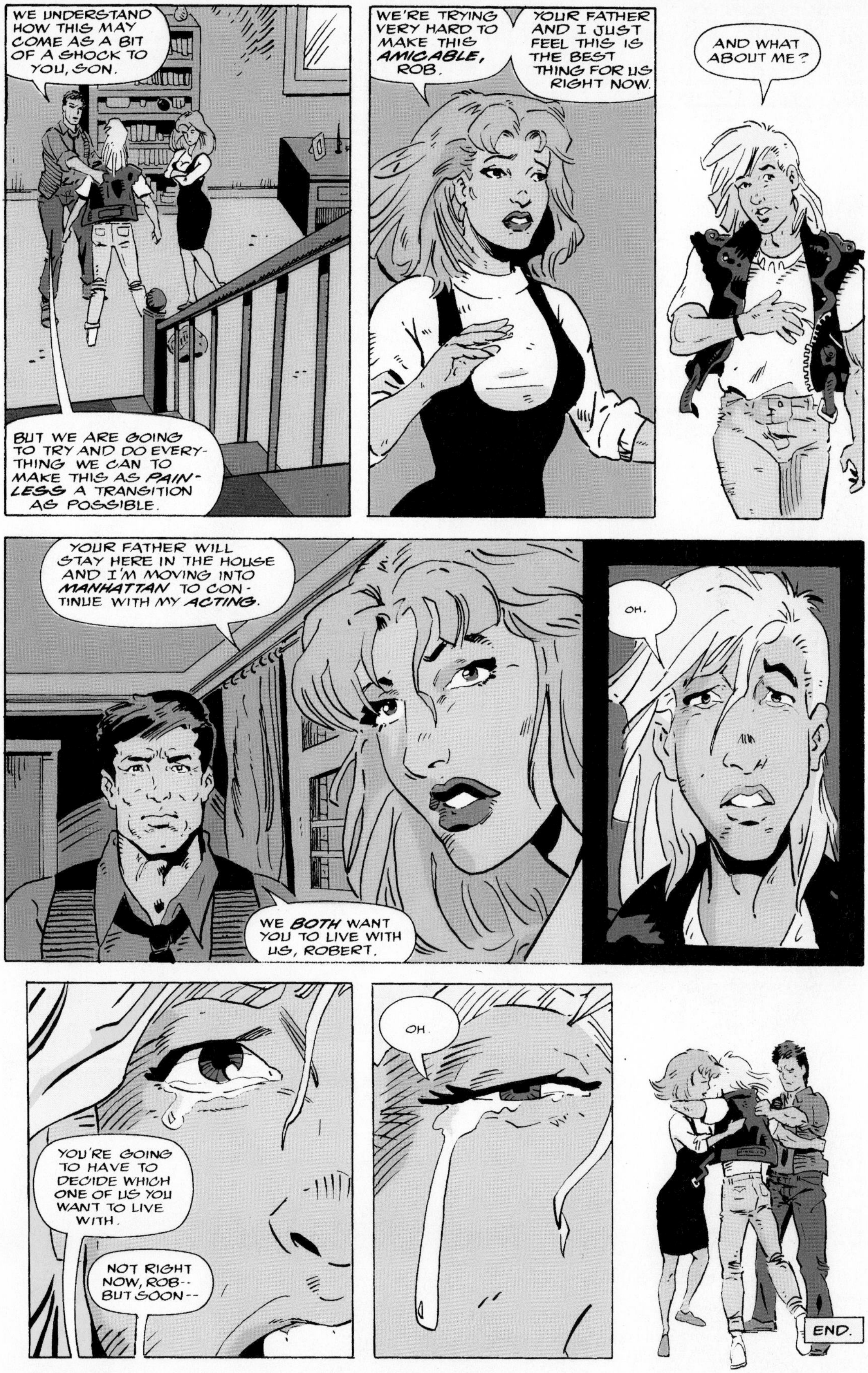

WE UNDERSTAND HOW THIS MAY COME AS A BIT OF A SHOCK TO YOU, SON.
BUT WE ARE GOING TO TRY AND DO EVERYTHING WE CAN TO MAKE THIS AS PAINLESS A TRANSITION AS POSSIBLE.
WE'RE TRYING VERY HARD TO MAKE THIS AMICABLE, ROB.
YOUR FATHER AND I JUST FEEL THIS IS THE BEST THING FOR US RIGHT NOW.
AND WHAT ABOUT ME?
YOUR FATHER WILL STAY HERE IN THE HOUSE AND I'M MOVING INTO MANHATTAN TO CONTINUE WITH MY ACTING.
WE BOTH WANT YOU TO LIVE WITH US, ROBERT.
OH.
YOU'RE GOING TO HAVE TO DECIDE WHICH ONE OF US YOU WANT TO LIVE WITH.
NOT RIGHT NOW, ROB-- BUT SOON--
OH.
END.

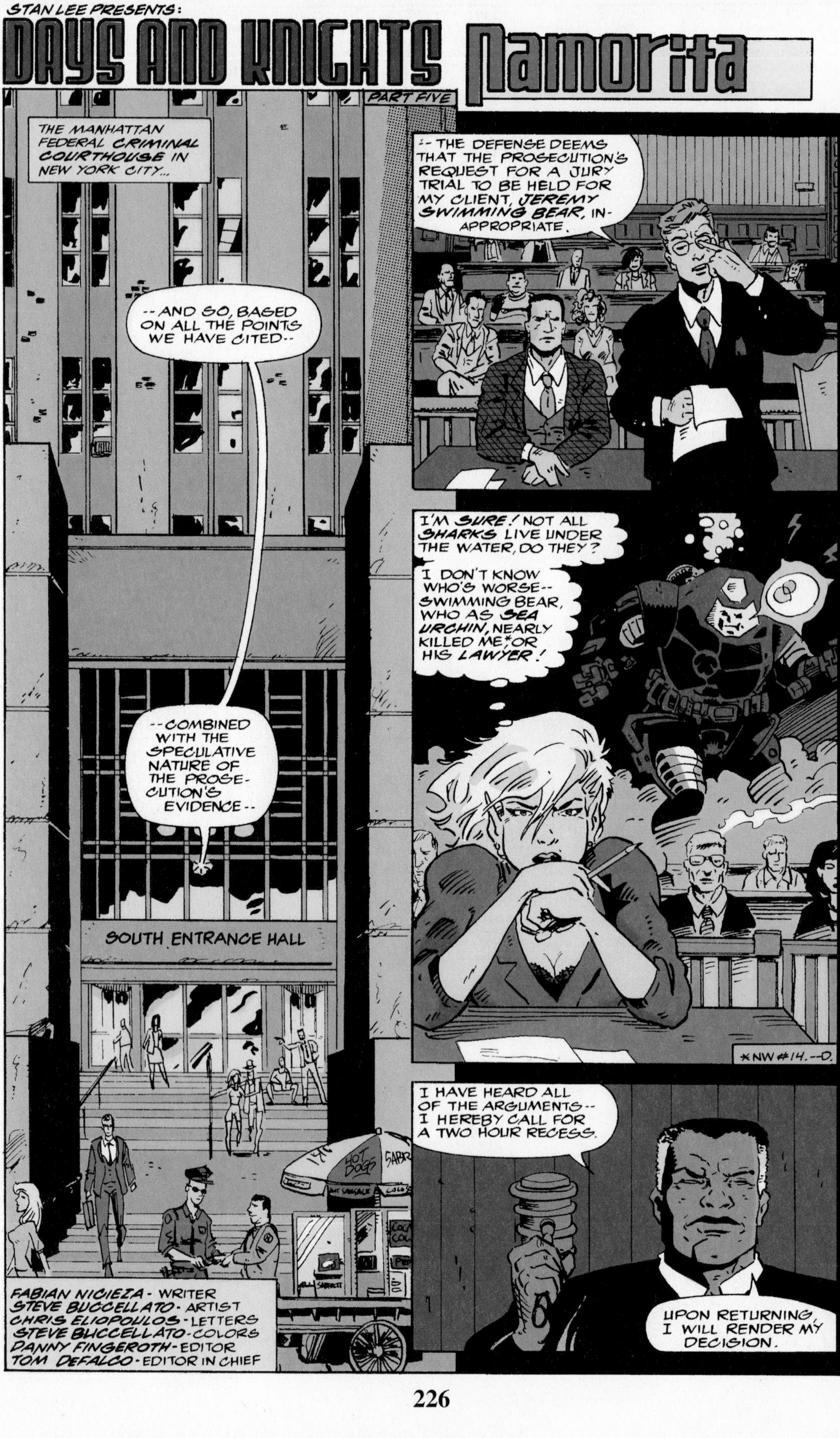
STAN LEE PRESENTS:
DAYS AND KNIGHTS
Namorita
PART FIVE
THE MANHATTAN FEDERAL CRIMINAL COURTHOUSE IN NEW YORK CITY...
--AND SO, BASED ON ALL THE POINTS WE HAVE CITED--
--COMBINED WITH THE SPECULATIVE NATURE OF THE PROSE-CUTION'S EVIDENCE--
--THE DEFENSE DEEMS THAT THE PROSECUTION'S REQUEST FOR A JURY TRIAL TO BE HELD FOR MY CLIENT, JEREMY SWIMMING BEAR, IN-APPROPRIATE.
I'M SURE! NOT ALL SHARKS LIVE UNDER THE WATER, DO THEY?
I DON'T KNOW WHO'S WORSE--SWIMMING BEAR, WHO AS SEA URCHIN, NEARLY KILLED ME,* OR HIS LAWYER!
*NW #14.--D.
SOUTH ENTRANCE HALL
HOT DOGS
I HAVE HEARD ALL OF THE ARGUMENTS--I HEREBY CALL FOR A TWO HOUR RECESS.
UPON RETURNING, I WILL RENDER MY DECISION.
FABIAN NICIEZA - WRITER
STEVE BUCCELLATO - ARTIST
CHRIS ELIOPOULOS - LETTERS
STEVE BUCCELLATO - COLORS
DANNY FINGEROTH - EDITOR
TOM DEFALCO - EDITOR IN CHIEF

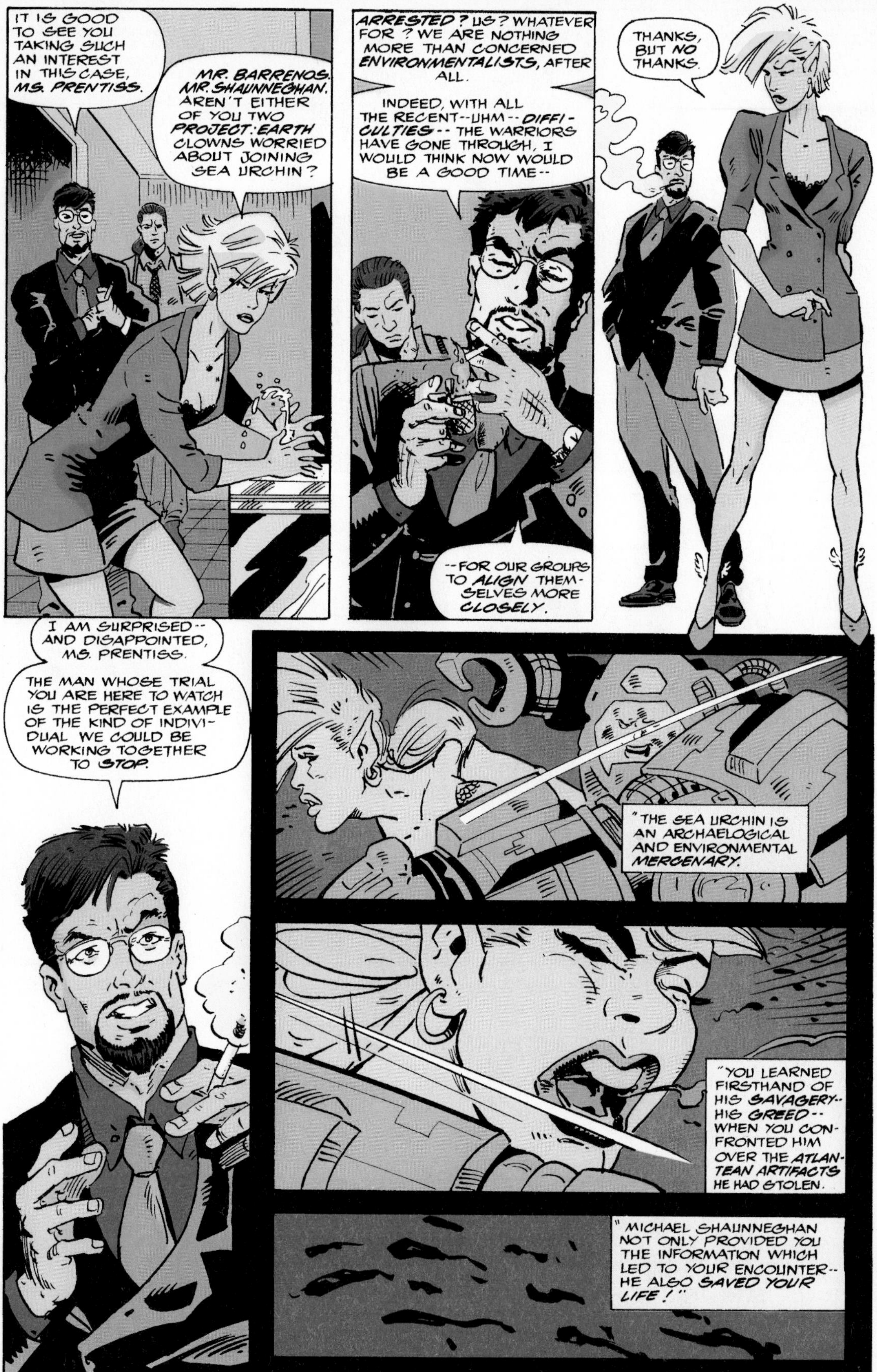
IT IS GOOD TO SEE YOU TAKING SUCH AN INTEREST IN THIS CASE, MS. PRENTISS.
MR. BARRENOS. MR. SHAUNNEGHAN. AREN'T EITHER OF YOU TWO PROJECT: EARTH CLOWNS WORRIED ABOUT JOINING SEA URCHIN?
ARRESTED? US? WHATEVER FOR? WE ARE NOTHING MORE THAN CONCERNED ENVIRONMENTALISTS, AFTER ALL.
INDEED, WITH ALL THE RECENT--UHM--DIFFICULTIES--THE WARRIORS HAVE GONE THROUGH, I WOULD THINK NOW WOULD BE A GOOD TIME--
--FOR OUR GROUPS TO ALIGN THEMSELVES MORE CLOSELY.
THANKS, BUT NO THANKS.
I AM SURPRISED--AND DISAPPOINTED, MS. PRENTISS.
THE MAN WHOSE TRIAL YOU ARE HERE TO WATCH IS THE PERFECT EXAMPLE OF THE KIND OF INDIVIDUAL WE COULD BE WORKING TOGETHER TO STOP.
"THE SEA URCHIN IS AN ARCHAELOGICAL AND ENVIRONMENTAL MERCENARY.
"YOU LEARNED FIRSTHAND OF HIS SAVAGERY--HIS GREED--WHEN YOU CONFRONTED HIM OVER THE ATLANTEAN ARTIFACTS HE HAD STOLEN.
"MICHAEL SHAUNNEGHAN NOT ONLY PROVIDED YOU THE INFORMATION WHICH LED TO YOUR ENCOUNTER--HE ALSO SAVED YOUR LIFE!"

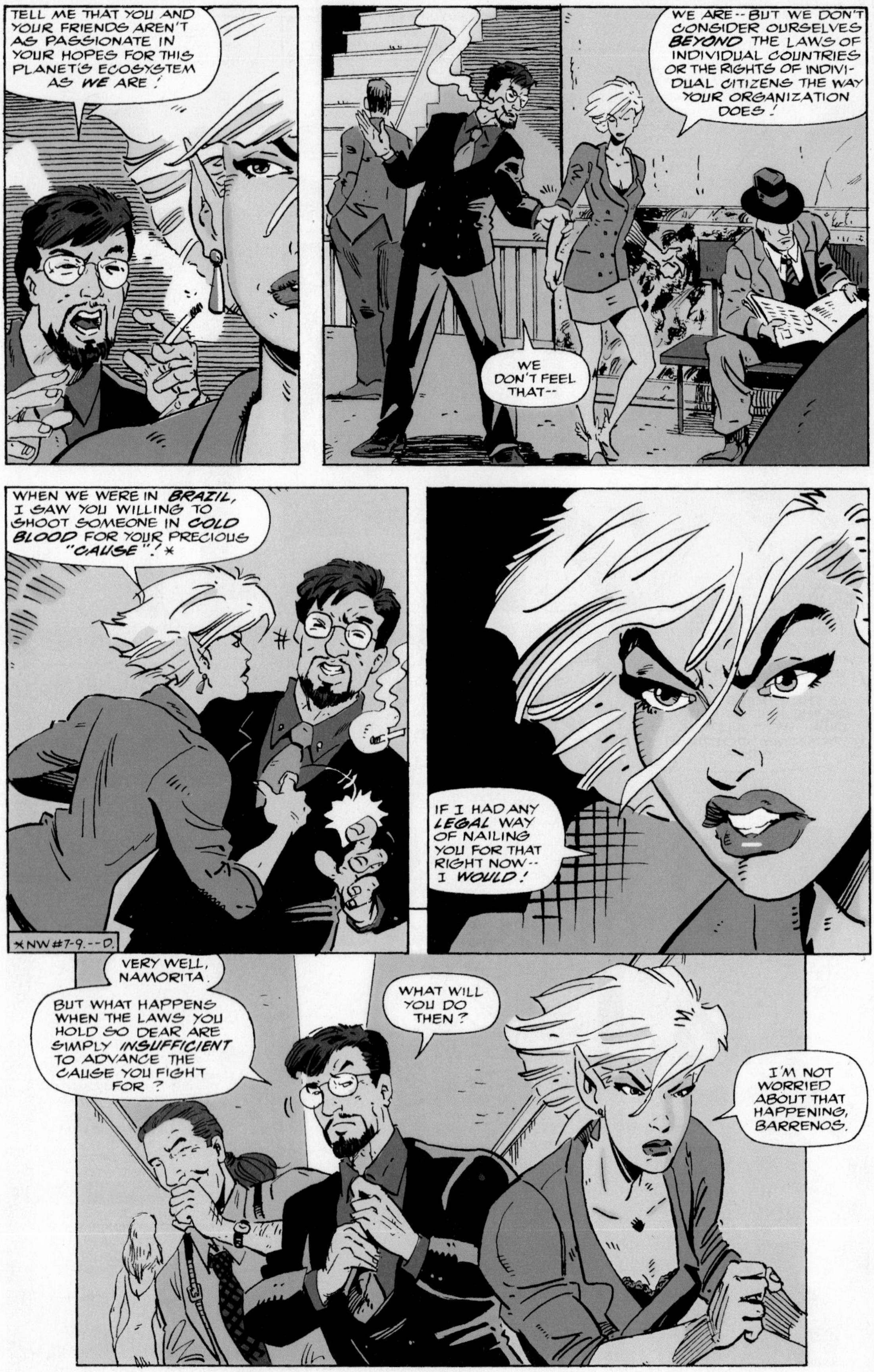
TELL ME THAT YOU AND YOUR FRIENDS AREN'T AS PASSIONATE IN YOUR HOPES FOR THIS PLANET'S ECOSYSTEM AS *WE* ARE!
WE DON'T FEEL THAT--
WE ARE--BUT WE DON'T CONSIDER OURSELVES *BEYOND* THE LAWS OF INDIVIDUAL COUNTRIES OR THE RIGHTS OF INDIVIDUAL CITIZENS THE WAY YOUR ORGANIZATION DOES!
WHEN WE WERE IN *BRAZIL*, I SAW YOU WILLING TO SHOOT SOMEONE IN *COLD BLOOD* FOR YOUR PRECIOUS *"CAUSE"*!*
*NW #7-9.--D.
IF I HAD ANY *LEGAL* WAY OF NAILING YOU FOR THAT RIGHT NOW-- I *WOULD*!
VERY WELL, NAMORITA.
BUT WHAT HAPPENS WHEN THE LAWS YOU HOLD SO DEAR ARE SIMPLY *INSUFFICIENT* TO ADVANCE THE CAUSE YOU FIGHT FOR?
WHAT WILL YOU DO THEN?
I'M NOT WORRIED ABOUT THAT HAPPENING, BARRENOS.

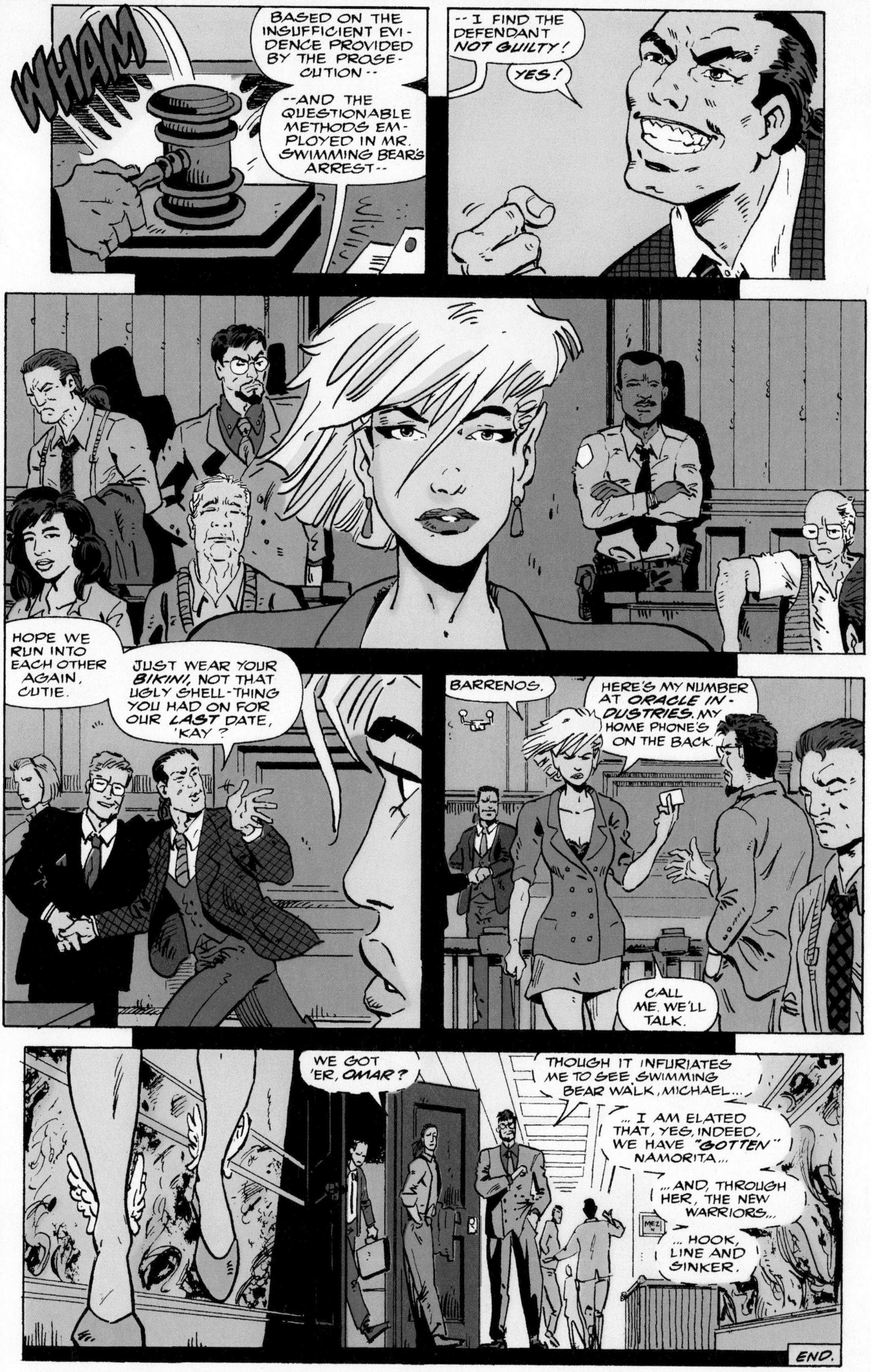
WHAM
BASED ON THE INSUFFICIENT EVIDENCE PROVIDED BY THE PROSECUTION --
--AND THE QUESTIONABLE METHODS EMPLOYED IN MR. SWIMMING BEAR'S ARREST--
-- I FIND THE DEFENDANT NOT GUILTY!
YES!
HOPE WE RUN INTO EACH OTHER AGAIN, CUTIE.
JUST WEAR YOUR BIKINI, NOT THAT UGLY SHELL-THING YOU HAD ON FOR OUR LAST DATE, 'KAY?
BARRENOS.
HERE'S MY NUMBER AT ORACLE INDUSTRIES. MY HOME PHONE'S ON THE BACK.
CALL ME. WE'LL TALK.
WE GOT 'ER, OMAR?
THOUGH IT INFURIATES ME TO SEE SWIMMING BEAR WALK, MICHAEL...
... I AM ELATED THAT, YES, INDEED, WE HAVE "GOTTEN" NAMORITA...
...AND, THROUGH HER, THE NEW WARRIORS...
... HOOK, LINE AND SINKER.
END.

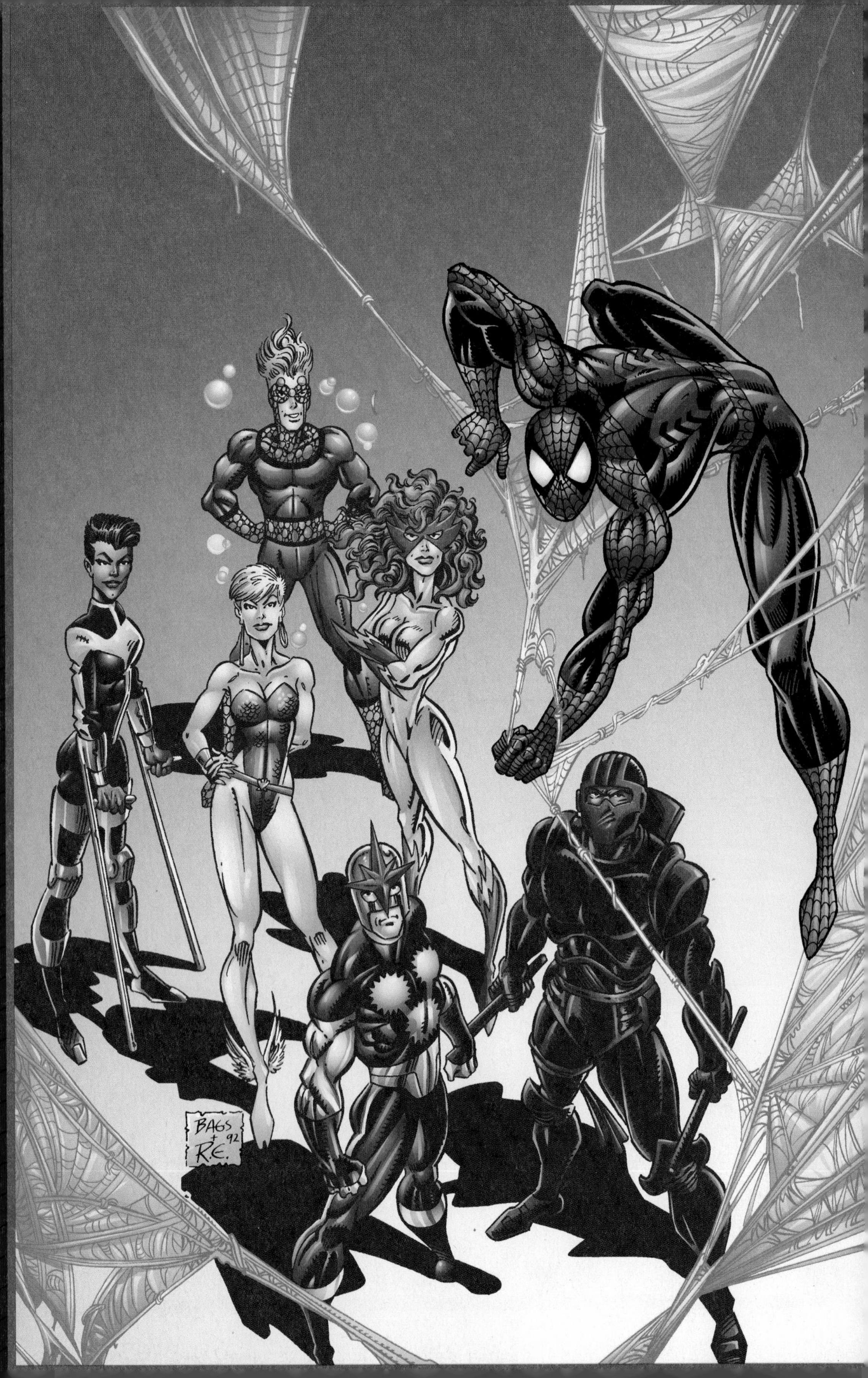
BAGS + '92 R.E.

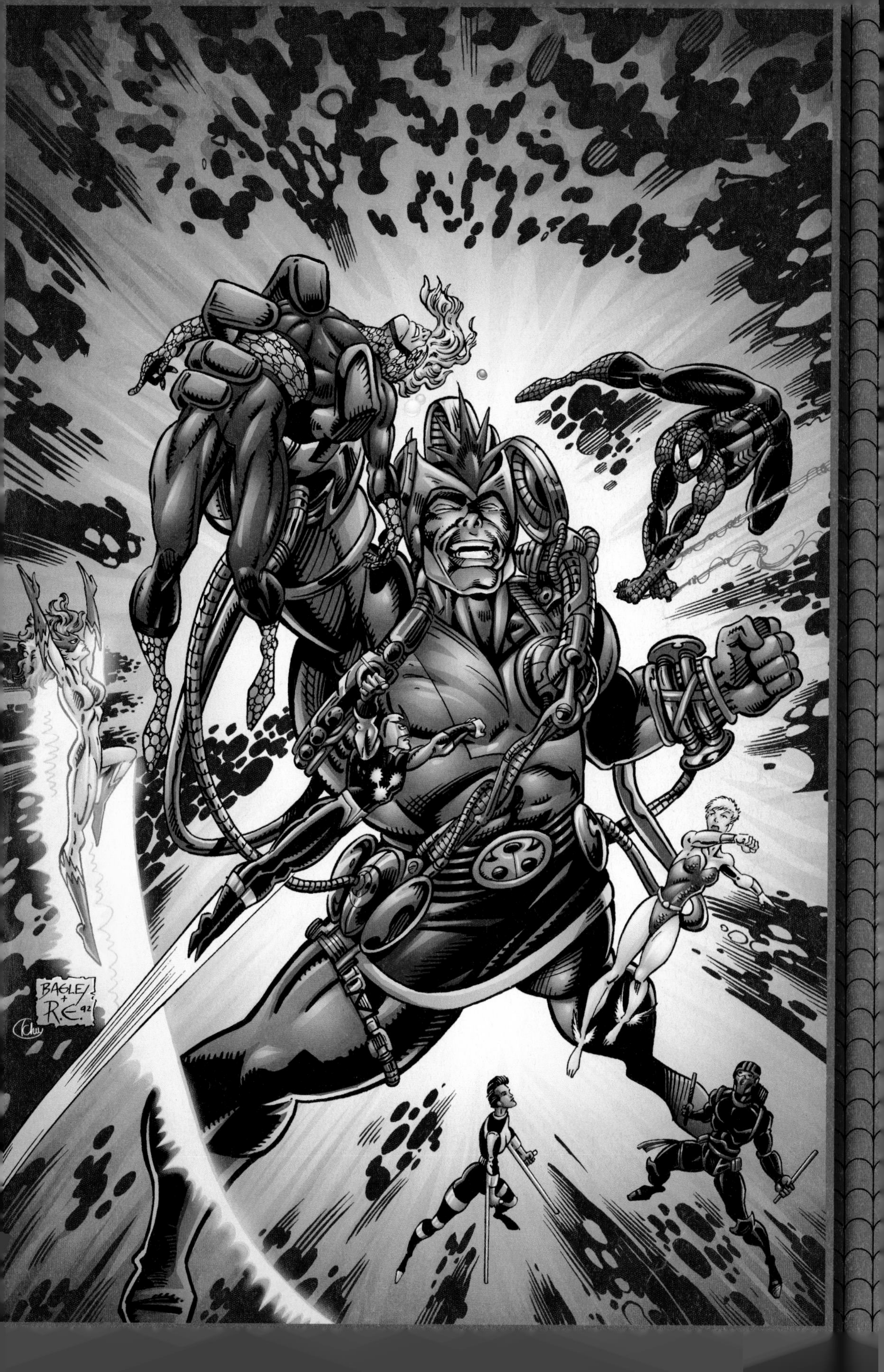
BAGLEY + R.E. '92

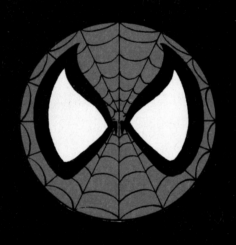